An Encyclopedia of South Carolina

Jazz & Blues Musicians

Tappin-Flcba
43 Lenox Ave. N.Y
JENKINS ORPHAN BAND Charlston S.C.

AN *Encyclopedia of* South Carolina JAZZ & BLUES Musicians

Benjamin Franklin V

THE UNIVERSITY OF SOUTH CAROLINA PRESS

Published by the University of South Carolina Press
Columbia, South Carolina 29208

www.sc.edu/uscpress

Manufactured in the United States of America

25 24 23 22 21 20 19 18 17 16
10 9 8 7 6 5 4 3 2 1

Library of Congress Cataloging-in-Publication Data can be found at http://catalog.loc.gov/.

ISBN: 978-1-61117-621-6 (cloth)
ISBN: 978-1-61117-622-3 (ebook)

Frontispiece: Edward Elcha and Percy Tappin, photograph postcard of the Jenkins Orphanage Band, Charleston, South Carolina, 1914. Silver and photographic gelatin on photographic paper; H × W: 3 1/2 × 5 3/8 in. (8.9 × 13.7 cm). Collection of the Smithsonian National Museum of African American History and Culture, 2014.63.88.1

To the music makers
and, as always,
to Jo, Abigail, Rebecca, Elizabeth, and Louisa

ALSO BY BENJAMIN FRANKLIN V

Commentaries on Jazz Musicians and Jazz Songs: A History of "Jazz in Retrospect" (2011)

Jazz and Blues Musicians of South Carolina: Interviews with Jabbo, Dizzy, Drink, and Others (2008)

Contents

Acknowledgments

Other than a travel grant to interview musicians in the 1980s, I neither requested nor received direct financial support for this project. I benefited enormously, though, from the resources of the University of South Carolina, including those of the Department of English, chaired by William E. Rivers and Nina Levine. I relied heavily on organizations within the university's library system, directed by Thomas F. McNally: the Interlibrary Loan Department (overseen initially by Marna Hostetler, then Amber Cook), the Reference Department (led by Sharon Verba), the School of Music Library (headed by Ana Dubnjakovic, following the tenure of Jennifer Ottervik), and the South Caroliniana Library (managed first by Allen Stokes and then by Henry Fulmer). Though I, alone, wrote the text and am responsible for everything in it, I could not have completed this book without the assistance of many people. Four librarians aided me to a degree I could not have expected: Debra C. Bloom, Local History Librarian, Richland County Public Library, Columbia, S.C.; Jeff Reid, Jr., Calhoun County Museum and Cultural Center, Saint Matthews, S.C.; Lorrey Stewart, South Caroliniana Library; and Susan Thoms, Spartanburg (S.C.) Public Libraries. Ever patient, Kesley Mumpower solved numerous computer problems. Alexander Moore, of the University of South Carolina Press, coddled me. Donald J. Greiner listened to numerous progress reports and commented insightfully about the introduction. Of the musicians documented herein, Gary Erwin (Shrimp City Slim), George Kenny, Drink Small, and John Williams helped me significantly. I am grateful to the individuals who permitted the publication of their photographs, but especially to Gene Tomko, who generously allowed me to use his copyrighted pictures. With apologies to anyone I overlooked, I thank the following people who assisted me: Iris Abney, Teddy Adams, Tee Alston, Karen Altman, Nancy Ames, George Anderson, J. T. Anderson, Alice Ansfield, Brent Appling, David Archer, Donna Arnold, Bob Ashley, Raymond Ausan, Laura Baines, Laurel Baker, Bert Barnett, Debra Basham, Bruce Bastin, Darla Baumli, Maeward Belk, Jerry Bell, Maria Beltran, Leslie Bennett, Michael Berry, Dorothy Bevill, Marilee Birchfield, Brian Bisesi, Sandra Bloodworth, Nancy Bolin, Matthew Bolton, Brett Bonner, Peter Box, Tobias Brasier, Olivia L. Bravo, Ward Briggs, Marc Brodsky, John Broven, Charlotte Pazant Brown, Karen Brown, Paul Brown, Phil Brown, Giacomo Bruzzo, Caspers Bull, Mary Bull, Beverly Bullock, William Lewis Burke, Jr., Patti Burns, Heinrich Buttler, Keith Byers, Trevor Cajiao, Gary J. Chaffee, Allan D. Charles, Kristin Charles-Scaringi, Noal Cohen, Sybil Coker, Ken Coleman, Terrye Conroy, Ashlie Conway, Robin Copp, Ursula Covay, Tracy Craft, Valerie Craft, Andy Craig, Jeni Dahmus, Dawn Dale, Avery L. Daniels, Isaac Davis, Jr., Ardie Dean, Jason Dean, Cynthia Dennis, Theresa Derrick, Sarah De Weever, Carlo Ditta, Lana S. Dixon, Judy Allen Dodson, Noreen M. Doughty, Samuel Douglas, Abe Duenas, Graham Duncan, William Durant, Richard Durlach, Andrew Dys, Bob Eagle, David Earl, Amy Edwards, Michael J. Edwards, Patricia Edwards, Halle Eisenman, Joanne Ellis, Mikael Elsila, Janie Erickson, Kris Esgar, Anna Evans, David H. Evans, Mary Jo Fairchild, Daniel R. Fallon, Angela Fama, Mary Faria, Charles Farley, Russell Feagin, Billy Feaster, Cheryl Ferguson, Laura Fisher, Greg Forter, Nancy Foster, Gordon Franklin, Amie Freeman, Adam French, George L. Frunzi, Krin Gabbard, Stephen D. Gailey, Frye Gaillard, Doris G. Gandy, Ken Garfield, Josh Garris, John Gasque, Tracie Gieselman-Holthaus, Kurt Goblirsch, Susan Godfrey, Kevin Goins, Marv Goldberg, Judy Goodwin, Winifred Goodwin, Miki Goral, Kathleen Gray, Brendan Greaves, Jeffrey P. Green, Aaron Greenhood, Maxine Griffin, Ramona L. Grimsley, Kim Gurekovich, Evan Haga, Rebecca Halpern, Friedrich Hamer, Lance Hanlin, Tayloe Harding, Leroy Pinckney Hardy, Jr., Cathy Harley, Jeff Harris, Britni Hartis, Jessica Harvey, Patrick J.

Harwood, Ayo Haynes, Constance J. Haynes, Joe Henderson, Lynn Henson, Marcos Hermes, Sara Herndon, Tim K. Hicks, Tim Higginbotham, Brendan Higgins, Meredith "Honi" Gordon Hillman, Laura Holden, Ellen Jane Hollis, Hunter Holmes, Joey Holmes, Nick Homenda, Lisa K. Hooper, Bertha Hope-Booker, Charlie Horner, Lisa Howdyshell, Jackson Howe, Brian M. Howle, Yvonne Hudgens, Michelle Hudson, Joanie G. Hunter, Stephanie Hunter, Harriett Hurt, Geraldine Ingersoll, Tanya Jackson, Sonia Jacobsen, Andrea Jarratt, Jan Jenson, Christine Johnson, Doris E. Johnson, Eartha Pinkney Johnson, Fred Johnson, Kevin Johnson, Phillip M. Johnson, Doris Johnson-Felder, Andrew Justice, Michael Katz, Red Kelly, Gerrick Kennedy, Marty Kesselman, Burt King, Charlene Knight, Ken Knox, Carrie Koerber, Robert G. Koester, Susan Koester, Amelia Koford, Katie E. Koon, Linda Koon, Mary Krautter, Jessica Krogman, Barbara J. Kukla, Cynthia Kutka, Marlise Langan, John Langellotti, David Lauderdale, John Laughter, Kevin LaVine, Eric S. LeBlanc, Brian Lee, John Lee, Maureen Lee, David Lewis, Johanna Lewis, David Lilly, Fredie Littles, Jr., Kimberly Littles, Wendi Loomis, Andrea Lorenzo-Luaces, Christopher Lornell, Peter B. Lowry, Lynn K. Lucas, Corwin Lucky, Brandon D. Lunsford, Maxine Lutz, Mary Mallaney, Barbara Mandeville, Tom Marcil, Bill Margulis, Autumn L. Mather, Chris Maume, Boncile McCollum, Emily S. McConnell, Patricia McCrea, Sarah Graydon McCrory, Sam McCuen, Tony McLawhorn, Betty McLin, Sarah McMaster, Cheryl McNeil, Erin McSherry, Cheryl Means, Lorraine Melita, Amanda Menard, Steve Mendoza, Nicholas G. Meriwether, Eva Mikusch, Phil X. Milstein, Dolores Minger, Loretto J. Mockabee, Patricia Mockabee, Joe Montague, Morgan Montgomery, Philip Montoro, Georgia Murphy, Christine Murray, Sarah Murray, David Nathan, Opal Louis Nations, David Ness, Dorianne Newkirk, Michelle Nimmons, Ed Nordine, Patrick O'Donnell, Megan Palmer, Gail C. Patterson, Rachel Pavlas, Jacqueline Peek Peace, Peter Penhallow, Derrin Perkins, Sherryl Peters, Angela Y. Peterson, Kay Peterson, Scott Phinney, Jose M. Pineiro, Karma Pippin, Patricia Poland, Christopher Popa, Maxine Porter, Beverly Pott, Rulinda Price, Roger O. Printup, Heather Pruitt, Anya Puccio, Darden Purcell, Bob Purse, Debbie Quick, Bill Randall, Eric Randall, Harri Rautiainen, Eddie Ray, Modestine Redden, Katherine Reeve, Richard Reid, Ilana Revkin, Zoe Rhine, Diane Rhodes, Marion C. Richards, Leah Richardson, John Ridley, Arnette Rivers, Peter James Roberts, Donald Robertson, Janet Robinson, Louester Robinson, Ron Rodney, Lauren Rogers, Baker Rorick, Clint Rosemond, Joseph A. Rosen, David S. Rotenstein, Tony Rounce, Tony Russell, Shannon Ryan, Angelo Salvo, Rainer Schneider, Colleen W. Seale, Cary Seaman, Linda Seitz, David Seubert, Neil Sharpe, Stanley E. Shealy, Nicole L. Shibata, David S. Shields, Jay Sieleman, Kristen Setzler Simensen, Timothy Simmons, Ree Simpson, Valerie Simpson, Jon Skinner, Harry Skoler, Susan Sliwicki, Clay Smith, Debra Smith, Fay Smith, Renee Smith, R. J. Smith, Susan Smith, Aaron Smithers, Kathy Snediker, Odell Staley, Chyrel Stalvey, Elaine Stefanko, Deborah Stewart, Tammy Strawbridge, Meg Stroup, Bill Sudduth, Harry Sullivan, Tim Swallow, Yuka Tadano, Mila Tasseva-Kurktchiev, Saddler Taylor, Tucker Taylor, John Tecklenburg, Allison Thiessen, Pamela Thomas, Bruce Thompson, Lish Thompson, Richard Thurmond, Joyce M. Tice, Art Tipaldi, Amy Trepal, Alex Trim, Matthew Turi, Amy Tuttle, Michael Ullman, Tut Underwood, Derik Vanderford, Brad Vickers, D. John Wagstaff, Irene Wainwright, Elijah Wald, Wolette R. Wales, Amanda Boyd Walters, Tom Warlick, J. T. Washington, Jackie Watkins, Tony Watson, Virginia Weathers, Todd Weeks, Christine Weislo, Dave Weld, Gaile Welker, Joya Wesley, Da-Renne P. Westbrook, Rebecca Westfall, Celeste Wiley, Albert Williams, Blondelle Williams, Calvernetta Williams, Lisa Williams, Dorianne Williams-Newkirk, Crystal Williamson, Cristi Wilson, Robert W. Winkley, Charles Winokoor, Jennifer Wochner, Theresa Wood, Leslie Wrenn, Debbie Yerkes, Anna Zacheri, T. Sam Ziady, and Karl Gert zur Heide.

Introduction

Of humble beginnings, jazz and blues long ago gained acceptance as vital, inventive musics, both nationally and internationally. This approval is evident in South Carolina, where jazz and blues are part of mainstream culture. They are performed in such venues as the Gaillard Auditorium in Charleston, the Koger Center in Columbia, the Peace Center in Greenville, and the Newberry Opera House, as well as at the Spoleto festival in Charleston. Annual blues festivals are held in Camden, Columbia, Denmark, and elsewhere; jazz and blues are featured in concerts produced by colleges and universities, some of which offer a jazz curriculum. The South Caroliniana Library at the University of South Carolina has an archive of the state's jazz and blues musicians, including the files created for this encyclopedia project, and the university's School of Music houses the Center for Southern African-American Music, which contains material relating to these performers. Books have been published about individual jazz and blues musicians from the Palmetto State, as well as about the Charleston jazz scene.[1] South Carolina Educational Television and ETV Radio broadcast these musics. At least partly because jazz and blues are so widely acknowledged, the names if not the music of Chris Potter and Drink Small, for example, are known to many of the state's arts devotees, who doubtless also are aware that these musicians are themselves South Carolinians. Yet aside from them and perhaps a dozen or so others, how many South Carolina jazz and blues performers are widely known even in their own state, except to the specialist or serious fan? Some music lovers surely know of Pink Anderson, Gary Davis, Jimmy Hamilton, and Buddy Johnson, but are they aware of Lottie Frost Hightower, Maceo Jefferson, Doug Quattlebaum, and Horace "Spoons" Williams, South Carolinians who are significant to one degree or another? They are among the hundreds of South Carolinians who contributed to the development of jazz and blues, the acceptance of which permits young performers to develop their art and contribute to the ongoing evolution of these musics. Because the obscurity of most South Carolina jazz and blues musicians makes their chronicling desirable, this encyclopedia documents as many of them as could be identified and as space permits.

Research on jazz and blues musicians of the Palmetto State, begun in the 1980s, benefited from the assistance of Thomas L. Johnson of the South Caroliniana Library and a grant from the South Carolina Committee for the Humanities (now known as the Humanities Council). The latter facilitated access to musicians for interviews that were broadcast on the South Carolina Educational Radio Network and published in *Jazz and Blues Musicians of South Carolina: Interviews with Jabbo, Dizzy, Drink, and Others* (2008). The desire to write an encyclopedia was inspired by the publication of *The South Carolina Encyclopedia* (2006). Edited by Walter Edgar, it has entries for important people and events from long before statehood through 2004. Yet because space limitations forced him to be more selective than he might have liked, the opportunity arose for others to write or edit encyclopedias about South Carolina topics that he could not deal with fully; sub-Edgar encyclopedias, they might be called. Long in the making, this encyclopedia of jazz and blues musicians is likely the first such book.

As Edgar's book had a length limit, so did this one. Because every musician who might qualify to be documented could not be accounted for, criteria were established for inclusion. To be considered a South Carolinian, one must have been born in the state or have lived in it for at least five years. This means that some musicians who were born in South Carolina are treated—Etta Jones, Lucky Thompson, and Webster Young, for example—even though they left the state as infants and had no recollection of having resided in it; this also means that some who lived here have been omitted because evidence does not prove that they did so for long enough to meet this definition of a resident. These include percussionist Emmanuel

Abdul-Rahim (resident of Charleston, born in New York), singer Irene Daye (resident of Greenville, born in Massachusetts), and drummer Ron Jefferson (resident of Orangeburg, born in New York), among others. Sometimes characterized as South Carolinians, the following musicians have not been documented because proof that they were born in the state or resided in it for at least five years is lacking: James Albert (Beans Hambone), James Alston, Scrapper Blackwell (born in Indiana), Arthur Briggs (born in Grenada), Sam (possibly named James) Butler (Bo-Weavil Jackson), Prince Cooper, John Faire, Herb Flemming (probably born in Montana), Dusty Fletcher (born in Iowa), Purvis Henson (probably born in Mississippi, though possibly in Texas), Freddie Jenkins (born in New York), Jack Johnson, Dennis McMillon, Scottie Nesbitt, Teddy Pendergrass (born in Pennsylvania), Danny Small, and George Washington (Bull City Red). Also excluded are some of the musicians Stanley Dance and Bruce Bastin mention as having performed with the Carolina Cotton Pickers because it has not been demonstrated that they were South Carolinians. Though the caption to a 1905 photograph of the Rabbit's Foot Minstrels baseball team identifies L. Adams (Columbia), Logan Littlejohn (Spartanburg), and Robert Prince (Bennetsville) as among its members, they have been omitted because no known evidence confirms that they were musicians.[2]

Some South Carolina musicians' siblings who were also musicians might be expected to be represented but are not because they do not qualify by birth or residency. Among them are Carl Martin (born in Virginia), half brother of Rowland; Francis Eugene Mikell, Jr. (born in Florida), brother of Otto; Red Prysock (born in North Carolina), brother of Arthur; and lyricist Ralph Freed (born in Vancouver, British Columbia, Canada), brother of Arthur.

Perhaps a dozen of the musicians who qualify as South Carolinians and who would have been treated are not. Five requested that they be omitted. One insisted on payment for his cooperation. Some musicians—or their representatives—were uncooperative or demanding beyond reason. One representative stated that attorneys would examine whatever was written about a certain musician. A few people refused to meet generous deadlines, despite reminders that they must be met. Without deadlines, the project could not have been completed.

As many South Carolina pre-jazz and pre-blues musicians as possible are included. *Pre-jazz* and *pre-blues* refer to nineteenth- and early twentieth-century music performed by brass bands and string bands, as well as that played in medicine and minstrel shows and vaudeville productions, all of which contributed to the musical potpourri from which jazz and blues emerged. Many of these musicians are identified by Lynn Abbott and Doug Seroff in *Out of Sight: The Rise of African American Popular Music, 1889–1895* (2002) and *Ragged but Right: Black Traveling Shows, "Coon Songs," and the Dark Pathway to Blues and Jazz* (2007). Some early musicians are mentioned in newspapers of interest primarily to blacks, including the *New York Age* (begun in 1887), the *Indianapolis Freeman* (1888), the *Chicago Defender* (1905), the *Pittsburgh Courier* (1907), and the *New York Amsterdam News* (1909). The *New York Clipper* (1853), which surveyed the broad entertainment industry, is a rich source of information. Bruce Bastin's *Crying for the Carolines* (1971) and especially *Red River Blues: The Blues Tradition in the Southeast* (1986) document bluesmen from the state. John Chilton's *A Jazz Nursery: The Story of the Jenkins' Orphanage Bands of Charleston, South Carolina* (1980) is the major source of information about musicians who played with the Jenkins Orphanage bands. This pamphlet is cited in entries for musicians about whom Chilton offers facts; in entries for those he merely names, he is not acknowledged. Even when next to nothing is known about them, orphanage musicians are included because they composed bands that were important, especially during the early decades of the twentieth century. Not only did they validate the vision and reward the commitment of the orphanage founders, Reverend Daniel Joseph Jenkins and his wife Lena, who wished to help poor black children become productive, self-sufficient citizens, but their music was so appealing that the bands traveled widely and were invited to perform at significant events, such as the inauguration of President Taft (1909) and the Anglo-American Exposition in London (1914); as a result they served as ambassadors for the orphanage and, by extension, Charleston and South Carolina. The bands were famous.

Almost all the musicians who could be identified as active before approximately 1960 are documented. There is selectivity to a degree with those who entered the scene later. Musicians who have recorded are usually included. Leaders are favored over sidemen and sidewomen, even though most jazz in particular would not have been played, let alone recorded, without the participation of accompanying musicians. Despite the importance of jazz educators, those who have not recorded are omitted. A musician's absence from this encyclopedia does not reflect a negative judgment about his or her music.

Jazz and blues are difficult to define, so much so that *The New Grove Dictionary of Jazz* (1994) required twenty-six double-columned, oversized pages to accommodate James Lincoln Collier's treatment of jazz and seven pages to characterize blues. In the first sentence of the blues essay, Paul Oliver and Barry Kernfeld state that no one definition of this music is possible; there is also no single definition of jazz. Rather than attempting to define these terms and apply the definitions to musicians to see if they qualify as performers of these musics, this volume considers as jazz and blues musicians those who are usually so regarded, as evidenced by their inclusion in publications devoted to jazz and blues. Because the term *blues* has evolved over time to incorporate musics known as rhythm and blues, doo-wop, and soul, musicians from these genres are included. Yet for reasons of space a line had to be drawn somewhere, and for this volume it is at gospel music, even though black religious music influenced both jazz and blues. Therefore this book does not document such important singers as Julius Cheeks (of the Sensational Nightingales) and Ira Tucker (of the Dixie Hummingbirds), both born in Spartanburg in the 1920s. Some individuals are treated, though, who were involved with jazz or blues but not primarily as musicians. These include dancers who improvised (Maceo Anderson, Peg Leg Bates, Charleston Brown, Snow Fisher, Aaron Palmer, and Prince Spencer), drum majors (Sunshine Anderson, Melvin Ellis, and Joseph Summers), lyricists (Arthur Freed and DuBose Heyward), record company owners (Hiram Johnson, Juggy Murray, Bobby Robinson, and Danny Robinson), and broadcasters (John Richbourg, Lloyd Smith, and Ray Smith), as well as a youthful conductor (John Garlington) and a nightclub proprietor (Ed Smalls).

Because locating birth and death dates of well-known figures may be done easily by consulting their entries in reference books and at online sites such as wikipedia.com, most people writing about them use the published dates in their own work. Unfortunately the dates—especially birth dates—are not always accurate, so errors are perpetuated. Some inaccuracies originate with the musicians themselves. During a 1987 interview the singer Arthur Prysock suggested that he was born in January 1929, the date recorded in every known source, including Leonard Feather's *Encyclopedia of Jazz in the Sixties.* He seemed to be about sixty, so his birth date was not questioned. It should have been. Prysock, Feather, and others were wrong, and acceptance of 1929 had consequences. The contents of *Jazz and Blues Musicians of South Carolina* were arranged chronologically according to musicians' birth dates, with Prysock placed between Etta Jones (presumably born in 1928, though possibly 1927) and Nappy Brown (October 1929). Yet after the book was published something seemed amiss. Because Prysock initially recorded in 1944 with the Buddy Johnson band, "They All Say I'm the Biggest Fool," his hit song from that session, was reviewed. After concluding that a fifteen-year-old would not likely have had such a mature, resonant baritone voice or have sung with a big-name band, his birth date was researched, and it was discovered that he was born in 1924. Obviously he misled people who wrote about him. He probably wanted to appear younger than he was so women, possibly thinking him available, would be inspired to hear him in live performance and buy his records. If he altered his age for commercial reasons, he was not the first entertainer to do so, nor would he be the last. Whatever his motivation, his ruse worked: 1929 became his accepted year of birth, including by writers for such respected newspapers as the *New York Times* and the *Independent* (London), who, in their obituaries of him, indicate that he was born then.

Research for this present book has tried to confirm every supposed fact about musicians' lives and careers, including birth and death dates, which was not easy. Wise but inconvenient South Carolina laws mandate that access to vital statistics records is subject to restrictions. Researchers must therefore rely on such unrestricted public documents as the census (available through 1940, with the exception of that for 1890, which was destroyed), draft registration cards, passport applications, ships' passenger lists, and the Social Security Death Index. Available at ancestry.com, these documents occasionally contain incorrect or conflicting information. When they do and it is impossible to determine when musicians were born or died, realities have been explained. These sources also contain presumed facts at odds with the beliefs of living musicians. When Joe Richardson was enumerated for the 1940 census, for example, his age was estimated as two years; yet he insists that he was born on 9 February 1940, two months before his family was enumerated. Surely his father, who provided the child's age, knew at least approximately when his son was born, though the enumerator might have entered the information incorrectly, recording two years rather than two months. In the Richardson entry both 1938 and 1940 are recorded as his possible birth year.

By providing correct birth and death dates, it was hoped that an example would be set for researchers involved in a project similar to this. One had already been set. Before the entries for this encyclopedia were completed, Bob Eagle and Eric S. LeBlanc's *Blues: A Regional Experience* (2013) was published.[3] When writing their book, begun in 1960, the authors used censuses through 1930, the Social Security Death Index, and other public documents to determine the birth and death dates of, mainly, black blues musicians born in the United States. For seemingly most musicians they identify the sources that helped them determine the dates. Because many of the documents they consulted were used for the encyclopedia, the same conclusions were usually reached, though not always. Eagle and LeBlanc offer precise birth dates for Baby Brooks, Bea Foote, and Lil McClintock, for example, while the dates for these musicians in the encyclopedia are less specific. (Possibly alone among published sources, their book records the correct birth date for Arthur Prysock.) Other researchers have drawn on these same documents when investigating their subjects, including Michael Gray for *Hand Me My Travelin' Shoes: In Search of Blind Willie McTell* and Tony Russell for *Country Music Originals: The Legends and the Lost* (both 2007), as well as Chuck Haddix for *Bird: The Life and Music of Charlie Parker* (2013).

Summaries of musicians' careers are based on information contained in such sources as scholarly books and essays, reliable jazz and blues encyclopedias, stories in jazz and blues periodicals, discographies, and newspaper articles, as well as in archives. Interviews with musicians were often helpful, though bassist Bill Crow cautions that "some jazz musicians entertain themselves by putting on the writers that interview them. As a result a number of articles in jazz magazines have carried phony historical items that were invented on the spur of the moment by the interviewees."[4] Generally reliable encyclopedias include but are not limited to the four volumes of Leonard Feather's *Encyclopedia of Jazz* (1955, 1960, 1966, 1976, the last written with Ira Gitler), Barry Kernfeld's *New Grove Dictionary of Jazz* (1994), and Feather and Gitler's *Biographical Encyclopedia of Jazz* (1999), plus Eagle and LeBlanc's *Blues: A Regional Experience,* though the last is not truly an encyclopedia because it contains mostly data, not articles.[5] Sheldon Harris's *Blues Who's Who: A Biographical Dictionary of Blues Singers* (1977) is a valuable resource. Despite the best efforts of these authors, their books contain errors and information of questionable accuracy, as is doubtless also the case with this book. Perfection is an ideal.

All entries use some version of this template:

Surname, Given Names (known as)
Instruments
Date of birth (place)–date of death (place)
S.C. residences: (years)
Text
Compositions
Recordings as Leader
Leaders Recorded With
Films
Awards
Website
References

When a heading does not apply to a musician it has been omitted. Entries are alphabetized according to performers' professional names but include the subjects' birth names when the professional names do not include birth surnames (Ironing Board Sam; Samuel Moore). These musicians' birth names are also listed alphabetically, with cross-references to the professional names (Moore, Samuel/*See* Ironing Board Sam). Names are treated mainly in the manner of Feather and Gitler's *Biographical Encyclopedia of Jazz,* as explained by Gitler on xv–xvi. When a musician is known by the complete first name, it is followed by the middle name, if any: Dixon, Ola Mae; when a musician is known by a diminutive or nickname, given and middle names appear within parentheses: Gillespie, Dizzy (John Birks); when a person is known by a middle name, the first name appears within parentheses: Simmons, (Samuel) Lonnie. When one is known by a professional name but also by an alternative professional name or alternative professional names, the alternative names follow the birth name within parentheses: Esquerita (Eskew Reeder; "Fabulash," "Magnificent Malochi," "S. Q."). When a musician is known primarily by birth name but has also been known by an alternative name or alternative names, the alternative names are placed within parentheses: Taggart, Joel Washington ("Blind Joel," "Blind Joe Donnell," "Blind Tim Russell," "Blind Jeremiah Taylor"). Norridge Mayhams presents a problem in this regard. Because he is identified as Norridge Mayhams on his early recordings, he is treated as such, though he is often named Norris the Troubadour on later ones.

Only individuals who wrote forty or more tunes (collaborators are not acknowledged) are identified as composers, with the exceptions of Theodore Bowman and Edmund Jenkins, who are special cases. In entries for musicians born before 1930 whose birth date is known but death date is not, a question mark appears in the space for the death date. This mark indicates that a performer is probably dead, though several such musicians were living as late as June 2015. In entries for people born after 1929 whose birth dates are known, the space for the death date is left blank for those who are not known to have died. In summaries of musicians' careers all state names are abbreviated, as is New York City (N.Y.C.).[6] Following career summaries a second paragraph is included when necessary to explain issues, especially concerning birth dates. For each category after the summaries the number of items is limited to fifty. Many of the musicians' compositions were identified at ascap.com and bmi.com, though the information at these sites is not always accurate, as is the case with the BMI listing for Joe Richardson. With recordings, single releases (78 or 45 r.p.m.) are indicated by placing titles within quotation marks; titles of albums (vinyl and CD) are italicized. When a musician recorded an album or albums and a single or singles in a calendar year, the album or albums are listed first. Albums of greatest hits and other collections are not accounted for unless they are part of a company's effort to release all or a substantial quantity of a musician's recordings, as Document Records does with blues musicians. The years recordings were made are specified; when they have not been determined release dates have been provided and noted. Films include those that were directed, though soundies, the equivalent of music videos made in the 1940s with minimal direction, are not accounted for, nor are videos of live performances. Under the heading "References," sources of useful information are identified. There are two kinds of references. Primary publications consist of writings entirely or mostly *by* the performers, including interviews; secondary publications, writings *about* the musicians. Other than referring to *The New Grove Dictionary of Jazz, Encyclopedia of the Blues, Blues Who's Who: A Biographical Dictionary of Blues Singers, Blues: A Regional Experience,* and *Jazz: New Orleans, 1885–1963: An Index to the Negro Musicians of New Orleans* in second paragraphs in the entries for, respectively, Bud Aiken, Gladys Bryant, Henry "Rufe" Johnson, Sylvia Mars, and Amos M. White, encyclopedias dealing specifically with jazz and blues musicians are not mentioned because readers of this book will likely already have consulted them. Such books have not been quoted. With only an exception or two, discographies are not cited. Discographical information may be found in Tom Lord's *Jazz Discography,* available electronically by subscription; in Leslie Fancourt and Bob McGrath's *The Blues Discography, 1943–1970* (2006); and in Robert Ford and Bob McGrath's *The Blues Discography [the Later Years], 1971–2000, a Selective Discography* (2011).

The musicians detailed in this encyclopedia range from the widely acclaimed (James Brown, Dizzy Gillespie) to the unknown (Columbus Williams, and many others). They include ones who helped create styles of music, including Piedmont blues (Willie Walker), bebop (Gillespie), soul (Brown), and funk (Fred Wesley), as well as the Motown sound (James Jamerson). Chris Smith and Theodore Bowman composed possibly the first song with "blues" in the title, "I've Got de Blues" (1901). Numerous big band musicians came from the state, including some, like Cat Anderson, who were wards of Jenkins Orphanage, probably the South Carolina institution responsible for the most jazz musicians, though what is now South Carolina State University also produced many, as has, more recently, the University of South Carolina. Broadcasting on WLAC (Nashville) in the 1950s, John Richbourg helped introduce rhythm and blues to a large audience. Gary Davis became important to the folk revival of the late 1950s and early 1960s. Chris Potter is one of the major jazz musicians of his generation. While these and other South Carolinians are significant figures, all the musicians identified in this book, including amateurs, warrant preservation in the written record. Alton Smith and Johnny Wilson are just two of the amateurs who inspired youngsters who became notable musicians, in their case Blood Ulmer. That is, the small state of South Carolina has produced an eclectic array of jazz and blues musicians, many of whom are herein documented.

NOTES

1. See, for example, *"Oh, What a Beautiful City": A Tribute to the Reverend Gary Davis (1896–1972) Gospel, Blues and Ragtime,* ed. Robert Tilling (Jersey, Channel Islands: Paul Mill Press, 1992); Warren W. Vaché, *Back Beats and Rim Shots: The Johnny Blowers Story* (Lanham, Md.: Scarecrow Press, 1997); Alyn Shipton, *Groovin' High: The Life of Dizzy Gillespie* (New York: Oxford University Press, 1999); Elijah Wald, *Josh White: Society Blues* (Amherst: University of Massachusetts Press, 2000); and R. J. Smith, *The One: The Life and Music of James Brown* (New York: Gotham Books, 2012); as well as Jack McCray, *Charleston Jazz* (Charleston, S.C.: Arcadia Publishing, 2007).
2. See Stanley Dance, *The World of Earl Hines* (New York: Scribner's, 1977), 263, and Bruce Bastin, "A Note on the Carolina Cotton Pickers," *Storyville* 95 (June–July 1981): 177–82. The photograph of the baseball team is reproduced in Lynn Abbott and Doug Seroff, *Ragged but Right: Black Traveling Shows, "Coon Songs," and the Dark Pathway to Blues and Jazz* (Jackson: University Press of Mississippi, 2007), 260.
3. After the entries were completed they were updated during the editorial process into June 2015 (the death of John Haynes and the Drink Small NEA award are the most recent events documented). No recording made after 2013 is included.
4. Bill Crow, *Jazz Anecdotes* (New York: Oxford University Press, 1990), 174. Crow's observation is confirmed by pianist Billy Taylor, who heard Charlie Parker providing incorrect information. Taylor "told of an afternoon visit that a journalist made to a club on the Street [52nd St.] where Parker was rehearsing his combo. Parker refused to answer his questions straight" (Peter Pullman, *Wail: The Life of Bud Powell* [N.p.: Peter Pullman, 2012], 402n1). Paul de Barros also confirms Crow's point: cornetist Jimmy McPartland "lied in jazz oral history interviews" about the suicide of his daughter (*Shall We Play That One Together? The Life and Art of Jazz Piano Legend Marian McPartland* [New York: St. Martin's, 2012], 245).
5. Because of space limitations or oversight, even some significant musicians are omitted from these books. Writing about South Carolinian Fud Livingston, for instance, Dick DuPage states that "it was surprising not to find his biographical sketch in Leonard Feather's 'Encyclopedia of Jazz'" ("Fud Livingston: A Triple Threat Man," *Record Research: The Magazine of Record Statistics and Information* 21 [January–February 1959], 3).
6. Throughout the text ampersands have been converted to *and* except in R&B, Q&A, and similar expressions; in such company and organization names as Faber & Faber and Rhythm & Blues Foundation; and in song titles—"C.C.&O. Blues" and "C.&N.W. Blues"—that include no spaces around the ampersand.

An Encyclopedia of South Carolina

Jazz & Blues Musicians

Acey, Johnny (John Acey Goudelock; "Johnny Chef")

Singer

3 September 1925 (probably Cherokee County, S.C., in or near Gaffney)–19 February 2009 (Macon, Ga.)

S.C. residence: Cherokee County, including Draytonville (probably 1925–at least until 1952)

During his S.C. years Goudelock sang with the Harmonizing Jubilee Singers. After settling in Jamaica, N.Y., in the 1950s, he worked as a cook for the N.Y.C. school system. As Johnny Acey he recorded off and on from 1958 to 1974 for such labels as Arrow, D.J.L., Falew (with his group, the Fingerpoppers), Fire (as Johnny Chef, a name indicating his profession), Fling, Smog City (with the Esquires Ltd.), and Stang. His recordings are included in compilations released by Charly, Funky Delicacies, and Past Perfect. Among his songwriting collaborators were Clarence L. Lewis, noted for having written "Ya Ya," and producer and record company owner Sylvia Robinson. He performed with the Rockaway Revue of Jamaica, N.Y., and with the Black Spectrum Theatre Company. Around 2004 he moved to Macon, Ga., where he died. He is buried in Georgia Veterans Memorial Cemetery, Milledgeville, Ga.

Johnny Acey; permission of Joanie G. Hunter

Acey was a half brother of harmonicaist Sharon Goudelock. Their surname is sometimes spelled Goudlock or Gowdlock. The spelling used in the singer's obituaries and on Acey's army enlistment form, as well as in the Social Security Death Index, which provides the birth date, has been adopted here. Sources identify Goudelock's birthplace as Gaffney, or near Gaffney, as do people who knew the singer. He was enumerated for the census on 11 April 1930 in Draytonville, about four miles from Gaffney. His obituary in the *Gaffney Ledger* states that he was born and reared in Cherokee County, which includes Gaffney and Draytonville. Though his daughter, Joanie G. Hunter, reported in a 2010 telephone conversation that he was born in Timber Ridge (York County), S.C., and was reared in Jonesville (Union County), S.C., this information has not been confirmed. When enlisting in the army on 1 December 1945 at Fort Benning, Ga., Goudelock indicated that he resided in Cherokee County, worked as a cook, and completed his education in grammar school; he attained the rank of TEC 5. He applied for a Social Security card in 1952 in S.C., where he presumably resided. Acey's recordings have been offered for sale on a CD-R as *My Home: The Complete Recordings!* Acey is sometimes confused with jazz pianist Johnny Acea.

Compositions

"Chicken Shack," "Christmas Keeps On Coming," "The Greatest Is You," "Hungry for Affection," "I Can't Stop Moving," "I'm Leaving," "It Wasn't Me," "I've Got the Blues," "Let's Make Love," "Love

Stay Away," "My Home," "Nobody's Woman," "Please Don't Go," "Say, Oh Yes," "Stay Away Love," "Tears," "This Town," "Watchman," "Why," "You," "You Walked Out," "You Went Too Far"

Recordings as Leader

"Be Fair to Me" (1958), "Our Love Is Over" (1958), "Please Don't Go" (1959), "Why" (1959), "Baby Please Come Back" (1962; as Johnny Chef), "Can't Stop Moving" (1962; as Johnny Chef), "I Go into Orbit" (1962), "What Am I Going to Do" (1962), "At the Same Time" (1963), "Don't Deceive Me" (1963), "The Greatest Is You" (1963; vocal and instrumental versions on different sides), "Stay Away Love" (1963; with the Fingerpoppers), "You Walked Out" (1963; with the Fingerpoppers), "Don't Deceive Me" (1964), "Forever More" (1968), "My Home" (1968), *My Home* (ca. 1968), "Christmas Keeps On Coming," two parts (1974; with the Esquires Ltd.)

References

SECONDARY: "John Acey Goudelock," *Macon (Ga.) Telegraph,* 24 February 2009, sec. A, p. 5 (obituary); "John Acey Goudelock," *Gaffney (S.C.) Ledger,* 25 February 2009, sec. A, p. 8 (obituary); Sir Shambling [John Ridley], "Johnny Acey," http://sirshambling.com/artists_2012/A/johnny_acey/index.php (2012; accessed 21 May 2014) (states incorrectly that Acey recorded with Wilhelmina Gray).

Aiken, Bud (Lucius Eugene)

Trombone, trumpet

Possibly 1896 (probably Charleston, S.C.)–21 August 1927

S.C. residence: Charleston (possibly 1896–late 1910s)

A ward of Jenkins Orphanage, Aiken played in its bands by approximately 1912 and performed with one of them in England in 1914. At the institution he helped teach Julius "Geechie" Fields to play the trombone. By the late 1910s he was a professional musician, touring with J. W. Brownlee's minstrel show and, ca. 1920, with the Florida Blossoms Company. During 1921 he was on the road with Fletcher Henderson, backing Ethel Waters. He played with Wilbur Sweatman's organization in the early 1920s, possibly touring with it in 1923. In 1924 he led the Jazz Syncopators, which broadcast over WHN in N.Y.C.

Aiken was the brother of trumpeter Gus Aiken; the surname is sometimes spelled Aitken. Some sources indicate that there were three Aiken brothers who were musicians—Augustus, Eugene, and Lucius. There were only two: Augustus (Gus) and Lucius Eugene (Bud). They were enumerated for the census with their parents and two sisters in Charleston on 11 June 1900. This document indicates that Lucius Aiken was born in S.C. in September 1896. The passenger list of the *Campania,* which transported him to England in May 1914, records his age as nineteen; the list of the *St. Louis,* which returned him to N.Y.C. in September 1914, indicates that he was born on 27 February 1896. John Chilton states that Aiken was born around 1900. Aiken registered twice for the draft during World War I. On one registration card, completed on an unspecified date in Orangeburg, S.C., he identified himself as Eugene Lucius, stated that he was born in Atlanta, Ga., on 5 September 1895, and noted that he was a musician traveling with J. W. Brownlee's minstrel show. The other card, completed in N.Y.C. on 12 September 1918, records his name as Lucius Eugene and birth date as 4 September 1897 (no birthplace is indicated); it also notes that he then worked as leader of the Jenkins Orphanage band. Aiken's death date is specified in the Gus Aiken entry in *The New Grove Dictionary of Jazz,* ed. Barry Kernfeld (New York: St. Martin's, 1994), 9.

Leaders Recorded With

Ethel Waters (1921), possibly Essie Whitman (1921), Perry Bradford (1923), Gulf Coast Seven (1923), Mary Jackson (1923), Ethel Ridley (1923), Wilbur Sweatman (1924), Louise Vant (1925)

References

SECONDARY: "Evening Post Radio Time-Table," *New York Evening Post,* 7 April 1924, p. 12; Richard Hadlock, *Jazz Masters of the Twenties* (New York: Macmillan, 1965), 196; John Chilton, *A Jazz Nursery: The Story of the Jenkins' Orphanage Bands of Charleston, South Carolina* (London: Bloomsbury Book Shop, 1980), 52; Garvin Bushell, as told to Mark Tucker, *Jazz from the Beginning* (Ann Arbor: University of Michigan Press, 1988), 28, 33, 38–39; Lynn Abbott and Doug Seroff, *Ragged but Right: Black Traveling Shows, "Coon Songs," and the Dark Pathway to Blues and Jazz* (Jackson: University Press of Mississippi, 2007), 302, 378; Mark Berresford, *That's Got 'Em! The Life and Music of Wilbur C. Sweatman* (Jackson: University Press of Mississippi, 2010), 139–40, 145.

Aiken, Gus (Augustus)

Trumpet

Late 1890s (probably Charleston, S.C.)–1 April 1973 (New York, N.Y.)

S.C. residence: Charleston (late 1890s–ca. 1920)

A ward of Jenkins Orphanage, Aiken was a member of its band that performed in *Uncle Tom's Cabin* in N.Y.C. (1913) and of another that played the next year at the Anglo-American Exposition in London. He influenced the style of Jabbo Smith, another ward. Upon leaving the institution by 1920, he played with the Florida Blossoms Company and the Tennessee Ten before touring with James P. Johnson, Arthur S. Ray, and Fletcher Henderson, the last backing Ethel Waters. He traveled to Cuba with Gonzell(e) White's organization in 1923 and in 1929 toured with a band affiliated with the Drake and Walker Company of black vaudevillians. Earl Hines admired Aiken's ability to produce a sound close to that of the human voice. As a sideman Aiken played on some notable recordings, including Louis Armstrong's "Mahogany Hall Stomp" (1936) and Buddy Johnson's "They All Say I'm the Biggest Fool" (1944). He led his own band from the 1940s into the 1960s, though it apparently never recorded; in the mid-1940s it played at the Penthouse in N.Y.C.

Aiken was the brother of musician Bud Aiken; the surname is sometimes spelled Aitken. Though every public document consulted relating to Gus Aiken uses the given name Augustus, some sources spell it Augustine. Documents record various dates for the trumpeter's birth. Conducted in Charleston on 11 June, the 1900 census indicates that he was born in July 1898. The passenger list of the *Campania,* which transported him to England in May 1914, identifies his age as seventeen; the list for the *St. Louis,* which returned him to N.Y.C. in September, notes that he was born on 26 July 1899 in Charleston. When Aiken sailed from Havana to N.Y.C. aboard the *Orizaba* in December 1923, for the passenger list he provided a birth date of 26 July 1900. The Social Security Death Index states that he was born on 26 July 1903. Any birth date after 11 June 1900 is incorrect because Aiken was enumerated that day for the census. This document specifies S.C. as his birthplace; the passenger list of the *Orizaba* records it as N.Y.C.

Leaders Recorded With

Eliza Christmas Lee (1921), Daisy Martin (1921), Lavinia Turner (1921), Ethel Waters (1921), Essie Whitman (1921), Perry Bradford (1923), Lena Wilson (1923), Mamie Smith (1924), Charlie Johnson (1925), Louise Vant (1925), Clara Smith (1927), Luis Russell (1931, 1934), Louis Armstrong (1935–1936), Sidney Bechet (1941), Roy Eldridge (1944), Buddy Johnson (1944), WNYC Festival (1949)

References

SECONDARY: Advertisement for Penthouse, *New York Post,* 28 June 1946, p. 43; Richard Hadlock, *Jazz Masters of the Twenties* (New York: Macmillan, 1965), 52, 196; Stanley Dance, *The World of Earl Hines* (New York: Scribner's, 1977), 22, 90; John Chilton, *A Jazz Nursery: The Story of the Jenkins' Orphanage Bands of Charleston, South Carolina* (London: Bloomsbury Book Shop, 1980), 14, 31, 52; Howard Rye, "Visiting Fireboys: The Jenkins' Orphanage Bands in Britain," *Storyville* 130 (1987): 137–43; Garvin Bushell, as told to Mark Tucker, *Jazz from the Beginning* (Ann Arbor: University of Michigan Press, 1988), passim; Chip Deffaa, *Voices of the Jazz Age: Profiles of Eight Vintage Jazzmen* (Urbana: University of Illinois Press, 1990), 193; Laurie Wright, "Pieces of the Jigsaw: Gus Aiken," in *Storyville 1996/7,* ed. Laurie Wright (Chigwell, Essex, England: L. Wright, 1997), 188–90; Lynn Abbott and Doug Seroff, *Ragged but Right: Black Traveling Shows, "Coon Songs," and the Dark Pathway to Blues and Jazz* (Jackson: University Press of Mississippi, 2007), 302, 378.

Aitken, Virgil

Trumpet

S.C. residence: Charleston (at least mid-1940s)

Apparently a ward of Jenkins Orphanage, Aitken played in its bands ca. 1945.

Aitken's surname might be spelled Aiken. This musician's relationship, if any, to Bud Aiken and Gus Aiken, whose surname is sometimes spelled Aitken, has not been determined.

Alberti, Bob (Robert Lewis)

Piano, organ, keyboards, arranger, conductor

1 December 1934 (Brooklyn, N.Y.)–

S.C. residences: Hilton Head (1993–2006), Bluffton (2006–)

Enamored of and adept at music from an early age, Alberti led a band in high school and studied with Teddy Wilson. He left school to become

Bob Alberti; photograph by Sally Stevens, permission of Bob Alberti

a professional musician, initially as pianist with Charlie Spivak, then with Louis Prima and Jerry Gray before joining Les Brown in Los Angeles. There he worked for ABC television for seven years before affiliating for twenty-three years with NBC, including as sometime pianist with the *Tonight Show* band. He became musical director for Bob Hope, a position he held for over two decades beginning in 1972; he served in similar capacity for various television programs. He was a personal conductor for such singers as Keely Smith and Kay Starr. Upon moving to S.C., Alberti became active on the local jazz scene and recorded as both leader and sideman.

Recordings as Leader

Pastels: Keyboard Interpretations by Bob Alberti (1987), *Nice 'n' Easy* (1995), *Everything I Love* (1997), *Christmas Favorites* (2001), *The Masters* (2002), *Solo* (2006)

Leaders Recorded With

Charlie Spivak (1952–1953), Les Brown (1972), Marcia Chastain (1992), Lynn Roberts (1995, 2001, 2009), Jim Belt (1998), Rose Bonanza (1998–1999), Penney Petersen (2001), Diane Linscott (2007)

Website

www.bobalberti.com (accessed 21 May 2014)

References

PRIMARY: Bob Alberti, *Up the Ladder and over the Top: Memoirs of a Hollywood Studio Musician* (Hilton Head, S.C.: privately published, 2003).

SECONDARY: Dick Mariotte, "Acclaimed Pianist Now Calls Island His Home," *Hilton Head (S.C.) News*, 3 November 1993, sec. B, p. 4.

Allen, Doris

Singer, drums

18 February 1940 (Windsor, S.C.)–28 November 2007 (Aiken, S.C.)

S.C. residences: Windsor (1940–1942), Montmorenci (1942–1967, 1984–2007), North Augusta (1967–1969)

Allen began singing professionally in 1967 with Leroy Lloyd and the Dukes, a band she later used on her recordings. She sang in a female vocal group while living in Conn. (1969–1984). After returning to S.C. she performed with various bands, including one led by Festus Williams, until retiring from music in 2005. She is buried in the Thankful Grove Baptist Church Cemetery, Windsor, S.C.

Compositions

"Candy from a Baby," "Hanging Heavy in My Mind," "Kiss Yourself for Me"

Recording as Leader

A Shell of a Woman: The Legendary Playground Sessions (1969, 1986; includes duets with Big John Hamilton)

Reference

SECONDARY: "Doris Allen," *Aiken (S.C.) Standard*, 2 December 2007, sec. A., p. 6 (obituary).

Allen's Brass Band

Beaufort, S.C.

Active by 1890 and presumably led by someone named Allen, this band was apparently formed to support the political activities of Robert Smalls, noted for liberating himself and others from slavery. It often led Smalls's Memorial Day march to the National Cemetery in Beaufort, where Smalls would speak. It participated in other parades, including one to celebrate S.C. troops departing for the Spanish-American War, as well as funeral processions. It initially played concert and military music, but, later, also jazz. Active into the 1950s, it performed in such cities as Augusta and Savannah, Ga.

References

SECONDARY: "The Stage," *Indianapolis Freeman: An Illustrated Colored Newspaper,* 20 December 1890, p. 6; Gerhard Spieler, "Brass Band Part of Beaufort Heritage," *Beaufort (S.C.) Gazette,* 16 April 1976, p. 7.

Allison, Mose John, Jr.

Piano, trumpet, singer, composer
11 November 1927 (Tippo, Miss.)–?
S.C. residence: Hilton Head (1999–?)

Allison began piano lessons at age five and wrote his first song while in grade school. In high school he played trumpet in the marching band and formed a group, the Feet Warmers. After serving in the army and attending the University of Mississippi, in 1950 he became a professional musician with the Nat Garner Trio, though he subsequently enrolled at Louisiana State University, from which he received a bachelor's degree in 1952. He toured with the Garner Trio (named for Nat Cole and Erroll Garner) before moving in 1956 to N.Y.C., where he played in lofts. He entered what might be called the big time when he affiliated that year with Al Cohn. The next year he formed a trio that played mainly blues, including some of his composing. He absorbed this form while growing up in Miss. With the trio he recorded for the initial time as leader; the resulting album, *Back Country Suite,* was so well received that other recordings quickly followed, and his reputation as pianist—then singer—soon became established. He recorded prolifically through the 1990s, mostly with major record labels: Prestige, Columbia, Atlantic, Elektra Musician, Blue Note, and Verve. Though he continued performing after moving to Hilton Head, he recorded little. His music has influenced the likes of John Mayall, Van Morrison, Bonnie Raitt, Pete Townshend, Bill Wyman, and the Yardbirds.

Compositions

"Ask Me Nice," "Autumn Song," "Back Down South," "Barefoot Dirt Road," "Blues," "City Home," "Creekbank," "Cuttin' Out," "Days Like This," "Devil in the Cane Field," "Don't Forget to Smile," "Ever Since I Stole the Blues," "Ever Since the World Ended," "Everybody Cryin' Mercy," "Feel So Good," "The Foolkiller," "Gimcracks and Gewgaws," "Hello There, Universe," "Hittin' on One," "How Does It Feel to Be Good Lookin'," "How Much Truth," "I Don't Worry 'bout a Thing," "If You Live," "If You're Goin' to the City," "I'm Alive," "I'm Not Talking," "It Didn't Turn Out That Way," "Jus' Like Livin'," "Kiddin' on the Square," "Let It Come Down," "Look Here," "Middle Class White Boy," "New Parchman," "Nightclub," "No Trouble Livin'," "One of These Days," "Parchman Farm," "Perfect Moment," "Puttin' Up with Me," "Saritha," "Swingin' Machine," "Tell Me Something," "Top Forty," "Transfiguration of Hiram Brown," "Western Man," "What's Your Movie," "Wild Man on the Loose," "Young Man," "Your Mind Is on Vacation," "Your Molecular Structure"

Recordings as Leader

Back Country Suite (1957), *Local Color* (1957), *Creek Bank* (1958), *Ramblin' with Mose* (1958), *Young Man Mose* (1958), *Autumn Song* (1959), *Transfiguration of Hiram Brown* (1959), *I Love the Life I Live* (1960), *V-8 Ford Blues* (1961), *I Don't Worry about a Thing* (1962), *Swingin' Machine* (1962), *The Word from Mose* (1964), *Mose Alive!* (1965), *Wild Man on the Loose* (1965), *I've Been Doin' Some Thinkin'* (1968), *Hello There, Universe* (1969), *Western Man* (1971), *Mose in Your Ear* (1972), *Your Mind Is on Vacation* (1976), *Pure Mose* (probably late 1970s), *Lessons in Living* (1982), *Middle Class White Boy* (1982), *Ever Since the World Ended* (1987), *My Backyard* (1989), *The Earth Wants You* (1993), *Gimcracks and Gewgaws* (1997), *Tell Me Something* (1997), *The Mose Chronicles—Live in London* (2000; two CDs), *The Way of the World* (2009)

Leaders Recorded With

Al Cohn–Bob Brookmeyer (1956), Al Cohn (1957), Stan Getz (1957), Al Cohn–Zoot Sims (1959–1961), Manhattan Jazz All-Stars (1959), David X. Young (1959)

Films

The Score (2001), *Mose Allison: Ever Since I Stole the Blues* (2005)

Awards

Long Island Music Hall of Fame (2006); Blues Marker, Mississippi Blues Trail, Tippo, Miss. (2012); National Endowment for the Arts Jazz Masters Award (2013)

Website

http://moseallison.com/ (accessed 21 May 2014)

References

PRIMARY: Dom Cerulli, "Mose Allison's Country-Style Jazz," *Down Beat* 25 (1 May 1958): 19, 41 (substantial comments by Allison); Mose Allison, "Speaking My Mind," *Crescendo* 4 (March 1966): 16 (though announced as an interview with Les Tomkins, no words by Tomkins are present); David W. Johnson, "Mose: The Allison Viewpoint," *Zoo World: The Music Magazine* 64 (1 August 1974): 33 (interview); Bob Ness, "Mose Allison," *Coda* 12 (April 1975): 6–7 (interview); Fred Truitt, "Mose Allison: Interview," *Cadence* 8 (September 1982): 11–15; Paul Zollo, "Legends of Songwriting: Mose Allison: Jazz Songs in Anti-time," *SongTalk: The Songwriters Newspaper,* Spring 1988, pp. 10, 23–24 (interview); Kevin B. Long, "Mose Allison Interview," *Cadence* 15 (December 1989): 5–10, 22; Richard Skelly, "Mose Allison: Forever a Free Spirit," *Goldmine* 266 (5 October 1990): 48, 50, 52, 152 (this issue is also designated volume 16, number 20) (interview); Wayne Enstice and Paul Rubin, *Jazz Spoken Here: Conversations with Twenty-Two Musicians* (Baton Rouge: Louisiana State University Press, 1992), 1–15.

SECONDARY: Neil Tesser, "An Interview with Mose Allison," *Chicago Reader,* 16 August 1974, pp. 8–10 (despite the title and the fact that the piece includes comments by Allison, this article is more a narrative by Tesser than an interview with Allison); Robert Palmer and Roberta Palmer, "Sounds," *Penthouse* 8 (February 1977): 40–42 (comments by Allison); John Detro, "Mose Allison: 'Backyard' Bluesman," *JazzTimes* 20 (June 1990): 9 (comments by Allison); Patti Jones, *One Man's Blues: The Life and Music of Mose Allison* (London: Quartet Books, 1995); Greg Cahill, "Sly Sage," *Northern California Bohemian,* http://www.metroactive.com/papers/sonoma/02.22.01/allison-0108.html (22–28 February 2001; accessed 21 May 2014) (comments by Allison).

Alston, Herbert A.

Trumpet

Ca. 1925 (N.Y. or S.C.)-?

S.C. residence: Charleston (by 1935-probably early 1940s)

A ward of Jenkins Orphanage, Alston performed in its bands ca. 1940. By 1945 he lived in Tampa, Fla., where he worked as a musician.

Conducted at the orphanage on 21 May, the 1940 census estimates Alston's age as fifteen, indicates that the musician lived in Charleston in 1935, records his middle initial, and names N.Y. as his state of birth. He is identified as a musician in the 1945 Florida census, which specifies S.C. as his birthplace. If he was the Herbert Alston who last resided in Moncks Corner, S.C., and died on 29 November 2005, then he was born on 26 April 1925, according to the Social Security Death Index.

Anderson, Alvin Lewis

See Anderson, Little Pink

Anderson, Buster (James)

Trombone

30 September 1915 (Georgetown, S.C.)-?

S.C. residences: Georgetown (1915-no later than late 1920s), Charleston (by late 1920s-probably after 1930)

A ward of Jenkins Orphanage, Anderson played in its bands in the late 1920s and performed with one of them in England in 1929.

The passenger list of the *Columbus,* which transported the orphanage band to Plymouth, England, in April 1929, records Anderson's age as fifteen. The list of the *Majestic,* which returned the group to N.Y.C. in June, specifies the musician's birth date and place.

References

SECONDARY: John Chilton, *A Jazz Nursery: The Story of the Jenkins' Orphanage Bands of Charleston, South Carolina* (London: Bloomsbury Book Shop, 1980), 39, 52; Howard Rye, "Visiting Fireboys: The Jenkins' Orphanage Bands in Britain," *Storyville* 130 (1987): 137–43.

Anderson, Cat (William Alonzo)

Trumpet

12 September 1916 (S.C., possibly Greenville)-30 April 1981 (Norwalk, Calif.)

S.C. residences: possibly Greenville (1916-1920), Charleston (1920-1932)

At age four Anderson was placed in Jenkins Orphanage, where he gained a degree of proficiency on several instruments. In the institution's bands he played trumpet, the instrument of his idol, Louis Armstrong. Beginning in 1929 he toured with orphanage bands along the Atlantic coast. He and other musicians left the institution in 1932 as struggling professionals, possibly returning there

Cat Anderson, Aquarium Club, N.Y.C., between 1946 and 1948; reproduced from the William P. Gottlieb Collection, Library of Congress, Music Division

when work was scarce. The next year they formed the Carolina Cotton Pickers. After leaving it in 1935 he played with several groups—including the Sunset Royals, in time led by Doc Wheeler, with which he blossomed—before joining Duke Ellington in 1944. He left this organization in 1947 to lead his own band and freelance, though he returned to Ellington three years later. Again he departed (in 1959) but reunited with Ellington for the last time in 1961. After leaving Ellington in 1971 Anderson settled in the Los Angeles area, where he gave music lessons and played with various groups. During the 1970s he toured Europe at least twice and lived in Paris for several months. He appears in the movie *Blazing Saddles* with the Count Basie band, though the music on the sound track was performed by studio musicians. Anderson is known primarily for playing high notes that added tonal color to Ellington's band but that struck some listeners as garish. Such playing may be heard on many recordings, including "El Gato," his feature with the band. His playing is typically more restrained on recordings with leaders other than Ellington, as well as on sessions he led.

California, Death Index, 1940–1997, records Anderson's birth date as 12 September 1916 and death date as 30 April 1981. It also notes that the trumpeter was born in S.C. to a woman surnamed Gardener and identifies his middle name as Alonzo. Evidence that he was born in Greenville, S.C., as numerous sources claim, is lacking. He appears to be absent from the 1920 census, though he was enumerated at the orphanage on 2 April 1930; this document estimates his age as thirteen. Sources indicate that he attended what is now South Carolina State University in the 1930s, but school records do not confirm this affiliation.

Compositions

"Blue Jean Beguine," "Do It Yourself," "El Gato," "A Gathering in a Clearing," "How about That Mess," "Mountain Air," "Night Train to Memphis," "On the Way Up," "Open Mike," "The Prowling Cat," "Swingin' the Cat," "Waiting for Duke"

Recordings as Leader

"Cat's Boogie" (1947), "For Jumpers Only" (1947), "I Gotta Go, Baby" (1947), "Swingin' the Cat" (1947), "Black-Eyed Blues" (1949), "Caruba" (1949), "Cat's in the Alley" (1949), "Home Town Stomp" (1949), *Cat Anderson Plays at 4 A.M.* (1958; also titled *Cat Anderson and the Ellington All-Stars* and *Ellingtonians in Paris*), *Cat on a Hot Tin Horn* (1958; also titled *Cat's in the Alley*), *A Flower Is a Lovesome Thing* (1959; also titled *Ellingtonia*), *A 'Chat' with Cat* (1964), *Cat Anderson, Claude Bolling and Co.* (1965), "I Cover the Waterfront" (1970), "Ramona" (1970), *Cat Speaks* (1977), *Cat Anderson Plays W. C. Handy* (1978), *Cat Anderson–François Guin and Les Four Bones* (1979), *Ellington Moods* (1979), *Old Folks* (1979)

Leaders Recorded With

Doc Wheeler (1941–1942), Duke Ellington (1944–1946, 1950–1959, 1961–1970), Lionel Hampton (1944, 1959, 1977–1979), Wynonie Harris (1948), Coronets (1951), Johnny Hodges (1956–1957, 1961, 1964, 1967), Mercer Ellington (1958–1959), Billy Strayhorn (1958), Tubby Hayes (1964), Lawrence Brown (1965), Earl Hines (1966), Paul Gonsalves (1970), Bobby Bryant (1971), Carmen McRae (1971–1972, 1979), Joe Williams (1971–1972), Gene Ammons (1972), Quincy Jones (1972, 1976), Charles Mingus (1972), *Newport in New York '72*, Diana Ross (1972), Bill Berry (1974, 1976), Louis Bellson (1975, 1977), Ernestine Anderson (1976), Benny Carter (1977, 1979), Swing Limited

Corporation (1978), Booty Wood (1978), Claude Bolling (1979), Georges Brassens (1979), Jazz Vagabonds (1979), Trumpet Kings (1979)

Film

Blazing Saddles (1974)

References

PRIMARY: Stanley Dance, *The World of Duke Ellington* (New York: Scribner's, 1970), 144–53 (substantial comments by Anderson); Cat Anderson, *The Cat Anderson Trumpet Method: A Systematic Approach to Playing High Notes* (Sherman Oaks, Calif.: Gwyn Publishing, 1973).

SECONDARY: Edward Kennedy Ellington, *Music Is My Mistress* (Garden City, N.Y.: Doubleday, 1973), 216; John Chilton, *A Jazz Nursery: The Story of the Jenkins' Orphanage Bands of Charleston, South Carolina* (London: Bloomsbury Book Shop, 1980), 24, 31, 33, 40–42, 44, 50, 52 (comments by Anderson); Bruce Bastin, "A Note on the Carolina Cotton Pickers," *Storyville* 95 (June–July 1981): 177–82; Eddie Lambert, "Cat Anderson," part 1, *Jazz Journal International* 35 (June 1982): 16–18; Eddie Lambert, "Cat Anderson," part 2, *Jazz Journal International* 35 (July 1982): 10–11; James Lincoln Collier, *Duke Ellington* (New York: Oxford University Press, 1987), passim; *The Duke Ellington Reader,* ed. Mark Tucker (New York: Oxford University Press, 1993), passim; Alexandre Rado, "Cat Anderson: The Musician and the Man," *The International Duke Ellington Music Society Bulletin* 4 (February 1995): 3–4, 8; Scott Yanow, *The Trumpet Kings: The Players Who Shaped the Sound of Jazz Trumpet* (San Francisco: Backbeat Books, 2001), 20–22.

Anderson, Charles

Ca. 1915–?
Trumpet
S.C. residence: Charleston (by late 1920s–early 1930s)

A ward of Jenkins Orphanage, Anderson played in its bands and later became a professional musician. In the 1930s he recorded with Boots and His Buddies, led by drummer Boots Douglas, as well as possibly with Earl Hines during the next decade.

Anderson's age was estimated as fifteen when the musician was enumerated for the census at the orphanage on 2 April 1930.

Leaders Recorded With

Boots and His Buddies (1935–1938), possibly Earl Hines (1947)

Anderson, Eugene

Drums
S.C. residence: Charleston (at least early 1900s)

Apparently a ward of Jenkins Orphanage, Anderson played in its bands ca. 1906. He probably became a professional musician, though he apparently never recorded. According to James P. Johnson, Anderson's "specialty was drumming on the wall" (27).

Reference

SECONDARY: Tom Davin, "Conversations with James P. Johnson," *Jazz Review* 2 (September 1959): 26–27.

Anderson, Kip

Singer, keyboards, broadcaster
Probably 24 January of 1938, but possibly of 1941 (Starr, S.C.)–29 August 2007 (Anderson, S.C.)
S.C. residences: Starr (1938 or 1941–1960s, ca. 1987–2007), Columbia (1960s, 1977–ca. 1987)

As a child Anderson sang in the Pleasant Grove Missionary Baptist Church in Iva. Discovered by the gospel singer Edna Gallmon Cooke, he toured with her during summers in the mid-1950s. Early in his recording career he affiliated with some small labels, including two he formed with Charles Derrick in the 1960s, Tomorrow and True-Spot; but he also recorded for major companies, such as Sharp, a subsidiary of Savoy, and Checker, a subsidiary of Chess. In the 1960s he worked as a disc jockey in Columbia, S.C., and then in Fayetteville, N.C. In the mid-1970s he began serving a ten-year sentence in the Central Correctional Institution in Columbia; there he and other prisoners formed a gospel quartet. When released he resumed his career as a disc jockey, became vice president of Electric City Records, and returned to recording, including some gospel songs released on his own Lorna label and an album with Nappy Brown. Most of his recordings might best be characterized as soul, or rhythm and blues. He is buried in the Pleasant Grove Missionary Baptist Church Cemetery, Iva.

Some sources record Anderson's birth year as 1938; others, as 1941. Though his name has been rendered Kipling Taquana Anderson, the 1940 census is the only public document located that records what might be his name, Thurmon K. Anderson. A two-year-old by this name was enumerated with his family on 12 April in Hall Township (which includes Iva and Starr), Anderson County. If Kip Anderson was born in the late 1930s, he was probably this person. If he was born after his family was enumerated, Thurmon was his brother.

Compositions

"Dog Don't Wear No Shoes," "Here Am I," "Here I Am, Try Me," "The Home Fires Are Brighter," "I Can't," "I Could'a Been Sleepin'," "I Done You Wrong," "I Feel Good," "If That Don't Make You Cry," "I'll Get Along," "I'm Gonna Cry," "I'm Out of Love," "I Wanna Be the Only One," "I Went Off and Cried," "I Will Cry," "A Knife and a Fork," "Oh My Linda," "Soul," "Stop These Tears," "Take It Like a Man," "Tell Her I Love Her," "That's When the Crying Begins," "Till Your Love Is Mine," "Wonderful," "You'll Lose a Good Thing"

Recordings as Leader

"The Home Fires Are Brighter" (1959), "I Wanna Be the Only One" (1959, 1966), "Oh My Linda" (1960), "Till Your Love Is Mine" (1960), "I Feel Good" (1962), "I Will Cry" (1962), "I Can't" (1964), "I Done You Wrong" (1964), "I'll Get Along" (1964), "That's When the Crying Begins" (1964), "Here I Am, Try Me" (1965), "If That Don't Make You Cry" (1965), "I Get Carried Away" (1965), "Tell Her I Love Her" (1965), "Woman, How Do You Make Me Love You?" (1965), "A Knife and a Fork" (1966), "Take It Like a Man" (1966), "Without a Woman" (1966), "I'm Out of Love" (1967), "You'll Lose a Good Thing" (1967), "Blue Moon" (1967 or 1968), "Unchained Melody" (1967 or 1968), "I Went Off and Cried" (1968), "Letter from My Darling" (1968), "That's All I Can Do" (1968), "Watch You Work It Out" (1968), *The Best of Kip Anderson and the Soul Aggregation* (ca. 1969), "Jesus Sings with Me," two parts (1989), "He Never Left Me Alone" (1991), "I Could'a Been Sleepin'" (1991), *A Dog Don't Wear No Shoes* (1992), *A Knife and a Fork* (1993), *Best of Both Worlds: 12 Rockin' Blues' [sic] Classics* (1996; with Nappy Brown), *The Doll and the White Roses* (2002 or 2003)

Leaders Recorded With

Al Browne (1963), Jimmy Brown (1967), Flashbacks (2001)

Award

Best Blues Album of the Year, Carolina Beach Music Awards (1997; for *Best of Both Worlds*, with Nappy Brown)

References

SECONDARY: Martin Goggin, "Kip Anderson: South Carolina Soulman," *Juke Blues* 52 (Winter 2002–2003): 46–51 (comments by Anderson); Charmaine Smith-Miles, "Musician Kip Anderson, an Anderson County Native, Dies," *Anderson (S.C.) Independent-Mail*, 29 August 2007, sec. A, pp. 1–2 (obituary); Mike Atherton, "Kip Anderson," *Blues and Rhythm: The Gospel Truth* 224 (November 2007): 12 (obituary); Opal Louis Nations, "The Charles Derrick Story: With Forays into the Careers of Kip Anderson, Drink Small and the Spiritualaires," *Blues and Rhythm: The Gospel Truth* 242 (September 2009): 16–20.

Anderson, Little Pink (Alvin Lewis)

Guitar, singer

13 July 1954 (Spartanburg, S.C.)-

S.C. residences: Spartanburg (1954-1972, 1979-1983, 1984-1994, 1996-2000, 2002, 2005-2006), Columbia (1972-1979), Enoree (1994-1995), Ridgeland (1995-1996)

Anderson was involved with music from infancy. Around age three he danced at fairs to the music of his father, Pink Anderson, and before turning ten played guitar with his father on a recording made by Samuel Charters. He grew up knowing Peg Leg Sam (Arthur Jackson), who had worked in

Little Pink Anderson, King Biscuit Blues & Gospel Festival, Helena, Ark., 10 October 2003; permission of the photographer, Gene Tomko

medicine shows with Pink Anderson. He dropped out of school in the eighth grade and toured with Clarence Carter before turning fifteen. Anderson was incarcerated from 1972 to 1979, and again in the mid-1990s. He quit playing in 1979 but resumed in 1997, performing at festivals, sometimes with Freddy Vanderford, who learned to play the harmonica from Peg Leg Sam. Often he performed tunes associated with his father. Anderson suffered a stroke in 2005. Though his roots are in S.C., he has lived in Tenn., Ga., N.C., Calif., N.J., D.C., and, since 2006, S.Dak.

Compositions

"I Just Want to Go," "Pain," "Sittin' Here Singing the Blues," "Willie Mae"

Recordings as Leader

Blues Legacy (1997; with Freddie Vanderford; privately issued), *Carolina Bluesman* (ca. 2001), *Sittin' Here Singing the Blues* (ca. 2005, ca. 2008), *Bagwell and Pink* (ca. 2010; with David Bagwell; privately issued), *Little Pink Live at the National Music Museum* (2011; privately issued)

Leaders Recorded With

Pink Anderson (1961 or 1962), Clarence Carter (1970s)

Website

http://littlepink.20m.com/ (accessed 21 May 2014)

References

SECONDARY: Peter Cooper, *Hub City Music Makers: One Southern Town's Popular Music Legacy* (Spartanburg, S.C.: Holocene, 1997), 44–63 (comments by Anderson); Linda Carron, "Alvin Anderson: Little Pink's Blues," *Living Blues* 137 (January–February 1998): 26–29 (comments by Anderson); Ray M. Stiles, "Blues on Stage: Alvin 'Little Pink' Anderson," www.mnblues.com/review/littlepink.html (1998; accessed 21 May 2014); Peter Cooper, "Little Pink Anderson," in *Music Makers: Portraits and Songs from the Roots of America*, ed. Timothy Duffy (Athens, Ga.: Hill Street Press, 2002), 17; Larry Benicewicz, "Little Pink Anderson: In His Father's Footsteps," www.bluesart.at/Neue Seiten/Little%20Pink%20Anderson.html (ca. 2006; accessed 21 May 2014); Steve Leggett, "Little Pink Anderson," www.allmusic.com/artist/little-pink-anderson-p724801/biography (undated; accessed 21 May 2014).

Anderson, Maceo E.

Dancer

Possibly 3 September 1910 (Fla., probably Lakeland, though conceivably Charleston, S.C.)–4 or 5 July 2001 (Los Angeles, Calif.)

S.C. residence: Charleston (by 1912–at least until 1924)

Anderson began dancing professionally with the act of Ida Mae Chadwick after moving to N.Y.C. from Charleston in the mid-1920s. He and two other young men soon formed a dance team that in 1927, with the addition of another dancer, became the Four Step Brothers, with which Anderson performed until it disbanded in the 1960s, other than when serving in the army in the 1940s. During its early years the group was associated with Duke Ellington, who composed "The Mystery Song" for the dancers. They were known for challenge dancing: one man danced while the others provided rhythmic accompaniment by clapping; each solo dancer tried to outdo the others. Concurrent with his involvement with the Four Step Brothers, Anderson operated a dance school in Los Angeles, beginning in the 1940s. He is buried in Palm Memorial Park Cemetery, Henderson, Nev.

The Social Security Death Index indicates that Anderson was born in 1909 and died on 4 July 2001. His grave marker, which identifies his birth date as 3 September 1910 and death date as 5 July 2001, includes the words "Watch your step, brother." When enumerated for the census in Charleston on 3 January 1920, his age was estimated as ten; in N.Y.C. on 22 April 1930, as eighteen; in N.Y.C. on 15 April 1940, as twenty-eight. When he enlisted in the army on 26 February 1943, he stated that he was born in 1910. The 1920 census indicates that he was born in S.C., though the other censuses and his military enlistment form state that he was born in Fla. His family was enumerated for the 1910 census in Lakeland, Fla., on 23 April. Because his name is absent from this document, he was born after this date. The Anderson family is documented in the Charleston city directory from 1912 to 1924.

Films (All with the Four Step Brothers)

Barber Shop Blues (1933), *When Johnny Comes Marching Home* (1942), *Hi, Buddy* (1943), *It Ain't Hay* (1943), *Rhythm of the Islands* (1943), *Greenwich Village* (1944), *That's My Gal* (1947), *Here Come the Girls* (1953), *The Patsy* (1964)

Awards

Hollywood Walk of Fame (1988; as member of the Four Step Brothers); Oklahoma City University's Living Treasure in American Dance Award (1993); Flo-Bert Award (1994)

References

PRIMARY: "Inquiring Photographer," *Chicago Defender,* 7 April 1965, p. 15 (daily edition) (Anderson answers the question, "What do you consider Chicago's biggest race problem?"); Rusty E. Frank, *Tap! The Greatest Tap Dance Stars and Their Stories, 1900–1955* (New York: William Morrow, 1990), 211–16 (mainly a narrative by Anderson).

SECONDARY: "Change Steps for Army," *New York Age,* 1 April 1944, p. 10; Jennifer Dunning, "Maceo Anderson, 90, Tap Dancer, Is Dead," *New York Times,* 14 July 2001, sec. A, p. 13 (obituary); Lewis Segal, "Maceo Anderson; Tap Dancer Who Broke Color Line," *Los Angeles Times,* 17 July 2001, sec. B. p. 11 (national edition) (obituary); Melba Huber, "Tappin' In: Maceo Anderson: From Cotton Boat to Cotton Club," http://www.melbasdance.com/MelbasTapColumns/tabid/64/articleType/ArticleView/articleId/97/Maceo-Anderson-From-Cotton-Boat-to-Cotton-Club.aspx (September 2001; accessed 21 May 2014) (comments by Anderson); Frank Cullen, *Vaudeville Old and New: An Encyclopedia of Variety Performers in America* (New York: Routledge, 2007), 1: 398–400.

Anderson, Pink (Pinkney)

Guitar, singer

Probably late 1900 (probably Waterloo Township, Laurens County, S.C.)–12 October 1974 (Spartanburg, S.C.)

S.C. residences: Waterloo Township, Laurens County (probably 1900–no later than 1909), Laurens Township, Laurens County (by 1909–1915 or 1916), Spartanburg (1915 or 1916–1974, with absences)

After learning the rudiments of guitar playing as a child, Anderson became adept after receiving instruction from Simmie Dooley in Spartanburg ca. 1916. Beginning in 1917, for almost three decades Anderson toured with W. R. Kerr's Indian Remedy Company, a medicine show headquartered in Spartanburg. With this organization he honed his skills as an entertainer. During these years on the road he was in Spartanburg sporadically. While there in the 1920s he teamed with Dooley, with whom he recorded four tunes in Atlanta at a session for Columbia (1928). Locally in the 1920s and 1930s Anderson also played in a string band. After Kerr went out of business in the mid-1940s, Anderson toured with other medicine shows. In 1950 he was recorded playing with one such show; this music was released on Riverside. Anderson became recognized in the early 1960s as a result of albums released on Bluesville, all recorded by Samuel Charters. This flurry of recording activity occurred during a national blues revival. The Englishman Syd Barrett used Pink and the first name of bluesman Floyd Council to name his band Pink Floyd, which became popular in the 1960s. Michael B. Smith considers Anderson "one of the king-pins of Palmetto blues" (27). Anderson, who suffered a stroke ca. 1964, is buried in Lincoln Memorial Gardens, Spartanburg.

Sources give conflicting information about Anderson's residences during the musician's formative years. Conducted in Waterloo Township, Laurens County, on 22 June, the 1900 census indicates that the Anderson family consisted of the parents and four children; Pink was not one of them, even though he would then have been four months old if what is thought to be his birth date (12 February 1900) is correct. When enumerated for the next census on 29 April 1910, the family resided in Laurens Township, Laurens County; Pink's age is recorded as ten. The earliest Spartanburg city directory that mentions the family of John and Evalina Anderson, including Pink, is that of 1916. Conducted on 12 January, the 1920 census indicates that the family of four, including Pink, then resided in Spartanburg and that he worked in a wood (lumber) yard; his age was estimated as nineteen.

Compositions

"Beat It to the Woods If You Can," "Cook Good Salad," "South Forest Boogie," "Travelin' Man"

Recordings as Leader

"C.C.&O. Blues" (1928; with Simmie Dooley), "Every Day in the Week Blues" (1928; with Simmie Dooley), "Gonna Tip Out Tonight" (1928; with Simmie Dooley), "Papa's 'Bout to Get Mad" (1928; with Simmie Dooley), *American Street Songs* (1950, with some songs by Gary Davis; also titled *Gospel, Blues and Street Songs*), *Ballad and Folksinger* (1961), *Carolina Blues Man* (1961), *Carolina Medicine Show Hokum and Blues* (1961–1962), *Medicine Show Man* (1961), "Old Cotton Fields of Home" (1961 or 1962; with Little Pink Anderson), "Weeping Willow

Blues" (1961 or 1962), "No Name Blues" (1972; unissued), "Stranger Blues" (1972; unissued)

Award

Spartanburg Music Trail Marker (2011)

References

SECONDARY: Bruce Bastin, *Crying for the Carolines* (London: Studio Vista, 1971), 79–82; "Pink Anderson," *Spartanburg (S.C.) Herald*, 16 October 1974, sec. B, p. 12 (obituary); "Pink Anderson," *Living Blues* 20 (March–April 1975): 57 (obituary); Bruce Bastin, "From the Medicine Show to the Stage: Some Influences upon the Development of a Blues Tradition in the Southeastern United States," *American Music* 2 (Spring 1984): 29–42; Bruce Bastin, *Red River Blues: The Blues Tradition in the Southeast* (Urbana: University of Illinois Press, 1986), 182–83; Peter Cooper, *Hub City Music Makers: One Southern Town's Popular Music Legacy* (Spartanburg, S.C.: Holocene, 1997), 44–63; Michael B. Smith, *Carolina Dreams: The Musical Legacy of Upstate South Carolina* (Beverly Hills, Calif.: Marshall Tucker Entertainment, 1997), 27–29, 171.

Anderson, Sunshine (James)

Drum major

S.C. residence: Charleston (possibly late 1920s–at least into early 1930s)

Apparently a ward of Jenkins Orphanage, Anderson was drum major for its bands ca. 1930.

Reference

SECONDARY: Bruce Bastin, "A Note on the Carolina Cotton Pickers," *Storyville* 95 (June–July 1981): 177–82.

Antrum, (Theodore) Roosevelt

Guitar, singer

Probably between 1903 and 1910 (probably Hodges, S.C.)–21 May 1948 (Charlotte, N.C.)

S.C. residence: probably Hodges (possibly as early as 1903, but no later than 1910–at least until 1920)

Antrum recorded four songs at a 1937 session in Charlotte, N.C. Bruce Bastin says that the "unknown guitarist" backing Antrum plays "remarkably like Blind Boy Fuller"; several sources indicate, without evidence, that Antrum was that guitarist. Bastin thinks that Antrum, who was no older than around age thirty-three when he recorded, "sounds to be an older singer" influenced by Fuller. He is buried in York Memorial Cemetery, Charlotte, N.C.

Antrum's age was estimated as six when the youth was enumerated for the census in Hodges on 29 April 1910; as thirteen when enumerated in Greenwood County in January (possibly the 24th) 1920. North Carolina, Deaths, 1931–1994, estimates that he was born in 1910. His surname is sometimes spelled Antrim.

Recordings as Leader (All 1937)

"Complaint to Make," "I Guess You're Satisfied," "No Use Worrying," "Station Boy Blues"

Reference

SECONDARY: Bruce Bastin, *Red River Blues: The Blues Tradition in the Southeast* (Urbana: University of Illinois Press, 1986), 198.

Arnold, John Henry ("Big Man," "Blind Man")

Guitar, singer

Possibly 19 May 1878 (Greenville County, S.C., possibly Dunklin Township)–4 March 1939 (Greenville, S.C.)

S.C. residences: Greenville County, including Dunklin Township, Greenville, and Greer (1878–no later than 1900, probably not before 1901–1939, with absences), Sullivan Township, Laurens County (at least 1900)

The blind Arnold was the first musician Josh White served as lead boy, or guide, and the meanest man White ever knew. A grocer in Greer at least in the 1910s, he was primarily a street musician who performed religious songs in Greenville and possibly elsewhere in S.C. In the early 1920s he traveled to Ga. and Fla.; in 1924 he was in Chicago. He was, according to White, a powerful singer but a poor guitarist. Despite making money from his music and conceivably other enterprises (White claimed that Arnold owned two racehorses in Greenville), Arnold sometimes slept in fields and was jailed for vagrancy. He is buried in the New Prospect Baptist Church Cemetery, Princeton, S.C.

Arnold's places of birth and death and death date come from his death certificate. His birth date is from his World War I draft registration card. When this card was completed on 12 September 1918, Arnold identified himself as a musician and grocer living in Greer; it indicates that he was blind in both eyes. He was enumerated for the 1880 census in Dunklin Township on 22 June. By the time of the 1900 census (21 June), he was a farm laborer living in Sullivan Township, near Princeton; this document indicates that he was born in May 1878. When enumerated in May 1910 he was again in Dunklin Township; a decade later (24 January 1920), he lived in Greenville.

References

SECONDARY: Avery S. Denham, "Preacher in Song," *Collier's* 118 (16 November 1946): 44, 72–73; Robert Shelton and Walter Raim, *The Josh White Song Book* (Chicago: Quadrangle Books, 1963), 16–19; Max Jones, "Josh White Looks Back 2," *Blues Unlimited* 56 (September 1968): 15–16; Bruce Bastin, *Red River Blues: The Blues Tradition in the Southeast* (Urbana: University of Illinois Press, 1986), 167–68; Elijah Wald, *Josh White: Society Blues* (Amherst: University of Massachusetts Press, 2000), 9–16, 18–19, 22, 302.

Arnold, Mac (McAlvin)

Bass, gas can and slide guitars, singer
30 June 1942 (Ware Place community, near Pelzer, S.C.)–
S.C. residences: Ware Place (1942–1946), Fork Shoals community, near Pelzer (1946–1956, 1990–), Greenville (1956–1964)

Influenced by church music during his youth, Arnold performed with Jay Floyd and the Shamrocks while attending Bryson High School in Fountain Inn, S.C.; James Brown occasionally played piano with the group. In the mid-1960s Arnold moved to Chicago, where he performed on bass with John Lee Hooker, A. C. Reed, Otis Spann, and Muddy Waters. After touring for a year with Waters, Arnold formed the Soul Invaders but left Chicago for Los Angeles in 1969. There he helped produce the television program *Soul Train* from 1971 until 1975. While still with *Soul Train* he became, in 1973, a freelance tape editor who worked until 1982 for such corporations as American Broadcasting Company and 20th Century Fox. For studios in Van Nuys, Calif., he edited audio tape from 1982 to 1989. Returning to S.C., he settled in the Fork Shoals community and drove distribution trucks for Belk department store until retiring in 2001. He returned to music in 2004. Since 2007 the Handlebar in Greenville has hosted the Mac Arnold Cornbread and Collard Greens Blues Festival. In 2010 he formed the I Can Do Anything Foundation to support music and the arts in public schools.

Compositions

"Ain't Sugar Coatin'," "Backbone and Gristle," "Blow till You Blow," "Brand New Chevrolet," "Buster," "Cackalacky Twang," "The Garden Song," "Gas Can Story," "Gitty Up," "Holdin' On to Lettin' Go," "I Believe," "I Can Do Anything," "I'm a Country Man," "I Refuse," "Lonely Scarecrow," "Love and Relations," "Mean to Me," "Swing My Way Back Home," "Things I Don't Need," "Too Much," "Tractor Song," "True to You," "U Dawg Gone Right," "Where I've Been," "Wrong"

Recordings as Leader

Nothin' to Prove (2005), "Get Me Back to the Country" (2005), *Backbone and Gristle* (2008), *Country Man* (2009), *Live at the Grey Eagle* (2010)

Leaders Recorded With (All 1966)

John Lee Hooker, Otis Spann, Muddy Waters

Film

Nothing to Prove: The Story of Mac Arnold's Return to the Blues (2009)

Mac Arnold, Pocono Blues Festival, Lake Harmony, Pa., 27 July 2007; permission of the photographer, Gene Tomko

Awards

Jean Laney Harris Folk Heritage Award (2006); honorary degree, University of South Carolina (2014)

Website

www.macarnold.com (accessed 21 May 2014)

References

PRIMARY: Michael Buffalo Smith, "Blues Comeback of the Year: Mac Arnold," http://www.swampland.com/articles/view/title: mac_arnold (July 2006; accessed 21 May 2014) (interview).

SECONDARY: Tim Holek, "Mac Arnold: Cornbread and Collard Greens," *Living Blues* 193 (December 2007): 18–25 (comments by Arnold); Brian S. Kelley, *Mac Arnold: Plate Full o' Blues* (N.p.: Blurb/Brian S. Kelley, 2009) (this book consists of Kelley's photographs of Arnold and Adam N. Kelley's introduction titled "The Greater Blues Experience: Mac Arnold and Plate Full o' Blues"); Robin Tolleson, "Overtones: Artist Mac Arnold Plays 'Feel Good' Blues," http://www.blueridgenow.com/article/20110429/ARTICLES/104291000?p=1&tc=pg (29 April 2011; accessed 21 May 2014) (comments by Arnold); Charmaine Smith-Miles, "The Mighty Mac: Mac Arnold Dishes on a Life Performing Blues Music," *Anderson (S.C.) Independent-Mail,* 4 May 2015, sec. A, pp. 3–4 (also available as "Mac Arnold Dishes on a Life Playing the Blues" at http://www.independentmail.com/news/0504-storytellermac_64595260 [accessed 10 May 2015]) (comments by Arnold).

Arnold, Vince

Violin

S.C. residence: Anderson (before and probably after 1895)

Arnold was valued so highly in 1895 that an anonymous writer mentioned him as a standard to which young black fiddlers could only aspire.

Reference

SECONDARY: "Disgraceful Mimicry—The Old and the Young Negro Compared," *Atlanta Voice of Missions by Way of the Cross,* August 1895, p. 2.

Asbury, Willie

Singer

Probably S.C.

S.C. residence: Orangeburg (by 1910–at least until 1913)

In 1910 Asbury toured with the Claflin University Student Singers as a humorist and dialect reader, and probably as a singer. He sang in and toured with the Claflin University Quintet, at least in 1913.

Reference

SECONDARY: "News of the Churches," *Nassau County Review* (Freeport, N.Y.), 15 July 1910, p. 1.

Ashford, Nick (Nickolas)

Composer, singer, percussion

4 May 1941 (probably Fairfield County, S.C.)–22 August 2011 (New York, N.Y.)

S.C. residence: probably Fairfield County (1941–probably early 1940s)

As an infant Ashford moved with his family from S.C. to Mich.; from there he located, as an adult, to N.Y.C., where he intended to become a dancer. At a Harlem church in 1964 he met seventeen-year-old Valerie Simpson, with whom he soon began writing songs, sometimes in collaboration with Josephine Armstead, including on "Let's Go Get Stoned," which became a hit for Ray Charles. As a result of their early work Ashford and Simpson affiliated with Motown Records in 1966. There they had their greatest writing success, composing songs popularized by Marvin Gaye and Tammi Terrell ("You're All I Need to Get By"), Gladys Knight ("Didn't You Know You'd Have to Cry

Nick Ashford; photograph by Timothy White, permission of Valerie Simpson

Sometime"), the Marvelettes ("Destination: Anywhere"), Smokey Robinson ("Who's Gonna Take the Blame"), Diana Ross ("Ain't No Mountain High Enough" and "Reach Out and Touch Somebody's Hand"), the Supremes ("Some Things You Never Get Used To"), and others. They also produced recordings for this company. The pair left Motown in 1973, contracted with Warner Brothers, and began singing as Ashford and Simpson. They married the next year. They gained greatest popularity as a vocal duo in the 1980s. All the while they continued writing songs for themselves and other performers. In 1996 they opened the Sugar Bar lounge in N.Y.C. Ashford and Simpson sing on the sound tracks of *Bad Boys* (1983), *Body Rock* (1984), *Gimme an "F"* (1984), *54* (1998), *Ghost World* (2001), and *The 40-Year-Old Virgin* (2005).

Ashford's birth and death dates come from the Social Security Death Index. All sources consulted indicate that Ashford was born in Fairfield, S.C. There is no such town, though the state has a Fairfield County.

Compositions

"Ain't No Mountain High Enough," "Ain't Nothing but a Maybe," "Ain't Nothing Like the Real Thing," "Anywhere," "Believe in Me," "Bend Me," "The Boss," "Bourgie, Bourgie," "California Soul," "Caretaker," "Clouds," "Cry Like a Baby," "Destination: Anywhere," "Destiny," "Didn't You Know You'd Have to Cry Sometime," "Drink the Wine," "Genius I," "Gimme Something Real," "I Don't Need No Doctor," "I'll Be There for You," "I'm Every Woman," "Is It Still Good to Ya," "It Came to Me," "It'll Come, It'll Come, It'll Come," "I Wanna Be Selfish," "Keep It Comin'," "The Landlord," "Let's Go Get Stoned," "Missing You," "My House," "Never Had It So Good," "One Step at a Time," "Over and Over," "Reach Out and Touch Somebody's Hand," "Release Me," "Remember Me," "Ride-O-Rocket," "Sell the House," "Shoe, Shoe Shine," "Solid," "Somebody Told a Lie," "Some Things You Never Get Used To," "So So Satisfied," "Surrender," "Taste of Bitter Love," "Tell It All," "Tried Tested and Found True," "Who's Gonna Take the Blame," "You're All I Need to Get By," "Your Precious Love"

Recordings as Leader (All with Valerie Simpson; These Are Release Dates, Not Necessarily Recording Dates)

Gimme Something Real (1973), *I Wanna Be Selfish* (1974), *Come as You Are* (1976), *Send It* (1977), *So So Satisfied* (1977), *Is It Still Good to Ya* (1978), *Stay Free* (1979), *A Musical Affair* (1980), *Performance* (1981), *Street Opera* (1982), *High Rise* (1983), *Real Love* (1986), *Love or Physical* (1989), *Been Found* (1996; with Maya Angelou), *The Real Thing* (2008)

Leaders Recorded With

Quincy Jones (1977–1978), Stu Gardner (1987)

Film

New Jack City (1991)

Awards (All with Valerie Simpson)

Christopher Brennan Award (1992); Rhythm & Blues Foundation Pioneer Award (1999); Songwriters Hall of Fame (2002)

References

PRIMARY: Nickolas Ashford and Valerie Simpson, *The Best of Ashford and Simpson* (Hialeah, Fla.: Columbia Pictures, 1977) (music and lyrics by Ashford); "Interview: Ashford and Simpson—Renowned Songwriting and Production Duo," http://claytonperry.com/2009/01/30/interview-ashford-simpson-renowned-songwriting-and-production-duo/ (2009; accessed 21 May 2014).

SECONDARY: Ben Sisario, "Nick Ashford, of Motown Writing Duo, Dies at 70," *New York Times,* 23 August 2011, sec. A, p. 23 (obituary); Fred Bronson, "Nick Ashford's Chart Legacy: From Diana Ross and Marvin Gaye to Method Man and Jessica Simpson," http://www.billboard.com/biz/articles/news/1173363/nick-ashfords-chart-legacy-from-diana-ross-and-marvin-gaye-to-method-man (24 August 2011; accessed 21 May 2014); Andy Greene, "Nick Ashford, Motown Hitmaker," *Rolling Stone* 1,139 (15 September 2011): 30 (obituary); Greg Kot, "Valerie Simpson on Nick Ashford: 'I'm Not Used to Him Not Being Here Yet,'" *Chicago Tribune,* 17 November 2011, arts and entertainment sec., p. 1.

Askew, Fleming or Flemming

Trumpet

Probably early 1920s, but possibly 1 May 1923 (S.C.)–21 February 1995

S.C. residences: Reaves Township, Marion County (conceivably early 1920s, but by 1930–no later than 1935), Charleston (by 1935–early 1940s)

A ward of Jenkins Orphanage, Askew played in its bands in the late 1930s and early 1940s. He served in the navy 1943–1946 and recorded at least once. Both of his compositions were copyrighted in 1950.

Askew's age was estimated as five when he was enumerated for the census in Reaves Township, Marion County, on 26 April 1930. At estimated age eighteen he was enumerated for the 1940 census at the orphanage on 21 May; this document notes that in 1935 he lived in Charleston. Both censuses state that he was born in S.C. and spell his given name Flemming; all other sources consulted spell it Fleming. Both the Social Security Death Index and Department of Veterans Affairs BIRLS Death File, 1850–2010, specify his birth date as 1 May 1923 and record his death date. He last resided in Richmond, Va.

Compositions

"Bullfrog Hump," "A Woman Is Never Satisfied"

Leader Recorded With

Ray Charles (1950)

Reference

SECONDARY: John Chilton, *A Jazz Nursery: The Story of the Jenkins' Orphanage Bands of Charleston, South Carolina* (London: Bloomsbury Book Shop, 1980), 52.

B

Barbour, Lee David

Guitar

19 January 1977 (Davenport, Iowa)–

S.C. residences: Summerville (1982–1993, 2001–2002), North Myrtle Beach (1993–1996), Columbia (1996–2001), Charleston (2002–)

Though he began piano lessons at age seven, Barbour became seriously interested in music at fifteen, when he started playing the guitar. After being graduated from Green Sea–Floyds High School in Green Sea, S.C. (1995), he attended the University of South Carolina, from which he received a bachelor's degree in jazz performance (2001). He served as adjunct professor of jazz guitar at the College of Charleston (2002–2006) and taught at the New York City Guitar School (2008–2009). In addition to playing with local groups such as Gradual Lean, he toured with Cary Ann Hearst, headed the group Caravan (which played primarily gypsy music), and co-led Illuminati Outro. He teaches guitar, is active on the Charleston music scene, and promotes such new projects as Post-cobra and Barbour + Kaler + Jenkins.

Compositions

"Ape Naked," "Black Forest Waltz," "Black Lipstick," "Blues for America," "Café Lullaby," "Expectation 2," "4 Times 1," "Guinevere," "Miles from Michelle," "Mindful of a Memory," "Monolith," "A Night in Samois," "Q's Blues," "Rebekah," "Rememory," "Return of the Lean," "Samba de Nenge," "Scarlet Circle," "White Devil," "Wolf Blitzer"

Recordings as Leader

A Night in Samois (2004; by Caravan), *Live at the Simons Center* (2006; by Illuminati Outro), *Songs*

Lee Barbour; photograph by Reese Moore, permission of Lee Barbour

for Singing (2006–2007; with Joe Beck), *Nonfiction* (2010–2011)

Website

http://leebarbour.com/ (accessed 21 May 2014)

References

PRIMARY: Erica Jackson Curran, "String Theorist," *Charleston* 28 (April 2014): 60 (also available at http://charlestonmag.com/features/string_theorist [accessed 21 May 2014]) (interview).

SECONDARY: Catherine Brennan, "Unlikely Bedfellows: Local Jazz Meets Digital Media," *Charleston (S.C.) Post and Courier,* 24 April 2003, sec. F, p. 19 (comments by Barbour); Jack McCray, "Barbour Makes Music the Focus for This Show," *Charleston (S.C.) Post and Courier,* 15 April 2004, sec. F, p. 9 (comments by Barbour); Jack McCray, "Barbour Mastering the Genres," *Charleston (S.C.) Post and Courier,* 10 March 2005, sec. F, p. 7; Jack McCray, "Gypsy Swing Keeps 'Caravan' Grooving," *Charleston (S.C.) Post and Courier,* 21 December 2006, sec. E, p. 4 (comments by Barbour); T. Ballard Lesemann, "Lee Barbour Makes a Wild Statement," http://www.charlestoncitypaper.com/charleston/lee-barbour-makes-a-wild-statement/Content?oid=4016949 (15 February 2012; accessed 21 May 2014).

Bash, Walter

Alto horn, saxophone

1910 (Cordesville, S.C.)-before 1980

S.C. residences: Cordesville (1910-no later than 1919), Charleston (by 1919-1932)

A ward of Jenkins Orphanage beginning in 1919, Bash played in its bands from ca. 1926 into 1932, even though he had been discharged from the school in 1930. He toured with the bands from 1928 into 1930, performed with the institution's quartet in N.Y.C. in 1928, and played with the Carolina Cotton Pickers during the 1930s. Ultimately he resided in Baltimore, Md.

John Chilton, who provides Bash's place and year of birth, indicates that Bash had died by the time Chilton completed his manuscript. It has not been determined if the Walter Bash enumerated for the 1940 census in Baltimore at estimated age thirty-eight was the musician.

Leader Recorded With

Carolina Cotton Pickers (1936–1937)

References

SECONDARY: "Colored Military Men Get Together at Large Banquet," *New York Age,* 14 April 1928, p. 10; John Chilton, *A Jazz Nursery: The Story of the Jenkins' Orphanage Bands of Charleston, South Carolina* (London: Bloomsbury Book Shop, 1980), 41, 52; Bruce Bastin, "A Note on the Carolina Cotton Pickers," *Storyville* 95 (June–July 1981): 177–82.

Bates, Peg Leg (Clayton)

Dancer, singer

11 October 1907 (Fountain Inn, S.C.)-6 December 1998 (Simpsonville, S.C.)

S.C. residences: Fountain Inn (1907-ca. 1910), Fairview Township, Greenville County (ca. 1910-at least until 1920)

Possibly as early as age five Bates danced in establishments and on the streets, generating money for his family. A mill accident in the late 1910s mangled his left leg, which was amputated below the knee. Outfitted with a wooden leg, he resumed dancing within two years. By age fifteen he was a professional, touring with minstrel shows, then carnivals, before performing in vaudeville. In the mid-1920s he joined the Dashing Dinah Company of Eddie Leonard, a soft-shoe dancer. With this group Bates traveled to N.Y.C., where he was discovered by impresario Lew Leslie, who cast him in *Blackbirds of 1928,* a revue that ran for several months in Paris. Back in the United States he resumed touring and ultimately established himself in N.Y.C., where he performed in notable venues, including important theaters and Harlem clubs, including the Cotton Club. He danced in Australia in 1938 and, subsequently, with major jazz bands, such as those led by Duke Ellington and Count Basie. He was with *Atlantic City Follies of 1945* and *Bronze Follies of 1946.* Bates was especially active in 1949, when he performed in Ken Murray's revue *Blackouts,* appeared on television for the initial time, and became a charter member of the Copasetics, an organization of mostly musicians dedicated to preserving the memory of Bill "Bojangles" Robinson. He went on to perform on television with some frequency, including over twenty times on a popular program hosted by Ed Sullivan. In the early 1950s in Kerhonkson, N.Y., he opened the Peg Leg Bates Country Club, which attracted a black clientele; with this enterprise he possibly became the first black resort owner in the United States. He was active in Ulster County, N.Y., civic life and ca. 1960 was president of Buster Entertainment Enterprise.

He was responsible for some of the dance steps of the vocal group the Temptations. Bates performed in *Tappin' Uptown* in 1982 and *The Joint Is Jumpin'* in 1995. In a performance of "Come Sunday" at the 2005 New York City Tap Festival, Jason Samuels Smith honored Bates by dancing with one leg stiff. Maurie Orodenker characterizes Bates as "a solid show-stopper with his monopod stepology, particularly when going into his acro bits." Honored in his hometown of Fountain Inn on 5 December 1998, he died the next day. He is buried in Palentown Cemetery, Rochester, Ulster County, N.Y.

Some sources incorrectly record Bates's death date as 8 December 1998.

Film

The Dancing Man: Peg Leg Bates (1991)

Awards

Human Relations Award of Radio Station WGHQ (1964); Flo-Bert Award (1991); Order of the Palmetto (1998); International Tap Dance Hall of Fame (2005); N.Y. Route 209 from Spring Glen to Ulster is named the Clayton "Peg Leg" Bates Memorial Highway; a life-sized statue of Bates is located in Fountain Inn.

References

PRIMARY: "The Talk of the Town," *New Yorker* 19 (20 November 1943): 17–21 (substantial comments by Bates); Rusty E. Frank, *Tap! The Greatest Tap Dance Stars and Their Stories, 1900–1955* (New York: William Morrow, 1990), 46–51 (mainly a narrative by Bates).

SECONDARY: Maurie Orodenker, "Shangri-La, Philadelphia," *Billboard* 57 (29 December 1945): 34; "Peg Leg Bates to Open Resort; Closes $50,000 Catskill Deal," *New York Age*, 1 November 1952, p. 32; C[aroline] S. C[oleman], "Peg Leg Bates," in *History of Fountain Inn*, comp. Caroline S. Coleman and B. C. Givens (Fountain Inn: Tribune-Times, ca. 1965), 60–62; James Haskins, *Black Dance in America: A History through Its People* (New York: HarperCollins, 1990), 87–89; Aïda Rogers, "Survival of the Greatest: Tap Dancer Peg Leg Bates Took His Place among the Very Best," *Sandlapper: The Magazine of South Carolina* 1 (January–February 1990): 57–59; Anthony Slide, *The Encyclopedia of Vaudeville* (Westport, Conn.: Greenwood, 1994), 27; Jacqui Malone, *Steppin' on the Blues: The Visible Rhythms of African American Dance* (Urbana: University of Illinois Press, 1996), 122; Vanita Washington, "Dance Legend Dies Hours after State Honors Him," *Greenville (S.C.) News*, 7 December 1998, sec. A, pp. 1, 4; "'Peg Leg' Bates, Entertainer, Was 91," *Greenville (S.C.) News*, 8 December 1998, sec. B, p. 4 (obituary); "Peg Leg Bates, One-Legged Dancer, Dies at 91," *New York Times*, 8 December 1998, sec. B, p. 10 (obituary); Frank Cullen, *Vaudeville Old and New: An Encyclopedia of Variety Performers in America* (New York: Routledge, 2007), 1: 80–81; Constance Valis Hill, *Tap Dancing America: A Cultural History* (New York: Oxford University Press, 2010), 164–68, 186–87.

Baxter, Quentin E.

Drums

28 August 1971 (Charleston, S.C.)-

S.C. residences: Charleston (1971-1989, 1992-), Columbia (1989-1992)

Baxter began playing percussion instruments around age five and, through high school, followed his parents' example by performing on drums at the Mount Zion Fire Baptized Holiness Church

Quentin Baxter; photograph by Reese Moore, permission of Quentin Baxter

in Charleston Heights. He also played in school bands. After studying pharmacy at the University of South Carolina (1989–1992), he received a degree in music theory and composition from the College of Charleston (1998), where he is an adjunct professor. He plays in Charleston with the group Gradual Lean and leads the group Emanon; also there in 2012 he helped establish the club the Mezz. Baxter, who has performed internationally, is also a recording engineer.

Composition

"Brother Blake"

Recording as Leader

The New Foundation (2013; with Marcus Amaker)

Leaders Recorded With

Teddy Adams (2000, 2002), Frank Duvall (2000), Savannah Jazz Orchestra (2000), Robert Lewis (2002), Monty Alexander (2003), René Marie (2004, 2006, 2010–2011, 2013), Junko Takeo (2006), Duda Lucena (2008), *Seeking: A Concert Dedicated to the Painting "Seeking"* (2008), Lee Barbour (2010), Charleston Jazz Initiative Legends Band (2010), Mark Sterbank (2010–2011, 2013), Charlton Singleton (2013)

Films

Brass Tacks (2004), *Song of Pumpkin Brown* (2007)

Award

Eddie Ganaway Distinguished Alumni Award, College of Charleston (2008)

Website

baxtermusic.com and quentinbaxter.com (accessed 21 May 2014)

References

SECONDARY: Clay Barbour, "Quentin Baxter: Jazz Drummer, Composer, Instructor Plays Every Beat," *Charleston (S.C.) Post and Courier,* 16 February 2002, sec. F, pp. 1, 3; Brittany McKeithan, "Touring the World to the Beat of His Own Drum," http://harwoodp.people.cofc.edu/facfocus/Faculty_Articles/BaxterArticle.htm (2005; accessed 21 May 2014); T. Ballard Lesemann, "The Baxter Factor," *Charleston (S.C.) City Paper,* http://www.charlestoncitypaper.com/charleston/feature-story-zwnj-the-baxter-factor/Content?oid=1107259 (15 November 2006; accessed 21 May 2014) (comments by Baxter); Jack McCray, *Charleston Jazz* (Charleston, S.C.: Arcadia Publishing, 2007), 111, 116, 127.

Beckum, Jimmy (Bernard James; "Big Jim")

Singer

22 February 1930 (Privateer, S.C.)–9 February 2001 (Columbia, S.C.)

S.C. residences: Privateer (1930–no later than ca. 1940), Sumter (possibly mid-1970s–2001)

At an undetermined date probably in the 1930s Beckum left S.C. for N.Y.C., where he received his schooling. In the mid-1940s he joined the Brooklyn Crusaders, a gospel quintet that briefly performed as the Varieteers before dissolving. He then sang with the Drifters (not the famous group of this name that recorded for Atlantic Records). The Drifters became the Majors, for which Beckum sang lead, as he did with the Schemers, which he joined in 1954 after the Majors disbanded. He is best known as one of the Harptones, a doo-wop/rhythm-and-blues group with which he performed in 1955–1956, 1961, 1964, and 1970–1972. He sings lead on the Harptones' recordings of "I've Got a Notion," "You Know You're Doing Me Wrong," and "You're Going to Need My Help Someday" and shares the lead with Willie Winfield on "Sunset." The group's recording of "Life Is but a Dream," with Beckum, is on the sound track of *Goodfellas* (1990). Upon returning to S.C. he sang in the choir at the Mulberry Baptist Church, Sumter, and for many years hosted radio programs in Sumter, including *Gospel View Caravan* on WQMC, the station of Morris College. Beckum is buried in the cemetery of his church.

Beckum's birth and death dates come from his obituary. The Beckum entry at http://www.findagrave.com/cgi-bin/fg.cgi?page=gr&GSln=beckum&GSfn=bernard&GSbyrel=all&GSdy=2001&GSdyrel=in&GSob=n&GRid=15909683&df=all& records an incorrect death date (accessed 21 May 2014). A claim that Beckum's Drifters sang on the radio program *Arthur Godfrey's Talent Scouts* has not been confirmed, though a group of white singers named the Drifters appeared on it in 1953.

Compositions

"Come On Up to My Room," "You Ran Away with My Heart" (also titled "You Ran Away from My Heart")

Leaders Recorded With

Majors (1951), Brownie McGhee (1951; with the Majors), Harptones (1955, 1961, 1964), Peggy Farmer (ca. 1955; with the Harptones), Ruth McFadden (1956; with the Harptones)

Award

Vocal Group Hall of Fame (2002; as member of the Harptones)

References

SECONDARY: Phil Groia, "The Majors," *Bim Bam Boom: The Magazine Devoted to the History of Rhythm and Blues* 1 (February–March 1972): 33 (comments by Beckum); James A. McGowan, *Hear Today! Here to Stay!* (Saint Petersburg, Fla.: Sixth House, 1983), 8–9, 63–65; "Bernard J. Beckum," *Sumter (S.C.) Item*, 13 February 2001, sec. A, p. 11 (obituary); Marv Goldberg, "The Harptones," http://www.uncamarvy.com/Harptones/harptones.html (2009; accessed 21 May 2014); Marv Goldberg, "The Majors," http://www.uncamarvy.com/Majors/majors.html (2009; accessed 21 May 2014) (comments by Beckum); Jason Ankeny, "The Harptones," http://www.allmusic.com/artist/the-harptones-mn0000076322 (undated; accessed 21 May 2014); "The Four Fellows," http://soldierboy.50megs.com/McGowan/fourfellows.htm (undated; accessed 21 May 2014); Opal Louis Nations, "Harptones Group Biography," ed. R. J. Cita, http://www.theoriginal-harptones.com/frameset.htm (undated; accessed 21 May 2014); Jay Warner, "The Harptones," http://www.vocalhalloffame.com/inductees/the_harptones.html (undated; accessed 21 May 2014).

Belden, Bob (James Robert)

Saxophone, piano, arranger, producer
31 October 1956 (Evanston, Ill.)–
S.C. residence: Goose Creek (late 1950s–probably 1973)

Reared in Goose Creek, Belden was graduated from what is now the University of North Texas in 1978, at which time he became a professional musician, initially with the band of Woody Herman. After playing with Donald Byrd in the early and mid-1980s, he performed with Mel Lewis and wrote music for movies. As leader and sideman he recorded for Blue Note in the 1990s. Also that decade he established the group Animation, which, with shifting personnel, continues performing, though it was largely inactive during the first years of the new century. On *Black Dahlia,* inspired by James Ellroy's novel of this title and possibly his major recording, he is backed by an orchestra of over sixty pieces, including such soloists as Lawrence Feldman, Tim Hagans, and Joe Lovano. He recorded albums of tunes written by the Beatles, Carole King, Prince, and Sting; this tendency to refashion familiar music led to his adding Indian and Spanish elements to compositions by Miles Davis. For Columbia he produced many releases, including Davis's *The Complete Bitches Brew Sessions* (1998), *The Cellar Door Sessions 1970* (2005), and *The Complete On the Corner Sessions* (2007), as well as reissues of individual albums, such as Herbie Hancock's *Sextant* (1998). In February 2015 Belden and Animation became the first American musicians to perform in Iran since its 1979 revolution.

Compositions

"Black Dahlia," "Call It What You Want To," "City of Angels," "Danza d'Amore," "Déjà Vu," "Elegy," "Genesis," "One for Dee Dee," "101 North," "Rites of Passage," "Tale of Two Souls," "Transparent Heart," "The Treasure," "Treasure Island," "Zanzibar"

Recordings as Leader

Treasure Island (1989), *La Cigale* (1990), *Straight to My Heart: The Music of Sting* (1991), *Prince Jazz* (1992), *Puccini's Turandot* (1992), *When Doves Cry: The Music of Prince* (1993; also titled *Purple Rain*), *Shades of Blue* (1994), *Shades of Red* (1994–1995), *Strawberry Fields* (1996), *Tapestry* (1997), "Blue Xmas" (1997; with Bob Dorough), *Re-animation Live!* (1999; with Tim Hagans), *Black Dahlia* (2000), *Agemo* (2006; remix of *Asiento*), *Asiento* (2006; by Animation), *Three Days of Rain* (2006), *Miles from India: A Celebration of the Music of Miles Davis* (2008), *Miles Español: New Sketches of Spain* (2011), *Transparent Heart* (2011)

Leaders Recorded With

North Texas State University Lab Band (1978), Woody Herman (1979), Paul Guerrero (1980), Glenn Wilson (1987), Red Rodney (1989–1990), McCoy Tyner (1992), Tim Hagans (1994, 1998), Denise Jannah (1994), Joey Calderazzo (1995), Herbie Hancock (1996), Joe Henderson (1996), Paquito d'Rivera (1998), Gary Smulyan (1999), Philip Bailey (2001), Classical Jazz Quartet (2002), James Moody (2003), Nicholas Payton (2005)

Film

Miles Electric: A Different Kind of Blue (2004)

Awards

Grammy Awards for best album notes and best production of a historical album (1996; for Miles Davis and Gil Evans, *The Complete Columbia Studio Recordings*); Grammy Award for best album notes (1998; for Miles Davis, *Quintet, 1965–'68*); Distinguished Alumnus Award, University of North Texas (2007)

References

PRIMARY: Bill Milkowski, "From Puccini to Prince: Bob Belden," *Down Beat* 61 (1 December 1994): 38–41 (interview); Robin Tolleson, "Bob Belden: Jazz Meets Pop," *Mix: Professional Audio and Music Production*, http://mixonline.com/mag/audio_bob_belden_jazz/ (1999; accessed 21 May 2014) (interview); Bill Milkowski, "Bob Belden: Riddle Me This," *JazzTimes* 30 (December 2000): 56–61 (substantial comments by Belden); Bob Belden, "Marchel Ivery (9.13.38–10.30.07)," *JazzTimes* 38 (March 2008): 42 (also available at http://issue.jazztimes.com/articles/25517-marchel-ivery-9-13-38-10-30-07 [accessed 21 May 2014]); Bob Belden, "Top Five Neglected Jazz Masterpieces," http://www.npr.org/2008/07/29/93013105/top-five-neglected-jazz-masterpieces (29 July 2008; accessed 21 May 2014); Bob Belden, "Teo Macero 10.30.25—2.19.08," *JazzTimes* 39 (March 2009): 43–44 (also available at http://jazztimes.com/articles/21278-teo-macero [accessed 21 May 2014]); Brent Butterworth, "Bob Belden: A Second Chance for Surround?," *JazzTimes* 40 (October 2010): 44–45 (interview excerpts); Bob Belden, "Artist's Choice: Bob Belden on Duke Pearson," http://jazztimes.com/articles/28499-artist-s-choice-bob-belden-on-duke-pearson (23 September 2011; accessed 21 May 2014); "Bob Belden Remembers Pete Rugolo," *JazzTimes* 24 (March 2012): 45–46; Jeff Dayton-Johnson, "Bob Belden: Jazz Adventurer," http://www.allaboutjazz.com/bob-belden-jazz-adventurer-bob-belden-by-jeff-dayton-johnson.php?page=1#.VBWY36MiBM8 (28 January 2013; accessed 21 May 2014) (interview); Bob Belden, "Bob Belden Remembers Donald Byrd," http://jazztimes.com/articles/73865-bob-belden-remembers-donald-byrd (14 February 2013; accessed 21 May 2014); Bruce Lindsay, "Profiles," *Jazz Journal* 66 (February 2013): 3, 6 (substantial comments by Belden); Anthony Kahn, "Bob Belden: An Uncontrollaby [*sic*] Analytical Mind," *JazzTimes* 43 (March 2013): 16–19 (also available as "Before and After with Bob Belden: An Uncontrollably Analytical Mind" at http://jazztimes.com/articles/76338-before-after-with-bob-belden [accessed 21 May 2014]) (Belden comments about recordings); "Bob Belden Remembers Jazz Reissue Producer Seth Rothstein," http://jazztimes.com/articles/96468-bob-belden-remembers-jazz-reissue-producer-seth-rothstein (12 July 2013; accessed 21 May 2014).

SECONDARY: Jeff Tamarkin, "Bob Belden: Eastern Promise," *JazzTimes* 38 (June 2008): 56–60 (also available at http://jazztimes.com/articles/17993-bob-belden-eastern-promise [accessed 21 May 2014]) (comments by Belden); Jack McCray, "Goose Creek Native Pushes Envelope for Global Appeal," *Charleston (S.C.) Post and Courier*, 20 July 2008, sec. G, pp. 1, 7 (comments by Belden); Bill Milkowski, "Back on Tracks," *JazzTimes* 41 (September 2011): 12–14; Thomas Erdbrink, "Rebirth of the Cool: American Music Makes a Return to Iran," *New York Times*, 24 February 2015, sec. A, p. 6 (national edition) (also available at http://www.nytimes.com/2015/02/24/world/rebirth-of-the-cool-american-music-makes-a-return-to-iran.html?_r=0 [accessed 26 March 2015]) (comments by Belden).

Benford, Bill (William Charles)

Tuba

Probably 18 April or 30 November 1900 (probably Charleston, S.C., though possibly Charleston, W.Va.)-?

S.C. residence: Charleston (probably 1900, but by 1913–ca. 1919)

A ward of Jenkins Orphanage, Benford performed with its bands in N.Y.C. (in *Uncle Tom's Cabin*) in 1913 and in England the next year. After leaving the institution probably before 1920, he settled in N.Y.C. as a professional musician. In a band nominally led by Willie Gant, ca. 1921 he played in Harlem at Leroy's, one of the first N.Y.C. jazz clubs. He is on Ethel Waters's first hit recording, "Down Home Blues" (1925). By the next year he was again in England, where he recorded with the Plantation Orchestra. Back in N.Y.C. he led a band that impressed Jelly Roll Morton to the degree that the pianist used some of its members, including Benford, at recording sessions.

Benford was the brother of drummer Tommy Benford. The passenger list of the *St. Louis*, which transported Benford from Liverpool to N.Y.C. in 1914, records his birth date as 18 April 1900; that for the *Homeric*, which he took from Southampton, England, to N.Y.C. in 1927, indicates that he was born on 30 November 1900. John Chilton states that Benford was born in 1902 in Charleston, W.Va. He was enumerated for the N.Y. state census in N.Y.C. on 1 June 1925 (estimated age twenty-five) and in N.Y.C. for the federal census on 28 April 1930 (twenty-nine) and 8 April 1940 (thirty-nine). Both federal censuses identify his occupation as musician and indicate that he was born in S.C.

Leaders Recorded With

Gulf Coast Seven (1925), Ethel Waters (1925), Thomas Morris (1926), Plantation Orchestra (1926), Jelly Roll Morton (1928, 1930), Bubber Miley (1930)

References

SECONDARY: John Chilton, *A Jazz Nursery: The Story of the Jenkins' Orphanage Bands of Charleston, South Carolina* (London: Bloomsbury Book Shop, 1980), 53; Howard Rye, "Visiting Fireboys: The Jenkins' Orphanage Bands in Britain," *Storyville* 130 (1987): 137–43; Garvin Bushell, as told to Mark Tucker, *Jazz from the Beginning* (Ann Arbor: University of Michigan Press, 1988), 28; Edward Ball, *The Sweet Hell Inside: A Family History* (New York: William Morrow, 2001), 106; Benjamin Franklin V, *Jazz and Blues Musicians of South Carolina: Interviews with Jabbo, Dizzy, Drink, and Others* (Columbia: University of South Carolina Press, 2008), 1–7.

Benford, Tommy (Thomas P.)

Drums

Probably 5 or 19 April 1905 (probably Charleston, S.C., though possibly Charleston, W.Va.)–24 March 1994 (Mount Vernon, N.Y.)

S.C. residence: Charleston (probably 1905, but by 1913–ca. 1921)

A ward of Jenkins Orphanage, Benford studied music there with Alonzo Mills. Upon leaving the institution he played with minstrel shows, carnivals, and circuses before performing with Diyaw Jones in Chicago. At the request of his brother, tubaist Bill, Benford left the Edgar Marton burlesque show ca. 1922 and joined his sibling in N.Y.C. There he performed with various groups, including a month with Duke Ellington's band as a replacement for the leader's infirm drummer, Sonny Greer. In 1932 Benford went to Europe with Sy Devereaux. He returned to the United States the next year but later that decade settled in Europe. In 1941 he went back to his homeland, where he played with numerous groups. He visited Europe in the early 1960s as a member of the revue *Jazz Train* and several times in the 1970s with Clyde Bernhardt. He was the initial musician Bob Greene selected for a band that, in the 1970s and 1980s, recreated the music of Jelly Roll Morton, with whom Benford had recorded. With this group he again traveled to Europe. Peter Watrous believes that along with Sidney Catlett, Benford "shaped early jazz drumming," and Whitney Balliett credits Benford with being one of the earliest modern drummers.

The Social Security Death Index records Benford's birth date as 19 April 1905. The passenger list of the *Exeter,* which transported the drummer to the United States in 1941, indicates that he was born on 5 April 1905 in Charleston, W.Va. Though Benford states in an interview published in 1982 that he was born in Charleston, W.Va., the 1920 and 1930 censuses record his birthplace as S.C.

Leaders Recorded With

Charlie Skeete (1926), Jelly Roll Morton (1928, 1930), Bubber Miley (1930), Coleman Hawkins (1937), Eddie Brunner (1938), Bill Coleman (1938), Alix Combelle (1938), Greta Keller (1938), Willie Lewis (1938, 1941), Orchestre Musette Victor (1938), Eddie South (1938), Louis Bacon (1939), Freddy Johnson (1939), Joe Turner (1939), Gus Viseur (1939), Pigmeat Markham (1945), Snub Mosley (1946), Pops Foster (undetermined date in the 1940s), Sidney Bechet (1949), Bob Wilbur (1949, 1977–1978), Jimmy Archey (1951–1952), Marty Grosz (1951), Rex Stewart (1953), Dick Wellstood (1954, 1978), Linda Hopkins (1960), Franz Jackson (1968), Pat Flowers (1972), Clyde Bernhardt (1973, 1975, 1977), Harlem Blues and Jazz Band (1973, 1975, 1979–1982), Preston Jackson (1973), Bob Greene (ca. 1974, 1982), Graham Stewart (1976), Soprano Summit (1977), Maxine Sullivan (1977), Dick Hyman (1978), Stan McDonald (1982–1983)

References

PRIMARY: Peter Carr et al., "Have Drum, Will Travel: An Interview with Tommy Benford," *Storyville* 100 (April–May 1982): 124–29; Whitney Balliett, *Jelly Roll, Jabbo, and Fats: 19 Portraits in Jazz* (New York: Oxford University Press, 1983), 45–51 (reprinted in Balliett's *American Musicians: Fifty-Six Portraits in Jazz* [New York: Oxford University Press, 1986], 47–51) (narrative by Benford); Peter Carr et al., "Have Drum, Will Travel: An Interview with Tommy Benford," *Storyville* 111 (February–March 1984): 105–7; Benjamin Franklin V, *Jazz and Blues Musicians of South Carolina: Interviews with Jabbo, Dizzy, Drink, and Others* (Columbia: University of South Carolina Press, 2008), 1–7.

SECONDARY: "Two Veteran Jazzmen Bring Special Verve to Home Office," *We the People* 23 (22 September 1969) (newsletter of the firm Merrill Lynch, Pierce, Fenner

& Smith; reproduced in Jack McCray, *Charleston Jazz* [Charleston, S.C.: Arcadia Publishing, 2007], 54) (comments by Benford); John Chilton, *A Jazz Nursery: The Story of the Jenkins' Orphanage Bands of Charleston, South Carolina* (London: Bloomsbury Book Shop, 1980), 15, 27, 31, 50, 52–53 (comments by Benford); Peter Watrous, "Tommy Benford, Jazz Dummer [*sic*], 88; Played with Stars," *New York Times*, 29 March 1994, sec. D, p. 22 (obituary); Edward Ball, *The Sweet Hell Inside: A Family History* (New York: William Morrow, 2001), 257–60, 348.

Bennett, Daniel

Tuba

Ca. 1914 (N.C., probably Wilmington)-before 1981

S.C. residence: Charleston (probably 1925-probably mid-1930s)

A ward of Jenkins Orphanage, Bennett played in its bands ca. 1930.

Bennett was the brother of trombonist Freddie Bennett. Bennett's age was estimated as sixteen when the musician was enumerated for the census at the orphanage on 2 April 1930. Bruce Bastin indicates that Bennett had died by the time Bastin completed his manuscript.

References

SECONDARY: John Chilton, *A Jazz Nursery: The Story of the Jenkins' Orphanage Bands of Charleston, South Carolina* (London: Bloomsbury Book Shop, 1980), 53; Bruce Bastin, "A Note on the Carolina Cotton Pickers," *Storyville* 95 (June–July 1981): 177–82.

Bennett, Freddie (Frederick)

Trombone, possibly trumpet

Mid-1910s (Wilmington, N.C.)-?

S.C. residence: Charleston (1925-1936)

A ward of Jenkins Orphanage, Bennett played in its bands in the early 1930s and then led one of them. After moving to N.Y.C. in 1936 he performed with various groups, including one led by Luis Russell, though he apparently never recorded. Ultimately he returned to the South.

Bennett was the brother of tubaist Daniel Bennett. Though John Chilton notes that Bennett was born in 1916, his age was estimated as sixteen when he was enumerated for the census at the orphanage on 2 April 1930. It has not been determined if the trumpeter Freddie Bennett who played with the band of Buster Jackson in 1939 was the Bennett from the orphanage. See "Albany, N.Y.," *New York Age*, 11 March 1939, p. 9.

Reference

SECONDARY: John Chilton, *A Jazz Nursery: The Story of the Jenkins' Orphanage Bands of Charleston, South Carolina* (London: Bloomsbury Book Shop, 1980), 53.

Benton, Brook (Benjamin Franklin Peay)

Singer, composer, arranger

19 September 1931 (Lugoff, S.C.)-9 April 1988 (New York, N.Y.)

S.C. residence: Lugoff (1931-1948, briefly ca. 1950, ca. 1987-1988)

As a youth Benjamin Peay sang in church and then with the Camden Jubilee Singers. In 1948 he moved to N.Y.C., where he sang with gospel groups including the Langfordaires and the Jerusalem Stars; the latter included Bill Pinkney. Peay joined the Sandmen ca. 1954 and soon became known as Brook Benton. He remained relatively obscure until recording for Mercury Records beginning in the late 1950s, which is also when he began writing songs with Clyde Otis. For Mercury he recorded most of his major hits, including "Endlessly," "It's Just a Matter of Time," and "Thank You, Pretty Baby," plus "A Rockin' Good Way" and "Baby (You've Got What It Takes)," duets with Dinah Washington. He co-composed all these songs except the last, as well as ones popularized by other singers, such as "Looking Back" (by Nat Cole) and "A Lover's Question" (by Clyde McPhatter). Additionally he arranged music, including "Thirty Days" for McPhatter. His last major hit was "A Rainy Night in Georgia," recorded in 1969 for Cotillion, a subsidiary of Atlantic Records. Benton sings the title songs in the movies *Walk on the Wild Side* (1962) and *A House Is Not a Home* (1964). Toward the end of his life he attempted, unsuccessfully, to establish a boys' music camp in Lugoff. He is buried in the cemetery of the Unity Family Life Center (the former Ephesus United Methodist Church), Lugoff.

Compositions

"Ain't Givin' Up Nothing," "Ambush," "Baby, I Love You," "Boll Weevil Song," "Come On, Baby, Let's Go," "Crazy in Love with You," "Don't Call Me,

I'll Call You," "Don't Walk Away from Me," "Endlessly," "Everything," "Flighty," "Forgotten," "For My Baby," "He'll Understand," "Honey Bee," "How Many Times," "Hurtin' Inside," "I Don't Know," "If Only I Had Known," "I Just Want to Love You," "I'll Take Care of You," "I'm Coming to See You," "In a Dream," "The Intoxicated Rat," "It's a Wonder," "It's Just a Matter of Time," "Johnny O," "Kiddio," "Let Me Fix It," "Lie to Me," "Looking Back," "A Lover's Question," "Mark My Word," "My Last Dollar," "No Matter What I Do," "One Love Too Many," "A Rockin' Good Way," "Sailor Boy's Love Song," "Send Back My Heart," "So Close," "Tell Me Now or Never," "Thank You, Pretty Baby," "That's Love," "Wake Up," "What a Kiss Won't Do," "What Is a Woman without a Man," "With All of My Heart," "You Precious Thing," "Your Love Alone," "You Went Back on Your Word, Little Girl"

Recordings as Leader (These Are Release Dates, Not Necessarily Recording Dates)

"The Kentuckian Song" (1955), "Ooh" (1955), "Bring Me Love" (1956), "Give Me a Sign" (1956), "Love Made Me Your Fool" (1956), "Some of My Best Friends" (1956), "All My Love Belongs to You" (1957), "The Wall" (1957), *Brook Benton* (1959), *Brook Benton at His Best!!!!* (1959), *Endlessly* (1959), *It's Just a Matter of Time* (1959), *I Love You in So Many Ways* (1960), *Songs I Love to Sing* (1960), *The Two of Us* (1960; with Dinah Washington), *The Boll Weevil Song and 11 Other Great Hits* (1961), *If You Believe* (1961), *Brook Benton* (1962; sometimes referred to as *There Goes That Song Again*), *Singing the Blues—Lie to Me* (1962), *Best Ballads of Broadway* (1963), *Born to Sing the Blues* (1964), *On the Countryside* (1964), *This Bitter Earth* (1964), *My Country* (1966), *Laura, What's He Got That I Ain't Got* (1967), *That Old Feeling* (1968), *Do Your Own Thing* (1969), *Brook Benton Today* (1970), *Home Style* (1970), *The Gospel Truth* (1971), *Story Teller* (1972), *Something for Everyone* (1973), *Brook Benton Sings a Love Story* (1975), *Mister Bartender* (1976), *This Is Brook Benton* (1976), *Makin' Love Is Good for You* (1977), *Brook Benton Sings the Standards* (1980), *Beautiful Memories of Christmas* (1983), *Soft* (1984)

Leaders Recorded With

Sandmen (1955), Lincoln Chase (1955; with the Sandmen), Chuck Willis (1955; with the Sandmen), Bo Thorpe (1984)

Film

Mister Rock and Roll (1957)

Awards

Order of the Palmetto (1985); Carolina Beach Music Awards Hall of Fame (2007); South Carolina Entertainment and Music Hall of Fame (date unknown)

Websites

www.bridgeplayasanjuan.com/brook_benton/33rpmlp.html (accessed 21 May 2014); www.secondhandlps.de/interpreten/index/0/showip/106/Brook-Benton.html (accessed 21 May 2014); janicesbluesalley.com/brook_benton.html (accessed 21 May 2014)

References

SECONDARY: Rodney Welch, "Brook's Back," *Camden (S.C.) Chronicle-Independent,* 6 November 1987, sec. A, pp. 1, 4; Howard W. French, "Brook Benton, Singer of Hit Tunes Known for His Ballads, Dies at 56," *New York Times,* 11 April 1988, sec. D, p. 13 (obituary); "Brook Benton Remembered as a Smooth Soul Singer," *Camden (S.C.) Chronicle-Independent,* 13 April 1988, sec. A, pp. 1, 10; Rodney Welch, "This Is Brook Benton," *Camden (S.C.) Chronicle-Independent,* 22 April 1988, sec. B, pp. 1, 4 (comments by Benton); Jim Tatum, "Remembering Brook Benton," *Camden (S.C.) Chronicle-Independent* 30 December 2005, sec. A, pp. 1, 6; Marv Goldberg, "The Sandmen," www.uncamarvy.com/Sandmen/sandmen.html (2009; accessed 21 May 2014).

Bilbro, Bert Hunter

Harmonica, singer

27 March of either 1888 or 1889 (Clinton, Miss.)–8 September 1951 (Chester, S.C.)

S.C. residence: Chester (ca. 1921–1951)

By late 1929 Bilbro's year-old recording of "C.&N.W. Blues" was considered famous ("Old Time Musical Convention to Be Held in Rock Hill"). Apparently on the basis of its success, Okeh, the label that released it, recorded him again, in Atlanta, where he had initially recorded. He recorded once more, in 1931 for RCA Victor in Charlotte, N.C. In addition to making music, Bilbro, a cotton field laborer, was a comedian. Reviewing a 1929 convention of fiddlers in York, S.C., a Rock Hill newspaper characterized his performance this way: "Bert Bilbro, blackface comedian of Chester, kept the audience in an uproar of laughter with his tricks and stunts.

Many persons expressed the opinion that Mr. Bilbro can act more like a negro than a negro himself" ("Prizes Divided at Fiddlers Meeting"). He is buried in section V, plot 2190, Evergreen Cemetery, Chester.

Bilbro's name is usually rendered, incorrectly, D. H. "Bert" Bilbro. His 1917 draft registration card records the name Burt H. Bilbro. This document, which he signed with an X, identifies his birth date as 27 March 1889; his grave marker specifies it as 27 March 1888. The census charts his movement. When enumerated in mid-June 1900 (birth date recorded as March 1889), he lived in Oxford, Ala.; on 22 April 1910 (estimated age twenty), in Lanett, Ala.; on 9 January 1920 (estimated age thirty), in Columbus, Ga. (where he also resided when his 1917 draft registration card was completed); on 9 April 1930 (estimated age forty-two; identified as Bert H. Bildro), in Chester, S.C. He estimated his age as fifty-two when enumerated in Chester on 4 April 1940. Obituaries note that he lived in Chester for thirty years.

Recordings as Leader

"C.&N.W. Blues" (1928), "Mohana Blues" (1928), "The Mocking Bird" (1929; unissued), "The Old Cherry Tree, Sweet Marie" (1929; unissued), "We're Gonna Have a Good Time Tonight" (1929), "Yes, Indeed I Do" (1929), "Chester Blues" (1931), "Locomotive Blues" (1931; unissued)

References

SECONDARY: "Prizes Divided at Fiddlers Meeting," *Rock Hill (S.C.) Evening Herald,* 29 October 1929, p. 1; "Old Time Musical Convention to Be Held in Rock Hill," *Rock Hill (S.C.) Evening Herald,* 8 November 1929, p. 3; "Heart Attack Is Fatal to Bert Hunter Bilbro," *Chester (S.C.) Reporter,* 10 September 1951, p. 1 (obituary); "Bert Hunter Bilbro Died Saturday," *Chester (S.C.) News,* 13 September 1951, p. 17 (obituary); Pete Lowry, "Bert Bilbro," *Blues Unlimited* 115 (September–October 1975): 3; "Early White Blues Harp," www.patmissin.com/articles/BRQ6.html (2007; accessed 21 May 2014).

Bing, Bill (Cleveland, Though Possibly Willie)

Singer, guitar

26 December 1922 (S.C., probably Barnwell County)–23 January 2014 (Augusta, Ga.)

S.C. residence: Barnwell County (probably early 1920s–no later than early 1940s)

When Bing was discharged from the army in 1945, he helped form the King Odom Quartet, a rhythm-and-blues group made up of South Carolinians. When it disbanded in 1954 he joined the Golden Gate Quartet, singing with it only that year. He ultimately settled in Augusta, Ga.

Bing was a brother of singer Isaiah Bing. His birth and death dates come from the Social Security Death Index. His age was estimated as six when he was enumerated for the census in Barnwell County on 28 April 1930; as seventeen when enumerated in Barnwell County on 22 April 1940. Both censuses record his given name as Cleveland. When enlisting in the army on 2 November 1942 as Willie, he stated that he was born in 1921.

Leader Recorded With

King Odom Quartet (1948, 1950–1952)

References

SECONDARY: "Spotlight on the King Odom Four, Part One!," http://www.vocalgroupharmony.com/Lucky.htm (2003; accessed 21 May 2014); "Spotlight on the King Odom Four, Part Two!," http://www.vocalgroupharmony.com/Im_Look.htm (2003; accessed 21 May 2014); Marv Goldberg, "The King Odom Quartet," http://www.uncamarvy.com/KingOdomQuartet/kingodomquartet.html (2009; accessed 21 May 2014) (comments by Bing); "Spotlight on Savannah Churchill, Part Two of Two," http://www.vocalgroupharmony.com/3ROWNEW/WhyWasIBorn.htm (2010; accessed 21 May 2014); "In Rememberance [*sic*] of . . . Isaiah Bing," http://www.toddbaptista.com/remember.html (2013; accessed 21 May 2014); "Uncommon Labels, Part One," http://www.vocalgroupharmony.com/4ROWNEW/AmazinWillieMays.htm (2013; accessed 21 May 2014); Todd Baptista, "In Rememberance [*sic*] of . . . Cleveland 'Bill' Bing, Baritone with Golden Gate Quartet, King Odom Four, Dies at 91," http://www.toddbaptista.com/remember.html (2014; accessed 21 May 2014) (obituary).

Bing, Isaiah S.

Singer

27 January 1926 (S.C., probably Barnwell County)–3 September 2008 (Metter, Ga.)

S.C. residence: Barnwell County (probably 1926–1943)

Bing sang with the Ashley Plantation Singers in S.C. before moving to N.Y.C. in 1943. There he performed with the gospel group Southern Trumpeters in the mid-1940s until helping form the King

Odom Quartet, a rhythm-and-blues group made up of South Carolinians. When it disbanded in 1954 he joined the Larks, remaining with this group until its dissolution the next year. Subsequently he worked for the N.Y.C. Housing Authority before moving to Fort Lauderdale, Fla., where he painted houses. He retired to Ga. in the late 1980s. His body was cremated.

Bing was a brother of singer Bill Bing. His birth and death dates come from the Social Security Death Index. His age was estimated as fourteen when he was enumerated for the census in Barnwell County on 22 April 1940; this document records the singer's middle initial. His age suggests that he might be the Turner S. Bing, estimated age four, who was enumerated with his family in Barnwell County on 28 April 1930. It has not been confirmed that the singer was born Isaiah Samuel Bing, Jr., as is sometimes claimed.

Leaders Recorded With

King Odom Quartet (1948, 1950–1952), Larks (1954–1955; two songs released as by the Kings)

Film

Rhythm and Blues Revue (1955; with the Larks)

References

SECONDARY: "Spotlight on the King Odom Four, Part One!," http://www.vocalgroupharmony.com/Lucky.htm (2003; accessed 21 May 2014); "Spotlight on the King Odom Four, Part Two!," http://www.vocalgroupharmony.com/Im_Look.htm (2003; accessed 21 May 2014); "Isiah [*sic*] Bing," *Savannah (Ga.) Morning News,* 6 September 2008, sec. B, p. 3 (also available at http://www.similarsites.com/goto/savannahnow.com?pos=16&s=10 [accessed 21 May 2014]) (death notice); Marv Goldberg, "The King Odom Quartet," http://www.uncamarvy.com/KingOdomQuartet/kingodomquartet.html (2009; accessed 21 May 2014) (comments by Bing); Marv Goldberg, "The Larks," http://www.uncamarvy.com/Larks/larks.html (2009; accessed 21 May 2014); "Spotlight on Savannah Churchill, Part Two of Two," http://www.vocalgroupharmony.com/3ROWNEW/WhyWasIBorn.htm (2010; accessed 21 May 2014); "In Rememberance [*sic*] of . . . Isaiah Bing," http://www.toddbaptista.com/remember.html (2013; accessed 21 May 2014) (comments by Bing) (obituary); "Uncommon Labels, Part One," http://www.vocalgroupharmony.com/4ROWNEW/AmazinWillieMays.htm (2013; accessed 21 May 2014); Todd Baptista, "In Rememberance [*sic*] of . . . Cleveland 'Bill' Bing, Baritone with Golden Gate Quartet, King Odom Four, Dies at 91," http://www.toddbaptista.com/remember.html (2014; accessed 21 May 2014).

Blake, William Leroy

Trombone, tuba, singer

October 1886 (Charleston, S.C.)–1958

S.C. residences: Charleston (1886–ca. 1910, early to mid-1920s–1950s), possibly Sumter (possibly mid-1910s)

A ward of Jenkins Orphanage, Blake played in its bands. In 1909 he performed a vocal solo at a concert by the institution's Orphan Brass Band and Jubilee Concert Company in Poughkeepsie, N.Y. After leaving the orphanage he traveled with theatrical productions until approximately 1917. He is probably the W. L. Blake who played with the Rabbit's Foot Minstrels in 1910 and Silas Green from New Orleans, a tent show, in 1916, as well as the William Blake who played with Prof. Murdock's Band and Minstrels in 1913. He reportedly studied music at Morris College, possibly in the mid-1910s. In 1920 he returned to the orphanage as band director, a position he held into the 1950s. In 1929 he accompanied the institution's band to London, where it performed in *Porgy.* He encouraged young Freddie Green to consult music books in Blake's library.

Conducted at the orphanage on 28 June, the 1900 census records Blake's birth date. The musician was initially listed in the Charleston city directory in the mid-1920s and was no longer in it by 1950. John Chilton records Blake's year of death.

References

SECONDARY: "Jenkins Band Makes Big Hit," *Poughkeepsie (N.Y.) Daily Eagle,* 13 July 1909, p. 5; Stanley Dance and Helen Dance, "The Freddie Green Interview," www.freddiegreen.org/interviews/dance.html (1977; accessed 21 May 2014); John Chilton, *A Jazz Nursery: The Story of the Jenkins' Orphanage Bands of Charleston, South Carolina* (London: Bloomsbury Book Shop, 1980), 34, 37, 39–41, 49, 53; Lynn Abbott and Doug Seroff, *Ragged but Right: Black Traveling Shows, "Coon Songs," and the Dark Pathway to Blues and Jazz* (Jackson: University Press of Mississippi, 2007), 364, 374, 380; Jack McCray, *Charleston Jazz* (Charleston, S.C.: Arcadia Publishing, 2007), 89.

Blowers, Johnny (John Garrett, Jr.)

Drums

21 April 1911 (Spartanburg, S.C.)–17 July 2006 (Westbury, N.Y.)

S.C. residence: Spartanburg (1911–1930)

Born to a piano-playing mother and a drums-playing father, Blowers began playing drums around age eight. After completing tenth grade at Frank Evans High School in Spartanburg, in October 1930 he moved to Fla., where he performed in a band while completing high school in Fort Myers. He then traveled with bands and, for two years, attended Oglethorpe University. After moving to N.Y.C. in 1937 he played with Bobby Hackett at Nick's, joined the band of Bunny Berigan, toured with Ben Bernie, and affiliated briefly with Jan Savitt. He recorded prolifically during the 1940s, including with major jazz musicians; he is on Billie Holiday's initial recording of "Lover Man" (1944). He also appeared on recordings intended for a general audience, including Perry Como's "Til the End of Time" (1945) and Ray Noble's "Linda" (1946), featuring Buddy Clark. For Columbia Records he recorded off and on with Frank Sinatra from 1944 to 1951, including on "It Never Entered My Mind" (1947). Also in the 1940s he served as a studio musician for radio networks; in 1947 the Johnny Blowers Club operated for three months in Astoria, Queens, N.Y. Though he continued playing with jazz musicians in the 1950s, he also backed such singers as Eddie Fisher and Andy Williams; he played on television programs, initially on NBC and then on ABC. During the 1960s he gave drum lessons, recorded jingles, played with society orchestras, and worked as a disc jockey, all while performing jazz occasionally. He drummed in the Broadway show *Follies* in the early 1970s. Beginning in 1986 he toured with the Harlem Blues and Jazz Band. He recorded for the last time in 1991, at a session he led.

Blowers's middle name is sometimes spelled Garett. Though the drummer's Spartanburg high school records indicate that Blowers was born in 1909, the Social Security Death Index specifies 21 April 1911. School records identify his last grade completed and the date he moved to Fla.

Recordings as Leader

"Blue and Broken" (1947), "Club Blowers Shuffle" (1947), "Dry Your Tears for Me, Dear" (1947), "Forever in Your Heart" (1947), "Git" (1947), "One Way Blues" (1947), "Rainbow Serenade" (1947), "This Game of Love" (1947), "Waiter—Pasta—Fazoo" (1947), "Alabama Jubilee" (1952), "Ten Little Fingers and Ten Little Toes" (1952), *Johnny Blowers and His Giants of Jazz* (1991)

Leaders Recorded With

Bob Pope (1936–1937, 1940), Bunny Berigan (1938), Bobby Hackett (1938), Teddy Wilson (1938), Ben Bernie (1939), Jan Savitt (1940), Ella Fitzgerald (1943, 1951), Red Norvo (1943), Perry Como (1944–1946), Eddie Condon (1944–1945, 1947, 1967), Billie Holiday (1944), Yank Lawson (1944–1945), Frank Sinatra (1944–1948, 1950–1951), Louis Armstrong (1945, 1949–1950), Pearl Bailey (1945, 1947), Billy Butterfield (1945), Don Byas (1945), Bing Crosby (1945), Harry "The Hipster" Gibson (1945), Woody Herman (1945), Ray Noble (1945–1946), Hazel Scott (1945, 1947), Al Sears (1945), Bill Stegmeyer (1945), Georg Brunis (1946), Peggy Lee (1946), Frankie Trumbauer (1946), Joe Marsala (1947, 1957), Modernaires (1947), *This Is Jazz* (1947; broadcast of Rudi Blesh's radio program), Bon Bon (late 1940s), Mel Tormé (1949–1950), Bobby Colt (1950), Anita O'Day (1950), Artie Shaw (1950, 1952), Cy Walter (1950), Tamara Hayes (1951), Sy Oliver (1951), Arthur Prysock (1951), Stuyvesant Stompers (1951), Trudy Richards (1952), Sauter-Finegan (1952), Sidney Bechet (1953), Bruce Prince-Joseph (1957), Eddie Barefield (1973), Warren Vaché, Sr. (1977), Pee Wee Erwin (1981), Barbara Lea (1983), Harlem Blues and Jazz Band (1986)

Films

Saturday Night Swing Club (1938), *The Last of the First* (2003)

Award

Spartanburg Music Trail Marker (2011)

References

PRIMARY: Chip Deffaa, "Portraits: Johnny Blowers," *Modern Drummer* 9 (July 1985): 38–40 (substantial comments by Blowers).

SECONDARY: Bertram Finch, "Spartanburg Drummer Wins National Acclaim," *Sunday Spartanburg (S.C.) Herald-Journal,* 18 September 1938, p. 12; Warren W. Vaché,

Back Beats and Rim Shots: The Johnny Blowers Story (Lanham, Md.: Scarecrow Press, 1997); Nat Hentoff, "Johnny Blowers: Riding the Rhythm Wave at 91," *JazzTimes* 32 (May 2002): 190 (comments by Blowers); Nat Hentoff, "Reading, Writing and Rhythm: Johnny Blowers, Part Two," *JazzTimes* 32 (June 2002): 130 (comments by Blowers); "John G. Blowers Jr.," *Westbury (N.Y.) Times*, 3 August 2006, p. 32 (obituary).

Blue Scotty (Milford Kenneth Scott)

Piano, organ, singer

25 November 1937 (probably Williamston, S.C.)–

S.C. residence: probably Williamston (1937–no later than 1945, mid-1950s)

Scott was reared partly in Toledo, Ohio, where he began playing piano ca. 1945. Probably in Williamston in the mid-1950s, he performed with the Composers; upon moving to Chicago he played with the Continentals. He was in the army from probably 1958 into 1964; during this period he entertained troops in England with Scotty's Quintet. After discharge he resided in Tex., Ariz., and Calif. before settling in Lake Charles, La. (1965). There he made his only recordings and performed with the Larks and the Soul Senders.

With one exception sources consulted indicate that Scott was born in Williamston, S.C. The exception is Mike Leadbitter, who spoke with the musician. Leadbitter states that Scott was born in Williamston, N.C., and that in the 1950s he broadcast on a radio station in "nearby Anderson." Approximately 165 miles separate Williamston and Anderson, N.C. The distance between Williamston, N.C., and Anderson, S.C., is almost four hundred miles. If Scott in fact broadcast in an Anderson that is near a Williamston, these towns, separated by only fourteen miles, are located in S.C.

Recordings as Leader (All 1969)

"Lonely Love Blues," "Lonesome Blues," "Shame, Shame on You," "Those Old Happy Days," "True Love Blues"

Leaders Recorded With

Chester Randle's Soul Sender's [*sic*] (ca. 1968), Rockin' Sidney Simien (1969)

Reference

SECONDARY: Mike Leadbitter, notes to *Those Old Happy Days: 1960s Blues from the Gulf* (1974; Flyright 513).

Bogan, Ted (Theodore R.)

Guitar, bass, singer

Probably 10 May 1910 (Spartanburg County, S.C.)–29 January 1990 (Detroit, Mich.)

S.C. residence: Spartanburg County, including Spartanburg town (1910–no later than 1930)

Mainly a guitarist, Bogan was self-taught, though he was presumably influenced by the playing of Spartanburg residents Pink Anderson and Simmie Dooley. He apparently toured with the Dr. Mines Medicine Show before joining Howard Armstrong and Carl Martin to form a string band that, after the addition of Bill Ballinger, became known as the Four Keys. Headquartered in Knoxville, Tenn., and under different names, this group was active in the early 1930s. Bogan, Armstrong, and Martin then moved to Chicago, where they continued working together, though Armstrong left the group around 1934. After possibly serving in the army during World War II, Bogan was, musically, mostly inactive until the mid-1960s, when he played in Chicago. In the early 1970s he began touring and then recording, including with Martin and Armstrong. This group—the last of the black string bands with musicians who began playing in the 1920s—performed internationally in the 1970s under the auspices of the United States Department of State.

Public documents contain conflicting information about Bogan's birth date. The Social Security Death Index records it as 10 May 1909. However, the 1910 census (conducted on 20 April) does not mention a Theodore residing with the Bogan family of Reidville Township, Spartanburg County. The musician's birth date is usually given as 10 May 1910. If this is accurate, as seems likely, Bogan was born three weeks after his family was enumerated for the census. And if this is the case he was probably born in Reidville Township. At the time of the next census (late January 1920), the family, including ten-year-old Ted, lived in Spartanburg. He left Spartanburg before 11 April 1930, the date the Bogans were enumerated for the next census, which does not mention him as living with the family.

Composition

"Ain't Doin' Bad Doin' Nothing"

Recordings as Leader

"I'm Through with You" (1934; with Louie Bluie [Howard Armstrong]), "State Street Rag" (1934),

"Ted's Stomp" (1934), "There's Nothing in This Wide, Wide World for Me" (1934), "Mary, Run to the Window" (1965), "West Virginia Blues" (1965), "Worried All the Time" (1965), *The Barnyard Dance* (1972; with Howard Armstrong and Carl Martin), *The New Mississippi Sheiks* (1972; with Sam Chatmon, Carl Martin, and Walter Vinson), "Hoodoo Blues" (1972; with Howard Armstrong and Carl Martin), "Seaboard Stomp" (1972), *Martin Bogan and Armstrong* (1974), *That Old Gang of Mine* (1975, 1977; with the Armstrongs and Carl Martin)

Leaders Recorded With

Bumble Bee Slim (Amos Easton) (1934), Steve Goodman (1975), Howard Armstrong (1985)

Film

Louie Bluie (1985)

References

PRIMARY: Allen Larman, "Martin, Bogan, and Armstrong," *Folkscene* 4 (July–August 1975): 12–14, 21 (interview).

SECONDARY: Paige Van Vorst, "String Jazz with Seasoning," *Mississippi Rag* 1 (March 1974): 4–5; Beulah Gilbreath, "Martin, Bogan and Armstrong Play in the Tradition of 30 Years Ago," *Elkins (W.Va.) Inter-Mountain,* 28 July 1978, p. 2; Jerry Gilbert, "Old Legends Never Die," *Melody Maker* 53 (14 October 1978): 55 (comments by Bogan); Bruce Bastin, *Red River Blues: The Blues Tradition in the Southeast* (Urbana: University of Illinois Press, 1986), 302–3; Chris Smith, "Ted Bogan, Thomas Burt, George Jackson," *Blues and Rhythm: The Gospel Truth* 52 (May 1990): 22 (obituary); Erin Kelly and Alva Noe, "An Interview with 'Louie Bluie' W. Howard Armstrong," *Blues Review Quarterly* 7 (1992–1993): 26–33; Chris Durman, "African American Old-Time String Band Music: A Selective Discography," *Notes: Quarterly Journal of the Music Library Association* 64 (June 2008): 797–810 (see especially 800, 807).

Bolton, Robert

Baritone horn

S.C. residence: Charleston (at least mid-1930s)

A ward of Jenkins Orphanage, Bolton played in its bands in the mid-1930s.

Bonds, Will

Probably guitar

Possibly S.C.

S.C. residence: possibly Greenville (at least early 1910s)

In the early 1910s Bonds played in a Greenville string band that included Gary Davis and Willie Walker. He taught Davis the tune "Candyman."

References

SECONDARY: Bruce Bastin, *Red River Blues: The Blues Tradition in the Southeast* (Urbana: University of Illinois Press, 1986), 171; *"Oh, What a Beautiful City": A Tribute to the Reverend Gary Davis (1896–1972) Gospel, Blues and Ragtime,* ed. Robert Tilling (Jersey, Channel Islands: Paul Mill Press, 1992), 8.

Bouchillon, Charlie (Charles G.)

Violin

18 May 1906 (Anderson County, S.C.)-September 1979 (West Palm Beach, Fla.)

S.C. residences: Anderson County, probably Williamston (1906-no later than 1910), Anderson (by 1910-ca. 1916), Greenville (ca. 1916-mid-1920s, ca. 1931-ca. 1943), Kingstree (mid-1920s-ca. 1931)

Bouchillon worked primarily as a clerk. With brothers Chris and Uris, he was a member of the Bouchillon Trio that, in 1925, recorded four tunes for Okeh, though only "She Doodle Dooed" was released. The next year, as the Greenville Trio, they recorded two songs for Columbia that have not been released; at the conclusion of this session they recorded two tunes under Chris Bouchillon's leadership that were released, "Talking Blues" (without Charlie) and "Hannah."

Bouchillon's S.C. residences come from the census and Greenville city directories.

Recordings as Leader

"She Doodle Dooed" (1925; with the Bouchillon Trio), unissued recordings (1925–1926; with the Bouchillon Trio and Greenville Trio)

Leader Recorded With

Chris Bouchillon (1926)

Bouchillon, Chris (Christopher Allen)

Mandolin, singer/speaker

21 August 1893 (Oconee County, S.C.)-18 September 1968 (West Palm Beach, Fla.)

S.C. residences: Oconee County (1893-no later than 1900), Williamston (by 1900-no later than 1910), Anderson (by 1910-ca. 1916), Greenville (ca. 1916-mid-1920s, ca. 1931-ca. 1959), Kingstree (mid-1920s-ca. 1931)

Bouchillon worked primarily as a machinist. Inspired by his banjo-playing father, John, Chris played the mandolin. He initially recorded for Okeh in 1925 as part of the Bouchillon Trio with his brothers Charlie and Uris. Of the four tunes recorded, only one was released, "She Doodle Dooed," on which Chris Bouchillon sings in a typical country manner. At his next session, for Columbia he recorded "Talking Blues" (1926), which established his reputation and initiated the musical genre known as talking blues in which such notables as Woody Guthrie, Johnny Cash, and Bob Dylan occasionally performed. Claims have been made that spoken hot rod recordings of the 1950s and 1960s, as well as rap music, may be traced to this recording. Legend indicates that Bouchillon recorded "Talking Blues" at the suggestion of a Columbia representative who disliked his singing but enjoyed listening to the musician speak. Despite the success of this recording, Bouchillon sings the lyrics to many, but not most, of his other recordings, including the song on the flipside of "Talking Blues," "Hannah." He recorded "New Talking Blues" in 1928. Though he lived to age seventy-five, his recording career was limited to the period 1925–1928 in Atlanta. He is buried in Graceland Cemetery, Greenville, S.C.

Bouchillon's S.C. residences come from the census and Greenville city directories.

Composition

"She Doodle Dooed"

Recordings as Leader

"She Doodle Dooed" (1925; with the Bouchillon Trio), unissued recordings (1925–1926; with the Bouchillon Trio and Greenville Trio), *Chris Bouchillon: The Original Talking Blues Man* (1926–1928), "A Bull Fight in Mexico" (1927), "Chris Visits the Barber Shop" (1927), "I Got Mine" (1928), "Speed Maniac" (1928)

Website

www.wikitree.com/wiki/Bouchillon-1 (accessed 21 May 2014)

References

SECONDARY: "C. A. Bouchillon," *Greenville (S.C.) News*, 20 September 1968, p. 10 (obituary); Tony Russell, *Blacks Whites and Blues* (New York: Stein and Day, 1970), 17–18; Bruce Bastin, *Red River Blues: The Blues Tradition in the Southeast* (Urbana: University of Illinois Press, 1986), 42, 197; Charles Wolfe, notes to *Chris Bouchillon: The Original Talking Blues Man* (1987; Old Homestead Records OHCS-181); Pat Harrison, notes to *Chris Bouchillon: The Original Talking Blues Man,* included in *Tom Darby and Jimmie Tarlton* (2005; JSP Records JSP 7746-D); Malcolm Jones, "Snake-Oil Music: On Medicine Shows and Other Forms of Homemade Entertainment," *American Scholar* 75 (Spring 2006): 118–24; Tony Russell, *Country Music Originals: The Legends and the Lost* (New York: Oxford University Press, 2007), 77–78.

Bouchillon, Ethel Mae Waters

Speaker

16 January 1903 (Atlanta, Ga.)–2 January 1980 (West Palm Beach, Fla.)

S.C. residences: Greenville (ca. 1923–mid-1920s, ca. 1931–ca. 1959), Kingstree (mid-1920s–ca. 1931)

In 1924 Ethel Mae Waters married Chris Bouchillon as her second husband. During World War II and later she worked primarily as a machinist. She recorded once, on "Adam and Eve" (1928), with the record label identifying the performers as Mr. and Mrs. Chris Bouchillon. On this recording she serves as interlocutor, setting up her husband's punch lines, but providing some of her own. Though they recorded this dialogue in four

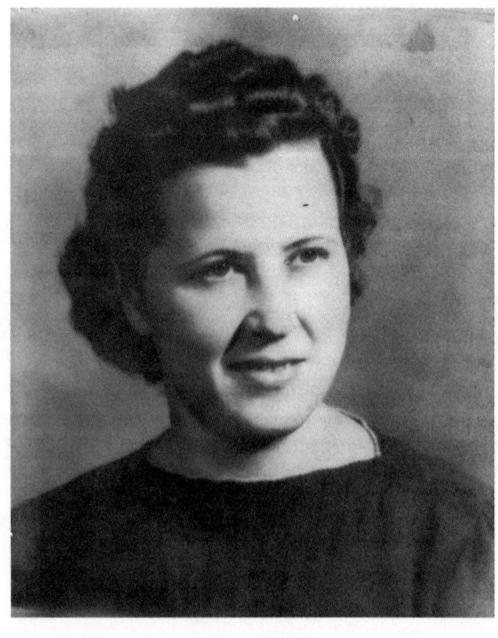

Ethel Bouchillon; permission of Valerie Craft

parts, only two parts were released. She is buried in Graceland Cemetery, Greenville, S.C.

Bouchillon's S.C. residences come from the census and Greenville city directories.

Recording as Leader

"Adam and Eve" (1928; with Chris Bouchillon)

Website

www.wikitree.com/wiki/Waters-141 (accessed 21 May 2014)

Reference

SECONDARY: "Ethel Mae Bouchillon," *Palm Beach (Fla.) Post,* 4 January 1980, sec. D, p. 11 (obituary).

Bouchillon, (John) Uris

Guitar

18 February 1898 (Anderson County, probably Williamston, S.C.)-18 January 1974 (Palm Beach County, Fla.)

S.C. residences: Anderson County, probably Williamston (1898-no later than 1910), Anderson (by 1910-ca. 1916), Greenville (ca. 1916-mid-1920s, ca. 1931-ca. 1952), Kingstree (mid-1920s-ca. 1931)

Bouchillon worked primarily as a machinist. With brothers Charlie and Chris, he was a member of the Bouchillon Trio that, in 1925, recorded four tunes for Okeh, though only "She Doodle Dooed" was released. The next year, as the Greenville Trio, they recorded two songs for Columbia that have not been released; at the conclusion of this session they recorded two tunes under Chris Bouchillon's leadership that were released, including "Talking Blues" (without Charlie), which established Chris's reputation. Uris provided instrumental accompaniment on all of Chris's recordings, with the exception of "Hannah."

Bouchillon's S.C. residences come from the census and Greenville city directories.

Recordings as Leader

"She Doodle Dooed" (1925; with the Bouchillon Trio), unissued recordings (1925–1926; with the Bouchillon Trio and Greenville Trio)

Leader Recorded With

Chris Bouchillon (1926–1928)

Website

www.wikitree.com/wiki/Bouchillon-4 (accessed 21 May 2014)

References

SECONDARY: "John U. Bouchillion [*sic*]," *Palm Beach (Fla.) Post-Times,* 20 January 1974, sec. B, p. 6 (obituary); "J. U. Bouchillon Sr.," *Greenville (S.C.) News-Piedmont,* 20 January 1974, sec. C, p. 10 (obituary).

Bowen, Ichabod Marcy

Singer

Probably 19 July 1896 (Spartanburg, S.C.)-probably 15 March 1968 (N.Y.)

S.C. residences: Spartanburg (probably 1896-possibly 1913), Orangeburg (at least 1913)

Bowen sang with the Claflin University Quintet, at least in 1913. He served as an army private during World War I. A resident of N.Y.C. by 1918, he worked as an elevator operator (1925), apartment house porter (1930), and watchman at a highway construction site (1940). He is buried in site 3439, section 2W, Long Island National Cemetery, Farmingdale, N.Y.

Bowen's place and 1896 date of birth come from the singer's World War I (1918) and World War II (1942) draft registration cards, as well as a delayed birth certificate issued in N.Y.C. in 1943. The 1900 and 1910 censuses indicate that Bowen was born in 1897 (in March, according to the earlier census). The 1925 N.Y. state census specifies that he was then twenty-five years old (enumerated on 1 June). The 1930 federal census estimates his age as twenty-nine (enumerated on 17 April). The Social Security Death Index notes that when he died, his last known residence was Jamaica/Saint Albans, N.Y. This document records his birth date as 19 July 1896 and death date as 15 March 1968, though at least two less reliable sources indicate that he died four days later.

Bowers, David C. ("Boots")

Singer, bass

23 January 1928 (S.C., probably Barnwell County)-23 October 1995

S.C. residence: Barnwell County (1928-no later than 1944)

In N.Y.C. by 1944, Bowers sang tenor for gospel groups the Southern Trumpeters (1944) and the Skylight Singers (1945). Soon he sang bass with rhythm-and-blues groups, initially the King Odom Quartet (1947–1954). Subsequently he sang with the Larks, of which he was a founding member, the Ravens, and the Buccaneers. He quit performing in the late 1950s. Bowers solos on the Larks' recording of "The World Is Waiting for the Sunrise," as well as on the group's performance of this song in the movie *Rhythm and Blues Revue.* He settled in Brooklyn, N.Y.

Bowers's birth and death dates and middle initial come from the Social Security Death Index. The singer was enumerated for the 1930 census in Four Mile Township, Barnwell County; for the 1940 census, in Richland Township, Barnwell County.

Leaders Recorded With

Bible Tone Gospel Quartet (mid-1940s), King Odom Quartet (1948, 1950–1952), Larks (1954–1955; two songs released as by the Kings), Ravens (1956–1957)

Film

Rhythm and Blues Revue (1955; with the Larks)

References

SECONDARY: Marv Goldberg, "The Ravens, Part 4," http://www.uncamarvy.com/Ravens/ravens04.html (1999; accessed 21 May 2014); "Spotlight on the King Odom Four, Part One!," http://www.vocalgroupharmony.com/Lucky.htm (2003; accessed 21 May 2014); "Spotlight on the King Odom Four, Part Two!," http://www.vocalgroupharmony.com/Im_Look.htm (2003; accessed 21 May 2014); Marv Goldberg, "The Du Droppers," http://www.uncamarvy.com/DuDroppers/dudrop.html (2009; accessed 21 May 2014); Marv Goldberg, "The King Odom Quartet," http://www.uncamarvy.com/KingOdomQuartet/kingodomquartet.html (2009; accessed 21 May 2014); Marv Goldberg, "The Larks," http://www.uncamarvy.com/Larks/larks.html (2009; accessed 21 May 2014); Marv Goldberg, "The Ravens, Part 3," http://www.uncamarvy.com/Ravens/ravens03.html (2009; accessed 21 May 2014); "Spotlight on Savannah Churchill, Part Two of Two," http://www.vocalgroupharmony.com/3ROWNEW/WhyWasIBorn.htm (2010; accessed 21 May 2014); "In Rememberance [*sic*] of . . . Isaiah Bing," http://www.toddbaptista.com/remember.html (2013; accessed 21 May 2014); "Uncommon Labels, Part One," http://www.vocalgroupharmony.com/4ROWNEW/AmazinWillieMays.htm (2013; accessed 21 May 2014); Todd Baptista, "In Rememberance [*sic*] of . . . Cleveland 'Bill' Bing, Baritone with Golden Gate Quartet, King Odom Four, Dies at 91," http://www.toddbaptista.com/remember.html (2014; accessed 21 May 2014).

Bowie, Prince

Mellophone, saxophone
Ca. 1925 (S.C.)–?
S.C. residence: Charleston (at least late 1930s–at least into early 1940s)

A ward of Jenkins Orphanage, Bowie played in its bands in the late 1930s and early 1940s.

Bowie's age was estimated as fifteen when the youth was enumerated for the census at the orphanage on 21 May 1940.

Bowman, Theodore Albert

Composer, singer
Probably mid-to-late 1870s (Charleston, S.C.)–13 December 1932
S.C. residence: Charleston (probably mid-to-late 1870s–ca. 1895)

In the 1890s Bowman performed in a medicine show with his musical partner, Chris Smith. They settled in N.Y.C., performing in vaudeville and composing songs as Smith and Bowman; Bowman mostly wrote the lyrics. Their compositions were sung by such vaudevillians as Bonita (Pauline des Landes), Harry Brown, Ethel Carter, A. H. Dougherty, Lizzie B. Raymond, and Claude Thardo. After Bowman moved to Boston and married Cora Terry in 1908, the spouses formed the team of Bowman and Terry and worked on the Mass. vaudeville circuit from 1909 to 1911. He sang with the Melrose Comedy Four in 1912; two years later he managed the Beacon Quartet in Boston. After serving in the navy from 1917 to 1919 he was employed as a railroad porter, at least in 1920. His last known performance was in 1926 with Jimmy Cooper's Darktown Frolics in Washington, D.C.

Because the 1900 census (conducted in N.Y.C. on 14 June) is the earliest known public document to record Bowman's birth date (October 1875), it is the most likely accurate of the several documents indicating when the composer was born. His age was estimated as thirty-one when he was enumerated in Boston on 5 January 1920; as fifty when enumerated in N.Y.C. on 23 April 1930. Massachusetts Marriages, 1841–1915, notes that at the time of his 1908 marriage, Bowman was thirty.

Compositions

"Ain't Dat an Awful Feeling!," "Ain't That You Maggie?," "Anna, Let Me Hear from You," "Car'lina Lou," "Coon's Day in May," "Diana Brown," "Good Evening, Emmaline," "Good Morning Carrie!," "The Humming Coon," "I Ain't Got No Time to Spare," "I Ain't Poor No More," "I'm Not 'Lowed to Answer Letters," "In the Jungle I'm a Queen," "It Ain't No Fault of Mine," "I've Got de Blues," "I Wants to Pick a Bone with You," "Johanna or 'Choose the One That You Love the Best!,'" "Liza, or You Only You," "Ma Clementina," "Mame, or the Mountain Maid," "Mind Your Own Business and I'll Mind Mine," "Mister Moon Kindly Come Out and Shine," "My Salinda Brown," "Nobody but You," "Oh Missus Sue Blue," "Since I Heard from Home," "Two Is Company and Three Is a Crowd," "When Mister Sun Gets Married to Miss Moon," "While the Rain Am Falling," "Write Yo' Baby Every Day," "Your Face Looks Familiar to Me"

References

SECONDARY: Tom Fletcher, *100 Years of the Negro in Show Business* (New York: Burdge, 1954), 50, 147; Benjamin Franklin V, "Chris Smith and the Bowmans," *Music Reference Services Quarterly* 15 (2012): 240–62.

Boyd, Don (Donald Edward)

Trombone

30 November 1921 (Beckley, W.Va.)–16 December 2005 (Columbia, S.C.)

S.C. residence: Columbia (1977–2005)

Upon finishing high school in Beckley, W.Va., Boyd became a professional musician, playing initially with Glen Gray's Casa Loma band and then with Harry James. For three years during World War II he was involved in musical activities while serving in the army air force. After leaving the military he joined the band of Les Brown, whose female vocalist was Doris Day; he is on Brown's recording of "I've Got My Love to Keep Me Warm," arranged by Skip Martin. After freelancing in N.Y.C. Boyd returned to Beckley, where he led a band and taught. He retired to S.C., where he was part of the Columbia music scene.

Leaders Recorded With

Casa Loma (1942), Harry James (1942–1943), Les Brown (1946–1947)

Film

Probably *Best Foot Forward* (1943)

Reference

SECONDARY: "Donald E. Boyd," *Columbia (S.C.) State*, 18 December 2005, sec. B, p. 4 (obituary).

Bradley, Herman

Drums, singer

2 June 1908 (Charleston, S.C.)–24 July 1998 (Albany, N.Y.)

S.C. residence: Charleston (1908–probably early 1910s)

As a child Bradley moved from Charleston to Newark, N.J. There, beginning in 1933, he led the Rhythm Dons, a band that became popular locally and was known for winning band battles. Its members included Ike Quebec and Jabbo Smith. Some musicians, including Al Cooper, left Bradley's group in 1937 to form the Savoy Sultans, which became the intermission band at the Savoy Ballroom in N.Y.C. Active into the 1980s, Bradley is buried in Albany Rural Cemetery, Menands, N.Y.

Bradley's birth and death dates come from the Social Security Death Index.

Leaders Recorded With

Wynonie Harris (1950), Freddie Mitchell (1950, 1952), Joey Thomas (1951), Mr. Sad Head (1953), Eddie Durham (1974)

Herman Bradley; permission of Barbara J. Kukla

References

SECONDARY: Barbara J. Kukla, *Swing City: Newark Nightlife, 1925–50* (Philadelphia: Temple University Press, 1991), 91, 142–43, 188 (comments by Bradley); "Herman Bradley," *Albany (N.Y.) Times Union*, 30 July 1998, sec. B, p. 6 (obituary).

Brazel, Gerald

Trumpet, flugelhorn
11 August 1962 (New York, N.Y.)–
S.C. residence: Saint Helena Island (1976–)

Brazel received an undergraduate degree from Berklee College of Music in 1984 and a master's from Lehman College in 2007. Though he has performed with many notable musicians, including Lionel Hampton from 1987 to 1994, he is best known for his affiliation with Lester Bowie for a decade beginning in 1989. When Bowie's health failed in 1999 Brazel became musical director of Bowie's group Brass Fantasy, a position he retains. He backed Digable Planets on "Rebirth of Slick (Cool Like Dat)," which won a Grammy Award for Best Rap Performance by a Duo or Group (1994). Though Brazel directs bands at Beach Channel High School and Channel View School for Research, both in Rockaway Park, N.Y., he maintains a home in S.C.

Leaders Recorded With

Rhythm Team (1987), Lester Bowie (1989–1990, 1992, 1997), Art Ensemble of Chicago (1990), Digable Planets (1992, 1994), Greg Osby (1993), Mighty Sparrow (1996, 1998, 2000, 2002), Pucho Brown (1999–2000, 2003–2004), Seleno Clarke (1999, 2003), Guru (2000)

Films

Malcolm X (1992), *Piñero* (2001)

Website

http://home.earthlink.net/~brassfantasy (accessed 21 May 2014)

Briggans, Eunice

See Brigham, Eunice Henry

Briggs, J. T. ("Preacher")

Guitar
Possibly 15 April 1904 (probably Union County, S.C.)–3 January 1983 (Spartanburg, S.C.)
S.C. residences: Union County (possibly 1904–at least until 1920, but no later than 1935), Spartanburg Township, Spartanburg County (by 1935–1983)

Briggs helped teach Henry "Rufe" Johnson to play the guitar.

Briggs's birth date comes from the Social Security Death Index; the nickname, from the obituary. For the 1910 (estimated age six) and 1920 (fifteen) censuses, Briggs was enumerated in Bogansville Township, Union County. He was enumerated for the 1930 and 1940 censuses in Spartanburg Township, Spartanburg County; for them he was estimated as twenty-one and thirty-seven, respectively.

Gerald Brazel, La Viola Café, Cedarhurst, N.Y., 31 October 2010; permission of the photographer, Bill Margulis, and Gerald Brazel

References

SECONDARY: Pete Lowry, notes to Henry "Rufe" Johnson, *The Union County Flash!* (1973; Trix 3304); Bruce Bastin, *Red River Blues: The Blues Tradition in the Southeast* (Urbana: University of Illinois Press, 1986), 193; "J. T. Briggs," *Spartanburg (S.C.) Herald-Journal,* 4 January 1983, sec. A, p. 5 (obituary).

Briggs, Pete (Peter)

Bass, tuba

Possibly ca. 1900 or ca. 1904 (probably S.C., possibly Charleston)–possibly 1970s

S.C. residence: possibly Charleston (ca. 1900 or ca. 1904–no later than 1921)

Briggs became a professional musician by 1921. All his recordings were made during the period 1927–1930, first in Chicago and then in N.Y.C. On recordings with Louis Armstrong he helped provide the rhythmic foundation (always on tuba) for some of the most valued jazz recordings, including "Potato Head Blues" and "Black and Blue." He was a regular member of the Jim Jam Jazzers (led by George Long) and Lucky Boy Minstrels, as well as bands led by Carroll Dickerson, Edgar Hayes, Vernon Andrade, and Herman Autrey. After leaving Autrey in 1944 he gave up music for farming.

Briggs was possibly related to trumpeter Arthur Briggs, who was not a South Carolinian. Sources indicate, without evidence, that Pete Briggs was born in Charleston ca. 1900 or ca. 1904. He might have taught music at Jenkins Orphanage, though no document consulted confirms his affiliation with this institution. The Social Security Death Index records the August 1965 death of a Peter Briggs who was born on 16 April 1902 and whose Social Security card was issued by the state of N.Y. It has not been determined if this person was the musician Pete Briggs. Without evidence Horst P. J. Bergmeier and Rainer E. Lotz state that Briggs died in the 1970s.

Leaders Recorded With

Louis Armstrong (1927, 1929), Carroll Dickerson (1928), Jelly Roll Morton (1930)

References

SECONDARY: "Jim Jam Jazzers," *Billboard* 33 (3 December 1921): 65; Horst P. J. Bergmeier and Rainer E. Lotz, "James Arthur Briggs," *Black Music Research Journal* 30 (Spring 2010): 95.

Brigham, Eunice Henry

Trumpet

9 April 1898 (Savannah, Ga.)–?

S.C. residence: Charleston (by 1906–probably late 1910s)

A ward of Jenkins Orphanage beginning in 1906, Brigham played in the school's bands starting ca. 1910 and performed with one of them in London in 1914. He helped teach Jabbo Smith to play the trumpet. Upon leaving the institution he performed with unknown groups before touring, from 1923 to 1930, with Frank Penman's Blue Melody Boys, Huntington's Minstrels, the Rabbit's Foot Minstrels, Alphonso Trent, and Ruby Williams. He is not known to have recorded.

Brigham's date and place of birth come from the passenger list of the *St. Louis,* which transported the orphanage band from Liverpool to N.Y.C. in September 1914. This list spells his surname Briggans. The passenger list for the *Campania,* which took the group to England in May, records it as Bruggan.

References

SECONDARY: John Chilton, *A Jazz Nursery: The Story of the Jenkins' Orphanage Bands of Charleston, South Carolina* (London: Bloomsbury Book Shop, 1980), 53; Howard Rye, "Visiting Fireboys: The Jenkins' Orphanage Bands in Britain," *Storyville* 130 (1987): 137–43.

Briscoe, Sylvester

Trombone, tuba

Probably ca. 1903 (Ky.)–before 1980

S.C. residence: Charleston (by early 1920s–mid-1920s)

A ward of Jenkins Orphanage, Briscoe played in its bands in the early 1920s. Leaving the institution at mid-decade (by 1926 he lived in Louisville, Ky.), he went on the road as a professional musician. With John Williams's Syncopators ca. 1926, his performance of "Tiger Rag"—playing trombone with his foot on the slide and other antics—was so spectacular that it inspired Mary Lou Williams, the band's pianist, to adopt flashy elements in her playing. From 1927 into the 1930s he was with the Hardy Brothers and groups led by Jordan Embry, Bennie Moten, and Blanche Calloway. He apparently never recorded.

Briscoe was a brother of pianist Dan Briscoe, who was not a South Carolinian. Sylvester Briscoe has not been located in the censuses of 1900, 1910, and 1940. At estimated age seventeen he was enumerated for the census in the Industrial School of Reform, Jefferson, Ky., on 9 January 1920; at estimated age twenty-seven, in Richmond, Ky., on 15 April 1930. He and his wife, Bessie, had two roomers when enumerated in 1930: Joseph Fleming and John Jackson, both musicians. John Chilton states that Briscoe was born around 1900 and had died by the time Chilton completed his manuscript.

References

SECONDARY: John Chilton, *A Jazz Nursery: The Story of the Jenkins' Orphanage Bands of Charleston, South Carolina* (London: Bloomsbury Book Shop, 1980), 26, 41, 53; Linda Dahl, *Morning Glory: A Biography of Mary Lou Williams* (New York: Pantheon, 1999), 48.

Brockman, (Marion) Brooks

Cornet, singer

4 May, probably 1880s (Laurens, S.C.)–15 June 1947 (Los Angeles, Calif.)

S.C. residences: Laurens (1880s–1903), Charleston (1903–no later than 1914), Columbia (at least 1914)

A ward of Jenkins Orphanage beginning in 1903, Brockman played in its bands. In Poughkeepsie, N.Y., in 1909, he sang a solo at a concert by the institution's Orphan Brass Band and Jubilee Concert Company. He became a bandmaster at the orphanage ca. 1912. Upon leaving this institution he moved to Columbia, S.C. In either 1917 or 1918 he began playing at the Plaza cabaret (previously the Cabaret Garden) in Calgary, Alberta, Canada; the Plaza probably dismissed him because of a policy that replaced black musicians with white ones. By 1930 he resided in Santa Barbara, Calif. He is buried in section D, Live Oak Cemetery, Monrovia, Calif.

Various dates have been recorded for Brockman's birth. One of his two World War I draft registration cards appears to specify the date of 4 May 1889 (the year is indistinct); the other indicates 4 May 1891. His age was estimated as forty-three when he was enumerated for the census in Santa Barbara on 16 April 1930. The California Death Index identifies the date as 4 May 1887, while his grave marker specifies the year 1883. He is absent from the Columbia city directories published during the 1910s.

References

SECONDARY: "Jenkins Band Makes Big Hit," *Poughkeepsie (N.Y.) Daily Eagle*, 13 July 1909, p. 5; "New Plaza Orchestra of White Artists Dispense Jazz Music," *Morning Albertan* (Calgary), 20 December 1920, p. 2; "Colored Musicians No Longer at Plaza," *Morning Albertan* (Calgary), 22 December 1920, p. 5; John Chilton, *A Jazz Nursery: The Story of the Jenkins' Orphanage Bands of Charleston, South Carolina* (London: Bloomsbury Book Shop, 1980), 20–21, 53.

Brooks, Baby (Roosevelt)

Guitar, singer

Possibly 2 June, probably between 1902 and 1906 (Greenville, S.C.)–4 January 1987 (Macon, Ga.)

S.C. residence: Greenville (between 1902 and 1906–probably at least until 1970)

Brooks played in the manner of Willie Walker. Around 1930 he was part of a trio with Baby Tate and Joe Walker that performed in the Greenville area. He largely quit playing by the mid-1960s, though in 1970 Peter Lowry recorded him performing seven tunes, including one, "Come Back Baby," with Tate backing him.

Baby Brooks (right), with Baby Tate, Spartanburg, S.C., 1970; permission of the photographer, Peter B. Lowry

Brooks was a nephew of guitarist Sam Brooks. Documents provide conflicting information about Brooks's birth year. When the guitarist was enumerated for the census in Greenville on 9 April 1930, his age was estimated as twenty-four. Georgia, Death Index, 1933–1998, records his age at death as eighty-three. The Social Security Death Index indicates that he was born on 2 June 1902.

Recordings as Leader (All 1970; All Unissued)

"Brook's [*sic*] Comeback Blues," "Come Back Baby," "Git It," "My God Going to Shake My Righteous Hand," "Nearer My God to Thee," "Paris Rag," "Put Me Down"

References

SECONDARY: Bruce Bastin and Pete Lowry, "Tricks Ain't Workin' No More: Blues from the South-East," *Blues Unlimited* 78 (December 1970): 11; Bruce Bastin, *Crying for the Carolines* (London: Studio Vista, 1971), 71–73; Bruce Bastin and Pete Lowry, "Blues from the South-East (Sequel 3): 'Tricks Ain't Workin' No More,'" *Blues Unlimited* 80 (February–March 1971): 15; Bruce Bastin and Pete Lowry, "Blues from the South-East (Sequel 5): 'Tricks Ain't Workin' No More,'" *Blues Unlimited* 82 (June 1971): 14; Bruce Bastin, *Red River Blues: The Blues Tradition in the Southeast* (Urbana: University of Illinois Press, 1986), 173–77.

Brooks, Sam

Guitar, singer

Possibly ca. 1908 (probably S.C., possibly Greenville)–possibly 1966 (possibly Clemson, S.C.)

S.C. residence: Greenville (by 1913–)

Beginning in the 1910s or 1920s in the Greenville area, where he lived as early as 1913, Brooks served his first cousin Willie Walker as guide and second guitarist. Each recorded but once: together in 1930 in Atlanta for Columbia. They recorded four tunes, though only "Dupree Blues" and "South Carolina Rag" (the latter in two takes) were released; "Da Da Da" and "Rider Blues" remain unissued. Stephen Calt et al. note that "Dupree Blues" is "one of the earliest recorded versions of the 'blues ballad.'" Brooks was known for chewing tobacco while singing.

Brooks was an uncle of guitarist Baby Brooks. The Columbia files record Sam Brooks's given name as David. Stephen Calt and John Miller state that Brooks died in 1966. It has not been determined if Brooks was the Sam Brooks who was estimated as age twelve when enumerated for the census in Greenville on 19 January 1920, or the Sam Brooks who was estimated as thirty-one when enumerated in Spartanburg on 2 May 1940 (this document notes that he resided in Spartanburg in 1935). These two Sam Brookses might be the same person. The one enumerated in Spartanburg worked as a laborer for a lumber company. South Carolinian Samuel D. Brooks, a semiskilled worker in the manufacturing of paper products, enlisted in the army on 26 October 1942 in Newark, N.J.; his birth year was recorded as 1909. No known evidence indicates that he was the musician.

Leader Recorded With

Willie Walker (1930)

References

SECONDARY: Stephen Calt et al., notes to *East Coast Blues, 1926–1935* (1968; Yazoo L-1013); Bruce Bastin and Pete Lowry, "Tricks Ain't Workin' No More: Blues from the South-East," *Blues Unlimited* 78 (December 1970): 11; Bruce Bastin, *Crying for the Carolines* (London: Studio Vista, 1971), 72–73; Stephen Calt and John Miller, notes to *Mama Let Me Lay It on You, 1926–1936* (1974; Yazoo L-1040); Bruce Bastin, *Red River Blues: The Blues Tradition in the Southeast* (Urbana: University of Illinois Press, 1986), 175–77, 185.

Brown, Arthur

Singer

S.C. residence: Charleston (1930s)

A ward of Jenkins Orphanage, Brown sang with its bands in the 1930s.

Brown, Charles

Alto horn

Possibly 14 October 1902, though possibly ca. 1905 (probably Greenville, S.C.)–?

S.C. residences: Greenville (possibly 1902 or ca. 1905–no later than 1914), Charleston (by 1914–at least into early 1920s)

A ward of Jenkins Orphanage, Brown played in its bands beginning in 1914, when he performed with one of them in England.

Brown's date and place of birth come from the passenger list of the *St. Louis,* which transported the orphanage band from Liverpool to N.Y.C. in

September 1914. John Chilton states that Brown was born in London, England. His age was estimated as fifteen when he was enumerated for the census at the orphanage on 9 January 1920.

References

SECONDARY: John Chilton, *A Jazz Nursery: The Story of the Jenkins' Orphanage Bands of Charleston, South Carolina* (London: Bloomsbury Book Shop, 1980), 53; Howard Rye, "Visiting Fireboys: The Jenkins' Orphanage Bands in Britain," *Storyville* 130 (1987): 137–43.

Brown, Charleston (Russell)

Dancer

Ca. 1906 (probably S.C., presumably Charleston)–?

S.C. residence: presumably Charleston (ca. 1906–no later than 1910)

In N.Y.C. ca. 1920, Brown was known for performing a Geechie dance on street corners and in clubs such as Leroy's. It became known as the Charleston, presumably because it originated with Brown, whose nickname was Charleston. (Without equivocation Garvin Bushell credits Brown with introducing the dance to N.Y.C.) At the request of the producer, Brown's dance was performed in *Runnin' Wild* (1923) to the music of "Charleston," which James P. Johnson wrote for the show. Around this time Brown, Joe Peterson, and Reuben Brown formed the Three Browns, a dance group that featured acrobatics, such as the splits; Charleston Brown's specialty was the knee-drop. The Three Browns danced at Balaban and Katz theaters in Chicago and toured as far west as California; the men performed with Duke Ellington at the Kentucky Club in N.Y.C. As a result of seeing the group at the Capitol Palace, a N.Y.C. club, Count Basie considered Charleston Brown "the undisputed champion Charleston dancer in Harlem."

Brown's age was estimated as three when the youth was enumerated for the census in N.Y.C. on 21 April 1910; as ten when enumerated there for the N.Y. state census on 1 June 1915. When enumerated in N.Y.C. for the federal census on 9 January 1920 and 7 or 8 April 1930, his ages were estimated, respectively, as fourteen and twenty-five. The 1930 census notes that Brown then worked as a dancer in a theater. The 1910 census states that he was born in S.C.; the 1920 and 1930 censuses, in N.Y. He is absent from the 1940 census. It has not been proven that Brown was born in S.C. However, because both his parents were born in the state, because the earliest census in which he appears (1910) identifies S.C. as his birthplace, and because he was nicknamed Charleston, he was probably born in S.C., in or near Charleston. Though at least one source states that the Three Browns disbanded in 1926, evidence proves otherwise. See the Sheboygan Theatre advertisement in *Sheboygan (Wis.) Press,* 29 September 1928, p. 21. Clovis E. Semmes indicates that the dancers performed at the Regal Theater in Chicago in the 1930s.

References

SECONDARY: Willie "The Lion" Smith, with George Hoefer, *Music on My Mind: The Memoirs of an American Pianist* (Garden City, N.Y.: Doubleday, 1964), 96–97; Marshall Stearns and Jean Stearns, *Jazz Dance: The Story of American Vernacular Dance* (New York: Macmillan, 1968), 145–46, 271; *Good Morning Blues: The Autobiography of Count Basie,* as told to Albert Murray (New York: Random House, 1985), 52; Garvin Bushell, as told to Mark Tucker, *Jazz from the Beginning* (Ann Arbor: University of Michigan Press, 1988), 28; Clovis E. Semmes, *The Regal Theater and Black Culture* (New York: Palgrave/Macmillan, 2006), 85.

Brown, Clinton

Baritone horn, drums

Probably January 1897 (Manning, S.C.)–?

S.C. residences: Manning (probably 1897–early 1910s), Charleston (early 1910s–at least until 1918)

A ward of Jenkins Orphanage, Brown played in its bands in the 1910s, including the one that performed in England in 1914.

Brown could easily be confused with his brother. On 5 June 1918 in Sumter, S.C., the musician, an employee of the orphanage, registered for the draft. On the registration card he indicated that his nearest relative is Clenton Brown, of Springfield, Mass. On this same date, Clenton Brown registered for the draft in Springfield, Mass.; on the registration card he noted that his nearest relative is his twin brother, Clinton Brown, of Charleston, S.C. On their registration cards, Clinton Brown recorded a birth date of 2 January 1897; Clenton, of 24 January 1897. For the passenger list of the *St. Louis,* which transported the orphanage band from Liverpool to N.Y.C. in September 1914, Clinton Brown identified his birth date as 2 August 1898.

Reference

SECONDARY: Howard Rye, "Visiting Fireboys: The Jenkins' Orphanage Bands in Britain," *Storyville* 130 (1987): 137–43.

Brown, Edward

Trombone

3 August 1896 (Charleston, S.C.)–?

S.C. residence: Charleston (1896–after 1914)

A ward of Jenkins Orphanage, Brown played in its bands in the 1910s, including the one that performed in London in 1914. In time he served the institution as assistant bandmaster.

Brown's date and place of birth come from the passenger list of the *St. Louis,* which transported the orphanage band from Liverpool to N.Y.C. in September 1914.

References

SECONDARY: John Chilton, *A Jazz Nursery: The Story of the Jenkins' Orphanage Bands of Charleston, South Carolina* (London: Bloomsbury Book Shop, 1980), 53; Howard Rye, "Visiting Fireboys: The Jenkins' Orphanage Bands in Britain," *Storyville* 130 (1987): 137–43.

Brown, James

Trumpet

S.C. residence: Charleston (by mid-1930s–at least into early 1940s)

Apparently a ward of Jenkins Orphanage, Brown played in its bands in the 1930s and early 1940s.

Reference

SECONDARY: John Chilton, *A Jazz Nursery: The Story of the Jenkins' Orphanage Bands of Charleston, South Carolina* (London: Bloomsbury Book Shop, 1980), 53.

Brown, James Joseph ("Godfather of Soul")

Singer, keyboards, dancer, composer

3 May 1933 (Barnwell, S.C.)–25 December 2006 (Atlanta, Ga.)

S.C. residences: Barnwell and vicinity (1933–1938), Beech Island (1979–1988, 1991–2006), Columbia (1988–1991)

Brown moved from S.C. to Augusta, Ga., by the late 1930s. Musically precocious, he there formed the Cremona Trio at age twelve; this group performed primarily gospel music, but also blues and pop. Before turning twenty he joined the band of his friend Bobby Byrd that evolved into the Famous Flames, which signed with King Records and recorded for the first time in 1956. The initial release, "Please, Please, Please," became a hit. "Try Me" (1958) was even more popular, reaching first position on the rhythm-and-blues charts. In 1962 Brown gave what is regarded as his greatest performance, a midnight show at the Apollo Theater that, when the music was released, established him as a major performer, one whose combination of rhythm and blues, soul, and gospel music—plus great energy—proved electrifying. Mainly because of this concert, Brown began performing in major venues, not just clubs and roadhouses. His reputation was enhanced with the 1965 release of "Papa's Got a Brand New Bag" and "I Got You (I Feel Good)," both of which reached the top of the rhythm-and-blues charts and ranked high on the pop charts. More hits followed, including "It's a Man's Man's Man's World" (1966), "Cold Sweat" (1967), "Say It Loud—I'm Black and I'm Proud" (1968), "Make It Funky" (1971), and "My Thang" (1974). By permitting a 1968 Boston performance to be televised, he helped ease racial tensions following the assassination of Dr. Martin Luther King, Jr.; during the concert he encouraged calm. He entertained troops in Vietnam in 1968 and the next year performed at the inauguration of President Nixon. Around this time his music evolved from soul to funk, with the assistance of instrumentalists Bootsy Collins, Pee Wee Ellis, Maceo Parker, and Fred Wesley. He performed in Africa several times, including in 1974 as headliner at the music festival held in conjunction with the Muhammad Ali–George Foreman boxing match. Though by the mid-1970s his appeal lessened in the United States, he had significant bookings abroad. His performance in *The Blues Brothers* (1980) led to a revival of popularity in his own country; subsequently he had such major hits as "Living in America" (1985) and "I'm Real" (1988). In recent years many performers have sampled his music. The movie *Get On Up* (2014) is based on Brown's life. A musical icon, Brown is buried at Beech Island, S.C.

Compositions

"Ain't It Funky Now," "Ain't That a Groove," "All I Need," "America Is My Home," "And I Do Just What I Want," "Baby, You're Right," "Blackenized,"

"Chonnie-on-Chon," "Cold Sweat," "Damn Right I'm Somebody," "Doing It to Death" (also titled "Gonna Have a Funky Good Time"), "Everything," "Funky Drummer," "Funky President," "Get on the Good Foot," "Get Right," "Get Up," "Ghetto Supastar," "The Grunt," "Hot," "Hot Pants," "I Don't Mind," "I Got the Feelin'," "I Got You (I Feel Good)," "I Know You Got Soul," "It's a Man's Man's Man's World," "King Heroin," "Licking Stick—Licking Stick," "Lost Someone," "Make It Funky," "Mashed Potatoes U.S.A.," "Mind Power," "Mother Popcorn," "My Thang," "Out of Sight," "Papa Don't Take No Mess," "Papa's Got a Brand New Bag," "The Payback," "Please, Please, Please," "Say It Loud—I'm Black and I'm Proud," "Shout and Shimmy," "Soul Power," "Soul President," "Super Bad," "Talkin' Loud and Sayin' Nothing," "There Was a Time," "Think (about It)," "Time Is Running Out Fast," "Try Me," "Unity"

Recordings as Leader (With the Exceptions of Brown's Collected Singles and Albums That Provide Recording Dates in the Title, These Are Release Dates, Not Necessarily Recording Dates)

The Singles (during the period 1956–1981; eleven two-CD sets), *Please Please Please* (1958), *Soul Pride: The Instrumentals, 1960–1969, Think* (1960), *Live at the Apollo* (1963), *Showtime* (1964), *Grits and Soul* (1965), *James Brown and His Famous Flames Sing Christmas Songs* (1966), *Cold Sweat* (1967), *Live at the Garden* (1967), *I Can't Stand Myself* (1968), *Live at the Apollo,* vol. 2 (1968), *Say It Live and Loud: Live in Dallas 08.26.68, Soulful Christmas* (1968), *Gettin' Down to It* (1969), *James Brown Plays and Directs the Popcorn* (1969), *Say It Loud—I'm Black and I'm Proud* (1969), *Funk Power 1970: A Brand New Thang, It's a New Day So Let a Man Come In* (1970), *Sex Machine* (1970), *Soul on Top* (1970), *Hot Pants* (1971), *Love Power Peace: Live at the Olympia, Paris, 1971, Revelation of the Mind* (1971), *There It Is* (1972), *Black Caesar* (1973), *The Payback* (1973), *Hell* (1974), *Dead on the Heavy Funk: 1975–1983, Sex Machine Today* (1975), *Jam 1980's* (1978), *Soul Syndrome* (1980), *In the Jungle Groove* (1986), *James Brown's Funky People* (1986), *Motherlode* (1988), *Live at Chastain Park* (1990), *Messing with the Blues* (1990), *Star Time* (1991), *Live at the Apollo 1995, Foundations of Funk* (1996), *Make It Funky* (1996), *ROR: James Brown Live* (1997), *Live at Studio 54* (1999), *The Next Step* (2002), *Ultimate Remixes* (2002), *A Family Affair* (2007), *Jazz* (2007), *Ultimate Showman: Live in Concert* (2007), *Twist* (2011)

Leaders Recorded With

Tammi Montgomery (later Terrell) (1962), Anna King (1963), Fred Wesley and the J.B.'s (1973)

Films

The T.A.M.I. Show (1964), *Ski Party* (1965), *The Phynx* (1970), *The Blues Brothers* (1980), *Doctor Detroit* (1983), *Rocky IV* (1985), *When We Were Kings* (1996), *Soulmates* (1997), *Blues Brothers 2000* (1998), *Holy Man* (1998), *Beat the Devil* (2002), *The Tuxedo* (2002), *Undercover Brother* (2002), *Paper Chasers* (2003), *Glastonbury* (2006), *Soul Power* (2008), *Sid Bernstein Presents . . .* (2010)

Awards

Georgia Music Hall of Fame (1983); Rock and Roll Hall of Fame (1986); Grammy Lifetime Achievement Award (1992); Rhythm & Blues Foundation Pioneer Award (1993); Hollywood Walk of Fame (1997); Songwriters Hall of Fame (2000); Kennedy Center Award (2003); United Kingdom Music Hall of Fame (2006); Order of the Palmetto (date unknown); South Carolina Entertainment and Music Hall of Fame (date unknown)

References

PRIMARY: James Brown, with Bruce Tucker, *James Brown, the Godfather of Soul* (New York: Macmillan, 1986); James Brown, *I Feel Good: A Memoir of a Life of Soul* (New York: New American Library, 2005).

SECONDARY: Geoff Brown, *The Life of James Brown* (New York: Omnibus Press, 1996); Douglas Wolk, *Live at the Apollo* (New York: Continuum, 2004); Anne Danielsen, *Presence and Pleasure: The Funk Grooves of James Brown and Parliament* (Middletown, Conn.: Wesleyan University Press, 2006); John Grooms, "Live from the Revival, It's James Brown!," in *Making Notes: Music of the Carolinas,* ed. Ann Wicker (Charlotte: Novello Festival Press, 2008), 111–13; *The James Brown Reader: 50 Years of Writing about the Godfather of Soul,* ed. Nelson George and Alan Leeds (New York: Plume, 2008); James Sullivan, *The Hardest Working Man: How James Brown Saved the Soul of America* (New York: Gotham Books, 2008); Don Rhodes, *Say It Loud! My Memories of James Brown, Soul Brother No. 1* (Guilford, Conn.: Lyons Press, 2009); Marc Myers, "James Brown: The Singles," www.jazzwax.com/2011/10/james-brown-the

-singles.html (2011; accessed 21 May 2014); R. J. Smith, *The One: The Life and Music of James Brown* (New York: Gotham Books, 2012).

Brown, John

Trombone, trumpet
September 1889 (S.C.)–?
S.C. residence: Charleston (by 1900–at least into 1910s)

A ward of Jenkins Orphanage beginning in 1900, Brown played in its bands and, ca. 1910, became its bandmaster.

Brown's birth date comes from the 1900 census, which was conducted at the orphanage on 28 June.

Reference

SECONDARY: John Chilton, *A Jazz Nursery: The Story of the Jenkins' Orphanage Bands of Charleston, South Carolina* (London: Bloomsbury Book Shop, 1980), 53.

Brown, Kathy (Katherine Ann)

Singer
5 August 1960 (Chadbourn, N.C.)–
S.C. residence: Cross (1995–)

Kathy Brown; photograph by Dorothy Shi, permission of Kathy Brown

Brown moved from N.C. to Washington, D.C., in the mid-1960s and to N.Y.C. in 1968. At age nine she began singing in her church choir, though in time she became enamored of and influenced by such singers as Aretha Franklin and Patti LaBelle. She was graduated from Wingate High School in Brooklyn and attended Manhattan College. After singing around town with the group Sweet Cinnamon, during the early 1990s she began performing and recording as a single. Since touring Europe in the 1990s she has spent approximately half her time there and half in S.C. She is popular as a singer of club music, with several of her recordings, including "Turn Me Out," reaching the upper levels of the dance and club charts.

Brown is a niece of singer Shirley Caesar, who is not a South Carolinian.

Compositions

"Don't Give Up," "Feel the Music," "Get Down on the Dance Floor," "Give It Up," "Give Me Your Love," "Got to Be Forever," "I Can't Deny," "Joy," "Love and Pain," "Love Is Not a Game," "Love Peace and Harmony," "Never Again," "Party People," "Power," "Rage," "Satisfied," "Show Me," "Somebody to Love," "Tell Me Why," "Turn Me On," "Turn Me Out," "Voodoo Magic"

Recordings as Leader (These Are Release Dates, Not Necessarily Recording Dates)

"Can't Play Around" (1993), "I Appreciate" (1995), "Turn Me Out" (1995), "Make Me Feel Like Singing" (ca. 1998), "Happy People" (1999), "Joy" (1999), "Give It Up" (2001), "Over You" (2001), "Sooky Sooky" (2001), "You Give Good Love" (2002), "Never Again" (2003), "Share the Blame" (2003), "Voodoo Magic" (2003), "Dare Me" (2006), "Get Another Love" (2006), "Light Up My Life" (2008; with Danism), "Sound of the City" (2008; with the White Knights), "Feel the Music" (2010), "Gotta Hold On" (2010), "Love and Pain" (2010), "Show Me How to Love" (2011; with Micky Moore), "Tell Me Why" (2011), "Believe in Yourself" (2013; with Marlon D), "Forever" (2013), "Give Me Your Love" (2013), "Gotta Keep On" (2013; with Gianfranco), "Not This Time" (2013; with Namy), "Somebody to Love" (2013; with Artificial Intelligence)

Leaders Recorded With (These Are Release Dates, Not Necessarily Recording Dates)

Warren Clark (2001), J. Majik (2001, 2003), Gloria Gaynor (2002), Major Boys (2004), J. Majik and Wickaman (2005, 2007), Soul Central (2005), Jerry Ropero and Michael Simon (2007), Dan-E-Mc (2013)

Reference

PRIMARY: "Kathy Brown—Artists [*sic*], Singer, Songwriter and Big Time Vocal Diva!," http://vimeo.com/61536277 (undated; accessed 21 May 2014) (video interview).

Brown, Maxine

Singer

Possibly 18 August 1938 (Kingstree, S.C.)–

S.C. residence: Kingstree (probably 1939–probably mid-1940s)

Brown lived in Kingstree until apparently being kidnapped and taken to N.Y.C. to live with her mother, who was previously unknown to her. Mahalia Jackson and the Five Blind Boys of Alabama were among her early musical influences. In the mid-1950s she helped establish the Royaltones, a gospel group; after it disbanded she joined the pop group Treys, which became the Manhattans. Her career as a single began in 1960; soon she had hits with "All in My Mind" and "Funny." "Oh No Not My Baby" (1964) and "We'll Cry Together" (1969) were other popular successes. Mid-decade, she recorded a series of duets with Chuck Jackson. She seldom recorded after the 1960s, though she released the self-produced *From the Heart* in 2005. Around 2002 she teamed with Beverly Crosby and Ella Garrett as the Wild Women to perform in the revue *Wild Women Don't Have the Blues.* Known primarily as a soul singer, Brown performs various kinds of music, including jazz and blues. Also an actor, she appeared in the stage productions *Don't Bother Me, I Can't Cope* (1974) and *Manhattan Towers* (2001).

Though Brown has stated that she has no middle name, sources identify her as Maxine Ella Brown. She has not been located in the 1940 census. At least one source identifies her birth date as 27 April 1932, though this is the date sometimes given for the country singer Maxine Brown.

Compositions

"All in My Mind," "Finding Love," "Funny," "I.O.U.," "Keep On Keeping On," "Let Me Give You My Lovin'," "Love Is in Command," "Love Is There Right under Your Nose," "Since I Found You," "Too Long Out in the Cold," "Walking through the Raindrops"

Recordings as Leader (These Are Release Dates, Not Necessarily Recording Dates)

"Harry Let's Marry" (1960), "After All We've Been Through" (1961), "Heaven in Your Arms" (1961), *The Fabulous Sound of Maxine Brown* (1962), "If I Knew Then" (1962), "If You Have No Real Objections" (1962), "I Got a Funny Kind of Feeling" (1962), "I Kneel at Your Throne" (1962), "My Time for Cryin'" (1962), "Life Goes On Just the Same" (1963), *Spotlight on Maxine Brown* (1964), "Put Yourself in My Place" (1964), *Saying Something* (1965; with Chuck Jackson), "One Step at a Time" (1965), "Anything You Do Is Alright" (1966), "Let Me Give You My Lovin'" (1966), "One in a Million" (1966), "The Secret of Livin'" (1966), *Hold On, We're Coming* (1967; with Chuck Jackson), *Out of Sight* (1968), "Soul Serenade" (1968), *We'll Cry Together* (1969), "From Loving You" (1969), "Love in Them There Hills" (1969), "Always and Forever" (1971), "Make Love to Me" (1971), "I.O.U." (1972), "Treat Me Like a Lady" (1972), *From the Heart* (2005)

Award

Rhythm & Blues Foundation Pioneer Award (1991)

Website

http://www.maxinebrown.com/ (accessed 21 May 2014)

References

PRIMARY: David Freeland, *Ladies of Soul* (Jackson: University Press of Mississippi, 2001), 138–65 (interview); Seamus McGarvey, "Maxine Brown: Come Full Circle," *Juke Blues* 54 (Autumn–Winter 2003): 20–22 (interview); William S. Gooch, "Maxine Brown: Still Here and Still Hot," http://www.newyorkcool.com/archives/2007/August/interview_Maxine_Brown.htm (2007; accessed 21 May 2014) (interview); John Broven, *Record Makers and Breakers: Voices of the Independent Rock 'n' Roll Pioneers* (Urbana: University of Illinois Press, 2009), 373–78 (substantial comments by Brown); David Cole, "From the Heart," *In the Basement* 61 (Spring 2011): 18–25 (interview); Arlene

Corsano, *Thought We Were Writing the Blues but They Called It Rock and Roll* (Tenafly, N.J.: ArleneChristine, 2014), 150–51 (substantial comments by Brown).

Brown, Melvin

French horn

Ca. 1918 (S.C.)-?

S.C. residence: Charleston (probably late 1920s-at least into mid-1930s)

A ward of Jenkins Orphanage, Brown played in its bands at least in the early 1930s.

Brown's age was estimated as twelve when the youth was enumerated for the census at the orphanage on 2 April 1930; this document records his birthplace.

Reference

SECONDARY: Bruce Bastin, "A Note on the Carolina Cotton Pickers," *Storyville* 95 (June–July 1981): 177–82.

Brown, Nappy (Napoleon Brown Culp)

Singer, composer

12 October 1929 (Charlotte, N.C.)-20 September 2008 (Charlotte, N.C.)

S.C. residence: Pomaria (1977-ca. 2002, and possibly briefly later)

As a youth Brown sang in church and in the early 1940s formed the Traveling Sons of Harmony. In time he performed with such gospel groups as the Golden Bells, the Selah Jubilee Singers, and the Heavenly Lights. Influenced by such musicians as Cab Calloway and Louis Jordan, he began singing rhythm and blues in the mid-1950s. He affiliated with Savoy Records, for which he recorded over fifty tunes from 1954 into the 1960s; one of his earliest recordings, "Don't Be Angry," became his biggest hit. During this period he toured in shows with such singers as Big Maybelle and Jackie Wilson. His activities for two decades beginning in the early 1960s are vague, though he reportedly worked as an elephant handler in a circus and as a custodian. After being rediscovered in the early 1980s, Brown recorded frequently (though he did not record for a decade after 1996), toured internationally, and received several awards. Though he claimed to have written "The Right Time" (also titled "Night Time Is the Right Time"), which he recorded in 1957 and Ray Charles did the next year, this tune appears to have evolved from a 1937 recording of "The Right Time" by Roosevelt Sykes. Brown's recording of "Piddly Patter Patter" is on the sound track of *Cry Baby* (1990). Brown is buried in Gethsemane Memorial Gardens, Charlotte.

Compositions

"Ain't No Way," "Baby It's All Over," "Blues You Are," "Brush Up," "Bye Bye Baby," "Come Over Here," "Deep Sea Diver," "Don't Be Angry," "Don't Hurt No More," "Down in the Alley," "Do You Know the Man," "Every Shut Eye Ain't Sleepin'," "Fishin' Blues," "Get Along," "Give Me Your Love," "Happy Am I," "I Cried Like a Baby," "I'm a Wild Man," "I'm Gonna Get You," "I'm Too Cool," "I'm with You All the Way," "In the Darkest Hour," "I've Had My Fun," "I Want to Live," "Jesus Said It," "Keep On Pleasin' You," "Keep the Faith," "Land I Love," "Lemon Squeezin' Daddy," "The Lock on the Door," "Lonely and Blue," "Love Me Like You Used to Do," "Mary Lou," "Never Too Late," "One More Time," "Open Up That Door," "Small Red Apples," "So Glad I Don't Have to Cry No More," "Something Gonna Jump Out the Bushes," "Still Holdin' On," "Take Care of Me," "Things Have Changed," "This Is My Prayer," "Top of Her Lungs," "Way Back," "Wella Wella Baby-La," "What's Come over You Baby," "You Must Be Crazy," "You Showed Me Love," "You Were a Long Time Coming"

Recordings as Leader

"Is It True, Is It True" (1954), "I Wonder" (1954), "That Man" (1954), "Two Faced Woman" (1954), "Don't Be Angry" (1955), "It's All Yours" (1955), "It's Really You" (1955), "Just a Little Love" (1955), "Piddly Patter Patter" (1955; also titled "Pitter Patter"), "Sittin' in the Dark" (1955), "There'll Come a Day" (1955), "Wella Wella Baby-La" (1955), "Am I?" (1956), "I Cried Like a Baby" (1956), "I'm Getting Lonesome" (1956), "Little by Little" (1956), "Love Baby" (1956), "Open Up That Door" (1956), "Because I Love You" (1957), "Bye Bye Baby" (1957), "Goody-Goody-Gum-Drop" (1957), "If You Need Some Lovin'" (1957), "I'm Gonna Get You" (1957), "I'm in the Mood" (1957), "Oh, You Don't Know" (1957), "Pretty Girl" (1957), "The Right Time" (1957), "It Don't Hurt No More" (1958), "Skiddy Roe" (1958), "You're Gonna Need Someone" (1958), "For Those Who Love" (1959), "I Cried

Like a Baby" (1959), "It's All Right Now" (1959), "So Deep" (1959), "This Is My Confession" (1959), *Thanks for Nothing* (1969), *When I Get Inside* (ca. 1977; with the Southern Sisters), *I Done Got Over* (1983), *Tore Up* (1984), *Something Gonna Jump Out the Bushes!* (1987), *Just for Me* (1988), *Deep Sea Diver* (1989), *Apples and Lemons* (1990), *Aw! Shucks* (1991), *Jus' Messin' 'Round* (1992), *Napolean [sic] Brown and the Faithful Workers* (1993), *I'm a Wild Man* (ca. 1993), *Who's Been Foolin' You* (ca. 1994–1995), *Best of Both Worlds: 12 Rockin' Blues' [sic] Classics* (1995; with Kip Anderson), *Long Time Coming* (ca. 2007)

Leaders Recorded With

Possibly the Jubilators (1950; this group is also known as the Selah Jubilee Singers), Sultans (1952), Heavenly Lights (1954), Bell Jubilee Singers (early 1970s)

Awards

Best Blues Album of the Year, Carolina Beach Music Awards (1997; for *Best of Both Worlds,* with Kip Anderson); Great Master Blues Artist, Blues Hall of Fame (2002); Outstanding Achievement Award, Carolina Beach Music Awards (2006); Nappy Brown Day in South Carolina (2008)

References

PRIMARY: Les Quinn, "A Natter with Nappy," *Blues and Rhythm: The Gospel Truth* 27 (March 1987): 19–20 (interview); Seamus McGarvey and Stuart Colman, "Nappy Brown: That Man!," *Juke Blues* 9 (Summer 1987): 11–15 (combines interviews by McGarvey and Colman); Scott M. Bock, "Nappy Brown: Lemon Squeezin' Daddy," *Living Blues* 191 (August 2007): 12–19 (mainly a narrative by Brown); Benjamin Franklin V, *Jazz and Blues Musicians of South Carolina: Interviews with Jabbo, Dizzy, Drink, and Others* (Columbia: University of South Carolina Press, 2008), 47–54.

SECONDARY: "Nappy Brown and the Heartfixers Tour: What Happened?," *Juke Blues* 10 (Autumn 1987): 5; Tut Underwood, "Nappy Brown's Zingy Trail of Blues," *Sandlapper: The Magazine of South Carolina* 9 (Winter 1998–1999): 17–19; J. C. Marion, "Nappy Brown—A Forgotten Original," http://home.earthlink.net/~jaymar41/NapBrown.html (1999; accessed 21 May 2014); Opal Louis Nations, "The Gospel Side of Nappy Brown," *Big City Blues* (December 2004–January 2005): 16–18; Gene Tomko, "The Right Time for Nappy Brown," *Charlotte Magazine* 13 (March 2008): 55–60 (comments by Brown); Ben Sisario, "Nappy Brown, 78, Blues and R&B Singer," *New York Times,* 25 September 2008, sec. B, p. 7 (obituary); Tony Russell, "Nappy Brown: 1950s Blues and R&B Singer Resurgent in the 80s and Last Year," *Guardian* (London), 26 September 2008, p. 47 (obituary); Billy Vera, "Nappy Brown," *Blues and Rhythm: The Gospel Truth* 234 (November 2008): 11 (obituary); Gene Tomko, "Nappy Brown," *Living Blues* 198 (December 2008): 66–67 (obituary); "Nappy Brown," *Juke Blues* 66 (Winter 2008): 60 (comments by Brown) (obituary); Billy Vera, "Nappy Brown Update," *Blues and Rhythm: The Gospel Truth* 236 (February 2009): 19; Arlene Corsano, *Thought We Were Writing the Blues but They Called It Rock and Roll* (Tenafly, N.J.: ArleneChristine, 2014), 93–96.

Bruggan, Eunice

See Brigham, Eunice Henry

Bryant, Gladys Lillian

Singer

Probably 21 December of a year from 1901 to 1904 (Aiken, S.C.)–?

S.C. residence: Aiken (probably sometime from 1901 to 1904–no later than 1922)

In 1922 at the Winter Garden Building in N.Y.C., Bryant sang in the chorus of *The Plantation Room Revue,* starring Florence Mills. The next year she accompanied Mills and others to England, where they staged *From Dover Street to Dixie* and where, along with Edith Wilson, she apparently became the first blues singer to perform. Also in 1923 she recorded six songs for Paramount Records, backed on some by Porter Grainger and on others by a band led by Fletcher Henderson. She sang in the chorus of Noble Sissle and Eubie Blake's *The Chocolate Dandies* (1924).

On her 1923 passport application Bryant indicated that she was born in Aiken, S.C., on 21 December 1901. The passenger list for the *Veendam,* on which she sailed from Southampton, England, to N.Y.C. in September 1923, records her birth date as 21 December 1902. She married the dancer Arthur Bryson in 1924; the 1930 census notes that she wed at age twenty. Conducted on 2 April, this census, which estimates her age as twenty-six, reveals that she then lived with her mother, Ora, now surnamed Gilchrist. Paul Vernon's statement that Bryant was, in 1952, the first person to perform the blues on television (on Groucho Marx's *You Bet Your Life*) has not been confirmed. Vernon might mistake Bryant for Gladys Bentley, who played and sang "Them There Eyes," which is not a blues, on this program in 1958. See Vernon's "Television," in *Encyclopedia of the Blues,* ed. Edward Komara (New York: Routledge, 2006), 2: 963–68.

Recordings as Leader (All 1923)

"Beale Street Woman," "Darktown Flappers Ball," "Laughin', Cryin' Blues," "Tired o' Wailin' Blues," "Triflin' Blues," "You've Got to See Mama Every Night"

References

SECONDARY: J. A. Jackson, "The Plantation Room Reopens," *Billboard* 34 (7 October 1922): 48; "Married," *Chicago Defender,* 31 May 1924, p. 8 (national edition); Mark Hale, "Early American Jazz in the UK," http://www.network54.com/Forum/27140/message/1023290033/early+American+jazz+in+the+UK (5 June 2002; accessed 21 May 2014).

Bryson, Peabo (Robert Peapo)

Singer, guitar, percussion, composer
13 April 1951 (Greenville, S.C.)–
S.C. residence: Greenville (1951–ca. 1967)

Exposed to music at home and at Greenville concerts, Bryson began performing at age fourteen with a group led by Al Freeman. In the late 1960s he became a full-time professional with Moses Dillard's band, with which he remained for approximately five years. He wrote material for and produced the sessions that resulted in music for his initial album, released by Bash Records. After signing with Capitol in 1977 he became a successful soul balladeer: His early albums feature such songs as "Feel the Fire" and "I'm So into You." Subsequently he recorded for Elektra, Capitol again, Columbia, Private Music, and Peek. Despite success as a soloist (including many songs that appeared on the rhythm-and-blues charts), he gained possibly greater acclaim for his duets with several female singers, including Natalie Cole, Roberta Flack, and Nancy Wilson. He sings on the sound tracks of *Bustin' Loose* (1981), *Bad Boys* (1983), *D.C. Cab* (1983), *Romantic Comedy* (1983), *Beauty and the Beast* (1991), *Aladdin* (1992), *Barney's Great Adventure* (1998), and *Big Boys* (2002) and performed at the 2005 JVC Jazz Festival. Other performers have sampled some of his recordings, including "Here We Go" at least a dozen times.

Compositions

"All My Love," "Ballad for D.," "Born to Love," "Catch 22," "Crosswinds," "Did You Ever Know?," "Don't Touch Me," "Feel the Fire," "A Fool Already Knows," "Friction," "Give Me Your Love," "Go for It," "Hold On to the World," "If It's Really Love," "I Found Love," "I Love the Way You Love," "I'm in Love," "I'm So into You," "It's Just a Matter of Time," "Let the Feeling Flow," "Light the World," "Like I Need You," "Love Has No Shame," "Love in Every Season," "Love Is a Waiting Game," "Love Is on the Rise," "Lover's Paradise," "Love Walked Out on Me," "Love Will Find You," "Make the World Stand Still," "Move Your Body," "My Heart Belongs to You," "Reaching for the Sky," "Remember When (So Much in Love)," "Same Old Love," "She's a Woman," "Shower You with Love," "Slow Dancin'," "Smile," "Straight from the Heart," "There Ain't Nothin' Out There," "There's No Guarantee," "Tonight," "Turn the Hands of Time," "Underground Music," "We Don't Have to Talk (about Love)," "When Will I Learn?," "Why Don't You Make Up Your Mind?," "You," "You Don't Have to Beg"

Recordings as Leader (These Are Release Dates, Not Necessarily Recording Dates)

Peabo (1976), *Crosswinds* (1978), *Reaching for the Sky* (1978), *We're the Best of Friends* (1979; with Natalie Cole), *Live and More* (1980; with Roberta Flack), *Paradise* (1980), *I Am Love* (1981), *Don't Play with Fire* (1982), *Turn the Hands of Time* (1982), *Born to Love* (1983; with Roberta Flack), "D.C. Cab" (1983), *Straight from the Heart* (1984), *Take No Prisoners* (1985), *Quiet Storm* (1986), *Positive* (1988), *All My Love* (1989), *Can You Stop the Rain* (1991), "Beauty and the Beast" (1991; with Celine Dion), "Garden Scene" (1992), "I Have Dreamed" (1992), "We Kiss in a Shadow" (1992), "A Whole New World (Aladdin's Theme)" (1992; with Regina Belle), "You Are My Home" (1992; with Linda Eder), *Through the Fire* (1994), "Loving You" (1995; with Nancy Wilson), "Pretty Woman" (1995), *It's Christmas!* (1996; with Sandi Patty), *Peace on Earth* (1997; reissued with a few different selections as *Christmas with You*), *Really Love* (1998), *Unconditional Love* (1999), *Missing You* (2007)

Leaders Recorded With

Kip Anderson (1967), Moses Dillard (1972), Michael Zager (1975), Melissa Manchester (1980),

Kenny G. (1993), Peter Nero (1995), Larry Coryell (1996), Fourplay (1996)

Awards

Grammy Award (1992; for "Beauty and the Beast," with Celine Dion); Grammy Award (1993; for "A Whole New World [Aladdin's Theme]," with Regina Belle)

References

PRIMARY: David Nathan, "Peabo Bryson: The Sky's the Limit . . . ," *Blues and Soul* 251 (9–22 May 1978): 20–21 (also available at http://www.soulmusic.com/index.asp?S=3&T=3&ART=1491 [accessed 21 May 2014]) (mostly a narrative by Bryson based on an interview with him); David Nathan, "Peabo Bryson Comes into His Own . . . ," *Blues and Soul* 270 (30 January–12 February 1979): 8–9 (also available at http://www.soulmusic.com/index.asp?S=3&T=3&ART=1492 [accessed 21 May 2014]) (mostly a narrative by Bryson based on an interview with him); Jay S. Jacobs, "Peabo Bryson: Feel the Fire," http://www.popentertainment.com/bryson.htm (1999; accessed 21 May 2014) (substantial comments by Bryson).

SECONDARY: Joanna Rubiner, "Peabo Bryson: Singer, Songwriter, Producer," in *Contemporary Musicians: Profiles of the People in Music,* ed. Julia M. Rubiner (Detroit: Gale Research, 1994), 11: 26–28.

Cadett, Wilmot

Trumpet

4 June 1909 (S.C., probably Charleston)–14 August 1989

S.C. residence: Charleston (probably 1909–at least into early 1930s)

A ward of Jenkins Orphanage, Cadett played in its bands in the late 1920s and early 1930s. By 1935 he was in a group led by Hartley Toots in Miami; by 1939 he was the high-note specialist with the band of Snookum Russell.

Cadett's birth and death dates come from the Social Security Death Index, which identifies Bronx, N.Y., as the musician's last known residence. Cadett lived with his parents when he was enumerated for the census in Charleston on 15 April 1910 (estimated age eleven months) and 5 January 1920 (ten years). He is presumably the Wm. Cadette, estimated age seventeen, who was enumerated at the orphanage on 2 April 1930. His surname is sometimes spelled Cadet, or Cadette.

References

SECONDARY: "Hartley Toots and Band Hit," *Chicago Defender,* 23 November 1935, p. 9 (national edition); "They Play Jazz and They Play It 'Hot,'" *Pittsburgh Courier,* 22 July 1939, p. 20 (Cadett's given name is spelled Wilmar); Bruce Bastin, "A Note on the Carolina Cotton Pickers," *Storyville* 95 (June–July 1981): 177–82.

Calhoun, Lucy

S.C. residence: Charleston (possibly by late 1930s–at least into early 1940s)

Apparently a ward of Jenkins Orphanage, Calhoun played in its bands in the early 1940s, though her instrument is not known.

Callaham, (Andrew) Bernard

17 February 1895 (Society Hill, S.C.)–5 April 1919 (Columbia, S.C.)

S.C. residences: Society Hill (1895–no later than 1910), Darlington (by 1910–no later than mid-1910s), Charleston (mid-1910s), Seneca (at least 1917), Columbia (Camp Jackson) (by 1919)

Apparently a ward of Jenkins Orphanage, Callaham played with its band in England in 1914. His instrument is not known.

The given name of nineteen-year-old Callaham on the passenger list of the *Campania,* which transported the orphanage band to England in May 1914, is difficult to read. (His name is absent from the passenger list of the *St. Louis,* which returned the group to N.Y.C. in September.) It appears to be Bernd. If so the musician was Andrew Bernard Callaham, who was enumerated for the census in Barnwell on 4 June 1900 (estimated age five) and in Darlington in April 1910 (possibly on the 10th; estimated age fifteen). When he registered for the draft in Oconee County, S.C., on 30 May 1917, he identified his race as Ethiopian and indicated that he was born in Society Hill on 17 February 1895.

At the time of his registration he taught at Seneca Institute, Seneca. When he died of appendicitis on 5 April 1919 at Camp Jackson, Columbia, he was a second lieutenant in the army. His body was removed to Allendale, S.C., where it is possibly buried.

Reference

SECONDARY: Howard Rye, "Visiting Fireboys: The Jenkins' Orphanage Bands in Britain," *Storyville* 130 (1987): 137–43.

Campbell, Richard

Ca. 1907 (S.C.)–?

S.C. residence: Charleston (by 1910s–at least until 1920)

A ward of Jenkins Orphanage, Campbell played in its bands in the 1910s, though his instrument is not known.

When enumerated for the census at the orphanage on 9 January 1920, Campbell's age was estimated as twelve. This document indicates that the musician was born in S.C.

Captain Luke (Luther Mayer, Jr.)

Singer

18 January 1927 (Newberry County, S.C.)–12 May 2015 (Winston-Salem, N.C.)

S.C. residences: Newberry County (1927–no later than 1930), Greenville (by 1930–no later than 1935), outside Clinton (by 1935–ca. 1941)

When Mayer was a child an uncle introduced him to the blues. By the early 1950s he sang in a church choir in Winston-Salem, N.C., where he moved ca. 1941, as well as with the Veteran Harmonizers, a gospel quartet from the same church. He performed the blues in local roadhouses during the 1960s and 1970s, in the latter decade with Guitar Gabriel (Robert Lewis Jones). Their partnership extended into the 1990s, including with Brothers in the Kitchen, a group that also included Tim Duffy. Following the death of Guitar Gabriel (1996), Cool John Ferguson replaced him, and the group—Mayer, Duffy, and Ferguson—was billed as the Music Makers. Mayer also teamed with guitarist Macavine Hayes. Mayer became known as Captain Luke because he regularly wore a captain's cap. He co-wrote the theme for the movie *Xu Bing's Tobacco Project Virginia* (2011). He is buried in Evergreen Cemetery, Winston-Salem, N.C.

Mayer's date and place of birth come from his draft registration card, completed in Winston-Salem, N.C., probably in 1945. This document records a middle name of Bookmon, though because it is placed within quotation marks it might be a nickname. Publications about the musician state, without evidence, that he was born in Greenville, S.C.; they do not agree on when in 1927 he was born, though not one records the date of 18 January. Mayer was enumerated for the 1930 census in Greenville and for the 1940 census at RFD #1, Clinton, where he also lived in 1935. The 1930 census indicates that his name has the suffix Jr. His CD *"Old Black Buck"* includes all of *Outsider Lounge Music,* four selections from *One of These Days,* and an additional song.

Compositions

"Backbone," "Dog and Cat Fight," "Kingfish Story," "Not My Type of Song," "Old Black Buck," "Serve Me Right," "Short-Haired Woman Blues"

Recordings as Leader

"Angels of Mercy" (1990s), "Dog and Cat Fight" (1990s), "Freight Train Boogie" (1990s), "I Don't Want No Woman" (1990s), "Kingfish Story" (1990s), "Rainy Night in Georgia" (1990s), *Outsider Lounge Music* (2001; with Cool John Ferguson), *One of These Days* (2008)

Leader Recorded With

Guitar Gabriel (1991)

Film

Toot Blues (2008)

References

SECONDARY: Wesley Wilkes, "Luther 'Captain Luke' Mayer," in *Music Makers: Portraits and Songs from the Roots of America,* ed. Timothy Duffy (Athens, Ga.: Hill Street Press, 2002), 100–103 (comments by Mayer); Larry Benicewicz, "Blues from the Drink House, Part 1: Captain Luke," http://www.bluesartstudio.at/NeueSeiten/BLUES%20FROM%20THE%20DRINK%20HOUSE, vol.1-2007.html (September 2007; accessed 21 May 2014) (comments by Mayer); Charlie Shelton, "Remembering Captain Luke, A Local Blues Legend," http://wunc.org/post/remembering-captain-luke-local-blues-legend (12 May 2015; accessed 16 May 2015); Cliff Bellamy, "Music Maker Artist 'Captain Luke' Dies," *Winston-Salem (N.C.) Herald-Sun,* 13 May 2015, sec. A, p. 6

(also available at http://www.heraldsun.com/news/showcase/x219727527/Music-Maker-artist-Captain-Luke-dies [accessed 16 May 2015]) (obituary).

Carolina Slim (Elijah Staley)

Guitar, drums, bass, singer

15 September 1926 (near Denmark, S.C.)–16 February 2014 (Jamaica, N.Y.)

S.C. residence: near Denmark (1926–early 1940s)

As a teenager known as Stud, Staley left S.C. for Augusta, Ga. There the owner of the bicycle shop where he worked called him Slim, then Carolina Slim to distinguish him from another worker named Slim. The sobriquet stuck. (He is not the N.C. bluesman Carolina Slim who was born Edward P. Harris [1923–1953]). Staley served in the army for an undetermined period during the Korean War, beginning in 1950. In N.Y.C. he joined Musicians Union, Local 802 (1960), and in time drummed with such blues performers as Big Maybelle, Wilbert Harrison, John Lee Hooker, and Brownie McGhee. In the late 1980s he began playing Piedmont blues in subway stations in N.Y.C. and became a member of Music under New York, which is part of the Metropolitan Transit Authority's Arts for Transit program. He also performed blues and gospel music at various private functions in the greater N.Y.C. area. He appears in Madonna's video "Secret" (1994). He is buried in Calverton National Cemetery, Calverton, N.Y.

Film

Elijah and Jeremiah (2013)

References

SECONDARY: Randy Kennedy, "A Great Gig: $1.50, Standing-Room Only," *New York Times*, 4 June 2002, sec. B, p. 3; George Kalogerakis, "A Platform for the Blues," *New York Times*, 6 October 2002, sec. E, pp. 26, 28; Ricky Gordon, "Carolina Slim: A Musician and Patriot Turns 80," *Allegro* 106 (November 2006): 19; "Fellow Musicians Honor Slim, an American Classic," *International Musician* 105 (February 2007): 20; James Barron, "He Played Blues Concerts Where the Admission Was Subway Fare," *New York Times*, 21 February 2014, sec. A, p. 22 (late edition) (also available at http://www.nytimes.com/2014/02/21/nyregion/he-played-blues-underground-where-admission-price-was-subway-fare.html?_r=0 [accessed 21 May 2014]) (obituary).

Carter, Wilbur

Trumpet, trombone

7 December 1920 or ca. 1922 (Charleston, S.C.)–26 July 1987 (Schenectady, N.Y.)

S.C. residence: Charleston (1920 or ca. 1922–at least into early 1940s)

A ward of Jenkins Orphanage, Carter played in its bands from the early 1930s until his release from the institution in 1941. Thereafter he lived for an undetermined period with his mother in Charleston. By the early 1950s he moved to Schenectady, N.Y., where he continued playing and lived the remainder of his life. He is buried in grave 1, range 5, lot 365, Parkview Cemetery, Schenectady.

Carter's 1920 birth date comes from the Social Security Death Index. When the musician was enumerated for the census at the orphanage on 2 April 1930, his age was estimated as eight; when enumerated there on 21 May 1940, as eighteen.

References

SECONDARY: "Wilbur Carter, Musician, 66," *Schenectady (N.Y.) Gazette*, 28 July 1987, p. 23 (obituary); Jack McCray, *Charleston Jazz* (Charleston, S.C.: Arcadia Publishing, 2007), 56; Jack McCray, "African American Music in Charleston, South Carolina, and Surrounding Areas: 1942–1968," in *Encyclopedia of African American Music*, ed. Emmett G. Price III et al. (Santa Barbara: Greenwood, 2011), 3: 179.

Cedar Creek Sheik (Philip McCutchen)

Guitar, singer

14 February 1910 (S.C.)–October 1964 (probably S.C., possibly Sampit Township, Georgetown County)

S.C. residences: unknown location (1910–no later than 1920), Suttons Township, Williamsburg County (by 1920–no later than 1930), Sampit Township, Georgetown County (by 1930–possibly 1964)

As Cedar Creek Sheik, McCutchen recorded ten tunes in Charlotte, N.C., in 1936, all released on Bluebird. Some of them, such as "Buy It from the Poultry Man," are bawdy. Because of the nature of his voice, which Tony Russell characterizes as "high, almost expressionless," one significant researcher, Bruce Bastin, thinks the singer white, while another, Russell, considers him black. The census (for 1920 and 1930) indicates that he was black. The musician's recording name probably derives from Cedar Creek of Suttons Township, Williamsburg County, S.C.

McCutchen's birth and death dates come from the Social Security Death Index. Sometimes McCutchen's given name is spelled Phillip and his surname, McCutcheon. The spellings used here come from the musician's Form SS-5, by which he applied for a Social Security card. On this document the person completing the form (the 1930 census reveals that McCutchen was illiterate) wrote the name Phillip McCutcheon but deleted one of the "l"s from the given name and the "o" from the surname. At the time of the 1920 census McCutchen resided in Suttons Township, Williamsburg County, and ten years later in Sampit Township, Georgetown County, where he worked as a farm laborer. His Form SS-5 indicates that in 1937 he resided at RFD 2, outside Andrews, which could be in Sampit Township. Bruce Bastin believes that he was "apparently from Andrews" (197), though it has not been determined if Bastin means that McCutchen was born there or resided there around the time he made his recordings, or both. He has not been located in the 1940 census.

Recordings as Leader (All 1936)

"Buy It from the Poultry Man," "Don't Credit My Stuff," "Don't Use That Stuff," "Ford V-8," "I Believe Somebody's Ridin' My Mule," "Jimmy Shut His Store Doors," "Mary Had a Little Lamb," "She's Totin' Something Good," "Watch the Fords Go By," "What a Pity"

References

SECONDARY: Tony Russell, *Blacks Whites and Blues* (New York: Stein and Day, 1970), 101; Bruce Bastin, *Red River Blues: The Blues Tradition in the Southeast* (Urbana: University of Illinois Press, 1986), 195, 197.

Chaney, Babe

Guitar
Possibly ca. 1903 (S.C.)-?
S.C. residence: probably Butler Township, Greenville County (probably at least 1910, though probably earlier and later)

Chaney, who did not record, taught Georgian Joe Parr to play chords. The black Chaney and white Parr toured together from 1951 to 1955.

A Babe Channey, estimated age seven, was enumerated for the census in Butler Township, Greenville County, in April 1910; the day is indecipherable. He was probably the guitarist.

References

SECONDARY: George Mitchell, "The Street Singer," *Atlanta (Ga.) Gazette,* 11 August 1976, p. 7; Bruce Bastin, *Red River Blues: The Blues Tradition in the Southeast* (Urbana: University of Illinois Press, 1986), 187–88.

Charleston Camp-Meeting Shouters

See Original Charleston Camp-Meeting Shouters

Charleston Quartet

Presumably Charleston, S.C.

In January 1892 the Charleston Quartet joined D. W. McCabe's Minstrels, with which it performed in Cuba and Mexico. In May McCabe abandoned his sixty-person company in Monterrey, Mexico. Friends assisted the group in reaching Laredo, Tex., where the troupe gave two performances to generate money for its subsistence.

References

SECONDARY: "Variety, Minstrel and Circus," *New York Clipper,* 6 February 1892, p. 795; "Variety and Minstrelsy," *New York Clipper,* 28 May 1892, p. 181.

Checker, Chubby (Ernest Evans)

Singer
3 October 1941 (Spring Gully, S.C.)-
S.C. residence: Spring Gully (1941–ca. 1950)

Though born in S.C., by age ten Ernest Evans lived in Philadelphia. Discovered by Dick Clark, he signed with Cameo and recorded as Chubby Checker for its subsidiary, Parkway Records. His first recording, "The Class," features imitations of popular singers. In 1960 he recorded "The Twist," a blues written by Hank Ballard that became the number one tune in the country and his signature song. As a result of its popularity he recorded other dance songs, though only one, "Pony Time" (a blues composed by Don Covay), reached first position on the music charts. Checker recorded frequently during the 1960s, but only occasionally thereafter. He became popular on the oldies circuit. Though he is in some halls of fame, a movement to have him inducted into the Rock and Roll Hall of Fame has so far failed.

Compositions

"Autobahn Baby," "Do the Limbo Rock," "Original Master of the Dance Hall Beat," "Texas Twist," "That's What It Takes"

Recordings as Leader

"The Class" (1959), "Schooldays, Oh, Schooldays" (1959), "Dancing Dinosaur" (1960), "The Hucklebuck" (1960), "Those Private Eyes" (1960), "Toot" (1960), "The Twist" (1960), "Whole Lotta Shakin' Goin' On" (1960), "Dance the Mess Around" (1961), "The Fly" (1961), "Gonna Be Alright" (1961), "Jingle Bell Rock" (1961; with Bobby Rydell), "Let's Twist Again" (1961), "Oh Susannah" (1961), "Pony Time" (1961), "That's the Way It Goes" (1961), "Twistin' U.S.A." (1961), "Dancin' Party" (1962), "Get Myself Together" (1962), "La Paloma Twist" (1962), "Let's Limbo Some More" (1962), "Limbo Rock" (1962), "Popeye (the Hitchhiker)" (1962), "Slow Twistin'" (1962; with Dee Dee Sharp), "Twenty Miles" (1962), "Birdland" (1963), "Black Cloud" (1963), "Loddy Lo" (1963), "Surf Party" (1963), "Twist It Up" (1963), "Hey, Bobba Needle" (1964), "Lazy Elsie Mollie" (1964), "Lovely Lovely" (1964), "She Wants t' Swim" (1964), "You Better Believe" (1964), "Discotheque" (1965), "Everything's Wrong" (1965), "Let's Do the Freddy" (1965), "Hey You! Little Boo-Ga-Loo" (1966), "Looking at Tomorrow" (1966), "Her Heart" (1967), "Karate Monkey" (1967), "Back in the U.S.S.R." (1969), "Reggae My Way" (1973), "She's a Bad Woman" (1974), "The Rub" (1976), "Running" (1981), "Harder Than Diamond" (1982), "Read You Like a Book" (1986), "Knock Down the Walls" (2008)

Films

Teenage Millionaire (1961), *Twist around the Clock* (1961), *Don't Knock the Twist* (1962), *Ring-a-Ding Rhythm!* (1962), *Die Ganze Welt Ist Himmelblau* (also titled *Rote Lippen Soll Man Küssen*) (1963), *The Comedy Man* (1964), *Let the Good Times Roll* (1973), *Purple People Eater* (1988), *Twist* (1992), *Calendar Girl* (1993), *The Wages of Spin* (2008), *Wildwood Days* (2008)

Awards

Grammy Award (1962; for "Let's Twist Again"); Order of the Palmetto (1987); South Carolina Entertainment and Music Hall of Fame (possibly 1994); Grammy Hall of Fame (2000; for "The Twist"); Rhythm & Blues Foundation Pioneer Award (2006)

Website

www.chubbychecker.com/ (accessed 21 May 2014)

References

SECONDARY: Jim Dawson, *The Twist: The Story of the Song and Dance That Changed the World* (Boston: Faber & Faber, 1995), passim; John Broven, *Record Makers and Breakers: Voices of the Independent Rock 'n' Roll Pioneers* (Urbana: University of Illinois Press, 2009), 429–32; Otis R. Taylor, Jr., "The Twist and Chubby Checker," *Columbia (S.C.) State*, 25 September 2011, sec. A, pp. 1, 14–15; Otis R. Taylor, Jr., "This Is Home," *Columbia (S.C.) State*, 25 September 2011, sec. E, pp. 1, 3.

Childers, Virgil

Guitar, singer

Ca. 1901 (Blacksburg, S.C.)–10 December 1939 (Shelby, N.C.)

S.C. residence: Blacksburg (ca. 1901–1939)

In Charlotte, N.C., Childers recorded six tunes for Bluebird in 1938. Bruce Bastin believes that "his style [is] unlike any other Carolina artist's although aurally of the region" (198). Listening to the recordings led Bastin to conclude that the musician "could well have been white" (199). Childers's death certificate, which spells his given name Vergil, indicates that Childers was "negro." This document notes that he was "shot by Shelby Policeman while trying to excape," and reveals that he died from "gun shot wounds in leg and abdomen." He foretells his manner of death in "Travelin' Man" ("he wouldn't give up 'til the police shot him down").

Childers's death certificate notes that the musician resided in Blacksburg, specifies his death date and birth and death places, and records that he died at age thirty-eight.

Recordings as Leader (All 1938)

"Dago Blues," "Preacher and the Bear," "Red River Blues," "Somebody Stole My Jane," "Travelin' Man," "Who's That Knockin' at My Door"

References

SECONDARY: Bruce Bastin, *Red River Blues: The Blues Tradition in the Southeast* (Urbana: University of

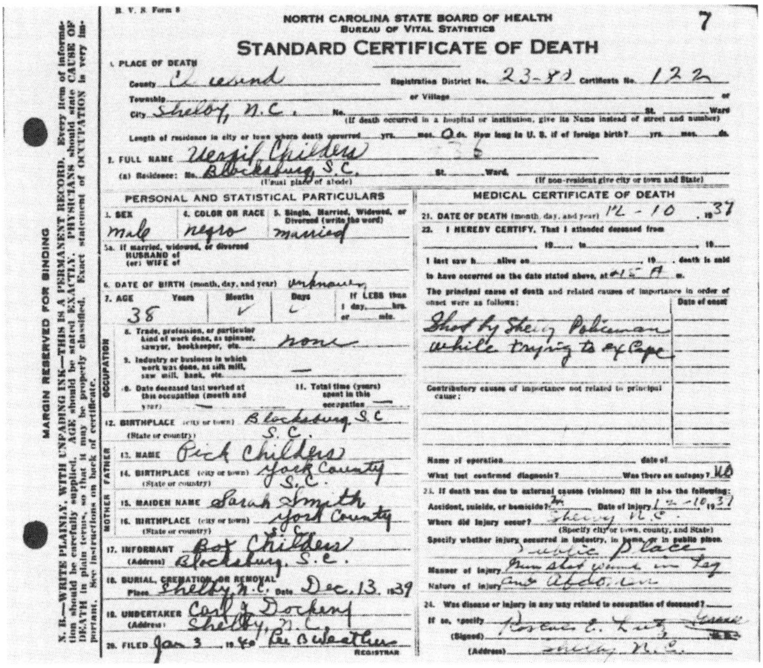

N. B.—WRITE PLAINLY, WITH UNFADING INK—THIS IS A PERMANENT RECORD. Every item of information should be carefully supplied. AGE should be stated EXACTLY. PHYSICIANS should state CAUSE OF DEATH in plain terms, so that it may be properly classified. Exact statement of OCCUPATION is very important. See instructions on back of certificate.

MARGIN RESERVED FOR BINDING

B. V. S. Form 8

NORTH CAROLINA STATE BOARD OF HEALTH
BUREAU OF VITAL STATISTICS

STANDARD CERTIFICATE OF DEATH 7

1. PLACE OF DEATH
County Cleveland Registration District No. 23-83 Certificate No. 122
Township or Village
City Shelby, N.C. No. St. Ward (If death occurred in a hospital or institution, give its Name instead of street and number)
Length of residence in city or town where death occurred yrs. mos. 0 ds. How long in U. S. if of foreign birth? yrs. mos. ds.

2. FULL NAME Virgil Childers
(a) Residence: No. Blacksburg, S.C. St. Ward. (Usual place of abode) (If non-resident give city or town and State)

PERSONAL AND STATISTICAL PARTICULARS
3. SEX male 4. COLOR OR RACE negro 5. Single, Married, Widowed, or Divorced (write the word) married
5a. If married, widowed, or divorced HUSBAND of (or) WIFE of
6. DATE OF BIRTH (month, day, and year) unknown
7. AGE Years 38 Months ✓ Days ✓ If LESS than 1 day, hrs. or min.
8. Trade, profession, or particular kind of work done, as spinner, sawyer, bookkeeper, etc. none
9. Industry or business in which work was done, as silk mill, saw mill, bank, etc. —
10. Date deceased last worked at this occupation (month and year) — 11. Total time (years) spent in this occupation —
12. BIRTHPLACE (city or town) Blacksburg S.C. (State or country) S.C.
13. NAME Pick Childers
14. BIRTHPLACE (city or town) York County (State or country) S.C.
15. MAIDEN NAME Sarah Smith
16. BIRTHPLACE (city or town) York County (State or country)
17. INFORMANT Bob Childers (Address) Blacksburg, S.C.
18. BURIAL, CREMATION, OR REMOVAL Place Shelby N.C. Date Dec. 13. 1939
19. UNDERTAKER Carl & Dockery (Address) Shelby, N.C.
20. FILED Jan 3 1940 Lee B. Weathers REGISTRAR

MEDICAL CERTIFICATE OF DEATH
21. DATE OF DEATH (month, day, and year) 12 - 10 1937
22. I HEREBY CERTIFY, That I attended deceased from 19 to 19
I last saw h alive on 19, death is said to have occurred on the date stated above, at 4:15 A m.
The principal cause of death and related causes of importance in order of onset were as follows: Date of onset
Shot by Shelby Policeman while trying to escape
Contributory causes of importance not related to principal cause:
Name of operation date of
What test confirmed diagnosis? Was there an autopsy? no
23. If death was due to external causes (violence) fill in also the following:
Accident, suicide, or homicide? ho Date of injury 12-10 1937
Where did injury occur? Shelby N.C. (Specify city or town, county, and State)
Specify whether injury occurred in industry, in home, or in public place. public place
Manner of injury gun shot wound in leg
Nature of injury and abdomen
24. Was disease or injury in any way related to occupation of deceased?
If so, specify (Signed) Roscoe E. Lutz Coroner
(Address) Shelby, N.C.

Virgil Childers, death certificate

Illinois Press, 1986), 198–99; "Virgil Childers Lyrics," http://weeniecampbell.com/yabbse/index.php?topic=7907.0 (2013; accessed 21 May 2014).

Chocolate Thunder

See Rodney, Linda Sullivan

Christopher, Homer C.

Accordion, guitar, violin

8 February 1905 (Beech Spring Township, Spartanburg County, S.C.)–28 November 1977 (Daytona Beach, Fla.)

S.C. residences: Beech Spring Township, Spartanburg County (1905–after 1910, but no later than 1920), Austin Township, Greenville County (by 1920–1923), Chick Springs, Greenville County (1923–1934), Anderson (1935–ca. 1939)

In the 1920s Christopher performed at square dances in the Greenville-Spartanburg area and at mid-decade began playing on the radio in these cities. After recording two tunes with his wife, Katherine, in 1926, Christopher recorded only in 1927, with accordionist Raney Van Vynckt; Christopher played guitar. The two men, who occasionally played the blues, performed together until 1934, when Christopher joined the Crazy Buckle Busters; the group broadcast on radio station WBT in Charlotte, N.C. From Charlotte in 1935, he moved to Anderson, S.C., where he played on WAIM. Returning to Charlotte ca. 1939, he joined the Briarhoppers, with which he remained for approximately a decade. During the 1940s he performed with the Tennessee Ramblers (from N.C.) and played with such country musicians as Judy Canova, Pee Wee King, Bill Monroe, and Minnie Pearl. In Charlotte ca. 1950 he affiliated with the Surf Riders, with which he performed until moving to Daytona Beach, Fla., in 1956. There he continued playing until his health declined in the mid-1960s. At least forty of Christopher's performances preserved on cassette tape have not been released. Bruce Bastin implies that in going from Greenville to Atlanta to record for Columbia, first with his wife and then with Van Vynckt, Christopher might have helped establish a connection that resulted in the Atlanta recordings of Spartanburg residents Pink Anderson and Simmie Dooley. He is buried in the Taylors First Baptist Church Cemetery, Taylors, S.C.

Christopher's S.C. residences through 1930 come from the census and his daughter, Marion C. Richards.

Compositions

"Lost Mamma Blues," "Roses in the Moonlight," "Spartanburg Blues"

Recordings as Leader

"After the Ball" (1926; with Katherine Christopher), "Southern Railroad" (1926; with Katherine Christopher), "Alabama Jubilee" (this and all subsequent recordings 1927; all with Raney Van Vynckt), "Drifting Back to Dreamland," "Farewell to Thee," "Going Slow" (two versions), "Hilo March," "Hometown Rag," "Lost Mamma Blues" (two versions), "March in D," "Old Fashioned Waltz," "Red Wing," "Sleep, Baby, Sleep," "Spartanburg Blues," "Waiting for the Robert E. Lee"

References

SECONDARY: Nat Green, "American Folk Tunes: Cowboy and Hillbilly Tunes and Tunesters," *Billboard* 56 (4 November 1944): 66; "Homer Christopher," *Spartanburg (S.C.) Journal,* 30 November 1977, sec. A, p. 3 (obituary); Tony Russell, "Homer Christopher and the Rise and Fall of the Piano Accordion," *Old Time Music* 33 (Summer 1979–Spring 1980): 15–17; Bruce Bastin, *Red River Blues: The Blues Tradition in the Southeast* (Urbana: University of Illinois Press, 1986), 184; Tom Warlick and Lucy Warlick, *The WBT Briarhoppers: Eight Decades of a Bluegrass Band Made for Radio* (Jefferson, N.C.: McFarland, 2008), passim.

Christopher, (Martha) Katherine Raines

Guitar, piano

21 June 1903 (outside Greer, S.C.)–15 April 1997 (Rome, Ga.)

S.C. residences: outside Greer (1903–1923), Chick Springs, Greenville County (1923–1934), Anderson (1935–ca. 1939)

A graduate of Taylors (S.C.) High School, Katherine Raines attended classes at Furman University and became a teacher. As a young woman she played several instruments and gave piano lessons. Because a musician scheduled to record with her husband, Homer Christopher, in Atlanta in 1926 was unable keep his commitment, she replaced him. The couple recorded two tunes, with her playing guitar and him playing violin; the record labels identify the musicians as "Homer Christopher and Wife." Bruce Bastin implies that in going from Greenville to Atlanta to record for Columbia, the Christophers might have helped establish a connection that resulted in the Atlanta recordings of Spartanburg residents Pink Anderson and Simmie Dooley. Later Katherine Christopher became a dressmaker. She is buried in the Taylors First Baptist Church Cemetery, Taylors, S.C.

Homer Christopher and Katherine Raines Christopher, wedding day, 23 September 1923; permission of Marion C. Richards

Christopher's S.C. residences come from the 1930 census and her daughter, Marion C. Richards.

Recordings as Leader (Both 1926; with Homer Christopher)

"After the Ball," "Southern Railroad"

References

SECONDARY: Tony Russell, "Homer Christopher and the Rise and Fall of the Piano Accordion," *Old Time Music* 33 (Summer 1979–Spring 1980): 15–17; Bruce Bastin, *Red River Blues: The Blues Tradition in the Southeast* (Urbana: University of Illinois Press, 1986), 184; "Mrs. Katherine R. Christopher," *Rome (Ga.) News-Tribune,* 16 April 1997, sec. A, p. 2 (obituary).

Claflin University Plantation Melody Quintet

Orangeburg

At least from 1897 into 1904 this group of jubilee singers toured as far north as Maine and as far west as Calif. In addition to religious songs the quintet sang secular, topical ones, such as "The Hero of Manila." A notice in the *Jefferson County (N.Y.) Journal* notes that "this band of singers has won universal praise wherever it has appeared" and identifies the singers' mission: "This company of student singers, under the direction of the president [Lewis M. Dunton], is undertaking to raise funds to meet urgent and imperative needs of the institution."

References

SECONDARY: "Local Record," *Jefferson County (N.Y.) Journal,* 16 August 1898, p. 5; "Plantation Melodies," *Syracuse (N.Y.) Courier,* 13 September 1898, p. 5; "Local Paragraphs," *Baldwinsville (N.Y.) Gazette and Farmers' Journal,* 15 September 1898, p. 1; Blinzy L. Gore, *On a Hilltop High: The Origin and History of Claflin College to 1984* (Spartanburg, S.C.: Reprint Company, 1994), 134.

Claflin University Quintet

Orangeburg

Presumably beginning around 1905 this group of jubilee singers toured in order to raise funds for Claflin University, where the vocalists were students. Stephen J. Herben wrote about the singers in 1908: "During the last three vacations a company of students from the university has traveled extensively in the Northern States, presenting the needs of the work, singing delightful plantation melodies which have charmed all who have heard them. The company of singers has taken collections and subscriptions for the building fund of the university. As a result of their labors four buildings have been erected and additional equipments have been provided" (8). A Claflin quartet, not a quintet, performed at least once in 1909; the *Christian Educator* indicates that these four men sang "songs, hymns, and plantation melodies." The quintet sang in Indianapolis at the First National Convention of Methodist Men (1913). The author of "The Convention Music" identifies the singers as Willie Asbury, Ichabod Bowen, John Dangerfield, Edmund Palmer, and Arthur Rivers; pianist Lulu Hunt was their accompanist. In 1916 the *Northwestern Christian Advocate* noted that the group "was known throughout the United States for their wonderful Negro melodies." One of its programs included "Banjo Song," "I Knew the Lord," "The New Dixie," "We Shall Rise," "When the Morning Comes," and the song for which it was best known, "The Old Flag Never Touched the Ground."

References

SECONDARY: S[tephen] J. H[erben], "Claflin University," *Epworth Herald* (Chicago), 1 February 1908, pp. 6–8 (consecutively numbered 922–24); untitled notice, *Christian Educator: A Quarterly Magazine of Facts* 19 (November 1909): 4; "The Convention Music," in *Militant Methodism: The Story of the First National Convention of Methodist Men,* ed. David G. Downey et al. (Cincinnati: Methodist Book Concern, [1913]), 374; "A Great Anniversary," *Northwestern Christian Advocate* 64 (26 April 1916): 23 (consecutively numbered 431); Blinzy L. Gore, *On a Hilltop High: The Origin and History of Claflin College to 1984* (Spartanburg, S.C.: Reprint Company, 1994), 132; Vivian Glover, *Men of Vision—Claflin College and Her Presidents* (Orangeburg, S.C.: Claflin College, 1995), 85; Lynn Abbott and Doug Seroff, *Out of Sight: The Rise of African American Popular Music, 1889–1895* (Jackson: University Press of Mississippi, 2002), 461.

Clark(e), Erskine

Drums, trumpet

Probably 1914 or 1915 (Fla.)–11 December 1929 (Charleston, S.C.)

S.C. residence: Charleston (after 1919, but by 1924–1929)

A ward of Jenkins Orphanage beginning in 1924, Clark(e) played in its bands in the late 1920s.

Clark(e)'s age was estimated as six when the youth was enumerated for the census in Dade County, Fla., on 24 June 1920. His death certificate identifies him as a "school boy" and a "musician," notes that he was born in Fla., estimates his age at death as fourteen, records when and where he died, and states that he succumbed to pneumonia. It indicates that he is buried in Lincoln Park, S.C., but such a place has not been located.

References

SECONDARY: John Chilton, *A Jazz Nursery: The Story of the Jenkins' Orphanage Bands of Charleston, South Carolina* (London: Bloomsbury Book Shop, 1980), 54; Bruce Bastin, "A Note on the Carolina Cotton Pickers," *Storyville* 95 (June–July 1981): 177–82.

Clark's Brass Band

See Professor Clark's Brass Band

Coker, Dolo (Charles Mitchell)

Piano

Possibly 16 November 1927, December 1927, or January 1928 (probably Florence, S.C.)–13 April 1983 (Los Angeles, Calif.)

S.C. residence: Florence (probably 1927 or 1928–ca. 1944)

Coker learned to play saxophones beginning at age nine and the piano at thirteen. After attending Mather Academy in Camden, S.C., he studied music in Atlanta for an undetermined period, though apparently briefly, before moving in the mid-1940s to Philadelphia, where he resided for a decade. There he attended the Landis School of Music, played in clubs with Ben Webster, and was the pianist in a band led by Jimmy Heath that included such musicians as John Coltrane and Benny Golson. He toured with Sonny Stitt from 1954 to 1957 and lived for a time in N.Y.C. After accompanying Philly Joe Jones to San Francisco in late 1959, he remained in Calif. Soon after moving to Los Angeles in 1960, he worked with Dexter Gordon for eighteen months; together they recorded the album *The Resurgence of Dexter Gordon* and appeared in Jack Gelber's *The Connection* (1961). On the record and in the play they performed several of Coker's compositions. Despite being musically active in Calif., he did not record from 1963 through 1967 and from 1969 through 1973. His career blossomed during the second half of the 1970s, when he led sessions that resulted in four albums for Xanadu. The year he died his widow established the Charles (Dolo) Coker Jazz Scholarship Foundation, Inc., which benefits high school and college students; one noted scholarship recipient is Nicaraguan pianist and composer Donald Vega. Coker is buried in lot 778, Pineview, grave A, Inglewood Park Cemetery, Inglewood, Calif.

Sources identify Coker's birthplace as Atlantic City, N.J., Hartford, Conn., and Philadelphia, Pa. California, Death Index, 1940–1997, which records it as N.J. without specifying a town, has two entries for him with identical information: one as Charles Mitchell Coker; the other, as Dolo Charles Coker. He was enumerated as Charlie Mitchel for the 1930 census, which was conducted in Florence, S.C., on 22 April. At that time he lived with his grandfather Wilson Coker (estimated age seventy); his mother, Elizabeth Coker (thirty and single); and his brother, George H. Coker (fifteen). The census notes that his grandfather had adopted him. California, Death Index, 1940–1997, states that Coker's mother's name is Mitchell, which was probably her married name and therefore his birth surname. The 1930 and 1940 censuses state that he was born in S.C. All the sources consulted that record his birth date use 16 November 1927. His estimated age in the 1930 census, though, is two years, three months; if this is accurate—the specificity suggests it is—he was born in either December 1927 or January 1928. The 1940 census (conducted in Florence on 26 April) estimates his age as twelve. So despite reports to the contrary, Coker was almost certainly born in S.C., probably in Florence, possibly in December 1927 or January 1928. In all likelihood, when he was adopted his probable birth surname became his middle name and his surname became that of his grandfather and the maiden name of his mother: Charles Mitchell Coker. His official residence likely remained Florence when he attended school in Camden.

Compositions

"Affair in Havana," "All Alone," "Captain Kidd," "Do I Love Her?," "Dolo," "Duck All Over Town," "El Tiante," "Field Day," "Jumping Jacks," "Just You," "Lady Hawthorne, Please," "Let's Pull Ourselves Together," "Lovely Lisa," "Mr. October," "Night Flight to Dakar," "Not Just to Be in Love Again," "Reflections," "Royal Madness," "Sadly, as I Drift Alone," "Sine and Cosine," "Spectrum," "Stepper," "Sweet Coke," "Tale of Two Cities," "There Is No Other Way," "The Things You Never Said," "Third Down," "Urbane"

Recordings as Leader

California Hard (1976), *Dolo!* (1976), "'Round Midnight" (1976), *Third Down* (1977), *All Alone* (1979), "Not Just to Be in Love Again" (1980)

Leaders Recorded With

Sonny Stitt (1957, 1976), Philly Joe Jones (1959), Dexter Gordon (1960), Art Pepper (1960), Junior Cook (1961), Sonny Forriest (1961), Les McCann (1961), Curtis Amy (1962), Dupree Bolton (1962), Richard Boone (1968), Teddy Edwards (1974), Richie Kamuca (1974), Red Rodney (1974), Sonny Criss (1975), John Rinaldo (1975), Harry Edison (1976–1977), Frank Butler (1977–1978), Sam Noto

(1978), *Xanadu at Montreux,* vols. 1, 3–4 (1978), *Night Flight to Dakar* (1980), *Xanadu in Africa* (1980), John Collins (1982)

Website

www.dolocokerjazz.org (accessed 21 May 2014)

References

SECONDARY: Tom Reed, *The Black Music History of Los Angeles—Its Roots* (Los Angeles: Black Accent on L.A. Press, 1992), 222; Scott Yanow, *Bebop* (San Francisco: Miller Freeman, 2000), 253–54.

Conger, Larry (Laurence Henry)

Cornet, trumpet, violin, singer
30 July 1926 (Marysville, Calif.)-?
S.C. residence: Camden (1957-)

As a youth Conger studied piano and violin. Later he played the C-melody saxophone before focusing on trumpet, which became his main instrument and on which he performed during his high school years with the Royal Tigers. He was with a Modesto, Calif., junior college band for a year before joining the air force. Shortly after being discharged he played music cross country en route to Ithaca, N.Y., where he studied engineering at Cornell University. Unhappy with the school's music program, he transferred to Ithaca College, from which he was graduated in 1953. After returning to Calif. he performed with Morris Taylor and the Sierra Melody Gang before becoming a music teacher, initially in Hopland, then in Williams, and then in Ukiah. He gave up teaching in 1957 to join the band of Turk Murphy, with which he remained for a year and a half. Thereafter he worked in industrial real estate, ultimately in S.C., where he played violin in the Greenville symphony (1958–1960), led the Two Rivers band from 1965 into 1970, and was active on the traditional music scene in the midlands.

Compositions

"Low Country Blues," "Two Rivers Rag"

Recordings as Leader

Carolina Jazz (1965), *Sailing Along* (1966), *Low Country Jazz* (1967), *Up the River to Jazztown* (1969; also titled *Larry Conger and His Two Rivers Jazz Band*), *Daddy-Do* (1970), *The Carolina Jazz Society Proudly Presents the House Band and Larry Conger* (late 1970s)

Leaders Recorded With

Turk Murphy (1957–1958), Don Ewell (1965), Art Hodes (1965), Jean Kittrell (1966), Tony Parenti (1966)

Reference

PRIMARY: Mary Lee Hester, "A South Carolina Jazz Gentleman," *Mississippi Rag* 27 (June 2000): 25–26, 28–30, 48 (mainly a narrative by Conger).

Larry Conger (trumpet), with the Turk Murphy band (Murphy, far right), N.Y.C., August 1957; permission of Larry Conger

Corley, Johnnie J., Jr.

See Fantastic Johnny C

Covay, Don (James Donald Randolph; "Pretty Boy")

Composer, singer, guitar

24 March of 1935 or 1936 (Orangeburg, S.C.)–31 January 2015 (Valley Stream, N.Y.)

S.C. residence: Orangeburg (1936–1948)

In 1948 the Randolph family moved from Orangeburg to Washington, D.C., where some of the children formed a gospel group. While in high school Randolph sang with a doo-wop group, the Rainbows; later he performed with the Bachelors. In the mid-1950s he became known as Don Covay. At his first recording session as leader he was backed by the Upsetters, the band of Little Richard, whom Covay served as part-time driver. Though he recorded frequently and with moderate success for two decades, he is most important as a composer. Chubby Checker's version of his "Pony Time" (1961) reached number one on the pop and rhythm-and-blues charts. More hit recordings of his compositions followed, including "Chain of Fools" (by Aretha Franklin), "I'm Hanging Up My Heart for You" (by Solomon Burke), and "Letter Full of Tears" (by Gladys Knight). Covay's compositions have been performed on over twenty sound tracks, including those of *The Graduate* (1967; "Mercy, Mercy"), *Hairspray* (1988; "Pony Time"), and *The Pelican Brief* (1993; "Chain of Fools"). In 2006 Shanachie Entertainment released *Back to the Streets: Celebrating the Music of Don Covay,* a CD featuring Covay's songs performed by the likes of Gary U.S. Bonds, Robert Cray, Iggy Pop, Jimmy Witherspoon, and Ron Wood.

Most sources record Covay's birth date as 24 March 1938. When the composer was enumerated for the census in Orangeburg on 19 April 1940, his age was estimated as five years. During a telephone conversation on 10 July 2012, his daughter Ursula Covay stated unequivocally that he was born on 24 March 1936; she also confirmed that he left Orangeburg with his family in 1948. Almost all sources render Covay's given names Donald James. The only public document consulted that notes his first name is the 1940 census, which calls the child James Randolph.

Compositions

"Believe It or Not," "Black Woman," "Can't Stay Away," "Chain of Fools," "Come See about Me," "Continental Twist," "Daddy Loves Baby," "Demonstration," "Don Covay Boogie," "Don't Play with Love," "Fine Sister," "Forty Days, Forty Nights," "Hold On," "Hungry for You," "I Don't Know What You've Got (but It's Got Me)," "I'm Coming Down with the Blues," "I'm Gonna Cry," "I'm Gonna Take What He's Got," "I'm Hanging Up My Heart for You," "I Told You," "It's Better to Have," "I Was Checking In," "Keep Doin' What You're Doin'," "Letter Full of Tears," "Long Tall Shorty," "Mad Dog Blues," "Mercy, Mercy," "Mister Twister," "No Tell Motel," "One Woman's Man," "Overtime Man," "Pony Time," "Put Yourself in My Place," "Rumble in the Jungle," "Seesaw," "Somebody's Got to Love You," "Sookie, Sookie," "Soul Meeting," "Take This Hurt off Me," "Temptation Was Too Strong," "That's How It Feels," "Think about It," "Three-Time Loser," "Tongue Tied," "Tonight's the Night," "Travelin' in Heavy Traffic," "Usual Place," "You Can Run but You Can't Hide," "You're Good for Me," "Your Latest Fool"

Recordings as Leader (These Are Release Dates, Not Necessarily Recording Dates)

"Bip Bop Bip" (1957; as Pretty Boy), "Paper Dollar" (1957; as Pretty Boy), "Believe It or Not" (1958; as Pretty Boy), "Betty Jean" (1958; as Pretty Boy), "Beauty and the Beast" (1959 or 1960), "'Cause I Love You" (1959 or 1960), "I'm Coming Down with the Blues" (1960), "Mary Lee" (1960), "Hand Jive Workout" (1961), "Love Boat" (1961), "Pony Time" (1961), "See about Me" (1961; official title, "Come See about Me"), "I'm Your Soldier Boy" (1962), "One Little Boy Had Money" (1962), "The Popeye Waddle" (1962), "You Picked Me" (1962), "Do the Bug" (1963), "Wiggle Wobble" (1963), *Mercy!* (1964), "Ain't That Silly" (1964), "Turn It On" (1964), *See-Saw* (1965), "Somebody's Got to Love You" (1966), "Temptation Was Too Strong" (1966), "Watching the Late Late Show" (1966), "I Was There" (1967), "Shingaling '67" (1967), "Chain of Fools" (1968), "Prove It" (1968), "Soul Time" (1968; by Soul Clan, a collective including Covay), "That's How It Feels" (1968; by Soul Clan), *The House of Blue Lights* (1969), "Black Woman" (1969), "C. C. Rider Blues" (1969), "Ice Cream Man" (1969), "Sweet Pea" (1969), *Country Funk* (1970),

Different Strokes for Different Folks (1970), "Sookie, Sookie" (1970), "Soul Stirrer" (1970), *Super Dude I* (1973), *Hot Blood* (1975), *Travelin' in Heavy Traffic* (1976), "No Tell Motel" (1976), "Once You Have It" (1976), "Right Time for Love" (1976), *Funky YoYo* (1977), "Back to the Roots" (1977), "Badd Boy" (1980), *Adlib* (2000)

Leaders Recorded With

Rainbows (possibly 1955–1956, 1960, 1962, possibly 1963), Ray Bryant (1961), King Curtis (1961), Soldier Boys (date unknown; released 1962), Solomon Burke (1964), Little Richard (1965), Rolling Stones (1985), Angela Strehli (date unknown; released 1993)

Award

Rhythm & Blues Foundation Pioneer Award (1994)

Website

http://www.doncovay.com/home.html (accessed 15 May 2015)

References

PRIMARY: Bill Dahl, "Have Mercy: Don Covay," *Living Blues* 155 (January–February 2001): 26–33 (Covay's comments from a telephone interview incorporated into Dahl's narrative).

SECONDARY: Robert Palmer, "A Reunion of Soul Clan at the Savoy Tonight," *New York Times,* 24 July 1981, sec. C, p. 24 (also available at http://www.nytimes.com/1981/07/24/arts/pop-jazz-a-reunion-of-soul-clan-at-the-savoy-tonight.html [accessed 21 May 2014]) (comments by Covay); "Mercy Mercy: Seamus McGarvey Meets Up with Don Covay," *Juke Blues* 47 (Summer 2000): 18–21 (comments by Covay); Red Kelly, "Don Covay and the Goodtimers—Temptation Was Too Strong (Atlantic 2357)," http://redkelly.blogspot.com/2007/04/don-covay-goodtimers-temptation-was-too.html (2007; accessed 21 May 2014); Kory Grow, "Don Covay, Influential R&B Artist and Songwriter, Dead at 78," *Rolling Stone,* http://www.rollingstone.com/music/news/don-covay-influential-r-b-artist-songwriter-dead-76-20150203 (3 February 2015; accessed 15 February 2015) (obituary); Richard Williams, "Don Covay Obituary," http://www.theguardian.com/music/2015/feb/04/don-covay (4 February 2015; accessed 15 February 2015); Bruce Weber, "Don Covay, 78, Performer and Writer of R&B Hits," *New York Times,* 7 February 2015, sec. D, p. 7 (also available at http://www.nytimes.com/2015/02/07/arts/music/don-covay-performer-and-writer-of-rb-hits-dies-at-78.html?_r=0 [accessed 15 February 2015]) (obituary); Peter Wolf, "The Soul Man's Soul Man," *Rolling Stone* 1,230 (12 March 2015): 16.

Craig, Ralph Francis

Bass trombone

29 May 1925 (Newport, Ky.)–1 May 2004 (Columbia, S.C.)

S.C. residences: Columbia (1992–1996), Swansea (1996–2004)

Craig spent most of his formative years in Norwood, Ohio. After serving in the army (1943–1946), he studied at the Cincinnati Conservatory of Music, from which he received a degree in 1949. He became a professional musician. After touring with bands from 1949 into 1957, he lived in N.Y.C. for five years, in Minneapolis in 1963, and in Chicago from 1964 into 1992. During his Chicago years he and his wife had a business, A La Carte, that made customized cassette tapes, called Go-Kart tapes, for children's entertainment in cars. They discovered, brought to Chicago, and managed Bonnie Herman, who became a member of Singers Unlimited. Craig served as a clinician for Olds trombones, for which he designed a variant of the P-24G instrument. Following his master's degree in social work from Loyola University in Maywood, Ill. (late 1980s), he worked with alcoholics and their adult children. After moving to Columbia in 1992, he became active on the music scene in the midlands. His body was cremated.

Recordings as Leader (Both Unissued)

Something Special (ca. 1979), *Lakeshore Cowboy* (ca. 1984)

Leaders Recorded With

Ralph Flanagan (1950–1954), Sam Donahue (1955, 1957–1958), Ralph Marterie (1955), H. P. Lovecraft (mid-1960s), Joe Morello (1969, ca. 1977), Dick Shory (1970), Jerry Butler (early 1970s), Jerry Butler and Brenda Lee Eager (early 1970s), Les Hooper (1973, 1977), Ju-Par Universal Orchestra (mid-1970s), Malcolm Tomlinson (mid-1970s), Bobby Christian (late 1970s), Rockie Robbins (late 1970s), Roger Pemberton (1980)

Reference

SECONDARY: "Ralph Craig," *Columbia (S.C.) State,* 2 May 2004, sec. B, p. 4 (obituary).

Crawford, Rosetta Smalls

Singer, piano

23 January 1904 (Charleston, S.C.)–January 1969 (New York, N.Y.)

S.C. residence: Charleston (1904–probably no later than early 1920s)

Though she recorded little, Crawford, a blues singer, performed songs written by the likes of Perry Bradford and James P. Johnson and was backed by such musicians as Johnson, Sidney Bechet, Clarence Williams, and, at his last recording session, Tommy Ladnier. At the New School in N.Y.C. in 1932, she sang in *From Sun to Sun,* produced by Zora Neale Hurston and arranged by Porter Grainger. In 1939 she toured with Mae West's troupe and appeared in *Blackbirds of 1939,* in which she performed "Thursday" with Lena Horne, Bobby Evans, and Taps Miller. The next year she sang in Donald Heywood's musical *South American Cruise* and was named, by unidentified music critics, as the vocalist most likely to succeed Bessie Smith as the major blues singer. At least in the late 1930s and early 1940s, she performed on radio programs broadcast both nationally (on the NBC *Maxwell House Show Boat* with the Hall Johnson Choir) and locally (*The Harlem Serenade* on WMCA in N.Y.C.).

Crawford's dates of birth and death come from the Social Security Death Index. As Rosetta Smalls, Crawford was estimated as age five when enumerated for the census in Charleston on 18 April 1910. She was widowed by the time she was enumerated for the 1930 census in N.Y.C. The statement in "'Don't Get Me High' Girl with Mae West" that she recorded "Don't Get Me High" and "St. Louis Blues" has not been confirmed.

Recordings as Leader

"Down on the Levee Blues" (1923), "If You Don't, I Know Who Will" (1923; unissued), "Lonesome Mama Blues" (1923), "Misery" (1926), "Two-Faced Man" (1926), "Double-Crossin' Papa" (1939), "I'm Tired of Fattenin' Frogs for Snakes" (1939), "My Man Jumped Salty on Me" (1939), "Stop It, Joe" (1939)

References

SECONDARY: Floyd G. Snelson, Jr., "Newsy Newsettes," *Pittsburgh Courier,* 26 March 1932, sec. A, p. 6; "She's Star," *Chicago Defender,* 18 February 1939, p. 19 (national edition); Lucien H. White, "'Blackbirds of 1939'—A Harlem Rhapsody—Makes Its Advent into New York at the Hudson Theatre," *New York Age,* 18 February 1939, p. 7; "'Don't Get Me High' Girl with Mae West," *Chicago Defender,* 15 April 1939, p. 21 (national edition); "Stars That Shine," *Chicago Defender,* 15 April 1939, p. 21 (national edition); Floyd G. Snelson, "Harlem: 'Negro Capitol of the Nation,'" *New York Age,* 9 March 1940, p. 4; "Donald Heywood Opus Shortened," *Pittsburgh Courier,* 9 March 1940, p. 21; "New Find Tops," *Chicago Defender,* 31 August 1940, p. 21 (national edition).

Dangerfield, John Henry

Singer

Probably 1897 or 1898 (Sumter, S.C.)–31 March 1935 (Wheeling, W.Va.)

S.C. residences: Sumter (probably 1897 or 1898–no later than 1900), McMillan Township, Florence County (by 1900–no later than 1910), Orangeburg (by 1910–at least until 1920)

Dangerfield sang with the Claflin University Quintet, at least in 1913. Following graduation from Claflin he received a degree from Meharry Medical School in Nashville, Tenn. In 1926 he established a medical practice in Wheeling, W.Va., where he died of acute uremia. He is buried in Orangeburg Cemetery, Orangeburg, S.C.

When enumerated for the census in McMillan Township, Florence County, on 1 June 1900, Dangerfield was estimated as age two years; for the census in Orangeburg on 15 April 1910, as twelve. When enumerated in Orangeburg on 8 January 1920 and in Wheeling on 14 April 1930, he was estimated as twenty and thirty, respectively. His death certificate and grave marker record his birth date as 2 March 1900; the death certificate notes his birthplace. Had Dangerfield been born on 2 March 1900, he would have been three months old when

John Dangerfield, death certificate

enumerated for the census that year. The person providing information to the enumerator would not likely have stated that a newborn was two years old. Therefore Dangerfield was probably born in 1897 or 1898.

References

SECONDARY: "J. Dangerfield Passes Sunday," *Wheeling (W.Va.) News-Register,* 1 April 1935, p. 2 (obituary); "Dangerfield Rites Will Be Held Today," *Wheeling (W.Va.) News-Register,* 2 April 1935, p. 2.

Daniels, Holland Wrightson ("Toby")

Trumpet and other instruments

2 October 1917 (Charleston, S.C.)–21 October 1997 (Charleston, S.C.)

S.C. residences: Charleston (1917–probably 1935, probably ca. 1941–1997), Orangeburg (probably 1935–1939), Florence (by 1939–1940)

In the 1930s Daniels played with the bands of Jenkins Orphanage, which his father served as president. With degrees from what is now South Carolina State University (bachelor's) and New York University (master's), he became an educator in Charleston, though he remained active in music. He reportedly organized the first band at Burke High School (1941), where he taught mathematics. He served as principal of several Charleston schools from 1955 until 1985 and in 1961 succeeded his father as president of the orphanage. He is buried in Sunset Memorial Gardens, North Charleston, S.C.

Daniels was the brother of trumpeter Paul Daniels. Daniels's birth and death dates come from the Social Security Death Index.

References

SECONDARY: "District Election," *Charleston (S.C.) News and Courier,* 17 May 1977, sec. A, p. 6; John Chilton, *A Jazz Nursery: The Story of the Jenkins' Orphanage Bands* of Charleston, South Carolina (London: Bloomsbury Book Shop, 1980), 33, 54 (comments by Daniels); Dawn Brazell, "Charleston Pays Tribute to Jazzmen at Garden Theatre," *Charleston (S.C.) News and Courier*, 6 October 1986, sec. B, p. 1; "Retired Principal Holland Daniels Dies," *Charleston (S.C.) Post and Courier*, 22 October 1997, sec. B, p. 2 (obituary); "Daniels," *Charleston (S.C.) Post and Courier*, 24 October 1997, sec. B, p. 2 (death notice); Edmund L. Drago, *Charleston's Avery Center: From Education and Civil Rights to Preserving the African American Experience*, ed. and revised by W. Marvin Dulaney (Charleston: History Press, 2006), 204.

Daniels, Ira

Trumpet

Ca. 1915 (Fla.)–?

S.C. residence: Charleston (1922–at least into early 1930s)

A ward of Jenkins Orphanage beginning in 1922, Daniels played in its bands in the early 1930s.

Daniels's age was estimated as fifteen when the musician was enumerated for the census at the orphanage on 2 April 1930; this document notes that he was born in Fla.

Reference

SECONDARY: John Chilton, *A Jazz Nursery: The Story of the Jenkins' Orphanage Bands of Charleston, South Carolina* (London: Bloomsbury Book Shop, 1980), 54.

Daniels, Julius

Guitar, singer

20 November 1901 (Denmark, S.C.)–18 October 1947 (Charlotte, N.C.)

S.C. residence: Denmark (1901–1912)

Daniels was one of the earliest Southeastern bluesmen to record. His recording career was limited to two sessions, to the year 1927, to the company Victor, and to the city of Atlanta. Though he sings and plays guitar on his recordings, he was accompanied by guitarists Bubba Lee Torrence at the first session and Wilbert Andrews at the second. He performed, but did not record, with Blind Gussie Nesbitt. Daniels was apparently the first person to record "Crow Jane Blues," a traditional tune, though the label on his recording credits him as its composer. His recordings are included in anthologies of blues and folk music; RCA Victor (London) released four of his performances on an extended-play record in 1965. Musicians who have recorded Daniels's tunes include Bull City Red (George Washington), the duo John Cephas and Phil Wiggins, Chris Smither, and Eleanor Ellis. The first annual Julius Daniels Memorial Blues Festival was held in Denmark, S.C., in 2010.

Sources indicate that from 1912 to 1930 Daniels lived in Pineville, Berkeley County, S.C. If he

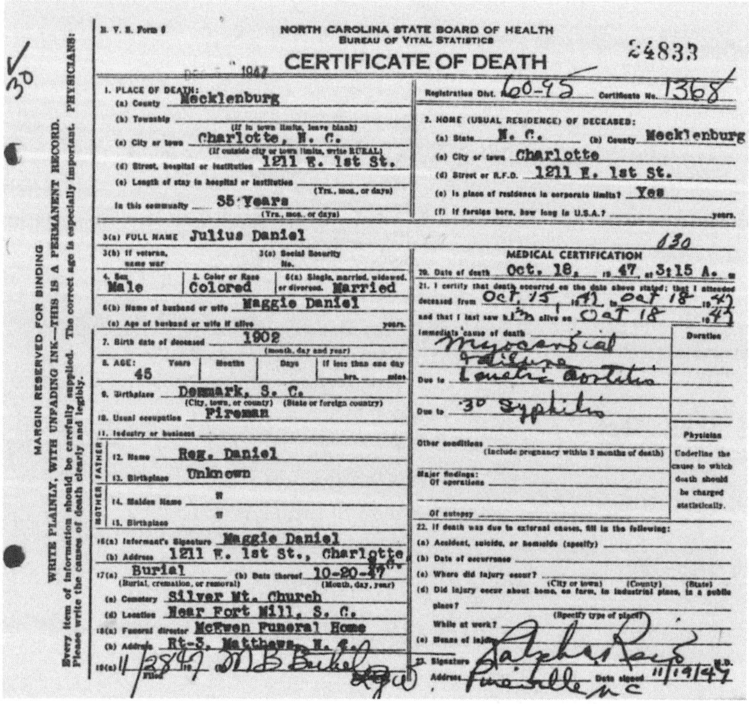

B. V. S. Form 6

NORTH CAROLINA STATE BOARD OF HEALTH
BUREAU OF VITAL STATISTICS

CERTIFICATE OF DEATH

24833

MARGIN RESERVED FOR BINDING

WRITE PLAINLY, WITH UNFADING INK—THIS IS A PERMANENT RECORD.

Every item of information should be carefully supplied. The correct age is especially important. PHYSICIANS: Please write the causes of death clearly and legibly.

1. PLACE OF DEATH: (a) County Mecklenburg
(b) Township
(c) City or town Charlotte, N. C.
(d) Street, hospital or institution 1211 E. 1st St.
(e) Length of stay in hospital or institution
In this community 35 Years

Registration Dist. 60-95 Certificate No. 1368

2. HOME (USUAL RESIDENCE) OF DECEASED:
(a) State N. C. (b) County Mecklenburg
(c) City or town Charlotte
(d) Street or R.F.D. 1211 E. 1st St.
(e) Is place of residence in corporate limits? Yes
(f) If foreign born, how long in U.S.A.? years.

3(a) FULL NAME Julius Daniel

3(b) If veteran, name war 3(c) Social Security No.

4. Sex Male 5. Color or Race Colored 6(a) Single, married, widowed, or divorced. Married

6(b) Name of husband or wife Maggie Daniel

(c) Age of husband or wife if alive years.

7. Birth date of deceased 1902 (month, day and year)

8. AGE: Years 45 Months Days If less than one day hrs. mins.

9. Birthplace Denmark, S. C. (City, town, or county) (State or foreign country)

10. Usual occupation Fireman

11. Industry or business

FATHER 12. Name Reg. Daniel
13. Birthplace Unknown

MOTHER 14. Maiden Name "
15. Birthplace "

16(a) Informant's Signature Maggie Daniel
(b) Address 1211 E. 1st St., Charlotte

17(a) Burial (Burial, cremation, or removal) (b) Date thereof 10-20-47 (Month, day, year)
(c) Cemetery Silver Mt. Church
(d) Location Near Fort Mill, S. C.

18(a) Funeral director McEwen Funeral Home
(b) Address Rt-3, Matthews, N. C.

19(a) 11/28/47 Filed

MEDICAL CERTIFICATION

20. Date of death Oct. 18, 19 47, at 3:15 A. M.

21. I certify that death occurred on the date above stated; that I attended deceased from Oct. 15, 1947, to Oct 18, 1947 and that I last saw him alive on Oct 18, 1947

Immediate cause of death Myocardial failure

Due to Luetic aortitis

Due to 30 Syphilis

Other conditions (include pregnancy within 3 months of death)

Major findings: Of operations

Of autopsy

Duration

Physician Underline the cause to which death should be charged statistically.

22. If death was due to external causes, fill in the following:
(a) Accident, suicide, or homicide (specify)
(b) Date of occurrence
(c) Where did injury occur? (City or town) (County) (State)
(d) Did injury occur about home, on farm, in industrial place, in a public place? (Specify type of place)
While at work?
(e) Means of injury

23. Signature M.D.
Address Pineville NC Date signed 11/19/47

Julius Daniels, death certificate

resided in Pineville, it was probably in the town of this name in N.C. The medical certification on Daniels's death certificate is signed by Ralph Reid of Pineville, N.C. The death certificate indicates that Daniels lived in Charlotte for the last thirty-five years of his life. It records his name as Julius Daniel; the labels on his recordings identify him as Julius Daniels. The Social Security Death Index uses the name Julious Daniels.

Compositions

"Can't Put the Bridle on That Mule This Morning," "My Mamma Was a Sailor," "Ninety-Nine Year Blues"

Recordings as Leader (All 1927)

"Can't Put the Bridle on That Mule This Morning," "Crow Jane Blues," "I'm Goin' to Tell God How You Doin'," "My Mamma Was a Sailor," "Ninety-Nine Year Blues," "Richmond Blues," "Slippin' and Slidin' up the Golden Street"

References

SECONDARY: Tony Russell, *Blacks Whites and Blues* (New York: Stein and Day, 1970), 43, 45; Bruce Bastin, *Crying for the Carolines* (London: Studio Vista, 1971), 86–89; Bruce Bastin, *Red River Blues: The Blues Tradition in the Southeast* (Urbana: University of Illinois Press, 1986), 195–97.

Daniels, Paul

Trumpet

Ca. 1907 (Charleston, S.C.)–?

S.C. residence: Charleston (ca. 1907–at least until 1942)

In the 1930s Daniels played with the bands of Jenkins Orphanage, which his father served as president. He became a public school teacher and possibly a band director.

Daniels was the brother of trumpeter Holland Daniels. The 1910 census and his 1942 military enlistment form record his middle initial as F; the 1930 census, as G. If it was G, the name was probably Gabasie, the middle name of his father. If so then he was probably Paul G. Daniels, Jr. His age was estimated as three when he was enumerated for the census on 20 April 1910; as twelve when enumerated on 7 January 1920; as twenty-one when enumerated on 9 April 1930; as thirty-three when enumerated on 20 April 1940. For all censuses he was enumerated in Charleston. His military enlistment form (completed 4 July 1942) indicates that he was born in 1906.

Reference

SECONDARY: John Chilton, *A Jazz Nursery: The Story of the Jenkins' Orphanage Bands of Charleston, South Carolina* (London: Bloomsbury Book Shop, 1980), 33, 54.

Dantzler, Isaac

Alto horn

Ca. 1890 (S.C.)–?

S.C. residence: Charleston (by 1900–possibly late 1910s, but probably no later than 1920)

A ward of Jenkins Orphanage, Dantzler played in its bands in the 1910s.

Dantzler's age was estimated age ten when the youth was enumerated for the census at the orphanage on 28 June 1900. He might be the Isaac Dantzler who was enumerated for the federal census on 5 January 1920 (estimated age thirty-one; the name is seemingly spelled Isice Dantuler), the N.Y. state census on 1 June 1925 (thirty-five), and the federal census on 4 June 1930 (forty). For all these censuses he was enumerated in N.Y.C. According to New York Abstracts of World War I Military Service, 1917–1919, this person, with the middle initial P. and born in Charleston, entered the army on 20 October 1914 (at age twenty-six and four-twelfths) and was discharged on 4 June 1920. He lived in N.Y.C. when completing his World War II draft registration card in 1942; for it, he recorded his birth date as 27 May 1888. Following his death on 7 January 1955, he was buried at site 1,256, section X, Long Island National Cemetery, Farmingdale, N.Y. Alternatively the musician could be the Nickerlus I. Dantzler, estimated age twenty, who was enumerated for the census in Orangeburg, S.C., on 23 April 1910. As another alternative he might be the Isaac Dantzler, born in Jedburg, S.C., whose twins died in Summerville, S.C., in September 1941 (as recorded in South Carolina Deaths, 1915–1943). An Isaac Dantzler has not been located in the 1940 census.

Dash, (St.) Julian Bennett

Saxophone, clarinet, arranger

9 April 1916 (Charleston, S.C.)–25 February 1974 (New York, N.Y.)

S.C. residence: Charleston (1916–1934)

During his years at Avery Institute in Charleston (class of 1934), Dash performed locally with the Nighthawks. In 1935 and 1936 he played in bands at Alabama State Teachers College, which he attended on a music scholarship. Leaving college to study embalming in N.Y.C., he led a band there in the late 1930s but soon joined Erskine Hawkins, who also had led a band at Alabama State. Dash remained with Hawkins until the mid-1950s. In 1939 Dash, Hawkins, and William Johnson composed "Tuxedo Junction." Hawkins's recording of this tune became so popular that Hawkins made it his theme song; it became even more widely known from Glenn Miller's recording (1940). After leaving Hawkins, Dash played in Harlem in the mid-1960s and led his own group in the early 1970s. He is buried in the Humane and Friendly Society Cemetery, Charleston.

Compositions

"Blue Sea," "Deacon Dash," "Double Shot," "House Party," "Nobody Met the Train," "Rhythm Punch," "Tuxedo Junction," "Two Shades of Blue," "Was It a Lie?," "Yes, No"

Recordings as Leader

"Creamin'" (1950), "Going Along" (1950), "Long Moan" (1950), "My Silent Love" (1950), "Blue Velvet" (1951), "Can't Understand It" (1951), "Coolin' with Dash" (1951), "Creamin' Boogie" (1951), "Cry" (1951), "Dance of the Mother Bird" (1951), "Dashin' In" (1951), "Devil's Lament" (1951), "For Squares Only" (1951), "Holiday in Cuba" (1951), "Hot Rod" (1951), "It's All Over Again" (1951), "Open Up Those Pearly Gates" (1951), "Preachin'" (1951), "Somebody's Gone" (1951), "Deacon Dash" (1953), "Fire Water" (1953), "So Let It Be" (1954), "Zig Zag" (1954), "Rhumba Punch" (1955), "Zero" (1955), *A Portrait of Julian Dash* (1970)

Leaders Recorded With

Erskine Hawkins (1938–1953, 1955), International Sweethearts of Rhythm (1944), Jimmie Mitchell (1950), Bobby Smith (1950), Carmen Taylor (1951), Buck Clayton (1953–1954, 1956), Melvin Smith (1953), Jimmy Rushing (1967), Jay McShann (1972)

References

PRIMARY: Olivier Keller, "Julian Dash," *Bulletin du Hot Club de France* 71 (October 1957): 3–4 (interview; in French).

SECONDARY: "Two Veteran Jazzmen Bring Special Verve to Home Office," *We the People* 23 (22 September 1969) (newsletter of the firm Merrill Lynch, Pierce, Fenner & Smith; reproduced in Jack McCray, *Charleston Jazz* [Charleston, S.C.: Arcadia Publishing, 2007], 54; also see 47–53) (comments by Dash); Dottie Ashley, "Panel to Discuss Contributions of Jazz Saxophone Great," *Charleston (S.C.) Post and Courier*, 27 June 2004, sec. E, p. 2.

Davis, Gary ("Blind Gary," "Rev. Gary")

Guitar, banjo, harmonica, singer

30 April of either 1896 or 1897 (Laurens County, S.C.)–5 May 1972 (Hammonton, N.J.)

S.C. residences: Laurens County (1896 or 1897–ca. 1900), Gray Court (ca. 1900–1911), Greenville (1911–1916, 1917–ca. 1924), Cedar Spring (1916–1917)

Mostly sightless a few weeks after birth, Davis taught himself to play the harmonica by age six but soon learned to perform on guitar and banjo. As a child he played at the Center Raven Baptist Church in Gray Court. From ca. 1911 to 1914 he

Gary Davis; permission of the photographer, Peter B. Lowry

belonged to a string band in Greenville; among its members was Willie Walker, who taught Davis to play guitar in the Piedmont style, of which Davis became one of the most important practitioners. He picked with his thumb and index finger. After becoming totally blind by 1914 or 1915, he attended the South Carolina School for the Deaf and the Blind (Cedar Spring) for the 1916–1917 school year. By the mid-1920s he lived in Asheville, N.C., from where he moved to Durham, N.C., ca. 1931, all the while performing as an itinerant musician. N.C. businessman J. B. Long discovered Davis and arranged for him to record for American Record Corporation in N.Y.C., which he did in 1935, both solo and with Blind Boy Fuller and Bull City Red (George Washington). Ordained a minister of the Free Baptist Connection Church in Washington, N.C., in 1937, he became known as Rev. Gary Davis. After moving to N.Y.C. in the early 1940s, he worked as a street musician and gave guitar lessons. In time he performed in concerts and in the mid-1950s began recording frequently. Generally considered a player of the holy blues—though how frequently he played the actual blues is open to question—as time passed he limited his playing largely to gospel music. Aspiring musicians gravitated to him, especially during the folk revival of the late 1950s and early 1960s, when he taught the likes of Ry Cooder, Dave Van Ronk, and Bob Weir. His music—which includes elements from the black church, marches, square dances, and other sources—influenced such performers as Bob Dylan and Taj Mahal. En route to a performance in Newtonville, N.J., he died of a heart attack. He is buried in Rockville Cemetery, Lynbrook, N.Y.

The Social Security Death Index indicates that Davis was born on 30 April 1897, not 1896, as is usually recorded. Confusion surrounds the dates Davis attended school in Cedar Spring. Though his application is dated 26 August 1914, he entered in 1916, staying one school year. See *Sixty-Eighth Annual Report of the South Carolina School for the Deaf and the Blind, Cedar Spring, S.C.* (Columbia, S.C.: Gonzales & Bryan, 1917), 18. Cedar Spring is now part of Spartanburg.

Compositions

"Baby, Let Me Lay It on You," "The Boy Was Kissing the Girl," "Cocaine Blues," "Cross and Evil Woman Blues," "Death Don't Have No Mercy," "I'm Throwin' Up My Hands," "Lo! I Be with You Always," "Lord, Search My Heart," "She's Funny That Way," "There's a Destruction in This Land," "Walkin' Dog Blues," "Whistlin' Blues," "You Got the Pocket Book, I Got the Key," "You Got to Go Down"

Recordings as Leader

The Complete Early Recordings of Rev. Gary Davis (1935, 1949), "Civil War Parade" (ca. 1945), "I Cannot Bear My Burden by Myself" (1949), "I'm Gonna Meet You at the Station" (1949), "Guitar Solo" (ca. 1950), *If I Had My Way: Early Home Recordings* (1953), *The Singing Reverend* (1954), *The Sun of Our Life: Solos, Songs, a Sermon, 1955–1957, American Street Songs* (1956, with some songs by Pink Anderson; also titled *Gospel, Blues and Street Songs*), *Pure Religion and Bad Company* (1957), *Demons and Angels* (1958–1959, 1962–1966), *Harlem Street Singer* (1960), *Pure Religion!* (1960), *A Little More Faith* (1961), *Say No to the Devil* (1961), *Blues and Ragtime* (1962–1968), *In Concert: Children of Zion* (1962), *Ragtime Guitar* (1962–1970), *The Guitar and Banjo of Reverend Gary Davis* (1964), *The Reverend Gary Davis at Newport* (1965), *Live and Kickin'* (1967), *Bring Your Money, Honey!* (1968), *O, Glory: The Apostolic Studio Sessions* (1969), *Delia—Late Concert Recordings 1970–1971, The Legendary Reverend Gary Davis 1971: Blues and Gospel, Live at Cambridge 1971*

Leaders Recorded With

Bull City Red (George Washington) (1935), Blind Boy Fuller (1935)

Films

Blind Gary Davis (1964), *Black Roots* (1970)

Awards

North American Folk Alliance Lifetime Achievement Award (2003); Blues Foundation Hall of Fame (2009)

Website

www.reverendgarydavis.com/ (accessed 21 May 2014)

References

PRIMARY: Richard A. Noblett et al., "The Reverend Gary Davis," *Blues Unlimited* 25 (September 1965): 10–11 (interview); Stephen T. Rye et al., "The Rev. Gary Davis: An Interview, Part 1," *Blues Unlimited* 38 (November 1966): 5–6; Stephen T. Rye et al., "The Rev.

Gary Davis," *Blues Unlimited* 39 (December 1966): 12 (interview).

SECONDARY: Stefan Grossman, *Rev. Gary Davis: The Holy Blues* (New York: Robbins Music/Chandos Music, 1970); Bruce Bastin, *Crying for the Carolines* (London: Studio Vista, 1971), 66, 69–71; Robert Tilling, "Rev. Gary Davis," *Blues Unlimited* 93 (July 1972): 15 (comments by Davis); Woody Mann, *Six Black Blues Guitarists* (New York: Oak Publications, 1973), 71–83; Bob Tilling, "I'm Here to Love You, You Understand!," *Blues Unlimited* 100 (April 1973): 42–43 (comments by Davis); Kip Lornell, "Part Two: Albany Blues," *Living Blues* 15 (Winter 1973–1974): 22–26 (see especially 26); Stefan Grossman, *Rev. Gary Davis/Blues Guitar* (New York: Oak Publications, 1974); Bruce Bastin, *Red River Blues: The Blues Tradition in the Southeast* (Urbana: University of Illinois Press, 1986), 166–67, 170–73; Larry Cohn, "Harlem and Past Memories," *Juke Blues* 10 (Autumn 1987): 7; Mary Katherine Aldin, "Living the Country Blues: Reverend Gary Davis," *Living Blues* 86 (May–June 1989): 43; Stefan Grossman, *Masters of Country Blues Guitar: Rev. Gary Davis* (Miami: CPP/Belwin, 1991) (republished as *Early Masters of American Blues Guitar: Rev. Gary Davis* [Van Nuys, Calif.: Alfred Publishing, 2007]); Stefan Grossman, "The Guitar Styles and Techniques of Rev. Gary Davis," *Blues Revue Quarterly* 1 (July 1991): 20–21; *"Oh, What a Beautiful City": A Tribute to the Reverend Gary Davis (1896–1972) Gospel, Blues and Ragtime,* ed. Robert Tilling (Jersey, Channel Islands: Paul Mill Press, 1992); Robert Tilling, "I Never Was Shy around None of Them Guitar Players," *Blues and Rhythm: The Gospel Truth* 69 (May 1992): 7; Robert Tilling, "Eagle Rocking Blues," *Blues and Rhythm: The Gospel Truth* 108 (April 1996): 12–14; Chris Smith, "A Number That (Almost) No Man Could Number," *Blues and Rhythm: The Gospel Truth* 118 (April 1997): 7; Robert Tilling, "Reverend Gary Davis on Compact Disc," *Blues and Rhythm: The Gospel Truth* 123 (October 1997): 10–12; Robert Tilling, "I Never Was Shy around None of Those Guitar Players," *Blues and Rhythm: The Gospel Truth* 169 (May 2002): 18–20 (this article is different from the one of similar title that Tilling published in 1992); Stephen Criswell, "Davis, Rev. Gary (1896–1972)," in *Encyclopedia of African American Music,* ed. Emmett G. Price III et al. (Santa Barbara: Greenwood, 2011), 1: 274–75.

Davis, Isaac ("Son")

Trumpet, singer

15 April 1929 (Morrisville Village, outside Andrews, S.C.)–28 May 2012 (Morrisville Village, S.C.)

S.C. residence: Morrisville Village (1929–2012)

An electrician by trade, Davis sang in choirs at Saint John A.M.E. Church, Andrews, and led the Old Morrisville Brass Band. He is buried in the cemetery of his church.

Reference

SECONDARY: "Isaac Davis, Sr., Andrews," *Kingstree (S.C.) News,* 13 June 2012, sec. A, p. 6 (obituary).

Davis, M. L.

Singer

S.C. residence: Charleston (at least 1909)

A ward of Jenkins Orphanage, Davis soloed in Poughkeepsie, N.Y., with the institution's Orphan Brass Band and Jubilee Concert Company (1909). A reviewer characterized her voice as "exceptionally clear and bell like."

Reference

SECONDARY: "Jenkins Band Makes Big Hit," *Poughkeepsie (N.Y.) Daily Eagle,* 13 July 1909, p. 5.

Davis, Raymond ("Sting Ray")

Singer

29 March 1940 (Sumter, S.C.)–5 July 2005 (New Brunswick, N.J.)

S.C. residences: Sumter (1940–possibly ca. 1945), Greenville (ca 1993–ca. 1996)

After leaving S.C. as a child Davis lived in Brooklyn, N.Y., before moving to Plainfield, N.J., in 1958. He sang with the Del-Larks in the early 1960s and then with the Parliaments, led by George Clinton. The Parliaments struggled, not finding success until "(I Wanna) Testify" became popular in 1967. In 1970 the group changed its name to Parliament and formed another band, Funkadelic; the two, which played funk and psychedelic rock, existed concurrently. The former featured horns; the latter, guitars. Davis subsequently sang with the Temptations and in the late 1990s toured with three former members of the Parliaments as the Original P.

Davis's birth and death dates come from the Social Security Death Index.

Composition

"Funky Dollar Bill"

Leaders Recorded With (with the Exception of the Date for the Temptations, These Are Release Dates, Not Necessarily Recording Dates)

Parliaments (1960, 1965–1969), Del-Larks (ca. 1960); Funkadelic (1970, 1972, 1974, 1976, 1978–

1979), Parliament (1970, 1974–1980), George Clinton (1982), Zapp (1982–1983), Temptations (1995)

Award

Rock and Roll Hall of Fame (1997; as member of Parliament and Funkadelic)

References

PRIMARY: David Mills et al., *George Clinton and P-Funk: An Oral History,* ed. Dave Marsh (New York: Avon, 1998), passim (interview excerpts); Paul Doyle, "Interview: Ray Davis, from the Original P," http://vermontreview.tripod.com/Interviews/raydavis.htm (undated; accessed 21 May 2014).

SECONDARY: Pierre Perrone, "Ray Davis: Independent Obit (Funkadelic Singer)," https: //groups.google.com/forum/?fromgroups=#!topic/alt.obituaries/xXYqNNqqw64 (2005; accessed 21 May 2014); Charlie Horner, with Pamela Horner, "Doo Wop and Soul in the Birthplace of Funk: The Story of Sammy and the Del Larks," *Echoes of the Past* 86 (Winter 2008): 11–20 (also available at www.classicurbanharmony.net/Del%20Larks%20Story%20edit.pdf [accessed 21 May 2014]) (comments by Davis).

Dean, Stephen

Drums

Ca. 1923 (S.C.)-?

S.C. residence: Charleston (possibly ca. 1923, but by 1935-at least into early 1940s)

A ward of Jenkins Orphanage, Dean played in its bands from the mid-1930s into the early 1940s.

Dean's age was estimated as seventeen when the musician was enumerated for the census at the orphanage on 21 May 1940; this document indicates that he was born in S.C. and that he lived in Charleston in 1935. When South Carolinian Stephen O. Dean enlisted in the army on 12 May 1943 at Fort Jackson, Columbia, S.C., he said that he was twenty-two. It has not been determined if he was the musician.

Delaney, Tom (Thomas Henry)

Composer, piano, singer

Possibly 14 September 1879 (Charleston, S.C.)-probably 22 December 1963 (Baltimore, Md.)

S.C. residence: Charleston (1879-no later than 1910)

While a ward of Jenkins Orphanage, Delaney formed the Springfield Minstrels, which reportedly toured with the institution's band. In time he became one of the first wards to make a name for himself as an entertainer and musician. He was a vaudevillian from ca. 1910 into the 1920s, including for a time with Pearl Mason, his wife. He played piano for and possibly managed Ethel Waters (1920s). Sometime after appearing regularly with John J. Quigley at Steeplechase Park in Brooklyn (late 1920s and early 1930s), he reduced his activities as a performing musician, though he remained at least minimally active into the 1950s. Delaney is best known and most significant as a composer. "The Jazz Me Blues" has been recorded hundreds of times, including initially in 1921 by, in sequence, Lillyn Brown, the Original Dixieland Jazz Band, Bix Beiderbecke, and Lucille Hegamin. His compositions have been recorded by such musicians as Louis Armstrong, Ma Rainey, Bessie Smith, Clara Smith, Mamie Smith, and Fats Waller. Delaney is buried in Mount Auburn Cemetery, Baltimore, the city in which he settled in the early 1930s.

Though such documents as his World War II draft registration card and the Social Security Death Index indicate that Delaney was born on 14 September 1889, his age was estimated as nine months when he was enumerated for the census in Charleston on 1 June 1880. When enumerated in Baltimore on 8 April 1940, he gave his age as sixty-one. His death date is usually recorded as 16 December 1963. The obituary published in the *Baltimore Afro-American* on Saturday, 28 December 1963, states that Delaney "died at home Sunday." The Sunday before the 28th was the 22nd.

Compositions

"Absent Minded Blues," "Bow-Legged Mama," "Charleston Geechie Dance," "Cootie for Your Tootie," "Death House Blues," "Down Home Blues," "Everybody's Blues," "Everybody Wants to Go to Heaven but Nobody Wants to Die," "Follow the Deal on Down," "Georgia Stockade Blues," "Give Me That Old Slow Drag," "Good Times up in Harlem," "Graveyard Love," "Hard Boiled Papa," "Honey Where You Been So Long?," "I Don't Care Where You Take It," "If I Lose, Let Me Lose," "I Love You Daddy but You Don't Mean Me No Good," "I'm a Back-Bitin' Mama," "I'm a Good Hearted Mama," "I'm Leavin' Just to Ease My Worried Mind," "I've Cried My Last Time over You," "I Wanna Jazz Some More," "The Jazz Me Blues,"

"Let the Good Times Roll," "Log Cabin Blues," "Low Down Mama Blues," "Meet Me up in Harlem," "Miss Lizzie Can't Strut No More," "Mournful Blues," "Move It On Out of Here," "Mr. Leader Man Swing That Band," "Never Drive a Beggar from Your Door," "New York Glide," "Nobody Knows the Way I Feel This Morning," "Parson Jones," "Police Blues," "Poon Tang," "Sinful Blues," "Slow and Steady," "Somethin' Goin' On Wrong," "South Bound Blues," "Strollin' down Pennsylvania Avenue," "Thing Called Love's Done Made a Fool Out of Me," "Troublesome Blues," "Walk That Broad," "When I Get Blues," "When I Leave This Time Baby," "Working Man Blues," "You May Go but You'll Come Back Some Day"

Recordings as Leader (All 1925)

"Bow-Legged Mama," "Georgia Stockade Blues," "I'm Leavin' Just to Ease My Worried Mind," "Parson Jones"

References

PRIMARY: Thurman Grove and Mary Grove, "Notes on Tom Delaney," *Record Changer* 3 (May 1944): 17, 39–41 (substantial comments by Delaney); E. B. Rea, "True Blues: 'Certain Feeling' Needed to Put Blues in Song, Says Tom Delaney," *Baltimore Afro-American*, 16 October 1948, magazine sec., p. 9 (substantial comments by Delaney).

SECONDARY: "Thomas Delaney, Songwriter, Dies," *Baltimore Afro-American*, 28 December 1963, p. 16 (obituary); John Chilton, *A Jazz Nursery: The Story of the Jenkins' Orphanage Bands of Charleston, South Carolina* (London: Bloomsbury Book Shop, 1980), 13, 54; Edward Ball, *The Sweet Hell Inside: A Family History* (New York: William Morrow, 2001), 179–83; Robert Deis, "The Heavenly Conundrum Popularized by a Song: 'Everybody Wants to Go to Heaven, but Nobody Wants to Die,'" http://www.quotecounterquote.com/2011/11/everybody-wants-to-go-to-heaven-but.html (11 April 2013; accessed 21 May 2014).

Derrick, Charles D., Jr.

Broadcaster, producer, manager, record company owner, singer

30 January 1927 (Lexington, S.C.)–23 August 2006 (Lexington, S.C.)

S.C. residence: Lexington (1927–1945, 1954–2006)

Following his army service (1945–early 1950s), Derrick matriculated at Kittrell College in Raleigh, N.C., where he began his radio career in 1953. After returning to Lexington the next year and enrolling at Allen University, he broadcast *Wings of Faith* on WOIC in Columbia; on this station in 1957 he began broadcasting *Dial Derrick*, which featured rhythm and blues. In 1955 he formed the Spiritualaires, with which he sang bass, recorded, and toured. He left this group to manage the singer Kip Anderson. In 1957 Derrick established the first of his record labels, Derrick. Others included Nation-Wide, Roadway, Tomaria, Tomorrow, and True Spot. In the late 1960s he formed a publishing and production company, Chitlin Music, which became Tomaria Music. His Platter Shops distributed records to stores in central S.C. He also worked as field representative for congressmen Floyd Spence and Joe Wilson. Derrick is buried in Spring Hill Cemetery, Lexington.

Compositions

"Can't Hide Sinner," "Family Prayer," "Here Am I," "Here I Am, Try Me," "Home Fires Are Brighter," "I Can't," "I Done You Wrong," "If That Don't Make You Cry," "I Get Carried Away," "I'll Get Along," "I'm Going on to Glory," "It Is a Weak Man That Cries," "I Wanna Be the Only One," "A Knife and a Fork," "Lay This Body Down," "Let Me Be the Only One," "Little Girl, Don't You Cry," "Lost Pride," "Money You Never Get Tired Of," "No Need to Cry," "Only Fool," "Soul," "Stop These Tears," "Talkin' 'bout Love," "Time Waits for No One," "Who's That Knocking at My Door?," "Woman, How Do You Make Me Love You Like I Do?"

Leader Recorded With

Spiritualaires (1955)

References

SECONDARY: "Charles D. Derrick Jr.," *Lexington County (S.C.) Chronicle and the Dispatch-News*, 31 August 2006, sec. A, p. 12 (obituary); Opal Louis Nations, "The Charles Derrick Story: With Forays into the Careers of Kip Anderson, Drink Small and the Spiritualaires," *Blues and Rhythm: The Gospel Truth* 242 (September 2009): 16–20.

Dillard, Moses Chriswell, Jr.

Guitar, singer, arranger, composer, producer

30 September 1946 (Greenville, S.C.)–14 July 1993 (Nashville, Tenn.)

S.C. residence: Greenville (1946–ca. 1966, possibly 1970–1971)

Dillard was involved in various aspects of music. He led groups, performed as sideman, composed and arranged, and from 1977 into 1980 operated a publishing company, Moses Dillard Music, in Nashville. In 1972 his group featured the singer Peabo Bryson. His most jazz-oriented recording is probably "Tribute to Wes [Montgomery]," on the album *Now!* Among the recording sessions he produced in whole or in part, one by New Faith is possibly the most noteworthy. In 1992 Warner Brothers released a CD by this gospel group that Dillard assembled from among inmates at the Tennessee State Penitentiary, Nashville. He gave up music for religion. With degrees from American Baptist College and Vanderbilt University, he was ordained in 1985. Cynthia Wilson-Felder dedicated her CD *New Songs of Zion* (1993) to Dillard, who is buried in section I, Garden of the Last Supper, Greenville Memorial Gardens, Piedmont, S.C.

Compositions

"Across the Sky," "Best of Me," "Bring Your Dreams to Me, Boy," "Cheating, Teasing, Misleading," "Cosmic Melody," "Deviled Egg," "Don't Ask Me Why," "Fairytales Come True," "Filet of Fatback," "Funk Encounter," "Get It While It's Hot," "Get Out of My Heart," "Give Love a Good Name," "Good Stuff," "Groovin' with You," "Here Come the Rattlesnakes," "Here We Go," "I Feel It Coming," "I Have a World of Love for You," "I Know I'm Satisfied," "I'll Pay the Price," "I Promise to Love You," "I've Got to Find a Way to Hide My Hurt," "Just for the Moment," "Let Me Hip You to the Streets," "Let's Make It a Party," "Nashville Gospel," "Nashville Soul," "One Woman Lover," "Perfect Love Affair," "Put It on the Line," "Rock on the Block," "Shuck and Jive," "Soul over Easy," "Stand by Me," "Take Good Care of My Lady," "They Don't Want Us Together," "This Is the Day," "Touch Me on My Hot Spot," "Tutty Frutty Booty Is Good When It's Hot," "Unlucky Guy," "We Fell in Love While Dancing," "We Gotta Come Together," "We'll Understand It Better," "Wha'cha See in Me?," "What's Better Than Love," "What Would It Take," "Woke Up Dis Mornin'," "You Just Can't Laugh It Off," "You've Got Me Dancing in My Sleep"

Recordings as Leader (These Are Release Dates, Not Necessarily Recording Dates)

"Go Way Baby" (1964), "I'll Pay the Price" (1964), "Pretty as a Picture" (1964), "They Don't Want Us Together" (1964, 1967; the latter with Joshua Dillard), "Get Out of My Heart" (1967; with Joshua Dillard), "My Elusive Dreams" (1967; with Joshua Dillard), "What's Better Than Love" (1967; with Joshua Dillard), *Now!* (1969), "Cheating, Teasing, Misleading" (1971; with Martha Starr), "I've Got to Find a Way to Hide My Hurt," two parts (1971), "Our Love Is True" (1971), "Thank God for This Thing Called Love" (1971), "You Can't Laugh It Off" (1971; with Martha Starr), "I Promise to Love You" (1972), "We Gotta Come Together" (1972), "Good Stuff" (1974), "Theme from Love Joy" (1974), "Filet of Fatback" (1975), "Wha'cha See in Me?" (1975), "Fairytales Come True" (1977; with Lorraine Johnson), "Here We Go" (1977; with Lorraine Johnson), "If You Don't Mean It, Don't Touch Me" (1977), "I Got My Mind Together" (1977), *Frisky* (1979; with Jesse Boyce), *Juice* (1979; with Jesse Boyce), *We're in This Thing Together* (1980; with Jesse Boyce)

Leaders Recorded With

Possibly Golden Wings (ca. early 1960s), Arthur Conley (1967), Jackie Hairston (1967), Oscar Toney, Jr. (1967), Mighty Sam McLain (1968), Sons of Moses (1968), James and Bobby Purify (1969), Lorraine Johnson (1977–1978), Saturday Night Band (1978–1979), Al Green (1982, 1986)

References

SECONDARY: Robert K. Oermann, "Singing Prisoners Need Another Miracle," *Florence (Ala.) Times Daily,* 4 July 1992, sec. A, p. 8; "Rev. Moses C. Dillard," *Greenville (S.C.) News,* 17 July 1993, sec. A, p. 7 (also available at http://www.findagrave.com/cgi-bin/fg.cgi?page=pv&GRid=39311759 [accessed 21 May 2014]) (obituary); Joe DePriest, "Musician Moses Dillard Was Always on the Go, Friend Recalls," *Charlotte (N.C.) Observer,* 18 July 1993, Gaston Observer sec., p. 2; Bruce Eder, "Moses Dillard," http://www.allmusic.com/artist/moses-dillard-mn0000593044 (undated; accessed 21 May 2014).

Ola Dixon; permission of the photographer, Joseph A. Rosen

Dixon, Ola Mae

Drums, singer
14 February 1943 (Marion, S.C.)–
S.C. residence: Marion (1943–1963)

Dixon entered the blues scene in the late 1960s as a singer with Charles Walker; soon she became a percussionist after teaching herself to play drums. During her affiliation with Walker she apparently operated a record store in Bronx, N.Y. Following his death in 1975 she joined Paul Oscher. She toured with Jimmy Rogers in 1980 and performed for several years in the 1980s with Luther "Guitar Junior" Johnson. Also that decade she played with the House Rockers and in N.Y.C. performed regularly at the Mondo Cane Bar and belonged to the house band at the Abilene Café, where she backed such musicians as Magic Slim and Pinetop Perkins. Though she mostly retired from music in the early 1990s in order to devote herself to church work, in 2001 she led a band at the Columbia Pike Blues Festival in Arlington, Va., and performed at the House of Blues in Boston. Peter Watrous observes that Dixon "has the secret that many more technically adept drummers don't have: she knows that certain rhythms, when combined with the right tempos, chase away problems."

Recordings as Leader

"Charles! From Ola to You" (1975), *Labor of Love* (1998–1999)

Leaders Recorded With

Charles Walker (1973–1974), Paul Oscher (1975), Big Walter Horton (1980), Luther "Guitar Junior" Johnson (1998), Louisiana Red (2000)

References

SECONDARY: Peter Watrous, "Pop: Houserockers, Blues," *New York Times,* 21 January 1988, sec. C, p. 24; Brian Bisesi, "Ola Dixon: 'She's the Drummer?,'" *Big City Rhythm and Blues* 18 (October–November 2012): 32; "Ola Dixon," http://www.severnrecords.com/site/artistDetail.asp?AID=18 (undated; accessed 21 May 2014); "Ola Dixon: *Labor of Love,*" http://www.severnrecords.com/site/albumDetail.asp?RID=5 (undated; accessed 21 May 2014).

Doctor, Joseph

See Washboard Doc

Dogan, Nathaniel

Piano
Probably ca. 1903 (probably Greenville, S.C.)–?
S.C. residence: Greenville (probably ca. 1903–probably no later than 1930)

In 1930 for Vocalion, Dogan accompanied singer Lee Green on two songs, "I Don't Care If the Boat Don't Land" and "Wash Day and No Soap."

When enumerated for the census in Greenville, S.C., on 26 April 1910, the Dogan family consisted of parents Luther and Mary and children Gomer, Booker, Lissie, and Charlie. A decade later the parents were probably dead because they are absent from the 1920 census. When it was conducted in Greenville County on 15 January, Booker, Elizabeth, and Charlie, as well as their brother Nathaniel, were enumerated; Gomer is not mentioned. (This census spells the surname Dogans.) At the time of the 1910 census Gomer's age was estimated as seven; in 1920 Nathaniel's was estimated as eighteen. Gomer and Nathaniel are almost certainly the same person. When enumerated for the census in East Saint Louis, Ill., on 9 April 1930, Nathaniel

Dogan, who worked as a music teacher, was estimated to be age twenty-seven. Though his birthplace is identified as Md., this census states that his parents were born in S.C. His wife, Alberta, probably provided the information to the enumerator. As Nat Doogan, the musician was enumerated on 20 April 1940 in East Saint Louis, where he worked on street construction as a laborer. This document estimates his age as thirty-six and records S.C. as his birthplace.

Leader Recorded With

Lee Green (1930)

Dooley, Simmie (Simeon; "Blind Simmie")

Guitar, kazoo, singer

1880s, possibly June 1887 (Hartwell, Ga.)–17 January 1961 (Spartanburg, S.C.)

S.C. residence: Spartanburg (not before 1917–1961)

A guitarist admired by Gary Davis and others, the blind Dooley apparently toured for a season or two with Doc Harper's medicine show. As a street musician he played mostly in the Spartanburg area. Upon meeting Pink Anderson possibly in the late 1910s and teaching the youngster to master some chords, he and Anderson began playing together; they also recorded together at Dooley's only recording session. Dooley might have quit playing music in the 1930s. He is buried in an unmarked grave in the East Spartanburg Cemetery.

The 1900 census indicates that Dooley was born in June 1887. When asked his birth date while registering for the draft on 2 August 1917, he said, "Don't know." When enumerated for the census on 2 April 1940, he estimated his age as fifty. His death notice in the *Spartanburg Herald* states that Dooley died at seventy-eight.

Composition

"C.C.&O. Blues"

Recordings as Leader (All 1928; with Pink Anderson)

"C.C.&O. Blues," "Every Day in the Week Blues," "Gonna Tip Out Tonight," "Papa's 'Bout to Get Mad"

References

SECONDARY: "Simmie Dooley," *Spartanburg (S.C.) Herald,* 18 January 1961, p. 3 (death notice); Bruce Bastin, *Crying for the Carolines* (London: Studio Vista, 1971), 79, 85; Bruce Bastin, *Red River Blues: The Blues Tradition in the Southeast* (Urbana: University of Illinois Press, 1986), 172, 174, 182–86; Peter Cooper, *Hub City Music Makers: One Southern Town's Popular Music Legacy* (Spartanburg, S.C.: Holocene, 1997), 47–48; Jerry Zolten, *Great God A'mighty! The Dixie Hummingbirds: Celebrating the Rise of Soul Gospel Music* (Oxford: Oxford University Press, 2003), 56–57.

Downing, Zeno

Trombone

S.C. residence: Charleston (1930s)

Apparently a ward of Jenkins Orphanage, Downing played in its bands in the 1930s.

Drayton, Charles Exodus

Singer

Mid-1880s (Charleston, S.C.)–?

S.C. residences: Charleston (mid-1880s–no later than 1900), Orangeburg (by 1900–at least until 1907)

While a student at Claflin University (by 1900–1907), Drayton, a baritone, toured with its vocal groups. Later he joined the Transcontinental Southland Jubilee Quartet before becoming a member of Hann's Jubilee Singers in the mid-1910s. Probably in 1917 Drayton proposed forming a quartet drawn from the membership of William A. Hann's organization in order to make money performing when Hann's group was on vacation. This quartet became known as the Four Harmony Kings, with which Drayton spent most if not all of the remainder of his career. This group gained some celebrity by 1918 and the next year affiliated, briefly, with James Reese Europe before returning to touring as an independent group. In Mechanics Hall, Boston, Drayton was in the dressing room of Europe when Herbert Wright killed Europe there on 9 May 1919. Drayton testified at Wright's trial. In 1921 the Four Harmony Kings joined the cast of Noble Sissle and Eubie Blake's *Shuffle Along,* the first successful black musical; during its run Paul Robeson sang with the quartet when one of its members was ill. The group remained with the show when it toured in 1923 and 1924. By the time it joined Sissle and Blake's *Chocolate Dandies* (1924), Drayton had left the Four Harmony Kings, though he rejoined in 1925 when the group was reconstituted following the dissolution of the original quartet. That year the men sailed to Europe, where they remained for an extended period. When the quartet broke up in 1933, three of the members, including Drayton, continued as a group. In spring 1938 Drayton returned to the United States, probably to his home in Cincinnati. Tim Brooks states that the Four Harmony Kings were, arguably, "the most prominent black quartet of their era, possibly the most popular prior to the debut of the Mills Brothers" (463).

Drayton's given names are sometimes recorded as Exodus Charles, sometimes as Charles Exodus. It has not been determined which is correct: he was graduated from the preparatory program at Claflin University as Exodus Charles Drayton and wrote a 1928 article as Chas. E. Drayton. The 1900 census (conducted in Orangeburg on 21 June) identifies him as Exodus, indicates that he was then a student at Claflin, and notes that he was born in S.C. in March 1887. His draft registration card (completed in Chicago on 7 September 1918) records the given name as Exodus and identifies his birth date as 16 May 1884. When, as Charles Exodus, he married Lillian Elizabeth Fuller in Hamilton, Ohio, on 28 April 1919, he stated that he was born in S.C., gave his birth year as 1886, and recorded his age as thirty-three. For the passenger list of the *Paris,* on which he departed Southampton, England, for N.Y.C. on 30 March 1938, Charles Exodus specified 29 August 1887 as his birth date, noted that he was born in Charleston, and said that he resided in Cincinnati, which is probably where his wife lived during his absence.

Recordings as Leader (All as Member of the Four Harmony Kings)

"One More Ribber to Cross" (1919; as Lieut. Jim Europe's Four Harmony Kings), "Swing Low, Sweet Chariot" (1919; as Lieut. Jim Europe's Four Harmony Kings), "Ain't It a Shame" (1921, 1926), possibly "Aunt Hagar's Children Blues" (1921), "Doan You Cry, Ma Honey" (1921), "Goodnight Angeline" (1921), "Love's Old Sweet Song" (1921), possibly "St. Louis Blues" (1921), "Sweet Adeline" (1921), "A Calliope Yodel" (1926), "De Gospel Train" (1926), "Dis Wicked Race" (1926), "Heabben" (1926), "Jesus Moves in de Middle ob de Air" (1926), "Joshua Fought the Battle of Jericho" (1926), "Little David Play on Your Harp" (1926), "Long Ago Lullaby" (1926), "Rolling and Rocker Dem in His Arms" (1926), "Beautiful" (1929), "Dixie Dawn" (1929), possibly "He's Got His Eyes on Me" (1929), possibly "Let's Go Down in Jordan" (1929), possibly "The Queen Street Rag" (1929), "Shout Hallelujah! 'Cause I'm Home" (1929), "When Eliza Rolls Her Eyes" (1929), possibly "You Got to Know How to Love" (1929)

References

PRIMARY: Chas. E. Drayton, "'The Four Harmony Kings' and Their Origin Discussed," *Los Angeles California Eagle,* 21 September 1928, pp. 1, 3.

SECONDARY: *Catalogue of Claflin University, Orangeburg, S.C., 1904–5* (Orangeburg: Claflin University Press, 1905), 84; *Annual Catalogue of Claflin University, Orangeburg, S.C., 1906–1907* (Orangeburg: Claflin University Steam Press, [1907]), 70, 115; Noble Lee Sissle, "Memoirs of Lieutenant 'Jim' Europe," typescript, ca. 1942, African American Odyssey, American Memory Collection, Library of Congress, 230–34, http://memory.loc.gov/cgi-bin/query/r?ammem/aaodyssey:@field(NUMBER+@band(musmisc+ody0717)) (accessed 21 May 2014); Ray Funk, "Three Afro-American Singing Groups," in *Under the Imperial Carpet: Essays in Black History, 1780–1950,* ed. Rainer Lotz and Ian Pegg (Crawley, England: Rabbit Press, 1986), 150–55; Reid Badger, *A Life in Ragtime: A Biography of James Reese Europe* (New York: Oxford University Press, 1995), 215–17, 222; Sheila Tully Boyle and Andrew Bunie, *Paul Robeson: The Years of Promise and Achievement* (Amherst: University of Massachusetts Press, 2001), 99–100; Tim Brooks, *Lost Sounds: Blacks and the Birth of the Recording Industry, 1890–1919* (Urbana: University of Illinois Press, 2004), 452–63.

Drayton, Joseph

Drums, trombone

Ca. 1914 (S.C.)-?

S.C. residence: Charleston (by 1930–at least into early 1930s)

A ward of Jenkins Orphanage, Drayton played in its bands in the 1930s.

Drayton's age was estimated as sixteen when the musician was enumerated for the census at the orphanage on 2 April 1930. He was possibly the Joseph Drayton, estimated age twenty-five, who was enumerated in Aiken, S.C., on 14 May 1940; this census indicates that this person also resided in Aiken in 1935 and in 1940 worked as a hospital orderly. Several black Joseph Draytons were born in S.C. ca. 1914. Most of them received little if any schooling; the one in Aiken completed four years of high school, which, if he was the musician, he would have done at the orphanage.

Dreher, Clarence M.

Probably 27 November of either 1891 or 1892 (Darlington, S.C.)–?

S.C. residences: Darlington (probably 1891 or 1892–no later than 1900), Orangeburg (by 1900–no later than 1910), Columbia (by 1910–no later than early 1910s), Charleston (by early 1910s–possibly late 1910s)

Possibly a ward of Jenkins Orphanage, Dreher played in its bands in the 1910s, including the one that performed in England in 1914. His instrument is not known.

Dreher's place and 1892 date of birth come from the passenger list of the *St. Louis,* which transported the orphanage band from Liverpool to N.Y.C. in September 1914. When enumerated for the census in Orangeburg on 6 June 1900, Dreher's birth date was identified as November 1891; conducted in Columbia on 22 April, the 1910 census records the middle initial of Dreher, estimated age eighteen. If he was born in 1891 or 1892, he played with the orphanage band at least in his early twenties, which suggests that he might then have been on the institution's staff.

Reference

SECONDARY: Howard Rye, "Visiting Fireboys: The Jenkins' Orphanage Bands in Britain," *Storyville* 130 (1987): 137–43.

Drew, Patti

Singer

29 December 1944 (Charleston, S.C.)–

S.C. residence: Charleston (1944–probably mid-to-late 1940s)

After leaving Charleston when young, Drew lived in Nashville before locating to Evanston, Ill., in 1956. Following her time singing lead with the Drew-Vels and recording under her own name in the mid-1960s, she signed with Capitol Records, which released four of her albums in successive years beginning in 1967. The reception of the first three led to her extensive touring. On the fourth she sings Richard Evans's arrangements of ballads and gentle swingers backed by a big band and strings. Mainly considered a rhythm-and-blues or soul singer, she was the first vocalist to record Neil Sedaka's "Workin' on a Groovy Thing." After retiring from music in 1971, she made one recording, a single about the football accomplishments of O. J. Simpson (1975), and apparently sang briefly with the group Front Line (1980s).

Composition

"Just Because"

Recordings as Leader (These Are Release Dates, Not Necessarily Recording Dates)

"Sufferer" (1965), "Where Is Daddy?" (1965), "It's All Over Now" (1966), "Mirror, Mirror" (1966), *Tell Him* (1967), *Workin' on a Groovy Thing* (1968), *I've Been Here All the Time* (1969), "He's the One" (1969), "Which One Should I Choose?" (1969), *Wild Is Love* (1970), "I'm Calling" (1970), "It's Just a Dream" (1970), "The Mighty O. J." (1975)

Leader Recorded With (These Are Release Dates, Not Necessarily Recording Dates)

Drew-Vels (1963–1965)

References

SECONDARY: Robert Pruter, "Evanston Soul: Patti Drew and the Drew-Vels," *Record Exchanger* 26 (1978): 22–24 (this issue is also designated volume 5, number 4) (reworked, with comments by Drew added, as "Beach Music from Historic Charleston to Windy Chicago . . . the Patti Drew Story," *It Will Stand* 3 [1981]: 14–15; also reworked, with no Drew comments, in Pruter's *Chicago Soul* [Urbana: University of Illinois Press, 1991], 169–70); "Working on a Groovy Thing!—The Patti Drew Story," http://www.soulfulkindamusic.net/articlepattidrew.htm (2007; accessed 21 May 2014); Andrew Hamilton, "The Drew-Vels," http://www.allmusic.com/artist/the-drew-vels-mn0001275465 (undated; accessed 21 May 2014).

Earl(e), Eugene

Trombone, tuba
Mid-1910s (Asheville, N.C.)-before 1980
S.C. residence: Charleston (1927-at least into early 1930s)

A ward of Jenkins Orphanage beginning in 1927, Earl(e) played in its bands into the early 1930s. He performed with the Carolina Cotton Pickers, beginning in 1933. Earl(e)'s age was estimated as fifteen when the musician was enumerated for the census at the orphanage on 2 April 1930; this document notes that he was born in N.C. The North Carolina Birth Index, 1800–2000, records that a boy surnamed Earle, but with no given name indicated, was born on 10 March 1917. It has not been determined if he was Eugene Earl(e). John Chilton states that Earl(e) was born in Asheville, N.C., ca. 1917, and had died by the time Chilton completed his manuscript.

Leader Recorded With

Carolina Cotton Pickers (1936–1937)

References

SECONDARY: John Chilton, *A Jazz Nursery: The Story of the Jenkins' Orphanage Bands of Charleston, South Carolina* (London: Bloomsbury Book Shop, 1980), 54; Bruce Bastin, "A Note on the Carolina Cotton Pickers," *Storyville* 95 (June–July 1981): 177–82.

Eclipse Brass Band

Charleston

On 26 April 1893 this fifteen-piece band performed in a parade celebrating the fiftieth anniversary of the Odd Fellows of Charleston.

Reference

SECONDARY: "Solving the Race Problem," *Indianapolis Freeman: An Illustrated Colored Newspaper,* 6 May 1893, p. 5.

Ellis, Jimmy (James Thomas, II)

Singer
15 November 1937 (Rock Hill, S.C.)-8 March 2012 (Rock Hill, S.C.)
S.C. residence: Rock Hill (1937-1958, 2000-2012)

Ellis began singing at the Cross Road Baptist Church and Saint Mary's Catholic Church, both in Rock Hill. After forming the Four Knights, he toured with Bobby Plair. Following graduation from Emmett Scott High School (1958) he settled in Philadelphia, where he sang nights and weekends while working as a handyman. He joined the Cordells, later named the Whirlwinds, and yet later known as the Exceptions. By 1972 Ellis and another member of the Exceptions joined two members of the Volcanoes to form the Trammps, a group that helped popularize disco. Ellis was its lead singer. In *Saturday Night Fever,* John Travolta dances to the group's recording of "Disco Inferno," which features Ellis. "Hold Back the Night" is another of the group's notable recordings. Ellis's body was cremated.

Composition

"Heartbeat"

Leaders Recorded With

Cordells (1961), Whirlwinds (1961, 1963), Exceptions (mid-1960s), Trammps (1970s)

Award

Grammy Award for singing on "Disco Inferno," which is on the sound track of *Saturday Night Fever,* which received a Grammy Award for Album of the Year (1979)

Website

http://thetrammps.net/index.html (accessed 21 May 2014)

References

SECONDARY: Dan Huntley, "A Return to the Music of Home," *Charlotte (N.C.) Observer,* 15 October 2000, sec. Y, p. 1 (comments by Ellis); Denyse C. Middleton, "Grammy to Gospel, Passion Still Burns," *Rock Hill (S.C.) Herald,* 24 October 2005, sec. A, pp. 1, 6 (comments by Ellis); Karen Bair, "Singing for a Higher Calling," *Rock Hill (S.C.) Herald,* 7 May 2007, sec. B, p. 1; Andrew Dys, "The Voice of 'Disco Inferno' Dies at 74," *Rock Hill (S.C.) Herald,* 9 March 2012, sec. A, pp. 1, 4; Daniel E. Slotnik, "Jimmy Ellis, 74, Lead Singer in Dance Band Trammps," *New York Times,* 9 March 2012, sec. B, p. 15 (national edition) (also available as "Jimmy Ellis Dies at 74; Lead Singer in Dance Band Trammps" at http://www.nytimes.com/2012/03/09/arts/music/jimmy-ellis-74-lead-singer-in-dance-band-trammps.html [accessed 21 May 2014]) (obituary); "James T. Ellis," *Rock Hill (S.C.) Herald,* 11 March 2012, sec. B, p. 2 (obituary); Andrew Dys, "Star's Song Resounds at Memorial," *Rock Hill (S.C.) Herald,* 17 March 2012, sec. A, pp. 1, 7; "Jimmy Ellis," *Blues and Rhythm: The Gospel Truth* 269 (May 2012): 26 (obituary).

Ellis, McKinley T.

Guitar, ukulele, singer
6 May 1918 (McDowell County, W.Va.)–26 August 1982 (Greenville, S.C.)
S.C. residence: Greenville (ca. 1931–1982)

Ellis moved from W.Va. to Greenville ca. 1931. Soon thereafter he began playing with Baby Tate, with whom and Washboard Willie Young he was part of the first band of black musicians (the Carolina Blackbirds) to play on the local radio station (1932). A left-handed guitarist who retained the standard stringing of his instrument, he performed popular music (such as "Besame Mucho" and "The Sheik of Araby") as well as the blues. He served in the army 1942–1945. Reunited in 1970, Ellis and Tate recorded music that has not been released. Ellis is buried in Walcott Cemetery in the Brutontown community, Greenville.

Ellis's birth and death dates come from the Social Security Death Index. The musician's birthplace is recorded in *The Official Roster of South Carolina Servicemen and Servicewomen in World War II, 1941–46* (N.p.: State Budget and Control Board, n.d.), 2: 1263. Ellis lived in Browns Creek Magisterial District, McDowell County, W.Va., as late as 5 April 1930, the day he was enumerated there for the census.

Leader Recorded With

Baby Tate (1970; unissued)

References

SECONDARY: Bruce Bastin and Pete Lowry, "Tricks Ain't Workin' No More: Blues from the South-East," *Blues Unlimited* 78 (December 1970): 11; Bruce Bastin, *Crying for the Carolines* (London: Studio Vista, 1971), 75; "McKinley Ellis," *Greenville (S.C.) News,* 28 August 1982, sec. C, p. 6 (obituary); Bruce Bastin, *Red River Blues: The Blues Tradition in the Southeast* (Urbana: University of Illinois Press, 1986), 177, 187, 192.

Ellis, Melvin ("Prezzy")

Drum major
Ca. 1906 (S.C.)–?
S.C. residence: Charleston (by 1920–probably at least into early 1920s)

A ward of Jenkins Orphanage, Ellis was associated with its bands in the 1920s.

Ellis's age was estimated as thirteen when the youth was enumerated for the census at the orphanage on 9 January 1920; this document notes that he was born in S.C. He might be the Melvin Ellis, estimated age thirty-two, who was enumerated in April 1940 in Holly Hill, S.C., where he also resided in 1935.

Erwin, Gary Anthony

See Shrimp City Slim

Esquerita (Eskew Reeder; "Fabulash," "Magnificent Malochi," "S. Q.")

Piano, singer
20 November 1938 (Greenville, S.C.)–23 October 1986 (New York, N.Y.)
S.C. residence: Greenville (1938–ca. 1953, mid-1950s)

Though at least one source claims that he was born in New Orleans, Eskew Reeder was born in Greenville, S.C. By age ten he was playing piano in a Greenville church. He apparently completed his schooling at the end of the ninth grade at Sterling High School. Upon leaving home, probably in 1953, he toured with gospel groups, most importantly the Heavenly Echoes, from Brooklyn, with which he recorded, as pianist, in 1955. He then toured the Southeast before returning to Greenville, where he played at the Owl's Club and was discovered ca. 1957 by Paul Peek, with whom he recorded, as pianist, in 1958. This same year he signed with Capitol Records and became known as Esquerita. His recordings for this label are, in their manic nature, similar to ones by Little Richard. (Little Richard credits Esquerita with teaching him to play the piano well and inspiring him to sport a pompadour.) He also recorded for Everest, Instant, Vee-Jay (backing Little Richard, with Jimi Hendrix as fellow sideman), Triumph, Okeh, Cross-Tone, and Brunswick (with Esquerita identified as Magnificent Malochi and with Dr. John on organ). Recordings he made for Norton (1958) and Motown (1963) have not been released, nor have those on which he performed as sideman with Bobby Jones (1958), Joe Jones and Reggie Hall (1963), and Earl King (1963). In the early 1970s he formed a group (with, among others, Charles Neville and Jerry Katz) that played regularly in N.Y.C. Indigent, he apparently made money working as a parking lot attendant and washing the windshields of cars stopped at Brooklyn intersections. Though several sources suggest that as Mark Malochi he was incarcerated at Rikers Island in N.Y.C., prison records do not support this contention or reveal that a person named Eskew Reeder was ever confined there. He is reportedly buried on Hart Island, Bronx County, N.Y. After Esquerita's death Mick Jones wrote and recorded the tune "Esquerita."

Though some sources maintain that Esquerita was born Steven Quincy Reeder, Jr., and others note that his birth name was Eskew Reeder, Jr., available evidence indicates that he was born Eskew Reeder, the same name as his father. The Social Security Death Index, for example, identifies him as such. This document records that he was born in S.C. on 20 November 1938, not 1935, the year claimed by almost all other sources consulted.

Compositions

"Alone," "Baby, You Can Depend on Me," "Believe Me When I Say Rock and Roll Is Here to Stay," "Dew Drop Inn," "Esquerita and the Voolah," "The Flu," "Freedom Blues," "Get Back Baby," "Gettin' Plenty of Lovin'," "Golly Golly, Annie Mae," "Hey Miss Lucy," "I Got to Learn," "Laid Off," "Oh Baby," "Please Come on Home," "The Rock-a-Round," "Rockin' the Joint," "Sarah Lee," "Seven Days and Seven Nights," "She Left Me Crying," "Southern Style," "There's Gotta Be a Way," "This Thing Called Love," "What Was Wrong," "Why Did It Take You So Long," "You Can't Pull Me Down"

Recordings as Leader

Esquerita: Collector's Series (also titled *Rockin' the Joint*) (1958; contains all the songs recorded for Capitol, including on the albums *Esquerita!* and *Wild Cat Shakeout*), *Vintage Voola* (1958), *I Never Danced Nowhere* (1962), "We Had Love" (1962; as Eskew Reeder), "Johnny Little" (1963; as Eskew Reeder), *Sock It to Me Baby* (1965), *Sinner Man: The Lost Session* (1966), "I Want to Know" (1966; as S. Q. Reeder), "Just in Time" (1966; as S. Q. Reeder), "Tell the World about You" (1966; as S. Q. Reeder), "Two Ton Tessie" (1966; as S. Q. Reeder), "You Better Believe in Me" (1967; as Eskew "Esque-Rita" Reeder), "As Time Goes By" (1968; as Magnificent Malochi), "Mama, Your Daddy's Come Home" (1968; as Magnificent Malochi)

Leaders Recorded With

Heavenly Echoes (1955), Paul Peek (1958), Rio Rockers (1958), Willie B. (1962), Eskerettes (1962), Little Richard (1964, 1967–1968, 1970), John Hammond (1970)

Website

http://koti.mbnet.fi/wdd/esquerita.htm (accessed 21 May 2014)

References

PRIMARY: Billy Miller, "Esquerita! The Voola Is Back!!!," *Kicks* 3 (1983): 4–8 (interview).

SECONDARY: Charles White, *The Life and Times of Little Richard, the Quasar of Rock* (New York: Harmony Books, 1984), 29–30; Johnny Carter, "Who Was Esquerita?," *Rockin' 50s* 6 (June 1987): 23; Keith Briggs, "Esquerita," *Blues and Rhythm: The Gospel Truth* 30 (July 1987): 7–8 (obituary); V. Vale, "Norton Records," in *Incredibly Strange Music* 1 (San Francisco: Re/Search Publications, 1993), 52–65 (see especially 58–59); Michael B. Smith, *Carolina Dreams: The Musical Legacy of Upstate South Carolina* (Beverly Hills, Calif.: Marshall Tucker Entertainment, 1997), 25–26, 172; Pierre Monnery and Jay Halsey, "The Magnificent Malochi: The Esquerita Story," *Blues and Rhythm: The Gospel Truth* 270 (June 2012): 12–20 (includes discography).

Evans, Ernest

See Checker, Chubby

Fantastic Johnny C (Johnnie J. Corley, Jr.)

Singer

Possibly 20 or 28 April 1939, or 28 April 1943 (Greenwood, S.C.)–14 March 2002 (probably Norristown, Pa.)

S.C. residence: Greenwood (1939 or 1943–probably ca. 1956)

After serving in the air force Corley settled in Norristown, Pa., where he operated heavy equipment and possibly resided for the remainder of his life. There producer Jesse James discovered him singing in church, became his manager, and composed songs for him. "Boogaloo down Broadway" was his biggest hit, reaching the top ten on both the rhythm-and-blues and pop charts; he performed it (lip-syncing) on *American Bandstand.* He sang at the Apollo Theater in 1967. Corley is buried in Indiantown Gap National Cemetery, Annville, Pa.

The Social Security Death Index records birth (28 April 1939) and death (14 March 2002) dates for Johnnie J. Corley. The Indiantown Gap National Cemetery indicates that Johnnie Corley, Jr., was born on 20 April 1939. All other sources consulted state that Corley was born on 28 April 1943 and spell the given name Johnny. His apparent absence from the 1940 census might indicate that the 1939 birth dates are incorrect.

Recordings as Leader (These Are Release Dates, Not Necessarily Recording Dates)

The Fantastic Johnny C. Singles Collection, 1967–1973, Boogaloo down Broadway (1968), "Good Love" (1970), "Let's Do It Together" (1970), "Peace Treaty" (1970), "You've Got Your Hooks in Me" (1970)

References

SECONDARY: "Marvelettes, Pips in Rocky G Apollo Show," *New York Amsterdam News,* 28 October 1967, p. 20; "Fantastic Johnny C," http://badcatrecords.com/BadCat/FANTASTICjohnN.Y.C.htm (undated; accessed 21 May 2014); Andrew Hamilton, "Fantastic Johnny C," http://www.allmusic.com/artist/the-fantastic-johnny-c-mn0000053882 (undated; accessed 21 May 2014).

Fawks, John

Violin

S.C. residence: Columbia (before and probably after 1895)

Fawks was valued so highly in 1895 that an anonymous writer used him as a standard to which young black fiddlers could only aspire.

Reference

SECONDARY: "Disgraceful Mimicry—The Old and the Young Negro Compared," *Atlanta Voice of Missions by Way of the Cross,* August 1895, p. 2.

Felix, Delbert Eugene

Bass

13 October 1957 (Frogmore, Saint Helena Island, S.C.)-

S.C. residences: Frogmore (1957-1975, 1979-1981, 1992-2004), Hilton Head (2004-)

The son of a high school band director, Felix took piano lessons as a child but became seriously attracted to music upon receiving an electric bass guitar at age eight. He was exposed to jazz in high school. After matriculating at Florida A&M University, he attended Florida State University, where he began playing the bass. He became a professional musician after studying at the Berklee School of Music, Boston, in 1977 and 1978. While in the navy (1981–1986), he performed in its band. He was the initial bassist in Branford Marsalis's quartet, with which he played for three years beginning in 1986. He is active on the music scene in and around Hilton Head.

Leaders Recorded With

Doug Carn (ca. 1976), Back Bay Boppers (1980), Berklee International Dues Band (1980), Branford Marsalis (1987–1988), Courtney Pine (1989), Freddy Cole (1992), Billy Cobham (ca. 1992), Bill Scarlett (1993), Bob Alberti (1995), Chris Potter (2005)

References

SECONDARY: David Lauderdale, "Musician Helps the Lowcountry Beat Go On," *Hilton Head (S.C.) Island Packet,* 24 May 2011, sec. A, p. 3; Michael Paskevich, "Meant to Be: Around the World and Back Again Was Just the Beginning for Delbert Felix," *Hilton Head Monthly* 5 (April 2013): 148–49 (also available as "Meant to Be: The Next Phase in Delbert Felix's Life Starts Now" at http://www.hiltonheadmonthly.com/events/arts-entertainment/2354-meant-to-be-the-next-phase-in-delbert-felix-s-life-starts-now [accessed 21 May 2014]) (comments by Felix).

Fennell, Ellory

Trombone

S.C. residence: Charleston (at least 1930s)

Apparently a ward of Jenkins Orphanage, Fennell played in its bands in the 1930s.

Ferguson, Cool John

Guitar, piano, singer, composer

3 December 1953 (Beaufort, S.C.)-

S.C. residence: Beaufort (1953-1996, 2007-)

Able to play the guitar at age three, Ferguson soon performed gospel music, including with the Ferguson Sisters, a group made up of three of his siblings. As a young teenager he played locally with a band led by Earl Davis. After forming the group Soul

Cool John Ferguson, Lincolnton, N.C., 25 March 2011; permission of the photographer, Gene Tomko

Connection around age sixteen, he headed another band, Plastic Society, before touring with the evangelist Reverend Ike (Frederick Eikerenkoetter)—all before finishing high school. Soon after being graduated from Beaufort High School in 1972, he rejoined Davis and was generally active on the local music scene. For five years he played with Stephen Best and the Soul Crusaders before having an extended solo engagement at a Beaufort club ca. 1980. Thereafter he traveled widely, including with tent revivals. Upon moving to Durham, N.C., in the mid-1990s, he played with Captain Luke (Luther Mayer) and Tim Duffy in the group Music Makers and worked for the Music Maker Relief Foundation as director of creative development. Subsequently he made a living from music while residing in Atlanta (2002–2004), Durham (2004–2007), and Beaufort (2007–).

Most sources incorrectly identify Saint Helena Island, S.C., as Ferguson's birthplace.

Compositions

"Australia," "Big Storm," "Black Mud Boogie," "The Cat Ate the Rat, the Rat Ate the Wizard," "Charleston Blues," "Chunk of Funk," "Come On Back to Me," "Cool John Blues," "Cootie's Jam," "Cootie's Testimony," "Did You Ever See a One-Eyed Woman Cry," "Durham Blues," "Esperanza," "False Love," "Foolin' Around in the Barn," "Golden Girl," "Good Man Gone Bad," "Gris Gris Isle," "Gullah Getaway," "Having Fun," "Here Comes Floyd," "If Harry," "I Love You," "I Think about You Daily," "It's True," "It's You That I Love," "Keep It Confidential," "Kickin' It," "Let Me Be Your Man," "Low Down Blues," "Marina," "Mister Brown," "No Hidin' Place," "Passing Time," "Patterson Avenue," "Pre-Alex Stomp," "Russian Funk," "Send Up My Timbers," "Serious, Serious Sadness," "Sixteen Years," "Song for Brenda," "Straight Church," "Strollin' by the Waterfront" (sometimes titled "Strollin' on the Waterfront"), "Tater Done," "Tell You a Story," "Uncle Johnny," "Who Did That?"

Recordings as Leader

"Song for Brenda" (1990s), "Strollin' on the Waterfront" (1990s), "Patterson Avenue" (1999), *Outsider Lounge Music* (2001; with Captain Luke [Luther Mayer]), *Guitar Heaven* (2004), *Cool John Ferguson* (2005), *Cool Yule* (2005), *Who Did That?* (2006), *With These Hands* (2007)

Leaders Recorded With

Carl Rutherford (2001), Pura Fé (2004), Lightnin' Wells (2005), Little Pink Anderson (ca. 2005), Lee Gates (2006), Dave McGrew (2006), John Dee Holeman (2009)

Film

Toot Blues (2008)

Website

www.cooljohnferguson.com (accessed 21 May 2014)

References

PRIMARY: Mark Coltrain, "You Can Groove or You Can Slide: Cool John Ferguson's Winding Road," *Living Blues* 183 (March–April 2006): 30–35 (mainly a narrative by Ferguson).

SECONDARY: Wesley Wilkes, "Cool John Ferguson," in *Music Makers: Portraits and Songs from the Roots of America,* ed. Timothy Duffy (Athens, Ga.: Hill Street Press, 2002), 54–57 (comments by Ferguson); David Menconi, "A Master of Blues Finds His Home," *Raleigh (N.C.) News and Observer,* 17 August 2003, sec. D, pp. 1, 4 (comments by Ferguson); Cathy Carter Harley, "Cool John Ferguson, Other Musicians Get Ready for Beaufort 26th Annual Gullah Festival," *Hilton Head (S.C.) Island Packet,* 24 May 2012, sec. C, p. 1 (also available as "Cool John Ferguson Gets Ready to Play 26th Annual Gullah Festival" at http://www.islandpacket.com/2012/05/23/2079411_cool-john-ferguson-gets-ready.html [accessed 21 May 2014]) (comments by Ferguson).

Ferguson, H-Bomb (Robert Percell; "Cobra Kid")

Piano, singer, maracas, marimba, dancer, composer
Possibly May 1929 (Charleston, S.C.)–26 November 2006 (Blue Ash, Ohio)
S.C. residence: Charleston (1929–ca. 1947)

Ferguson took piano lessons at an early age and played the instrument in church. Before turning twenty he was discovered by trumpeter Cat Anderson. In time he traveled to N.Y.C. with the Ted Anderson band and toured with Roy Milton. Ferguson was especially active recording during the first half of the 1950s, when his "Good Lovin'" apparently attained a degree of popularity. (His early singing style was influenced most by Wynonie Harris.) At approximately this same time he toured with B. B. King. Around 1957 he moved to Cincinnati, where he resided for the remainder of his life. Upon largely retiring from performing in the 1970s, he worked as a garbage truck driver. After resuming his career in the early 1980s, he appeared on the cover of *Living Blues* (1986) and performed at various festivals, including the 1992 Chicago Blues Festival and several European ones. Part of his success in live performance resulted from his outlandish appearance: He wore wigs that were often garish; sometimes he performed in a hula skirt and, occasionally, with a boa constrictor around his neck. Following his death from emphysema and cardiopulmonary disease, his body was cremated.

Though Ferguson told Steven C. Tracy that he was born in either 1930 or 1931, 9 May 1929 is usually recorded as his birth date. Exclusive of the day, it is probably confirmed by the 1930 census. Conducted in Charleston on 4 April, it records his age as ten months. He was estimated as ten years old when enumerated for the census in Charleston on 8 April 1940. He is possibly the Robert P. Ferguson who served as pantryman on ships sailing between N.Y.C. and Europe from no later than 1946 at least into 1948.

Compositions

"Ain't Like That," "Baby, Don't Go," "Baby, Please," "Big City Blues," "Blue Shadows Falling," "Bookie's Blues," "Bottom of the Glass," "Caldonia Is Back," "Don't Leave Me," "Feel Like I Do," "Fooling Around," "Gettin' Down," "Give It Up," "Good Lovin'," "Good Time Gal," "Hard Lovin' Woman" (also titled "Hard Lovin' Women"), "Heart in My Hand," "Hot Kisses," "I Ain't Gonna Run," "I Got a Love," "I Had a Dream," "I Love My Baby," "I'm Gone, I'm Gone," "I'm So Lonely," "It's Midnight Hour," "Josephine," "Leavin' You Tomorrow," "Life Is Hard," "Lonesome Avenue," "Meatloaf," "Medicine Man," "Midnight Ramblin' Tonight," "Moon Shine on Me," "My Brown Frame Baby," "New Way Blues," "On My Way," "Over You Losin' My Mind," "Rain Rain Rain," "Roamin' Blues," "Rock, H-Bomb, Rock," "Shake and Bake," "Shake Your Apple Tree," "She Don't Want Me," "She's Been Gone," "Tortured Love," "Trip with a Statue," "Weekend Honky Tonk Cowboy," "Wine Headed Woman," "Woodpecker," "Work for My Baby"

Recordings as Leader

"Hard Lovin' Woman" (1950; as Bob Ferguson), "I'm Gone, I'm Gone" (1950; as Bob Ferguson), "Jumpin' and Shoutin'" (1950; as Bob Ferguson), "Wine Head" (1950; as Bob Ferguson), "Blow Mr. Singleton" (1951), "Feel Like I Do" (1951), "Gone with the Wind" (1951), "Good Lovin'" (1951), "Good Time Gal" (1951), "I Love My Baby" (1951), "My Love" (1951), "On My Way" (1951), "Preachin' the Blues" (1951), "Rock, H-Bomb, Rock" (1951), "Slowly Goin' Crazy" (1951), "Sundown Blues" (1951), "Big City Blues" (1952), "Bookie's Blues"

(1952), "Give It Up" (1952), "Hot Kisses" (1952), "Life Is Hard" (1952), "My Fine Brown Frame Baby" (1952), "New Way Blues" (1952), "Tortured Love" (1952; with Varetta Dillard), "Work for My Baby" (1952), "Every Night" (1953), "Nanny Miss Fanny" (1953), "She's Been Gone" (1953), "You Made Me Baby" (1953), "Don't Leave Me" (1957), "She Don't Want Me" (1957), "Boogie Down" (1958), "Cryin' over You" (1958), "Little Tiger" (1958), "No Sackie Sack" (1958), "Rain Rain Rain" (1958), "Spaghetti and Meat Balls" (1958), "I'm So Lonely" (1960), "Lady Queen" (1960), "Mary, Little Mary" (1960), "The Mess Around" (1960), "Midnight Ramblin' Tonight" (1960), "Heart in My Hand" (1985), "I Ain't Gonna Run" (1985), "Lonesome Avenue" (1985), "Shake and Bake" (1985), *Bad Times Blues* (1989), "I Had a Dream" (1989), "Medicine Man" (1989), *Wiggin' Out* (1993)

Leaders Recorded With

Varetta Dillard (1952), Andy Kirk (1954), George Thorogood (1986)

Film

The Life and Times of H-Bomb Ferguson (2006)

Awards

Michael W. Bany Lifetime Achievement Cammy (2003; a Cammy is the Cincinnati Area Music Award); H-Bomb Ferguson Day in Cincinnati (17 October 2006); Cincinnati Entertainment Awards Music Hall of Fame (2007)

References

PRIMARY: Barry Lee Pearson, "'One Day You're Gonna Hear about Me': The H-Bomb Ferguson Story," *Living Blues* 69 (1986): 15–21, 24–26 (interview; includes discography); Mick Rainsford, "Rock H-Bomb Rock: The H-Bomb Ferguson Story," *Blues and Rhythm: The Gospel Truth* 148 (April 2000): 8–14 (interview).

SECONDARY: David S. Rotenstein, "H-Bomb Ferguson: A Man, His Blues, and His Wig," *Footnotes: Atlanta's Music and Entertainment Weekly*, 1 December 1990, pp. 8, 15 (comments by Ferguson); Steven C. Tracy, *Going to Cincinnati: A History of the Blues in the Queen City* (Urbana: University of Illinois Press, 1993), 154–64 (comments by Ferguson); "Ferguson, Robert 'H-Bomb,'" *Cincinnati Enquirer*, 28 November 2006, sec. B, p. 4 (obituary); Rebecca Goodman, "Legendary Blues Singer 'H-Bomb' Ferguson, 77, Shaped Modern Music," *Cincinnati Enquirer*, 28 November 2006, sec. B, p. 4; Larry Nager, "Beneath the Wig: Remembering the Explosive H-Bomb Ferguson," *Cincinnati Magazine* 50 (February 2007): 90–93; Dave Penny, "Obituaries: H-Bomb Ferguson," *Blues and Rhythm: The Gospel Truth* 216 (February 2007): 18; Brian Baker, "The H-Bomb That Never Stopped Exploding: More Than a Local Blues Novelty, H-Bomb Ferguson Was a True Original," *Cincinnati City Beat*, 14–20 November 2007, pp. 26, 28; Larry Birnbaum, *Before Elvis: The Prehistory of Rock 'n' Roll* (Lanham, Md.: Scarecrow Press, 2013), 280–81; Christina Ferguson, with Michael Reilly, "H-Bomb Ferguson: 'I'm H-Bomb Ferguson, the Mother's Son, and after Me There Damn Sure Ain't Gonna Be None!!,'" http://members.nuvox.net/~on.lboyd/hbbio.htm (undated; accessed 21 May 2014) (comments by Ferguson).

Ferguson, Jim (James Warner)

Bass, singer

10 December 1950 (Jefferson City, Mo.)–

S.C. residences: Columbia (1952–1956), West Columbia (1956–1981)

At age four Ferguson began singing in church; though he continued doing so, he did not take voice lessons until around age sixteen. He continued them into his college years. As a freshman at the University of South Carolina, he began studying the bass and soon performed locally with such musicians as Johnny Helms and Terry Rosen. Taking a few months off from school, he toured with the New Christy Minstrels. Upon moving temporarily to N.Y.C. in 1978, he was mentored by Chuck Israels, Red Mitchell, and other notable bassists. After receiving undergraduate (1980) and graduate (1981) degrees from the University of South Carolina, he moved to Nashville, where he remains and where he works as a freelancer and studio musician. He toured over the years as bassist and singer with Crystal Gayle and performed as staff singer with the Statler Brothers. He taught at Belmont University in Nashville (1983–1990) before teaching bass and voice at Middle Tennessee State University, beginning in 1998.

Compositions

"Come Home to Red," "Not Just Another Pretty Bass," "Walkin' the Dog," "What's a Guy Supposed to Do?," "When the Night Is Done"

Recordings as Leader

Not Just Another Pretty Bass (1997), *Deep Summer Music* (2000), *Haunted Heart* (2005; with Mundell Lowe)

Jim Ferguson; photograph by Kathryn Simpson Brashears, permission of Jim Ferguson

Leaders Recorded With

David Allyn (1976, 1981), Maxine Sullivan (1980–1981), Lenny Breau (1982), Stephane Grappelli (1985), k. d. lang (ca. 1988), Kenny Rogers (1989), Slim Whitman (1989), Donna McElroy (ca. 1989), Donna Ulisse (1990), B. B. Watson (1991), Brenda Lee (ca. 1991), Crystal Gayle (1992–1993, ca. 1995, ca. 1997, 1999), Lisa Stewart (1992), Al Jarreau (ca. 1992), Eddy Arnold (ca. 1993), Pete Fountain (ca. 1993), Kathie Lee Gifford (ca. 1993), Ronnie Milsap (ca. 1993, 2001), BeBe and CeCe Winans (ca. 1993), Robin Anderson (1994), Gatlin Brothers (1994), Kathy Troccoli (ca. 1994, 2010), Don McLean (ca. 1995, 2000), Devon Sinclair (ca. 1995), Danny Davis (ca. 1996), Tom T. Hall (1997), Jo-El Sonnier (1997), Tanya Savory (ca. 1997), April Barrows (1998–2000), Julia Rich (1998, 2000, 2002–2003, 2008), Lorrie Morgan (ca. 1998), Red Hot Big Band (ca. 1999, ca. 2007), Jeff Steinberg (2000, ca. 2004, ca. 2013), Billy Gilman (ca. 2000), Jack Jezzro (2001, ca. 2009–ca. 2011), Richard Sudhalter (2001), Lane Brody (ca. 2002), Camille Harrison (ca. 2002), Rachael Price (2003), Karen Johns (2005), Benita Hill (2006), Joe Settlemires (ca. 2006), Justin Thompson (ca. 2006), Jerry Krahn (ca. 2007), Beegie Adair (2010), Bruce Dudley (ca. 2010), Halie Loren (ca. 2010), Jaimee Paul (ca. 2010–ca. 2011), Barbara Lea (ca. 2012)

Website

http://jimfergusonmusic.com/ (accessed 21 May 2014)

References

SECONDARY: Terry Teachout, "A Bassist Who Is No Mean Tenor," *New York Times*, 8 August 1999, sec. AR, pp. 29, 31; Joel Siegel, "Jim Ferguson," *JazzTimes* (April 2001): 30–31.

Fields, Geechie (Julius P.)

Trombone

Presumably 31 December 1903 (S.C.)-?

S.C. residence: Charleston (by 1915-ca. 1924)

A ward of Jenkins Orphanage beginning in 1915, Fields learned to play the trombone from Bud Aiken and Jake Frazier. After leaving the institution ca. 1924 he settled in N.Y.C. as a professional musician. In addition to recording with several luminaries, including Jelly Roll Morton, he played in bands led, successively, by Earle Howard, Charlie Skeete, and Bill Benford. Upon retiring from music he apparently became involved in boxing as a coach and trainer. He was reportedly once married to the singer Myra Johnson, who recorded with Jimmy Lunceford and Fats Waller, among others.

John Chilton states that Fields was born in Ga. His age was estimated as twenty-six when he was enumerated for the census in N.Y.C. on 2 May 1930; this document records his middle initial, notes that he was then a musician, and indicates that he was born in S.C. It has not been determined if he was the Julius Fields who played with Silas Green from New Orleans, a tent show, in the late 1930s and 1940.

Leaders Recorded With

Thomas Morris (1926), Jelly Roll Morton (1928, 1930), James P. Johnson (1929), Clarence Williams (1929–possibly 1930)

References

SECONDARY: John Chilton, *A Jazz Nursery: The Story of the Jenkins' Orphanage Bands of Charleston, South Carolina* (London: Bloomsbury Book Shop, 1980), 54; Lynn Abbott and Doug Seroff, *Ragged but Right: Black Traveling Shows, "Coon Songs," and the Dark Pathway to Blues and Jazz* (Jackson: University Press of Mississippi, 2007), 382.

Fisher, Snow (George)

Dancer, singer, drummer

11 November 1890 (Charleston, S.C.)–8 January 1938 (Brussels, Belgium)

S.C. residence: Charleston (1890–no later than mid-1910s)

Fisher left Charleston at an undetermined date, though he lived in Chicago by the mid-1910s. Around this time Spencer Williams wrote "Shim-Me-Sha-Wabble" for Fisher to perform at the Elite Café; Fisher's name appears in its lyrics. Fisher's performance led to a dance craze known as the shimmy. In time Fisher moved to N.Y.C. He performed in musical revues throughout the 1920s, dancing in such productions as *Bandanna Land* (1922), *Sheik of Harlem* (1923), *Dixie to Broadway* (1924), *Red Hot Mama* (1926), *Africana* (1927, with his partner, Pickaninny Hill), *Land of Syncopation* (1928), *Bojangles' Revels* (1929), and *Brown Skin Models of 1930*. He was known for his interpretation of "Shine," also titled "That's Why They Call Me Shine." Probably in 1930 or 1931 he moved to Europe, where he lived first in France, then Belgium. In Paris he formed a band, the Harlomarvels, that played in several European countries, including Spain and Switzerland. His sidemen included trumpeter Julio Cueva and saxophonist Cle Saddler. At least in 1935, he emceed at the Nest, a London club. He died of pneumonia.

In "Across the Pond," Edgar A. Wiggins identifies Fisher's birth date. Information about Fisher and Spencer Williams comes from the unpublished research of Karl Gert zur Heide.

References

SECONDARY: Spencer Williams, *Shim-Me-Sha-Wabble* (New York: Stern, 1917) (sheet music); "Eve Lynn Chats 'bout Society and Folks," *Pittsburgh Courier*, 28 February 1925, p. 19; Observer, "At Harlem Theatres," *New York Amsterdam News*, 14 August 1929, p. 9; Street-Wolf of Paris [Edgar A. Wiggins], "Montmartre," *Chicago Defender*, 1 September 1934, p. 12 (national edition); Leonard G. Feather, "The London Lowdown," *New York Amsterdam News*, 7 September 1935, p. 7; "Snow Fisher Is Back in Paris," *Chicago Defender*, 31 July 1937, p. 10 (national edition); Teddy Drayton, "Snow Fisher Dies in Brussels," *Chicago Defender*, 12 February 1938, p. 9 (national edition) (obituary; a brief statement about and a photograph of Fisher appear on p. 1); "Out of Billy Rowe's Harlem Note Book," *Pittsburgh Courier*, 12 February 1938, p. 11; Edgar A. Wiggins, "Across the Pond," *Chicago Defender*, 12 February 1938, p. 9 (national edition); Spencer Williams, "Basin Street Blues: The Cradle of Swing Was Right Back in New Orleans in the 1900's," *Rhythm* 13 (February 1939), 76, 78, 80; Bricktop [Ada Smith], with James Haskins, *Bricktop* (New York: Atheneum, 1983), 12; Dulcila Cañizares, "El olvidado Julio Cueva," *Signos: En la expressión de los pueblos* 46 (2001), 5–22 (see especially 11) (in Spanish).

Foote, Bea (Beatrice Harrisson Pugh)

Singer

Probably 3 September of, probably, 1896, but possibly of 1898 (probably S.C.)–?

S.C. residence: unknown location (1896 or 1898–no later than 1900)

Foote was active on the N.Y.C. music scene by 1925, when she departed for Paris as a member of the troupe La Revue Nègre, which included young Josephine Baker; she returned to the United States in March 1926. In November 1927 she appeared in Irvin C. Miller's *Blue Baby* at the Lincoln Theatre in Harlem, where she also performed, the next year, in Addison Carey's production of *Headin' for Harlem*. She was affiliated with Smalls Paradise in 1930. In April 1937 she performed at Club Crystal Caverns in Washington, D.C. She made all her recordings in 1938; Buster Bailey, J. C. Higginbotham, Sammy Price, and Charlie Shavers were among her accompanying musicians. Though several of the songs have sexual content, she is best known for the first tune she recorded, "Weed," which describes the effects of marijuana. By 1940 she was possibly no longer an entertainer, or possibly even alive; that year Floyd G. Snelson asked, in his newspaper column,

"Where are the glamour girls of yesteryear?" Foote is one about whom he wonders.

Foote was the half sister of drummer George Jenkins, who was not a South Carolinian. When she was enumerated as Beatrice Harrisson for the census in Wilmington, N.C., on 18 June 1900, her birth date was identified as September 1896. Her age was estimated as twelve when she was enumerated as Battrice Pugh in Wilmington on 18 April 1910. As Beatrice Foote, presumably her married name, she was enumerated for the census in Norfolk, Va., on 6 January 1920; her age was estimated as twenty-two. All these censuses indicate that she was born in S.C. Foote returned to the United States from France in March 1926 on the *De Grasse;* its passenger list records 3 September 1898 as her birth date and identifies her birthplace as Sarbora, N.C. When she tried but failed to enter Canada at Lacolle, Quebec, in 1932, she gave her age as thirty and birthplace as Va.

Recordings as Leader (All 1938)

"Baby, Ain't You Satisfied?," "Could Be You," "I Want a Long Time Daddy," "Jive Lover," "Satisfied," "Try and Get It," "Weed"

References

SECONDARY: advertisement for the Lincoln Theatre, *New York Amsterdam News,* 23 November 1927, p. 13; advertisement for the Lincoln Theatre, *New York Amsterdam News,* 15 February 1928, p. 15; "Club Chats," *New York Amsterdam News,* 26 March 1930, pp. 4–5; "In the Nation's Capital," *New York Amsterdam News,* 10 April 1937, p. 22; Floyd G. Snelson, "Harlem: 'Negro Capitol of the Nation,'" *New York Age,* 10 February 1940, p. 4; Allan McMillan, "Allan's Alley," *New York Amsterdam News,* 31 March 1951, p. 22.

Foster, Tommie (Thomas)

Piano

Ca. 1893 or 3 June 1896 (probably Jonesville, S.C.)–?

S.C. residence: Jonesville (probably ca. 1893 or 1896–after 1948)

Characterized by Pete Lowry and Bruce Bastin as among the Union County party pianists, Foster helped inspire Henry "Rufe" Johnson to play the piano ca. 1933.

Foster's age was estimated as seventeen when the musician was enumerated for the census on 21 April 1910 in Jonesville; as twenty-eight when enumerated on 10 January 1920 in Union County; as thirty-seven when enumerated on 8 April 1930 in Jonesville; and as forty-six when enumerated on 4 April 1940 in Jonesville. His draft registration card, completed on 5 June 1917, indicates that he was born on 3 June 1896. According to South Carolina, Deaths, 1944–1955, Foster survived his wife, Icie, who died on 21 June 1949.

References

SECONDARY: Pete Lowry, notes to Henry "Rufe" Johnson, *The Union County Flash!* (1973; Trix 3304); Bruce Bastin, *Red River Blues: The Blues Tradition in the Southeast* (Urbana: University of Illinois Press, 1986), 193.

Fowler, Craig

Guitar

S.C. residence: possibly Gray Court (ca. 1902)

Fowler was the first person to teach Gary Davis to play a guitar chord. Davis considered him a "remarkable" guitarist.

Reference

SECONDARY: *"Oh, What a Beautiful City": A Tribute to the Reverend Gary Davis (1896–1972) Gospel, Blues and Ragtime,* ed. Robert Tilling (Jersey, Channel Islands: Paul Mill Press, 1992), 8.

Frazier, Jake (Jacob William)

Trombone

1897, or a few years later (Charleston, S.C.)–?

S.C. residences: Charleston (1897, or a few years later–probably no later than 1919), Columbia (probably by 1919–at least until 1920, but no later than 1921)

A ward of Jenkins Orphanage, Frazier played in its bands in the 1900s and 1910s and performed with one of them in England in 1914. At the institution he helped teach Julius "Geechie" Fields to play the trombone. He became a professional musician. At least in early 1920 he performed with a theater band in Columbia. By 1921 he resided in N.Y.C., where he recorded with female blues singers that year and again from 1924 into 1926, the period of his greatest recording activity. He played in bands led by Will Marion Cook, Willie Gant, Fate Marable, Arthur S. Ray, and Gonzell(e) White, as well as in an organization affiliated with the Drake and Walker Company of black vaudevillians. He traveled to Cuba with White in 1923.

The passenger list of the *St. Louis,* which transported the orphanage band from Liverpool to N.Y.C. in September 1914, indicates that Frazier was born in Charleston on 23 December 1897. When enumerated for the census in Columbia on 9 January 1920, he gave his age as nineteen; he was then rooming with fellow musician Ossie Gary, who was doubtless the cornetist O. C. Gary. The passenger list of the *Orizaba,* which took Frazier from Havana to N.Y.C. in late 1923, records that he was born in Charleston on 27 September 1900. His age was estimated as twenty-three when he was enumerated for the N.Y. state census in N.Y.C. on 1 June 1925. He is probably the Jacob Frazier, presumably born in September 1897, who was enumerated with his family in Charleston on 4 or 5 June 1900.

Compositions

"Jake's Weary Blues," "Louisville Blues"

Recording as Leader

"Jake's Weary Blues" (1925)

Leaders Recorded With

Eliza Christmas Lee (1921), Daisy Martin (1921), probably Lavinia Turner (1921), probably Charles Booker (1924), Helen Gross (1924–1925), Rosa Henderson (1924–1926), Kansas City Five (1924–1925), Viola McCoy (1924), Josie Miles (1924–1925), Julia Moody (1924), Monette Moore (1924–1925), probably Nettie Potter (1924), Six Black Diamonds (1924), Clementine Smith (1924–1925), Mamie Smith (1924), Original Jazz Hounds (1925–1926), Alberta Perkins (1925), Buddy Christian (1926), Maggie Jones (1926)

References

SECONDARY: John Chilton, *A Jazz Nursery: The Story of the Jenkins' Orphanage Bands of Charleston, South Carolina* (London: Bloomsbury Book Shop, 1980), 54; Garvin Bushell, as told to Mark Tucker, *Jazz from the Beginning* (Ann Arbor: University of Michigan Press, 1988), 23, 28.

Frazier, Theodore

S.C. residence: Charleston (probably late 1920s–at least into early 1930s)

Apparently a ward of Jenkins Orphanage, Frazier played in its bands in the early 1930s, though his instrument is not known.

Free, Ron (Ronald Guy)

Drums

15 January 1936 (Charleston, S.C.)–

S.C. residences: Charleston (1936–1951, ca. 1967–1975, 1989–1991), Isle of Palms (ca. 1960, ca. 1984–ca. 1985), North Charleston (ca. 1960–ca. 1967), Mount Pleasant (ca. 1985–ca. 1989)

Free left high school to tour with the trio of Tommy Weeks and then played with a carnival band. He moved to N.Y.C. in the mid-1950s; there he took drum lessons and performed in *Shoestring '57,* an off-Broadway production. He became part of the jazz scene, playing in lofts and clubs, touring with the likes of Lennie Tristano, rooming with such musicians as Elvin Jones and Ben Tucker, and recording. He left this scene around 1960, when he returned to the Charleston area, where he played occasionally, as he did in San Diego after moving there in 1975. He again relocated to the Charleston area ca. 1984 and currently resides in Hot Springs, Va.

Recordings as Leader

The Search for Truth (1991; by Free Expression), *Concepts* (2009; by Triologue, with Bob Bowen and Royce Campbell)

Leaders Recorded With

Chris Connor (1957), Sal Salvador (1957), Mose Allison (1958–1959), Lee Konitz (1959), Elmer Gibson (1994), Hod O'Brien (2003), Royce Campbell (2008–2009, 2012)

Films

Love Crimes (1992), *Chasers* (1994)

References

PRIMARY: Benjamin Franklin V, *Jazz and Blues Musicians of South Carolina: Interviews with Jabbo, Dizzy, Drink, and Others* (Columbia: University of South Carolina Press, 2008), 120–29; Ron Free, "The Parade," http://www.jazzloftproject.org/blog/general/the-parade-by-loft-drummer-ron-free (2010; accessed 21 May 2014).

SECONDARY: Sam Stephenson, "What Happened to Ronnie Free?," *Oxford American* 34 (July–August 2000): 34–39 (comments by Free); Sam Stephenson, *The Jazz Loft Project: Photographs and Tapes of W. Eugene Smith from 821 Sixth Avenue, 1957–1965* (New York: Knopf; Durham, N.C.: Center for Documentary Studies, Duke University, 2009), passim (includes a segment titled "What Happened to Ronnie Free?" [113–15] that is mostly different from Stephenson's essay of identical title in *Oxford American*) (comments by Free).

Freed, Arthur

Lyricist, piano, singer
9 September 1894 (Charleston, S.C.)–12 April 1973 (Bel Air, Calif.)
S.C. residence: Charleston (1894–no later than 1897)

As a child Freed moved with his family from Charleston to Seattle, Wash., where he began piano lessons at age six. He started writing songs at Phillips Exeter Academy in N.H. Soon after being graduated in 1914 he worked as a piano player for a music publisher in Chicago. As a singer he toured for a season with the Marx Brothers before joining vaudevillian and composer Gus Edwards ("By the Light of the Silv'ry Moon"). Freed collaborated on songs with Edwards's musical director, Louis Silvers. After serving in the army (1918–1919), Freed resumed writing with others, mainly as lyricist, and settled in Los Angeles. He and Nacio Herb Brown, his most frequent composing partner, wrote tunes for movies, including *Broadway Melody* (1929); *Hollywood Revue of 1929; Going Hollywood* (1933), starring Bing Crosby; *Broadway Melody of 1936;* and *Broadway Melody of 1938.* Some of Freed's songs were popular with jazz musicians and jazz-influenced singers, especially in the 1930s, though several of them have proven enduringly popular, such as "I Cried for You," written with Gus Arnheim and Abe Lyman. In the late 1930s he gave up songwriting for producing movies. He began this part of his career with *The Wizard of Oz* (1939); two of his films, *An American in Paris* (1951) and *Gigi* (1958), won the Academy Award for best picture. He is interred in Garden of Memories, Honor-Lawn Crypt 418, Hillside Memorial Park, Culver City, Calif.

Freed was a brother of lyricist Ralph Freed ("How about You?"), who was not a South Carolinian. Though the census 1910–1940 estimates that Arthur Freed was born in 1895, his actual birth date is 9 September 1894, as proven by "Charleston Archive—Birth Records from the City of Charleston 1877–1926," vol. 17 ("Return of White Births in the City of Charleston, S.C. 1891–1896"). This source confirms Freed as his surname, though some sources record it as Grossman, his mother's maiden name. "Charleston Archive" is located in the CCPL/South Carolina History Room, Charleston County Public Library. In an interview with Robert Rohauer, Freed states that his family moved from Charleston when he "was too young to remember" (2). The Freeds left Charleston no later than 1897, when Arthur's brother Victor was born in Colorado.

Compositions

"After Sundown," "All I Do Is Dream of You," "Alone," "Blondy," "Broadway Melody," "Broadway Rhythm," "A Bundle of Old Love Letters," "Chant of the Jungle," "Cinderella's Fella," "Coffee Time," "Come Out, Come Out, Wherever You Are," "Everybody Sing," "Fit as a Fiddle," "Good Morning," "Hold Your Man," "I Cried for You," "I'm Feelin' Like a Million," "It Looks Like Love," "It's Winter Again," "It Was So Beautiful," "I've Got a Feelin' You're Foolin'," "Louisiana," "Love Songs of the Nile," "The Moon Is Low," "My Wonderful One, Let's Dance," "A New Moon Is over My Shoulder," "On a Sunday Afternoon," "Only Love Is Real," "Our Big Love Scene," "Our Love Affair," "Pagan Love Song," "Should I?," "Sing before Breakfast," "Singin' in the Rain," "Smoke Dreams," "Sun Showers," "Temptation," "This Heart of Mine," "The Wedding of the Painted Doll," "We'll Make Hay While the Sun Shines," "When Buddha Smiles," "When Winter Comes," "Would You?," "You and I," "You Are My Lucky Star," "Your Broadway and My Broadway," "You're Simply Delish," "Yours and Mine," "Your Words and My Music," "You Were Meant for Me"

Awards

Irving G. Thalberg Award (1951; awarded by the Academy of Motion Picture Arts and Sciences); Honorary Academy Award for Distinguished Service (1968); Songwriters Hall of Fame (1972)

References

PRIMARY: *A Tribute to Arthur Freed,* ed. Robert Rohauer (New York: Gallery of Modern Art, 1967), 2–5 (interview); John Kobal, *People Will Talk* (New York Knopf, 1985), 634–53 (interview).

SECONDARY: Hugh Fordin, *M-G-M's Greatest Musicals: The Arthur Freed Unit* (New York: Da Capo), 1996.

Frost, Lottie

See Hightower, Lottie Frost

G

Gaffney, Howard Leon

Trumpet

17 April 1913 (Wayne County, W.Va.)–13 October 1987

S.C. residences: Limestone (by 1920–no later than 1930), Gaffney (by 1930–no later than early 1930s)

Following his tenure with the band of Jimmy Livingston, Gaffney received a music scholarship to Oglethorpe University, where he played in a group led by Doug Youngblood and that included Johnny Blowers. In 1935 Gaffney and Blowers joined Bob Pope's organization, ultimately headquartered in Charlotte, which played primarily in the Southeast. Gaffney remained a musician at least into the mid-1940s, when he performed with Harry Cool.

The 1920 census (conducted in Limestone, S.C.) indicates that Gaffney was born in W.Va.; the 1930 census (in Gaffney, S.C.), in Va.; the 1940 census (in N.Y.C.), in S.C. Gaffney was born in Wayne County, W.Va., on 17 April 1913, as documented in the Wayne County Indexed Register of Births.

Leaders Recorded With

Bob Pope (1936), Teddy Powell (1940–1941), Bob Zurke (1940)

References

SECONDARY: "Harry Cool," *Billboard* 58 (15 June 1946): 41, 43; Warren W. Vaché, *Back Beats and Rim Shots: The Johnny Blowers Story* (Lanham, Md.: Scarecrow Press, 1997), 12, 18–19.

Gardiner, Robert Aman

Saxophone

12 December 1966 (Columbia, S.C.)–

S.C. residences: Columbia (1966–1970, 1985–1990, 1999–2002), Sumter (1970–1976), Anderson (1976–1979), Cheraw (1979–1985), Newberry (1997–1999), Irmo (2002–)

Gardiner began playing saxophone in his school's band at age twelve. During each of his four high school years in Cheraw, he was selected for the all-state band. After receiving an undergraduate degree in music from the University of South Carolina in 1990, he served for four years in the air force, playing in its band. Gardiner received a master's degree from DePaul University (1997) and a doctorate from the University of South Carolina (2008). He taught music at several public schools and at Claflin University before affiliating with Lander University, where he currently teaches. He founded and directed the Columbia Jazz Orchestra (active 2004–2010), leads his own quartet, and plays regularly with the Palmetto Concert Band. Though primarily a jazz musician, he also performs classical, rhythm-and-blues, salsa, and popular music.

Compositions

"Automatically Hip," "Fabulous Friday," "Flick," "James Brown," "Monk's Corner," "Soul of Confidence," "Superman," "Swing Valley," "Van Gogh Double Espresso," "Waynesville"

Recording as Leader

Soul of Confidence (2010)

Leaders Recorded With

Air Mobility Command Band (1990, 1993), Clark Terry (1995), DePaul University Jazz Ensemble (1996), Bobby Sanders (1996), Palmetto Concert Band (1998, 2000, 2008), Lunch Money (2009)

Website

http://robertgardinermusic.com (accessed 21 May 2014)

References

SECONDARY: Susan Gilmour, "Gardiner Leads the Band," *Cheraw (S.C.) Link*, 16 October 2007, sec. A, p. 13 (comments by Gardiner); Otis R. Taylor, Jr., "'Soul of

Robert Gardiner, Blue Martini, Columbia, S.C., 2004; photograph by Jerry Cover, permission of Robert Gardiner

Confidence,' CD Release a Seminal Moment for Professor," *Columbia (S.C.) State,* 27 May 2011, sec. E, p. 3 (comments by Gardiner); Patrick Wall, "The Robert Gardiner Quartet," *Columbia (S.C.) Free Press,* 1–7 June 2011, p. 56 (comments by Gardiner); Michelle Laxer, "Lander Professor Gardiner Jazzes It Up with Confidence," *Greenwood (S.C.) Index-Journal,* 26 June 2011, sec. D, pp. 1–2 (comments by Gardiner).

Garland, Hank (Walter Louis; "Sugarfoot")

Guitar, mandolin

11 November 1930 (Cowpens, S.C.)–27 December 2004 (Orange Park, Fla.)

S.C. residence: Cowpens (1930–1946)

Garland began playing the guitar at age six. Discovered at fourteen, he moved to Nashville two years later; there he was mentored by Billy Byrd and joined the band of Cowboy Copas before leading his own sessions and becoming a studio musician. Considered a virtuoso, he recorded with many notable performers, including the Everly Brothers ("Bye, Bye Love" and "Wake Up, Little Susie"), Roy Orbison ("Only the Lonely"), and Elvis Presley ("Are You Lonesome Tonight," "It's Now or Never," and "Little Sister," among other popular songs). An admirer of Charlie Christian and Django Reinhardt, Garland learned to play jazz rhythm from Barry Galbraith. With the likes of Gary Burton and Joe Morello as sidemen, he made jazz recordings in 1959–1960. A 1961 automobile accident almost killed him, caused severe brain damage, and essentially ended his career. He claimed to have written "Jingle Bell Rock" with Bobby Helms. The movie *Crazy* (2008) is based on Garland's life. Garland is buried in the Garden of Everlasting Life, Jacksonville Memory Gardens, Orange Park, Fla.

The album *The Unforgettable Guitar of Hank Garland* includes *Subtle Swing,* plus additional material. The two-CD *Move! The Guitar Artistry of Hank Garland* contains *Velvet Guitar, Jazz Winds from a New Direction,* and *Subtle Swing,* as well as supplementary selections. The five-CD *Legendary Guitarist Hank Garland* comprises *Velvet Guitar, Jazz Winds from a New Direction, The Unforgettable Guitar of Hank Garland, Jazz in New York,* and *The Carousel Club, Printer's Alley, Nashville, Tn. February 27, 1959.*

Compositions

"Baby Guitar," "Byrdland Guitar," "Ed's Place," "Guilty Tears," "Hands of God," "Hank's Dream," "Hello World," "I'll Just Say Goodnight to You," "Jaywalk," "Love Hangover," "Midnight Blues," "Pork-Chop Stomp," "Riot Chous" (also titled "Riot Chorus"), "Sentimental Dream," "Seventh and Union," "Sock Hop Baby," "Steel Guitar Fever," "Sugarfoot Boogie," "Sugarfoot Rag," "Sugarfoot Rag Square Dance," "Tangleweed," "Three-Four, the Blues," "Why Not," "Wiggle Waggle"

Recordings as Leader

Hank Garland and His Sugar Footers (1949–1951), "Guitar Polka," (1952), "Tea for Two" (1952), "Boo-Hoo" (1953), "Brazil" (1953), "Have You Ever Been Lonely" (1953), "Make Believe" (1953), "Moonlight on the Colorado" (1953), "Steel Guitar Rag" (1953), *The Carousel Club, Printer's Alley, Nashville, Tn. February 27, 1959, Velvet Guitar* (1959), "Ed's Place" (1959), "Polka Dots and Moonbeams" (1959), "Secret Love" (1959), "Some of These Days" (1959), *Jazz in New York* (ca. 1959–1960), *Jazz Winds from a New Direction* (1960), *Subtle Swing* (1960)

Leaders Recorded With

Paul Howard (1946), Cowboy Copas (1947–1949, 1958), Grandpa Jones (1947, 1949, 1961), Autry Inman (1948–1949), Eddie Crosby (1949), Red Foley (1949–1950, 1953), Anita Carter (1951, 1960), Eddie Hill (1951–1952), Webb Pierce (1951, 1953–1958), Eddy Arnold (1952, 1954), Justin Tubb (1953–1958), Wilburn Brothers (1953, possibly 1957), Mac Wiseman (1953–1955, 1957, 1960–1961), Grady Martin (1954–1956), Eddie Bond (1955), Jim Reeves (1955, 1957–1961), Faron Young (1955–1961), Doug Kershaw (1956–1958, 1960), Marty Robbins (1956, 1960–1961), Wilf Carter (1957), Patsy Cline (1957, 1959–1960), Little Jimmy Dickens (1957, 1959–1960), Everly Brothers (1957–1960), Lefty Frizzell (1957–1958, 1961), Ferlin Husky (1957), Brenda Lee (1957–1961), Ronnie Self (1957, 1959–1960), Carl Smith (1957–1959), Porter Wagoner (1957–1961), Browns (1958–1961), Billy "Crash" Craddock (1958, 1960), Carl Dobkins, Jr. (1958–1961), Melvin Endsley (1958–1959, possibly 1960, 1961), Don Gibson (1958–1961), Louvin Brothers (1958–1960), Moon Mullican (1958–1959), Elvis Presley (1958–1961), Conway Twitty (1958), Kitty Wells (1958), Johnny Horton (1959–1960), Hank Locklin (1959–1960),

Skeets McDonald (1959–1960), Skeeter Davis (1960), George Hamilton IV (1960–1961), Roy Orbison (1960–1961), Burl Ives (1961), Stonewall Jackson (1961), Sonny James (1961), Jerry Lee Lewis (1961), Patti Page (1961)

Awards

Hollywood Rock Walk of Fame (1997); Spartanburg Music Trail Marker (2011)

References

PRIMARY: Toy Caldwell, "An Interview with Hank Garland," *Guitar Player* 15 (January 1981): 80.

SECONDARY: Rich Kienzle, "Hank Garland: Legendary Country-Jazz Artist," *Guitar Player* 15 (January 1981): 76–78, 80, 84, 86 (comments by Garland); Peter Cooper, *Hub City Music Makers: One Southern Town's Popular Music Legacy* (Spartanburg, S.C.: Holocene, 1997), 24–29; Michael B. Smith, *Carolina Dreams: The Musical Legacy of Upstate South Carolina* (Beverly Hills, Calif.: Marshall Tucker Entertainment, 1997), 16–19, 172–73; John Fordham, "Influence and Confluence," in *Masters of Jazz Guitar,* ed. Charles Alexander (London: Balafon Books, 1999), 60–63; Ron Word, "Legendary Guitarist Hank Garland Now Lives Quiet Life," *Miami (Fla.) Herald,* 10 July 2004, sec. B, p. 3 (comments by Garland); Ron Word, "Legendary Guitarist Hank Garland Dies," *Miami (Fla.) Herald,* 28 December 2004, sec. B, p. 5 (obituary); Jason Spencer, "Musical Pioneer, Cowpens Native Hank Garland Dead at 74," *Spartanburg (S.C.) Herald-Journal,* 29 December 2004, sec. A, p. 1 (also available at http://www.goupstate.com/article/20041229/NEWS/412290327?template=printpicart [accessed 21 May 2014]) (obituary).

Garlington, John C.

Conductor

14 November 1903 (Laurens, S.C.)–?

S.C. residences: Laurens (1903–no later than early 1910s, by 1920–), Charleston (by early 1910s–no later than 1920)

A ward of Jenkins Orphanage, Garlington conducted its band during performances, beginning at approximately age ten, though Alonzo Mills was the real leader. He accompanied the band to England in 1914.

Garlington's date and place of birth come from the passenger list of the *St. Louis,* which transported the orphanage band from Liverpool to N.Y.C. in September 1914. When enumerated for the census in Laurens on 21 January 1920 (estimated age fifteen), Garlington worked as a house painter.

References

SECONDARY: Howard Rye, "Visiting Fireboys: The Jenkins' Orphanage Bands in Britain," *Storyville* 130 (1987): 137–43; Edward Ball, *The Sweet Hell Inside: A Family History* (New York: William Morrow, 2001), 105.

Garrison, Ame or Amy (Amelia L.)

Saxophone, trombone, violin, clarinet, organ, accordion

17 January 1909 (Charleston, S.C.)–22 August 1997 (East Orange, N.J.)

S.C. residence: Charleston (1909–no later than mid-1920s)

Garrison left Charleston at an undetermined date but completed high school in Newark, N.J., where she apparently resided for the remainder of her life. There she organized a band in which she played trombone, though the saxophone soon became her primary instrument. In Newark in the late 1930s she headed the Sirens of Swing before touring with the International Sweethearts of Rhythm around 1942. The musicians in both these bands were female. Later that decade she was playing again in Newark with Three (sometimes Four) Chucks and a Chick, pleasing audiences with "Mule Train" in particular. She is buried in Fairmount Cemetery, Newark.

Garrison's birth and death dates and middle initial come from the Social Security Death Index. The death date is confirmed in the two pieces published in the *Newark Star-Ledger.* In *Swing City,* Barbara J. Kukla identifies Garrison's birthplace as Charleston, S.C.; in "Amelia 'Ame' Garrison, Swing Era Musician, 89," as Newark, N.J. The 1930 and 1940 censuses indicate that she was born in S.C.

References

SECONDARY: Barbara J. Kukla, *Swing City: Newark Nightlife, 1925–50* (Philadelphia: Temple University Press, 1991), 118, 196–97, 229, 233; "Garrison—Amelia 'Ame,'" *Newark Star-Ledger,* 26 August 1997, p. 48 (death notice); Barbara Kukla, "Amelia 'Ame' Garrison, Swing Era Musician, 89," *Newark Star-Ledger,* 27 August 1997, p. 31 (obituary); D. Antoinette Handy, *The International Sweethearts of Rhythm: The Ladies Jazz Band from Piney Woods Country Life School,* revised edition (Lanham, Md.: Scarecrow Press, 1998), 144, 152, 155–56.

Gary, O. C.

Cornet

Ca. 1901 (S.C.)–?

S.C. residences: Charleston (by early 1910s–probably no later than 1919), Columbia (probably 1919–at least until 1920)

A ward of Jenkins Orphanage, Gary played in its bands during the 1910s and became a professional musician. At least in early 1920 he performed with a theater band in Columbia.

Gary is doubtless the Ossie Gary who was enumerated for the census in Columbia on 9 January 1920, when he was rooming with trombonist Jake Frazier. This document records his age as eighteen and indicates that he was born in S.C.

Gary, Sam (Samuel, Jr.)

Singer

Possibly 19 February 1915 (Bainbridge, Ga.)–20 July 1986 (New Ellenton, S.C.)

S.C. residence: New Ellenton (ca. 1966–1986)

Gary was trained as a chef. He was part of the ensemble in *John Henry,* which was produced on Broadway in 1940; Paul Robeson played the lead, and Josh White portrayed Blind Lemon. Gary's career is linked to White's. In 1940 Gary was a member of Josh White and His Carolinians. The next year Gary and White performed with the Almanac Singers, which also included Lee Hayes, Millard Lampell, and Pete Seeger. This group recorded two albums: *Songs for John Doe* and *Talking Union.* Gary and White were involved with political leftists, going so far as to belong, briefly, to the Communist Party, though they joined chiefly for social reasons. Gary and White gave concerts in London for BBC (1951). Gary was most active recording in the mid-1950s, when his only album was released and he appeared on White's *Josh at Midnight* and *Josh White Comes a-Visitin'.* He reportedly sings on the sound track of the movie *Lost Lagoon* (1958). He quit performing professionally upon moving to New Ellenton, though he then sang in church. Following his death in a home fire, he was buried in the Thankful Grove Missionary Baptist Church Cemetery, Williston, S.C.

The singer's birth date comes from the Social Security Death Index.

Recording as Leader

Sam Gary Sings (1955)

Leaders Recorded With

Almanac Singers (1941), Josh White (1941, 1955–1956)

References

SECONDARY: Dorothy Schainman Siegel, *The Glory Road: The Story of Josh White* (San Diego: Harcourt Brace Jovanovich, 1982), passim; Fran Chapman, "Sunday Afternoon Fire Leaves Aiken Man Dead," *Aiken (S.C.) Standard,* 21 July 1986, sec. B, p. 1; "Samuel Gary," *Aiken (S.C.) Standard,* 21 July 1986, sec. B, p. 8 (obituary); "Services Today for Singer Samuel Gary," *Aiken (S.C.) Standard,* 23 July 1986, sec. B, p. 7; "Samuel Gary," *Aiken (S.C.) Standard,* 25 July 1986, sec. A, p. 4; Martha Norris, "A Life Full of Music, Children, and Love," *Aiken (S.C.) Standard Magazine,* 18 January 1987, pp. 6–7; Elijah Wald, *Josh White: Society Blues* (Amherst: University of Massachusetts Press, 2000), passim.

Gary, Sam (Sammie or Sammy Lee, Jr.)

Guitar, singer

8 January 1944 (Columbia, S.C.)–20 August 1979 (Columbia, S.C.)

S.C. residence: Columbia (1944–1979)

Gary and singer Bill Johnson formed the duo Sam and Bill in 1962. After recording at mid-decade Gary left Johnson and played guitar with the Soul Brothers. The Sam and Bill duo continued with Sam (not Sammy) Davis, Jr., replacing Gary. After losing or severely injuring a finger in an automobile accident, Gary learned to play the guitar in a new manner. Gloria Fowles (later Gloria Gaynor) recorded Gary's "Let Me Go Baby" as the B side of her first release (1966). Following his murder at the Last Chance Saloon in Columbia, Gary was buried in Palmetto Cemetery, Columbia.

Compositions

"Beautiful Baby," "Don't Give Up," "From These Hills," "It Ain't Never Gonna Die," "Let It Burn," "Let Me Go Baby," "Something's Wrong," "Treat Me Right," "Trying to Find Her," "Understanding," "You Better Stop Messing Around," "You Can't Go Half Way"

Recordings as Leader (All with Sam and Bill; with Bill Johnson)

"Beautiful Baby" (1965), "For Your Love" (1965), "Fly Me to the Moon" (1966), "Treat Me Right" (1966)

Leader Recorded With

Kip Anderson (1963; this session is sometimes credited to Al Browne)

References

SECONDARY: "Sam and Bill," *Blues and Soul: Monthly Music Review* 1 (October 1967): 4–5; "Sammie L. Gary Jr.," *Columbia (S.C.) State,* 22 August 1979, sec. D, p. 5 (obituary); "Man Charged in Saloon Shooting," *Columbia (S.C.) State,* 23 August 1979, sec. C, p. 9; "Sam and Bill," http://indangerousrhythm.blogspot.com/2007/01/sam-bill_116767561978708739.html (2007; accessed 21 May 2014); Sir Shambling [John Ridley], "Sam and Bill," http://www.sirshambling.com/artists_2012/S/sam_&_bill/index.php (2012; accessed 21 May 2014).

Gibbs, William

Cornet, baritone horn

Probably 5 May 1898, though possibly ca. 1901 (Charleston, S.C.)–?

S.C. residence: Charleston (probably 1898–1910s)

A ward of Jenkins Orphanage, Gibbs played in its bands during the 1910s and performed with one of them in London in 1914. A professional musician active at least until 1930, he reportedly played at Smalls Paradise in N.Y.C.

Gibbs's 1898 date and place of birth come from the passenger list of the *St. Louis,* which transported the orphanage band from Liverpool to N.Y.C. in September 1914. It spells the surname Gibbes. When enumerated for the census in N.Y.C. on 2 April 1930, Gibbs indicated that he was born in S.C. and identified himself as a musician. This document estimates his age as twenty-nine.

Reference

SECONDARY: John Chilton, *A Jazz Nursery: The Story of the Jenkins' Orphanage Bands of Charleston, South Carolina* (London: Bloomsbury Book Shop, 1980), 54.

Gill, Tommy (Thomas Lee, Jr.)

Piano, arranger

11 August 1964 (Charleston, S.C.)–7 August 2014 (Charleston, S.C.)

S.C. residence: Charleston and vicinity (1964–1981, off and on 1988–1993, 1993–2014)

Gill began piano lessons at age five. Though he attended James Island High School, he finished high school in Denton, Tex., in 1982. The next year he moved to Boston, where he received a certificate in piano technology from the New England Conservatory of Music (1986); there he took piano lessons from Jaki Byard and Fred Hersch. He worked as an apprentice piano technician at Tanglewood in Lenox, Mass. (1986), with Steinway & Sons in N.Y.C. (1986–1988), and in Los Angeles (1988–1993). After returning to S.C. as a full-time resident, he completed his bachelor's degree at the College of Charleston (1993), where he taught as adjunct professor of music from 1994 until his death. He was musical director and pianist with Gilmore Entertainment Group (1995–1999) and Moranz Entertainment Group (1999–2010). In 2010 the Charleston Jazz Orchestra performed his arrangement of *Rhapsody in Blue,* with Gill on piano.

In her 2001 article Dottie Ashley refers to "Gill's just-released CD" *Going Overboard* (2001), though it remains unissued. Gill intended to title this planned CD *Underway.*

Compositions

"Around the Bend," "Fury of the Sound," "Indian Cove," "Overboard," "Swingin' on the Hook," "Underway," "Waterway Dolphin"

Leaders Recorded With

Danny Leonard (1982), Mark Masters (1990, 1993), Ron Free (1991), Para Ti (1999), Brad Moranz (2003), Seacoast Choir (2003), Robert Williams (2008), Charleston Jazz Initiative Legends Band (2010), Mark Sterbank (2010–2011), Charlton Singleton (2011)

References

SECONDARY: Dottie Ashley, "Songs Are Inspired by Composer's Harrowing Night at Sea," *Charleston (S.C.) Post and Courier,* 11 November 2001, sec. E, p. 2 (comments by Gill); Dottie Ashley, "Charleston Won't Sound the Same without Tommy Gill," *Charleston (S.C.) Post and Courier,* 9 August 2014, sec. Editorial/Opinion, p. 19 (also available at http://www.postandcourier.com/article/20140809/PC1002/140809424 [accessed 25 January 2015]) (comments by Gill); Adam Parker, "Local Jazz Pianist Dies at 49," *Charleston (S.C.) Post and Courier,* 9 August 2014, south sec., p. 4 (as "Tommy Gill, Charleston Jazz Pianist, Dies at 49," also available at http://www.postandcourier.com/article/20140808/PC1610/140809489 [accessed 25 January 2015]) (obituary).

Gillespie, Dizzy (John Birks)

Trumpet, conga drum, singer, composer, arranger
21 October 1917 (Cheraw, S.C.)–6 January 1993 (Englewood, N.J.)
S.C. residence: Cheraw (1917–1933)

The most important and famous jazz musician born in S.C., Gillespie was exposed to music at home by his father (who played the piano in a local band), at church, and then at Robert Smalls School in Cheraw. Though he attended Laurinburg Institute, he received little musical instruction at this N.C. school that he entered in 1933. There he practiced playing the trumpet alone or with trombonist Norman Powe, a cousin who was also from Cheraw. In 1935 he left Laurinburg to join his mother in Philadelphia. He quickly found work as a professional musician, initially with Frankie Fairfax. Upon moving to N.Y.C. he affiliated with Teddy Hill, with whom he made his first recordings in 1937. His playing with Hill and other leaders early in his career was influenced by Roy Eldridge. Of the big bands he played with, he was with Cab Calloway's the longest (1939–1941); one of his notable solos with this organization is on "Pickin' the Cabbage" (1940), which he composed and arranged. In the early 1940s he was one of the young musicians experimenting with new approaches to music in Harlem, either at Monroe's Uptown House or Minton's Playhouse, or both. Recordings exist of him playing at Minton's with Charlie Christian, Kenny Clarke, and other musicians essential to the development of what would become known as bebop, or bop, a music characterized by advanced harmonics (including dissonance), unexpected accents, sometimes blistering speed, and a new role for the rhythm section. Mostly it was played by small groups. In 1943 Gillespie joined the Earl Hines band, which included such modern musicians as Charlie Parker and Oscar Pettiford, as well as singers Billy Eckstine and Sarah Vaughan. He left Hines for a new band formed by Eckstine (1944); it, too, included young instrumentalists. Soon thereafter he began leading combos, which allowed greater freedom than big bands for experimental playing. With them he made some of his most virtuosic and enduring recordings, including "All the Things You Are," "Anthropology," "Be-Bop," "Blue 'n' Boogie," "Dizzy Atmosphere," "52d Street Theme," "Hot House," "Night in Tunisia," "Salt Peanuts," and "Shaw 'Nuff." In 1945 Gillespie and Parker formed a combo that gave a masterful performance at Town Hall in N.Y.C. and, at Billy Berg's Club in Hollywood, exposed West Coast musicians to bop. During the second half of the 1940s Gillespie led a big band that toured Scandinavia in 1948, with a side trip to Paris by way of Belgium. The recording of its performance at Salle Pleyel (Paris) demonstrates its—and Gillespie's—brilliance, though the band's quality soon declined. With his large ensemble, which included the conga player Chano Pozo, Gillespie established the genre known as Afro-Cuban jazz. The trumpeter formed his own record company, Dee Gee, in 1951; headquartered in Detroit, it recorded and released material by him as well as by such musicians as Milt Jackson and Annie Ross. With Charlie Parker, Bud Powell, Charles Mingus, and Max Roach, he participated in what some listeners consider the greatest jazz concert, one performed at Massey Hall in Toronto (1953). From 1953 to 1961 he was affiliated with record companies owned by Norman Granz (Norgran, Clef, and Verve), for which he recorded

Dizzy Gillespie, 52d St. and 6th Ave., N.Y.C., between 1946 and 1948; reproduced from the William P. Gottlieb Collection, Library of Congress, Music Division

with big bands and combos. For the United States Department of State he formed a band that toured the Middle East and South America in the mid-1950s. Thereafter he mainly fronted small groups, usually quintets or sextets, with a 1960s quintet featuring James Moody being especially noteworthy. In the early 1970s he toured with Giants of Jazz, a sextet that included Art Blakey, Thelonious Monk, Al McKibbon, Sonny Stitt, and Kai Winding. He made his last major recordings with another of Granz's labels, Pablo (1974–1982). These include performances from the Montreux Jazz Festival in Switzerland, as well as a duet session with Oscar Peterson and a quartet date with Count Basie. In time the radical of the 1940s became an elder statesman revered for his music and engaging personality. In 1964 Gillespie announced his mock candidacy for the presidency of the United States. Fourteen years later at a White House jazz festival, he coaxed President Carter into participating in a performance of "Salt Peanuts" with him and Max Roach. Cheraw honored Gillespie with a parade (1959), the key to the city (1983), and a seven-foot bronze statue (2002). He is buried in Flushing Cemetery, Flushing, N.Y.

Gillespie was the father of singer Jeanie Bryson, who is not a South Carolinian. He is sometimes mistakenly credited with appearing in the movie *Tall, Tan and Terrific* (1946).

Compositions

"Algo Bueno" (also titled "Woody'n You"), "Anthropology," "Back to the Land," "Be-Bop," "Birks' Works," "Blue 'n' Boogie," "Blues for Bird," "Blues for Norman," "Brother K," "Caprice," "Carambola," "The Champ," "Con Alma," "Cubana Be," "Cubana Bop," "Diggin' Diz," "Dizzy Atmosphere," "Emanon," "Follow the Leader," "Good Dues Blues," "Groovin' High," "Guarachi Guaro," "He Beeped When He Shoulda Bopped," "Hey Pete, Let's Eat Mo Meat," "I Waited for You," "Jump Did Le Ba," "Kush," "Little David," "Lorraine," "Manteca," "Montreux Blues," "Night in Tunisia" (also titled "Interlude"), "Olé," "Olinga," "One Bass Hit," "Ool Ya Ku," "Oop Bop Sh'Bam," "Ow!," "Pickin' the Cabbage," "Salt Peanuts," "Shaw 'Nuff," "Steeplechase," "Swing Low, Sweet Cadillac," "Tanga," "That's Earl, Brother," "Things to Come," "Tour de Force," "Two Bass Hit," "Wheatleigh Hall," "You Got It"

Recordings as Leader (Albums Only)

Diz and Getz (1953), *Quintet of the Year* (1953), *Afro* (1954; also titled *Manteca*), *Roy and Diz* (1954), *Tour de Force* (1955), *For Musicians Only* (1956), *World Statesman* (1956), *Birks' Works* (1957), *Dizzy Gillespie at Newport* (1957), *Duets* (1957), *The Greatest Trumpet of Them All* (1957), *Sonny Side Up* (1957), *"Have Trumpet, Will Excite!"* (1959), *Gillespiana* (1960), *A Portrait of Duke Ellington* (1960), *Carnegie Hall Concert* (1961), *The New Continent* (1961–1962), *Perceptions* (1961), *Dizzy on the French Riviera* (1962), *New Wave!* (1962), *Dizzy Gillespie and the Double Six of Paris* (1963), *Dizzy Goes Hollywood* (1963), *Something Old, Something New* (1963), *The Cool World* (1964), *Jambo Caribe* (1964), *The Melody Lingers On* (1966), *Jazz for a Sunday Afternoon* (1967), *Swing Low, Sweet Cadillac* (1967), *Cornucopia* (1969), *My Way* (1969), *The Real Thing* (1969–1970), *Sweet Soul* (1969–1970), *Dizzy Gillespie and the Mitchell Ruff Duo in Concert* (1971), *Giants* (1971), *Portrait of Jenny* (1971), *Dizzy Gillespie's Big 4* (1974), *Afro-Cuban Jazz Moods* (1975), *Bahiana* (1975), *The Dizzy Gillespie Big 7 at the Montreux Jazz Festival 1975*, *Dizzy's Party* (1976), *Dizzy Gillespie Jam: Montreux '77*, *Free Ride* (1977), *The Gifted Ones* (1977), *Digital at Montreux, 1980*, *Musician—Composer Raconteur* (1981), *"To a Finland Station"* (1982), *Endlessly* (1987), *Bird Songs* (1992), *To Bird with Love* (1992), *To Diz with Love* (1992)

Leaders Recorded With

Teddy Hill (1937), Cab Calloway (1939–1941), Lionel Hampton (1939, 1945), Charlie Christian (1941), Pete Brown (1942), Woody Herman (1942–1943, 1979), Les Hite (1942), Lucky Millinder (1942), Duke Ellington (1943, 1952, 1957, 1965), Charlie Parker (1943, 1945–1948, 1950–1952), Billy Eckstine (1944, 1972), Coleman Hawkins (1944, 1956), John Kirby (1944), Boyd Raeburn (1944–1946), Sarah Vaughan (1944–1945, 1951, 1953, 1986), Georgie Auld (1945), Slim Gaillard (1945), Clyde Hart (1945), Joe Marsala (1945), Red Norvo (1945), Oscar Pettiford (1945), Wilbert Baranco (1946), Ray Brown (1946), Jazz at the Philharmonic (1946–1947, 1954–1958, 1960, 1966), Tony Scott (1946), Metronome All-Stars (1947, 1949–1950), Barry Ulanov (1947), Kenny Clarke (1948), Dinah Washington (1948), Don Byas (1952), Norman Granz (1953–1954), Stan Kenton (1953, 1955),

Benny Carter (1954, 1976, 1987), Teddy Wilson (1955), Bud Powell (1960), Count Basie (1961), Quincy Jones (1964, 1989), Cal Tjader (1964–1965, 1972), Gil Fuller (1965), T-Bone Walker (1966, 1973), Carmen McRae (1970, 1976), Giants of Jazz (1971–1972, 1974), Charles Mingus (1972), Oscar Peterson (1974, 1977, 1980), Big Joe Turner (1974), Roy Eldridge (1975), Teresa Brewer (1978, 1991), Illinois Jacquet (1980), Bill Russo (1983), Arnett Cobb (1987)

Films

Jivin' in Be-Bop (1946; an excerpt was released in 1947 as *Harlem Rhythm*), *Harlem Dynamite* (1949), *The Cool World* (1964), *Dizzy Gillespie* (1965), *La Rumba* (1978), *A Night in Havana: Dizzy Gillespie in Cuba* (1989), *El Invierno en Lisboa* (1991), *A Great Day in Harlem* (1994), *The Spitball Story* (1997)

Awards (Selected)

Honorary degree, Rutgers University (1970); honorary degree, Chicago Conservatory of Music (1978); honorary degree, University of South Carolina (1980); honorary degree, Clark College (1982); honorary degree, Clark University (1988); Commander, French Arts and Letters Order (1989); Grammy Lifetime Achievement Award (1989); honorary degree, Berklee College of Music (1989); National Medal of Arts (1989); Kennedy Center Honors Award (1990); honorary degree, Columbia University (1991); honorary degree, Wilkes University (1992); Nesuhi Ertegun Hall of Fame (2004)

Website

http://www.dizzygillespie.com/ (accessed 21 May 2014)

References

PRIMARY: Dizzy Gillespie, with Gene Lees, "The Years with Yard," *Down Beat* 28 (25 May 1961): 21–23; Mike Bourne, "Fat Cats at Lunch: An Interview with Dizzy Gillespie," *Down Beat* 39 (11 May 1972): 16–17; Stanley Crouch, "Dizzy Gillespie: A Players Interview," *Players* 2 (January 1976): 18–24, 96, 98; Zane Knauss, "Dizzy Gillespie," in *Conversations with Jazz Musicians* (Detroit: Gale Research, 1977), 63–76; Dizzy Gillespie, with Al Fraser, *To Be, or Not . . . to Bop: Memoirs* (Garden City, N.Y.: Doubleday, 1979); Laurent Clarke and Franck Verdun, *Dizzy Atmosphere: Conversations avec Dizzy Gillespie* (N.p.: Institut National de l'Audioviseul, 1990) (in French); Wayne Enstice and Paul Rubin, *Jazz Spoken Here: Conversations with Twenty-Two Musicians* (Baton Rouge: Louisiana State University Press, 1992), 171–84; Charles Graham, *The Great Jazz Day* (New York: Da Capo, 2000), 38–39 (reminiscence by Gillespie); Studs Terkel, *And They All Sang: Adventures of an Eclectic Disc Jockey* (New York: New Press, 2005), 152–56 (Gillespie narrative from 1982); Benjamin Franklin V, *Jazz and Blues Musicians of South Carolina: Interviews with Jabbo, Dizzy, Drink, and Others* (Columbia: University of South Carolina Press, 2008), 24–31.

SECONDARY (because of the great number of publications about Gillespie, only books that focus entirely or mostly on him are included, plus an obituary): Michael James, *Dizzy Gillespie* (London: Cassell, 1959); Raymond Horricks, *Dizzy Gillespie and the Be-Bop Revolution* (New York: Hippocrene, 1984); Barry McRae, *Dizzy Gillespie: His Life and Times* (New York: Universe Books, 1988); *Dizzy: John Birks Gillespie in His 75th Year*, ed. Lee Tanner (San Francisco: Pomegranate Artbooks, [ca. 1992]); Peter Watrous, "Dizzy Gillespie, Who Sounded Some of Modern Jazz's Earliest Notes, Dies at 75," *New York Times*, 7 January 1993, sec. D, p. 20 (obituary); Alyn Shipton, *Groovin' High: The Life of Dizzy Gillespie* (New York: Oxford University Press, 1999); Ken Vail, *Dizzy Gillespie: The Bebop Years, 1937–1952* (Lanham, Md.: Scarecrow Press, 2003); Donald L. Maggin, *Dizzy: The Life and Times of John Birks Gillespie* (New York: HarperEntertainment, 2005).

Gilliard, Amos

Trombone

Probably ca. 1885–?

S.C. residence: Charleston (by 1891–ca. 1902, possibly 1919–possibly early 1920s)

A ward of Jenkins Orphanage beginning in 1891, Gilliard performed with its band in England four years later. In 1903 and 1904 he played with the Rabbit's Foot Minstrels (he was featured on the tune "Eiffel Tower"); in 1904, with Rusco and Holland's Georgia Minstrels; by 1906, with the Florida Blossoms Company; by 1912, with Allen's New Orleans Minstrels. In 1917 he joined James Reese Europe's band that, when stationed in Europe during World War I, became famous as the 369th Regiment Hell Fighters. He also performed in the 816th Pioneer Regiment Brass Band, led by Amos M. White. After the war he played with Silas Green from New Orleans, a tent show, before presumably teaching music at the orphanage at least in 1919 and 1920. During the mid-1920s he led a jazz group at a resort near Lake Okeechobee, Fla.

The passenger list of the *Paris,* which transported the orphanage band to England in September 1895, states that Gilliard was then age four; the list for the *Teutonic,* which returned the group to the United States the next month, indicates that he was ten. West Virginia, Deaths Index, records the death of Amos L. Gilliard in Cabell County on 4 October 1935; it indicates that he was born in Charleston, S.C., in 1885. This person was probably the musician.

Leader Recorded With

James Reese Europe (1919)

References

SECONDARY: Joe Miller, "Another Old Timer," *Chicago Defender,* 14 March 1925, p. 6; Amos White, as told to Bertrand Demeusy, "The Amos White Musical Career," *Record Research: The Magazine of Record Information and Statistics* 69 (July 1965): 3, 10; John Chilton, *A Jazz Nursery: The Story of the Jenkins' Orphanage Bands of Charleston, South Carolina* (London: Bloomsbury Book Shop, 1980), 23–24, 54; Howard Rye, "Visiting Fireboys: The Jenkins' Orphanage Bands in Britain," *Storyville* 130 (1987): 137–43; Stephen L. Harris, *Harlem's Hell Fighters: The African-American 369th Infantry in World War I* (Washington, D.C.: Brassey's, 2003), 75–76; Lynn Abbott and Doug Seroff, *Ragged but Right: Black Traveling Shows, "Coon Songs," and the Dark Pathway to Blues and Jazz* (Jackson: University Press of Mississippi, 2007), passim.

Gillum, Charles

Trumpet

Ca. 1922 (S.C., possibly Greenville)–?

S.C. residences: Greenville (possibly ca. 1922, but by 1935–no later than 1940), Charleston (by 1940–at least into early 1940s)

A ward of Jenkins Orphanage, Gillum played in its bands in the late 1930s and early 1940s.

Gillum was the brother of saxophonist Christopher Gillum. Gillum's age was estimated as eighteen when the musician was enumerated for the census at the orphanage on 21 May 1940; this document identifies S.C. as his birthplace and notes that in 1935 he lived in Greenville. It has not been determined if he was the Charles Gillum who recorded in the 1950s with such singers as Camille Howard, Helen Humes, and Jimmy Witherspoon.

Gillum, Christopher

Saxophone

Ca. 1923 (S.C., possibly Greenville)–?

S.C. residences: Greenville (possibly ca. 1923, but by 1935–no later than 1940), Charleston (by 1940–at least into early 1940s)

A ward of Jenkins Orphanage, Gillum played in its bands in the late 1930s and early 1940s.

Gillum was the brother of trumpeter Charles Gillum. Gillum's age was estimated as seventeen when the musician was enumerated for the census at the orphanage on 21 May 1940; this document identifies S.C. as his birthplace and notes that in 1935 he lived in Greenville.

Gillum, Paul

S.C. residence: Charleston (at least early 1940s)

Apparently a ward of Jenkins Orphanage, Gillum played in its bands in the early 1940s, though his instrument is not known. From Charleston he moved to Chicago.

It has not been determined if Gillum was related to the musicians Charles Gillum and Christopher Gillum, orphanage wards.

Ginyard, J. C. (Caleb Nathaniel, Jr.)

Singer

Probably November 1908 (probably Caw Caw Township, Calhoun County, S.C.)–11 August 1978 (Basel, Switzerland)

S.C. residences: probably Caw Caw Township, Calhoun County (probably 1908–1914), near Riley (1914–1918), Saint Matthews (1918–1920), Columbia (1920–1922), Orangeburg (1922)

As a youth Ginyard sang in church as a member of the congregation; by the early 1930s he became a professional singer. Both a lead tenor and, later, baritone, during his long career he performed with jubilee quartets that sang doo-wop/rhythm and blues, as well as gospel music. In the 1930s he established the Royal Harmony Singers (also known as the Florida Boys), which evolved into the Jubalaires (or Jubilaires). In Calif. this group was filmed for several soundies and appeared in a movie. Upon leaving the Jubalaires, in 1947 Ginyard established the Dixieaires (also known as Angel Voices), which lasted until 1950 or 1951, though he soon revived the group with different personnel. Active at the same time as the Du Droppers, which he formed in 1952, the reconstituted Dixieaires remained together until the mid-1950s. The Du Droppers' recordings of "I Wanna Know" and "I Found Out" reached near the top of the rhythm-and-blues charts, while the single of "Dead Broke" and "Speed King" was the first release of Groove Records, a subsidiary of RCA Victor. When Ginyard quit the Dixieaires and Du Droppers ca. 1955, he joined the Golden Gate Quartet, which became the first group to entertain United Nations Emergency Forces in Egypt (1957). The singers settled in Europe in 1959. After leaving this quartet in 1971 he resided in Basel, Switzerland, where he continued performing, including as a singing waiter.

Some sources record the singer's name as Julius Caleb Ginyard; others, as Junior Caleb Ginyard. Conducted in Caw Caw Township, Calhoun County, on 20 May 1910, the census uses the name Junior and indicates that the child's age was then one year, six months. Conducted in Amelia Township, Calhoun County, on 6 January 1920, the next census records Ginyard's name as Julian and estimates his age as ten. The Social Security Death Index uses the name Caleb Ginyard. Marv Goldberg explains that as a youth Ginyard was called Junior Caleb because his father was Caleb Ginyard, Sr.; Junior Caleb became shortened to J. C. The singer discusses his name on the first page of *My Name Is Caleb N. Ginyard.* He believed he was born on 15 January 1910. The Dixieaires that recorded in 1954 consisted of three-quarters of the Du Droppers; this group of Dixieaires was apparently assembled for this single recording session for Harlem Records ("I'm Not Like I Used to Be" and "Traveling All Alone").

Compositions

"Can't Do Sixty No More," "The Eternal Light," "I Know That You and I Will Never Meet Again," "I Wanna Know," "Joe Louis Is a Fightin' Man," "Speed King"

Leaders Recorded With

Royal Harmony Singers (1941–1942), Jubalaires (1944, 1946–1947), Andy Kirk (1945; with the Jubalaires), Dixieaires (ca. 1947–ca. 1952, 1954), Du Droppers (1952–1955), Sunny Gale (1953; with the Du Droppers), Big John Greer (1953; with the Du Droppers), Golden Gate Quartet (1957, 1964)

Film

Ebony Parade (1947; with the Jubalaires)

Awards

United in Group Harmony Hall of Fame (1998; as member of the Jubalaires); Vocal Group Hall of Fame (1998; as member of the Golden Gate Quartet)

References

PRIMARY: Caleb N. Ginyard III, *My Name Is Caleb N. Ginyard: A Father and Son Autobiography of a Spiritual Music Genius* (Hanover Twp., Pa.: n.p., 2002).

SECONDARY: "Famed Quartet UNEF-Bound," *Pacific Stars and Stripes,* 12 April 1957, p. 8; Karen Caplan, "The Jubalaires," http://www.ugha.users5.50megs.com/UGHA/ughahof98.htm (1998; accessed 21 May 2014); J. C. Marion, "Once Again, Too Soon: The Du Droppers," http://home.earthlink.net/~jaymar41/Dudroppers.html (1999; accessed 21 May 2014); "Previous Vocal Group Record of the Week," http://www.vocalgroupharmony.com/UntilYou.htm (2001; accessed 21 May 2014); Marsha Grant, "The Du Droppers Page (Featuring J. C. Ginyard)," http://www.vocalgroupharmony.com/dudrpprs.htm (2002; accessed 21 May 2014); Opal Louis Nations, notes to *Jubalaires: The Singing Waiters, 1947–1948* (2003; Heritage HT CD 48); Jerry Lynott, "In Tune with His Father," *Wilkes-Barre (Pa.) Times Leader,* 18 July 2004, sec. A, p. 3; Jay Warner, *American Singing Groups: A History from 1940s to Today* (Milwaukee: Hal Leonard, 2006), 169–71; Marv Goldberg, "The Du Droppers," http://www.uncamarvy.com/DuDroppers/dudrop.html (2009; accessed 21 May 2014) (comments by Ginyard); Tony Cummings, "The Dixieaires: A Neglected Jubilee Gospel Group Who Once Made the R&B Charts," http://www.crossrhythms.co.uk/articles/music/The_Dixieaires_A_neglected_jubilee_gospel_group_who_once_made_the_RB_charts/42225/p1/ (2010; accessed 21 May 2014); "Doo-Wop: Biography Groups and Discography," http://doo-wop.blogg.org/themes-_du_droppers-237445.html (2010; accessed 21 May 2014).

Glenn, Howard Lindbergh

Trumpet, trombone

Ca. 1929 (S.C., probably Burns Township, Dorchester County)–?

S.C. residences: Burns Township, Dorchester County (probably ca. 1929–at least until 1935, but no later than 1940), Charleston (by 1940–)

A ward of Jenkins Orphanage, Glenn presumably played in its bands at least in the early 1940s.

Glenn was the brother of trumpeter Sadie Glenn. As Lindbergh Glenn, age zero, he was enumerated with her for the census in Burns Township, Dorchester County, on 2 April 1930. His age was estimated as eleven when he was enumerated at the orphanage on 21 May 1940 as Howard L. Glenn; this document identifies S.C. as his birthplace and notes that in 1935 he lived in rural Dorchester County. John Chilton's statement that in the early 1940s Glenn served as a band director at the orphanage has not been confirmed. If Glenn was born ca. 1929, Chilton's claim seems improbable.

Reference

SECONDARY: John Chilton, *A Jazz Nursery: The Story of the Jenkins' Orphanage Bands of Charleston, South Carolina* (London: Bloomsbury Book Shop, 1980), 54.

Glenn, Sadie Thomasina

Trumpet

Ca. 1927 (probably Burns Township, Dorchester County, S.C.)–?

S.C. residences: Burns Township, Dorchester County (probably ca. 1927–at least until 1935, but no later than 1940), Charleston (by 1940–)

A ward of Jenkins Orphanage, Glenn played in its bands in the mid-1940s.

Glenn was the sister of musician Howard Glenn. The correct ordering of her given names has not been determined. Her age was estimated as three when she was enumerated as Thomasina Glenn for the census in Burns Township, Dorchester County, on 2 April 1930. It was estimated as thirteen when she was enumerated as Sadie T. Glenn at the orphanage on 21 May 1940; this document indicates that in 1935 she lived in rural Dorchester County. Both censuses identify S.C. as her birthplace.

Glenn, William Henry

Singer

22 August 1886 (Charleston, S.C.)–?

S.C. residence: Charleston (1886–no later than 1906)

An entertainer by 1906 when, as Willie Glenn, he was a comedian with the Florida Blossoms Company, Glenn is best known for his partnership with Walter Jenkins in the team of Glenn and Jenkins that lasted from probably 1917 at least into 1950. The pair became known for acting as two porters in "Working for the Railroad," a routine that included "Broom Blues." They performed in Europe in 1921 and 1922 and appeared on the first Radio-Keith-Orpheum Hour, broadcast nationally in 1929 on NBC. For four years beginning in the early 1920s, they were accompanied by the blues guitarist Lonnie Johnson. The team performed in Earl Dancer's *Africana* (1927), starring Ethel Waters, as well as in Leonard Harper's *Midnight Steppers of 1927* and *Hot Feet* (1930). A reviewer characterizes the pair's act as having "a novel line of humor, jazz blues and freak dancing" (advertisement for Glenn and Jenkins). In 1939 the team successfully sued the Cotton Club for breach of contract.

A Glenn and Jenkins scrapbook is housed in the New York Public Library, Schomburg Center, Manuscripts & Archives, Sc MG 599. It has not been determined if the S.C.-born William H. Glenn who died in Northampton, Mass., on 1 July 1972 was the vaudevillian.

References

SECONDARY: "A Note or Two," *Chicago Defender,* 24 August 1918, p. 6; advertisement for Glenn and Jenkins, *Variety,* 25 March 1921, p. 37; M.H.S., "Vaudeville," *New York Clipper,* 25 January 1922, p. 9 (under "Palace"); "Glenn and Jenkins among Few to Win Nitery Wage Suit," *New York Amsterdam News,* 30 March 1940, p. 16; "Form 2nd Unit for Vets Hospital Show," *Pittsburgh Courier,* 7 January 1950, p. 18; Lonnie Johnson, "From End to End," in *Conversation with the Blues,* by Paul Oliver (Cambridge: Cambridge University Press, 1965), 140; Marshall Stearns and Jean Stearns, *Jazz Dance: The Story of American Vernacular Dance* (New York: Macmillan, 1968), 150, 244; Lynn Abbott and Doug Seroff, *Ragged but Right: Black Traveling Shows, "Coon Songs," and the Dark Pathway to Blues and Jazz* (Jackson: University Press of Mississippi, 2007), 264, 290.

Glover, Candice Rickelle

Singer

22 November 1989 (Beaufort, S.C.)–

S.C. residence: Saint Helena Island (1989–)

A 2008 graduate of Beaufort High School who began singing as a child, Glover performs various kinds of music, including jazz and blues. Her first single, "I Am Beautiful," was released on the day she became the 2013 American Idol on a television talent program. As a result of winning this award, she sang the National Anthem at the 2013 Memorial Day concert at the United States Capitol.

Composition

"I Am Beautiful"

Recording as Leader

Music Speaks (2013)

Awards

American Idol (2013); Candice Glover Day in South Carolina (4 May 2013)

References

SECONDARY: Cathy Carter Harley, "From St. Helena Island to 'American Idol,'" *Hilton Head (S.C.) Island Packet*, 18 March 2012, sec. C, pp. 1–2 (also available as "Singer Candice Glover Goes from St. Helena Island to 'American Idol'" at http://www.islandpacket.com/2012/03/18/2003112_singer-candice-glover-goes-from.html [accessed 21 May 2014]) (comments by Glover); Jon Caramanica, "For 'Idol,' a Mild Finale to a Bumpy Season," *New York Times*, 18 May 2013, sec. C, pp. 1, 7; Gerrick D. Kennedy, "'Idol' Finds Her True Voice," *Los Angeles Times*, 19 March 2014, sec. D, p. 6 (also available as "'Idol' Winner Candice Glover Talks about Her New Album, 'Music Speaks'" at http://www.latimes.com/entertainment/music/posts/la-et-ms-idol-candice-glover-album-music-speaks-20140306,0,6688393.story#axzz2y162qz7j [accessed 21 May 2014]) (comments by Glover).

Glover, James

Saxophone
Ca. 1925 (S.C., possibly Summerville)-?
S.C. residences: Summerville (possibly ca. 1925, but by 1935–no later than 1940), Charleston (by 1940–at least into early 1940s)

A ward of Jenkins Orphanage, Glover played in its bands from the mid-1930s into the early 1940s.

Glover's age was estimated as fifteen when the musician was enumerated for the census at the orphanage on 21 May 1940; this document indicates that he was born in S.C. and that in 1935 he lived in Summerville.

Godfrey, Rickey Eugene

Guitar, keyboards, singer
29 November 1956 (Greenville, S.C.)-
S.C. residences: Greenville (1956–1962, 1971–1993), Spartanburg (1962–1971)

Born blind, Godfrey began his schooling at the South Carolina School for the Deaf and the Blind in 1962. The next year he began lessons in voice and piano. He started playing the guitar in 1971 and studied classical guitar from 1972 to 1975; in time he became enamored of and influenced by Rick Derringer, Django Reinhardt, and Johnny Winter. In 1972 he joined a band for the first time, the rock group Fresh Licks. Two years later he affiliated with Garfeel Ruff, which recorded for Capitol. He played briefly with Junior Walker and the All Stars in 1978. During the 1980s he performed with various groups, including one led by Sonny Turner (1982–1983). Early the next decade he played with Five Wheel Drive before moving to Nashville (1993), where he performed regularly with Donna Fargo (1995–1999) and Sam Moore (2000–2002) and freelanced. He backed Linda Rodney at the 2010 Montreal Jazz Festival. His music has been warmly received, especially in his home state, as

Rickey Godfrey, Hard Rock Café, Nashville, 18 November 2012; photograph by Danusia Bois of the Nashville Blues Society, permission of Rickey Godfrey

indicated by his Carolina Beach Music Awards. Godfrey is the brother of musician Ronnie Godfrey.

Compositions

"Baby, Let It All Hang Out," "Blonde Leading the Blind," "Choice Is Yours," "Clifford Woman," "Doing the Best I Can," "Don't Argue in the Kitchen," "Don't Get Your Honey Where You Get Your Money," "Fools Way Out," "Get Your Business Straight," "God Only Knows," "Good Mistake," "Heart on Fire," "Help Yourself to Me," "I Got the Hots for You," "I Remember Annie Mae," "It Can Happen to You," "It's a Good Night to Drink," "It's Football Time in Tennessee," "I Want Me a Nasty Woman," "Johnny Jones," "Let's Fall Back in Love," "Let's Get Busy," "Let the Tail Wag the Dog," "Love Injection," "Music City Blues," "My Knees Are Getting Sore," "Pine Needles Don't Cry," "Plummer Man," "Romance without Finance," "Shagadelic," "Shag Beach Party," "Shag to a Shuffle," "She Shot a Hole in My Soul Again," "Take a Look," "Will You Marry Me?," "You're So Good for Me," "You Won't Have Far to Fall"

Recordings as Leader

Garfeel Ruff (1978), *The Hitter* (1978; movie sound track by Garfeel Ruff), *Born to Play* (1979; by Garfeel Ruff), *Let the Big Dog Eat* (1983; as Rick E. Godfrey), *Good Godfrey* (from 1984 to 1999; with Ronnie Godfrey), *Soul Sensations* (2002; selections by both Godfrey and the Sugar Bees), "I Hear the Bells" (2004), "Shoe Shoppin'" (2004), "Boogie-Woogie Santa Claus" (2005), *Once in a Lifetime Love* (2006), "Runnin' Out of Time" (2007), *Nasty Man* (2010)

Leaders Recorded With

Joyous Perrin (1983), Sonny Turner (1983), Rob Cassels (1984), Bill Pinkney (1984), Harvey Willis (1984), Len Barry (1989), Amy Watkins (1998–1999), Sugar Bees (2001), Clifford Curry (2002, 2006), Jennifer Licko (2004), Johnny Lee (2005), Preston Shannon (2006), Linda Rodney (2009)

Awards

Best Duo Recording and Best Collaboration, Carolina Beach Music Awards (2003; for "Never Let You Go," with Andrew Keesee); Best Group, Carolina Beach Music Awards (2004); Best Group Album of the Year, Carolina Beach Music Awards (2004; for *Soul Sensations*); Best Song, Carolina Beach Music Awards (2004; for "Can't Change My Heart"); Best Group, Carolina Beach Music Awards (2006); Best Group Album of the Year, Carolina Beach Music Awards (2006; for *Once in a Lifetime Love*)

Website

http://www.myspace.com/therickeygodfreyband (accessed 21 May 2014)

References

PRIMARY: Michael B. Smith, *Carolina Dreams: The Musical Legacy of Upstate South Carolina* (Beverly Hills, Calif.: Marshall Tucker Entertainment, 1997), 120–22 (interview) (additional comments by Godfrey on 113–19); Michael B. Smith, "Out of the Darkness, a Beautiful Light Cometh," http://www.swampland.com/articles/view/title: ricky_godfrey (2002; accessed 21 May 2014) (interview); Brian M. Howle, "The Nicest 'Nasty Man' You'll Ever Hear: Musician/Vocalist Rickey Godfrey," *Alternatives NewsMagazine: The NewsMagazine for Young Professionals* 25 (4–18 November 2010): 23, 26–27 (also available at http://bhowle.wordpress.com/2010/11/01/the-nicest-'nasty-man'-you'll-ever-hear-musicianvocalist-rickey-godfrey/ [accessed 21 May 2014]) (interview).

SECONDARY: Michael Staton, "Rickey Godfrey," *Industry Mega-Scene*, June 2010, p. 17 (comments by Godfrey).

Goins, Elder James

Guitar, singer

18 July 1921 (Greenbriar area of Fairfield County, near Winnsboro, S.C.)–27 July 2006 (near Ridgeway, S.C.)

S.C. residences: Greenbriar area of Fairfield County, near Winnsboro (1921–ca. 1926), Simpson (ca. 1926–ca. 1941), near Ridgeway (ca. 1941–2006)

A carpenter by trade, Goins performed with his wife, Pauline, as a vocal duo. They were discovered by Tim and Denise Duffy, who helped them financially, recorded them, and arranged for them to perform their raw, emotional music at festivals. Goins is buried in the Evergreen Memorial Gardens, Winnsboro, S.C.

Goins's birth and death dates come from the Social Security Death Index. For the 1930 and 1940 censuses Goins was enumerated in Fairfield Township #9, Fairfield County. "Elder James Goins" identifies his church as the Spiritual Holiness Church of Simpson. In a telephone conversation on 24 January 2013, his widow reported that it is the Spiritual Way Seventh Day Adventist Holiness

Church of Simpson. His obituary indicates that he was pastor of the Spiritual Way Seventh Day Adventist Church #2, the same church mentioned in the program from his funeral. The program, which also records his birth date, is in Fairfield County African American Obituaries, vol. 5, at the South Carolina Room, Fairfield County Library, Winnsboro. Unissued recordings by the Goinses are housed in the Timothy Duffy Collection (#20044), Southern Folklife Collection, Louis Round Wilson Special Collections, University of North Carolina, Chapel Hill.

Recordings as Leader (with Mother Pauline Goins)

Recorded Raw (1997), "Prayed" (probably 1997)

Film

Toot Blues (2008)

References

SECONDARY: "Elder James Goins," in *Music Makers: Portraits and Songs from the Roots of America,* ed. Timothy Duffy (Athens, Ga.: Hill Street Press, 2002), 68–69; "James Goins," *Columbia (S.C.) State,* 31 July 2006, sec. B, p. 4 (obituary).

Goins, Mother Pauline Singleton

Singer

Possibly 27 October 1925 (between Ridgeway and Winnsboro, S.C.)–?

S.C. residences: between Ridgeway and Winnsboro (possibly 1925–ca. 1941), near Ridgeway (ca. 1941–)

Goins and her husband, James, performed as a vocal duo. They were discovered by Tim and Denise Duffy, who helped them financially, recorded them, and arranged for them to perform their raw, emotional music at festivals.

Goins identifies her birth date as 27 October 1925, which is possible because her age was estimated as four when she was enumerated for the census in Township 04, Fairfield County, on 8 April 1930. Yet when she was enumerated at the same place on 17 May 1940, her age was estimated as thirteen. Unissued recordings by the Goinses are housed in the Timothy Duffy Collection (#20044), Southern Folklife Collection, Louis Round Wilson Special Collections, University of North Carolina, Chapel Hill.

Recordings as Leader (with Elder James Goins)

Recorded Raw (1997), "Prayed" (probably 1997)

Film

Toot Blues (2008)

Reference

SECONDARY: "Elder James Goins," in *Music Makers: Portraits and Songs from the Roots of America,* ed. Timothy Duffy (Athens, Ga.: Hill Street Press, 2002), 68–69.

Goodwin, Dick (Gordon Richard)

Trumpet, piano, composer, arranger

22 January 1941 (Cape Girardeau, Mo.)–

S.C. residence: Columbia (1973–)

Goodwin led a coast guard band (1958–1962) before enrolling at the University of Texas, Austin, from which he received degrees in 1965 (bachelor's), 1967 (master's), and 1969 (doctoral). As an undergraduate he was instrumental in creating the university's jazz program. After earning his Ph.D. he remained at the university as a professor until 1973, when he accepted a position at the University of South Carolina, where he established a doctoral program in composition and spent the remainder of his teaching career. He is one of the most active musicians on the local jazz scene, as leader, player, and composer.

Compositions

"Ann Street," "April 30th," "Birthday Boy," "Bong," "Boop Music," "Brown-Eyed Child," "Bump and Grind," "Cantata for Soul Sister and Jazz Band," "Caught with an Uppercut," "Characters," "Crash Jr.," "Diz," "El Caribe," "The Gold Commode," "Grey Day, February," "Harshly, as in a Morning Freight Train," "How Did We Get Here?," "Installments," "Jabbo," "Jammin' a Classic," "Janie's a Charmer," "Jazz Legs," "Jazz Miniatures," "Lady on the Mountain," "The Left One," "Lickety Split," "Marc's Mark," "Miss Information," "Mr. Peacock's Lament," "Oh, Yes You Can," "The Old Wine Bottle," "100 in the Shade," "The Provincial Correspondent (to the Wall Street Journal)," "Samba Nueva," "Sarah's Song," "Shadow Man," "Something about Duke," "Street of Caracas," "Sure Shot (Ian's Samba)," "A Swing through Time," "These Are the Years," "The Thinker," "Thus Spake Cocky," "Up Swing," "Wednesday Afternoons," "Weeping Crystal," "What I Think of When I Think of Bye Bye

Blackbird," "When He Gets Sweaty His Glasses Slide down His Nose Blues," "Xalapa," "Young Brother"

Recordings as Leader

Dick Goodwin Jazz Quintet (1978), *Studio Time* (2001), *Studio Time 2* (2006)

Leaders Recorded With

USC Faculty Jazz Quintet (1980), Roger Pemberton (1987), Mary Ann Hurst (2007), Doug Williams and Bunny Williams (2010–2012)

Award

Elizabeth O'Neill Verner Individual Artist Award (2001)

Website

www.goodwinmusics.com (accessed 21 May 2014)

References

PRIMARY: Benjamin Franklin V, *Jazz and Blues Musicians of South Carolina: Interviews with Jabbo, Dizzy, Drink, and Others* (Columbia: University of South Carolina Press, 2008), 143–59.

SECONDARY: Otis R. Taylor, Jr., "Dick Goodwin Strikes Up the Band," *Columbia (S.C.) State,* 28 December 2008, sec. E, pp. 1, 3; Anita Baker, "The Dick Goodwin Big Band, Making Music in the Midlands since 1970s," *Columbia (S.C.) Star,* 27 January 2012, p. 8; Jerry Ford, *Dreamers: Entertainers from Small Town to Big Time* (Cape Girardeau, Mo.: Southeast Missouri State University Press, 2012), 78–82.

Goodwin, Henry Clay

Trumpet, singer

Probably 2 January 1907 (probably Columbia, S.C.)–2 July 1979 (New York, N.Y.)

S.C. residence: probably Columbia (1907–no later than ca. 1922)

While a high schooler in Washington, D.C., Goodwin replaced Sidney DeParis in the local band of Sam Taylor. He next joined the organization of Claude Hopkins that toured Europe in 1925 with La Revue Nègre, which included young Josephine Baker. Probably in 1926 he and trombonist Daniel Doy left Hopkins to play in Paul Wyer's band in Argentina but relocated to the United States after five months because of Doy's poor health. If, as he claimed, Goodwin formed the Bellhop Band ca. 1927, he soon resumed life as a sideman with the groups of Elmer Snowden and Cliff Jackson. Again he went to Europe, this time with Lucky Millinder (1933); then, after freelancing in N.Y.C., he returned to Europe, now with Edgar Hayes (1938). Back in N.Y.C. in the 1940s he played with such leaders as Sidney Bechet, Cecil Scott, and Art Hodes. With a group led by Mezz Mezzrow, Goodwin performed at what is considered the first significant jazz festival, the one held in Nice, France, in 1948. He played in Europe for the last time with the band of Jimmy Archey (1952). Goodwin was inspired initially by trumpeter Johnny Dunn. Gunther Schuller characterizes Goodwin as "a most assured swing stylist and specialist in the plunger and growl."

The trumpeter's date and place of birth are in dispute. When enumerated for the census in N.Y.C. in April 1930, Goodwin stated that he was born in S.C. and estimated his age as twenty-three. The passenger list of the *Columbus,* on which he sailed from Bremen to N.Y.C. in April 1938, records that he was born in Columbia, S.C., on 2 January 1907, the date also specified in the Social Security Death Index. Though Goodwin misstates the year he played in Europe with Claude Hopkins (in "Music Is My Business," he says 1924, when it was 1925), he notes that he was eighteen at the time. However, several sources indicate that he was born in Columbia on 2 January 1910, a year that seems improbable because he would have been fifteen when traveling to Europe with Claude Hopkins

Henry Goodwin (left), with Sandy Williams, Times Square (?), N.Y.C., ca. July 1947; reproduced from the William P. Gottlieb Collection, Library of Congress, Music Division

in 1925. Despite declaring in 1930 that he was born in S.C. and in 1938 that he was born in Columbia, Goodwin states in "Music Is My Business" that he was born in Washington, D.C. No public document that records Washington as his birthplace or 1910 as his year of birth has been located. He might be the Henry Goodwin who was enumerated for the census in April 1910 in Columbia when eight months old and residing with his parents, James and Josephine Goodwin, at the home of his maternal grandmother, Julia Nelson. Despite Goodwin's claim that he formed the Bellhop Band, the article "Bellhop Band Here" notes that in December 1927 Goodwin was a member of this group led by pianist Silas Carter. A paragraph appended to "Music Is My Business" indicates that Goodwin composed "Edgar Steps Out." Broadcast Music, Inc. (BMI), a performing rights company, identifies its composer as Edgar Hayes.

Leaders Recorded With

Possibly Paul Wyer (ca. 1926), Lieut. Matt's Rhapsodists (1927), Cliff Jackson (1930), Edgar Hayes (1937–1938), Kenny Clarke (1938), Slim Gaillard (1940), Sidney Bechet (1941–1942, 1949), Pat Flowers (1946), Pops Foster (1946), Creole George Guesnon (1946), Art Hodes (1946), Bob Wilber (1949), Jimmy Archey (1951–1952), Willie "The Lion" Smith (1953, 1957), Lucille Hegamin (1961), Memphis Cotton Carnival (1971)

References

PRIMARY: Henry Goodwin, "Music Is My Business," *Jazz Record* 43 (April 1946): 7–8.

SECONDARY: "Bellhop Band Here," *Baltimore Afro-American*, 17 December 1927, p. 7; Mike Pinfold, "The Forgotten Ones—Henry Goodwin," *Jazz Journal International* 36 (December 1983): 13; Gunther Schuller, *The Swing Era: The Development of Jazz, 1930–1945* (New York: Oxford University Press, 1989), 421; Scott Yanow, *The Trumpet Kings: The Players Who Shaped the Sound of Jazz Trumpet* (San Francisco: Backbeat Books, 2001), 173–74.

Goodwin, Ralph Norman ("Iron Fingers")

Piano

24 January 1924 (Columbia, S.C.)–3 March 2011 (Prosperity, S.C.)

S.C. residences: Columbia (1924–1974), Prosperity (1974–2011)

As a child Goodwin learned to play piano from his sister; he never took formal lessons. After being graduated from Columbia High School and serving in the army during World War II, he sold medical supplies and equipment for the entirety of his working life. Concurrently he played piano in the S.C. midlands, initially with Snuffy Jenkins and His Hired Hands, a country group, but also with jazz combos. In time he performed with the Jazztones and Dick Goodwin. Known affectionately as Iron Fingers, he helped found the Carolina Jazz Society in 1958.

Leaders Recorded With

Knights of Dixieland (1962), Larry Conger (1965–1966, 1969), Ernie Carson (1971), Joe Darensbourg (1972)

Reference

SECONDARY: "Ralph Goodwin," *Columbia (S.C.) State*, 5 March 2011, sec. B, p. 4 (obituary).

Goudelock, John Acey

See Acey, Johnny

Goudelock, Sharon

Harmonica

Early or mid-1910s (probably Draytonville, S.C.)–before 1986 (probably Draytonville, S.C.)

S.C. residence: Draytonville (probably early or mid-1910s–no later than 1985)

Goudelock apparently played the blues and gospel music, though he probably never recorded.

Bruce Bastin's claim that Goudelock (whose surname Bastin spells Gowdlock) was the brother of guitarist Jack Goudlock has not been substantiated. According to the 1930 census Sharon Goudelock was a half brother of singer John Acey Goudelock, also known as Johnny Acey. Their surname is sometimes spelled Goudlock or Gowdlock. The spelling used in the newspaper obituaries of John Acey Goudelock, in his army enlistment record, and in the Social Security Death Index has been used here. Sharon's given name is sometimes spelled Sharron. Goudelock's age was estimated as six when the youth was enumerated for the census on 2 January 1920; as nineteen when enumerated 11 April 1930; as twenty-five when enumerated on 6 May 1940. All these censuses were conducted in

Draytonville Township, Cherokee County. Bastin indicates that Goudelock died before Bastin finished writing his book.

Reference

SECONDARY: Bruce Bastin, *Red River Blues: The Blues Tradition in the Southeast* (Urbana: University of Illinois Press, 1986), 190.

Goudlock, Jack (John R.)

Guitar, singer

Early-to-mid-1890s (Union County, S.C.)–13 October 1977 (Asheville, N.C.)

S.C. residence: Union County (early-to-mid-1890s–at least until 1920)

Goudlock played the country blues and recorded four tunes, all at one session for RCA Victor in Charlotte, N.C., in 1931. He partnered occasionally with Blind Gussie Nesbitt, who performed on two of Goudlock's recordings, though only the ones Goudlock played unaccompanied were released. In 1918 and 1919 he served in the army. He is buried in Riverside Cemetery, Asheville.

Bruce Bastin's claim that Goudlock (whose surname Bastin spells Gowdlock) was the brother of harmonicaist Sharon Goudelock has not been substantiated. Jack Goudlock's obituary, which provides the middle initial, and the Social Security Death Index spell the musician's surname Goudlock, the spelling adopted here; this same spelling is used in *The Official Roster of South Carolina Soldiers, Sailors and Marines in the World War, 1917–18* (N.p.: n.p., ca. 1929), 2: 1,371, where the given name is spelled Johnie. The 1900 census states that Goudlock was born in June 1892. His age was estimated as nineteen when he was enumerated for the census in Santuc Township, Union County, on 25 April 1910; as twenty-five when enumerated in the same place on 19 January 1920; as thirty-four when enumerated in Asheville, N.C., on 9 April 1930; as forty-five when enumerated in the same place on 8 April 1940. The Social Security Death Index identifies his birth date as 30 May 1894; his death date comes from his obituary. Sources state that he lived in Cross Keys, S.C. Though he might have resided there after the 1920 census was conducted and before moving to N.C. before 1930, until 1920 he lived with his parents and siblings in Santuc Township, Union County, S.C., which does not incorporate Cross Keys. His obituary states, incorrectly, that he lived for sixty-five years in Buncombe County (which includes Asheville), N.C.

Recordings as Leader (All 1931)

"Have You Been Converted?" (unissued), "Poor Jane Blues," "Rollin' Dough Blues," "You'd Better Mind" (unissued)

References

SECONDARY: Bruce Bastin, *Crying for the Carolines* (London: Studio Vista, 1971), 22; "John Goudlock," *Asheville (N.C.) Citizen,* 17 October 1977, p. 8 (obituary); Bruce Bastin, *Red River Blues: The Blues Tradition in the Southeast* (Urbana: University of Illinois Press, 1986), 189–90, 197, 233–34.

Graham, Zacharias

Trombone

S.C. residence: Charleston (at least mid-1930s)

Apparently a ward of Jenkins Orphanage, Graham played in its bands in the mid-1930s.

The city directory records a Zacharias Graham living in Charleston in 1891. If he was the father of the musician, as seems likely, then the child was probably born in Charleston.

Grant, Isiah Alexander

Singer

Ca. 1886 (possibly S.C. or Fla.)–1920 (Louisville, Ky.)

At least in 1908 Grant, a baritone, sang with the orchestra of Professor Dick Anderson that toured with the Rabbit's Foot Minstrels. That summer in Shelby, N.C., he was badly burned in a fire in the company's train car. A ballad singer, he offered a rendition of "The Fairest Flower of All" that reportedly led to encores on a regular basis. In 1913 he married Leola B. "Coot" Pettigrew, with whom he formed the act Grant and Grant. They performed with C. W. Park's Musical Comedy Company by August 1914; the next year they were with Alexander Tolliver's Smart Set Company, a variety show billed as "The Greatest Colored Show on Earth." The Smart Set group also included Ma Rainey, Clara Smith, and Trixie Smith, all of whom became significant blues singers, as did, to a lesser degree, Coot Grant.

Grant's birthplace has not been determined, though a 1908 *Indianapolis Freeman* article about the Rabbit's Foot fire states that the singer is "from South Carolina." Without evidence John Henry

Vanco asserts that Grant was born in 1886 in Saint Petersburg, Fla. If Vanco is correct, then the statement in the *Freeman* could mean that Grant resided, but was not born, in S.C. Grant's name is sometimes rendered Isaiah Grant and Isiah I. Grant. The singer's full name, year and place of death, age at death, and estimated birth year are recorded in Kentucky, Death Records, 1911–1955.

References

SECONDARY: "Rabbit's Foot Minstrel Co.'s Car Burned," *Indianapolis Freeman: An Illustrated Colored Newspaper,* 22 August 1908, p. 5; Cal Wells, "Alexander Tolliver's Big Show," *Indianapolis Freeman: An Illustrated Colored Newspaper,* 27 May 1916, p. 4; John Henry Vanco, notes to *Coot Grant and Kid Wilson: Complete Recorded Works in Chronological Order, Volume 1, 1925–1928* (1997; Document Records DOCD-5563); Lynn Abbott and Doug Seroff, *Ragged but Right: Black Traveling Shows, "Coon Songs," and the Dark Pathway to Blues and Jazz* (Jackson: University Press of Mississippi, 2007), 122, 126, 262–64, 357.

Grate, Tommy (Thomas, Jr.)

Singer

17 October 1935 (possibly Beaufort, S.C.)-27 February 1998 (Anderson, S.C.)

S.C. residences: possibly Beaufort (possibly 1935-no later than 1940), Anderson County, including the town of Anderson (by 1940-no later than early 1950s, by mid-1960s-1998)

Grate sang bass with several doo-wop/rhythm-and-blues groups, initially with the Five Wings in 1954. When it disbanded the next year he joined the Vocaltones, then the Dubs, with which he performed into the mid-1960s. He is on the Dubs' biggest hit, "Could This Be Magic," and sings lead on the group's "Gonna Make a Change." He is buried in the Holly Springs Baptist Church Cemetery, Belton, S.C.

Grate was the brother of singer Miriam Grate. His birth and death dates come from the Social Security Death Index. His age was estimated as four when the youth was enumerated for the census in Pendleton Township, Anderson County, on 27 April 1940. The Brenda Lee with whom he recorded was not the popular singer of this name.

Leaders Recorded With

Five Wings (1955), Brenda Lee (1955), Billy Nelson (1955), Vocaltones (1955–1956), Dubs (1957–1963)

References

SECONDARY: Todd R. Baptista, *Group Harmony: Behind the Rhythm and the Blues* (New Bedford, Mass.: TRB Enterprises, 1996), 29–34, 165; "Thomas Grate Jr.," *Anderson (S.C.) Independent-Mail,* 1 March 1998, sec. A, p. 10 (obituary); Marv Goldberg, "The Dubs," http://www.uncamarvy.com/Dubs/dubs.html (2009; accessed 21 May 2014); Frank Fazio, "The Dubs," http://www.soulfulkindamusic.net/dubs.htm (undated; accessed 21 May 2014).

Green, Butler

Tuba

Mid-1880s (S.C.)-?

S.C. residence: Charleston (by 1890-at least into 1910s)

A ward of Jenkins Orphanage in the 1890s, Green played in its bands during that decade and into the 1910s. He performed with one of them in England in 1895.

The passenger list of the *Paris,* which transported the orphanage band to England in September 1895, records Green's age as nine; the list for the *Teutonic,* which returned the group to the United States the next month, specifies it as seven. Conducted at the orphanage on 28 June, the 1900 census indicates that the musician was born in May 1883. His relationship, if any, to cornetist Daniel Green has not been established. A Butler Green was enumerated for the census in Washington Township, McCormick County, S.C., on 10 February 1920; this document estimates his age as thirty-four and identifies S.C. as his birthplace. It has not been determined if this person was the musician.

References

SECONDARY: John Chilton, *A Jazz Nursery: The Story of the Jenkins' Orphanage Bands of Charleston, South Carolina* (London: Bloomsbury Book Shop, 1980), 55; Howard Rye, "Visiting Fireboys: The Jenkins' Orphanage Bands in Britain," *Storyville* 130 (1987): 137–43.

Green, Daniel

Cornet

September 1882, or mid-1880s (S.C.)-?

S.C. residence: Charleston (by 1890-)

A ward of Jenkins Orphanage, Green played in its earliest bands and performed with one of them in England in 1895. He became an assistant bandmaster at the institution.

The passenger list of the *Paris,* which transported the orphanage band to England in September 1895, records Green's age as nine; the list of the *Teutonic,* which returned the group to the United States the next month, specifies it as eleven. Conducted at the orphanage on 28 June, the 1900 census indicates that the musician was born in September 1882. His relationship, if any, to tubaist Butler Green has not been established.

References

SECONDARY: John Chilton, *A Jazz Nursery: The Story of the Jenkins' Orphanage Bands of Charleston, South Carolina* (London: Bloomsbury Book Shop, 1980), 55; Howard Rye, "Visiting Fireboys: The Jenkins' Orphanage Bands in Britain," *Storyville* 130 (1987): 137–43.

Green, Ed

Guitar

1890 (near Charleston, S.C.)–ca. 1971 (probably Glenn Dale, Md.)

S.C. residence: near Charleston (1890–ca. 1903, possibly ca. 1908–no later than ca. 1950)

Green played with a carnival as early as 1903. After leaving it he remained a professional musician, performing at dances, parties, and churches. By ca. 1950 he lived in Washington, D.C., where he worked as a house painter and occasionally played with Mississippi John Hurt. He recorded only one tune, "South Carolina Blues," which appears on the Flyright album *Another Man Done Gone . . .* In the notes to this release, Ed Morris characterizes Green's music: He "played sacred, blues and other secular music in a style that predated the earliest recorded black music. His music belonged to the period when Negro folk musicians were turning from banjo to the guitar. His is a style which includes a great many raps, taps and stretched bass strings."

Ed Morris notes that Green died in the Glendale Sanatorium, Washington, D.C. The existence of this facility has not been confirmed. Morris possibly refers to Glenn Dale Hospital, Glenn Dale, Md. Morris states that Green's son, Little Willie Green, recorded in Atlanta for Brunswick in 1928. It has not been determined if the son was born or spent significant time in S.C.

Recording

"South Carolina Blues" (1965)

References

SECONDARY: Ed Morris, quoted by Bruce Bastin in the brochure accompanying the album *Another Man Done Gone . . .* (1978; Flyright 528), 12–13; Bruce Bastin, *Red River Blues: The Blues Tradition in the Southeast* (Urbana: University of Illinois Press, 1986), 48, 315–16.

Green, Freddie (Frederick William; "Pep")

Guitar, singer

31 March 1911 (Charleston, S.C.)–1 March 1987 (Las Vegas, Nev.)

S.C. residence: Charleston (1911–1923, ca. 1929–1930)

After living his first dozen years in Charleston, Green resided with an aunt in N.Y.C. from 1923 until approximately 1929. He returned to Charleston when his mother died; while there he played banjo with a Jenkins Orphanage band, accompanying it on a 1930 tour of Maine. Instead of returning to Charleston, he settled in N.Y.C., where he resumed living with his aunt in Harlem. He first performed professionally in N.Y.C. in a trio at the Yeah Man Club, where he transitioned from banjo to guitar. He moved to the Exclusive Club and then to the Black Cat, where he was discovered by John Hammond, who arranged for him to audition for Count Basie. Impressed, Basie hired him in 1937, and Green remained with Basie for fifty years.

Freddie Green; permission of John C. Williams, Jr.

With this band he became known as the premier jazz rhythm guitarist (one who solely keeps time), which he is still considered. He, pianist Basie, bassist Walter Page, and drummer Jo Jones propelled the band. Because of their collective skill, they became known as the All-American Rhythm Section. Despite his decades with Basie, Green recorded with many instrumentalists and singers. He backed Billie Holiday, for example, on some of her most enduring recordings, such as "A Sailboat in the Moonlight' and "This Year's Kisses." He, himself, sings on "Them There Eyes" (1938), a famous recording by the Kansas City Six, featuring Lester Young. His composition "Corner Pocket" has been recorded over a hundred times.

Compositions

"Back and Forth," "Bustin' Suds," "Corner Pocket" (also titled "Until I Met You"), "The Countess," "Crossfire," "The Daly Jump," "A Date with Ray," "Down for Double," "Feed Bag," "Freddie's Tune," "Free and Easy," "Free Eats," "Green Is Blue," "High Tide," "I Ain't Mad at You," "I Don't Know Yet," "Jumpin' for Maria," "Little Red," "Paging Mr. Green," "Right On," "Swingin' Back," "Up in the Blues," "You're the Best"

Recordings as Leader

"Get Lucky" (1945), "I'll Never Be the Same" (1945), "I'm in the Mood for Love" (1945), "Sugar Hips" (1945), *Mr. Rhythm* (1954), *Rhythm Willie* (1975; with Herb Ellis)

Leaders Recorded With

Mildred Bailey (1937), Count Basie (1937–1987), Billie Holiday (1937–1940, 1950, 1952, 1954), Teddy Wilson (1937–1938), Ida Cox (1938–1939), Benny Goodman (1938), Kansas City Five (1938), Kansas City Six (1938–1939), Pee Wee Russell (1938), Lionel Hampton (1939), Glenn Hardman (1939), Joe Sullivan (1940), Metronome All Stars (1941), Dicky Wells (1943), Kansas City Seven (1944), Earle Warren (1944), Lester Young (1944), Lucky Thompson (1945), Benny Carter (1946), Illinois Jacquet (1946–1947, 1952), Jimmy Rushing (1946, 1955, 1963), Sir Charles Thompson (1947, 1954), Dinah Washington (1948–1951, 1957), Sarah Vaughan (1950, 1954, 1958, 1960, 1981), Paul Quinichette (1951–1952, 1956–1959), Eddie "Lockjaw" Davis (1952), Charlie Parker (1952), Buck Clayton (1953–1954, 1956), Tony Scott (1953, 1956–1957), Joe Newman (1954–1956, 1958), Brother John Sellers (1954), Al Cohn (1955), Jo Jones (1955, 1976), Nat Pierce (1955–1956), Buddy Rich (1955), Sonny Stitt (1955), Ruby Braff (1956), Seldon Powell (1956), Big Joe Turner (1956, 1972), Frank Wess (1956–1957), Lambert, Hendricks, and Ross (1957), Gerry Mulligan (1957), Eddie "Cleanhead" Vinson (1957), Nat Cole (1958), Harry Edison (1958), Coleman Hawkins (1958), Zoot Sims (1958), Ray Charles (1959–1960), Joe Williams (1959, 1971, 1977), Woody Herman (1962)

Films

Rhythm and Blues Review (1955), *The Last of the Blue Devils* (1979)

Award

New Jersey Jazz Society American Jazz Hall of Fame (1998)

Website

www.freddiegreen.org/ (accessed 21 May 2014)

References

PRIMARY: Bill Coss, "Swing Is Here to Stay: Interviews with the Basie Band," *Jazz Today* 2 (August 1957): 17–19; Max Jones and Sinclair Traill, "Freddie Greene and Those 'Rhythm Waves,'" *Melody Maker* 32 (16 November 1957): 5 (interview); Freddie Green, "In My Opinion," *Jazz Journal* 15 (June 1962): 15–16; Stanley Dance, *The World of Swing* (New York: Scribner's, 1974), 1: 13–17 (interview); Stanley Dance and Helen Dance, "The Freddie Green Interview," www.freddiegreen.org/interviews/dance.html (1977; accessed 21 May 2014).

SECONDARY: Dom Cerulli, "Freddie Greene," *International Musician* 60 (1962): 26–27 (comments by Green); Raymond Horricks, *Count Basie and His Orchestra: Its Music and Its Musicians* (Westport, Conn.: Negro Universities Press, 1971), 124–32; John Chilton, *A Jazz Nursery: The Story of the Jenkins' Orphanage Bands of Charleston, South Carolina* (London: Bloomsbury Book Shop, 1980), 41–42, 55; Stanley Dance, *The World of Count Basie* (New York: Scribner's, 1980), passim; James Condell, "Freddie Green: Mister Rhythm," *Coda* 219 (April–May 1988): 6–8; Lewis Hay Dickert, Jr., "An Analysis of Freddie Green's Style and His Importance in the History of Jazz Guitar" (Ph.D. dissertation, University of Memphis, 1994); Thomas Johnson, "'Count Basie's Left Hand' Comes to the Caroliniana," *Caroliniana Columns* (Fall 1999): 4–5, 11; David Ness, "Freddie Green," *Jazz Educators Journal* 32 (November 1999): 43–45, 47; Michael Pettersen, "Distilling Big Band Guitar: The Essence of Freddie Green," *Down Beat* 67 (October 2000): 93; Edward Ball, *The Sweet Hell Inside: A Family History* (New York: William Morrow, 2001), 314–17, 348–49.

Greene, (Samantha) Madeline

Singer

30 May of either 1921 or 1922 (Saint Matthews, S.C.)–30 May 1976 (Cleveland, Ohio)

S.C. residence: Saint Matthews (1921 or 1922–ca. 1924)

Around age two Greene moved with her family from Saint Matthews to Cleveland, Ohio, where she spent most of her life. While a student at John Jay High School, she sang at various Cleveland venues, including Cedar Gardens, a popular club. After winning a beauty pageant in Cleveland in 1937, she performed at the Cotton Club in Cincinnati, where she was discovered. Later that year she recorded with Earl Hines. She sang with the Jeter-Pillars Orchestra at Club Plantation in Saint Louis ca. 1938; there she met Benny Goodman, who signed her to a two-year contract in 1939. After touring northern states with his band, she had racial problems in the South as a result of singing with a white group. To spare her, Goodman voided the contract and arranged for her to join Hines's band, which she did in 1940; Billy Eckstine was its male vocalist. That year at the Hines recording session that produced Eckstine's "Jelly, Jelly," which became a hit, Greene recorded "Everything Depends on You." She was with Hines when his organization included Dizzy Gillespie and Charlie Parker, who were in the process of creating a music that became known as bebop. Hines's second pianist, Sarah Vaughan, succeeded Greene as singer with this band in 1943. During the mid-1940s Greene was with Lionel Hampton; late that decade she sang, but did not record, with Erskine Hawkins. After retiring from band singing she performed mainly in Cleveland well into the 1950s. She is buried in lot 2-16, section 56, Lake View Cemetery, Cleveland.

Madeline Greene, with Earl Hines, probably early 1940s; permission of Eric Randall

During a telephone conversation (15 October 2013), Greene's son, Bill Randall, reported that his mother was born on 30 May 1922 and died on her birthday; some sources record her birth date as 31 May 1922. The 1930 census indicates that when she was enumerated on 10 April in Cleveland, she was eight years old, which, if accurate and if she was born on 30 or 31 May, means that she was born in 1921. This year of birth, 1921, is recorded in Ohio, Death Index, 1908–1932, 1938–1944, and 1958–2007, where she is identified by her married name, Madelin [*sic*] G. Randall, though she was divorced from Willie Randall, a saxophonist she met in the Earl Hines band. This document also records her death date. Despite Allan McMillan's statement that Greene would record in 1951, consulted documents do not confirm that she did. Some sources suggest that she recorded with Coleman Hawkins. She did not. Confusion on this point probably arose because Earl Hines's 1941 recording of "It Had to Be You," featuring Greene, appears on the reverse of Hawkins's 1939 recording of "Body and Soul," as issued on Bluebird 30-0825. Her compositions are preserved in the Dallas Bartley material, Katherine G. Lederer Collection [M035], Department of Special Collections and Archives, Missouri State University, Springfield, Mo.

Compositions

"It's a Hit," "Left with an Empty Heart," "Little Sister Susie," "Sharecropper," "A Stranger," "What Would You Do?," "You're the Greatest"

Recordings as Leader (Both 1950)

"Be Sure," "I've Got a Right to Be Blue"

Leaders Recorded With

Earl Hines (1937, 1940–1942), Jimmy Mundy (1939), Lionel Hampton (1944, 1946)

References

SECONDARY: "To Sing with Goodman's Orchestra," *Indianapolis Recorder,* 27 May 1939, sec. 1, p. 1; "Colored Girl Signs with Goodman Ork," *Durham (N.C.) Carolina Times,* 3 June 1939, pp. 1, 8; "She's Some Good Looker," *Evansville (Ind.) Argus,* 13 December 1940, p. 1; Dave Dexter, Jr., "Hines Hits Broadway and Tears It Apart!," *Down Beat* 8 (15 February 1941): 3; Allan McMillan, "Allan's Alley," *New York Amsterdam News,* 17 February 1951, p. 22; Bob Williams, "Elks Once Picked Madeline Swinging Star of the 40's," *Cleveland (Ohio) Call and Post,* 20 August 1966, sec. C, p. 6 (also available at http://www.vocalgroupharmony.com/3ROWNEW/SheAlways.htm [accessed 21 May 2014]) (comments by Greene); Stanley Dance, *The World of Earl Hines* (New York: Scribner's, 1977), passim; Alyn Shipton, *Groovin' High: The Life of Dizzy Gillespie* (New York: Oxford University Press, 1999), 109, 113; "Ladies of R&B, Part Five," http://www.vocalgroupharmony.com/Sally.htm (2005; accessed 21 May 2014) (also titled "Previous Vocal Group Record of the Week"); "Previous Vocal Group Record of the Week #601," http://www.vocalgroupharmony.com/ROWNEW/Evrythng.htm (2009; accessed 21 May 2014); "Previous Vocal Group Record of the Week #725," http://www.vocalgroupharmony.com/4ROWNEW/BeSure.htm (2011; accessed 21 May 2014).

Griffin, Della (Ardella Gilliam, Della Simpson)

Singer, drums, saxophone, organ
Probably 12 June 1923 (probably Newberry, S.C.)–?
S.C. residences: probably Newberry (probably 1923–no later than 1935), unknown location(s) (after 1942–no later than 1949)

At an undetermined date Ardella Gilliam moved to N.Y.C., where she grew up and attended high school. Before becoming a teenager she demonstrated talent as a dancer and singer; in time she became a proficient drummer and saxophonist. In 1950 or 1951 as Della Simpson, she and Frances Kelly formed the Enchanters, a female rhythm-and-blues vocal quartet that in 1952 became the Dell-Tones (sometimes spelled Dell Tones or Dell-tones), named for Simpson, the lead singer. One of its members was Gloria Alleyne, who became known as Gloria Lynne. The Dell-Tones united with the Orioles in 1957 to record as the Kings and Queens. When the Dell-Tones dissolved that year, Simpson toured as a single before retiring from music four years later. She returned to it as Della Griffin in 1973, when she accepted an engagement at a Harlem club, the Blue Book, that lasted until 1987. On all her recordings made after the 1950s, she sings standards and is backed by jazz musicians.

Griffin's birth name, Ardella Gilliam, comes from the 1940 census, for which she was enumerated in N.Y.C. in April; it indicates that she resided there in 1935. Early in her career she performed as Della Simpson, the surname being that of her husband (Jimmy Simpson, who managed the Enchanters and the Dell-Tones), though following her second marriage (to musician Paul Griffin possibly in 1961) she became known as Della Griffin, a name she retained after marrying her third husband, Jimmy Walker. Most documents consulted record 12 June 1925 as her birth date; at least one source identifies it as 6 December 1925, while "Vocalists Wore 'Hot' Duds, Victim Charges" records her age in 1956 as twenty-eight. Writing in 1981, Al Morris confirms that Griffin believed she was born in June. The most credible evidence about when she was born is in the 1940 census, for which her father stated that she was then sixteen. If this information is correct and if she was born in June, then she was born in 1923. All sources consulted identify Newberry as the singer's birthplace, though supporting evidence is lacking. The Gilliam family has not been located in the 1930 census. Aural evidence does not support William Sutherland's claim that Griffin appears on Dakota Staton's CD *Darling Please Save Your Love for Me* (1991, though Sutherland dates it 1994).

Recordings as Leader

Della Griffin Sings (ca. 1974), *I'll Get By* (1990), *Travelin' Light* (1992), *The Very Thought of You* (1996)

Leaders Recorded With

Possibly Frank Humphries (probably early 1950s; as Della Simpson), Enchanters (1951; as Della Simpson), Dell-Tones (1953–1955; as Della Simpson), Kings and Queens (1957; as Della Simpson), Etta Jones (1989), Houston Person (1994)

References

SECONDARY: "Vocalists Wore 'Hot' Duds, Victim Charges," *New York Age Defender,* 23 June 1956, p. 7; Al Morris, "Theatre Briefs," *New York Amsterdam News,* 20 June 1981, p. 33; William Sutherland, "Della Griffin: Jazz and R&B Pioneer (Part 1)," http://content.yudu.com/Library/A1oddy/DellaGriffinJazzandR/resources/index.htm?referrerUrl=http%3A%2F%2Ffree.yudu.com%2Fitem%2Fdetails%2F187676%2FDella-Griffin-Jazz-and-R-B-Pioneer (2006; accessed 21 May 2014); William Sutherland, "Della Griffin: Jazz and R&B Pioneer (Part 2)," http://ezinearticles.com/?Della-Griffin:-Jazz-and-RandB-Pioneer-%28Part-2%29&id=274156 (2006; accessed 21 May 2014); Marv Goldberg, "The Enchanters/Delltones," http://www.uncamarvy.com/Enchanters/enchanters.html (2009; accessed 21 May 2014).

Guitar Slim (James Stephens)

Guitar, piano, organ

Probably 10 March 1915 (probably in or near Pauline, S.C.)–10 February 1991 (Greensboro, N.C.)

S.C. residence: in or near Pauline (probably 1915–no later than ca. 1929)

Stephens played the pump organ by age five; by seven he was adept at piano. Quitting school in the third grade, he worked to help support his family of tenant farmers. He mastered the guitar while traveling with a medicine show as a comedian and pianist, beginning ca. 1929. Thus began a life of itinerancy. In 1953 he settled in Greensboro, N.C., where he worked as a landscaper and performed miscellaneous chores. He played at the 1980 National Folk Festival, Wolf Trap Farm, Va. Late in his life the Piedmont Blues Preservation Society of Greensboro promoted him by arranging international engagements (1986), as well as local ones (such as at the 1987 Carolina Blues Festival). He is buried in Maplewood Cemetery, Greensboro.

The Social Security Death Index, North Carolina Death Collection, 1908–2004, and most other sources record Stephens's birth date as 10 March 1915; David Nelson states that Stephens was born on 4 March 1910.

Recordings as Leader

Greensboro Rounder (1974–1975), "Come On Down to My House" (ca. 1975), "Wildwood Blues Speak" (1977 or 1978), "Your Close Friend" (1977 or 1978), "Bad Luck Blues" (1980), "Betty and Dupree" (1980), "Come On in My Kitchen" (1980), "Did You Get That Letter?" (1980), "Got to Find Me a Woman" (1980), "Hard-Headed Blues" (1980), "I'm Feelin' Lonesome" (1980), "Jazz Boogie" (1980), "Lonesome Home Blues" (1980), "Lookout Blues" (1980), "Lovin' Blues" (1980), "Lula's Back in Town" (1980), "Outdoor Weather Blues" (1980), "Walkin' Boogie" (1980), "What a Friend We Have in Jesus" (1980), "Won't You Spread Some Flowers on My Grave" (1980)

References

SECONDARY: Bruce Bastin, *Red River Blues: The Blues Tradition in the Southeast* (Urbana: University of Illinois Press, 1986), 194, 289 (Bastin refers to Stephens as Stephenson); Tom Steadman, "Greensboro Blues Veteran Guitar Slim Dies at Age 75," *Greensboro (N.C.) News and Record,* 11 February 1991, sec. B, p. 3 (obituary); Tom Steadman, "Blues Society Gambles on Holmes Brothers," *Greensboro (N.C.) News and Record,* 15 February 1991, weekend sec., p. 4; David Nelson, "James 'Guitar Slim' Stephens," *Living Blues* 97 (May–June 1991): 44 (obituary); "James 'Guitar Slim' Stephens," in *Music Makers: Portraits and Songs from the Roots of America,* ed. Timothy Duffy (Athens, Ga.: Hill Street Press, 2002), 151.

Hall, Jim (James Allen)

Drums, percussion, guitar

10 February 1939 (Charleston, W.Va.)–

S.C. residence: Columbia (1979–)

Hall played the ukulele by around age five, though within a few years he switched to guitar. Beginning ca. 1957 he played in local combos and bands, including one led by Ned Guthrie that featured drummer Butch Miles. After serving in the army (1958–1960), Hall enrolled at West Virginia Institute of Technology, where he began playing drums. For two years following his 1965 graduation, he taught music at Dunbar (W.Va.) High School. He received a master's degree from North Texas State University in 1970 and took additional courses there the next year. He taught music at Southwest Texas State University from 1971 until 1978 but took a leave of absence to teach as an adjunct at North Texas

State in 1978 and 1979. Then he accepted a teaching position at the University of South Carolina, from which he retired in 2001. In Columbia he has been active on the local jazz scene, especially as regular drummer in groups led by Dick Goodwin, with whom he had performed in Tex. He played guitar with the Jazz Guitar Summit (2009–2011).

Leaders Recorded With

North Texas State University One o'Clock Lab Band (1970–1971), Dick Goodwin (1978, 1980, 2003, 2006), Roger Pemberton (1986), Mary Ann Hurst (2007), Pete Neighbour (2009)

Hamilton, Jimmy (James)

Clarinet, saxophone, piano, arranger

Possibly 25 May 1917, though possibly ca. 1911 (Dillon, S.C.)–20 September 1994 (Saint Croix, Virgin Islands)

S.C. residence: Dillon (probably 1917, but possibly ca. 1911–possibly ca. 1922)

Hamilton's father was an amateur musician. Because of the presence of musical instruments in his house in Philadelphia, where the family moved from S.C., young Hamilton began experimenting with them, initially with a baritone horn. In time he joined the band of Frankie Fairfax as a trumpeter but during this tenure switched to clarinet, on which he was influenced by Benny Goodman. After moving to N.Y.C. he played with Teddy Wilson, Benny Carter, and other leaders. When he was with Dave Martin, Duke Ellington invited him to join his band to replace Chauncey Haughton, who had succeeded Barney Bigard as clarinetist. Though reluctant to accept because the band traveled so much and because he would be required to play tenor saxophone in addition to clarinet, Hamilton accepted the offer in 1943 and remained with Ellington for a quarter century. His notable recordings with Ellington include "Air-Conditioned Jungle" (1947) and *Far East Suite* (1966). After leaving Ellington in 1968 (his departure was noted in the jazz press), Hamilton moved, in time, to the Virgin Islands, though he occasionally returned to the United States to record and play at festivals. During much of the 1970s he and his group, including his pianist wife, Vivian, performed Fridays at the Holger Danske Hotel, Christiansted, Saint Croix; their music was broadcast live on radio station WSTX. (In 1945 Hamilton's wife recorded as Vivian Smith with Pigmeat Markham for Blue Note Records.) Gary Giddins states that Hamilton "was Artie Shaw's rival for the loveliest clarinet sound in big band music" (255). Hamilton is buried in the Saint Croix Botanical Gardens.

Jimmy Hamilton (left), with Harry Carney, Aquarium Club, N.Y.C., ca. November 1946; reproduced from the William P. Gottlieb Collection, Library of Congress, Music Division

Hamilton's death date and 1917 birth date come from the Social Security Death Index. The 1920 census documents a black youth in Dillon named James W. Hamilton. Estimated age eight when enumerated on 24 February, he was born in S.C. to William and Lula Hamilton. If he became the musician Jimmy Hamilton, as seems likely, then his accepted birth year, 1917, is incorrect.

Compositions

"Air-Conditioned Jungle," "Big Boy Blues," "Big Shoe," "Blues for Christmas," "Blues for Clarinet" (also titled "Blues for Clarinets"), "Blues in My Music Room," "Clarinet Melodrama," "Duet," "Fade Up," "Get Ready," "Hoppin John," "Madam Butterfly," "Meet the Frog," "Monologue" (also titled "Pretty and the Wolf"), "Mr. E-Z," "Night Mist Blue," "Nix It, Mix It," "Nodido," "Prelude to a Mood," "Salute to Charlie Parker," "Slapstick," "Theme for Trambeam," "Three J's Blues," "Tootie for Cootie," "Ultra Blue" (also titled "Ultra Violet"), "Waltz a Minute"

Recordings as Leader

"Blues for Clarinets" (1945), "Blues in My Music Room" (1945), "Old Uncle Bud" (1945), "Slapstick" (1945), "Big Fifty" (1953), "Love Comes but Once" (1953), "Rockaway Special" (1953), "The Tattooed Bride" (1953), *Accent on Clarinet* (1954; also titled

Jimmy Hamilton and His Orchestra, Jimmy Hamilton and the New York Jazz Quintet, and *Sweet but Hot*), *Clarinet in Hi Fi* (ca. 1954; also titled *Jimmy Hamilton and His Orchestra* and *Jimmy Hamilton and the New York Jazz Quintet*), *Swing Low, Sweet Clarinet* (1960), *Can't Help Swingin'* (1961), *It's about Time* (1961), *Rediscovered at the Buccaneer* (1985)

Leaders Recorded With

Jimmy Mundy (1939), Billie Holiday (1940–1942, 1952), Teddy Wilson (1940–1941), Chick Bullock (1941), Pete Brown (1942), Duke Ellington (1943–1968, possibly 1969), Sonny Greer (1944), Dwight "Gatemouth" Moore (1945), Esquire All-American Award Winners (1946), Esquire All Stars (1946), Al Hibbler (1947, 1951), Tyree Glenn (1949), Johnny Hodges (1950, 1954–1961, 1964, 1966–1967), Chubby Kemp (1950), Tony Pappa (1952), Harry Carney (1954), Oscar Pettiford (1954), Lucky Thompson (1954), Ben Webster (1954), Ralph Burns (1955), Buck Clayton (1956), Jazz Festival All Stars (1956), Mercer Ellington (1958–1959), Billy Strayhorn (1958), Swingville All Stars (1961), Lawrence Brown (1965), Ella Fitzgerald (1966), Earl Hines (1966), Manassas Jazz Festival (1968, 1973, 1983), Bull Run Blues Blowers (1972–1973), Clarinet Summit (ca. 1983, 1987), Any Ol' Time Jazz Band (1984), Clark Terry (1988)

Film

Boogie-Woogie Dream (1941)

Awards

Esquire's All American Hot Jazz Award (1946); winner in the *Down Beat* critics' and readers' polls (1969)

References

PRIMARY: Stanley Dance, *The World of Duke Ellington* (New York: Scribner's, 1970), 140–44 (within Dance's narrative, Hamilton details aspects of his career).

SECONDARY: "Jimmy Hamilton Quits Duke after 26 Years," *Down Beat* 35 (22 August 1968): 13; Edward Kennedy Ellington, *Music Is My Mistress* (Garden City, N.Y.: Doubleday, 1973), 220–21; Gary Giddins, *Rhythm-a-ning: Jazz Tradition and Innovation in the '80s* (New York: Oxford University Press, 1985), 119–22, 255; James Lincoln Collier, *Duke Ellington* (New York: Oxford University Press, 1987), passim; *The Duke Ellington Reader,* ed. Mark Tucker (New York: Oxford University Press, 1993), passim; Scott Yanow, *Bebop* (San Francisco: Miller Freeman, 2000), 200–1; Steve Voce, "Scratching the Surface . . . ," *Jazz Journal* 56 (November 2003), 12–13.

Hamilton, Lonnie, III

Saxophone
14 November 1927 (Charleston, S.C.)–?
S.C. residences: Charleston (1927–1947, 1955–), Orangeburg (1947–1951), Union (1953–1955)

Though not a ward of Jenkins Orphanage, Hamilton played in its bands in the mid-1940s. Following his 1951 graduation from what is now South Carolina State University, he served in the army for two years. He taught in Union, S.C. (1953–1955), before becoming an educator in Charleston; he remained such until retiring in 1987, serving the last twelve years as director of adult and community education. He received a master's degree from VanderCook College of Music in Chicago (1965) and was an elected member of the Charleston County Council (1970–1994). In 2005 he established a foundation that awards grants to help defray the college costs of high school graduates. A professional musician for most of his adult life, he leads his own groups and performs as sideman, primarily in the Charleston area.

Hamilton's papers are in the Avery Research Center for African American History and Culture, Charleston.

Composition

"Ugly Ways Blues"

Leader Recorded With

Charleston Jazz Initiative Legends Band (2010)

Film

Rich in Love (1992)

References

SECONDARY: John Chilton, *A Jazz Nursery: The Story of the Jenkins' Orphanage Bands of Charleston, South Carolina* (London: Bloomsbury Book Shop, 1980), 48–49, 55 (comments by Hamilton); Adam Ferrell, "Charleston Jazz History Enlivened," *Charleston (S.C.) Post and Courier,* 31 March 2003, sec. B, pp. 1, 5; Jack McCray, *Charleston Jazz* (Charleston, S.C.: Arcadia Publishing, 2007), 81, 108; Asmith [*sic*], "Lonnie Hamilton, III: A Lowcountry Icon," http://www.patriotspoint.org/news_events/lonnie-hamilton-iii-a-lowcountry-icon/ (19 February 2013; accessed 21 May 2014) (comments by Hamilton).

Hardison, Alex

Trumpet
Ca. 1905 (Ga.)-?
S.C. residence: Charleston (by 1920–at least into early 1930s)

A ward of Jenkins Orphanage, Hardison played in its bands in the late 1920s and early 1930s.

Hardison was probably the brother of trombonist Leroy Hardison. His age was estimated as fourteen when the youth was enumerated for the census at the orphanage on 9 January 1920; this document identifies Ga. as his birthplace. His surname is sometimes spelled Hardeson.

Hardison, Leroy

Trombone
Ca. 1907 or 6 February 1910 (Ga.)-before 1980
S.C. residence: Charleston (by 1920–at least into early 1930s)

A ward of Jenkins Orphanage, Hardison played in its bands in the early 1930s; upon being released from the institution on the last day of 1930, he became a band instructor, probably at the orphanage. During much of the 1930s he played with the Carolina Cotton Pickers, a group he managed. He reportedly attended Florida Normal College.

Hardison was probably the brother of trumpeter Alex Hardison. His age was estimated as twelve when the youth was enumerated for the census at the orphanage on 9 January 1920; this document identifies Ga. as his birthplace. Bruce Bastin records the birth date 6 February 1910. John Chilton indicates that Hardison had died by the time Chilton completed his manuscript. Hardison's surname is sometimes spelled Hardeson.

Leaders Recorded With

Carolina Cotton Pickers (1936–1937), Cat Anderson (1947)

References

SECONDARY: Stanley Dance, *The World of Earl Hines* (New York: Scribner's, 1977), 262; John Chilton, *A Jazz Nursery: The Story of the Jenkins' Orphanage Bands of Charleston, South Carolina* (London: Bloomsbury Book Shop, 1980), 41, 55; Bruce Bastin, "A Note on the Carolina Cotton Pickers," *Storyville* 95 (June–July 1981): 177–82.

Hardy, Alonzo

Cornet, trumpet
Mid-to-late 1880s (Charleston, S.C.)-August 1970 (Philadelphia, Pa.)
S.C. residences: Charleston (mid-to-late 1880s–no later than 1910), Columbia (by 1910–no later than 1930, by 1940–ca. 1956)

A ward of Jenkins Orphanage beginning in 1895, Hardy became its musical director. He played in its band at the 1901 Pan-American Exposition in Buffalo, N.Y. According to Amos M. White, sometime later Scott Joplin told Hardy that if the orphanage band Hardy was leading at Young's Million Dollar Pier in Atlantic City, N.J., could perform the composer's rags well, Hardy could have them, presumably to play in subsequent performances. It did. Hardy reportedly attended college in S.C., though records at what is now South Carolina State University do not include his name. By 1910 he lived in Columbia, where he worked as an undertaker and owned a movie theater. By 1930 he resided in N.Y.C., where he was involved with the Elks Club, presumably in some capacity with its band. At least in 1932, as Professor Alonzo Hardy he led the band of the Manhattan Temple, number 93. He returned to Columbia by 1940 and moved to Thomasville, Ga., ca. 1956, before locating to Philadelphia.

Hardy was the father of saxophonist Leroy Pinckney Hardy. Hardy's age was estimated as twenty-five when the musician was enumerated for the census in Columbia on 18 April 1910; he then worked as an embalmer. His 1917 draft registration card indicates that he, a resident of Columbia, "can't say" his date of birth but records his birth year as 1886. It also notes that he has a wife and child; though not named, they were Estelle Pinckney Hardy and Leroy Pinckney Hardy. Alonzo and Estelle were ultimately divorced. He was estimated as forty-two when enumerated for the census in N.Y.C. on 6 April 1930; he was then an undertaker living as a roomer with Margie Hardy, presumably his wife, age twenty-five. He was estimated as forty-five when enumerated in Columbia on 8 April 1940; a widower, he then worked as an undertaker. John Chilton believes that Hardy was born in 1889. Jeffrey P. Green speculates that Hardy accompanied the orphanage band to London in 1914. If Amos M. White states correctly that Hardy spoke with Scott Joplin in N.J., the meeting occurred between 1909, when one of the newest of the rags Joplin gave Hardy was published (Henry Lodge's "Temptation Rag"), and 1913, the last year White played with the orphanage band. Chilton states that Eugene Mikell was musical director of the band that played in Atlantic City. If musical director and band leader were separate positions, White and Chilton probably correctly identify the men's roles with the band. Chilton states that Hardy attended the Seneca (S.C.) Institute and what is now South Carolina State University.

References

SECONDARY: "Music News," *New York Amsterdam News*, 4 May 1932, p. 9; "Thousands Attend Funeral Hon. Thos. H. Pinckney," *Columbia (S.C.) Palmetto Leader*, 4 January 1936, p. 1; Amos M. White, interview by William Russell, 23 August 1958, four reels of tape and a typed summary, Hogan Jazz Archive, Tulane University, New Orleans, p. 19 of summary (also available at http://musicrising.tulane.edu/uploads/transcripts/a.%20white%2008-23-1958.pdf [accessed 21 May 2014]); John Chilton, *A Jazz Nursery: The Story of the Jenkins' Orphanage Bands of Charleston, South Carolina* (London: Bloomsbury Book Shop, 1980), 13, 33, 55; Jeffrey P. Green, *Edmund Thornton Jenkins: The Life and Times of an American Black Composer, 1894–1926* (Westport, Conn.: Greenwood, 1982), 23, 38.

Hardy, Leroy Pinckney

Saxophone

September of 1912, or possibly of 1911 (Columbia, S.C.)–25 December 1989 (Washington, D.C.)

S.C. residence: Columbia (1911 or 1912–no later than 1929, 1936–1959)

Hardy performed a saxophone solo on "Somebody's Knocking at Your Door" at the 1928 commencement exercises at Hampton Normal and Agricultural Institute. Soon thereafter he lived in N.Y.C., where he attended New York University–Washington Square College during the 1930 spring semester. With N.Y.C. as his home base, he toured with bands, including in Europe. All his recordings date from 1931, when he played at four sessions led by Blanche Calloway. Probably the first all-male band led by a woman, it included such musicians as Cozy Cole, Clyde Hart, and Ben Webster. Following the 1936 death of his grandfather Thomas Hamilton Pinckney, also a musician, Hardy returned to Columbia to help operate the family funeral home.

Leroy Hardy (standing saxophonist), with a navy band; permission of Leroy Hardy, Jr.

During World War II he served as a musician in the navy, attaining the rank of Musician, First Class. He stopped playing the saxophone professionally by 1948. He is buried in plot 23, 1223, Quantico National Cemetery, Quantico, Va., along with his wife, Pearle Victoria Hardy.

Hardy was the son of musician Alonzo Hardy. The author of "Thousands Attend Funeral Hon. Thos. H. Pinckney" states that Hardy "is a graduate of Hampton Institute, Va."; college records show that he was enrolled only for the 1926–1927 school year and do not indicate that he received a degree. These records identify Columbia as his home, his birth date (11 September 1911), and his parents. His mother was Estelle, daughter of Thomas Hamilton Pinckney. His age was estimated as fifteen when he was enumerated for the census in N.Y.C. on 11 April 1930. Because he recorded the following year, this age seems too young. The passenger list for the *Rex,* which transported him from Villefranche to N.Y.C. in October 1933, notes that he was born in 1911 on the 22nd of an unspecified month. His grave marker records a birth date of 22 September 1912, which his son, Leroy Pinckney Hardy, Jr., confirms.

Leader Recorded With

Blanche Calloway (1931)

References

SECONDARY: "Mary E. Smith Wins Geo. W. Blount Prize," *New York Age,* 9 June 1928, p. 2; "Thousands Attend Funeral Hon. Thos. H. Pinckney," *Columbia (S.C.) Palmetto Leader,* 4 January 1936, p. 1.

Harper, (William) Emerson ("Geechie")

Saxophone, clarinet, oboe

Possibly 28 February of 1897 or 1898 (Columbia, S.C.)–?

S.C. residences: Columbia (possibly 1897 or 1898–ca. 1902, at least April 1910), Charleston (ca. 1902–no later than early 1910, after April 1910–no later than 1918)

Apparently a ward of Jenkins Orphanage beginning ca. 1902, Harper played with its band in England in 1914 and taught music at the institution. By 1918 in N.Y.C., he was with Leroy Smith's Society Orchestra, with which he remained for seventeen years. Clarinetist Garvin Bushell considered him "about the best soloist Leroy had." Harper also performed with other bands and was one of the first blacks to play in a N.Y.C. radio orchestra. He was with Fletcher Henderson during the mid-1940s. He gave composition lessons to Margaret Bonds, noted pianist, composer, and arranger; he freelanced in N.Y.C. during the 1950s and 1960s.

The musician's age was estimated as eleven and birthplace as S.C. when Harper was enumerated for the census in Columbia on 19 April 1910. The passenger list of the *St. Louis,* which transported the orphanage band from Liverpool to N.Y.C. in September 1914, specifies a birth date of 28 February 1897 and birthplace as Columbia. His 1918 draft registration card indicates that he was born on 28 February 1898. His age was estimated as thirty-seven and his birthplace as S.C. when he was enumerated for the census in N.Y.C. on 15 April 1930; his age was estimated as fifty-three and his birthplace as Kans. when enumerated in N.Y.C. on 6 April 1940. He and his wife served as surrogate parents to the young Langston Hughes; together in 1947, Harper and Hughes bought a home in Harlem on E. 127th St., where Hughes created many of his literary productions. To the Harpers, Hughes dedicated *The Big Sea* (1940), the first volume of his autobiography. See Arnold Rampersad, *The Life of Langston Hughes* (New York: Oxford University Press, 1986, 1988), two vols., passim.

Composition

"I'm Marching Down Freedom Road" (also titled "Freedom Road")

Leaders Recorded With

Leroy Smith (1921, 1924, 1928), possibly Clara Smith (1929), Edith Wilson (1929), Fletcher Henderson (1944–1945)

References

PRIMARY: Emerson Harper, as told to Bertrand Demeusy, "Le Roy Smith and His Band," *Jazz Monthly* 170 (April 1969): 5–7.

SECONDARY: "New Year Rides in on Avalanche of Gay Parties," *New York Amsterdam News,* 9 January 1943, p. 8; John Chilton, *A Jazz Nursery: The Story of the Jenkins' Orphanage Bands of Charleston, South Carolina* (London: Bloomsbury Book Shop, 1980), 17, 55; Howard Rye, "Visiting Fireboys: The Jenkins' Orphanage Bands in Britain," *Storyville* 130 (1987): 137–43; Garvin Bushell, as told to Mark Tucker, *Jazz from the Beginning* (Ann Arbor: University of Michigan Press, 1988), 17; Helen Walker-Hill, *From Spirituals to Symphonies: African-American Women Composers and Their Music* (Westport, Conn.: Greenwood, 2002), 152.

Harrington, Hamtree (James Carl)

Singer, monologist, ukulele, dancer

11 January of either 1891 or 1894 (Columbia, S.C.)–probably 1954

S.C. residence: Columbia (1891 or 1894–no later than 1908)

Harrington joined a carnival as a teenager. In the 1910s he toured in vaudeville with Maude Mills, whom he wed in 1916. When their marriage dissolved five years later, he teamed with Cora Green for the remainder of the decade. They performed in *Dixie to Broadway* (1924–1925), starring Florence Mills, his former sister-in-law; when Mills became ill, Harrington and Green replaced her in the London production of *Blackbirds of 1927;* Harrington also appeared in *Blackbirds of 1939*. He made all his recordings in the 1920s. He worked as a single during the 1930s, performing in revues with such singers as Alberta Hunter, Clara Smith, and Ethel Waters, and acting in several movies, including ones featuring Nina Mae McKinney and Waters. He helped found the Negro Actors' Guild of America. A serious painter and photographer who operated a N.Y.C. photography studio in the 1930s and 1940s, Harrington remained an entertainer at least until 1952.

The birthplace and 1891 birth date come from Harrington's 1942 draft registration card, which records the middle name Hamtree; the 1894 birth date is from the passenger list of the *Homeric,* on which the entertainer sailed from Southampton, England, to N.Y.C. in October 1927 as James Carl Harrington. The latter document identifies his birthplace as Columbia, D.C. [*sic*]. His age was estimated as thirty-five when he was enumerated for the census in N.Y.C. on 9 April 1930. Though his death year is usually identified as 1956, Alvin Chick Webb, writing in 1954, mentions the "recent deaths of Garland Wilson and Hamtree Harrington."

Recordings as Leader

"I'm Gone, Dat's All" (1923; unissued), "Voodoo" (1923; unissued), "Waitin' for the Evenin' Mail" (1923; unissued), "Cash on Delivery" (1924), "Nobody Ever Let Me in on Nothin'" (1924), "Fly Round, Young Ladies, Fly Round" (1925), "If I Can't Come In, Don't Let Nobody Come Out" (1925; with Cora Green), "Last Go Round" (1925), "Murder in the First Degree" (1925), "Sweet Georgia Brown" (1925), "You're Talking to the Wrong Man Now" (1925)

Leader Recorded With

Dixie Jubilee Singers (1924)

Films

Starland Revue, No. 11 (1922), *Gayety* (1929), *His Woman* (1931; also titled *Blind Cargo*), *Mills Blue Rhythm Band* (1933), *Rufus Jones for President* (1933), *Bubbling Over* (1934), *The Devil's Daughter* (1939), *Keep Punching* (1939)

References

PRIMARY: Hamtree Harrington, "'Canned Music' Rouses Wrath of Jobless Musicians and Actors," *New York Amsterdam News,* 19 December 1936, p. 18.

SECONDARY: "Ever Hear of 'Syncopating Shoes'? Well, Hear Them Now," *Chicago Defender,* 15 July 1922, p. 6 (national edition) (comments by Harrington); Bob Slater, "Theatrical Jottings," *New York Age,* 7 July 1923, p. 6; "James C. Harrington," *New York Amsterdam News,* 6 March 1929, p. 6; "Admitted to the Museum," *New York Amsterdam News,* 18 September 1929, p. 9; Roi Ottley, "This Hectic Harlem," *New York Amsterdam News,* 24 January 1934, p. 9; "Great Comedian Calls It Quits—Photographer Now," *Pittsburgh Courier,* 4 June 1938, p. 13; Alvin Chick Webb, "Footlights and Sidelights," *New York Amsterdam News,* 12 June 1954, p. 22; Bill Egan, "Harrington, James Carl 'Hamtree,'" in *Encyclopedia of the Harlem Renaissance,* ed. Cary D. Wintz and Paul Finkelman (New York: Routledge, 2004), 1: 536–38; Frank Cullen, *Vaudeville Old and New: An Encyclopedia of Variety Performers in America* (New York: Routledge, 2007), 1: 488–89.

Harris, (Willie) Ralph

Trombone

Ca. 1924 (S.C.)–?

S.C. residence: Charleston (1930s–at least into early 1940s)

A ward of Jenkins Orphanage, Harris played in its bands in the 1930s and early 1940s.

The musician's age was estimated as sixteen when Harris was enumerated for the census at the orphanage on 21 May 1940; this document records his name as Willie R. Harris and S.C. as his birthplace. Chilton provides the name Ralph and indicates that the surname might be Harrison.

Reference

SECONDARY: John Chilton, *A Jazz Nursery: The Story of the Jenkins' Orphanage Bands of Charleston, South Carolina* (London: Bloomsbury Book Shop, 1980), 55.

Harvey, Aaron

Saxophone, clarinet

Possibly 19 May 1919 (Charleston, S.C.)-13 September 1988 (Charleston, S.C.)

S.C. residences: Charleston (possibly 1919-probably 1942, with absences; 1946-early-to-mid-1950s, with absences; by mid-1950s-1988); Orangeburg (early-to-mid-1950s)

Inspired by the Jenkins Orphanage bands, Harvey left high school in the eleventh grade to become a musician. Initially he played with the Carolina Stompers; then, with the Carolina Cotton Pickers. After serving in the army (1942–1946), he toured with Tiny Bradshaw. Giving up playing in 1948, he opened a record store in Charleston but soon resumed his schooling at what is now South Carolina State University; in time he received a law degree from LaSalle Extension University and became a magistrate in Charleston, where he also served as bandmaster at Burke High School. He is buried in the Emmanuel A.M.E. Church Cemetery, Charleston.

When enumerated for the census on 2 January 1920, Harvey was estimated as age two; on 4 April 1930, as ten; on 10 April 1940 (though he was absent when enumerated), as nineteen. All these censuses were conducted in Charleston. The birth date of 19 May 1919 is recorded in *The Official Roster of South Carolina Servicemen and Servicewomen in World War II, 1941–46* (N.p.: State Budget and Control Board, n.d.), 3: 1849. Though his obituary states that Harvey received undergraduate and graduate degrees from the University of South Carolina, the school has no record of his having attended.

Leader Recorded With

Possibly Carolina Cotton Pickers (1936–1937)

References

SECONDARY: Barbara S. Williams, "Negro Attorney Nominated for Charleston Magistrate," *Charleston (S.C.) News and Courier*, 25 April 1969, sec. A, pp. 1–2; John P. Algar, "Helping People Is Reward for Magistrate Harvey," *Charleston (S.C.) News and Courier*, 26 April 1970, sec. B, p. 10; Robert Small, "Judge Harvey: He Traded the Horn for a Gavel," *Charleston (S.C.) News and Courier*, 9 December 1979, sec. F, p. 3; Bruce Bastin, "A Note on the Carolina Cotton Pickers," *Storyville* 95 (June–July 1981): 177–82; "Former Charleston Magistrate Aaron Harvey Dies," *Charleston (S.C.) News and Courier*, 16 September 1988, sec. A, p. 7 (obituary).

Haynes, John L., Jr.

Bass

29 April 1918 (Clifton Forge, Va.)-9 June 2015 (Camden, S.C.)

S.C. residence: Camden (1950-2015)

Haynes played ukulele before switching to guitar. After moving from Clifton Forge to Waynesboro, Va., to accept a position with DuPont in 1939, he joined Joe Gleese's Melodiers, a local band, as guitarist. Following service in the navy (1943–1945), he rejoined the group, but as bassist. Thereafter he played only bass. When DuPont established a plant in Camden, Haynes, a maintenance supervisor, was transferred to it. He was active musically during his decades in S.C., playing with bands and combos, leading his own group, and performing with the Carolina Dixieland Jazz Society.

Leaders Recorded With

Larry Conger (1965–1966, 1969), Don Ewell (1965), Art Hodes (1965), Ralph Sutton (1966), Jimmy Farr (1968), Maxine Sullivan (1978, 1982), Banu Gibson (1982), Johnny Mince (1982), Carrie Smith (1982)

Reference

SECONDARY: "John L. Haynes Jr.," *Columbia (S.C.) State*, 11 June 2015, sec. C, p. 4 (obituary).

John Haynes, Strawberry Sky Recording Studio, Columbia, S.C., 27 August 1991; permission of Constance J. Haynes

Haywood, Joe Dean

Singer, drums

12 June 1939 (Cowpens, S.C.)–14 November 1996 (Spartanburg, S.C.)

S.C. residences: Cowpens (1939–mid-1940s), Spartanburg (mid-1940s–ca. 1964, 1988–1996)

As a youth Haywood sang in the J. W. Sanders Gospel Chorus at Island Creek Baptist Church, Cowpens, of which he was a member. Backed by the Fabulous Dobbs, he performed in a local talent contest in 1957; two years later he sang with the Dynamic Twisters. After leaving S.C. for N.Y.C. ca. 1964, Haywood had a brief professional singing career highlighted by his being the first person to record "Warm and Tender Love" (a song he might have written, though Bobby Robinson receives composer credit), which Percy Sledge covered with great success. Heywood sang it at the Apollo Theater in 1965. Though he returned to Spartanburg occasionally, he settled there permanently in 1988. There he drove taxis. His recording of "Strong Feeling" is on the sound track of *What Doesn't Kill You* (2008). Haywood is buried in an unmarked grave in the Haywood family plot in the Island Creek Baptist Church Cemetery.

Compositions

"First Breath of Spring," "Hand in Hand," "Hurry Hurry Hurry," "I'll Never Let You Go," "Let Me Whisper in Your Ear," "Let's Make It," "Sadie Mae," "Say You Will," possibly "Warm and Tender Love"

Recordings as Leader

"I Would If I Could" (1965), "Talk to Me Baby (Put Some Sugar in My Ear)" (1965), "Warm and Tender Love" (1965), "When You Look in the Mirror (You're Looking at the One I Love)" (1965), "I Love You, Yes I Do" (1965 or 1966), "It Takes the Dark to Make You See the Light" (1965 or 1966), "Let's Walk Together" (1965 or 1966), "Hand in Hand" (1967), "I Wanna Love You" (1967), "Let's Make It" (1967), "(Play Me) a Cornbread Song" (1967), "Sadie Mae" (1967), "Say You Will" (1967), "I Cross My Heart" (1967 or 1968), "I'm Walkin'" (1967 or 1968), "In Your Heart You Know I Love You" (1967 or 1968), "Strong Feeling" (1967 or 1968), "Debt of Love" (1968), "Ghost of a Love" (1968)

References

SECONDARY: Apollo Theater advertisement, *New York Amsterdam News,* 26 June 1965, p. 22; "Joe Dean Haywood," *Spartanburg (S.C.) Herald-Journal,* 16 November 1996, sec. B, p. 6 (obituary); Linda Conley, "Musician's Lost Story: Upstate Man Wrote Multiple Songs under Several Labels," www.goupstate.com/article/20120826/ARTICLES/208271004/1112 (2012; accessed 21 May 2014); Red Kelly, "Case One: Joe Haywood," http://souldetective.blogspot.com/2006/04/case-one-joe-haywood.html (2012; accessed 21 May 2014); Red Kelly, "The Update Project: Case One—Joe Haywood," http://souldetective.blogspot.com/2012/06/update-project-case-one-joe-haywood.html (2012; accessed 21 May 2014); Sir Shambling [John Ridley], "Joe Haywood," http://www.sirshambling.com/artists_2012/H/joe_haywood/index.php (2012; accessed 21 May 2014).

Helbing, Stockton Thomas

Drums, percussion

29 August 1980 (Saint Louis, Mo.)–

S.C. residence: Florence (1985–1998, 2004–2006)

Helbing, who began playing drums in the sixth grade, performed with the S.C. All-State Jazz Band in 1996 and 1997 while a student at West Florence High School, class of 1998. As a scholarship student at the University of North Texas, he studied with Ed Soph; he received a bachelor's degree from this institution in 2003. After touring with Maynard Ferguson as drummer and musical director (2002–2006), Helbing settled in Dallas, where he operates Armored Records. He is Artist in Residence at Southwestern Baptist Theological Seminary in Fort Worth, Jazz Artist in Residence at Oklahoma State University, and Music Director at Grace Fellowship Church in Paradise, Tex. He became the drummer for the band of Doc Severinsen in 2012.

Compositions

"As the Battle Wages On," "Battlestations and Escape Plans," "Brotha B," "A Certain Amount of Indiscretions," "Cool Man Jack," "Crazy Aquarius," "The Day After," "Early Departure," "For Nothing Is Secret," "Hardlining," "Headshot," "Kelsier," "Knows One to Take One," "Lineage," "The Morning Of," "The Night Before," "Oddball," "Orbital," "Overtime Loss," "Plans and Recreations," "Pwned!," "Shifty," "Suppose You Do," "Tel'aran'rhiod," "Transfer Notice," "Trask," "Turnpike," "Upright and Locked," "A Wintery Mix"

Stockton Helbing; photograph by Vladimir Kolopic, permission of Stockton Helbing

Recordings as Leader

Lodestar (2004), *For Nothing Is Secret* (2006), *Battlestations and Escape Plans* (2010–2011), *Crazy Aquarius* (2011), *Handprints* (2012)

Leaders Recorded With

Paul Tynan (2001, 2008), Standards Trio (2002), University of North Texas One o'Clock Lab Band (2002–2003), Noel Johnston (2003), Maynard Ferguson (2005–2006), Brian Mulholland (2005), Clay Ross (2005), Tyler Summers (2005, 2010), Ken Edwards (2006), Chip McNeill (2007), Andrea Smith (2007–2008), Bryan English (ca. 2007), Kevin Brunkhorst and Ryan Davidson (2008), Dan Cavanagh (2008), Neil Shah (2008), Darden Purcell (2009), YT little d (2009), Kris Berg (2010–2011, 2013), Sidney Thompson (2010), Madeline Enna (2011–2012), Anthony Plant (ca. 2011), Carry On (2012), Imperial Brass (2012), Johnny Beckett (2013), Susan Hanlon (2013)

Website

http://www.stocktonhelbing.com/ (accessed 21 May 2014)

References

PRIMARY: "Take Five with Stockton Helbing," http://www.allaboutjazz.com/php/article.php?id=41103#.UNxb_azjOtg (2011; accessed 21 May 2014); Benjamin Hawkins, "Jazz Drummer Trains Musical 'Chameleons,'" http://www.bpnews.net/printerfriendly.asp?Idaho=37686 (2012; accessed 21 May 2014) (substantial comments by Helbing).

Helms, Johnny (John N.)

Trumpet

10 February 1935 (Columbia, S.C.)-27 March 2015 (Columbia, S.C.)

S.C. residence: Columbia (1935-1954, 1955-1958, 1960-2015)

Helms was playing regularly in Columbia clubs and other local venues by age thirteen; by sixteen he led a group that performed as often as six nights a week. After enrolling at the University of South Carolina, he transferred to the University of Miami, where he played in the band as well as in local clubs and in nearby towns with the likes of Cannonball Adderley. After a year at Miami he returned to Columbia to teach but also to attend the University of South Carolina, from which he was graduated in 1973. He spent a year or two in Paterson, N.J., playing in the greater N.Y.C. area. Upon returning to Columbia in 1960 he remained there, though he occasionally played elsewhere, as at the JVC Jazz Festival in N.Y.C. and aboard the jazz cruise ship *Norway*. He was a major force behind Jazz on Main (also known as Main Street Jazz), an annual festival held in Columbia (1987–1997). Though tapes exist of Helms's playing, none of his music has been released commercially. His body was donated to the University of South Carolina School of Medicine.

References

PRIMARY: Benjamin Franklin V, *Jazz and Blues Musicians of South Carolina: Interviews with Jabbo, Dizzy, Drink, and*

Others (Columbia: University of South Carolina Press, 2008), 104–19.

SECONDARY: "John N. 'Johnny' Helms," *Columbia (S.C.) State*, 31 March 2015, sec. C, p. 3 (obituary).

Henderson, Earl

Banjo, guitar, ukulele

Ca. 1905 (probably Walterboro, S.C.)-?

S.C. residences: Walterboro (probably ca. 1905-possibly early 1920s), Charleston (possibly early 1920s-1924, ca. 1927-1928, 1934-ca. 1935, 1936-1942, 1942-1944, 1946-at least until 1980, and presumably until death)

Henderson began his musical career in 1926 with the Plantation Five; two years later he joined the band of Fess Mitchell, with which he remained into 1934. After reportedly attending a music school in Tyrone, Pa., he toured with the Carolina Cotton Pickers (1935–1936). Back in Charleston he established a group that performed locally in the late 1930s. During the period 1940–1944 he played with the Nighthawks, a Charleston band. After retiring from professional playing in the early 1950s, he taught music part-time.

References

SECONDARY: Robert Small, "Musician Gets Back to Basics," *Charleston (S.C.) News and Courier*, 13 April 1980, sec. E, p. 14 (comments by Henderson); Bruce Bastin, "A Note on the Carolina Cotton Pickers," *Storyville* 95 (June–July 1981): 177–82.

Henderson, James

S.C. residence: Charleston (at least early 1930s)

Apparently a ward of Jenkins Orphanage, Henderson played in its bands in the early 1930s, though his instrument is not known.

Heyward, (Edwin) Dubose

Lyricist, librettist

31 August 1885 (Charleston, S.C.)-16 June 1940 (Tryon, N.C.)

S.C. residence: Charleston (1885-1940, with absences)

From an established though not wealthy family (an ancestor, Thomas Heyward, Jr., signed the Declaration of Independence), Heyward dropped out of high school at age fourteen. He worked in insurance before devoting himself to literature; he and a few others formed the Poetry Society of South Carolina in 1920. "In some of his poems," Hollis Alpert writes, Heyward "had attempted to suggest rhythms similar to those of jazz and its form known as blues" (16); Alpert also notes that George Gershwin was smitten by Heyward's "apparent musical sensitivity" in the novel *Porgy* (45). Heyward and his wife, Dorothy, re-wrote the novel as a play, also titled *Porgy*, that was produced on Broadway (1927–1928, revived 1929) and became the basis for *Porgy and Bess* (1935). For this opera Heyward wrote the libretto and some lyrics to Gershwin's compositions, a few in collaboration with Ira Gershwin. Heyward alone was responsible for "My Man's Gone Now," "A Woman Is a Sometime Thing," and "Summertime," the last having been recorded well over a thousand times, including by, notably, Billie Holiday, Sarah Vaughan, and Louis Armstrong and Ella Fitzgerald. Stephen Sondheim believes that Heyward is "the author of the finest set of lyrics in the history of the American musical theater—namely, those of *Porgy and Bess*." Heyward is buried in Saint Philips Episcopal Church Cemetery, Charleston.

Though Ira Gershwin used some lines from Heyward's libretto in his lyrics to "I Loves You, Porgy," "Oh, I Can't Sit Down," and "A Red-Headed Woman," Heyward declined Gershwin's offer of co-composer credit. He contributed to the scenarios for the movies *The Emperor Jones* (1933) and *The Good Earth* (1937).

Compositions

"Bess, You Is My Woman Now," "Buzzard Song," "I Got Plenty o' Nuttin'," "It Ain't Necessarily So," "It Take a Long Pull to Get There," "My Man's Gone Now," "Summertime," "A Woman Is a Sometime Thing"

References (Only Those Relating to "Porgy and Bess")

PRIMARY: DuBose Heyward, *Porgy* (New York: Doran, 1925); DuBose Heyward and Dorothy Heyward, *Porgy: A Play in Four Acts* (Garden City, N.Y.: Doubleday, Page, 1927); DuBose Heyward, introduction, *Porgy: A Play in Four Acts*, by Heyward and Dorothy Heyward (Garden City, N.Y.: Doubleday, Doran, 1928), ix–xxi; DuBose Heyward, "Porgy and Bess Return on Wings of Song," *Stage* 13 (October 1935): 25–28 (also published in *A DuBose Heyward Reader*, 46–51); DuBose Heyward, George Gershwin, and Ira Gershwin, *The Theatre Guild Presents "Porgy and Bess"* (New York:

Gershwin Publishing, 1935) (lyrics by Heyward and Ira Gershwin; music by George Gershwin); *A DuBose Heyward Reader,* ed. James M. Hutchisson (Athens: University of Georgia Press, 2003).

SECONDARY: Frank Durham, *DuBose Heyward: The Man Who Wrote "Porgy"* (Columbia: University of South Carolina Press, 1954); William H. Slavick, *DuBose Heyward* (Boston: Twayne, 1981); Hollis Alpert, *The Life and Times of "Porgy and Bess": The Story of an American Classic* (New York: Knopf, 1990); James M. Hutchisson, *DuBose Heyward: A Charleston Gentleman and the World of "Porgy and Bess"* (Jackson: University Press of Mississippi, 2000); Stephen Sondheim on DuBose Heyward, in *Invisible Giants: Fifty Americans Who Shaped the Nation but Missed the History Books,* ed. Mark Carnes (New York: Oxford University Press, 2002), 150; Richard Crawford, "Where Did Porgy and Bess Come From?," *Journal of Interdisciplinary History* 36 (Spring 2006): 697–734.

Awards

Contemporary Verse Prize (1921; for the Poem "Gamesters All"); honorary degree, University of North Carolina (1928); honorary degree, College of Charleston (1929); National Institute of Arts and Letters (1937)

Higgins, Billy (William Weldon; "Jazz Caspar")

Singer

9 June 1888 (Columbia, S.C.)–19 April 1937 (New York, N.Y.)

S.C. residence: Columbia (1888–no later than ca. 1910)

Judged one of the twelve greatest black comedians by Langston Hughes and Milton Meltzer, Higgins performed in black vaudeville and musicals that appealed primarily to black audiences. An original member of the Billy King Stock Company in 1912, he starred with King that year in *Two Bills from Alaska.* He led the Bearcat Entertainers while serving in Europe with the 805th Infantry during World War I. With this troupe he sang such songs as "Shooting across the Rhine" and "There's a Great Day Coming When You Lay That Gang Plank Down" and recited a version of the Lord's Prayer with words reflecting current military realities. Later he starred in the revue *Cotton Land* (1924), for which James P. Johnson wrote the music, and performed in *Hot Chocolates* (1929), starring Louis Armstrong and with music by Fats Waller. He recorded duets with female blues singers during the 1920s. On "A to Z Blues" he sings what are considered among the most sadistic lyrics ever recorded. He apparently wrote both the music and words to "I'm Through with You (as I Can Be)," though as composer he was primarily a lyricist. He wrote the words (Benton Overstreet composed the music) to "There'll Be Some Changes Made," which has been recorded hundreds of times since its initial recording by Ethel Waters in 1921. Higgins is buried in Long Island National Cemetery, Farmingdale, N.Y.

It has not been determined if this performer was the Billy Higgins who appears in the movie *Scandals of 1933.*

Compositions

"Early in the Morning" (also titled "Early Every Mornin'"), "Georgia Blues," "I Don't Want Nobody That Don't Want Me" (also titled "I Don't Want You If You Don't Want Me"), "I'm Through with You (as I Can Be)," "Papa, Mama's All Alone Blues," "There'll Be Some Changes Made"

Recordings as Leader

"A to Z Blues" (1924; with Josie Miles), "Get Yourself a Monkey Man and Make Him Strut His Stuff" (1924; with Viola McCoy), "I Don't Want Nobody That Don't Want Me" (1924; with Viola McCoy), "I'm Done Done Done with You" (1924; with Josie Miles), "Keep On Going" (1924; once with Viola McCoy and once, as Jazz Caspar, with Kitty Brown), "Let's Agree to Disagree" (1924; with Josie Miles), "One of These Days" (1924; as Jazz Caspar, with Kitty Brown), "Picnic Time" (1924; with Josie Miles), "Satisfied" (1924; with Josie Miles), "Sweet Mandy" (1924; with Alberta Perkins, as Louella Jones), "Who Calls You Sweet Mama Now?" (1924; with Alberta Perkins, as Louella Jones), "Ain't Trustin' Nobody No More" (1925; with Alberta Perkins), "How Can I Miss You?" (1925; with Monette Moore, as Susie Smith), "I'm Tired of Beggin' You to Treat Me Right" (1925; with Alberta Perkins), "Levee Blues" (1925), "Nobody Else Can Take Your Place" (1925; with Alberta Perkins), "You Ain't Nothin' to Me" (1925; with Monette Moore, as Susie Smith), "Big Business," two parts (1929; with Ed Green)

Leader Recorded With

Josie Miles (1925)

References

SECONDARY: Paul S. Bliss, *Victory: History of the 805th Pioneer Infantry American Expeditionary Forces* (Saint Paul: Paul S. Bliss, 1919), 203–4; Langston Hughes and Milton Meltzer, *Black Magic: A Pictorial History of the Negro in American Entertainment* (New York: Prentice-Hall, 1967), 99, 336; Alec Wilder, *American Popular Song: The Great Innovators, 1900–1950* (New York: Oxford University Press, 1972), 28; Bernard L. Peterson, Jr., *The African American Theatre Directory, 1816–1960* (Westport, Conn.: Greenwood, 1997), 112–13; Frank Cullen, *Vaudeville Old and New: An Encyclopedia of Variety Performers in America* (New York: Routledge, 2007), 1: 510; "Songmasonry: There'll Be Some Changes Made," http://inkhornterm.blogspot.com/2009/07/songmasonry-therell-be-some-changes.html (16 July 2009; accessed 21 May 2014); Jan Souther, "Advertisers Use Music from the Past to Get Their Message Across," *Citizens' Voice* (Wilkes-Barre, Pa.), 13 March 2011, sec. C, p. 9.

Hightower, Lottie Frost

Piano

Possibly September 1891 (Charleston, S.C.)–after 1957

S.C. residence: Charleston (probably 1891–1917, with absences)

Lottie Frost began playing piano at age twelve and reportedly studied music at a conservatory in Boston. After returning to Charleston she became, in 1914, the pianist at the Dixieland Theater. Two years later she toured with Henry Wooden's Bon Tons. With Wooden, she and drummer Willie Richardson performed as a duo; their feature, "Memphis Blues," was a crowd favorite. Also in 1916 as a member of Willie Lewis's band she performed with the revue *Broadway Rastus* at the Strand Theater in Jacksonville, Fla. She taught music in Charleston in 1917. When Alexander Tolliver's Smart Set three-piece jazz group played there that year, she replaced its pianist and three months later, while on tour in W.Va., married its leader, trumpeter Willie Hightower. (Ma Rainey and Bessie Smith performed with the Smart Set at the same time as the Hightowers.) At the completion of this tour the couple briefly oversaw the orchestra of the Lincoln Theater in Cincinnati before returning to the road with C. W. Park's Colored Aristocrats. Still in 1917 they and drummer Willie Campbell constituted the jazz group that toured with the Augusta Mines-Boyd Harris Show. The Hightowers returned to Tolliver's group in 1919 and played again with Wooden's Bon Tons before settling in Chicago in 1921. There she led the Night Hawks (or Eudora Night Hawks), with which "she played good band piano," according to Johnny St. Cyr (16). She was active in Musicians Union, Local 208, serving as financial secretary at least for five years, beginning in 1923.

Hightower's birthplace is confirmed in Cook County, Illinois, Birth Certificates Index, 1871–1922, which documents the birth of her son, Thomas Hightower. It also notes that she was thirty when he was born (3 December 1922). When enumerated for the 1940 census in Chicago on 17 April, she gave her age as forty-eight and indicated that she was born in S.C. She is probably the Charlott E. Frost who was enumerated in Charleston on 2 June 1900; this census indicates that she was born in September 1891. Neither the Boston Conservatory nor the New England Conservatory of Music has a record of her, though the former did not keep student records during the time she would have attended. She might have studied in Boston with individuals associated with one or both of these institutions. On 29 December 1917 the *Indianapolis Freeman: An Illustrated Colored Newspaper* published a Christmas greeting from the Hightowers (p. 4). It indicates that during their performances they play "a few of their own original Jazz numbers, which will be published soon" and that "Mrs. Hightower ... is a feature of [*sic*] her own original numbers." Their compositions have not been identified. The greeting includes a photograph of Lottie Hightower and one of her husband. The 1918 Charleston city directory records her residence and occupation. Doc Cheatham indicates that Hightower served as president of Local 208 at an unspecified time; he also quotes her as saying that she was a graduate of Fisk University, though her attendance at this school has not been confirmed. For the 1940 census she indicated that she completed four years of high school. In 1927 the record company Black Patti released two tunes by Hightowers [*sic*] Night Hawks that feature her husband, though she does not appear on them. In recalling the Hightowers, Johnny St. Cyr states, incorrectly, that she was from Louisiana.

References

SECONDARY: "A Note or Two," *Chicago Defender,* 15 December 1917, p. 4 (big weekend edition); "At Liberty," *Chicago Defender,* 11 June 1921, p. 7 (national edition);

"Chiefs of America's Greatest Musical Organization," *Chicago Defender,* 12 June 1926, sec. A, p. 5 (national edition); Dave Peyton, "The Musical Bunch," *Chicago Defender,* 21 August 1926, p. 6 (national edition); Dave Peyton, "The Musical Bunch," *Chicago Defender,* 12 November 1927, pp. 6–7 (national edition); Willie Hightower, interview by William Russell, 3 June 1958, three reels of tape and a typed summary, Hogan Jazz Archive, Tulane University, New Orleans, pp. 20–29 of summary of reel 1, track 2 (comments by Lottie Frost Hightower); Johnny St. Cyr, "Jazz as I Remember It: Part Four; Chicago Days," *Jazz Journal* 20 (January 1967): 14–16; Adolphus "Doc" Cheatham, *I Guess I'll Get the Papers and Go Home: The Life of Doc Cheatham* (London: Cassell, 1996), 31; Lynn Abbott and Doug Seroff, *Out of Sight: The Rise of African American Popular Music, 1889–1895* (Jackson: University Press of Mississippi, 2002), 318; Peter Dunbaugh Smith, "Ashley Street Blues: Racial Uplift and the Commodification of Vernacular Performance in Lavilla, Florida, 1896–1916" (Ph.D. dissertation, Florida State University, 2006), 97; Lynn Abbott and Doug Seroff, *Ragged but Right: Black Traveling Shows, "Coon Songs," and the Dark Pathway to Blues and Jazz* (Jackson: University Press of Mississippi, 2007), 142, 150–51, 358, 398n249.

Hill, Bertha ("Chippie")

Singer, dancer

Probably ca. 1897 (S.C., possibly Charleston)–7 May 1950 (New York, N.Y.)

S.C. residence: possibly Charleston (probably ca. 1897–possibly 1910s)

Judged one of the twelve greatest black folk musicians by Langston Hughes and Milton Meltzer and considered one of the classic blues singers, Hill apparently began performing as a teenager. Though her life and career until 1925 lack documentation, she presumably danced in a show headlined by Ethel Waters in 1919 and toured as dancer and singer with Ma Rainey's Rabbit's Foot Minstrels in the early 1920s. She settled in Chicago by mid-decade. There she sang in clubs, as well as at the Palladium Dance Hall with King Oliver, and recorded with such musicians as Louis Armstrong, Georgia Tom (Thomas A. Dorsey), Lonnie Johnson, Richard M. Jones, and Tampa Red (Hudson Whittaker). Backed by Armstrong and Jones in 1926, she made what is probably the first recording of Jones's "Trouble in Mind." After touring with Lovie Austin in 1929 she largely retired from music, though she performed occasionally thereafter. Rediscovered by Rudi Blesh in 1946, she appeared on his *This Is Jazz* radio program, and he released her music on his Circle Records in 1946 and 1947. In the latter year she moved to N.Y.C., where she sang at such venues as Carnegie Hall, Jimmy Ryan's, Town Hall, and the Village Vanguard. She performed at the Bessie Smith Memorial Concert at Town Hall on the first day of 1948; in May she sang in Paris. Soon after Hill was killed by a hit-and-run driver in N.Y.C., Blesh, Eddie Condon, and Bob Maltz organized a memorial concert for her at Stuyvesant Casino, N.Y.C. Dan Burley thought her an "acid-tongued blues singer," while the author of "Singing for the Devil" considered her "one of the primitives of jazz" (80). She is buried in Lincoln Cemetery, Blue Island, Ill.

The date and place of the singer's birth cannot be determined with certainty. With one exception all sources consulted indicate, without evidence, that Hill was born on 15 March 1905. The exception is Bruce Bastin, who records "ca. 1900" ("From the Medicine Show to the Stage: Some Influences upon the Development of a Blues Tradition in

Bertha Chippie Hill, N.Y.C., between 1946 and 1948; reproduced from the William P. Gottlieb Collection, Library of Congress, Music Division

the Southeastern United States," *American Music* 2 [Spring 1984]: 30). Perhaps partly because she and Richard M. Jones composed "Pratt City Blues" (Pratt City is located outside Birmingham, Ala.), some sources claim that she was an Alabamian. In "Blues Singer Chippie Hill Killed by Car; Nab Driver," for example, Rudi Blesh refers to her as "Alabama-born." Ted Watson noted in 1974 that ca. 1930 the singer arrived in Chicago "from Birmingham[,] where she was well known in the night life circles" and that she often recorded there as Birmingham Bertha. Though it has not been confirmed that Hill ever performed as Birmingham Bertha (Ethel Waters recorded "Birmingham Bertha" in 1929) and no known evidence indicates that she resided in Ala. or recorded anywhere but Chicago and N.Y.C., she could have lived in Ala. before settling in Chicago, even though Blesh wrote in 1950 that she lived in N.Y.C., then Chicago, then N.Y.C. Most frequently, and without evidence, her birthplace is identified as Charleston, S.C. (She recorded "Charleston Blues.") The most likely reliable source of information about these topics is Hill herself. She estimated her age as forty-three when she was enumerated for the census in Chicago on 4 April 1940; this document, which identifies her as a nightclub entertainer, indicates that she was born in S.C. It also specifies her marital status as widow. Because she had been married and had children, one of whom was Ribichal Hill (who, according to "The Show Must Go On," died in Birmingham at age fifteen, probably in mid-January 1939), presumably she initially married a man named Hill and this was her married name; if so her maiden name has not been determined. (If unsubstantiated claims that she was the daughter of John Hill and Ida Jones are correct, then she was probably born Bertha Hill.) In a 1941 newspaper column Bob Hayes devotes a paragraph to Hill, noting that she is confined to her apartment and desires company because she "is lonesome." If he implies that she was then living alone, without a spouse, then he possibly validates her claim of widowhood. According to Barry Kernfeld she married John Offet in 1929; she wed him early the next decade, according to Daphne Duvall Harrison. Yet because Offet, who was born in 1905, did not die until the first day of 1988, according to the Social Security Death Index, widow Hill could not have married him until after she was enumerated for the 1940 census. The identity of the husband who predeceased her remains unknown. If the singer was born Bertha Hill in S.C., she could have been one of two people of this name. One, born in May 1898, was enumerated for the census in Berkeley County on 13 June 1900; she lived with her parents Smart (a farm laborer) and Victoria Hill and three older siblings. Another one was estimated age fourteen when enumerated in N.Y.C. on 15 January 1920; she and four siblings were the children of William and Cora Hill. There are also two married Bertha Hills who could be the singer. The wife of David Hill and mother of David Hill, Jr., one (state of birth not specified) was enumerated for the N.Y. state census in N.Y.C. on 1 June 1925; this document gives her age as twenty-seven. Another one, born in Ga. and estimated as age thirty-three, was enumerated for the federal census in Chicago on 4 April 1930 with husband James Hill and three children. No evidence found indicates that the singer was born or resided in Ga.

Compositions

"Pleadin' for the Blues," "Pratt City Blues"

Recordings as Leader

Complete Recorded Works 1925–1929 in Chronological Order, "Around the Clock Blues" (1946), "Black Market Blues" (1946), "Careless Love" (1946, 1947), "Charleston Blues" (1946), "How Long Blues" (1946, 1947), "Jailhouse Blues" (1946), "Mistreatin' Mr. Dupree" (1946), "Nobody Knows You When You're Down and Out" (1946), "Trouble in Mind" (1946), "Baby, Won't You Please Come Home" (1947), "Blues Improvisation" (1947), "Chippie's Blues" (1947), "Darktown Strutters' Ball" (1947), "Don't Leave Me, Daddy" (1947), "Lonesome Road" (1947), "Some of These Days" (1947)

Award

Newspaper Guild of New York Page One Award (1948)

References

SECONDARY: "The Show Goes On," *Chicago Defender,* 28 January 1939, p. 19 (national edition); Bob Hayes, "Here and There," *Chicago Defender,* 6 December 1941, p. 20 (national edition); "'Chippie' Hill, Blues Singer, to Make a Comeback," *New York Age,* 28 June 1947, p. 11; "Singing for the Devil," *Time* (15 September 1947): 78, 80 (comments by Hill); John McNulty, "Blues-Shouting Woman Out of the Past," *New York pm Daily,*

16 February 1948, p. 2; Peter Drew, "Bertha's Blues: 'Want You Boys to Remember One Gal Ain't Got It All,'" *Record Changer* 7 (April 1948): 11 (comments by Hill); Boris Vian, "Bertha 'Chippie' Hill," *Jazz Hot* 23 (Mai 1948): 5 (in French); Bob Aurthur, "Let the Good Times Roll," *Playback* 25 (February 1950): 3–4 (comments by Hill); "Blues Singer Chippie Hill Killed by Car; Nab Driver," *New York Age,* 13 May 1950, p. 2 (includes survey of Hill's career by Rudi Blesh); Dan Burley, "Highdown on the Lowdown," *New York Age,* 13 May 1950, p. 6; "Calendar of Events," *New York Amsterdam News,* 20 May 1950, p. 18; Vic Schuler, "Blues for Bertha," *Melody Maker* 26 (24 June 1950): 9; Rudi Blesh, *Shining Trumpets: A History of Jazz,* 4th ed. (London: Cassell, 1958), 137–39; Langston Hughes and Milton Meltzer, *Black Magic: A Pictorial History of the Negro in American Entertainment* (New York: Prentice-Hall, 1967), 336; Derrick Stewart-Baxter, *Ma Rainey and the Classic Blues Singers* (New York: Stein and Day, 1970), 72–74; Ted Watson, "Memoirs of Midnight Man: Early Show Days," *Chicago Defender,* 27 April 1974, sec. A, p. 4 (big weekend edition); Daphne Duval Harrison, *Black Pearls: Blues Queens of the 1920s* (New Brunswick: Rutgers University Press, 1988), 95, 232–34; Christopher Hillman and Roy Middleton, *Richard M. Jones: Forgotten Man of Jazz* (Tavistock, England: Cygnet Productions, 1997), passim; Barry Kernfeld, "Hill, Chippie," in *Harlem Renaissance Lives: From the African American National Biography,* ed. Henry Louis Gates, Jr., and Evelyn Brooks Higginbotham (New York: Oxford University Press, 2009), 262–63.

Hill, Wallace R.

Drums

Probably 26 February 1912 (Columbia, S.C.)–14 September 2003

S.C. residences: Columbia (probably 1912–no later than 1920), Charleston (by 1920–probably after 1930)

A ward of Jenkins Orphanage, Hill played in its bands in the late 1920s and performed with one of them in England in 1929. He became a professional musician or a music teacher, or both.

Hill's age was estimated as nine when the youth was enumerated for the census at the orphanage on 9 January 1920. The passenger list of the *Majestic,* which transported the institution's band from Southampton, England, to N.Y.C. in June 1929, indicates that he was born in Columbia on 26 February 1912. His army enlistment form (completed on 8 March 1943) identifies his civilian occupation as "musicians and teachers of music" and notes that he was born in 1912. The Social Security Death Index provides his middle initial and confirms that he was born on 26 February 1912. He last resided in Orange, N.Y. Though John Chilton identifies Wallace Hill (p. 39) and Walter Hills (p. 55) as orphanage musicians, they are apparently the same person, Wallace Hill.

References

SECONDARY: John Chilton, *A Jazz Nursery: The Story of the Jenkins' Orphanage Bands of Charleston, South Carolina* (London: Bloomsbury Book Shop, 1980), 39, 55; Howard Rye, "Visiting Fireboys: The Jenkins' Orphanage Bands in Britain," *Storyville* 130 (1987): 137–43.

Holland, Peanuts (Herbert Lee)

Trumpet, singer

Possibly 9 February 1906 (probably Va., though possibly N.C.)–7 February 1979 (Stockholm, Sweden)

S.C. residence: Charleston (by 1920–probably late 1920s)

Smitten by a Jenkins Orphanage band he heard perform in Norfolk, Va., where he lived with an aunt, Holland begged to be sent to the institution. After entering it probably in the late 1910s, he played in its bands. A professional musician by the late 1920s, he had his own band in the 1930s; during the 1940s he performed as sideman with such leaders as Coleman Hawkins, Fletcher Henderson, and Al Sears. His longest affiliation was with the band of Charlie Barnet (1941 or 1942–1946). With it Holland soloed and sang, though he was not a crooner. Mostly he performed novelty tunes, such as "Oh! Miss Jackson" (1942) and "E-Bob-O-Lee-Bob" (1945). He plays on Barnet's popular recording of "Skyliner" (1944). He led his own group in 1946 before joining the band of Don Redman later that year. He accompanied it to Europe, where he stayed, living the remainder of his life there, initially in France, later in Sweden. During his third of a century in Europe, he led his own combos and played as featured trumpeter with groups led by Europeans and visiting Americans.

All music sources consulted state that Holland was born in 1910. Public documents indicate otherwise. His age was estimated as three when he was enumerated for the census in Norfolk, Va., on 15 April 1910; this document states that he was born in Va. His age was estimated as twelve when he was enumerated at the orphanage on 9 January 1920; this census notes that he was born in N.C.

The Social Security Death Index records his birth date as 9 February 1906. His middle name has been rendered LeRoy.

Recordings as Leader

"Peanut Butter Blues" (1946, 1952), "For Sentimental Reasons" (1947), "Open the Door, Richard" (1947), "Put 'Em in a Box" (1948), "Teresa" (1948), "Archbishop" (1950), "Hired to Be Inspired" (1950), "Stardust" (1950), "Ba, Ba Vita Lamm" (1951), "Den Lille Ole Med Paraplyen" (1951), "I Forgot to Forget" (1951), "Just a Gigolo" (1951, 1952, 1959), "Basin Street Blues" (1952), "Black and Blue" (1952), "The Mooche" (1952), "St. Louis Blues" (1952), "Tea for Two" (1952), "When the Saints Go Marching In" (1952), "How High the Moon" (1957), "Jammin' the Blues" (1957), "St. James Infirmary" (1959)

Leaders Recorded With

Alphonso Trent (1930, 1933), Fletcher Henderson (1941), Charlie Barnet (1942–1946), Teddy Bunn (1945), Don Byas (1946–1947), Tyree Glenn (1946–1947), Don Redman (1946), Bob Henders (1947), Thore Jederby (1947), Glen Powell (1947–1948), Olle Johnny (1948), Guy Lafitte (1954), Mezz Mezzrow (1955), Maxim Saury (1955), Bud Powell (1959), Albert Nicholas (1963), Nelson Williams (1963)

Film

Sous-sol (1953)

References

SECONDARY: John Chilton, *A Jazz Nursery: The Story of the Jenkins' Orphanage Bands of Charleston, South Carolina* (London: Bloomsbury Book Shop, 1980), 28, 31, 41, 55 (comments by Holland); Scott Yanow, *The Trumpet Kings: The Players Who Shaped the Sound of Jazz Trumpet* (San Francisco: Backbeat Books, 2001), 193–94.

Holmes, Edward

Saxophone

Ca. 1927 (S.C.)–?

S.C. residences: Summerville (by 1935–no later than 1940), Charleston (by 1940–at least into early 1940s)

A ward of Jenkins Orphanage, Holmes played in its bands ca. 1940.

Conducted at the orphanage on 21 May 1940, the census notes that in 1935 Holmes resided in Summerville, estimates his age as thirteen, and indicates that he was born in S.C.

Holmes, Horace

Cornet, trumpet

Possibly 27 December 1902 (Charleston, S.C.)–?

S.C. residence: Charleston (possibly 1902–1918)

Holmes became a ward of Jenkins Orphanage in 1911. He was in the institution's band that performed in N.Y.C. (in a production of *Uncle Tom's Cabin*) in 1913 and that played in England the next year. He was apparently the greatest early influence on the trumpet style of Jabbo Smith, another ward. Upon leaving the institution in 1918 Holmes became a professional musician, initially working in theaters. After attending Morehouse College he formed a band in 1921 and moved to N.Y.C. three years later. He played with various groups, including ones led by Cliff Jackson and Elmer Snowden, and recorded with Ethel Waters and possibly Mamie Smith, two of the major singers of the time. He quit performing in the late 1920s in order to operate a music store. He is presumably the Horace Holmes who gave music lessons in N.Y.C. as late as 1958.

Holmes's date and place of birth come from the passenger list of the *St. Louis*, which transported the orphanage band from Liverpool to N.Y.C. in September 1914. The musician's age was estimated as sixteen when Holmes was enumerated for the census at the institution on 9 January 1920.

Leaders Recorded With

Possibly Mamie Smith (1924), Ethel Waters (1925), Viola McCoy (1927)

References

SECONDARY: "Parents Join Kids at Party Frolic," *New York Amsterdam News*, 22 February 1958, p. 27; John Chilton, *A Jazz Nursery: The Story of the Jenkins' Orphanage Bands of Charleston, South Carolina* (London: Bloomsbury Book Shop, 1980), 14, 55–56; Howard Rye, "Visiting Fireboys: The Jenkins' Orphanage Bands in Britain," *Storyville* 130 (1987): 137–43; Chip Deffaa, *Voices of the Jazz Age: Profiles of Eight Vintage Jazzmen* (Urbana: University of Illinois Press, 1990), 193.

Holmes, Nat (Nathaniel; "Georgetown")

Trumpet

16 August 1927 (Charleston, S.C.)–1 October 2005 (Elmira, N.Y.)

S.C. residences: Charleston and environs, including Georgetown (1927–at least into mid-1940s)

A ward of Jenkins Orphanage, Holmes played in its bands ca. 1940. Before settling in Elmira, N.Y., he lived in Philadelphia, where he played with Lionel Hampton, probably Purvis Henson, and conceivably others. Holmes, who worked for General Electric, operated Nat Holmes's School of Music. He is buried in Woodlawn Cemetery, Elmira, N.Y.

Holmes's dates and places of birth and death come from the Social Security Death Index and from his obituaries. The 1940 census, conducted at the orphanage on 21 May, identifies Georgetown as the musician's residence in 1935. The website obituary states that early in his career Holmes played with Henderson Pervis, though the existence of such a musician has not been confirmed. This person was probably the saxophonist Purvis Henson.

Leader Recorded With

Preston Love (1951)

References

SECONDARY: "Holmes, Nathaniel 'Georgetown,'" *Elmira (N.Y.) Star-Gazette,* 6 October 2005, sec. C, p. 4 (obituary); "Holmes, Nathaniel 'Georgetown,'" http://www.joycetice.com/obitcemc/wlobitho.htm (2007; accessed 21 May 2014) (obituary).

Holmes, Reuben Sam

Drums

Ca. 1924 (S.C.)-?

S.C. residence: Charleston (by 1935-at least into early 1940s)

A ward of Jenkins Orphanage, Holmes played in its bands in the early 1940s and probably in the late 1930s.

Conducted at the orphanage on 21 May, the 1940 census indicates that Holmes was born in S.C., estimates his age as sixteen, and notes that in 1935 he lived in Charleston.

Hooks, Robert

Alto horn

S.C. residence: Charleston (at least early 1930s)

Apparently a ward of Jenkins Orphanage, Hooks played in its bands in the early 1930s.

Howe, Jack Kenneth

Saxophone, clarinet

22 February 1907 (Oak Park, Ill.)-16 October 1992 (White Rock, S.C.)

S.C. residence: Chapin (late 1960s-1992)

Howe learned to play the saxophone by listening to recordings by the Wolverines, featuring Bix Beiderbecke. With the Princeton University Triangle Jazz Band, he participated in one of the first recordings by a collegiate jazz group. After completing his degree in 1930 he lived in Chicago, where he played at informal sessions led by Squirrel Ashcraft. During World War II he served in the navy as a code breaker; following the war he worked in Chicago for the C.I.A. before becoming a businessman. He moved to Chapin when his company relocated to S.C. An amateur musician, Howe was important as a jazz organizer. In Chicago in the early 1960s he assembled teenagers into the Windjammers, a group that recorded two albums. He organized other bands there and, later, in Chapin. He also provided bands for Princeton reunions, beginning in 1975. A founding member of the Sons of Bix, he is buried in the Saint Francis of Assisi Episcopal Church Cemetery, Chapin.

Leaders Recorded With

Princeton Triangle Jazz Band (1928; also known as the Equinox Orchestra), Squirrel Ashcraft (1930s, 1947, 1950–1953), Sons of Bix (1975–1981, early or mid-1980s), Maxine Sullivan (1978), Bob Haggart (1980–1981, 1986)

References

PRIMARY: Jack Howe, *Friends with Pleasure: A History of the Sons of Bix* (N.p.: n.p., n.d) (privately distributed); Benjamin Franklin V, *Jazz and Blues Musicians of South Carolina: Interviews with Jabbo, Dizzy, Drink, and Others* (Columbia: University of South Carolina Press, 2008), 8–16.

SECONDARY: "Jack Howe," *Columbia (S.C.) State,* 17 October 1992, p. B4 (obituary).

Hubbard, Lester or Leslie

Drums

S.C. residence: Charleston (at least during 1920s)

Apparently a ward of Jenkins Orphanage, Hubbard played in its bands in the 1920s and performed with the institution's quartet in N.Y.C. in 1928.

Hubbard's given name is recorded as Lester in John Chilton, *A Jazz Nursery: The Story of the Jenkins' Orphanage Bands of Charleston, South Carolina* (London: Bloomsbury Book Shop, 1980), 56; as Leslie in "Colored Military Men Get Together at Large Banquet." It has not been determined which name is correct.

Reference

SECONDARY: "Colored Military Men Get Together at Large Banquet," *New York Age*, 14 April 1928, p. 10.

Humphries, Bill (William Darlington)

Banjo

19 March 1927 (Allendale, S.C.)–18 April 1996 (New Orleans, La.)

S.C. residence: Allendale (1927–probably 1945)

After serving in the army (1945–1946), Humphries attended the University of Virginia, from which he received a degree in foreign affairs in 1951. He became a venture capitalist in New Orleans. There he played with the Crawford-Ferguson Night Owls, including on the riverboat *President* and at the Rex parade during Mardi Gras. He is buried in Swallow-Savannah Cemetery, outside Allendale.

Leader Recorded With

Crawford-Ferguson Night Owls (1965)

Reference

SECONDARY: "Businessman, Musician William Humphries Dies," *New Orleans Times-Picayune*, 20 April 1996, sec. B, p. 5 (obituary).

Hunt, Lulu (Lula M.)

Piano, singer

Probably 1880s (S.C.)–?

S.C. residences: unknown place, though conceivably Charleston (probably 1880s–no later than 1900), Charleston (by 1900–no later than ca. 1902), Orangeburg (by ca. 1902–no later than 1915, by 1921–at least until 1922)

Beginning ca. 1902 Hunt directed the Claflin University music department. She played piano for and toured with the Claflin University Quintet in 1913. She lived in N.Y.C. by the mid-1910s but returned to the Claflin faculty at least for the 1921–1922 school year. By the mid-1920s she was again in N.Y.C., where she led the Music and Dramatic Club Sextet and played piano for musical groups at the 137th St. Y.W.C.A. She performed at Claflin in June 1929 and taught at Clark University in 1929 and 1930. In N.Y.C. in the 1930s she served as president of the Claflin University Club.

Conducted in Charleston on 2 June, the 1900 census indicates that Hunt was born in S.C. in January 1882. The 1915 N.Y. state census, conducted in N.Y.C. on 1 June, estimates her birth year as 1887 and identifies her profession as music teacher. The 1925 N.Y. state census, conducted in N.Y.C. on 1 June, records her age as thirty, confirms that she was born in S.C., and names her profession as music teacher. Conducted in N.Y.C. on 2 April, the 1940 federal census estimates her birth year as 1888, states that she was born in S.C., and notes that she is an orphanage "cottage mo.," which might mean "cottage mother."

References

SECONDARY: "Y.W.C.A. Notes," *New York Age*, 2 July 1914, p. 7; "Record Breaking Attendance at the State A.M. College," *Chicago Defender*, 28 November 1914, p. 2 (big weekend edition); "W. 137th St. Y.W.C.A.," *Chicago Defender*, 17 October 1925, sec. A, p. 6 (national edition); "Business Girls' Club at 137th St. 'Y' Told of Employers' Sorrows," *New York Age*, 30 January 1926, p. 3; "Addresses Claflin University Meet," *Chicago Defender*, 22 June 1929, p. 11 (national edition); "Tid-Bits of New York Society," *Chicago Defender*, 16 August 1930, p. 11 (national edition); "Dr. and Mrs. L. H. Dunton Given Reception by Claflin Alumni in N.Y.," *New York Age*, 2 September 1933, p. 3; Vivian Glover, *Men of Vision: Claflin College and Her Presidents* (Orangeburg, S.C.: Claflin College, 1995), 87.

Hunter, Robert

Trumpet

S.C. residence: Charleston (probably by late 1920s–at least into mid-1930s)

Apparently a ward of Jenkins Orphanage, Hunter played in its bands ca. 1930.

Hurst, Mary Ann

Singer

21 February 1953 (Levittown, Long Island, N.Y.)–

S.C. residence: Camden (2006–)

Reared internationally (Germany, Japan, Thailand), as well in the United States, Hurst received an undergraduate degree from Gustavus Adolphus

Mary Ann Hurst; photo by Lin Gurley, permission of Mary Ann Hurst

College (1975) and a graduate degree from the University of Minnesota (1991); she also studied at Harvard University (1991–1992). In Minneapolis she sang with her own group, Mary Ann's Rainbow (1977). She performed in China (in clubs, at embassies, and with the Chinese-Japanese group Beijing Jazz) and Turkey (with Tuna Otenel, among others). While living in San Antonio beginning in 1996, she sang with Jim Cullum's band at The Landing; on active duty with the army in Hawaii, she performed regularly with guitarist Jeff Peterson. After moving to S.C. she frequently teamed with guitarist Richard Maxwell. The peripatetic nature of her singing career resulted from job assignments, both civilian and military.

Compositions (with the Exception of "My Head's OK but My Heart's Not Smart," for Which She Wrote the Music and Words, Hurst Translated, from Chinese, the Lyrics to All These Songs)

"Crescent Moon Rising," "Embroidered Pouch," "Herdsman Song," "Kanding Village Love Song," "Little Cabbage," "My Head's OK but My Heart's Not Smart," "Nanniwan," "North Wind Blows," "Sanshilipu Village," "Swallow," "Yi Meng Mountain"

Recordings as Leader (These Are Release Dates, Not Necessarily Recording Dates)

Cool Standards (2000), *Favorite Family Hymns* (2000; privately issued), *Chinese Folksongs in a Jazz Mode* (2001), *Jazz Lullabies* (2001; privately issued), *Jazzz . . . d* (2005), *Wishing on a Star* (2005), *Born under a Wand'rin' Star* (2007)

Website

http://www.maryannhurst.com/Site/Welcome.html (accessed 21 May 2014)

Reference

PRIMARY: Stina Björkell, "Mary Ann Hurst—Jazz, with a Hint of China," http://gbtimes.com/culture/music/mary-ann-hurst-jazz-hint-china (2009; accessed 21 May 2014) (substantial comments by Hurst).

Hutto, J. B. (Joseph Benjamin)

Guitar, drums, singer, composer

29 April 1926 (probably Williston Township, Barnwell County, S.C.)–12 June 1983 (Harvey, Ill.)

S.C. residence: Williston Township, Barnwell County (probably 1926–at least until 1930)

Hutto was introduced to music as a child in Augusta, Ga., where, in time, he and his siblings formed the Golden Crown Gospel Singers. Upon moving to Chicago in the 1940s he became serious about music and discovered the blues. By mid-decade he drummed with Johnny Ferguson's Twisters. He began playing guitar during this period and was influenced most heavily on the slide guitar by Elmore James. After serving in the military during the Korean War, he returned to Chicago, where he formed a group, the Hawks, with which he made his first recordings in 1954.

J. B. Hutto (second from right), Turner's Blue Lounge, Chicago, 1968; permission of the photographer, Robert G. Koester

Apparently unable to make a living playing music, he more or less abandoned it for a decade. After reestablishing the Hawks in 1965 he performed frequently at Turner's Blue Lounge in Chicago and recorded for various labels, including Delmark and Vanguard. Thereafter he toured extensively in the United States and Europe and lived for a time in Boston. He is known for his emotional guitar playing and occasionally incomprehensible singing, as well as for his colorful attire, including odd headgear, such as a fez. He influenced the playing of Lil' Ed Williams (his nephew) and Dave Weld.

Hutto's birth and death dates come from the Social Security Death Index. Without evidence sources identify both Elko and Blackville, S.C., as the musician's birthplace. Only one public document that places Hutto in S.C. has been located: the 1930 census, for which he was enumerated on 1 May in Williston Township, Barnwell County, where he was probably born. Williston Township is a rural area between Williston and Elko. This document discredits a claim that he moved to Augusta, Ga., in 1929.

Compositions

"Angel Face," "Black's Ball," "Bluebird," "Blues for Fonessa," "Blues Stay Away from Me," "Chicago Boogie," "Combination Boogie," "Come On Back Home," "Dim Lights," "Don't You Lie to Me," "Eighteen-Year-Old Girl," "Fifteen-Cent Phone Call," "Floating Fruit Boogie," "Girl I Love," "Going Ahead," "Goodnight Boogie," "Hip Shakin'," "J. B.'s Crawl," "Jealous Hearted Woman," "Leave Your Love in Greater Hands," "Little Girl Dressed in Blue," "Lone Wolf," "Love Retirement," "Lovin' You," "Lulubelle's Here," "Married Woman Blues," "My Heart Is Achin' to Love You," "My Kind of Woman," "New Hawk Walk," "Now She's Gone," "Pet Cream Man," "Please Help," "Radar," "Recycled Woman," "She's So Sweet," "Sloppy Drunk," "Soul Lover," "Speak My Mind," "Story of My Little Angel," "Stranger Blues," "That's the Truth," "Things Are So Slow," "Too Much Alcohol," "Tumbleweed," "Wild, Wild Woman," "You Don't Have to Go," "You Sure Hurt Me Bad"

Recordings as Leader

"Combination Boogie" (1954), "Dim Lights" (1954), "Lovin' You" (1954), "Now She's Gone" (1954), "Pet Cream Man" (1954), "Price of Love" (1954), "Things Are So Slow" (1954), "Goin' Ahead" (1965), "Married Woman Blues" (1965), "Please Help" (1965), "That's the Truth" (1965), "Too Much Alcohol" (1965, 1971), *J. B. Hutto and the Hawks* (1966), *Stompin' at Mother Blues* (1966, 1972), *Hawk Squat* (1968), "Come Back Home" (1970), "Speak My Mind" (1970), *Hip Shakin': Live in London* (1972), *Sidewinder* (1972), "Hear Me Cryin'" (1973), "Hipshakin'" (1973, 1977; the latter as "Hip Shakin'"), "I Have to Go" (1973), "Long Distance Call" (1973), *Blues for Fonessa* (1976), *Slide Guitar Master: Hip Shakin'* (1976–1977), *Boogie with J. B. Hutto and the Houserockers* (1977; later released as *Live 1977*, with three additional selections), "It's Too Much" (1977), "You Must Be Crazy" (1977), *Keeper of the Flame* (1979), *Live at Shaboo Inn, Conn. 1979*, *Bluesmaster* (late 1970s–early 1980s), *Hip Shakin' Music*, vol. 1 (late 1970s–early 1980s), *High and Lonesome* (1982), *Sideslinger* (1982), "I Feel So Good" (1982), *Slippin' and Slidin'* (1983; also titled *Rock with Me Tonight*)

Leader Recorded With

Brewer Phillips (1977, 1982)

Film

Chicago Blues (1971)

Awards

Blues Foundation Hall of Fame (1985, 2014; the latter for the album *Hawk Squat*)

Website

http://www.jbhutto.com/ (accessed 21 May 2014)

References

PRIMARY: Jim O'Neal and Amy van Singel, "J. B. Hutto," *Blues Unlimited* 71 (April 1970): 18–19 (interview); Dave Weld, "Living Blues Interview: J. B. Hutto," *Living Blues* 30 (November–December 1976): 14–24.

SECONDARY: Don Kent, "The Post-war Blues," *Blues Unlimited* 24 (July–August 1965): 12–13; Mike Rowe, "'The Hawk': J. B. Hutto," *Blues Unlimited* 36 (September 1966): 3–4; Dave Weld, "J. B. Hutto," *Living Blues* 57 (Autumn 1983): 12–13 (comments by Hutto) (obituary); "J. B. Hutto Would Play in Our Back Yard: Mike Stephenson Interviews Lil' Ed Williams," *Blues and Rhythm* 200 (June 2005): 30–31; Karen Nugent, "Remember J. B. Hutto?," *Boston Blues Society*, http://www.bostonblues.com/features.php?key=storyHutto (August 2007; accessed 21 May 2014); "Dave Weld Remembers J. B. Hutto," *Chicago Blues Guide*, http://chicagobluesguide.com/features/jb-hutto-by-weld/jb-hutto-weld-page.html (2010; accessed 21 May 2014).

I

Ironing Board Sam (Samuel Moore)

Piano, organ, singer

17 July 1939 (probably Ebenezer Township, York County, S.C.)–

S.C. residences: Ebenezer Township, York County (probably 1939–probably ca. 1955), Rock Hill area (ca. 2006–ca. 2008), Fort Mill (ca. 2008–2011)

A professional pianist by his mid-teens, Moore left S.C. ca. 1955. He then lived in Winston-Salem, Miami, Memphis (where he released tunes on his own Board Record label), Nashville (where he appeared on the *Night Train* television program in 1964 and 1965, sometimes as featured performer but usually backing other musicians), Chicago, Waterloo, and Los Angeles before settling in New Orleans in 1974. There he resided until 2003 and had his greatest, if modest, success: He played in the French Quarter and five times performed at the New Orleans Jazz & Heritage Festival. At the 1979 festival he played inside a water-filled tank, which led to his demonstrating this ability on the television program *Real People*. He moved from New Orleans to Jackson, Miss., and from there, ca. 2006, to outside Rock Hill before locating to Fort Mill two years later. He performed in Rock Hill at the 2010 Old Town Blues and Jazz Festival. In 2011 he moved to Chapel Hill, N.C. He entertains people not only with his music but also through visuals. Early in his career he built a button-board keyboard on an ironing board; later during performances he used an ironing board as a stand for an electric keyboard. He sometimes painted his ironing board in psychedelic colors and for a time decorated one with Christmas tree lights. He was occasionally backed by a battery-operated toy monkey playing drums. He performed inside a large jukebox of his own making (after listeners inserted coins, he played).

When enumerated for the census in Ebenezer Township, York County, on 9 April 1940, Samuel Moore was estimated as age zero years. This township was annexed into Rock Hill in the 1960s. *Double Bang!* includes new material from 2012 plus reissues of ten singles. In 2013 the site http://www.kickstarter.com/projects/tomciaburri/ironing-board-sams-tenth-a-music-documentary announced the publication of *Tenth,* a book of

Ironing Board Sam, Lincolnton, N.C., 25 March 2011; permission of the photographer, Gene Tomko

photographs of Sam limited to twenty copies signed by him and the photographers (accessed 21 May 2014). Its publication has not been confirmed.

Compositions

"Bound to Get There," "Chillin' Like an Ice Cube," "Hanky Panky Girl," "The Human Touch," "I Love You," "Ironing on the Baby Grand," "Jealous Hearted Man," "Non Support," "Raining in My Heart," "Shakin' Out," "Treat Me Right," "When You Brought Me You," "Wino"

Recordings as Leader

Double Bang! (1968–1970, ca. 1975, 2012; two CDs), "A Space Streaker" (1970), "Shakin' Out," two parts (1971), *The Ninth Wonder of the World of Music* (probably mid-1970s), "This Is a New Day" (1974 or 1975), "Baby, What You Want Me to Do" (1975), *The Human Touch* (1991), "Cherry Pie" (1995), "Why I Sing the Blues" (1995), *Going Up* (2011), *Ironing Board Sam and the Sticks* (2013)

Films

Big Bob Johnson and His Fantastic Speed Circus (1978), *Ironing Board Sam Returns* (2015)

References

SECONDARY: Hammond Scott, "'Steady Ironing Man': Ironing Board Sam," *Living Blues* 23 (September–October 1975): 32–33; Jeff Hannusch, "Ironing Board Blues," *Blues Access* 24 (Winter 1996): 18–21 (also available as "Ironing Board Blues: Ironing Board Sam's Human Touch" at www.bluesaccess.com/No_24/ironing.html [accessed 21 May 2014]) (comments by Ironing Board Sam); Gene Tomko, "Ironing Board Sam: I Played the Blues All My Life," *Living Blues* 211 (February 2011): 8–9; John Morthland, "Ironing Board Sam," http://www.musicmaker.org/artists/ironing-board-sam/ (2012; accessed 21 May 2014); Bryan C. Reed, "The Entertainer," *Indy Week* (Durham, N.C.), 6 March 2013, pp. 24–25 (also available as "Long a Rambler, Bluesman Ironing Board Sam Has Earned a New Lease on Fun" at http://www.indyweek.com/indyweek/long-a-rambler-bluesman-ironing-board-sam-has-earned-a-new-lease-on-fun/Content?oid=3368665&mode=print [accessed 21 May 2014]) (comments by Ironing Board Sam).

Irving, Porter

Guitar, singer

Probably late nineteenth century (possibly Laurens County, S.C.)–?

S.C. residence: possibly Laurens County (possibly late nineteenth century–)

A carnival musician, Irving was known for singing "Cocaine Blues" and "Delia." Gary Davis credits him with introducing Davis to the blues, presumably during the first decade of the twentieth century, probably in upstate S.C.

References

SECONDARY: Stefan Grossman, *Rev. Gary Davis/Blues Guitar* (New York: Oak Publications, 1974), 10–11; Anna Reith, "Cover to Cover: Cocaine Blues," http://annareith.wordpress.com/2012/07/01/cover-to-cover-cocaine-blues/ (2012; accessed 21 May 2014).

Jackson, Archie

Singer, guitar, violin

S.C. residence: Greenville area (by early 1920s–probably no later than 1930, with absences)

A street musician, Jackson performed in and around Greenville in the early 1920s. Though primarily a singer, he played guitar, sometimes using picks made from sardine cans; the resulting metallic sound permitted his playing to be heard beyond the rage of a finger-picked (or wood- or plastic-picked) instrument. Blind, he required a lead boy, or guide, one of whom was Josh White, whose playing Jackson influenced.

The Archie Jackson enumerated for the census in S.C. who most likely could have been the musician was, according to the 1900 census, born in February 1898; for this document he was enumerated in Grove Township, Greenville County, on 1 June. At estimated age twelve he was enumerated in the same place on 9 May 1910. Both censuses note that he was born in S.C. His death certificate states that he died in Greenville on 6 November 1930 at age forty; it indicates that he was born in Greenville. Single, he worked as a road constructor, a job that could conceivably be performed by a partially sighted person, though it is not certain if the musician had any vision. Because the 1910 census provides a space for indicating if individuals are blind and the space for Jackson is not marked, if this person was the musician he became blind or visually impaired after becoming a teenager. In *Red River Blues,* Bruce Bastin notes that Jackson was never a full-time resident of Greenville and that he left the town by 1931. If the musician was the youth enumerated for the 1900 and 1910 censuses in Grove Township, his disappearance from Greenville by 1931 resulted from his death in late 1930.

References

SECONDARY: Max Jones, "Josh White Looks Back (Part 1)," *Blues Unlimited* 55 (July 1968): 16–17; Bruce Bastin, *Crying for the Carolines* (London: Studio Vista, 1971), 67–68; Bruce Bastin, *Red River Blues: The Blues Tradition in the Southeast* (Urbana: University of Illinois Press, 1986), 167–68; Elijah Wald, *Josh White: Society Blues* (Amherst: University of Massachusetts Press, 2000), 19–20.

Jackson, Arthur

See Peg Leg Sam

Jackson, Charles

Trombone

Possibly 2 January 1913 (Gainesville, Fla.)-?

S.C. residence: Charleston (by late 1920s-at least until 1930)

A ward of Jenkins Orphanage, Jackson played in its bands at least in the late 1920s and performed with one of them in England in 1929.

The passenger list of the *Columbus,* which transported the orphanage band to Plymouth, England, in April 1929, records Jackson's age as fourteen. The list of the *Majestic,* which returned the group to N.Y.C. in June, identifies the birth date (2 January 1913) and place (Gainesville, Fla.). Jackson's age was estimated as seventeen when the musician was enumerated for the census at the institution on 2 April 1930.

Reference

SECONDARY: "Visiting Fireboys: The Jenkins' Orphanage Bands in Britain," *Storyville* 130 (1987): 137–43.

Jackson, Chuck (Charles)

Singer

22 July 1937 (Latta, S.C.)-

S.C. residences: Latta (1937-1950), Orangeburg (1956)

In 1950 Jackson moved from Latta to Pittsburgh to live with an aunt. There he listened to and was inspired by Art Blakey and Horace Silver and joined the 5 Mellows, a doo-wop group that became the 4 Dots. After singing in 1954 and 1955 with the Raymond Raspberry Singers, a gospel group, he attended what is now South Carolina State University, though he soon returned to Pittsburgh because of civil unrest in Orangeburg. For two years beginning in 1957 he sang with the Del Vikings, another doo-wop group, before pursuing a solo career, at the urging of Jackie Wilson, as a soul/rhythm-and-blues singer. He recorded for the initial time under his own name (as Charles Jackson) in 1959 and soon affiliated with Wand, a subsidiary of Scepter Records. For it, as Chuck Jackson, he had quick success with "I Don't Want to Cry" and especially "Any Day Now" before moving to Motown Records, for which he recorded "Are You Lonely for Me Baby" and other songs. Subsequent recordings include "I'm Needing You, Wanting You" for All Platinum Records. He recorded duets with Maxine Brown, Cissy Houston, and Tammi Terrell.

Jackson is a cousin of singer Ann Sexton. In an interview with Kelly Caldwell, Jackson indicates that for one semester he attended what is now South Carolina State University during a time of boycotts and riots in Orangeburg. There were significant ones in 1956.

Compositions

"Anymore," "Baby, I'll Get It," "Chuck's Soul Brothers Twist," "Don't Let Me Catch You Crying," "For All Time," "Going Back to My Baby's Love," "Go On Yak Yak," "I'd Never Get Over Losing You," "I Don't Want to Cry," "Is There Anything Love Can't Do?," "Just a Little Bit of Your Soul," "Just a Little Mixed Up," "Tears of Joy," "Turn Me Loose," "What You Gonna Say," "Yah"

Recordings as Leader (These Are Release Dates, Not Necessarily Recording Dates)

"Come On and Love Me" (1960; as Charles Jackson), "Ooh, Baby" (1960; as Charles Jackson), *"I Don't Want to Cry!"* (1961), "Hula Hula" (1961; as Charles Jackson), "I'm Yours" (1961; as Charles Jackson), "Mr. Pride" (1961; as Charles Jackson), "This Is It" (1961; as Charles Jackson), *Any Day Now* (1962), *Encore!* (1963), *Chuck Jackson on Tour* (1964), *Mr. Everything* (1965), *Saying Something* (1965; with Maxine Brown), *Dedicated to the King!!* (1966), *Tribute to Rhythm and Blues,* 2 vols. (1966), *The Early Show* (1967; with Tammi Terrell), *Hold On, We're Coming* (1967; with Maxine Brown), *Chuck Jackson Arrives!* (1968), *Goin' Back to Chuck Jackson* (1969), *Teardrops Keep Fallin' on My Heart* (1970), *Through All Times* (1974), *Needing You Wanting You* (1975), *The Great Chuck Jackson* (1977), *I Wanna Give You Some Love* (1980), "All Over the World" (ca. 1988), "Relight My Fire" (ca. 1989), *I'll Take Care of You* (1992; with Cissy Houston), *I'll Never Get Over You* (1998)

Leaders Recorded With

Del Vikings (1957, 1959; also known as the Versatiles), Gary U.S. Bonds (early 1980s)

Film

Boogie Man: The Lee Atwater Story (2008)

Awards

Rhythm & Blues Foundation Pioneer Award (1992); Joe Pope Pioneer Award (2009)

Website

http://www.chuckjackson.org/chuckj/ (accessed 21 May 2014)

References

PRIMARY: Kelly Caldwell, "Chuck Jackson: Soul Man Returns to Detroit," http://metrotimes.com/music/chuck-jackson-soul-man-returns-to-detroit-1.1236574 (2011; accessed 21 May 2014) (interview).

SECONDARY: Bill Dahl, *Motown: The Golden Years* (Iola, Wis.: Krause Publications, 2001), 258–60 (comments by Jackson); Mark Winegardner, "Chuck Jackson: Man with a Masterpiece," *Oxford American* 63 (2008): 112–14 (also available at http://groups.yahoo.com/group/Detroiters/message/47448 [accessed 21 May 2014]) (comments by Jackson); Marv Goldberg, "The Del Vikings," http://www.uncamarvy.com/DelVikings/delvikings.html (2011; accessed 21 May 2014); "Chuck Jackson," https: //sites.google.com/site/pittsburghmusichistory/pittsburgh-music-story/r-b-funk/chuck-jackson (undated; accessed 21 May 2014).

Jackson, Michael

S.C. residence: Charleston (at least 1930s)

Apparently a ward of Jenkins Orphanage, Jackson played in its bands in the 1930s, though his instrument is not known. He reportedly attended what is now South Carolina State University.

Reference

SECONDARY: John Chilton, *A Jazz Nursery: The Story of the Jenkins' Orphanage Bands of Charleston, South Carolina* (London: Bloomsbury Book Shop, 1980), 33, 56.

Jacobs, Charles

Saxophone, arranger

S.C. residence: Charleston (1930s)

Upon leaving Jenkins Orphanage, where he was a ward, Jacobs played with the Carolina Cotton Pickers.

Reference

SECONDARY: Stanley Dance, *The World of Earl Hines* (New York: Scribner's, 1977), 264.

Jamerson, James Lee

Bass

29 or 31 January 1936 or 29 January 1938 (Edisto Island, S.C., or Charleston, S.C.)–2 August 1983 (Los Angeles, Calif.)

S.C. residences: Edisto Island and Charleston (one place or the other 1936–1954)

Before he was a teenager Jamerson played the piano and trombone. After moving to Detroit in 1954 he learned the bass at Northwestern High School. By 1957 he was playing with local groups and soon began recording. He became a more or less regular session musician at Motown Records and a member of its rhythm section known as the Funk Brothers. By using jazz elements, including phrasing, Jamerson created a sound not previously heard in soulful popular music. Don Snowden notes that Jamerson "changed the fundamental role of the [bass] in a pop context from strict rhythm accompaniment to a throbbing, melodic style that made 'Motown bass lines' as much of a pop archetype as Chuck Berry guitar licks" (67). Indispensable to Motown, he played on many of the company's greatest hits, including "Ain't No Mountain High Enough" (Diana Ross), "Baby Love" (Supremes), "Back in My Arms Again" (Four Tops), "Come See about Me" (Supremes), "Dancing in the Street" (Martha and the Vandellas), "For Once in My Life" (Stevie Wonder), "I Can't Get Next to You" (Temptations), "I Heard It through the Grapevine" (both Marvin Gaye and Gladys Knight), "My Girl" (Temptations), "My Guy" (Mary Wells), "Please, Mr. Postman" (Marvelettes), and "Stop! In the Name of Love" (Supremes). Motown moved to Los Angeles in 1972; Jamerson soon followed, though his affiliation with the company ended in 1973. Thereafter he freelanced. He is buried in section 37, plot 265, grave 4, Woodlawn Cemetery, Detroit.

Jamerson's birthplace is in dispute. Some sources indicate Edisto Island; others, Charleston. Sources also do not agree on when he was born. Though the program distributed at his funeral states that Jamerson was born in Charleston on 29 January 1938, Dr. Licks states that the bassist's birth certificate records the date 29 January 1936 (*Standing in the Shadows of Motown,* 3). The Social Security Death Index indicates that he was born on

31 January 1936; California, Death Index, 1940–1997, on 29 January 1938.

Compositions

"Fever in the Funk House," "The Flick"

Recordings as Leader

Twistin' the World Around (1963; as member of the Funk Brothers, here identified as the Twistin' Kings), *That Motown Sound* (1965; released as by Earl Van Dyke and the Soul Brothers, who were really the Funk Brothers)

Leaders Recorded With

Five Daffs (ca. 1958), Marv Johnson (1959), Miracles (1959–1960, 1962–1965, 1967), John Lee Hooker (1961–1962), Marvelettes (1961–1962, 1964–1965, 1967), Temptations (1961–1969), Mary Wells (1961–1962, 1964), Marvin Gaye (1962–1967, 1969–1971), Martha (Reeves) and the Vandellas (1962–1965, 1967, 1969–1970), Stevie Wonder (1962, 1965–1969), Jerry Butler (ca. 1963, ca. 1968), Four Tops (1964–1967, 1970), Supremes (1964–1968), Isley Brothers (1965–1966, probably 1969), Edwin Starr (1965–1966, 1974), Jr. Walker (1965–1966, 1969), San Remo Golden Strings (mid-1960s), Chris Clark (1966), Contours (1966), Gladys Knight (1966–1973), Smokey Robinson (1966–1967, probably 1977), Marvin Gaye and Tammi Terrell (1967), Shorty Long (1967), Jackie Wilson (1967), David Ruffin (1968–1969), Jackson 5 (1969–1970), Originals (1969), Spinners (1970), Hues Corporation (1973), Houston Person (1973), Al Wilson (1973), Shirley Bassey (ca. 1974), Dennis Coffey (ca. 1974), Buddy Miles (ca. 1974), Joan Baez (1975), Fontella Bass (1975), Sylvers (1975), Bill Withers (1975), Hugo Montenegro (ca. 1975), Robert Palmer (ca. 1975, ca. 1992), Donald Byrd (1976), Pointer Sisters (1976), Billy Davis, Jr., and Marilyn McCoo (ca. 1976), Wah Wah Watson (ca. 1976), Jimmy Ponder (1977), Marlena Shaw (1977), John Handy (1978), Hubert Laws (1978), Joe Sample (1978), Bonnie Pointer (ca. 1978)

Awards

Rock and Roll Hall of Fame (2000); *Grammy Magazine* Lifetime Achievement Award (2004; awarded to the Funk Brothers); Fender Hall of Fame (2009); *Bass Player* Lifetime Achievement Award (2011)

References

PRIMARY: Dan Forte, "James Jamerson: Preeminent Motown Bassist," *Guitar Player* 13 (June 1979): 44–45, 133–34 (also available at http://www.ricksuchow.com/press-group-248.html, though without Forte's introductory comments and a Jamerson discography [accessed 21 May 2014]) (interview).

SECONDARY: Don Snowden, "Motown's Unsung Hero," *Los Angeles Times*, 28 August 1983, calendar sec., pp. 67, 91 (obituary); Marshall Crenshaw, "James Jamerson: 1938–1983," *Rolling Stone* 405 (29 September 1983): 60 (obituary); Nelson George, "Standing in the Shadows of Motown: The Unsung Session Men of Hitsville's Golden Era," *Musician* 60 (October 1983): 60–66 (also published in George's *Buppies, B-Boys, Baps and Bohos: Notes on Post-soul Black Culture* [New York: HarperCollins, 1992], 165–75) (comments by Jamerson); Nelson George, *Where Did Our Love Go? The Rise and Fall of the Motown Sound* (New York: St. Martin's 1985), passim; Dr. Licks [Allan Slutsky], *Standing in the Shadows of Motown: The Life and Music of Legendary Bassist James Jamerson* (Wynnewood, Pa.: Dr. Licks Publishing, 1989); Nelson George, "James Jamerson: Interview with a Ghost," in *The Bass Player Book*, ed. Karl Coryat (San Francisco: Miller Freeman Books, 1999), 164–69; Lars Bjorn, with Jim Gallert, *Before Motown: A History of Jazz in Detroit, 1920–1960* (Ann Arbor: University of Michigan Press, 2001), 201–2; Walter Rhett, "James Lee Jamerson: The Lowcountry's Musical Genius," *Charleston (S.C.) Chronicle*, 24 September 2003, p. 11; Jack McCray, *Charleston Jazz* (Charleston, S.C.: Arcadia Publishing, 2007), 94–99; Rick Suchow, "James Jamerson: Motown's Master of the Groove," *Bass Guitar Magazine* 41 (March–April 2009): 28–31 (also available at http://www.ricksuchow.com/press-group-249.html [accessed 21 May 2014]); Otis R. Taylor, Jr., "Amplified Funk," *Columbia (S.C.) State*, 22 July 2012, sec. E, pp. 1, 3.

Jefferson, Maceo Buckingham

Banjo, guitar, singer, arranger

14 July in late 1890s (Beaufort, S.C.)–14 June 1974 (Bridgeport, Conn.)

S.C. residences: Beaufort (late 1890s–no later than 1910), Charleston (by 1910–1916)

After being discharged from the navy on 24 December 1919, Jefferson began playing professionally with Frank Clarke in Norfolk, Va., though they soon relocated to Washington, D.C., where they performed at the Poodle Dog Café. During this period Jefferson studied counterpoint and harmony and wrote some arrangements for Russell

Wooding. By 1921 he was performing in N.Y.C. clubs and cabarets, including Perry's Japanese Garden, as well as with bands led by Wilbur Sweatman and others. His N.Y.C. recordings with Lucille Hegamin and Ethel Waters are the only ones he made in his own country. As a member of the Plantation Orchestra, he traveled to Europe in 1926 and remained there until the mid-1930s, working as a professional musician (including, in France, as a member of the New Yorkers and the Leon Abbey band in the late 1920s) and doing most of his recording. Upon returning to the United States in 1935, he played with Willie "The Lion" Smith and toured with W. C. Handy. Back in Europe in 1938 he led a band at La Grosse Pomme (the Big Apple), a Paris club operated by singer Adelaide Hall, and recorded for the last time at a session he led in Paris in 1941. Soon thereafter he was interned by the Nazis near Compiègne, France; after being liberated in 1944 he lived the remainder of his life in the United States, residing first in N.Y.C. but ultimately settling in Bridgeport, Conn.

Jefferson was the brother of trumpeter Warren Jefferson. Conducted in Beaufort on 9 June, the 1900 census records Jefferson's birth date as July 1898 and given name as Moses; the enumerator might have misunderstood the child's given name. The youth's age was estimated as eleven when Jefferson was enumerated for the census in Charleston on 18 April 1910. The Department of Veterans Affairs BIRLS Death File, 1850–2010, indicates that he was born on 14 July 1897; the Social Security Death Index, on 14 July 1898. The Connecticut Death Index, 1949–2001, estimates the year as 1899. Jefferson's middle name and information about his military service come from *The Official Roster of South Carolina Soldiers, Sailors and Marines in the World War, 1917–18* (N.p.: n.p., ca. 1929), 1: 561.

Compositions

"An-No-Bor Isle," "Bring 'Em Back Alive," "Chiquita," "I'm Afraid," "I've Been Where You're Goin'," "Let Me Know," "Pack Up Your Bags and Be Gone," "Ready for Love," "The Record Shop Song," "Shall We Remember," "So Big and Heavy," "Swing Time," "Taking My Time"

Recordings as Leader

"Isn't It Romantic?" (1932; unissued), "Crying for Love" (1933), "Look Who's Here" (1933), "Ready for Love" (1933), "Stormy Weather" (1933), "Au revoir, pays de mes amours" (1941), "Dis moi quand meme" (1941), "Pourquoi n'etes vous pas venue?" (1941), "Saut rhythme" (1941)

Leaders Recorded With

Lucille Hegamin (1922), Ethel Waters (1925), Plantation Orchestra (1926), Harry Jackson (1928–1930), Jack Hamilton (1928 or 1929), Arthur Briggs (1929), Louis Armstrong (1934), Willie Lewis (1937)

References

SECONDARY: J. A. Jackson, "Where Stage and Sermons Harmonize," *Billboard* 33 (5 March 1921): 41; A. F. Rosemond, "News of Our Entertainers in Europe," *New York Amsterdam News,* 21 March 1928, p. 9; "Notes from Paris," *Baltimore Afro-American,* 6 April 1929, p. 28; "N.Y. Musicians Please Royalty at 'La Pergola,'" *Chicago Defender,* 31 August 1929, p. 7; "Paris!," *Pittsburgh Courier,* 9 April 1938, p. 19; "Musician, Held by Nazis Tells of Life in Prison," *Chicago Defender,* 2 September 1944, p. 10 (national edition) (comments by Jefferson); Dan Burley, "Clothes and Other Lines," *New York Age,* 4 February 1950, p. 6; Frank Driggs, "Maceo B. Jefferson," *Storyville* 58 (April–May 1975): 140–43 (translated into French by François Desbrosses, this article also appears in *Bulletin du Hot Club de France* 557 [Novembre 2006]: 7–9); Horst P. J. Bergmeier and Rainer E. Lotz, "James Arthur Briggs," *Black Music Research Journal* 30 (Spring 2010): 128, 133–34, 142, 167, 171, 176.

Jefferson, Warren W.

Trumpet

Probably ca. 1904 (S.C., probably Beaufort)–after 1973

S.C. residences: probably Beaufort (possibly 1904–no later than 1910), Charleston (by 1910–no later than early 1930s)

At least in the late 1920s and early 1930s Jefferson played with the band of Eddie White that was headquartered in Philadelphia and included Jimmy Mundy. He then became a regular with Earl Hines, staying with him until 1936.

Jefferson was the brother of musician Maceo Jefferson, whom Warren survived. Jefferson's age was estimated as six when the youth was enumerated for the census in Charleston on 18 April 1910; this document records his middle initial. He is possibly the Warren Jefferson the Social Security Death Index identifies as having died in Bronx, N.Y., in July 1984 (other sources specify the day: 1 July); this person was born on 24 October 1904.

Leader Recorded With

Earl Hines (1933–1934)

References

SECONDARY: "Hines' Orchestra to Play for Our Party," *Chicago Defender,* 9 November 1935, p. 17 (national edition); Jack Ellis, "Orchestras," *Chicago Defender,* 16 May 1936, p. 23 (national edition); Dan Burley, "Back Door Stuff," *Chicago Defender,* 30 May 1936, p. 10 (national edition); Frank Driggs, "Maceo B. Jefferson," *Storyville* 58 (April–May 1975): 140–43 (translated into French by François Desbrosses, this article also appears in *Bulletin du Hot Club de France* 557 [Novembre 2006]: 7–9); Barbara J. Kukla, *Swing City: Newark Nightlife, 1925–50* (Philadelphia: Temple University Press, 1991), 230–31.

Jenkins, Edmund Thornton

Composer, bassoon, clarinet, oboe, organ, piano, trumpet, violin, singer

9 April 1894 (Charleston, S.C.)–12 September 1926 (Paris, France)

S.C. residence: Charleston (1894–1914, except when attending college)

Jenkins was a son of Lena James Jenkins and Daniel Joseph Jenkins, founders of Jenkins Orphanage. A leader of and performer with the institution's bands, he played with one of them in England in 1914. When it returned to Charleston he stayed in London, where he enrolled in the Royal Academy of Music, with which he remained affiliated into 1921. (Previously he studied at Avery Institute in Charleston and, from 1908 to 1914, at what is now Morehouse College in Atlanta.) He won several awards at the academy and edited the student magazine, *The Academite.* Mainly a classical composer, he played in the academy's orchestra but also in dance bands and theater bands. Around 1920 he declined an invitation to lead the Southern Syncopated Orchestra, which was touring Europe, though he led a band at the Queen's Hall Roof Garden in 1921. Jenkins returned to the United States in 1923 but the next year moved to Paris. There he published some of his compositions through his own company, the Anglo-Continental-American Music Press, and had some of his works performed. *Encyclopedia of African American Music* characterizes his *Charlestonia* as "one of the first symphonic compositions by an African American to utilize idioms and tunes from African American musical traditions" (3: 1018). He is buried in the Humane and Friendly Society Cemetery, Charleston.

Jenkins was the brother of trombonist Nathaniel Jenkins and trumpeter Stirling Jenkins.

Compositions (Only Those with Probable Folk or Quasi-jazz Elements)

American Folk Rhapsody (later titled *Charlestonia*), *Folk Rhapsody, Jungle Blues, The Saxophone Strut* (also titled *Milano Strut*)

Leaders Recorded With

Jack Hylton (1921), Queen's Dance Orchestra (1921)

Awards (All from the Royal Academy of Music)

Oliveria Prescott Prize (1917); Battison Haynes Prize (1918); Charles Lucas Prize (1918); Ross Scholarship (1919); Associate of the Royal Academy of Music (1921)

References

SECONDARY: John Chilton, *A Jazz Nursery: The Story of the Jenkins' Orphanage Bands of Charleston, South Carolina* (London: Bloomsbury Book Shop, 1980), 22–23, 56; Jeffrey P. Green, *Edmund Thornton Jenkins: The Life and Times of an American Black Composer, 1894–1926* (Westport, Conn.: Greenwood, 1982); Betty Hillmon, "In Retrospect: Edmund Thornton Jenkins; American Composer; At Home Abroad," *Black Perspective in Music* 14 (Spring 1986): 143–80; Jeffrey P. Green, "An American Band in London, 1914," *Musical Traditions* 9 (Autumn 1991): 12–17; Jeffrey P. Green, "Edmund Jenkins of South Carolina," *Black Music Research Journal* 30 (Spring 2010): 183–95; "*American Folk Rhapsody: Charlestonia* (1917), Edmund Thornton Jenkins (1894–1926)," in *Encyclopedia of African American Music,* ed. Emmett G. Price III et al. (Santa Barbara: Greenwood, 2011), 3: 1017–18; Jeffrey P. Green, "Edmund T. Jenkins of the Royal Academy of Music," www.jeffreygreen.co.uk/edmund-t-jenkins-of-the-royal-academy-of-music (undated; accessed 21 May 2014); Royal Academy of Music, "Prize Board. Oliveria Prescott Prize. 1910–32," http.apollo.ram.ac.uk/emuweb/pages/ram/display.php?irn=18866 (undated; accessed 21 May 2014).

Jenkins, Hezekiah (Zebedee Manigault)

Guitar, harmonica, singer

Possibly late 1880s (Columbia, S.C.)–17 May 1941 (Jamaica, N.Y.)

S.C. residence: Columbia (possibly late 1880s–probably early 1910s)

After serving as a porter in Columbia, Manigault entered vaudeville as a comic, probably in the early 1910s. As a result of performing the skit "Hezekiah Jenkins," he became known by this name. In time he teamed with such performers as Clifford Brooks, Amon Davis, Johnny Hudgins, Aaron Palmer, and Blanche Russell. Until settling in N.Y.C. no later than 1930, he toured, including with A. G. Allen's New Orleans Minstrels. His most enduring composition and recording inspired singer Maria Muldaur to state that filmmaker "Ken Burns could have done a three-hour documentary on the Great Depression and not come up with a more accurate and compelling description of it than is in this one song called 'The Panic Is On' by Hezekiah Jenkins" (Crowley). It has been revived by Muldaur on *Good Time Music for Hard Times* (2009) and Loudon Wainwright III on *10 Songs for the New Depression* (2010). In 1929 Bessie Smith recorded "I've Got What It Takes," which Jenkins wrote that year with Clarence Williams.

Manigault was the brother of entertainer Walter Manigault, known professionally as Walter Jenkins. On his 1917 draft registration card Zeb Manigault specified his birth date as 4 March 1888; on the 1918 card (as Zebedee Manigault), as 16 February 1883. When enumerated for the census in N.Y.C. on 2 April 1930, his age was estimated as forty. When enumerated on 3 April 1940 in Saint Anthony Hospital, Jamaica, N.Y., where he had been a patient at least since 1935, his age was estimated as forty-six. His obituary states that after quitting vaudeville, Manigault worked as a red cap in Pennsylvania Station, N.Y.C., and sang with "the famous Red Cap's Quartet." This group was known as the Grand Central Red Cap Quartet, which began recording in the 1930s. Perhaps Manigault sang with it even though he worked at a different railroad station. It has not been determined if he is on the recordings.

Compositions

"Change," "Curious Blues," "Florida Blues," "Hen Pecked Man," "I'm Gonna Pizen You," "I've Got What It Takes" (also titled "I Got What It Takes"), "Mouth Organ Blues," "My Own Rag" (also titled "Jenkinson Rag"), "The Panic Is On," "Poor Me," "Shout You Cats," "Sister, It's Too Bad," "You're Mine"

Recordings as Leader (All but the Last Two as Jenkins and Jenkins, with Dorothy Jenkins)

"Hen Pecked Man" (1924), "Mouth Organ Blues" (1924), "Fare Thee Well" (1925), "Sister, It's Too Bad" (1925), "Curious Blues" (1926), "Miserable Blues" (1926), "The Panic Is On" (1931), "Shout You Cats" (1931)

References

SECONDARY: "Zeb Manigault Veteran Actor, Passes Away," *New York Amsterdam Star-News,* 31 May 1941, p. 4 (obituary); Lynn Abbott and Jack Stewart, "The Iroquois Theater," *The Jazz Archivist: A Newsletter of the William Ransom Hogan Jazz Archive* 9 (December 1994): 2–20 (see especially 15–16); Lynn Abbott and Doug Seroff, *Ragged but Right: Black Traveling Shows, "Coon Songs," and the Dark Pathway to Blues and Jazz* (Jackson: University Press of Mississippi, 2007), 239, 241–43; Peter Crowley, "Maria Muldaur's 'Continuum of Life,'" http://www.lakeplacidnews.com/page/content.detail/id/502821/Maria-Muldaur-s-continuum-of-life-.html?nav=5066 (16 September 2010; accessed 21 May 2014).

Jenkins, Lucas

Ca. 1885–?

S.C. residence: Charleston (1890s)

Jenkins played in the Jenkins Orphanage bands at least in the 1890s and performed with one of them in England in 1895. His instrument is not known.

The passenger list of the *Paris,* which transported the orphanage band to England in September 1895, records Jenkins's age as ten; the list for the *Teutonic,* which returned the group to the United States the next month, specifies it as nine.

Reference

SECONDARY: Howard Rye, "Visiting Fireboys: The Jenkins' Orphanage Bands in Britain," *Storyville* 130 (1987): 137–43.

Jenkins, Nathaniel

Trombone

Ca. 1884 (probably Charleston, S.C.)–?

S.C. residence: Charleston (probably ca. 1884–at least into 1920s)

A son of Lena James Jenkins and Daniel Joseph Jenkins, founders of Jenkins Orphanage, Nathaniel Jenkins played in the institution's bands from the 1890s into the 1920s and performed with one of them in England in 1895.

Jenkins was the brother of composer Edmund Jenkins and trumpeter Stirling Jenkins. The passenger list of the *Paris,* which transported the orphanage band to England in September 1895, records Jenkins's age as eleven; the list for the *Teutonic,* which returned the group to the United States the next month, specifies it as four.

References

SECONDARY: Jeffrey P. Green, *Edmund Thornton Jenkins: The Life and Times of an American Black Composer, 1894–1926* (Westport, Conn.: Greenwood, 1982), 7, 22; Howard Rye, "Visiting Fireboys: The Jenkins' Orphanage Bands in Britain," *Storyville* 130 (1987): 137–43.

Jenkins, Robert

Saxophone
Ca. 1925 (S.C.)-?
S.C. residence: Charleston (by mid-1930s–at least into early 1940s)

Apparently a ward of Jenkins Orphanage, Jenkins played in its bands from ca. 1935 at least into the early 1940s.

Jenkins's age was estimated as fifteen when the youth was enumerated for the census at the orphanage on 21 May 1940; this document indicates that he was born in S.C.

Jenkins, Stirling Herbert

Trumpet, possibly trombone
Ca. 1883 (probably Charleston, S.C.)-1912 (possibly Washington, D.C.)
S.C. residence: Charleston (probably ca. 1883–probably early 1900s)

A son of Lena James Jenkins and Daniel Joseph Jenkins, founders of Jenkins Orphanage, Jenkins played in the institution's bands at least in the 1890s and performed with one of them in England in 1895. He also played at the University of Pennsylvania, where he studied dentistry, which he practiced in Washington, D.C.

Jenkins was the brother of composer Edmund Jenkins and trombonist Nathaniel Jenkins. The passenger list of the *Paris,* which transported the orphanage band to England in September 1895, records Jenkins's age as twelve; the list for the *Teutonic,* which returned the group to the United States the next month, specifies it as ten.

References

SECONDARY: Jeffrey P. Green, *Edmund Thornton Jenkins: The Life and Times of an American Black Composer, 1894–1926* (Westport, Conn.: Greenwood, 1982), 7, 22, 27; Howard Rye, "Visiting Fireboys: The Jenkins' Orphanage Bands in Britain," *Storyville* 130 (1987): 137–43.

Jenkins, Thaddeus ("Little Jabbo")

Trumpet
S.C. residence: Charleston (by 1920–at least into late 1920s)

A ward of Jenkins Orphanage beginning in 1920, Jenkins played in its bands in the 1920s and performed with the institution's quartet in N.Y.C. in 1928. He was a professional musician by 1931.

Leaders Recorded With

Eddie Deas (1931), Arthur Williams (1938)

References

SECONDARY: "Colored Military Men Get Together at Large Banquet," *New York Age,* 14 April 1928, p. 10; John Chilton, *A Jazz Nursery: The Story of the Jenkins' Orphanage Bands of Charleston, South Carolina* (London: Bloomsbury Book Shop, 1980), 56.

Jenkins, Walter (Walter Manigault)

Singer, harmonica
Possibly 9 March 1884 (Fairfield County, S.C.)-28 September 1953 (New York, N.Y.)
S.C. residences: Fairfield County (possibly 1884–possibly late 1880s), Columbia (possibly late 1880s–no later than 1915)

Manigault, who served as a porter in Columbia as late as 1909, entered vaudeville as Walter Jenkins by 1915. He is probably the Walter Jenkins who teamed with Philip Giles by 1917. He is best known for his partnership with William Glenn in the team of Glenn and Jenkins that lasted from probably 1917 at least into 1950. The pair became known for performing as two porters in "Working for the Railroad," a routine that included "Broom Blues." They performed in Europe in 1921 and 1922 and appeared on the first Radio-Keith-Orpheum Hour, broadcast nationally in 1929 on NBC. For four years beginning in the early 1920s, they were accompanied by the blues guitarist Lonnie Johnson. The team performed in Earl Dancer's *Africana* (1927), starring Ethel Waters, as well as in two productions by Leonard Harper, *Midnight Steppers of 1927* and *Hot Feet* (1930). In 1939 the team successfully sued the Cotton Club for breach of contract. A reviewer characterizes the pair's act as having "a novel line of humor, jazz blues and freak dancing" (advertisement for Glenn and Jenkins). M.H.S. states that Jenkins plays "the 'bluest' harmonica we've ever heard in vaudeville." The entertainer is buried in Evergreens Cemetery, Brooklyn, N.Y., burial number 377587.

Manigault was the brother of entertainer Zebedee Manigault, known professionally as Hezekiah Jenkins. Manigault's birth date comes from his 1918 draft registration card and the passenger lists of the *Ile de France* (12 May 1921) and *Celtic* (20 August 1922); the lists also indicate his birthplace. When enumerated for the N.Y. state census on 1 June 1915, however, the performer gave his age as twenty-three. A Glenn and Jenkins scrapbook is housed in the New York Public Library, Schomburg Center, Manuscripts & Archives, Sc MG 599.

References

SECONDARY: advertisement for Jenkins and Giles, *New York Clipper,* 21 February 1917, p. 26; "A Note or Two," *Chicago Defender,* 24 August 1918, p. 6; advertisement for Glenn and Jenkins, *Variety,* 25 March 1921, p. 37; M.H.S., "Vaudeville," *New York Clipper,* 25 January 1922, p. 9 (under "Palace"); "Glenn and Jenkins among Few to Win Nitery Wage Suit," *New York Amsterdam News,* 30 March 1940, p. 16; "Form 2nd Unit for Vets Hospital Show," *Pittsburgh Courier,* 7 January 1950, p. 18; "Veteran Comic Dies from Heart Ailment," *New York Amsterdam News,* 3 October 1953, p. 3 (obituary); Lonnie Johnson, "From End to End," in *Conversation with the Blues,* by Paul Oliver (Cambridge: Cambridge University Press, 1965), 140; Marshall Stearns and Jean Stearns, *Jazz Dance: The Story of American Vernacular Dance* (New York: Macmillan, 1968), 150, 244.

Jennings, Butler

Harmonica
Ca. 1902 (probably Jonesville, S.C.)–?
S.C. residence: Jonesville (probably ca. 1902–)

Jennings helped teach Peg Leg Sam (Arthur Jackson) to play the harmonica.

Jennings was enumerated twice for the 1910 census in Jonesville. The first time, he was with the family of his grandparents Mack and Julia Goudelock (enumerated 21 April); the second, with his brother-in-law Tony Murphy and his wife Clara Murphy (enumerated 4 May). For the first census his age was estimated as nine; for the second, as seven.

Reference

SECONDARY: Bruce Bastin, *Red River Blues: The Blues Tradition in the Southeast* (Urbana: University of Illinois Press, 1986), 190.

Jennings, Inez

Singer, dancer
25 November 1920 (Sumter, S.C.)–19 July 2002
S.C. residence: Sumter (1920–1922)

In the late 1920s Jennings's mother hosted house-rent parties in Newark, N.J.; there in 1936 Jennings sang and danced at Villa Maurice as an amateur. Subsequently she sang professionally at various Newark clubs and in such N.Y. cities as Albany, Troy, and Utica.

Jennings was a sister of comedian Fortune "Fats" Jennings (1914–1983), who was born in Sumter, S.C. Jennings's birth and death dates come from the Social Security Death Index. Barbara J. Kukla specifies when Jennings left Sumter for Newark.

Reference

SECONDARY: Barbara J. Kukla, *Swing City: Newark Nightlife, 1925–50* (Philadelphia: Temple University Press, 1991), 66, 201–2 (comments by Jennings).

Johnson, Billy (William Francis)

Composer, singer
Possibly 1867 (Charleston, S.C.)–12 September 1916 (Chicago, Ill.)
S.C. residence: Charleston (possibly 1867–possibly early 1870s)

As a child Johnson reportedly left Charleston with his family for Augusta, Ga., where he received his schooling. He began performing in minstrel shows in the early 1880s and in time wrote songs for them. By late 1894 he was with Billy Jackson's Colored Minstrels, which also included Bob Cole. Around this time Johnson affiliated with Cole's All-Star Stock Company. By 1896 Johnson and Cole were members of Black Patti's Troubadours, for which they wrote the skit "At Jolly Coon-ey Island." The next year they formed a partnership independent of Black Patti. In addition to performing and composing, the team of Cole and Johnson created *A Trip to Coontown* (initially produced in 1897), one of the earliest full-scale musical productions by blacks. A *Saturday Budget* review of this production indicates that Johnson (here named Tilly, not Billy) is "an artist to his fingers' tips." Because of the pair's ultimate popularity and the nature of some of the men's compositions, the two became known as "The Kings of Koondom," according to the *New York Times.* His years with Cole constituted Johnson's career apex. Their composition "La Hoola Boola" became the Yale University fight song, "Boola Boola." When the partnership dissolved in 1901 Johnson continued writing tunes, but his entertainment activities were less impressive than they had been with Cole. Sylvester Russell, then the major commentator on black entertainment, wrote in 1902 that Johnson provided "fuel, to feed the fire made hot by Cole"; he also thought that when the team broke up, Johnson was "left weeping in the wilderness over the prestige of the past and the loss of a superior partner." In 1907 Johnson staged the musical numbers in *Captain Rufus* and *In Zululand.* Four years later he performed in the musical *Dr. Herb's Prescription, or It Happened in a Dream.* After moving to Chicago he gave up show business for politics; because his new pursuit was unsuccessful, he returned to entertainment in partnership with Tom Brown. They produced and starred in *Twenty Miles from Home* (1914). Johnson performed for the last time in 1915, with the Pierot Minstrels. He died after falling from the balcony of the Pioneer Club in Chicago. Sylvester Russell was more enthusiastic about Johnson in 1916 than he had been in 1902. Following the entertainer's death Russell wrote that "Billy Johnson's career has been one of the most brilliant among actors of the American stage." Johnson is buried in section 5, lot 14, row 1, grave 37, Lincoln Cemetery, Blue Island, Ill.

Though the composer's death certificate indicates that Johnson was born in 1867 and died at age forty-nine, most sources record, without evidence, a birth year of 1858. Johnson is not one of the Johnsons who, in 1901, teamed with Bob Cole as Cole and the Johnson Brothers (these were the siblings J. Rosamond and James Weldon Johnson) or the Johnson of Cole and Johnson who formed a partnership in 1902 (this Johnson was Rosamond). He is also not the Billy B. Johnson who wrote songs with Chris Smith, among others, and who teamed with Estelle (Stella) Johnson in vaudeville as the Johnsons, sometimes in collaboration with Smith. Characterizing Johnson as "an artist to his fingers' tips" is not unique to the *Saturday Budget;* he is also so described in "Sherman Opera House, Newark," *Phelps (N.Y.) Citizen,* 1 February 1900, p. 3, and possibly elsewhere. "La Hoola Boola" was used as the theme for *The Adventures of Frank Merriwell,* a radio series. In his 1916 article about Johnson, Sylvester Russell attributes composership of several songs to him; on this topic Russell is unreliable.

Compositions

"The Black Four Hundred's Ball," "Charity Began at Home," "Chicken," "Christening of a Little Black Coon," "The Coontown Regiment Is Off to War," "The Czar of the Tenderloin," "The Famous Black Moguls," "Good-Bye Old Mexico," "I Belong to the Government Now," "I Can Stand for Your Color but Your Hair Won't Do," "I Don't Know Why I Love You," "I Hope These Few Lines Will Find You Well," "I Knowed You afore Your Hair Got Straight," "In Dahomey," "I Wonder What Is That Coon's Game," "La Hoola Boola," "The Luckiest Coon in Town," "Miss Amorinta Jackson's Promenade," "The Moon Has His Eyes on You," "Mr. Coon You're Alright in Your Place" (also titled "Mr. Coon You're All Right in Your Place"), "My Carolina Caroline," "My Leonora Lee," "The Naughty Bow-Wow," "No Coons Allowed!," "O-San," "Queen of Shinbone Alley," "The Red, White and Blue Is Calling You," "Since Bill Bailey Came Back Home," "Since Mandy Green's Got Opera on the Brain" (also titled "Since Mandy Green's Got Opera on Her Brain"), "Swing Me Honey, Swing Me," "There's a Warm Spot in My Heart for You Baby," "A Trip to Coontown," "The Trumpet in the Cornfield," "The Wedding of the Chinee and the Coon," "What a Real American Can Do," "When I Gets to Be the Ruling Power," "When the Chickens Go to Sleep," "When the War Is O'er," "Where the Ivy Leaves Grow Close beside the Door," "You'll Have to Choose Another Baby, Now," "The Zulu Hall of Fame"

References

SECONDARY: "Amusements: At the Bijou Theatre," *Reading (Pa.) Eagle,* 29 September 1895, p. 8 (this promotional statement for John W. Isham's Octoroons was published in at least one other newspaper: *Utica [N.Y.] Daily Press,* 20 November 1895, p. 5, col. 3); "Stage Notes of the Week," *New York Times,* 14 August 1898, p. 6; "A Trip to Coontown," *Saturday Budget* (Quebec), 22 October 1898, p. 4; Sylvester Russell, "Mr. Cole and the Johnsons," *Indianapolis Freeman: An Illustrated Colored Newspaper,* 16 August 1902, p. 5; Sylvester Russell, "Billy Johnson," *Indianapolis Freeman: An Illustrated Colored Newspaper,* 23 September 1916, p. 6; "Pioneers of the Stage: Memoirs of William Foster," ed. Theophilus Lewis, in *The Official Theatrical World of Colored Artists* 1 (April 1928): 40–42, 44–49; Eileen Southern, *Biographical Dictionary of Afro-American and African Musicians* (Westport, Conn.: Greenwood, 1982), 212; Thomas L. Riis, "'Bob' Cole: His Life and His Legacy to Black Musical Theater," *Black Perspective in Music* 13 (Autumn 1985): 135–50; Thomas L. Riis, *Just before Jazz: Black Musical Theater in New York, 1890–1915* (Washington, D.C.: Smithsonian Institution Press, 1989), 26, 28, 80, 84, 239–41; Thomas L. Riis, *More Than Just Minstrel Shows: The Rise of Black Musical Theatre at the Turn of the Century* (Brooklyn: Brooklyn College of the City University of New York, 1992), passim; Bernard L. Peterson, Jr., *A Century of Musicals in Black and White: An Encyclopedia of Musical Stage Works by, about, or Involving African Americans* (Westport, Conn.: Greenwood, 1993), passim; Samuel A. Hay, *African American Theatre: A Historical and Critical Analysis* (Cambridge: Cambridge University Press, 1994), 142, 145–46; Lynn Abbott and Doug Seroff, *Out of Sight: The Rise of African American Popular Music, 1889–1895* (Jackson: University Press of Mississippi, 2002), passim; Karen Sotiropoulos, *Staging Race: Black Performers in Turn of the Century America* (Cambridge: Harvard University Press, 2006), passim; Frank Cullen, *Vaudeville Old and New: An Encyclopedia of Variety Performers in America* (New York: Routledge, 2007), 1: 246–47; Paula Marie Seniors, *Beyond Lift Every Voice and Sing: The Culture of Uplift, Identity, and Politics in Black Musical Theater* (Columbus: Ohio State University Press, 2009), 14–19; Fred R. Shapiro, "You Can Quote Them," *Yale Alumni Magazine* 73 (September–October 2009): 57–58 (also available at http://www.yalealumnimagazine.com/articles/2552 [accessed 21 May 2014]); Krystyn R. Moon, David Krasner, and Thomas L. Riis, "Forgotten Manuscripts: A Trip to Coontown," *African American Review* 44 (Spring–Summer 2011): 7–24.

Johnson, Buddy (Woodrow Wilson)

Leader, composer, arranger, piano, singer

1 January 1915 (Darlington County, S.C.)–9 February 1977 (New York, N.Y.)

S.C. residence: Darlington County, including Darlington town (1915–no later than 1935)

Johnson reportedly played the piano as early as age five. In high school he wrote and played in musical revues. To pursue a career in music he moved to N.Y.C. in the mid-1930s; by the end of the decade he had toured Europe as pianist with the Cotton Club Revue. Upon returning to the United States he signed with Decca Records and recorded for the initial time; he remained with Decca until affiliating with Mercury in 1953. He began an extended engagement at the Savoy Ballroom in 1945. Largely because his band played danceable music, it was popular, as evidenced by its extensive touring. Not only did Johnson hire good musicians, including trumpeter Dupree Bolton and trombonist Slide Hampton, but two singers in particular enhanced the music: his sister Ella Johnson and Arthur Prysock. Johnson discovered and hired vocalist Etta Jones, though she did not record with him. Among his hits were "Hittin' on Me," "Please, Mr. Johnson," "Since I Fell for You," and "They All Say I'm the Biggest Fool." He composed all these songs, as well as many of the ones his band played. His recording of "When My Man Comes Home" is on the sound track of *Life* (1999). Johnson retired from the music business by the mid-1960s, presumably to become a minister. He is buried in Woodlawn Cemetery, Bronx, N.Y.

Johnson's birth date comes from the Social Security Death Index; the death date, from the musician's death notice. Conducted in N.Y.C. on 2 April, the 1940 census indicates that then and in 1935, Johnson lived in N.Y.C. with his siblings Ella Johnson and Hiram Johnson; the latter became a record company owner.

Compositions

"A-12," "Baby, Don't You Cry," "B. J. Blues," "Bring It Home to Me," "Buddy's Boogie," "Did You See Jackie Robinson Hit That Ball?," "Dr. Jive Jives," "Go Ahead and Rock," "Going to New York," "Hittin' on Me," "I Keep On Loving You," "I'll Dearly Love You," "I'm Just Your Fool," "I'm Stepping Out," "In There," "It's Obdacious," "I Wonder Where Our Love Has Gone," "Jeanette," "Keep Me Close to You," "Kool Kitty," "Let's Start All Over Again," "Like You Do," "My Humble Plea," "My Lonely Cabin," "No More Love," "Now You're Gone," "One of Them Good Ones," "One Thing I Never Could Do," "Please, Mr. Johnson," "Rock On," "Satisfy My Soul," "Save Your Love for Me,"

"Serves Me Right," "Since I Fell for You," "Small Taste," "South Main," "Stop Pretending," "That's How I Feel about You," "That's the Stuff You Gotta Watch," "There's No One Like You," "They All Say I'm the Biggest Fool," "This New Situation," "Troyon Swing," "Walk 'Em," "When My Man Comes Home," "Without the One You Love," "You'd Better Believe Me," "You Got It Made," "You'll Get Them Blues," "You're Everything My Heart Desires"

Recordings as Leader

"Reese's Idea" (1939), "Stop Pretending" (1939), "Please, Mr. Johnson" (1940), "Southern Echoes" (1940), "You Won't Let Me Go" (1940), "Boogie-Woogie's Mother-in-Law" (1941), "I'm Stepping Out" (1941), "New Please Mr. Johnson" (1941), "Southern Exposure" (1941), "Troyon Swing" (1941), "Uncle Eph's Dream" (1941), "I Ain't Mad with You" (1942), "I Done Found Out" (1942), "Let's Beat Out Some Love" (1942), "Stand Back and Smile" (1942), "Fine Brown Frame" (1944), "I Still Love You" (1944), "South Main" (1944), "They All Say I'm the Biggest Fool" (1944), "Opus Two" (1945), "Since I Fell for You" (1945), "Walk 'Em" (1945), "Far Cry" (1947), "Hey, Sweet Potato" (1947), "L'il Dog" (1947), "No, There'll Never Be Someone So Sweet as You" (1947), "Somebody's Knockin' at My Door" (1947), "You'll Get Them Blues" (1947), "Did You See Jackie Robinson Hit That Ball?" (1949), "Down Yonder" (1949), "That's What My Baby Said" (1949), "Dr. Jive Jives" (1950), "(Ever Since) the One Love's Been Gone" (1950), "I Cry" (1950), "You Got to Walk That Chalk Line" (1950), "Am I Blue?" (1951), "At Last" (1951), "A Handful of Stars" (1951), "Root Man Blues" (1951), "Baby, You're Always on My Mind" (1952), "Shufflin' and Rollin'" (1952), *Buddy and Ella Johnson, 1953–1964, Buddy Johnson Wails* (1957), *Go Ahead and Rock* (1958)

Leaders Recorded With

Skeets Tolbert (1941), Andrew Tibbs (1951), Ella Johnson (1954–1956)

References

SECONDARY: Mel Tapley, "Walkin' Rhythm's Buddy Johnson Leaves Hospital," *New York Amsterdam News,* 22 January 1977, sec. D, p. 2; "Johnson—Woodrow Buddy," *New York Times,* 10 February 1977, 42 (death notice); Dave Penny and Tony Burke, "Buddy Johnson—The Decca Years (1939–1952)," *Blues and Rhythm: The Gospel Truth* 1 (July 1984): 12–17 (includes discography); Dave Penny, "Walk 'Em Again," *Blues and Rhythm: The Gospel Truth* 40 (November 1988): 17–19, 21 (includes discography); Billy Vera, "Buddy Johnson: A Reassessment," *Blues and Rhythm: The Gospel Truth* 174 (November 2002): 8–9; J. C. Marion, "Walk 'Em: The Buddy Johnson Story," http://home.earthlink.net/~v1tiger/buddyj.html (2004; accessed 21 May 2014); J. C. Marion, "The Buddy Johnson Story: Part Two," http://home.earthlink.net/~v1tiger/buddyj2.html (2004; accessed 21 May 2014); Larry Birnbaum, *Before Elvis: The Prehistory of Rock 'n' Roll* (Lanham, Md.: Scarecrow Press, 2013), 178–80.

Johnson, Ella (Ella May or Ellamae)

Singer

Probably late 1910s (Darlington County, S.C.)–8 or 16 February 2004 (New York, N.Y.)

S.C. residence: Darlington County, including Darlington town (probably late 1910s–probably 1939)

When Buddy Johnson became successful in N.Y.C., he invited Ella Johnson, his sister, to join him there as singer with his band, which she did. She recorded for the initial time in 1940, with one of the songs, "Please, Mr. Johnson," becoming a hit, mainly in the black community. Other musical successes followed, always with her brother's band: "When My Man Comes Home" (1942), "That's the Stuff You Gotta Watch" (1944), "Hittin' on Me" (1953), and "I Don't Want Nobody" (1955). She was the first singer to record her brother's "Since I Fell for You" (1945), which was later recorded by many other vocalists, and "Did You See Jackie Robinson Hit That Ball?" (1949), which gained popularity in Count Basie's recording of it that same year. She was also the initial singer to record "Alright, Okay, You Win" (1955), which became associated with Joe Williams. In an age when some singers used their band affiliations to launch solo careers, Johnson sang only with her brother's group, other than at a few sessions she led, sometimes backed by Buddy Johnson's band. When her brother left the music business by the mid-1960s, she did, too. Her recording of "When My Man Comes Home" (1942), with her brother's band, is on the sound track of *Life* (1999). She is buried in Woodlawn Cemetery, Bronx, N.Y.

The Social Security Death Index indicates that Johnson was born on 19 November 1916 and died on 8 February 2004; all other sources consulted state that she died on 16 February 2004. Johnson was estimated as age two when she was enumerated for the census in Darlington County on 13 January 1920; as ten when enumerated in Darlington on 16 April 1930; as twenty-two when enumerated in N.Y.C. on 2 April 1940. Censuses identify her given name as Ella May (1920) and Ellamae (1930, 1940). The 1940 census reveals that then and in 1935, Johnson lived in N.Y.C. with her siblings Buddy Johnson and Hiram Johnson; the latter became a record company owner.

Recordings as Leader

"Darlin' Baby" (1945), "Since You Went Away" (1945), *Buddy and Ella Johnson, 1953–1964*

Leader Recorded With

Buddy Johnson (1940–1942, 1944–1945, 1947, 1949–1958, 1961)

Award

Rhythm & Blues Foundation Pioneer Award (1992)

References

SECONDARY: Mel Tapley, "Walkin' Rhythm's Buddy Johnson Leaves Hospital," *New York Amsterdam News,* 22 January 1977, sec. D, p. 2 (comments by Johnson); Dave Penny, "Walk 'Em Again," *Blues and Rhythm: The Gospel Truth* 40 (November 1988): 17–19, 21 (includes discography); Billy Vera, "Buddy Johnson: A Reassessment," *Blues and Rhythm: The Gospel Truth* 174 (November 2002): 8–9; "Ella Johnson, 86, Singer in Jazz Bands," *New York Times,* 20 March 2004, sec. B, p. 7 (obituary); Billy Vera, "Ella Johnson," *Blues and Rhythm: The Gospel Truth* 189 (May 2004): 11 (obituary); Richard Tapp, "Ella Johnson," *Juke Blues* 56 (Summer 2004): 64–65 (obituary).

Johnson, Henry ("Rufe")

Guitar, banjo, harmonica, piano, singer

Probably late 1908 (Union County, S.C.)–1 February 1974 (Union, S.C.)

S.C. residence: Union County, including Bogansville Township and Buffalo (probably 1908–1974)

Johnson lived his entire life in Union County. As a child he was known as Rooster, which evolved into Rufe. He learned to play the guitar around 1925 and the piano later. During the 1930s he sang on radio programs in Spartanburg (with the West Spring Friendly Four) and Union (with the Silver Star Quartet). He performed religious music until the early 1950s, when he embraced secular music, including the blues. Also until the early 1950s he worked as a farmer; thereafter, as a porter at the Wallace Thomson Hospital in Union. All of Johnson's recordings were made in the early 1970s. The only album devoted entirely to his music was released on Trix. During this same period Johnson and Peg Leg Sam (Arthur Jackson) had a regular program on the Union radio station and performed together elsewhere, including at Endangered Species, a club in Chapel Hill, N.C. Bruce Bastin states that Johnson "remains the finest country blues guitarist I've ever seen and heard" ("Truckin' My Blues Away," 211). Johnson died at the hospital where he worked and is buried in the Wyatts Chapel Baptist Church Cemetery, Buffalo, S.C.

Johnson was the brother of guitarist Roosevelt Johnson and a cousin of guitarist Thelmon Johnson. Though Johnson's birth date is most frequently given as 8 December 1908, the Social Security Death Index records it as 2 October 1908. When Johnson was enumerated for the census in Union County on 30 January 1920, his age was estimated as eleven; in Bogansville Township on 26 April 1930, as twenty-six. His death date comes from the obituaries published in Spartanburg and Union newspapers. The Johnsons were tenants on a farm between Union and Jonesville. It has not been confirmed that Johnson composed the tunes listed here, which Sheldon Harris credits to him in *Blues Who's Who: A Biographical Dictionary of Blues Singers* (New Rochelle, N.Y.: Arlington House, 1979), 282. The vinyl and CD releases of *The Union County Flash!* include the statement, "All compositions and arrangements by Henry Johnson." Though he might have written some of the tunes, he did not compose all of them. "Can't Keep from Cryin'" and "Rock Tonight Baby," recorded in Union in 1973, were released on *Another Man Done Gone*... (Flyright 528); the album cover indicates, incorrectly, that they were recorded in 1963. *Carolina Country Blues* (Flyright 505) preserves performances by five musicians at the 1973 Chapel Hill Festival in N.C. With eight selections, Johnson is the one most heavily represented. Recordings Johnson made in 1972 remain unissued.

Compositions

"Boogie Baby," "Had a Little Woman," "Join the Army," "Me and My Dog," "My Baby's House,"

"My Dog Blues," "Sittin' Down Thinkin'," "Union County Slide"

Recordings as Leader

The Union County Flash! (1972), "Can't Keep from Cryin'" (this and all subsequent recordings 1973), "Crow Jane," "Had a Little Woman," "Hey, Noah," "Me and My Dog," "My Mother's Grave Must Be Found," "Rock Tonight, Baby," "Sittin' Down Thinkin'," "Step It Up and Went," "Union County Slide," "Until I Found the Lord"

Leader Recorded With

Peg Leg Sam (1970, 1972)

References

SECONDARY: Kip Lornell, "Peg Pete and His Pals," *Living Blues* 11 (Winter 1972–1973): 27–29; "Henry Johnson," *Spartanburg (S.C.) Herald-Journal,* 3 February 1974, sec. A, p. 9 (obituary); "Henry Johnson," *Union (S.C.) Daily Times,* 4 February 1974, p. 5 (obituary); Pete Lowry, "Henry 'Rufe' Johnson, 1908–1974," *Living Blues* 17 (Summer 1974): 6 (obituary); Bruce Bastin, brochure accompanying the album *Another Man Done Gone . . .* (1978; Flyright 528), 8–9; Bruce Bastin, *Red River Blues: The Blues Tradition in the Southeast* (Urbana: University of Illinois Press, 1986), 188, 190, 192–94; Bruce Bastin, "Truckin' My Blues Away: East Coast Piedmont Styles," in *Nothing but the Blues: The Music and the Musicians,* by Lawrence Cohn et al. (New York: Abbeville, 1993), 205–31 (see especially 211–12, 231).

Johnson, Hiram

Record company owner, manager, promoter

18 December 1907 (Darlington County, S.C.)-February 1980

S.C. residence: Darlington County, including Darlington town (1907-no later than 1935)

By 1935 Johnson lived in N.Y.C., where he worked as a bootblack in 1940. At least in 1948 he served as a music publicist. During the mid-1950s he managed several doo-wop/rhythm-and-blues groups, including the Dovers, the Dubs (and its predecessors, the Marvels and the Five Wings), the Paragons, and the Shells. Though he established Johnson Records in 1957 apparently to release music by the Dubs, demand for the group's music so overwhelmed his distribution system that he arranged for Gone Records to distribute the Dubs' records. He sold his company later that year.

Johnson's birth and death dates come from the Social Security Death Index. Johnson was estimated as age three when he was enumerated for the census in Philadelphia Township, Darlington County, on 7 May 1910; as twelve when enumerated in Darlington County on 13 January 1920; as thirty-one when enumerated in N.Y.C. on 2 April 1940. The 1940 census indicates that in that year and in 1935 he lived in N.Y.C. with his siblings Buddy Johnson, the band leader, and Ella Johnson, the singer; it also identifies his occupation. Todd R. Baptista states that Johnson did not compose some of the songs credited to him.

Compositions

"Ain't That So," "Ain't You Got Music," "Baby, Oh Baby," "Come On, Baby," "Cry, Baby, Cry," "Deep Within," "Don't Ask Me to Be Lonely," "Don't Cry," "Early in the Evening," "Fine Little Girl," "For the First Time," "Gonna Make a Change," "Hold Me, Baby," "Hurry Up, Honey," "If I Had a Chance to Love You," "Is There a Love for Me?," "Limborino," "Love of Sylvia," "Made for Lovers," "My Cherie," "My Heart," "Please Be My Guy," "Pretty Little Girl," "Pretty Little School Girl," "She Wasn't Meant for Me," "Sippin' Soda," "Someone Up There," "Song in My Heart," "Such Lovin'," "That's All I Wanno Do," "Thief," "We're Goin' Out to Rock Tonight," "What's in an Angel's Eyes?," "Will You Miss Me?," "You Are My Angel"

References

SECONDARY: "Buddy's Brother Joins McCarthy," *New York Amsterdam News,* 27 March 1948, p. 25; Todd R. Baptista, *Group Harmony: Behind the Rhythm and the Blues* (New Bedford, Mass.: TRB Enterprises, 1996), 28–40; Marv Goldberg, "The Dubs," http://www.uncamarvy.com/Dubs/dubs.html (2009; accessed 21 May 2014).

Johnson, Jonas

12 August 1912 (Charleston, S.C.)-?

S.C. residence: Charleston (1912-at least until 1930)

A ward of Jenkins Orphanage, Johnson played in its bands at least in the late 1920s and performed with one of them in England in 1929. His instrument is not known.

The passenger list of the *Majestic,* which transported the orphanage band from Southampton, England, to N.Y.C. in June 1929, records Johnson's birth date and place. The musician's age was estimated as seventeen when Johnson was enumerated for the census at the institution on 2 April 1930.

Reference

SECONDARY: Howard Rye, "Visiting Fireboys: The Jenkins' Orphanage Bands in Britain," *Storyville* 130 (1987): 137–43.

Johnson, Roosevelt

Guitar

Ca. 1906 (Union County, S.C.)–?

S.C. residence: Union County, including Bogansville Township (ca. 1907–)

Johnson helped teach Henry "Rufe" Johnson, his brother, to play the guitar.

Johnson was a cousin of guitarist Thelmon Johnson. When enumerated for the census in Union County on 30 January 1920, he was estimated as age thirteen; in Bogansville Township on 26 April 1930, as twenty-four; in Union Township on 16 April 1940, as thirty-four.

References

SECONDARY: Pete Lowry, notes to Henry "Rufe" Johnson, *The Union County Flash!* (1973; Trix 3304); Bruce Bastin, *Red River Blues: The Blues Tradition in the Southeast* (Urbana: University of Illinois Press, 1986), 193.

Johnson, Thelmon

Guitar

1903 (S.C.)–27 August 1922 (Winston-Salem, N.C.)

Johnson helped teach Henry "Rufe" Johnson, his cousin, to play the guitar.

Johnson was a cousin of guitarist Roosevelt Johnson. His dates and places of birth and death come from his death certificate, which indicates that he died from typhoid fever.

References

SECONDARY: Pete Lowry, notes to Henry "Rufe" Johnson, *The Union County Flash!* (1973; Trix 3304); Bruce Bastin, *Red River Blues: The Blues Tradition in the Southeast* (Urbana: University of Illinois Press, 1986), 193.

Johnson, Wanda Jean

Singer

8 October 1963 (outside Belton, S.C.)–

S.C. residences: outside Belton (1963–1995), Anderson (1995–)

Reared in a musical family that sang in a Baptist church, Johnson, who works in law enforcement, performed with some siblings as the Johnson Sisters. After singing at blues jams, she became part of the group Cocktail Frank. Following her 1998 graduation from Southern Wesleyan University she joined Shrimp City Slim (1999–2013), with whom she appeared at numerous festivals and toured extensively, especially internationally.

Compositions

"Always," "Bad Case of the Blues," "Bath Water," "Believe Me, Baby," "Blue Ain't Nothin' but a Color," "Good Home Lovin'," "Heading North," "Hold What You Got," "I Apologize," "If I Rise in the Morning," "I'm Through with You," "Just Tell Me," "Love Food," "Move On," "The Pane," "The River," "Time to Get Over You"

Recordings as Leader

Call Me Miss Wanda (2003), *Natural Resource* (2006), *Hold What You Got* (2008)

Leader Recorded With

Cocktail Frank (1998; unissued)

Award

Tri-County Technical College Face of the 1990s (2012)

Wanda Johnson, Greenwood Blues Cruise, Greenwood, S.C., 9 July 2011; permission of the photographer, Gene Tomko

References

PRIMARY: Scott M. Bock, "I'm Just a Woman That Likes to Sing," *Living Blues* 198 (December 2008): 14–19 (narrative by Johnson).

SECONDARY: Lisa Garrett, "Wanda Johnson Named One of Tri-County's Faces of the Decades," http://www.tctc.edu/About_TCTC/Media/News_Releases/1990s_face_of_the_decades.xml (9 May 2012; accessed 21 May 2014) (comments by Johnson); Vincent Harris, "Wanda Johnson Is No Blues-Club Veteran, but She Sounds Like It," http://www.goupstate.com/article/20120606/ENT/206071007 (6 June 2012; accessed 21 May 2014) (comments by Johnson).

Johnson, William

Trombone

Possibly May 1888 (S.C.)–?

S.C. residence: Charleston (by 1895–at least into early 1900s)

A ward of Jenkins Orphanage, Johnson played in its bands from the 1890s into the early 1900s and performed with one of them in England in 1895.

The passenger list of the *Paris,* which transported the orphanage band to England in September 1895, records Johnson's age as seven; the list for the *Teutonic,* which returned the group to the United States the next month, specifies it as four (and spells the surname Johnston). Conducted at the orphanage on 28 June, the 1900 census indicates that the musician was born in S.C. in May 1888.

References

SECONDARY: John Chilton, *A Jazz Nursery: The Story of the Jenkins' Orphanage Bands of Charleston, South Carolina* (London: Bloomsbury Book Shop, 1980), 56; Howard Rye, "Visiting Fireboys: The Jenkins' Orphanage Bands in Britain," *Storyville* 130 (1987): 137–43.

Jones, Abraham

Baritone horn

June 1886 (S.C.)–?

S.C. residence: Charleston (at least 1890s–at least into early 1900s)

A ward of Jenkins Orphanage, Jones played in its bands in the early 1900s.

Jones's birth date and place come from the 1900 census, which was conducted at the orphanage on 28 June.

Jones, Etta

Singer

Possibly 1927 or 25 November 1928 (Aiken, S.C.)–16 October 2001 (Mount Vernon, N.Y.)

S.C. residence: Aiken (1927 or 1928–no later than 1930)

After leaving Aiken as an infant, Jones lived briefly in Detroit before, by 1930, locating to N.Y.C., where, and in its environs, she lived the rest of her life. Buddy Johnson discovered her at the Apollo Theater; though she toured with his band, she never recorded with it. She performed as a single at the Onyx Club, where she impressed Leonard Feather, who arranged for her initial recording session. In time she became a regular with Earl Hines. The album *Don't Go to Strangers* established her reputation as a sensitive interpreter of lyrics. After performing with Houston Person in the late 1960s, she and the saxophonist formed a musical team in the early 1970s that remained intact for the remainder of her career, though she also recorded with other leaders during the last five years of her life. She had productive associations with record companies Prestige, Muse, and HighNote. Influenced by Billie Holiday and Dinah Washington, Jones primarily sang standards, infusing them with a blues feeling.

No public document has been located indicating Jones's birth date; without evidence reference works identify it as 25 November 1928. Jones might be the Georgetta Jones enumerated for the census in N.Y.C. on 3 April 1930. Estimated age three and born in S.C., she was the daughter of Deliah Jones.

Recordings as Leader

"Blow Top Blues" (1944), "Evil Gal Blues" (1944), "Long, Long Journey" (1944), "Salty Papa Blues" (1944), "Solitude" (1945), "So Tired" (1945), "Among My Souvenirs" (1946), "Blues to End All Blues" (1946), "Mean to Me" (1946), "Osculate Me, Daddy" (1946), "Ain't No Hurry, Baby" (1947), "I Sold My Heart to the Junkman" (1947), "Misery Is a Thing Called Moe" (1947), "My Sleepy Head" (1947), "Overwork Blues" (1947), "The Richest Guy in the Graveyard" (1947), "This Is a Fine Time" (1947), "What Ev'ry Woman Knows" (1947), *Etta Jones Sings* (1957; also titled *The Jones Girl . . . Etta Sings Sings Sings*), *Don't Go to Strangers* (1960), *Hollar!* (1960–1962), *Something Nice* (1960), *So Warm* (1961), *From the*

Heart (1962), *Lonely and Blue* (1962), *Love Shout* (1962–1963), *Etta Jones Sings* (1965), *Etta Jones '75*, *Ms. Jones to You* (1976), *My Mother's Eyes* (1977), *If You Could See Me Now* (1978), *Don't Misunderstand: Live in New York* (1980), *Save Your Love for Me* (1980), *Love Me with All Your Heart* (1983), *Fine and Mellow* (1986), *I'll Be Seeing You* (1987), *Sugar* (1989), *Christmas with Etta Jones* (1990), *A Night in Roppongi* (1990), *Reverse the Charges* (1992), *At Last* (1993, 1995), *My Gentleman Friend* (1994), *The Melody Lingers On* (1997), *Etta Jones Sings the Songs of Buddy Johnson: My Buddy* (1998), *All the Way* (1999), *Easy Living* (2000), *The Way We Were: Live in Concert* (2000), *Etta Jones Sings Lady Day* (2001)

Leaders Recorded With

Floyd "Horsecollar" Williams (1945), Pete Johnson (1946), Earl Hines (1952), Gene Ammons (1962, 1973), Cedar Walton (1972), Houston Person (1973–1974, 1977, 1980, 1994), James Williams (1996), Ray Brown (1997–1998), Milt Jackson (1997), Junior Mance (1998), Dick Morgan (1998), Clark Terry (1999), Keter Betts (2000), Jeanie Bryson (2000), Vanessa Rubin (2000), John David Simon (2000), Gene Walker (2000)

Awards

Eubie Blake Jazz Award (1982); Grammy Hall of Fame (2008; for the album *Don't Go to Strangers*)

References

PRIMARY: Benjamin Franklin V, *Jazz and Blues Musicians of South Carolina: Interviews with Jabbo, Dizzy, Drink, and Others* (Columbia: University of South Carolina Press, 2008), 32–39.

SECONDARY: Mathew Bahl, "Remembering Etta Jones," http://www.allaboutjazz.com/php/article.php?id=24821&pg=1 (2007; accessed 21 May 2014).

Jones, Rufus ("Speedy")

Drums

Probably 28 May 1931 (Charleston, S.C.)–probably 18 April 1990 (Las Vegas, Nev.)

S.C. residences: Charleston (probably 1931–ca. 1953), Columbia (Fort Jackson) (ca. 1957)

As a youth Jones played trumpet, clarinet, violin, and saxophone before focusing on the drums. Though not a ward of Jenkins Orphanage, he played with its bands in the 1940s. He reportedly attended Florida A&M University briefly in the early 1950s but quit school to become a professional musician, initially with Lionel Hampton. After serving in the army he became active on the N.Y.C. music scene; he performed regularly at the Metropole. He drummed with Maynard Ferguson (1959–1963) before forming his own quintet, which was active in 1963 and 1964. He was with Count Basie in the mid-1960s before joining Duke Ellington (on recordings there was a brief period of overlap), with whom he was a regular from 1966 until 1973, when arthritic hands forced him to abandon playing. He is known for drumming at great speeds; his performance on "Kixx" with Ellington (1972) illustrates his ability to sustain interest in a drum solo. Bruce Klauber believes that Jones was, at his best, "one of the most flexible, sensitive, and swinging drummers" (92).

Though 27 May 1936 is the accepted date of the musician's birth, the Social Security Death Index indicates that Jones was born on 28 May 1931. When he was enumerated for the census in Charleston on 20 April 1940, his age was estimated as eight. His age is recorded as twenty-four on the passenger list of the *Liberté*, which transported members of the Lionel Hampton band to N.Y.C. from Le Havre, France, in March 1955. Though sources specify 25 April 1990 as his death date, the Social Security Death Index identifies it as a week earlier.

Recording as Leader

Five on Eight (1963)

Leaders Recorded With

Lionel Hampton (1954), Amos Milburn (1955), Buddy Johnson (1958, 1961), Chris Connor (1960–1961), Maynard Ferguson (1960–1963), Woody Herman (1960), Count Basie (1965, 1967), Al Grey (1965), Duke Ellington (1966–1973), Johnny Hodges (1967), Alice Babs (1973)

References

PRIMARY: Robert Barnelle, "Rufus 'Speedy' Jones," *Modern Drummer* 7 (November 1983): 76–80 (narrative by Jones).

SECONDARY: Edward Kennedy Ellington, *Music Is My Mistress* (Garden City, N.Y.: Doubleday, 1973), 402; John Chilton, *A Jazz Nursery: The Story of the Jenkins' Orphanage Bands of Charleston, South Carolina* (London: Bloomsbury Book Shop, 1980), 48, 56; Bruce Klauber, "What Do You Know About. . . ? Rufus 'Speedy' Jones," *Modern Drummer* 35 (August 2011): 90–92.

Jordan, (James) Taft

Trumpet, singer

Probably 15 February 1914 (S.C., probably Florence)–1 December 1981 (New York, N.Y.)

S.C. residence: probably Florence (probably 1914–no later than 1920)

Jordan learned to play the trumpet as a teenager in Norfolk, Va., where he performed through high school. After moving with his mother to Philadelphia, he played with the bands of Ted Tinsley, Billy Watson, Jimmy Gorham, and Doc Hyder. He joined Chick Webb in 1934; other than for a brief period with Willie Bryant, Jordan remained with Webb until the drummer's death (1939), and even beyond it when Ella Fitzgerald nominally led Webb's band. Probably in the early 1940s he formed a quintet that played in Harlem, including at the Savoy Ballroom; then, mid-decade, he was a regular with Duke Ellington. During the 1950s he worked as a studio musician at rhythm-and-blues recording sessions, including ones led by Lavern Baker and Ruth Brown. After affiliating with various groups he toured with Benny Goodman and played with the clarinetist at the Brussels World's Fair and Newport Jazz Festival, both in 1958. Subsequently he primarily freelanced, though in the 1960s he played in the pit band for *Hello, Dolly!* Mostly influenced by the playing of Louis Armstrong, Jordan also imitated his singing. He is on such significant recordings as Chick Webb and Ella Fitzgerald's "A-Tisket, a-Tasket" (1938), Ellington's *Black, Brown, and Beige* (1944), and Miles Davis's *Miles Ahead* (1957) and *Sketches of Spain* (1959).

Though 15 February 1915 is Jordan's accepted birth date, the Social Security Death Index indicates that the trumpeter was born on 15 February 1914. His age was estimated as five when he was enumerated for the census in Norfolk on 2 January 1920; this document reveals that he was born in S.C. Conducted in Norfolk on 10 April, the 1930 census estimates his age as fourteen and specifies S.C. as his birthplace. The 1940 census (conducted in N.Y.C. on 3 April) estimates his age as twenty-five, notes that he lived in N.Y.C. in 1935, and identifies Va. as his birthplace. All secondary sources consulted state that he was born in Florence, S.C. These assertions are probably correct because Jordan's mother, Annie Dunkin, was enumerated there for the census on 28 or 29 April 1910, estimated age fifteen. A claim that Jordan led a recording session for Aamco that was released in

Taft Jordan, Aquarium Club, N.Y.C., ca. 1946; reproduced from the William P. Gottlieb Collection, Library of Congress, Music Division

the 1950s has not been confirmed, but he plays on an Aamco recording of music from *Porgy and Bess,* led by George Rhodes (1958). He appears in Art Kane's 1958 photograph known as "A Great Day in Harlem." Also in this picture, Jordan's son, Taft Jordan, Jr., is seated on the curb next to Count Basie. See Charles Graham, 69, 72–73.

Recordings as Leader

"Devil in the Moon" (1935), "If the Moon Turns Green" (1935), "Louisiana Fairytale" (1935), "Night Wind" (1935), *The Moods of Taft Jordan* (1958–1959), "Indian Summer" (1959), "Young Man with a Horn" (1959), *Mood Indigo* (1961)

Leaders Recorded With

Alabama Washboard Stompers (1932), Washboard Rhythm Kings (1932–1933), Chick Webb (1933–1939), Ethel Waters (1934), Willie Bryant (1936, 1945), Ella Fitzgerald (1936–1941, 1951–1953, 1962, 1973), Duke Ellington (1943–1947), Herbie Fields (1944), Sonny Greer (1945), Doc Pomus (1945), Laurel Watson (1945), Al Hibbler (1946–1947, 1954), Johnny Hodges (1947), Sir Charles Thompson (1947), Ivory Joe Hunter (1949), Sarah Vaughan (1949), Sy Oliver (1950–1952), Pearl Bailey (1951–1953), Connee Boswell (1951), Bennie Green (1951), Blues Chasers (1952), Hadda Brooks (1952), Ruth Brown (1952–1953, 1960), Benny Carter (1952), Arthur Prysock (1952), Little Jimmy Scott (1952), Big Joe Turner (1952, 1959), George Williams (1953–1954), Louis Armstrong (1954), LaVern Baker (1954, 1957, 1960), Big Maybelle (1954), Steve Allen (1955), Dizzy Gillespie (1955), Al Sears (1955), Varetta Dillard (1956), André Persiany (1956), Miles Davis (1957, 1959–1960), Linda Hopkins (1957), Rex Stewart (1957–1959), Eugenie Baird (1958), Benny Goodman (1958), Red Prysock (1958), George Rhodes (1958), Dud Bascomb (1959–1960), Don Redman (1959), Dakota Staton (1959), Al "Jazzbo" Collins (1960), Swingville All Stars (1960), Eddie Barefield (1973), Norris Turney (1977)

Film

A Great Day in Harlem (1994)

References

PRIMARY: Stanley Dance, *The World of Swing* (New York: Scribner's, 1974), 1: 77–92 (narrative by Jordan); Johnny Simmen, "Sandy Williams: A Portrait," *Storyville* 116 (December 1984–January 1985): 48–69 (see especially 49) (Jordan's 1958 comments about Sandy Williams).

SECONDARY: Charles Graham, *The Great Jazz Day* (New York: Da Capo, 2000), 55; Scott Yanow, *The Trumpet Kings: The Players Who Shaped the Sound of Jazz Trumpet* (San Francisco: Backbeat Books, 2001), 215–16.

Keenan, Norman Dewey

Bass

23 November 1916 (Union, S.C.)–12 February 1980 (Brooklyn, N.Y.)

S.C. residence: Union (1916–probably 1930)

Born to musical parents, Keenan began taking piano lessons in Union and continued them after moving to Brooklyn, N.Y., at age thirteen. Approximately two years later he started playing bass. He and neighborhood friends formed a group, led by Joe Alston, that evolved into the Tiny Bradshaw band in the mid-1930s. Keenan left it in 1939 to join Lucky Millinder. Later that year or early in 1940 he affiliated with Henry Wells; he was with Earl Bostic from mid-1940 into 1941. In late 1941 he led a band that played at Smalls Paradise in N.Y.C. He joined Cootie Williams in early 1942 and stayed with him until Keenan was drafted into the army in 1944; he rejoined Williams upon being discharged in early 1946. He was with Eddie "Cleanhead" Vinson from 1947 to 1949, and with the Harlemaires later in 1949. In a trio with Carl Lynch and Clarence Williams, he played at the Village Vanguard from 1949 to 1957, when he became the full-time bassist for Harry Belafonte, with whom he remained into 1962. He then worked two seasons on the television program *Hootenanny.* He is best known for his years with Count Basie (mid-1960s–mid-1970s). He is buried in site 3094, section 5, Calverton National Cemetery, Calverton, N.Y.

Military records identify Keenan's middle initial as W. Keenan lived in Union as late as 4 April 1930, when he was enumerated there for the census. His statement that in the 1950s he recorded with such rhythm-and-blues groups as the Cardinals, Orioles, and Ravens has not been substantiated.

Leaders Recorded With

Cootie Williams (1942, 1944, 1946–1947), Bob Merrill (1947), Beatrice Reading (1953), Big Maybelle (1954), Harry Belafonte (1957–1959, 1961–1962), Miriam Makeba (ca. 1960), Chad Mitchell (ca. 1963), Count Basie (1965–1973), Frank Sinatra (1965–1966), Roy Eldridge (1966), Kay Starr (1968), Joe Williams (1971), Big Joe Turner (1972), Teresa Brewer (1973)

Film

Cootie Williams and His Orchestra (1943; series 1, number 2 of *Film Vodvil*)

References

PRIMARY: "Musicians Talking: Norman Keenan to Peter Vacher," *Jazz and Blues* 1 (April 1971): 12–15.

SECONDARY: "Keenan—Norman D.," *New York Times*, 17 February 1980, sec. 1, p. 44 (late edition) (death notice).

Kennedy, Arthur

Alto horn, mellophone, trumpet
Ca. 1909 (S.C.)-?
S.C. residence: Charleston (by 1920-at least into early 1930s)

A ward of Jenkins Orphanage, Kennedy played in its bands in the late 1920s.

Kennedy's age was estimated as ten when the youth was enumerated for the census at the orphanage on 9 January 1920; this document identifies his birthplace.

Kenny, George W., Jr.

Saxophone, flute, bass
3 December 1932 (Charleston, S.C.)-
S.C. residences: Charleston (1932-1951, 1959-), Orangeburg (1955-1959)

Kenny played in the band at Burke High School in Charleston. After service in the air force (1951–1955), he enrolled at what is now South Carolina State University, from which he received a degree in 1959. He became a music teacher in Charleston, first at Lang High School (1959–1962), then at C. A. Brown High School (1962–1985), next at Burke High School (1985–1987), and finally at Courtney Middle School (1987–1991). He performed in Charleston for decades, leading his own groups and playing with such leaders as David Archer and Jamie Harris.

In *A Jazz Nursery: The Story of the Jenkins' Orphanage Bands of Charleston, South Carolina* (London: Bloomsbury Book Shop, 1980), 56, John Chilton spells Kenny's surname Kinnie and states that the musician played with the institution's bands in the 1940s, a claim that Kenny, never a ward of the institution, denies.

Leaders Recorded With

Counts (1979), Andrea Dupree (1995), Charleston Jazz Initiative Legends Band (2010)

References

SECONDARY: Jack McCray, *Charleston Jazz* (Charleston, S.C.: Arcadia Publishing, 2007), passim; Jack McCray,

George Kenny; permission of George Kenny

“Cookin’ with Jazz Musician George Kenny,” http://www.postandcourier.com/apps/pbcs.dll/article?avis=CP&date=20090305&category=ARCHIVES&lopenr=303059829&Ref=Ark.&template=printart (2012; accessed 21 May 2014).

Kenyatta, Robin (Robert Prince Haynes)

Saxophone, flute, hand percussion, singer

6 March 1942 (Moncks Corner, S.C.)–28 October 2004 (Lausanne, Switzerland)

S.C. residence: Moncks Corner (1942–probably 1946)

At age four Robert Haynes moved from S.C. to N.Y.C. Enamored of the alto saxophone at fourteen, he mastered it to the degree that he played it in clubs following graduation from high school. In the army, which he joined in 1962, he performed in a military band; concurrently he learned to play other instruments and to compose and arrange. Upon returning to civilian life he affiliated with the band of Pucho Brown and became known as Robin Kenyatta, in honor of his political idol, Jomo Kenyatta of Kenya. He participated in Bill Dixon’s October Revolution concerts in 1964. For a decade beginning in the mid-1960s he recorded frequently—as leader and sideman—initially in the avant-garde mode. He moved to Paris in 1969 but in 1972 returned to N.Y.C., where he soon made his most notable recording, “Last Tango in Paris” (1973). In the late 1970s he settled in Lausanne, Switzerland, where he taught and from which he toured. After returning to the United States in 2002 he taught music at Bentley College in Waltham, Mass., beginning in 2003, and modestly reentered the scene with performances in Boston and N.Y.C. Kenyatta was adept at the blues, hard bop, free jazz, funk, and Caribbean music.

Robin Kenyatta, in Italy; permission of Ayo Haynes

Kenyatta’s birth name is sometimes rendered Prince Robert Haynes. Ayo Kenyatta Haynes states that her father became known as Robin Kenyatta following his military service; Valerie Wilmer believes that he adopted this name at age thirteen, which seems unlikely.

Compositions

“Angela,” “Another Freight Train,” “Bad Boy,” “Beggars and Stealers,” “Blue Robin,” “Blues for Mama Doll,” “Blues for Your Mama,” “The Booze and I,” “Calling on You,” “Calypso Girl,” “Cool Blue,” “Dig, Dig, Diggin’,” “Dream Bug,” “Encourage the People,” “Every Body’s Talkin’,” “Ghost Stories,” “Girl from Martinique,” “Gun the Honeydripper,” “Gypsy Man,” “Hello Blues,” “His Love,” “If She Can’t Do It,” “Inscrutable Miss ‘O,’” “Island Shakedown,” “I Think I Got the Blues,” “Jazz Dance,” “Little Blue Devil,” “Love Him and Surrender,” “Melodie Chinoise,” “Nairobi Hot 5,” “Reflective Silence,” “Swinging Regards,” “Terra Nova,” “Thank You Jesus,” “Two Bass Blues,” “We’ll Be So Happy,” “Xenia,” “You Know How We Do,” “Zulu Princess”

Recordings as Leader

Until (1966–1967), *Stompin’ at the Savoy* (1967, 1974), *Beggars and Stealers* (1969, 1975), *Girl from Martinique* (1970), *Gypsy Man* (1972), *Robin Kenyatta’s Free State Band* (1972), *Terra Nova* (1973), *Nomusa* (1975), *Encourage the People* (1976), *Take the Heat off Me* (1979), *Blues for Mama Doll* (1987), *Ghost Stories* (1991), *Cool Blue* (2001)

Leaders Recorded With

Valerie Capers (1965–1966), Jazz Composer’s Orchestra (1965), Bill Dixon (1966), Roswell Rudd (1966–1967), Sonny Stitt (1966), Andrew Hill (1967, 1975), Barry Miles (1967), Archie Shepp (1968), Alan Silva (1970–1971), Oscar Brown, Jr. (1973), Ted Curson (1974), Magma (1984)

References

SECONDARY: Valerie Wilmer, "Robin Kenyatta and the Gypsy Life," *Down Beat* 39 (20 July 1972): 13, 48 (comments by Kenyatta); Margalit Fox, "Robin Kenyatta, 62, Saxophonist Whose Jazz Sampled Many Styles," *New York Times*, 15 November 2004, sec. B, p. 9 (titled "Robin Kenyatta, 62, Composer of Jazz and an Alto Saxophonist, Dies," this obituary is also available at http://www.nytimes.com/2004/11/14/arts/music/14kenyatta.html?_r=0) [accessed 21 May 2014]); Ayo Kenyatta Haynes, "Versatile Reeds Player and Educator," http://www.jazzhouse.org/gone/lastpost2.php3?edit=1099496862 (2004; accessed 21 May 2014).

King, Mabel (Donnie Mabel Elizabeth Washington)

Singer

25 December 1932 (Charleston, S.C.)–9 November 1999 (Woodland Hills, Calif.)

S.C. residence: Charleston (1932–1933)

At age two months Mabel Washington moved with her family from Charleston to Bronx, N.Y. At an undetermined date she began her show business career as a singer, initially with the Sincere Four, a gospel group. Upon marrying she assumed the surname of her husband and retained it after divorcing him. As Mabel King she recorded in the 1950s for Rama Records and in the 1960s for Amy Records. In 1956 she, Clyde McPhatter, the Teenagers, the Cleftones, and others were featured in a show at the Apollo Theater; she performed at a Harlem dance with the Heartbeats, Billy Dawn, and others; and she was part of a ten-day Alan Freed show in Brooklyn that also featured, among others, Fats Domino, Big Joe Turner, and the Penguins. During this period she was considered a blues singer—a great one, according to James A. McGowan. She wrote songs with Raoul J. Cita and formed a publishing company with him, Sitma Music. She performed on the 1979 Easter Seal telethon. As an actor she became well known as the Wicked Witch of the West in the Broadway and movie versions of *The Wiz*, as Steve Martin's mother in *The Jerk*, and as the mother in the first two seasons of the television series *What's Happening!!* As a member of the chorus King is on the recording of the all-black production of *Hello, Dolly!* (1967). She sings "Don't Nobody Bring Me No Bad News" in *The Wiz* (film version) and on the sound track of *Love Is Not Enough* (1979); "March Blues," in the movie *Ganja and Hess*. Her body was cremated.

Compositions

"At a Table for Two," "At the Rink," "Carnival Theme," "How Much Do I Love You?," "I and I Are One," "I Could Cry," "I'll Be Seeing You in My Dreams," "I'm a Rolly Polly Baby," "I'm Gonna Change," "I'm Gonna Stick Like Glue to You," "I'm So in Love with You," "I Remember," "It's You," "I've Never Been in Love Before," "Love Eternally," "Lucky Me," "Massacra," "Our Destiny," "Our Love," "Please Believe I Love You," "Season of Love," "Second Hand Love," "Table Talking," "Tell Me," "That's Love," "That's What I Need," "That's Why I Dream," "Twilight," "We Are in Love," "We Got Love"

Recordings as Leader

"Alabama Rock 'n' Roll" (1956), "I'm Gonna Change" (1956), "Second Hand Love" (1956), "Symbol of Love" (1956), "Go Back Home Young Fella" (1962), "Lefty" (1962), "Love" (1962), "When We Get the Word" (1962), "I Could Cry" (1963), "Why Can't We Get Together" (1963)

Films

Don't Play Us Cheap (1973), *Ganja and Hess* (1973), *The Bingo Long Traveling All-Stars and Motor Kings* (1976), *Scott Joplin* (1977), *The Wiz* (1978), *The Jerk* (1979), *The Gong Show Movie* (1980), *Getting Over* (1981), *The Jerk, Too* (1984), *Black Vampire* (1988), *Scrooged* (1988), *Dead Men Don't Die* (1990)

References

PRIMARY: Robert H. Phillips, *Rising to the Challenge: Celebrities and Their Very Personal Health Stories* (Garden City Park, N.Y.: Avery, 1990), 143–48 (interview).

SECONDARY: Bill Simon, "Rhythm-Blues Notes," *Billboard* 63 (9 June 1956): 46; Clyde Reid, "Backstage," *New York Amsterdam News*, 16 June 1956, p. 28; Vashti McKenzie, "Mabel King Is Mama on 'What's Happening,'" *Washington (D.C.) Afro-American*, 12 April 1977, p. 11 (comments by King); "It's Happening for Mabel King," *Encore: American and Worldwide News* 6 (20 June 1977): 51–52 (comments by King); James A. McGowan, *Hear Today! Here to Stay!* (Saint Petersburg, Fla.: Sixth House, 1983), 77, 138, 177; Todd R. Baptista, *Group Harmony: Behind the Rhythm and the Blues* (New Bedford, Mass.: TRB Enterprises, 1996), 196; Nick Ravo, "Mabel King, 66, Who Played the Wicked Witch in 'The Wiz,'" *New York Times*, 18 November 1999, sec. B, p. 15 (obituary).

Kirkland, Leroy E.

Composer, arranger, producer, guitar, piano

Probably 10 February of either 1904 or 1906 (Columbia, S.C.)–6 April 1988 (New York, N.Y.)

S.C. residence: Columbia (probably 1904 or 1906–probably no later than 1907)

Though born in Columbia, Kirkland was reared in Jacksonville, Fla., where he worked as a butcher. At least in 1932 he played banjo with Belton's Florida Society Syncopators of West Palm Beach; apparently around 1940 he moved to N.Y.C. He joined the army in 1942; when stationed in Flora, Miss., he played guitar with and arranged for the base band. He affiliated with Erskine Hawkins's band as guitarist in 1944. In 1951 he helped found the Dreamers, a vocal group, and became rhythm-and-blues staff arranger for Savoy Records. He was affiliated with several other record companies, including Okeh and Mercury; for the Wheeler label he became head of artists and repertoire in 1952. A few years later he was musical director for shows produced by Alan Freed; in the early 1960s he was instrumental to the success of Ruby and the Romantics, a vocal group. He played in Cab Calloway's band in 1966. Late in life he focused on gospel music. Two of his compositions gained favor with jazz musicians: "Charleston Alley," recorded by the vocal group Lambert, Hendricks, and Ross and several times by Charlie Barnet, among others, and "Cloudburst," also by Lambert, Hendricks, and Ross, as well as by Count Basie, the Pointer Sisters, and others. Some of Kirkland's compositions have been performed on movie sound tracks, including those of *Kicking and Screaming* (1995; "All in My Mind"), *This Year's Love* (1999; "Stop the Wedding"), and *Burlesque* (2010; "Something's Got a Hold on Me"). The rapper Flo Rida samples the introduction to "Something's Got a Hold on Me" on "Good Feeling" (2011), which went platinum. Kirkland is buried in plot 8, 0, 10121, Calverton National Cemetery, Calverton, N.Y.

Columbia, S.C., is identified as Kirkland's birthplace in Florida, Deaths, 1877–1939, which documents Kirkland's stillborn son (1926). The birth date of 10 February 1904 (based on some military records) is noted at http://www.findagrave.com/cgi-bin/fg.cgi?page=gr&GSln=kirkland&GSfn=leroy&GSby=1904&GSbyrel=in&GSdy=1988&GSdyrel=in&GSob=n&GRid=878712&df=all& (undated; accessed 21 May 2014); that of 10 February 1906 is recorded in the Social Security Death Index. Estimated age twenty-three and identified as a musician, Kirkland was enumerated for the census in Jacksonville, Fla., on 1 April 1930. When he enlisted in the military he stated that he was born in S.C. in 1908 and indicated that his highest level of education was grammar school. He is probably the Leroy Kirkland, estimated age twenty-nine, who was enumerated for the census in N.Y.C. on 5 April 1940. This document reveals that he was born in S.C., concluded his education after the second grade, lived in Miami, Fla., in 1935, and worked as an auto mechanic. The leader Claude Cloud, with whom Kirkland recorded in 1954, might be a pseudonym, possibly for Kirkland.

Compositions

"After Hour Stuff," "Ain't No Use," "All in My Mind," "Battle Royal," "Betty, Dear," "Big Beat," "Boss Is Home," "Bump," "Charleston Alley," "Cloudburst," "Come Walk with Me," "Fish Roll," "Gabbin' Blues," "Good Feeling," "Good Lovin'," "Helpless Heart," "Here 'Tis," "I Can See Everybody's Baby," "If I Could Be Loved by You," "If I Could Spend My Life with You," "I Know Every Move You Make," "I Like Your Line," "I'll Be a Crybaby from Now On," "I Never Loved Anyone but You," "It's a Man's World," "I Wash My Hands," "Joogie Boogie," "Little Boy, You're Gonna Be Sorry," "Lollipop Baby," "Love Bank," "Mumbles Blues," "My Country Man," "No Sacrifice," "Old Spanish Town," "Paramount Rock," "Ride, Sammy, Ride," "Rock-a-Diddle Rock," "Rocking Red Riding Hood," "'Scuse Me, Baby," "Sloppin'," "Slow Boat to Monaco," "Something's Got a Hold on Me," "Stop the Wedding," "Think of Poor Me," "Till Dawn and Tomorrow," "Trombone Rock," "Waiting, Wanting," "Watch That Action," "Way Back Home," "We're Strollin'"

Recordings as Leader

"Caminemos" (1957), "Paramount Rock" (1957), "Rock-a-Diddle Rock" (1957), "Trombone Rock" (1957), "Get a Job" (1958), "La Dee Dah" (1958), "Strollin' the Cha Cha Cha" (1958), "The Walk" (1958), *Mashin' and All That Jazz* (1962)

Leaders Recorded With

Doc Wheeler (1941–1942), Erskine Hawkins (1944–1951, 1960), Cootie Williams (1944–1945),

Eddie Mack (1949, 1952), Bobby Smith (1949), Julian Dash (1951), Varetta Dillard (1951–1953, 1955), Hot Lips Page (1951), Big Maybelle (1952–1954), Hadda Brooks (1952), Ella Fitzgerald (1952), Bill Kenny (1952), Annie Laurie (1952), Danny Taylor (1952), Titus Turner (1952), Dolly Cooper (1953), Sammy Cotton (1953), Larry Darnell (1953), Carmen Taylor (ca. 1953), Baby Dee (1954), Claude Cloud (1954), Wilbert Harrison (1954), John Lee Hooker (1954), Lillian Leach (1954), Beatrice Reading (1954), Roamers (1954–1955), Mamie Thomas (1954), Ruth Brown (1955), Carnations (1955), Dreams (1955), Screamin' Jay Hawkins (1955, 1967), Doc Jones (1955), Little David (1955), Florence Wright (1955), Nappy Brown (1956), Dave Burton (1956), Barbie Gaye (1956), Little Terry (1956), Schoolboys (1956), Sam "The Man" Taylor (1956), King Curtis (1957), Lloyd "Fatman" Smith (1957), Twin-Tones (1957), Rollee McGill (ca. 1965)

References

SECONDARY: "Belton's Florida Band Ranks as One of Best in Nation," *Pittsburgh Courier,* 27 August 1932, p. 7; "Topflight Musicians Doing Patriotic Duty at Ordnance Plant," *New York Age,* 14 August 1943, p. 10; Jesse H. Walker, "Theatricals," *New York Amsterdam News,* 28 May 1966, p. 23; Robert Pruter, "Leroy Kirkland, 82, New York Arranger, Dies," *Goldmine* 205 (17 June 1988): 5 (this issue is also designated volume 14, number 13) (obituary); Norbert Hess, "Obituaries," *Juke Blues* 14 (Winter 1988–1989): 21.

Kitt, Eartha Mae

Singer

Probably mid-to-late 1920s (in or near North, S.C.)–25 December 2008 (Weston, Conn.)

S.C. residence: in or near North (probably mid-to-late 1920s–no later than 1935)

Kitt moved from S.C. to N.Y.C. at an undetermined date, but no later than 1935. There, after dropping out of the High School of Performing Arts, she began her show business career as a member of Katherine Dunham's dance company (1944). With it she performed on Broadway in *Carib Song* (1945) and *Bal Negre* (1946). With this ensemble in the late 1940s she traveled to Europe. There she left Dunham. In Paris she made her initial recordings, with a jazz trio led by Doc Cheatham, and was cast as Helen of Troy opposite Orson Welles (as Dr. Faustus) in *Time Runs . . .*, a one-act play written by Welles. After returning to the United States in 1951 she appeared in the revue *New Faces of 1952* and soon became established as an actor and singer; her recordings of "C'est si bon" and "Santa Baby" (both 1953) were hits. She performed on Broadway (*Mrs. Patterson* [1954–1955], *Shinbone Alley* [1958], *Jolly's Progress* [1959]) and in movies, and in the 1960s she appeared on television programs, including *I Spy* (1965). She became a popular-culture icon because of her role as Catwoman in the series *Batman* (1967–1968). As a result of losing engagements in the United States after speaking against the Vietnam War at a White House luncheon (1968), she worked mainly in Europe for almost a decade. She accepted an invitation from President Carter to sing at the White House in 1978; this same year she starred in the musical *Timbuktu!* Late in her career she again performed on Broadway (*The Wild Party* [2000], *Nine* [2003]) and resumed recording with jazz musicians, such as Jerry Bergonzi, Joachim Kühn, and Rolf Kühn. She performed as Billie Holiday in *Lady Day at Emerson's Bar and Grill* (1996),

Eartha Kitt; Library of Congress, Prints & Photographs Division, Carl Van Vechten Collection, LC-USZ62-128088

sang at the 2006 Monterey Jazz Festival, and gave an eightieth birthday concert at the 2007 JVC Jazz Festival. Her body was cremated.

Kitt did not know when she was born. She states in "The Rose" (1995) that her age "could be anywhere between sixty and seventy" (21). The Social Security Death Index records Kitt's birth date as 26 January 1926; the first two volumes of U.S. Public Records Index state that she was born on 26 January 1928. When Kitt was enumerated for the census in N.Y.C. on 8 April 1940, her age was estimated as fourteen. Several sources indicate that Benedict College students located Kitt's birth certificate, which reveals a birth date of 17 January 1927. The existence of this document has not been confirmed. The claim of Kitt's biographer, John L. Williams, that "Kitt's birth was registered on 17 January, 1927 in the small town of St Matthews," S.C. (4) has not been substantiated. Eartha Keitt, age one-and-a-half, lived with Thomas and Mary Keitt, identified as her parents and characterized as Negro, when enumerated for the census in Providence, S.C., on 2 April 1930. (Most sources, including Kitt, note that her unknown father was white.) Like North, the unincorporated Providence is in Orangeburg County. It has not been determined if Eartha Keitt was Eartha Kitt, who appears otherwise to be missing from the 1930 census.

Compositions

"Alone," "How Many Times," "I Had a Hard Day Last Night," "My Discarded Men"

Recordings as Leader (Albums Only)

Eartha-Quake (1950, 1952–1957, 1959–1960; 5 CDs containing all of Kitt's Kapp, RCA Victor, Seeco, and Swing recordings), *Bad but Beautiful* (released 1962), *Live at Tivoli* (1962; also titled *After Dark* and *C'est si bon Live in Tivoli*), *The Romantic Eartha* (released 1962; also titled *The Best of All Possible Worlds*), *Eartha Kitt Sings in Spanish/Canta en Español* (released 1965), *In Person at the Plaza* (1965), *Love for Sale* (released 1965; also titled *Eartha for Always*), *Sentimental Eartha* (released 1970), *I Love Men* (1981–1982), *I'm Still Here* (released 1989), *Live in London* (1989; 2 vols.), *The Nearness of You* (1989; also includes material by Ronnell Bey and Clark Terry), *Thinking Jazz* (1991), *Standards/Live* (1992), *Back in Business* (ca. 1994), *Live from the Café Carlyle* (2006), *Live at the Cheltenham Jazz Festival* (2008)

Leaders Recorded With

Doc Cheatham (1950), Marcus Miller (2004)

Films

Casbah (1948), *Parigi e Sempre Parigi* (1951; also titled *Paris Is Always Paris*), *New Faces* (1954), *The Mark of the Hawk* (1957), *Anna Lucasta* (1958), *St. Louis Blues* (1958), *Saint of Devil's Island* (1961), *Drei Männer Spinnen* (1962), *Synanon* (1965), *Uncle Tom's Cabin* (1965), *Up the Chastity Belt* (1971; also titled *The Chastity Belt*), *Lieutenant Schuster's Wife* (1972), *Friday Foster* (1975), *To Kill a Cop* (1978), *Butterflies in Heat* (1979), *All by Myself* (1982), *A Night on the Town* (1983), *The Serpent Warriors* (1985), *Dragonard* (1987), *Master of Dragonard Hill* (1987), *The Pink Chiquitas* (1987); *Erik the Viking* (1989), *Living Doll* (1990), *Ernest: Scared Stupid* (1991), *Boomerang* (1992), *Fatal Instinct* (1993), *Harriet the Spy* (1996), *I Woke up Early the Day I Died* (1998), *Feast of All Saints* (2001), *Anything but Love* (2002), *Holes* (2003), *Preaching to the Choir* (2005), *And Then Came Love* (2007)

Award

Hollywood Walk of Fame (1960)

Website

www.earthakitt.com (accessed 21 May 2014)

References

PRIMARY: Clare Powers, "Eartha Kitt Talks Turkey," *Down Beat* 20 (29 July 1953): 3, 6, 8 (substantial comments by Kitt); Leonard Feather, "The Blindfold Test," *Down Beat* 21 (14 July 1954): 21 (Kitt comments about recordings); Eartha Kitt, "My Experience with the Supernatural," *Science Fiction Digest* 1 (1954): 4–5; Eartha Kitt, *Thursday's Child* (New York: Duell, Sloan and Pearce, 1956); Eartha Kitt, *Alone with Me: A New Autobiography* (Chicago: Regnery, 1976); Eartha Kitt, *I'm Still Here* (London: Sidgwick & Jackson, 1989) (republished as *Confessions of a Sex Kitten* [New York: Barricade Books, 1991] and again as *I'm Still Here: Confessions of a Sex Kitten* [New York: Barricade Books, n.d.]); Eartha Kitt, "The Rose," in *What We Know So Far: Wisdom among Women*, ed. Beth Benatovich (New York: St. Martin's, 1995), 13–21; Eartha Kitt, with Tonya Bolden, *Rejuvenate! (It's Never too Late)* (New York: Scribner's, 2001).

SECONDARY: "Josh White Taught Her the Blues," *Melody Maker* 27 (20 January 1951): 6 (comments by Kitt); Reid E. Jackson, "What Kept Eartha Kitt Down in Down Beat Poll?," *Baltimore Afro-American*, 2 January 1954, p. 11; Alan Ebert, "Eartha!," *Essence* 9 (June 1978): 68–71, 139 (reprinted in Ebert's *Intimacies: Private Conversations with Very Public Women* [Raleigh, N.C.: Lightning Bug Press, 2001], 167–73) (comments by Kitt); Albert Williams, "Brilliant Blues," *Chicago Reader,* 3 May 1996, pp. 49–50; "Eartha Kitt Portrays Jazz Singer Billie Holiday in One-Woman Musical," *Jet* 90 (27 May 1996): 54–55 (comments by Kitt); Karen S. Schneider, with Cynthia Wang, "Eye of the Tigress," *People* 52 (25 October 1999): 131–32, 135–36 (also available at http://www.people.com/people/archive/article/0,,20129568,00.html [accessed 21 May 2014]) (comments by Kitt); Rob Hoerburger, "Eartha Kitt, a Performer Who Seduced Audiences Dies at 81," *New York Times,* 26 December 2008, sec. A, p. 37 (obituary); Phil Sarata, "Kitt Left Hometown of North 'in Tears,' Returned in Triumph," *Orangeburg (S.C.) Times and Democrat,* 27 December 2008, sec. A, pp. 1, 3; John L. Williams, *America's Mistress: The Life and Times of Eartha Kitt* (London: Quercus, 2012).

Koon, Jessie

Tuba

S.C. residence: Charleston (1920s)

Apparently a ward of Jenkins Orphanage, Koon played in its bands in the 1920s.

Kyer, Wilson Harrison ("Peaches")

Piano, leader

Probably 21 August of either 1888 or 1889 (Charleston, S.C.)-August 1982

S.C. residence: Charleston (probably 1888 or 1889-at least until 1900)

In 1912 and 1913 Kyer was musical director for the Smart Set Company, which produced *The Dark-Town Politician,* a musical comedy. Succeeded in this capacity by Luckey Roberts, Kyer toured with Corwell and Nye's Mississippi Minstrels and Musical Maids in 1913. That year in Philadelphia he married the singer Charlotte M. "Lottie" Gee, who later introduced "I'm Just Wild about Harry" in *Shuffle Along* (1921). They were divorced in 1924. In the early 1920s Kyer made his only known recordings, backing singers Ethel Waters and Lucille Hegamin. As a pianist in N.Y.C. he performed both classical (as a member of the Euphonic Trio in 1932, for example) and popular (including at a dance recital by Mura Dehn in 1943) music. He was most active as a band leader. No later than 1936 and at least through 1941, he led the Colonial Dance Orchestra, which was part of the Works Progress Administration Music Project. He also led the Brycollians in N.Y.C. (1941).

Documentation of Kyer's early and late years has not been located. When enumerated for the 1900 census in Charleston, Kyer lived with his parents, Edward and Isabella Kyer. No Charleston city directory after 1900 mentions this family. Kyer's 1917 and 1942 draft registration cards and the Social Security Death Index indicate that the musician was born on 21 August 1888; the 1900 census records the birth date as August 1889. His age was estimated as thirty-seven when he was enumerated for the N.Y. state census on 1 June 1925; as forty-one when enumerated for the federal census in N.Y.C. on 25 April 1930; as fifty-one when enumerated for the 1940 federal census in N.Y.C. on 9 April 1940. Aspects of Kyer's career from 1932 into 1943 may be documented through newspaper announcements of the musician's performances; see selected notices, below.

Compositions

"College March," "Darling Mine"

Leaders Recorded With

Ethel Waters (1921), Lucille Hegamin (1922)

References

SECONDARY: "World of Players," *New York Clipper,* 10 May 1913, p. 6 (under "Corwell and Nye's Mississippi Minstrels and Musical Maids"); "Concert Planned by Euphonic Trio," *Yonkers (N.Y.) Herald Statesman,* 20 September 1932, p. 11; "WPA Free Concerts," *New York Post,* 18 July 1936, p. 10 (under "Thursday, July 23"); "5 Concerts Listed for This Week by WPA Music Unit," *Brooklyn (N.Y.) Eagle,* 17 December 1940, p. 19; "By Way of Mention," *New York Age,* 26 April 1941, p. 5 (under "Progressive Club of Empire Lodge No. 5"); "Musicians Gather for Dance Recital," *Brooklyn (N.Y.) Eagle,* 9 May 1943, p. 32; Lynn Abbott and Doug Seroff, *Ragged but Right: Black Traveling Shows, "Coon Songs," and the Dark Pathway to Blues and Jazz* (Jackson: University Press of Mississippi, 2007), 116–18; Howard Rye, "Southern Syncopated Orchestra: The Roster," *Black Music Research Journal* 30 (Spring 2010): 33 (under "Gee, Lottie [Charlotte M.]").

Ladson, Samuel

S.C. residence: Charleston (1920s)

Apparently a ward of Jenkins Orphanage, Ladson played in its bands in the 1920s, though his instrument is not known.

Ladson's given name is recorded in John Chilton, *A Jazz Nursery: The Story of the Jenkins' Orphanage Bands of Charleston, South Carolina* (London: Bloomsbury Book Shop, 1980), 56. The musician could be the Samuel Ladson, estimated age five, who lived with his family on Saint Helena Island, S.C., when enumerated for the census on 21 April 1910. Conducted at the orphanage on 9 January, the 1920 census enumerates a Walter Ladson, estimated age thirteen. Whether Samuel Ladson and Walter Ladson are the same person has not been determined; nor has it been ascertained if the musician was the drugstore porter Samuel Ladson, born in S.C., who was enumerated for the 1930 census in N.Y.C. at estimated age twenty.

Leake, Henry

See Leeke (Leake), Henry

Lee, Henry

Mellophone

S.C. residence: Charleston (by late 1920s–at least into early 1930s)

Apparently a ward of Jenkins Orphanage, Lee played in its bands ca. 1930.

Leeke (Leake), Henry

Saxophone

Ca. 1919 (S.C.)–?

S.C. residence: Charleston (1930s)

A ward of Jenkins Orphanage, Leeke played in its bands in the 1930s.

When Leeke was enumerated for the census at the orphanage on 2 April 1930, his age was estimated as eleven; this document identifies his birthplace as S.C. In *A Jazz Nursery: The Story of the Jenkins' Orphanage Bands of Charleston, South Carolina* (London: Bloomsbury Book Shop, 1980), 56, John Chilton spells the surname Leake.

Lester, Henry

Violin

S.C. residence: Abbeville (before and probably after 1895)

Lester was valued so highly in 1895 that an anonymous writer used him as a standard to which young black fiddlers could only aspire.

Reference

SECONDARY: "Disgraceful Mimicry—The Old and the Young Negro Compared," *Atlanta Voice of Missions by Way of the Cross,* August 1895, p. 2.

Letman, Johnny (John Bernard)

Trumpet, singer

Probably 6 September 1915 (McCormick, S.C.)–17 July 1992 (New York, N.Y.)

S.C. residence: McCormick (probably 1915–no later than 1930)

Though Letman was born in S.C., he reportedly lived most of his formative years in Chicago, where he learned to play the trumpet and, in time, became a professional musician. His most notable early association was with Nat Cole (1933–1934). Letman stated that he, Letman, did the singing with this group and that Cole then never sang. From his subsequent home bases of Champaign, Ill., and Columbus, Ohio, he toured with bands before returning to Chicago in 1938; there he headed his own group (1939–1940). In 1943 he moved to Detroit, where he worked in an aircraft factory, but also played with Teddy Buckner. He next located to N.Y.C., where he began his recording career and lived the remainder of his life. He formed a trio in 1959 that appeared at the Metropole that year and in 1960. Around this same time he was a regular with trombonist Conrad Janis. He played in the pit bands of Broadway shows *Marathon '33* (1963–1964) and *Never Live over a Pretzel Factory* (1964) and toured France with Tiny Grimes in the late 1960s. In the mid-1980s he performed internationally with the New Orleans Blues Serenaders, the band from the musical *One Mo' Time.* Letman acknowledged the influence of Louis Armstrong above all others, though he was also inspired by Roy Eldridge. Albert J. McCarthy notes that Letman had the "ability to play a ballad in a lyrical manner without descending to sentimentality" (30).

Though 6 September 1917 is Letman's accepted birth date, the Social Security Death Index indicates that the trumpeter was born on 6 September 1915.

Recordings as Leader

Introducing Johnny Letman (1959; extended-play record), *The Many Angles of John Letman* (1960), *A Funky Day in Paris* (1968)

Leaders Recorded With

Lena Horne (1945), Phil Moore (1945–1947, 1953), Una Mae Carlisle (1946), Cab Calloway (1947, 1957–1958), Milt Buckner (1949), Joey Thomas (1951), Annie Laurie (1952), Earl Hines (1953, ca. 1977), Stuff Smith (1958), Joe Thomas (1958), Chubby Jackson (1959), Arnold Wiley (1959), Panama Francis (1960), Leroy Parkins (1960), Bernard Addison (1961), Tiny Grimes (1968), Cozy Cole (1977), Lionel Hampton (1977), Sammy Price (1977), Stan Rubin (1982–1983), New Orleans Blues Serenaders (1985–1986), Bruce Adams (1987), Red Richards (1987), Buck Clayton (1988), Lars Edegran (1990)

References

PRIMARY: Chip Deffaa, *Jazz Veterans: A Portrait Gallery* (Fort Bragg, Calif.: Cypress House, 1996), 14 (substantial comments by Letman).

SECONDARY: Albert J. McCarthy, "Johnny Letman," *Jazz Monthly* 1 (March 1960): 8–9, 30 (comments by Letman); Hugues Panassié, "Un grand tompette: Johnny Letman," *Bulletin du Hot Club de France* 102 (Novembre 1960): 3–4 (in French); Steve Voce, "Obituary: Johnny Letman," *Independent* (London), 25 July 1992, p. 14; Scott Yanow, *The Trumpet Kings: The Players Who Shaped the Sound of Jazz Trumpet* (San Francisco: Backbeat Books, 2001), 231.

Lewis, Robert Stephen

Saxophone
24 June 1971 (Moscow, Idaho)–
S.C. residence: Summerville (1999–)

Lewis grew up in a musical family in Kennewick, Wash., where he began piano lessons around age eight and saxophone lessons in middle school. During his high school junior year in Drøbak, Norway, he became seriously interested in jazz. As an undergraduate at the University of Idaho, from which he received a bachelor's degree in saxophone performance (1994), he played locally in rock, blues, and jazz bands. He freelanced while a graduate student at Western Michigan University (master's degree, 1997). In S.C. he affiliated with the College of Charleston, where he heads the jazz program. Concurrent with his academic duties, he plays regularly as leader and sideman, arranges and composes for and performs with the Charleston Jazz Orchestra, and is musical director for and plays with the Darius Rucker big band.

Compositions

"Clark," "Easy Rawlins," "Fearless Jones," "Finders Keepers," "First Day Back," "The Gift," "The Gloaming," "Hush," "Limestone," "Swagger," "Tuesday," "What Goes Up"

Recordings as Leader

Swagger (2000; with Frank Duvall), *Fearless Jones* (2002; with Frank Duvall), *First Takes* (2010; with Gerald Gregory and Ron Wiltrout)

Leader Recorded With

Jill Terhaar Lewis (2011)

Award

Down Beat Student Music Award for best jazz soloist (1998)

Website

http://lewisr.people.cofc.edu/Robert_Lewis,_jazz_saxophonist/Welcome.html (accessed 21 May 2014)

Reference

SECONDARY: Jack McCray, "Charleston Native and Saxist a Renaissance Man," *Charleston (S.C.) Post and Courier,* 28 July 2011, sec. E, p. 16.

Liberty, Jeff (Jeffrey William)

Guitar, singer, composer
14 May 1966 (Toronto, Ontario, Canada)–
S.C. residence: Columbia (1992–1996 [Fort Jackson], 2000–)

From Canada, Liberty moved to Omaha, Nebr., in 1982. While in the army (he served from 1984 to 1996), at age twenty he began playing guitar and became dedicated to the blues after listening to Muddy Waters's album *Hard Again.* The death of Stevie Ray Vaughan in 1990 deepened his commitment to the music. During his last army

Jeff Liberty, Lexington, S.C., 2014; photograph by David Black, permission of Jeff Liberty

assignment, at Fort Jackson, he was active on the Columbia blues scene. Following his discharge he went to Memphis, where he played with the Beale Street Cadillac Blues Band. After settling in Columbia, in 2002 he established the Jeff Liberty Band, which remains active. He performed at the 2013 Julius Daniels Blues Festival.

Compositions

"All My Might," "Broad St. Shorty's Breakfast Café," "Bye-bye, Baby," "Devil's Advocate," "Disturbing the Peace," "Dry Spell," "Flip the Switch," "Fried Baloney Samitch," "Girl Next Door," "A House That You Ain't Built," "I Ain't Worried," "I'll Keep My Soul," "I'm Doin' Right," "I Thought She Was a Woman," "I Told You So," "Jimmy's Shuffle," "Jump on It," "Keepin' Me in the Dark," "The Last Straw," "Lightnin' Man," "The Light of Love," "Little Child in My Soul," "Love, Tears, and Joy," "Pater Familius (Rubber Monkey's Uncle)," "Payday," "Preachin' the Blues," "Repossess My Love," "Rita's Swing," "Rollin' Away," "Rubber Monkey," "Second Wind," "Since I Seen the Last of You," "Suitcase at the Door," "The Tax of Bein' Free," "Tell Me That You Feel Like I Do," "Tell Me Why," "Temptation or Reward," "That Ring," "U Can't Find Me," "Walk on By," "We Ain't Supposed to Be," "Women Want Men," "You've Got to Find Some Other Way"

Recordings as Leader

The Tax of Bein' Free (2001), *Dry Spell* (2002), *I Told You So* (2003), *Motherless Chillin'* (2004; with Mike "Naz" Nazarenko), *Meat and Potatoes* (2006), *Live at Joe's* (2007), *Bus Songs* (2009)

Leader Recorded With

Shelley Magee (2005)

Website

http://www.jeffliberty.com (accessed 21 May 2014)

Ligon, Bert

Piano, keyboards, guitar, composer
16 April 1954 (Wichita Falls, Tex.)–
S.C. residence: Lexington (1991–)

Self-taught on piano and guitar, Ligon became a professional musician at nineteen. After touring with Maynard Ferguson in 1983 he settled in Dallas, Tex., where he formed a band and worked as composer, arranger, and studio pianist for most of the 1980s. Concurrently he attended the University of North Texas, receiving degrees in 1987 (undergraduate) and 1988 (graduate). There, in 1988, he taught jazz improvisation. After directing the jazz program at Richland Community College in Dallas (1989–1991), he affiliated with the University of South Carolina, where he heads the jazz program.

Compositions

"Arches," "Ariana," "Arrival," "Ash," "August Moon," "Big Foot Waltz," "Blue Mesa," "Body Language," "Bossa Azul," "Bossa Rojo," "Bossa Verde," "Brainstorm," "Broken Resolutions," "Cabaña Cubano," "La Calle Doce," "Capri," "Caracas," "Cascade," "Close to Home," "Dancer," "Dancing B-a-r-e," "Dawn," "Drive Time," "Duet for Cello and Piano," "Fancy That," "Far from Home," "Gypsy," "I'll Go Rhythms," "Mild-Mannered Reporter," "Missing You," "Moss," "Mr. T. J.," "Off Blue," "Open Secret," "Ouzel Falls," "Passenger," "Polosiano," "River Journey," "Saturday," "Saturn Moons," "Seabreeze," "Swing Break," "Take It Home," "Unicorn," "View from the Bridge"

Recordings as Leader

Condor (1980), *Dancing Bare* (1983), *Jazz Trio 2006* (with Renata Bratt and Martin Norgaard)

Leaders Recorded With

University of North Texas One o'Clock Lab Band (1988), University of North Texas Jazz Singers (1991), Pete Neighbour (2009), Robert Gardiner (2010)

References

PRIMARY: Bert Ligon, *Connecting Chords with Linear Harmony: A Study of Three Basic Outlines Used in Jazz Improvisation and Composition, Based on a Study of Hundreds of Examples from Great Jazz Artists* (Lebanon, Ind.: Houston Publishing, 1996); Bert Ligon, *Comprehensive Technique for Jazz Musicians* (Lebanon, Ind.: Houston Publishing, 1999); Bert Ligon, *Jazz Theory Resources: Tonal, Harmonic, Melodic, and Rhythmic Organization of Jazz* (Lebanon, Ind.: Houston Publishing, 2001), two vols.

Livingston, Fud (Joseph Anthony)

Saxophone, clarinet, arranger, piano, singer/speaker
10 April 1906 (Charleston, S.C.)–25 March 1957 (New York, N.Y.)
S.C. residence: Charleston (1906–ca. 1923, though also sporadically later)

Musically precocious, Livingston played the piano at age four; in time he became adept at reed instruments. He was inspired by the bands of Jenkins Orphanage and occasionally practiced with some of their musicians. At the Citadel he studied composition and arranging, though in 1923 he left the school without a degree to become a professional musician, initially with Tal Henry and then with Mark H. "Banjo" Goff. His arrangements for Ben Pollack, whose band he joined in Chicago in 1924, soon attracted attention. Within a few years of entering the N.Y.C. scene in 1927, he affiliated with the band of Paul Whiteman and composed—with Matty Malneck and Gus Kahn—"I'm Thru with Love," which became a standard. Livingston's excessive drinking caused professional problems, though he joined Jimmy Dorsey in 1935. Livingston's last regular band affiliation was with Bob Zurke in 1939–1940. Thereafter Livingston scuffled. Gunther Schuller characterizes him as "an astonishingly gifted arranger." Richard M. Sudhalter refers to Livingston's "writing Debussian harmonies into his musical miniatures" (136). In commenting about Joe Venuti's 1928 recording of "Doin' Things," Brad Kay states that Livingston's arrangement "has that Livingston transparency, swing and variety we now recognize as hallmarks of his best work" (13). Livingston is buried in Saint Lawrence Cemetery, Charleston.

Livingston was the brother of saxophonist Toots Livingston. The copyright entry for "I'm Thru with Love" spells the second word as indicated here.

Fud Livingston; permission of John Tecklenburg

Compositions

"Any Old Time (I'm Feeling Blue)," "Au Reet," "Easter Bells," "Feelin' No Pain," "Harlem Twist," "Hep-Tee-Hootie," "Humpty Dumpty," "Imagination," "I'm Thru with Love" ("J'en ai marre de l'amour"), "Inside on the Southside," "Lorraine," "Moo," "Never Too Late to Pray," "Pasa 'Qui Ba-Bee," "Remember I Love You," "Richmond, Va.," "Sax Appeal," "Springtime in Charleston," "There You Go," "Without a Penny in Your Pocket"

Recording as Leader

"Moo" (1932)

Leaders Recorded With

Ben Pollack (1924, 1926–1927), California Ramblers (1925), Earl Baker (1926), White Tops (1926), All-Star Orchestra (1927–1929), Arkansas Travelers (1927), Carl Fenton (1927), Miff Mole (1927–1928), Red Nichols (1927–1929), Charleston Chasers (1928–1929), Benny Goodman (1928), Lennie Hayton (1928), Jimmy McHugh (1928), Mendello's

Dance Orchestra (1928), Irving Mills (1928), Mississippi Maulers (1928), Joe Venuti (1928, 1930), Wabash Dance Orchestra (1928), Irving Brodsky (1929), Fred Elizalde (1929), Louisiana Rhythm Kings (1929), Dick McDonough (1929), Boyd Senter (1929), Frankie Trumbauer (1930), Paul Whiteman (1930), Jimmy Dorsey (1935–1937), Louis Armstrong (1936), Bing Crosby (1936–1937), Lily Pons (1936), Ginger Rogers (1936), Jerry Colonna (1938–1939)

References

SECONDARY: Dick DuPage, "Fud Livingston: A Triple Threat Man," *Record Research: The Magazine of Record Statistics and Information* 21 (January–February 1959): 3–4; Gunther Schuller, *The Swing Era: The Development of Jazz, 1930–1945* (New York: Oxford University Press, 1989), 810; Richard M. Sudhalter, *Lost Chords: White Musicians and Their Contribution to Jazz, 1915–1945* (New York: Oxford University Press, 1999), passim; Nathaniel Shilkret, *Sixty Years in the Music Business,* ed. Niel Shell and Barbara Shilkret (Lanham, Md.: Scarecrow Press, 2005), 64, 171, 173; Brad Kay, notes to *The Story of Joseph "Fud" Livingston* (2009; Jazz Oracle BDW-8060).

Livingston, Toots (Walter Francis, Jr.)

Saxophone, clarinet

28 October 1902 (Charleston, S.C.)–13 August 1931 (Mount Pleasant, S.C.)

S.C. residence: Charleston area (1902–1931, except when touring with bands in the 1920s)

Livingston learned to play various reed instruments while growing up in Charleston. He is possibly best known for his performance on "Somebody Stole My Gal" (1923), made at the first of his ten recording sessions with Ted Weems; these were also Weems's initial recording dates. Livingston is buried in Saint Lawrence Cemetery, Charleston.

Livingston was the brother of saxophonist Fud Livingston.

Leader Recorded With

Ted Weems (1923–1924)

Logan, Peter M. ("Hatsie")

Cornet and other instruments

Probably mid-to-late 1870s (Charleston, S.C.)–4 September 1907 (Charleston, S.C.)

S.C. residence: Charleston (probably mid-to-late 1870s–1907)

Presumably the first music instructor at Jenkins Orphanage, Logan probably also played in its bands. He is buried in the Humane and Friendly Society Cemetery, Charleston.

Logan's birthplace and date and place of death come from the musician's death certificate, which records Logan's occupation as musician. Conducted in Charleston on 2 June 1900, the census estimates that Logan was born in March 1878; the death certificate indicates that he died at age thirty-one, which is impossible if he was born in 1878. Either the birth date given in the census or implied on the death certificate (ca. 1876) is inaccurate; possibly both are. Because Logan died in 1907, he could not have led the orphanage band at the Anglo-American Exposition in London in 1914, though Jeffrey P. Green believes that he did.

Reference

SECONDARY: Jeffrey P. Green, *Edmund Thornton Jenkins: The Life and Times of an American Black Composer, 1894–1926* (Westport, Conn.: Greenwood, 1982), 22, 38–39.

Lovel, Joseph

S.C. residence: Charleston (probably by late 1920s–at least into early 1930s)

Apparently a ward of Jenkins Orphanage, Lovel played in its bands in the early 1930s, though his instrument is not known.

Lucky, Cab

Guitar, bass, harmonica, singer

1 October 1938 (Lamar, S.C.)–11 March 2011 (Brooklyn, N.Y.)

S.C. residence: Lamar (1938–mid-1960s)

Lucky was most active around 1980, when he appeared as sideman on recordings released by Spivey Records, operated by blues singer Victoria Spivey; music he recorded on a demonstration tape in 1983 has not been released. A variety store clerk in Brooklyn, he frequently performed in and around N.Y.C.

Lucky's birth and death dates come from the Social Security Death Index. Estimated age two, Lucky was enumerated for the census in Lamar on 24 April 1940. Recordings he reportedly made with soul musicians before 1980 have not been identified.

Compositions

"Mailman Blues," "Whiskey Blues"

Recordings as Leader

"Come On to My House" (1979), "Mama Don't Allow" (1979)

Leaders Recorded With

Washboard Doc (ca. 1978, 1980), Eunice Davis (1980), Screamin' Jay Hawkins (1981)

Reference

SECONDARY: Len Kunstadt, notes to Washboard Doc's *Early Morning Blues* (1980; L+R Records LR 42.010).

Mack, Freddie (Fred, Jr.; "Mr. Super Bad")

Leader, broadcaster, singer
Possibly 15 September 1934 (probably Bennetsville or Lester, S.C.)–11 January 2009 (Plains, Scotland)
S.C. residence: Marlboro County (1934–ca. 1947)

Mack boxed professionally from 1954 until 1965. He then turned to music, fronting the Freddie Mack Extravaganza in Great Britain before making television commercials for K-Tel Records as Mr. Super Bad beginning in 1974. A resident of Scotland, he became a disc jockey, initially in 1979 on Radio Clyde and later, in 2002 and 2003, on Clan FM in Lanarkshire. He toured as leader of a disco show.

Mack indicated that he was born in Bennettsville; Richard Mooney identifies Mack's birth date as 15 September 1934. A Fred Mack, Jr., estimated age five, was enumerated for the census on 29 April 1940 in Lester, which is approximately five miles from Bennettsville. If this child became the performer, as can be assumed, then the entertainer might have been born in Lester, not Bennettsville. Numerous sources incorrectly credit to Mack several K-Tel albums that are collections of previously released recordings by various musicians, not including him. After establishing the Scots Boxing Hall of Fame in 2001, Mack served as its president until his death. He stated that he attended the 1952 Olympics in Helsinki as an alternate boxer, one who would have participated had another American fighter been unable to perform. This claim is not substantiated in William H. Thomas, "Boxing: Report of Committee Chairman," in *United States 1952 Olympic Book: Quadrennial Report of the United States Olympic Committee,* ed. Asa S. Bushnell (New York: United States Olympic Association, 1953), 156–63. This source gives the results of all fights held in the Olympics boxing tryouts in Kansas City, Mo., in June 1952. Mack is not mentioned.

Recordings as Leader

The Fantastic Freddie Mack Show (1966), "People," two parts (1973; vocal and instrumental versions)

Leaders Recorded With

Ultrafunk (1974), Tight Fit (1981)

Films

Cleopatra (1963), *I Due Evasi di Sing Sing* (1964; also titled *Two Escape from Sing Sing*), *The Great Rock 'n' Roll Swindle* (1980)

References

PRIMARY: "Freddie Mack Mr. Superbad Interview, Part One," http://vimeo.com/16651875 (2008; accessed 21 May 2014) (video interview); "Freddie Mack aka Mr. Superbad, Part Two," http://vimeo.com/16684399 (2008; accessed 21 May 2014) (video interview); "Freddie Mack Extravaganza," http://www.california-ballroom.info/bands/freddie-mac.htm (undated; accessed 21 May 2014) (substantial comments by Mack).

SECONDARY: Richard Mooney, "Soul Star Mr. Superbad Talks about His First Love of Boxing," http://www.dailyrecord.co.uk/news/local-news/soul-star-mr-superbad-talks-2834934 (23 July 2008; accessed 21 May 2014) (comments by Mack); Brian Beacom, "Veteran Radio Clyde DJ Mr. Superbad Dies at 72; Freddie Mack was Boxer, Actor and R&B Singer in Larger-Than-Life Career," *Evening Times* (Glasgow, Scotland), 16 January 2009, news sec., p. 24 (obituary); Brian Donald, "Freddie Mack," *Herald* (Glasgow, Scotland), 17 January 2009, features sec., p. 17 (obituary).

Mack, Oscar Lee

Singer

Probably 30 May 1936 (probably Providence Township, Sumter County, S.C.)–7 June 1989 (Detroit, Mich.)

S.C. residence: Providence Township, Sumter County (probably 1936–no later than early 1960s)

In the early 1960s Mack worked as a handyman for Otis Redding, who probably arranged for Mack to record for Volt Records and Stax Records. Redding sings along with Mack on "Dream Girl." Around this time Mack sang in the Duncan Trio, backing vocalist James Duncan, and formed a duo with Steve Jackson that recorded two songs.

Michigan, Death Index, 1971–1996, records Mack's birth date as 30 May 1936; the Social Security Death Index, as 30 May 1938. When Mack was enumerated for the census in Providence Township, Sumter County, on 20 May 1940, his age was estimated as three. If this estimation is accurate and if he was born on 30 May, he was born in 1936.

Compositions

"Dream Girl," "I'm Glad It's Over"

Recordings as Leader (These Are Release Dates, Not Necessarily Recording Dates)

"Don't Be Afraid of Love" (1963), "I See My Baby Commin'" (1963), "Dream Girl" (1964), "You'll Never Know How Much I Love You" (1964), "Forever and Always" (mid-1960s; as Oscar and Steve, with Steve Jackson), "Hotdogs Peanuts Popcorn" (mid-1960s), "I'll Go on Lovin' You" (mid-1960s), "Shut Up" (mid-1960s; as Oscar and Steve, with Steve Jackson), "I'm Glad It's Over" (1968), "Put Out the Fire" (1968)

Leader Recorded With

James Duncan (released 1962)

References

SECONDARY: Sir Shambling [John Ridley], "Oscar and Steve," http://www.sirshambling.com/artists_2012/O/oscar_steve/index.php (2012; accessed 21 May 2014); Sir Shambling [John Ridley], "Oscar Mack," http://www.sirshambling.com/artists_2012/M/oscar_mack/index.php (2012; accessed 21 May 2014).

Mackey, Wes (Wesley)

Guitar, singer

12 December 1942 (Big State community, near Yemassee, S.C.)–

S.C. residence: Big State community, near Yemassee (1942–ca. 1959)

Introduced to music by his parents, who sang at home and listened to blues and gospel recordings, Mackey began playing the guitar around age ten. Approximately seven years later he left home for Augusta, Ga., where he became a professional musician, playing at juke joints with his group Guitar Wes and the Houserockers. Later in Augusta he performed with the Rock and Roll Kings before becoming an itinerant musician. In time he moved to Halifax, Nova Scotia, Canada, where he led the band Wes Mackey and the Brotherhood. After six years in Halifax he moved to Calgary, Alberta, before locating to Port Hardy, British Columbia, where he gave up playing music. He resumed performing upon moving to Nanaimo, near Vancouver; he also studied music there at Malaspina College. He lived briefly in Hong Kong and then

Wes Mackey; permission of the photographer, Angela Fama, and Wes Mackey

in Malaysia before settling in Vancouver. Most influenced by John Lee Hooker and Jimmy Reed, Mackey became a solo performer late in his career, augmenting his music with Roland PK5 bass pedals.

Compositions

"Angel Girl," "Be a Man, Boy," "Blues Rules," "Footsie Brown," "Full Moon in Lamanon," "Good Morning Blues," "In My Neighbourhood," "Journey," "Life Is a Journey," "Mr. Blues Album Blues," "Rapperswill," "Thank You Carolina," "Train," "Who Do Da Voodoo?"

Recordings as Leader

Bluesman (1994), *Second Chance* (2005), *Mr. Blues* (2006), *Beyond Words* (2009), *Good Morning Blues* (2011; with Cityreal), *Life Is a Journey* (2013)

Award

Honorary citizen, Lamanon, France

Website

http://www.wesmackey.com/wes_mackey_soul_bag_magazine.htm (accessed 21 May 2014)

References

PRIMARY: Georges Lemaire, "Wes Mackey: Au-Dela des Mots," *Soul Bag* 192 (Septembre 2008): 26–29 (narrative, in French, by Mackey) (also available, in English, as "Au-Dela des Mots [Beyond Words]" at http://www.wesmackey.com/wes_mackey_soul_bag_magazine.htm [accessed 21 May 2014]).

SECONDARY: Jack McCray, "Local Boy Makes Good at Blues Bash," *Charleston (S.C.) Post and Courier*, 12 February 2004, sec. F, pp. 8, 13 (comments by Mackey); Jill Fowler, "The Return of Wes Mackey," *Truro (Nova Scotia) Daily News*, 6 August 2009, p. 2.

Mancha, Steve (Clyde Darnell Wilson)

Singer, composer

25 December 1945 (Walhalla, S.C.)–8 January 2011 (Detroit, Mich.)

S.C. residence: Walhalla (1945–early 1950s)

Around age fifteen Clyde Wilson began singing in Detroit with the Jaywalkers, which also included Melvin Davis, Tony Newton, and David Ruffin. He recorded for the initial time with Two Friends, a duo with his high school classmate Wilburt Jackson. In the early 1960s he was contracted to Motown Records, began writing songs, and soon became known professionally as Steve Mancha. Mid-decade, he recorded for Wheelsville Records, then Groovesville, before affiliating with Groove City Records in the late 1960s. Mancha sang lead with 100 Proof Aged in Soul, including on "Somebody's Been Sleeping" (1970), which reached the top ten on the pop charts. Sometime after the early 1970s this rhythm-and-blues and soul singer turned to gospel music. His compositions have been recorded by Tammi Terrell ("Just Too Much to Hope For"), Terrell and Marvin Gaye ("Give a Little Love"), and the Monitors ("Number One in Your Heart"), among others.

With one exception all sources consulted indicate that the singer was born in Walhall, S.C., which does not exist. Some sources claim that the Wilson family left S.C. for Detroit in 1950; others, in 1954. It has not been determined which date, if either, is correct. Some sources spell the given name of Wilburt Jackson Wilbert.

Compositions

"Age Ain't Nothing but a Number," "As Long as Heaven Allows," "Bad Bill of Goods," "Best in Town," "Breakdown," "Clean Slate," "Come Back to My Arms," "Come in Out of the Rain," "Did My Baby Call?," "Don't Let Me Lose You," "Don't Make Me a Story Teller," "Doorman," "Family Reunion," "Give a Little Love," "Giving Up Your Love Is Like (Giving Up the World)," "The Harder You Love," "Hate Yourself in the Morning," "He's Beating Your Time," "I Could Never Hate Her," "I Don't Care," "If the World Should End Tonight," "I'm Gonna Let You Know," "I Need My Baby," "It's Unbelievable," "I've Come to Save You," "I Won't Love You and Leave You," "Just Can't Get Over This Feeling," "Just Keep On Lovin' Me," "Just Too Much to Hope For," "Keep the Faith," "Little Understanding," "A Love Like Yours," "Monday through Thursday," "More, More, More," "Need to Be Needed," "Not Enough Love to Satisfy," "Nothing Sweeter Than Love," "Number One in Your Heart," "Out of My Reach," "Save It," "She's Not Just Another Woman," "Since You Been Gone," "Some Other Man," "Straight Spittin'," "Sweet Baby," "Think before You Walk Away," "This One Is Mine," "Unyielding," "We Luv N.Y.," "You're Still in My Heart"

Recordings as Leader (These Are Release Dates, Not Necessarily Recording Dates)

"Family Reunion" (ca. 1960; as Two Friends, with Wilburt Jackson), "Just Too Much to Hope For" (ca. 1960; as Two Friends, with Wilburt Jackson), "Did My Baby Call" (1965), "She's So Good" (1965), "Whirlpool" (1965), "You're Still in My Heart" (1965), "Friday Night" (1966), "I Don't Want to Lose You" (1966), "Monday through Thursday" (1966), "Need to Be Needed" (1966), "Don't Make Me a Storyteller" (1967), "I Won't Love and Leave You" (1967), "Just Keep On Loving Me" (1967), "Sweet Baby, Don't Ever Be Untrue" (1967), "Hate Yourself in the Morning" (1969), "A Love Like Yours" (1969), "Deeper in Love" (ca. 1969), "If You'll Be My Girl" (1971; as Clyde Wilson), "Open Up" (1971; as Clyde Wilson), "It's All Over the Grapevine" (1986)

Leaders Recorded With (These Are Release Dates, Not Necessarily Recording Dates)

Laurence Faulkon (1962), Holidays (1966), Hot Wax (1969), New Holidays (1969), 100 Proof Aged in Soul (1969–1972), 8th Day (1971), Parliament (1971–1972), Freda Payne (1971)

References

SECONDARY: "I Don't Want to Lose You—Steve Mancha," http://bluesphotobman.blogspot.com/2012/12/i-don-want-to-lose-you-steve-mancha.html (2012; accessed 21 May 2014); Graham Finch, "Steve Mancha," http://www.soulfuldetroit.com/web15-Holidays/11-Steve-Mancha.htm (undated; accessed 21 May 2014) (comments by Mancha); Andrew Hamilton, "Steve Mancha," http://www.allmusic.com/artist/steve-mancha-mn0000042668 (undated; accessed 21 May 2014); "Steve Mancha," http://www.soulwalking.co.uk/Steve%20Mancha.html (undated; accessed 21 May 2014).

Manigault, Hezekiah

See Jenkins, Hezekiah

Manigault, Walter

See Jenkins, Walter

Mars, Johnny (John Robert)

Harmonica, bass, singer
7 December 1942 (Laurens, S.C.)–
S.C. residences: Laurens (1942–ca. 1947), unidentified place (late 1940s)

As a youth Mars moved frequently until settling at age fourteen in New Paltz, N.Y., following his mother's death. There he played in a blues band (Train Riders) and attended high school, which he completed in 1962. He was next affiliated with the psychedelic group Burning Bush. He formed the John Mars Band before moving, in 1967, to San Francisco, where he established Last Mile, which evolved into the Johnny Mars Blues Band. He remained in Calif. until moving to England in 1972. There he assumed leadership of and toured with the Sunflower Band. By 1978 he made Somerset, England, his home. He teaches music to children and performs on the European blues circuit, often with guitarist Michael Roach.

Compositions

"Early in the Morning," "Harp Funk," "Have You Heard about the Blues," "Home Sweet Home,"

Johnny Mars, Pocono Blues Festival, Lake Harmony, Pa., 26 July 2008; permission of the photographer, Gene Tomko

"I'm Hungry Blues," "It Takes Time," "Living in the Shadow," "Livin' in the Ghetto," "London Blues," "Remember?," "Stateside," "You Know the Rules"

Recordings as Leader

Blues from Mars (1972), *Johnny Mars and the Oakland Boogie* (ca. 1974), *Mighty Mars* (1980), *Life on Mars* (1981), "Horses and Places" (1981), "Mighty Mars" (1981), *Hot Lips Boogie* (1983), *Born under a Bad Sign* (1985), "Born under a Bad Sign" (1985), *Fire in the City* (1986; by Mars-Fenwick Band, with Ray Fenwick), "Smoking Out the Barons" (1986; by Mars-Fenwick Band, with Ray Fenwick), *Can You Hear Me?* (1992; with Big Fat Mama), *Stateside* (1993–1994), *King of the Blues Harp* (1994), *Guess Who* (2002), *Higer and Higer* (2006)

Leaders Recorded With

Art Hodes (1987), Do-Ré-Mi (1988), Bananarama (1990–1991), Barrelhouse Blues Orchestra (2003)

Website

www.johnnymars.com (accessed 21 May 2014)

References

PRIMARY: Steve Rye and Richard Noblett, "Blues from Mars," *Blues Unlimited* 104 (October–November 1973): 5, 16 (autobiographical sketch); Scott M. Bock, "Life on Mars," *Living Blues* 204 (December 2009): 26–32 (mainly a narrative by Mars).

SECONDARY: Chris Smith, "Blues from Mars," *Living Blues* 12 (Spring 1973): 13 (comments by Mars).

Mars, Sylvia

Singer, piano

Possibly ca. 1933 (Abbeville, S.C.)-

S.C. residence: Abbeville (possibly ca. 1933-no later than mid-1950s)

One of Mars's grandfathers was reportedly "one of the better down country blues singers in South Carolina" ("Spotlighting: Sylvia Mars"). At age five Mars began dancing on Abbeville streets to entertain and get money from mill employees leaving work. At an undetermined date she left S.C. for Boston, where she started singing professionally in 1956. There she was active on the folk/blues scene: singing in clubs (including Storyville and the Jewel Room of the Bostonian Hotel), coffeehouses, churches, hospitals, schools, and possibly other venues; performing at benefit concerts and on radio and television; and belonging to the Folksong Society of Greater Boston. On her sole album she sings blues, spirituals, and hymns. Some she performs solo; others, with guitar accompaniment; and still others, with guitar and harmonica backing. A schooled musician who studied piano and music theory for six years, she composed tunes that were published under an unknown pseudonym. Mars was active as late as 1973, when she performed at the Playboy Club in Kansas City, Mo.

The singer's name has not been located in public documents, including the 1940 census; if she wed, Mars might have been her married name. Her birth date and place come from Bob Eagle and Eric S. LeBlanc, *Blues: A Regional Experience* (Santa Barbara: Praeger, 2013), 289. The birthplace is also specified in the catalogue of Folk-Lyric Records, which released Mars's album. See http://www.popsike.com/SYLVIA-MARS-Blues-Walk-Right-In-RARE-FolkLyric-LP/4732651402.html (undated; accessed 21 May 2014). "Spotlighting: Sylvia Mars" provides evidence for determining the approximate recording date of *Blues Walk Right In:* Mars "has recently cut a record album . . . to be released by Folk Lyric in the near future." Her lyrics for the old tune "Alabama Bound" were published in "The Folk Process," *Sing Out! The Folk Song Magazine* 11 (October–November 1961): 43.

Composition

"Alabama Bound"

Recording as Leader

Blues Walk Right In (probably 1961 or 1962)

References

SECONDARY: "Spotlighting: Sylvia Mars," *Broadside* 1 (6 April 1962): 1; "Fun after Dark . . . Etc.," *Kansas City Star,* 4 March 1973, sec. F, p. 6. Mars is apparently mentioned in other issues of *Broadside,* though these references have not been located.

Martin, Albert ("Pepper")

Alto horn, saxophone

1910 (Asheville, N.C.)-before 1981

S.C. residence: Charleston (1925-mid-1930s)

A ward of Jenkins Orphanage beginning in 1925, Martin played in its bands in the late 1920s and early 1930s. Subsequently he was with the Carolina Cotton Pickers.

John Chilton records Martin's birth year. Bruce Bastin indicates that Martin had died by the time Bastin completed his manuscript.

Leader Recorded With

Carolina Cotton Pickers (1937)

References

SECONDARY: John Chilton, *A Jazz Nursery: The Story of the Jenkins' Orphanage Bands of Charleston, South Carolina* (London: Bloomsbury Book Shop, 1980), 57; Bruce Bastin, "A Note on the Carolina Cotton Pickers," *Storyville* 95 (June–July 1981): 177–82.

Martin, Bill (William Edward)

Bass guitar, cello, percussion, saxophone
21 May 1956 (Columbia, S.C.)–
S.C. residences: Columbia (1956–1974, 1978–1985), Greenville (1974–1978)

Though interested in music during his high school years, Martin was, aside from some piano and guitar lessons, self-taught. He received a degree from Furman University in 1978. As a graduate student at the University of South Carolina, he recorded *Blues for Chairman Mao* and *Graffiti.* On the first he plays several instruments including alto saxophone, an instrument he subsequently abandoned. After receiving a Ph.D. from the University of Kansas and becoming a philosophy professor at DePaul University in Chicago, he remained involved in music to the degree that he wrote books about it and continued playing bass guitar with rock groups and, solo, within the avant-garde context. On the instrument he was most influenced by Paul McCartney and Chris Squire.

Compositions

"Beyond the Fields We Know," "Blues for Chairman Mao," "Carlos," "Cello Solo" (I), "Cello Solo" (II), "Fela," "First It Lives," "LUPE Dance," "On Hearing the World Spin," "Parking Lot Shakedown," "Scurillous," "Sleepy Seed (The Legend of Ernie Banks)," "Steel Drum," "The Story of Graffiti"

Recordings as Leader

Blues for Chairman Mao (1981), *Graffiti* (1985)

References

PRIMARY (music books only): Bill Martin, *Music of Yes: Structure and Vision in Progressive Rock* (Chicago: Open Court, 1996); Bill Martin, *Listening to the Future: The Time of Progressive Rock, 1968–1978* (Chicago: Open Court, 1998); Bill Martin, *Avant Rock: Experimental Music from the Beatles to Björk* (Chicago: Open Court, 2002).

Martin, Fiddlin' (Frank or Franklin)

Guitar, violin
Probably between 1847 and 1860 (probably S.C., possibly Cherokee Township, Spartanburg County)–after 10 April 1910
S.C. residence: probably Cherokee Township, Spartanburg County (probably between 1847 and 1860–at least into 1880s)

Born a slave, Martin played with (and possibly formed) a string band in the Spartanburg area, probably in the 1880s. Among his children with his wife Harriet was Rowland Martin, who became a musician; among those with his second wife, Mary, was Carl Martin, who was born in Va. in 1906 and who also became a musician. With Howard Armstrong and Ted Bogan, Carl Martin continued the black string band tradition into the 1970s.

The census contains conflicting information about Martin. Conducted in Cherokee on 2 June, the 1880 census indicates that he was then twenty-seven; the husband of Harriet Martin; the father of two children, including Rowland; and a farmer. In the 1900 census (16 June), he is identified as fifty-two, the husband of Hattie (a nickname for Harriet) Martin, the father of three children, a brick mason, and a resident of High Shoals, N.C. The 1910 census (16 April) characterizes him as fifty; the husband of Mary Martin; the father of seven children, including Carl; a mason; and a resident of Richmond District, Va. The censuses of 1880 and 1900 record his given name as Frank and indicate that he was born in S.C.; the 1910 census specifies his given name as Franklin and birthplace as N.C.

References

SECONDARY: Allen Larman, "Martin, Bogan, and Armstrong," *Folkscene* 4 (July–August 1975): 12–14, 21; Bo Basiuk, "Interview with Carl Martin," *Blues Magazine* 1 (August 1975): 26–33; Mike Joyce and Bob Rusch, "Carl Martin: An Interview," *Cadence* 3 (August 1977): 17–20; "Carl Martin 1906–1979," *Living Blues* 43 (Summer 1979): 28–29, 40; Bruce Bastin, *Red River Blues: The Blues Tradition in the Southeast* (Urbana: University of Illinois Press, 1986), 172, 183, 301.

Martin, Rowland

Bass, guitar, mandolin, violin
Probably mid-to-late 1870s (S.C., probably Cherokee Township, Spartanburg County)-?
S.C. residence: Cherokee Township, Spartanburg County (probably mid-to-late 1870s-at least into 1880s)

Blind from glaucoma (though when the blindness occurred is not known), Martin mastered various string instruments and taught his half brother Carl Martin to play them; he inspired Howard Armstrong, Carl Martin's longtime musical partner, to play the violin. He formed a string band that performed throughout the Southeast, probably beginning in the 1910s. During the next decade the quartet—the two Martins, Armstrong, and Bill Ballinger—played on radio stations WNOX and WROL in Knoxville, where Rowland Martin and other family members resided. In 1930 a version of this group—the Martins, Armstrong, and perhaps another musician—recorded in Knoxville as the Tennessee Chocolate Drops; the music was released on Vocalion.

Martin was a son of musician Fiddlin' Martin. The 1880 and 1900 censuses spell Martin's given name Rowland; interviews with Carl Martin spell it Roland. Conducted in Cherokee Township, Spartanburg County on 2 June, the 1880 census identifies Martin's age as five; conducted in High Shoals, N.C., on 14 June, the 1900 census records his birth date as January 1878.

Recordings as Leader (Both 1930; with the Tennessee Chocolate Drops)

"Knox County Stomp," "Vine Street Drag"

References

SECONDARY: Allen Larman, "Martin, Bogan, and Armstrong," *Folkscene* 4 (July–August 1975): 12–14, 21; Bo Basiuk, "Interview with Carl Martin," *Blues Magazine* 1 (August 1975): 26–33; J. Roderick Moore and Kip Lornell, "On Tour with a Black String Band in the 1930s: Howard Armstrong and Carl Martin Reminisce," *Goldenseal: A Quarterly Forum for Documenting West Virginia's Traditional Life* 2 (October–December 1976): 9–12, 46–52; Mike Joyce and Bob Rusch, "Carl Martin: An Interview," *Cadence* 3 (August 1977): 17–20; "Carl Martin 1906–1979," *Living Blues* 43 (Summer 1979): 28–29, 40; Bruce Bastin, *Red River Blues: The Blues Tradition in the Southeast* (Urbana: University of Illinois Press, 1986), 172, 183, 301–2; Erin Kelly and Alva Noe, "An Interview with 'Louie Bluie' W. Howard Armstrong," *Blues Review Quarterly* 7 (1992–1993): 26–33.

Martin, Walter

Alto horn, saxophone
Ca. 1914 (Charleston, S.C.)-?
S.C. residence: Charleston (ca. 1914-at least into early 1930s)

A ward of Jenkins Orphanage beginning in 1927, Martin played in its bands in the late 1920s and early 1930s.

John Chilton specifies 1914 as Martin's birth year; conducted at the orphanage on 2 April, the 1930 census estimates the youth's age as fifteen. If, as Chilton indicates, Martin played with the institution's bands into the early 1930s, then he is probably not the alto saxophonist Walter Martin who recorded with Oliver Cobb in 1929, Eddie Johnson in 1932, and the Original St. Louis Crackerjacks in 1936.

Reference

SECONDARY: John Chilton, *A Jazz Nursery: The Story of the Jenkins' Orphanage Bands of Charleston, South Carolina* (London: Bloomsbury Book Shop, 1980), 57.

Mason, Lil (Lillian; "Blues Mistress," "Chicago's Sweetheart of the Blues," "Upstairs Lil")

Singer
7 February 1918 (Union, S.C.)-probably 19 February 1988 (Chicago, Ill.)
S.C. residence: Union (1918-possibly early 1920s)

Mason moved with her family from S.C. to Gary, Ind., before settling in Chicago, where she sang in clubs from the early 1940s at least into the mid-1960s. Backed by pianist Little Brother Montgomery, she recorded four songs for Okeh Records in 1944, though they have not been issued. Rondo Records released tunes from a 1946 session, but for the remainder of her career she recorded only once, a single in the early 1980s. She is buried in Oakland Memory Lane Cemetery, Dolton, Ill.

A claim that Mason was born Lillian Robertson has not been confirmed, though a girl of this name, estimated age three, was enumerated for the census in Union, S.C., on 2 February 1920. Robert L. Campbell and Robert Pruter state that the singer was born Lillian Mason. They also note that she died on 21 February 1988, though her obituary indicates that she died two days earlier.

Compositions

"How Fast Can You Boogie?," "Upstairs"

Recordings as Leader

"The Buggy Ride," two parts (1946), "How Fast Can You Boogie?" (1946), "Upstairs" (1946), "The Cabrini Green Song," two parts (1982)

References

SECONDARY: "Lillian 'Upstairs' Mason, 60, Blues Singer," *Chicago Sun-Times,* 23 February 1988, p. 61 (obituary); Robert L. Campbell and Robert Pruter, "Rondo," http://myweb.clemson.edu/~campber/rondo.html (5 June 2013; accessed 21 May 2014).

Mayer, Luther, Jr.

See Captain Luke

Mayhams, Norridge Bryant ("Norris the Troubadour")

Composer, singer, banjo, guitar, record company owner
Probably 17 August 1903 (Georgetown, S.C.)–22 July 1988 (Norwalk, Conn.)
S.C. residence: Georgetown (1903–ca. 1919)

After working as a cook on ships, including the *Lake Ellerslie* at least in July 1921, Mayhams became a professional musician, conceivably in the late 1920s. In N.Y.C. he formed a combo that played in speakeasies, performed at college bars, and broadcast on WMCA. He composed gospel, blues, and popular songs, including "We'll Build a Bungalow," which became well known in a recording by Johnny Long (1949) and later was used on the sound track of *The Group* (1966). It was also recorded by jazz musicians Sy Oliver (1949) and Bob Scobey (1957), as well as by the Smith Street Society Jazz Band (1999). His earliest recordings were released on major labels, including Decca. Many of his post-1930s recordings were done by the song-poem method: he paid a firm to create recordings of his songs, which he then released on his own labels (Co-ed and Mayhams Collegiate). On post-1936 recordings he is often identified as Norris the Troubadour. He established a publishing company, Sorority Fraternity; in 1962 he helped establish Brandes Records, for which he wrote songs. Most of his early recordings—sacred ("Crying Holy unto the Lord") and profane ("Ash Haulin' Blues")—have been released on CD, as have later recordings of undetermined dates.

Mayhams's birth and death dates, state of birth, and place of death come from Connecticut Death Index, 1949–2001, which spells the surname Mayhans; the Social Security Death Index (Mayhams) confirms the birth date and month and year of death. Estimated age twenty-seven, he was enumerated for the census in N.Y.C. on 5 April 1930; this document states that he then worked as a porter in a wholesale house and was born in S.C. The 1940 census, for which he was enumerated as Norbridge Mayhams in N.Y.C. on 8 April, indicates that he was born in N.C., estimates his age as thirty-six, and notes that he then worked as a musician. In *Experiences of a Collegiate Singer,* Mayhams states that he performed with the band of Chick Webb, though he does not indicate when. He told Pamela Raye Fiore in 1985 that he played banjo with Webb, beginning at age nineteen. Webb did not form his group until 1926. Though Mayhams is sometimes credited with having been affiliated with saxophonist Earl Bostic, on Co-ed he released "From Hopewell Junction" and "Ridehorsse-Ridehard,"

Norridge Mayhams, inlay of his guitar; photograph by Martin Keith/Veillette Guitars, permission of the guitar's owner, Baker Rorick

the labels of which identify Carl Bostic as the orchestra leader; Mayhams sings on the latter and possibly on the former. For proof that a Carl Bostic led a band (the Hot Shots), see St. Clair "Sinky" Bourne, "Follow the Activities: Calendar Girls," *New York Age,* 8 April 1933, p. 9. That Bostic was a saxophonist is documented in "Diton and 'Blackbirds' Stars Entertain at Vets.' Hospital," *New York Amsterdam News,* 24 April 1929, p. 12. For a discussion of song-poems, see Phil Milstein, "What Is This Song-Poem?," http://www.songpoemmusic.com/what_is.htm (2003; accessed 21 May 2014).

Compositions

"Be No Fool—Play It Cool—Stay in School," "Blue Am I," "But the Rock Rolls On," "Casey's Walk," "Dance Dance All Night Long," "Dance the Rattlesnakin Mama," "Fortitude," "From Hopewell Junction," "God's Heaven's Heavenly Grocery Store," "Grits and Gravy," "House in Bin," "I Am Back from Vietnam," "I'd Call This World a Heaven," "If I Could Call You Mine," "I've Got Soul Love Burning in My Heart," "Jeanie," "Jesus Will Soon Be Coming," "Listen to the Mocking Bird," "Mario and Josephine Joe," "Mary Ann McCarthy," "Midwifery," "Mint Julep Bloomin' Like a Tulip," "Mr. Guitar Man I Know You Can," "My College Girl," "My Minnesota Girl," "My S.O.S. to You," "Play It Smart Play It Hard" (also titled "Play It Hard—Play It Smart"), "Remember Me," "Ridehorsse-Ridehard," "Rock n' Rollin' Honey" (also titled "Rock 'n' Roll 'n' Honey"), "Runaway Heart" (also titled "Run Away Heart"), "Said G.I. Joe with a South Korean," "Seaboard, the Southern, and the A.C.L." (presumably later titled "The A.C.L. and the S.A.L."),"Singin' Sied the Showboy," "Stars in the Blue," "Surfing Is a Sight to See," "Surfing on a Swingin' Soiree," "Sweet Shirley," "The Wall Street Daily Cry," "We'll Build a Bungalow," "Wonderful Day," "Yam-tang, Yam-tang, Ranky-tang," "You Left Me Honey Honey," "You're My Surfer Girl Forever," "Zoomba Zoomba High Kicka Zoomba"

Recordings as Leader

Norridge Mayhams and the Blue Chips 1936: Complete Recorded Works in Chronological Order, "Chippin' Rock Blues" (1938; by the Hipp Cats), "It Must Be Jelly" (1938; by the Hipp Cats), "Talk about Jerusalem Mornin'" (1938; by Norris the Troubadour), "Winter Will Soon Be Over" (1938; by Norris the Troubadour), "Yam-tang, Yam-tang, Ranky-tang" (ca. 1948; by Norris the Troubadour), "I'd Call This World a Heaven" (1956; by Norris the Troubadour), "Remember Me" (1956; by Norris the Troubadour), *Our Centennial Album, 1776–1976* (dates unknown; by Norris the Troubadour Seaboard Coastliners), "Dance Dance All Night Long" (1979; by Seaboard Coastliners), "Sweet Shirley" (1979; by Seaboard Coastliners), "Jeanie" (1983; by Norridge and the Seaboard Coastliners), "Peas Puddin' Hot" (1983; by Norridge and the Seaboard Coastliners)

Leader Recorded With

Carl Bostic (possibly ca. 1945, possibly ca. 1949)

References

PRIMARY: Norris the Troubadour, *Experiences of a Collegiate Singer* (New York: n.p., 1947) (the 1974 edition, published by Sorority Fraternity Records Publications, identifies the author as N. B. [Norris the Troubadour] Mayhams); Pamela Raye Fiore, "Norridge Mayhams: Music Man," *Poughkeepsie (N.Y.) Journal,* 20 October 1985, sec. B, pp. 1–2 (substantial comments by Mayhams).

SECONDARY: L.H., "Mostly 'bout the Mayhams," *New York Age,* 5 November 1949, p. 29; Jesse H. Walker, "Theatricals," *New York Amsterdam News,* 7 July 1962, p. 17; "Mayhams Shows He's Still a Hit-Maker," *Billboard* 85 (23 June 1973): 8; Tony Russell, notes to *Norridge Mayhams and the Blue Chips 1936: Complete Recorded Works in Chronological Order* (1996; Document DOCD-5488); Phil Milstein, "Mayhams Mayhem," http://www.songpoemmusic.com/labels/mayhams.htm (2004; accessed 21 May 2014); Baker Rorick, "Great Acoustics: 1942 Gibson TG-7N," *Acoustic Guitar* 149 (May 2005): 98 (this issue is also designated volume 15, number 11); Bob Purse, "He'd Call This World a Heaven," http://bobpurse.blogspot.com/2009/06/hed-call-this-world-heaven.html (5 June 2009; accessed 21 May 2014); Bob Purse, "Mayhams Mayhem," http://bobpurse.blogspot.com/2009/10/mayhams-mayhem.html (22 October 2009; accessed 21 May 2014); Bob Purse, "Norris Mayhams: The Early Years," http://bobpurse.blogspot.com/2009_11_01_archive.html (29 November 2009; accessed 21 May 2014); Bob Purse, "One Year In!," http://bobpurse.blogspot.com/2009/12/one-year-in.html (30 December 2009; accessed 21 May 2014); Bob Purse, "Sing It, Norris!," http://bobpurse.blogspot.com/2011/03/sing-it-norris.html (5 March 2011; accessed 21 May 2014); Darryl Bullock, "Mayhams Mayhem," http://worldsworstrecords.blogspot.com/2011/09/mayhams-mayhem.html (23 September 2011; accessed 21 May 2014); Bob Purse, "A Great Norridge Mayhams

Find," http://bobpurse.blogspot.com/2012/01/great-norridge-mayhams-find.html (16 January 2012; accessed 21 May 2014); Bob Purse, "Norridge Mayhams Last Gasp," http://bobpurse.blogspot.com/2012/08/norridge-mayhams-last-gasp.html (2 August 2012; accessed 21 May 2014); Bob Purse, "An Unusual Calypso Record from Norridge Mayhams' Label (MP3's)," http://blog.wfmu.org/freeform/2013/03/an-unusual-calypso-record-from-norridge-mayhams-label.html (3 March 2013; accessed 21 May 2014).

Mazyck, Oscar

Drums

February 1890 (S.C.)–before 1980

S.C. residence: Charleston (at least early 1900s)

A ward of Jenkins Orphanage, Mazyck played in its bands in the early 1900s.

Mazyck's birth date and place come from the 1900 census, for which he was enumerated at the orphanage on 28 June. In *A Jazz Nursery: The Story of the Jenkins' Orphanage Bands of Charleston, South Carolina* (London: Bloomsbury Book Shop, 1980), 57, John Chilton indicates that Mazyck had died by the time Chilton completed his manuscript.

McClennan, George A.

Tuba

Ca. 1926 (S.C.)–?

S.C. residence: Charleston (by late 1930s–at least into early 1940s)

A ward of Jenkins Orphanage, McClennan played in its bands in the early 1940s and possibly in the late 1930s.

When enumerated for the census at the orphanage on 21 May 1940, McClennan estimated his age as fourteen; this document indicates that he was born in S.C.

McClintock, Lil

Guitar, singer

Mid-1880s (S.C., probably Laurens County)–after 1930, but no later than 1940 (probably Union County, S.C.)

S.C. residences: probably Laurens County (mid-1880s–no later than 1930), Union Township, Union County (by 1930–no later than 1940)

Burm Lawson of Union arranged for McClintock and Gussie Nesbitt to record on the same day in Atlanta for Columbia Records, which they did in December 1930. Paul Oliver suggests that McClintock fashioned songs out of fragments of other tunes, as may be observed on "Don't Think I'm Santa Claus." Expanding on Oliver's observation, Mike Ballantyne posits that this same song "is an excellent example (and one of the very few existing examples) of an early, twentieth century, medicine show singer's song-medley, and one that belongs almost solely to, and is a direct product of the shows." J. M. Mancini believes that McClintock's "Furniture Man" is a meditation on modernity.

When, as Lill McClintock, the musician was enumerated for the census in Hunter Township, Laurens County, on 15 January 1920, his age was estimated as thirty-six; that of his wife, Mamie, as thirty. Though his occupation as detailed in the census is difficult to read, he might then have been a helper in a drug store. The McClintocks were enumerated for the 1930 census on 8 April in Union Township, Union County, with their ages estimated as forty-four and forty, respectively; Lil then worked as a rock mason. Mamie McClintock was a widow when enumerated for the census in Union Township on 23 April 1940 at estimated age fifty. On 26 April 1910 a Mary McClintock, estimated age twenty, was enumerated for the census in Clinton with her husband, W. M. McClintock, estimated age twenty-four, who worked at odd jobs. (Many Marys are known as Mamie.) These censuses show a consistent birth year for the wife (ca. 1890) and age differential between the spouses (four or six years). If the musician and his wife were the couple enumerated for the 1920 and 1930 censuses, as surely they were, and if the Mary of the 1910 census was this woman, then Lil was probably W. M. McClintock. Neither Lil nor W. M. McClintock has been located in the 1900 census. A draft registration card completed in Laurens on 12 September 1918 relates to Lil McClintock. (Laurens is about fifteen miles from Clinton.) The line for the registrant's name reads "Lil For Doza Wm McClintock"; the signature line reads "Lil for Doza William McClintock." It has not been determined if this wording means that the person being registered was Lil McClintock, if Lil registered for Doza William McClintock, or something else. Perhaps the person's formal name was Doza William McClintock and "Lil For" means that he was commonly known as Lil. The person registering for the draft was a "mecanic" residing in Laurens who was born on 5 June 1883. Because he identified his nearest relative as Press McClintock of Spartanburg, S.C., he was probably not then married. If this is the case, then the W. M. McClintock enumerated with Mary for the 1910 census was not Lil. Alternatively if this person was then married, he was probably the W. M. McClintock who was enumerated with Mary in 1910. And if this is the case, then Lil was probably W. M. McClintock, whose given name was William. Issues relating to the 1910 census and the 1918 draft registration card remain unresolved.

Recordings as Leader (All 1930)

"Don't Think I'm Santa Claus," "Furniture Man" (two takes), "Mother Called Her Child to Her Dying Bed," "Sow Good Seeds"

References

SECONDARY: Chapman J. Milling, "Delia Holmes—A Neglected Negro Ballad," *Southern Folklore Quarterly* 1 (December 1937): 3–7; David Evans, "Lil McClintock," *Blues Unlimited* 40 (January 1967): 11; Paul Oliver, *Aspects of the Blues Tradition* (New York: Oak Publications, 1970), 39; Richard Raichelson, "Lil McClintock's 'Don't You Think I'm Santa Claus,'" *JEMF Quarterly* 6 (Autumn 1970): 132–34; Tony Russell, *Blacks Whites and Blues* (New York: Stein and Day, 1970), 43–44; Bruce Bastin, *Red River Blues: The Blues Tradition in the Southeast* (Urbana: University of Illinois Press, 1986), 188–89; J. M. Mancini, "'Messin' with the Furniture Man': Early Country Music, Regional Culture, and the Search for an Anthological Modernism," *American Literary History* 16 (Summer 2004): 208–37; Mike Ballantyne, "Lil McClintock, Blues and Medicine Shows," www.mikeballantyne.ca/mcclintock.php (2011; accessed 21 May 2014); Mike Greenblatt, "Sowing the Seeds of Love," *Goldmine* 828 (May 2013): 66 (this issue is also designated volume 39, number 6) (also available as "Lil McClintock Worked to Sow the Seeds of Love in His Blues Music" at http://www.goldminemag.com/article/lil-mcclintock-worked-to-sow-the-seeds-of-love-in-his-blues-music [accessed 21 May 2014]).

McCutchen, Philip

See Cedar Creek Sheik

McFadden, Ruth Naomi

Singer
31 July 1938 (Charleston, S.C.)–
S.C. residence: Charleston (1938–1951)

McFadden moved from Charleston to Harlem in 1951. There she sang in church but also with her mother on radio station WLIB with the Dorothy Rivers Singers. She took dancing lessons and attended a charm school. As a result of winning Amateur Hour at the Apollo Theater in 1955, she signed a contract with Old Town Records, which recorded her in 1956. That year in Brooklyn she performed as part of Alan Freed's Easter Jubilee of Stars, which included such groups as the Platters, the Teenagers, the Flamingos, and the Cleftones. Her contract with Old Town was voided so she could complete her studies at Charles Evans Hughes High School in N.Y.C., which she did in 1957. She recorded four songs for Tiara in 1958. Then she recorded sporadically into the early 1970s. Though she did not record subsequently, she frequently performed in

Ruth McFadden, Baby Grand Club, Harlem, early 1960s; permission of Tony Rounce

clubs. From the late 1960s into the mid-1970s she toured with Carl Holmes and the Commanders, including in Europe. During the 1970s and 1980s she sang with such society bands as those led by Peter Duchin, Skitch Henderson, and Lester Lanin. She attended Fordham University for a year in the 1980s. She has worked as a human resources assistant with a N.Y.C. law firm since 1987. Occasionally in the 1990s and early 2000s she performed with the Sheps, a vocal group.

Recordings as Leader

"Darling, Listen to the Words of This Song" (1956), "Dreaming Is No Good for You" (1956), "School Boy" (1956), "Since My Baby's Been Gone" (1956), "Teenage Blues" (1956), "Two in Love" (1956), "United We Stand" (1956), "You for Me" (1956), "At the Crossroads" (1958), "(I Wouldn't Be Where I Am) If You Hadn't Gone Away" (1958), "My Baby's Comin' Home" (1958), "You Must Come In at the Door" (1958), "Don't Take Your Love" (1961), "Lovin' Time" (1961), "Pencil and Paper" (1962), "Stop Playing That Song" (1962), "He Hurt Me Again" (1964), "It Could Be Sweet Again" (1964), "Do It Up Right" (1965), "I'll Cry" (1965), "Rover Rover" (1968), "Run Rover Run" (1968), "Ghetto Woman" (1972; two versions)

References

PRIMARY: John Broven, with Richard Tapp, "Angel in Harlem: The Ruth McFadden Story," *Juke Blues* 47 (Summer 2000): 32–39 (narrative by McFadden) (includes discography); George L. Frunzi, "An R&B Vocal Group Road Trip . . . Destination: New York City . . . and a Conversation with Ruth McFadden," *Echoes of the Past* 98 (Winter 2011): 19–23.

SECONDARY: John Broven, *Record Makers and Breakers: Voices of the Independent Rock 'n' Roll Pioneers* (Urbana: University of Illinois Press, 2009), 220–22 (comments by McFadden).

McGee, Evelyn

See Stone, Evelyn McGee

McGill, Benjamin

Trombone, tuba

Probably 12 March 1912 (Columbia, S.C.)–?

S.C. residences: Columbia (probably 1912–no later than 1924), Charleston (by 1924–probably no later than 1935)

A ward of Jenkins Orphanage, McGill played in its bands at least in the late 1920s and performed with one of them in England in 1929.

The passenger list of the *Majestic,* which transported the orphanage band from Southampton, England, to N.Y.C. in June 1929, identifies McGill's birth date and place. John Chilton notes that the musician moved from the orphanage to N.Y.C. If so he is probably the Benjamin McGill who was enumerated there on 16 April 1940; for this document he estimated his age as thirty-three and indicated that he also lived in N.Y.C. in 1935.

References

SECONDARY: John Chilton, *A Jazz Nursery: The Story of the Jenkins' Orphanage Bands of Charleston, South Carolina* (London: Bloomsbury Book Shop, 1980), 57; Howard Rye, "Visiting Fireboys: The Jenkins' Orphanage Bands in Britain," *Storyville* 130 (1987): 137–43.

McGill, Rollee

Saxophone, singer

Probably 29 December 1931 (Kingstree, S.C.)–11 October 2000 (Philadelphia, Pa.)

S.C. residence: Kingstree (probably 1931–ca. 1950)

During his years in Kingstree, McGill farmed with his family and performed with the Carolina Quartet Boys, a gospel group consisting of four McGill brothers. Though he attended Thomson High School, he did not progress beyond the eighth grade. After hearing a recording by Louis Jordan, he became interested in rhythm and blues. Upon moving to Philadelphia ca. 1950 he attended a music school for three years and organized some classmates into the Rhythm Rockers, later known as the Whippoorwills. With this group he recorded for the initial time at a session that produced "There Goes That Train," which reached the top ten on some rhythm-and-blues charts. Its success led to a contract with Mercury Records; subsequently he recorded for various minor labels. His most notable performance is on "Get a Job," by the Silhouettes, on which he plays the saxophone solo. This recording, which reached the first position on both the pop and rhythm-and-blues charts, is on the sound tracks of *American Graffiti* (1973), *Trading Places* (1983), and *Stand by Me* (1986). Concurrent with his musical activities, McGill worked as a machinist (1964–2000). He is buried in Greenmount Cemetery, Philadelphia.

Rollee McGill; permission of John Broven, John Broven Collection

Though McGill was estimated as age eight when enumerated for the census in Kingstree on 7 May 1940, he believed he was born on in 1934.

Compositions

"Blue Moon Melody" (also titled "Blue Moon Moon"), "Come Home," "Come On In," "Go On Little Girl," "I'm Not Your Square," "In My Neighborhood," "Let's Go," "A Moment of Love," "Night after Night," "Oncoming Train," "People Are Talking," "Rhythm Rockin' Blues," "Someday," "That's My Girl," "There Goes That Train," "There's Madness in My Heart," "You Can Keep It," "You Left Me Here to Cry"

Recordings as Leader

Rhythm Rockin' Blues (1954–1959, 1961, 1963, ca. 1965), "She's So Fine" (1959), "She's So Lovely" (1959), "Who Are You?" (1959)

Leaders Recorded With

Solomon Burke (1955), Sensations (1955), Turbans (1955), Silhouettes (1957)

References

PRIMARY: John Broven, with Richard Tapp, "The Story of Rollee McGill Rhythm Rockin' Man," *Juke Blues* 51 (Summer 2002): 14–19 (mostly a narrative by McGill).

SECONDARY: "Rollee McGill," http://articles.philly.com/2000-10-18/news/25587477_1_daughters-bow-ties-contracting (18 October 2000; accessed 21 May 2014) (obituary); Bill Dahl, notes to McGill's *Rhythm Rockin' Blues* (2009; Bear Family 15926).

McIntosh, Traps (Joseph)

Drums

S.C. residence: Charleston (possibly late 1890s–possibly early 1900s)

Apparently a ward of Jenkins Orphanage, McIntosh played in its bands ca. 1900. He moved from Charleston to N.Y.C., where his playing was admired, though he apparently never recorded. James P. Johnson considered McIntosh "the greatest drummer of all time" (27). He notes that McIntosh "used a small drum, bass drum and cymbal. His drumsticks were two chair rungs, whittled down. He played the cymbal with a stick. He had a [drum] roll that was like tearing toilet paper and he was a sensational exhibitionist, flying sticks and all. He'd hit the gong, toss his sticks into the air and go right into the groove" (27).

Reference

SECONDARY: Tom Davin, "Conversations with James P. Johnson," *Jazz Review* 2 (September 1959): 26–27.

McKenzie, Mac (Elias W.)

Violin

15 May 1916 (Charleston, S.C.)–3 May 2006 (Albany, N.Y.)

S.C. residence: Charleston (1916–ca. 1918)

Around 1918 McKenzie moved with his family from Charleston to N.Y.C., where as early as age eight he sang and danced in the Bowery. He played the drums before taking violin lessons in high school. Beginning in the mid-1930s he performed with tramp bands (funny clothes, kazoos, washboards) and led his own quintet, which played primarily jazz but also blues. By 1938 he electrified his violin. Though he continued performing after moving to Albany, N.Y., in 1941, he gave up playing in 1953. He served in the army in 1943. He is buried in Gerald B. H. Solomon Saratoga National Cemetery, Schuylerville, N.Y.

McKenzie's birth and death dates, place of death, and middle initial come from the Social Security

Death Index. Both Bruce Bastin and Kip Lornell record the birth year as 1915.

References

PRIMARY: Kip Lornell, "Albany Blues," *Living Blues* 14 (Autumn 1973): 25–27 (substantial comments by McKenzie).

SECONDARY: Bruce Bastin, *Red River Blues: The Blues Tradition in the Southeast* (Urbana: University of Illinois Press, 1986), 339 (comments by McKenzie).

McKinney, Nina Mae (Probably Nannie M. McKenna)

Singer

Early 1910s, but possibly 16 June 1912 (Lancaster, S.C.)–3 May 1967 (New York, N.Y.)

S.C. residence: Lancaster (early 1910s–ca. 1924)

McKinney was reared on or near the property of Colonel Leroy Springs, founder of what became Springs Industries. She attended Lancaster Normal and Industrial Institute but left Lancaster around age twelve. According to Alvin E. White her family resided briefly in Savannah, Ga., before moving to N.Y.C. After working as a dancer in Harlem clubs, she presumably appeared in the revue *Blackbirds of 1928*, which featured singer Adelaide Hall and dancer Bill "Bojangles" Robinson. She was discovered by the Hollywood director King Vidor, who cast her as Chick in *Hallelujah* (1929), in which she sings "(Gimme Dat) Old Time Religion," "St. Louis Blues," and "Swanee Shuffle," the last of which Irving Berlin wrote for this film. Success as Chick resulted in an MGM contract for McKinney. During a 1931 vaudeville tour with Willie "The Lion" Smith and Charles Ray, she sang "I Must Have That Man" and "Sleepy Time Down South." With the Eubie Blake band in *Pie, Pie, Blackbird* (1932), she sings "It Takes a Blackbird to Make the Sweetest Kind of Pie" and "Everything I Got Belongs to You." This same year in N.Y.C. she performed "Love, Nuts and Noodles" in the revue *Ballyhoo of 1932*. Apparently because her Hollywood career failed to blossom, in 1932 she moved to Europe, where she performed in cabarets and plays; on tour she was presented as the Black Garbo. In London she entertained King George V, performed at the Palladium, and was featured on BBC television. As perhaps a sign of her popularity in England, Lawrence (or Laurence) Wright (writing as Horatio Nicholls) included her likeness on the sheet music to his and Joseph George Gilbert's "She's Not as Black as She's Painted," published in London in 1937. In the mid-1930s, while abroad, she wed Jimmy Monroe, who, following their divorce, next married Billie Holiday. Back in the United States she sang with the band of Pancho Diggs that, in the early 1940s, became known as Nina Mae McKinney and Her Orchestra. She then returned to making movies until 1950. Little is known about her subsequent activities, though late in life she worked as a domestic. Her body was cremated.

Nina Mae McKinney; permission of Barbara J. Kukla

Of the many sources consulted, approximately half indicate that McKinney was born in 1912; about half, in 1913. One specifies 1909; one, 1917. She likely was the Nannie M. McKenna, estimated age eight and born in S.C., who was enumerated for the census in Lancaster on 14 January 1920. She lived with her grandmother Mary A. McKenna and Mary's son, Napolean. For the passenger list of the *Lafayette,* which sailed from Le Havre to N.Y.C. on 11 March 1931, McKinney stated that she was born in Lancaster on 16 June 1912. For the passenger list of the *Mooltan,* which departed London for Australia on 23 July 1937, she identified herself as Nina

Mae Monroe (McKinney) and gave her age as twenty-five. The 1940 census, conducted in N.Y.C. on 29 April, records that even though she was married (presumably to Jimmy Monroe), she resided with her parents, James Edwin Maynor (born in Ga.) and Georgia C. Maynor (born in S.C.). This document notes that she was born in S.C., completed one year of high school, lived in N.Y.C. in 1935, and worked as a motion picture actress; it estimates her age as twenty-seven. Her mother was almost certainly the Georgia McKinie who, when enumerated in Savannah, Ga., in January 1920, was estimated as age twenty-three and worked as a servant; married, she was born in S.C., as were her parents. This census does not identify her husband, though James Maynor was born in Savannah, according to his 1917 and 1942 draft registration cards, as well as his 1919 army discharge form. (He served from 2 August 1918 until 18 July 1919, mostly overseas.) His absence probably explains Georgia's presence in Savannah (initially, to live with her husband), why Nina Mae McKinney lived with her maternal grandmother in January 1920 (because her mother was unable to tend to her), and why she dwelled in Savannah after leaving Lancaster and before moving to N.Y.C. (to be reunited with her parents, following James's return—or to join her mother, with whom she traveled to be with James, who might have settled in N.Y.C. following discharge from the army). Conceivably Maynor was not McKinney's biological father. Without evidence Stephen Bourne identifies the father as Hal McKinney, a claim that seems unlikely, given the McKenna/McKinie/McKinney name on the maternal side of the entertainer's family. Some sources record Nina Mae McKinney's middle name as Mayme. Though McKinney sang in all but one of her movies made from 1929 to 1939—sometimes growling and scatting—and in live performances, little of her singing was recorded. She sings on three commercially issued recordings, two as vocalist with pianist Garland Wilson: "Minnie the Moocher's Wedding Day" and "Rhapsody in Love." They were made in Paris for French Brunswick. The third release, "Swanee Shuffle" (with a band led by Curtis Mosby), is from the sound track of *Hallelujah.* She speaks on Reverend A. W. Nix's "The Black Diamond Express to Hell," parts 5 and 6, recorded for Vocalion. She is possibly the Nannie McKinney who, in 1927, made two unreleased test pressings for Vocalion backed by pianist Porter Grainger: "Dyin' Crap Shooter's Blues" and "The Band'll Play Who'd a-Thought It." If she recorded these tunes and was born ca. 1912, she was precocious.

Recording as Leader

"Swanee Shuffle" (1929)

Leaders Recorded With

A. W. Nix (1930), Garland Wilson (1932)

Films

Hallelujah (1929), *Manhattan Serenade* (1929), *They Learned about Women* (1930), *Safe in Hell* (1931; also titled *The Lost Lady*), *Passing the Buck* (1932), *Pie, Pie, Blackbird* (1932), *Kentucky Minstrels* (1934), *BBC: The Voice of Britain* (1935), *Reckless* (1935), *Sanders of the River* (1935), *The Black Network* (1936), *The Lonely Trail* (1936), *Gang Smashers* (1938), *The Devil's Daughter* (1939), *Straight to Heaven* (1939), *Dark Waters* (1944), *Together Again* (1944), *The Power of the Whistler* (1945), *Night Train to Memphis* (1946), *Danger Street* (1947), *Pinky* (1949), *Copper Canyon* (1950)

Award

Black Filmmakers' Hall of Fame (1978)

Website

http://www.webring.org/go?ring=afroa&id=27&ac=NwkYB%B8%AC%9E%8B%FD%EB%DA%86co_KqtD%0C%FC%EC%85%DA%A5%BC%8E%97ju%5EYb%3F%03%11%A3%F6%CD%C6%B6%F3%82%95c%7C%40%5C(0%0E%16%E4%F3%C3%D8%B4&&go (accessed 21 May 2014)

References

SECONDARY: Richard Watts, Jr., "Sight and Sound," *New York Herald Tribune,* 17 June 1934, sec. V, p. 1; "From Hollywood," *Reading (Pa.) Eagle,* 16 February 1935, p. 9; "What Happened To: Nina Mae McKinney?," *Hue* 1 (February 1954): 19; Willie "The Lion" Smith, with George Hoefer, *Music on My Mind: The Memoirs of an American Pianist* (Garden City, N.Y.: Doubleday, 1964), 196–97; "Nina Mae McKinney Dead," *New York Amsterdam News,* 13 May 1967, p. 1 (obituary); Ralph Matthews, "Thinking Out Loud!," *Washington (D.C.) Afro-American,* 20 May 1967, p. 21; Alvin E. White, "Nina Mae McKinney, Star of Early Theatre, Buried," *Baltimore Afro-American,* 20 May 1967, p. 11; Marjorie Clinton McMurray, "Black Lancaster," *Tap Journal: A Community Magazine of Education and the Arts* 2 (Spring 1977): 18–21 (also see front cover and copyright page); Barbara J. Kukla, *Swing City: Newark*

Nightlife, 1925–50 (Philadelphia: Temple University Press, 1991), 82–83, 98, 194; Stephen Bourne, *Nina Mae McKinney: The Black Garbo* (Duncan, Okla.: Bear-Manor Media, 2011).

McNeill, Charles

S.C. residence: Charleston (by early 1930s–at least into mid-1930s)

Apparently a ward of Jenkins Orphanage, McNeill played in its bands in the early 1930s, though his instrument is not known.

McPherson, Joseph

Tuba
(Probably S.C.)–?
S.C. residence: Charleston (by early 1930s–at least into mid-1930s)

A ward of Jenkins Orphanage, McPherson played in its bands in the early 1930s.

References

SECONDARY: John Chilton, *A Jazz Nursery: The Story of the Jenkins' Orphanage Bands of Charleston, South Carolina* (London: Bloomsbury Book Shop, 1980), 57; Bruce Bastin, "A Note on the Carolina Cotton Pickers," *Storyville* 95 (June–July 1981): 177–82.

Mercury, George

S.C. residence: Charleston (by early 1930s–probably at least into mid-1930s)

Apparently a ward of Jenkins Orphanage, Mercury played in its bands in the early 1930s, though his instrument is not known.

Middleton, Frank

Probably mid-to-late 1880s (S.C.)–?
Alto horn
S.C. residence: Charleston (by 1895–at least into early 1900s)

A ward of Jenkins Orphanage, Middleton played in its bands from the mid-1890s at least into the early 1900s and performed with one of them in England in 1895.

The passenger list of the *Paris,* which transported the orphanage band to England in September 1895, records Middleton's age as four; the list for the *Teutonic,* which returned the group to the United States the next month, specifies it as seven. When Middleton was enumerated for the census at the institution on 28 June 1900, his birth date was identified as June 1886. If he was born in 1886, he might be the Frank Middleton, age forty-three, who died at John's Island, S.C., on 23 November 1929.

References

SECONDARY: John Chilton, *A Jazz Nursery: The Story of the Jenkins' Orphanage Bands of Charleston, South Carolina* (London: Bloomsbury Book Shop, 1980), 57; Howard Rye, "Visiting Fireboys: The Jenkins' Orphanage Bands in Britain," *Storyville* 130 (1987): 137–43.

Mikell, Francis Eugene

Conductor, teacher, cornet, violin, and other instruments
Ca. 1880 or 27 March 1885 (Charleston, S.C.)–19 January 1932 (Brooklyn, N.Y.)
S.C. residences: Charleston (ca. 1880 or 1885–probably mid-1890s, possibly ca. 1900–1902, ca. 1904–1909), Orangeburg (ca. 1902–ca. 1904)

Mikell studied at Tuskegee Institute before teaching reading, geography, and music at what is now South Carolina State University. For one season during the first years of the twentieth century, he toured with Mahara's Minstrels. He taught in Charleston at Jenkins Orphanage, where he directed the band that played in the parade for the inauguration of President Taft (1909). From 1910 at least into 1914 he was music director of the Globe Theatre in Jacksonville, Fla. Following that affiliation he led an orchestra at the Pekin Theatre in Chicago before teaching at the Bordentown Industrial School in N.J. In 1917 he enlisted in the National Guard and became bandmaster of and arranger for the 369th Regiment Hell Fighters Band, led by James Reese Europe. For this group he recruited Amos Gilliard, Herbert Wright, and Steven Wright. Mikell accompanied the band to Europe that year and conducted it when James Reese Europe was at the war front. Back in the United States he led the band following Europe's death in 1919. (Herbert Wright killed Europe.) In time he returned to his position at Bordentown, though he also taught elsewhere and occasionally led the Clef Club orchestra. When the orphanage band played at Hammerstein's Roof Garden in N.Y.C.

in 1924, he served as guest conductor. Amos M. White considered Mikell "the finest bandmaster [he] ever heard." Of Mikell's students, Benny Carter had the most illustrious career, though Freddie Jenkins played for years with Duke Ellington. Neither man was associated with Jenkins Orphanage. Mikell is buried in site 12002, section 2, Cypress Hills National Cemetery, Brooklyn, N.Y.

Mikell was the father of saxophonists Otto R. Mikell and Francis Eugene Mikell, Jr.; the latter was not a South Carolinian. The given name of the father is sometimes recorded as Francis; at other times, Eugene. Because a son was named Francis Eugene Mikell, Jr., the father was Francis Eugene Mikell. The grave marker of the senior Mikell indicates that this was his name and that he was born on 27 March 1885. His age was estimated as thirty when he was enumerated as Eugene for the census in Jacksonville, Fla., on 18 April 1910; as forty-five when enumerated as Francis for the N.Y. state census in N.Y.C. on 1 June 1925; as forty-six when enumerated as Francis for the federal census in Queens, N.Y., on 22 April 1930. Given his schooling realities and his teaching at what is now South Carolina State University (he is listed in its 1897–1904 catalogue as Eugene F. Mikell), his being forty-six in 1930 seems improbable. According to the 1910 census, he was born in S.C.; the 1930 census states that he was born in Cuba. Identified as a music teacher, Eugene F. Mikell is included in the 1902 Charleston city directory.

Compositions

"American Expeditionary Force," "Father, to Thy Dear Name," "Good Bye," "Great Camp Meeting Day," "Lackawanna"

Leader Recorded With

James Reese Europe (1919)

References

SECONDARY: "Here and There," *Washington (D.C.) Colored American,* 29 December 1900, p. 15; "Mikell Now Leader of 'Hell Fighters' Band," *New York Age,* 21 June 1919, p. 6; Lucien H. White, "Forming Boys' Bands," *New York Age,* 17 July 1920, p. 5; Lucien H. White, "Gene Mikell Is a Busy Teacher," *New York Age,* 1 January 1921, p. 5; "Lt. E. [*sic*] Eugene Mikell, Musician, Is Dead," *Brooklyn (N.Y.) Daily Eagle,* 21 January 1932, p. 17 (obituary); Lucien H. White, "F. Eugene Mikell, Well Known Musician, Dies in Navy Hospital," *New York Age,* 30 January 1932, p. 7 (obituary); Amos M. White, interview by William Russell, 23 August 1958, four reels of tape and a typed summary, Hogan Jazz Archive, Tulane University, New Orleans, p. 18 of summary (also available at http://musicrising.tulane.edu/uploads/transcripts/a.%20white%2008-23-1958.pdf [accessed 21 May 2014]); [Roger Ringo], "Reminiscing in Tempo with Freddie Jenkins," *Storyville* 46 (April 1973): 124–33 (Mikell's surname is spelled Michaels); Stanley Dance, *The World of Swing* (New York: Scribner's, 1974), 1: 136; John Chilton, *A Jazz Nursery: The Story of the Jenkins' Orphanage Bands of Charleston, South Carolina* (London: Bloomsbury Book Shop, 1980), 3, 13, 20, 23, 57; Jeffrey P. Green, *Edmund Thornton Jenkins: The Life and Times of an American Black Composer, 1894–1926* (Westport, Conn.: Greenwood, 1982), passim; Reid Badger, *A Life in Ragtime: A Biography of James Reese Europe* (New York: Oxford University Press, 1995), passim; Stephen L. Harris, *Harlem's Hell Fighters: The African-American 369th Infantry in World War I* (Washington, D.C.: Brassey's, 2003), 75, 78, 160, 220; Peter Dunbaugh Smith, "Ashley Street Blues: Racial Uplift and the Commodification of Vernacular Performance in Lavilla, Florida, 1896–1916" (Ph.D. dissertation, Florida State University, 2006), passim; Horst P. J. Bergmeier and Rainer E. Lotz, "James Arthur Briggs," *Black Music Research Journal* 30 (Spring 2010): 96.

Mikell, Otto Reginald

Saxophone, clarinet

17 February 1904 (Orangeburg, S.C.)–23 May 1970 (possibly Bloomfield, N.J.)

S.C. residences: Orangeburg (at least 1904), Charleston (possibly 1904–probably no later than 1909)

Because his father, Francis Eugene Mikell, was a musician and music teacher, Mikell grew up in a musical atmosphere. Player of several reed instruments, including the bass saxophone, he became a professional musician. In the mid-1920s he was with the house band at the Savoy Ballroom in N.Y.C., Leon Abbey's Savoy Bearcats. He was in Europe in 1930, presumably as a musician. He became a music teacher. Mikell is buried in grave 1, lot 254A, Mount Vernon section, Glendale Cemetery, Bloomfield, N.J.

Mikell was the brother of saxophonist Francis Eugene Mikell, Jr., who was not a South Carolinian. In 1930 Mikell sailed from Cherbourg, France, to N.Y.C. on the *Bremen.* Its passenger list indicates where and when he was born; the date is confirmed by the Social Security Death Index.

Leaders Recorded With

Savoy Bearcats (1926), Fess Williams (1926–1927), probably Noble Sissle (1943)

Reference

SECONDARY: "Abbey Got Cash and Praise from European Newspapers," *Baltimore Afro-American*, 6 September 1930, p. 8.

Miles, Josie (Josephine)

Singer

Ca. 1900 (Summerville, S.C.)–possibly 1950s or 1960s

S.C. residence: Summerville (ca. 1900–no later than 1922)

Though Miles recorded over fifty songs from 1922 to 1925, performed in a popular show, and possibly sang in another, little is known about her, other than that she was from Summerville and left there for N.Y.C. no later than 1922. That year she toured with Noble Sissle and Eubie Blake's *Shuffle Along*, the first successful black musical; in it she sang "31st Street Blues." The next year she supposedly performed in *Runnin' Wild*. Primarily considered a blues singer, she began recording in 1922 for Black Swan Records before affiliating with Gennett and other labels. She was backed by groups known as the Kansas City Five and the Choo Choo Jazzers; Jake Frazier, Fletcher Henderson, Bubber Miley, Joe Smith, and Rex Stewart were among her accompanying musicians. She recorded vocal duets with Billy Higgins (known as Jazz Caspar) in 1924. It has not been determined if Miles was the Missionary Josephine Miles who recorded for Gennett in 1928. Without evidence sources indicate that the singer died in a Kansas City automobile accident in the 1950s or 1960s.

Recordings as Leader

Complete Recorded Works in Chronological Order (1922–1925; two CDs)

References

SECONDARY: "South Carolina Girl Gets Exclusive Recording Contract," *New York Amsterdam News*, 7 November 1923, p. 3 (reprinted in *Los Angeles California Eagle*, 9 November 1923, p. 5) (probably written by Joe Davis, her manager, this article states, incorrectly, that Miles had not recorded before her relationship with Gennett); Bruce Bastin, with Kip Lornell, *The Melody Man: Joe Davis and the New York Music Scene, 1916–1978* (Jackson: University Press of Mississippi, 2012), 16–19, 21–24; Arwulf Arwulf [Theodore Grenier], "Josie Miles," http://www.allmusic.com/artist/josie-miles-mn0000831463 (undated; accessed 21 May 2014).

Miley, Bubber (James Wesley)

Cornet, trumpet

Possibly 2 April 1903 (Aiken, S.C.)–May 1932 (New York, N.Y.)

S.C. residence: Aiken (1903–ca. 1909)

At age six Miley moved from Aiken to N.Y.C., where, to help his family financially, he sang on the streets. He began trombone and cornet lessons at fourteen but a year later reportedly joined the navy, in which he supposedly served as a band boy for eighteen months. Soon after discharge he established the Carolina Five, which played at various N.Y.C. clubs. He then toured with the Sunny South show before joining the band of Mamie Smith, with which he made his first recordings in 1921. His most important affiliation, with the Duke Ellington band (initially called the Washingtonians), lasted from the middle through the late 1920s, when his irresponsible behavior caused Ellington to fire him. He played in Paris with Noble Sissle (1929). Upon returning to the United States, he was with Zutty Singleton and then Allie Ross before forming his own band, the Mileage Makers, in 1930. With it he played in Irving Mills's revue *Harlem Scandals* (1931) until tuberculosis forced him to give up playing; he died from the disease. Influenced most by Johnny Dunn and King Oliver, Miley is important for using a plunger mute to create exotic growls and "wa-wa"s that helped establish what became known as the jungle sound of Ellington's band. His playing made him, as James Lincoln Collier has written, "a major factor in creating the style that would make [Ellington's] group famous, and night after night he stirred up audiences so that people would walk out later remembering the band as much as the singers and dancers" (48). Such playing may be heard on recordings of tunes for which he and Ellington are identified as co-composers, including "Black and Tan Fantasy," "Creole Love Call," and "East St. Louis Toodle-Oo." These compositions, which remained in Ellington's book, were also performed by Miley's successors in the band, Cootie Williams and Ray Nance, whose styles Miley influenced.

Yet Miley was a significant soloist apart from his growling and "wa-wa"-ing. Barry McRae observes that Miley "was a master of the stop-time chorus and his solos could be as stark as a New Orleans primitive and equally as emotional."

Several 1903 dates have been recorded for Miley's birth; the one from the passenger list for the *Paris,* on which Miley returned to N.Y.C. from France in June 1929, is used here. Though more than one date has been given for his death in May 1932, it has not been determined which is correct. His military service has not been confirmed.

Compositions

"Black and Tan Fantasy," "Blue Harlem," "The Blues I Love to Sing," "Creole Love Call," "Doin' the Voom Voom," "Down in the Mouth Blues," "East St. Louis Toodle-Oo," "Goin' to Town," "Just for You," "Lenox Avenue Shuffle," "Sweet Man Joe," "Those Blues," "Will You Forgive Me"

Recordings as Leader (All 1930)

"Black Maria," "Chinnin' and Chattin' with May," "I Lost My Gal from Memphis," "Loving You the Way I Do," "The Penalty of Love," "Without You, Emaline"

Leaders Recorded With

Mamie Smith (1921–1922), Mary Jackson (1923), Thomas Morris (1923), Charles Booker (1924), Perry Bradford (1924), Duke Ellington (1924, 1926–1929), Helen Gross (1924), Rosa Henderson (1924), Lethia Hill (1924), Margaret Johnson (1924–1925), Kansas City Five (1924), Viola McCoy (1924), Hazel Meyers (1924), Josie Miles (1924–1925), Julia Moody (1924), Monette Moore (1924–1925), Alberta Perkins (1924), Nellie Potter (1924), Six Black Diamonds (1924), Clementine Smith (1924), Texas Blues Destroyers (1924), Alberta Hunter (1925), Sara Martin (1925–1926), Clarence Williams (1926), Evelyn Preer (1927), Martha Copeland (1928), Warren Mills (1928), Leo Reisman (1929–1931), Hoagy Carmichael (1930), Jelly Roll Morton (1930), King Oliver (1930)

Award

New Jersey Jazz Society American Jazz Hall of Fame (1996)

References

SECONDARY: Roger Pryor Dodge, "Bubber," *H.R.S. Society Rag,* October 1940, 10–14; Roger Pryor Dodge, "Bubber Miley," *Jazz Monthly* 4 (May 1958): 2–7, 32 (the two Dodge articles are reprinted in *Hot Jazz and Jazz Dance: Roger Pryor Dodge Collected Writings, 1929–1964,* ed. Pryor Dodge [New York: Oxford University Press, 1995], 84–89, 247–59); Gunther Schuller, *Early Jazz: Its Roots and Musical Development* (New York: Oxford University Press, 1968), 320–32; Barry McRae, "A B Basics No. 38: Bubber Miley," *Jazz Journal* 23 (February 1970): 39; Edward Kennedy Ellington, *Music Is My Mistress* (Garden City, N.Y.: Doubleday, 1973), 106; James Lincoln Collier, *Duke Ellington* (New York: Oxford University Press, 1987), passim; Gunther Schuller, *The Swing Era: The Development of Jazz, 1930–1945* (New York: Oxford University Press, 1989), passim; *The Duke Ellington Reader,* ed. Mark Tucker (New York: Oxford University Press, 1993), passim; Scott Yanow, *The Trumpet Kings: The Players Who Shaped the Sound of Jazz Trumpet* (San Francisco: Backbeat Books, 2001), 259–60; Jack Sohmer, "Miley, Bubber," in *Harlem Renaissance Lives: From the African American National Biography,* ed. Henry Louis Gates, Jr., and Evelyn Brooks Higginbotham (New York: Oxford University Press, 2009), 349–51; Bruce Bastin, with Kip Lornell, *The Melody Man: Joe Davis and the New York Music Scene, 1916–1978* (Jackson: University Press of Mississippi, 2012), passim.

Miller, Fred

Presumably S.C.
Guitar
S.C. residence: Sumter County, though possibly Sumter town (possibly by 1920-possibly 1940)

An itinerant musician, Miller is known solely for his relationship with the North Carolina blues shouter Richard "Big Boy" Henry, which began in 1933. Miller mentored the young Henry, taught him songs by the likes of Blind Boy Fuller, and formed a team with him. The duo played on street corners. In time Miller moved to N.Y.C., where Henry occasionally visited him in the late 1940s or early 1950s; there they again performed together.

A Fred Miller of Sumter County was enumerated for the census in 1920, 1930, and 1940. It has not been determined if this black farmer, born in S.C., was the guitarist; nor has it been ascertained if the Fred Miller who married Julia Weeks in Sumter in January 1920 was the musician.

Reference

SECONDARY: Tom Rankin, "Blues for Mr. President," *Southern Changes: A Chronicle of the Ongoing Struggle for Equality* 6 (1984): 12–13.

Miller, Johnny

See Stark, Cootie

Mills, Alonzo J.

Cornet

Early or mid-1890s (probably John's Island, S.C., though conceivably Charleston, S.C.)–possibly 27 May 1965

S.C. residences: probably John's Island (early or mid-1890s–no later than 1910), Charleston (possibly early or mid-1890s, but by 1910–probably at least until 1933)

A ward of Jenkins Orphanage, Mills played in its bands at least during the 1910s and 1920s. He led the one that played in *Uncle Tom's Cabin* in N.Y.C. in 1913; the next year he performed with the orphanage band in England. A tutor at the institution, he was praised by Jabbo Smith for offering substantial music instruction; he also taught Cat Anderson, who considered him strict. Mills played in the institution's bands that performed in *Porgy* in N.Y.C. (1927–1928) and London (1929).

Mills was the father of musician Alonzo J. Mills, Jr. Mills was enumerated for the census at the orphanage on 2 April 1910, though this document does not record his estimated age. The passenger list of the *St. Louis,* which transported the institution's band from England to N.Y.C. in September 1914, indicates that Mills was born on 12 November 1895 at John's Island, S.C. His middle initial comes from his World War I draft registration card, which, though undated, was probably completed in 1917. It indicates that he was born at John's Island in 1895 and that he was twenty-two when he filled out the form in Kershaw County, S.C. Estimated age twenty-four, Mills was enumerated for the census in Charleston on 15 January 1920; this document indicates that he was a musician who owned his own business. The passenger list of the *Columbus,* which took the orphanage band to Plymouth, England, in April 1929, records his age as thirty-five. The passenger list of the *Majestic,* which returned the group to N.Y.C. in June, identifies his birth date as 21 September 1895 and place as Charleston. He was enumerated for the census in N.Y.C. on 15 May 1930 and 2 April 1940. The first estimates his age as thirty-five (he then worked as a laborer in construction); the second, as forty-six (a railroad carman [cleaner]). When Mills completed a World War II draft registration card, probably in 1941, he recorded his birth date as 21 September 1893; he then lived in N.Y.C. and worked for the New York Central Railroad. He is probably the Alonzo J. Mills buried in section T, site 8490, Long Island National Cemetery, Farmingdale, N.Y. If so he served in World War I and attained the rank of corporal. The cemetery indicates that he was born on 23 September 1892 and died on 27 May 1965.

References

SECONDARY: John Chilton, *A Jazz Nursery: The Story of the Jenkins' Orphanage Bands of Charleston, South Carolina* (London: Bloomsbury Book Shop, 1980), 14–15, 24, 39, 57; Mike Joyce, "Jabbo Smith: Interview," *Cadence* 8 (May 1982): 11; Howard Rye, "Visiting Fireboys: The Jenkins' Orphanage Bands in Britain," *Storyville* 130 (1987): 137–43.

Mills, Alonzo J., Jr.

Probably clarinet

13 October 1919 (Charleston, S.C.)–1 January 1975

S.C. residence: Charleston (1919–probably at least until 1933)

Mills played in the Jenkins Orphanage bands that performed in *Porgy* in N.Y.C. in 1927–1928 and London in 1929. He was with the institution's quartet in N.Y.C. in 1928. He is, in all likelihood, the Alonzo Mills who soloed in Charleston at a benefit concert for the orphanage in October of, probably, 1933.

Mills was the son of cornetist Alonzo J. Mills. The Social Security Death Index records Mills's birth date, and month and year of death; the day of death comes from http://www.death-record.com/l/104281295/Alonzo-Mills (undated; accessed 21 May 2014).

References

SECONDARY: "Colored Military Men Get Together at Large Banquet," *New York Age,* 14 April 1928, p. 10; John Chilton, *A Jazz Nursery: The Story of the Jenkins' Orphanage Bands of Charleston, South Carolina* (London: Bloomsbury Book Shop, 1980), 39; Howard Rye, "Visiting Fireboys: The Jenkins' Orphanage Bands in Britain," *Storyville* 130 (1987): 137–43; Jack McCray, *Charleston Jazz* (Charleston, S.C.: Arcadia Publishing, 2007), 44.

Mills, Robert

Ca. 1919-?
S.C. residence: Charleston (by 1930-)

A ward of Jenkins Orphanage, Mills played in its bands in the 1930s, though his instrument is not known.

Estimated age eleven, Mills was enumerated for the census at the orphanage on 2 April 1930.

Mills, Thomas (?)

Ca. 1903-?
S.C. residence: Charleston (at least 1910s)

Possibly a ward of Jenkins Orphanage, Mills played in its bands in the 1910s, including the one that performed in England in 1914.

The musician's surname is conceivably Millie. The given name is abbreviated on the passenger list of the *Campania,* which transported the orphanage band to England in May 1914. It appears to be Thos., though Howard Rye interprets it as Thurs. This document specifies his age as eleven. Mills's name is absent from the list of the *St. Louis,* on which the group returned to N.Y.C. in September.

Reference

SECONDARY: Howard Rye, "Visiting Fireboys: The Jenkins' Orphanage Bands in Britain," *Storyville* 130 (1987): 137–43.

Milton, John

Tuba
S.C. residence: Charleston (at least 1920s)

Apparently a ward of Jenkins Orphanage, Milton played in its bands in the 1920s.

Minger, Pete (George Allen)

Trumpet, flugelhorn, piano, singer
22 January 1943 (Orangeburg, S.C.)-13 April 2000 (Pompano Beach, Fla.)
S.C. residence: Orangeburg (1943-mid-1960s)

Inspired initially by Louis Armstrong, Minger began playing professionally at fourteen. He attended several colleges and served in the army (1967–1969) before affiliating with Count Basie, with whom he played from 1970 to 1980, except for most of 1977. After receiving undergraduate and graduate degrees from the University of Miami in the 1980s, he performed and taught in southeastern Fla., though he also toured with the Philip Morris Superband and the band of Frank Wess. An ordained minister, he served as music director at the Solid Rock Family Worship Center in Fort Lauderdale. His dedication to religion is reflected in his last album, which features religious tunes he wrote. He is buried in section 429, site 698, Florida National Cemetery, Bushnell, Fla.

Compositions

"Ain't No Man o War," "Better Get Right with Jesus," "Blues for B. B." (also titled "Pete's Blues"), "Come to Me Sweet Jesus," "Get On Up," "He Carries Me through the Storm," "Holy Spirit," "I Know That Jesus Will Bring Me Through," "Jesus I Know (the Word)," "Jesus Take My Life (and Set Me Free)," "Jesus We Love You," "Look to the Sky (Jesus Is Coming Again)," "Paradise," "Praise the Lord," "Rebuke the Devour" [*sic*]

Recordings as Leader

Straight from the Source (1983; with additional material, titled *Minger Painting*), *Look to the Sky* (1992), *Through the Storm* (1999)

Leaders Recorded With

Count Basie (1970–1973, 1975–1980), Joe Williams (1971), Jazz at the Philharmonic (1972), Big Joe Turner (1972), Al Grey (1977), Chubby Jackson (1978), Milt Jackson (1978), Ella Fitzgerald (1979), Cleveland Eaton (1980), Alice Day (1981), Eddie Higgins (1982), University of Miami Concert Jazz Band (1983–1984), Neil Rogers (1984–1985), Nancy Reed (1986), Phil Urso (1986), Concord Festival All Stars (1990), Mel Tormé (1990), Frank Wess (1990), Arthur Barron (1994), Pete Brady (ca. 1990s), Billy Marcus (1996), Turk Mauro (1996), Billy Ross (1996), Melton Mustafa (1997), Keter Betts (1998)

Film

The Last of the Blue Devils (1979)

References

SECONDARY: Matt Schudel, "Trumpeter Pete Minger," *Fort Lauderdale (Fla.) SunSentinel,* 21 April 2000, sec. B, p. 7 (obituary); Scott Yanow, *The Trumpet Kings: The Players Who Shaped the Sound of Jazz Trumpet* (San Francisco: Backbeat Books, 2001), 261.

Mockabee, Rudy (Jesse Rudolph, Jr.)

Singer, drums

27 January 1944 (Cowpens, S.C.)–22 May 2013 (Huntsville, Ala.)

S.C. residence: Cowpens (1944–ca. 1969)

Growing up in Cowpens, Mockabee played drums in school bands, including one at Benjamin E. Mays High School in Pacolet, from which he was graduated in 1962. After performing with the Yakety Yaks, he sang for approximately a year with the Drifters. He settled in Huntsville, Ala., where he established a band that continued for the remainder of his life. In addition to leading his own group, during the period 2008–2010 he was the featured singer with the Flashbacks of Athens, Ala. He is buried in the Mount Calvary Baptist Church Cemetery, Cowpens.

Mockabee's birth date comes from the program distributed at the singer's funeral. It has not been confirmed that "Better Together," "Just Want to Be Your Friend," "Love Makes the Woman Shine," and "Lover My Love"—attributed to Mockabee and released on Crown Records in 2006—are actually by him.

Rudy Mockabee; permission of Loretto J. Mockabee

Recordings as Leader

"Cheer Up (Daddy's Coming Home)" (1969), "Sweet Thing" (1969), "Piece of My Heart" (1970), "Think about It" (1970)

Leaders Recorded With

Yakety Yaks (possibly 1968), Drifters (possibly 1969)

References

PRIMARY: Georgia Carter, "Music Is Life to Me," *Florence (Ala.) Times Daily,* 11 November 1983, sec. D, p. 1 (substantial comments by Mockabee).

SECONDARY: Brendan Greaves and Jason Perlmutter, notes to *Said I Had a Vision: Songs and Labels of David Lee* (2010; Paradise of Bachelors PoB-01); Sir Shambling [John Ridley], "Rudy Mockabee," http://www.sirshambling.com/artists_2012/M/rudy_mockabee/index.php (2012; accessed 21 May 2014); "Rudy Mockabee," *Spartanburg (S.C.) Herald-Journal,* 28 May 2013, sec. C, p. 2 (obituary).

Moore, Samuel

See Ironing Board Sam

Morant, Joey (Joseph Nathaniel)

Trumpet, cornet, flugelhorn, euphonium, guitar, bass, drums, singer

11 August 1938 (Charleston, S.C.)–

S.C. residences: Charleston (1938–1957, 1980–1990, 1992–1993), Orangeburg (1961)

Having been taught music at Henry P. Archer Elementary School in Charleston by Fletcher Linton, Morant received further instruction at Burke High School from Holland Daniels. After completing high school he moved to Boston, though he returned to S.C. to enroll in what is now South Carolina State University, which he attended for one semester in 1961. He served in the military (both army and marine corps) from 1962 to 1964 before matriculating at the University of Hartford, from which he received a degree in 1968. He toured with his own group until 1970, when he began a long-term engagement at the Tic Toc Club in Salisbury Beach, Mass. During this period he also worked as a sideman. He lived and performed in Calif. from 1974 to 1976 and then in N.Y.C. until 1980. He returned to Charleston to chair the MOJA Arts Festival but left in 1990 to play lead trumpet in the band at Merv Griffin's Resorts International in Atlantic

Joey Morant; permission of Joey Morant

City, N.J. Back in Charleston in 1992 he served for a year as director of the MOJA Arts Festival. After again playing with the band at Resorts International (1993–1996), he settled in the greater N.Y.C. area, where he remains. He performs regularly there as leader and with groups such as the Harlem Blues and Jazz Band, both in clubs and at prestigious venues such as the Waldorf-Astoria; he also performs internationally. At Ground Zero, site of the 2001 terrorist attacks in N.Y.C., he played "Star Spangled Banner" at the three-month anniversary of these events. He is known for his energetic, entertaining performances.

Compositions

"Bells on Your Toes," "Catfish Stew Blues," "Eat 'Em Up," "437 Race Street," "Good-Bye Mamma," "My Son Amadeus," "Patriotic Rag," "Ya Git Wat Yo Giv"

Recordings as Leader

"Chicken Talk" (1969), "Swamp Rat" (1969), *Better Late Than Never* (1992)

Leaders Recorded With

Lloyd Price (1963), Lainie Cooke (2003, 2007), Dennis Day (2008), Charleston Jazz Initiative Legends Band (2010)

Award

Harlem Jazz and Music Festival Instrumentalist of the Year (2003)

References

SECONDARY: Prentiss Findlay, "Joey Morant: Trumpeter Called 'Mr. Entertainment,'" *Charleston (S.C.) Post and Courier,* 7 November 1992, sec. E, pp. 1, 3; Jack McCray, *Charleston Jazz* (Charleston, S.C.: Arcadia Publishing, 2007), 75, 83, 103.

Morgan, Henry

Baritone horn
-before 1981
S.C. residence: Charleston (at least early 1930s)

A ward of Jenkins Orphanage, Morgan played in its bands in the early 1930s. Bruce Bastin states that Morgan had died by the time Bastin completed his manuscript.

Reference

SECONDARY: Bruce Bastin, "A Note on the Carolina Cotton Pickers," *Storyville* 95 (June–July 1981): 177–82.

Morrow, El (E. L.)

Guitar
Possibly 12 March of either 1905 or 1906 (Lancaster County, S.C.)-10 March 1954 (Charlotte, N.C.)
S.C. residence: Lancaster County, including Indian Land (1905 or 1906-no later than 1930)

On the two tunes Morrow is known to have recorded, he plays guitar, and Beans Hambone (James Albert) sings. Marshall Wyatt states that the record sold 385 copies. "Beans," which might be the first recording of a cigar-box guitar, generated interest over half a century later. Marcello Carlin notes that Morrow's tuning—"beyond individualistic"—permits one "to hear a new music fumbling its way into existence," a music that is played intentionally off key. He characterizes this recording as bearing "a startling beauty which transcends any imposed notions of thoughtlessness." On 28 October 2005 it was aired on *Mixing It,* a BBC program hosted by Mark Russell and Robert Sandall on Radio 3.

Morrow's places of birth and death come from North Carolina, Deaths, 1931–1994. This source indicates that Morrow was born on 12 March 1906; his 1942 draft registration card (which confirms his birthplace), on 12 March 1905. The musician is probably the A. L. Morrow, estimated age six, who was enumerated for the census at Indian Land, Lancaster County, on 16 or 18 April 1910. He was enumerated as E. L. Morrow, estimated age twenty-five, in Charlotte, N.C., on 11 April 1930. His draft registration card, signed with an X, records his height as five feet.

Recordings as Leader (Both 1931; with Beans Hambone)

"Beans," "Tippin' Out"

References

SECONDARY: Paul Oliver, *Songsters and Saints: Vocal Traditions on Race Records* (Cambridge: Cambridge University Press, 1984), 51, 53; Bruce Bastin, *Red River Blues: The Blues Tradition in the Southeast* (Urbana: University of Illinois Press, 1986), 197; Marshall Wyatt, notes to *Good for What Ails You: Music of the Medicine Shows, 1926–1937*, pp. 44, 51 (2005; Old Hat Records CD-1005); Marcello Carlin, review of *On Stage with the George Mitchell Minstrels*, http://nobilliards.blogspot.com/2009/04/george-mitchell-minstrels-on-stage-with.html (2009).

Motley, Frank, Jr. ("Dual-Trumpet," "Two Horn")

Trumpet, trombone, singer, composer

30 December 1923 (Cheraw, S.C.)–31 May 1998 (Durham, N.C.)

S.C. residences: Cheraw (1923–ca. 1940), Orangeburg (ca. 1940–ca. 1944)

Reared in Cheraw, Motley reportedly received an engineering degree from what is now South Carolina State University in 1944. Following service in the navy (1944–1946), he lived briefly in N.Y.C. before residing in Omaha, Nebr., from where he toured with territory bands led by Preston Love and Nat Towles. He possibly studied at the Chicago Conservatory of Music (1948–1950) before settling in Washington, D.C., where he presumably attended the Modern School of Music. Also in Washington he led a group, the Motley Crew; there, too, he recorded most frequently during his greatest period of activity, the 1950s. He and the Motley Crew played in Alaska in 1955; three years later he was part of a USO tour of Germany, the Middle East, and the South Pacific. Late that decade he moved to Canada, first Montreal and then Toronto, where he recorded for Paragon Records. In time he released music on his own label, Frank Motley. In 1984 he moved to Durham, N.C., where he lived the remainder of his life. Though Motley is best known for playing two trumpets simultaneously, Jay Bruder believes that he "was a translator [who] took swing, hard bop, and black pop influences and transformed them into pioneering rhythm and blues efforts" ("Two Horn Blues," part 2, 11).

Nothing about the contents of the CD *Honkin' at Midnight*, released in 2000, appears to have been published, though some of the thirty selections might be alternate takes of previously issued material.

Compositions

"All I Need Is Love," "Baby, Indeed I Do," "Bow-wow-wow," "Cadillac Blues," "Chickadee," "Chip's Groove," "Clap Hands," "Climbing Eiffel Tower," "Closing Time," "Cryin' All Alone," "Diggin' in the Ground," "Double or Nothing," "Dual Trumpet Blues," "Dual Trumpets Bounce" (also titled "Dual Trumpet Bounce"), "Ella's Ways," "Frantic Love," "Give Me One More Chance," "Go Man, Go," "Gossip in the Market," "Heartbreaker," "High and Low," "Hitchhikin'," "Hit the Ole Jackpot," "Honkin' at Midnight," "Hurricane Lover," "I Found Out," "I Love to Love You Baby," "I Was Framed," "JC's Theme," "Just Because My Love Is True," "Keep Your Head Up High," "Let Me Back in There Again," "Looking Ahead," "Never Would Have Made It," "New Hound Dog," "Nobody's Here," "Ouch," "Ride On," "Since My Love Has Gone," "Slave for You, Baby," "Stop Beating My Heart," "Swinging Along," "That Ain't Right," "T.V. Boogie Blues," "Two Horn Motley," "Undertaker," "We Ain't Gonna Ride No More," "What Can I Do?," "What's That Stuff Joe's Got," "You Got What It Takes"

Recordings as Leader

"Bow-wow-wow" (1951, 1954 or 1955), "Dual Trumpet Blues" (1951), "Fat Man" (1951), "Herbert's Jump" (1951), "That's All Right with Me" (1951), "Caravan" (1952), "Heavy Weight Baby" (1952), "I Found Out" (1952), "Dual Trumpets Bounce" (1952 or 1953), "Keep Your Head Up High" (1953), "What's That Stuff Joe's Got" (1953), "Curley's Lament" (1953 or 1954), "I'm Losing My Mind over You" (1953 or 1954), "Indeed I Do" (1953 or 1954), "Crying, Crying" (1954), "Frantic Love" (1954),

"I'm Gonna Miss You" (1954), "New Hound Dog" (1954), "Snatch It" (1954), "Boomerang Lover" (1954 or 1955), "Diggin' in the Ground" (1954 or 1955), "Don't Go" (1954 or 1955), "Double or Nothing" (1954 or 1955), "High and Low" (1954 or 1955), "Hitch Hikin'" (1954 or 1955), "Honkin' at Midnight" (1954 or 1955), "I Was Framed" (1954 or 1955), "JC's Theme" (1954 or 1955), "The Last Time" (1954 or 1955), "Memories of You" (1954 or 1955), "Motley's Jazz" (1954 or 1955), "What Can I Do?" (1954 or 1955), "When the Saints Go Marching In" (1954 or 1955), "Yeah Let's Fly" (1954 or 1955), *Honkin' at Midnight* (1950s–1960s), "Climbing Eiffel Tower" (1956), "Frankie and Johnny" (1956), "Give Me One More Chance" (1956), "Stop Beating My Heart" (1956), "Swinging Along" (1956), "Three Blind Mice" (1956), "Wanda Landa Landa" (1956), *Swingin' n' Rockin'* (ca. 1961), "Rock and Roll's Gotta Beat" (ca. 1961), "Space Age" (ca. 1961), "A Bunch of Bad Cats" (early 1960s), *Frank Motley and the Hitch-Hikers* (1970; also titled *Let It Be*), *Chip Dip* (1972), "Country Music" (ca. 1978), "Two Horn Motley" (ca. 1978)

Leaders Recorded With

Charlie Gonzales (also known as Bobby Prince) (1951), Heartbreakers (1951), Lloyd "Fat Man" Smith (1951), T. N. T. Tribble (1951–1952), Clefs (1952), Jimmy Crawford (1952–1953), Chords (1953), Twilighters (1953), Parakeets (possibly 1953, 1954), Angel Face (Elsie Kenley) (1953 or 1954, ca. 1956), Curley Bridges (1953 or 1954), possibly Rainbows (1953 or 1954), Ontarios (1954), Paul Crawford (1954 or 1955), Larry Ellis (early 1960s), Jackie Shane (1960s)

References

SECONDARY: "Frank Motley Sets Tour of the South," *Baltimore Afro-American*, 19 September 1953, p. 6; "Swinging Along," *Stars and Stripes*, 19 September 1958, p. 12; "USO Group Plays 1st Lebanon Date," *Stars and Stripes*, 24 September 1958, p. 9; Major Robinson, "New York Beat," *Jet* 14 (23 October 1958): 63; Professor Hi-Jinx, notes to *Frank Motley* (1986; Krazy Kat KK 805); Dave Penny, "Washington Bounce: Frank Motley and His Motley Crew," *Blues and Rhythm: The Gospel Truth* 28 (April 1987): 16–19 (includes discography); Jay Bruder, "Two Horn Blues: Frank Motley and the 'D.C.' R&B Sound: 1950–1960," part 1, *Blues and Rhythm: The Gospel Truth* 83 (October 1993): 4–7; Jay Bruder, "Two Horn Blues: Frank Motley and the 'D.C.' R&B Sound: 1950–1960," part 2, *Blues and Rhythm: The Gospel Truth* 84 (November 1993): 8–11; Bill Munson, "Frank Motley in Canada," *Blues and Rhythm: The Gospel Truth* 91 (August 1994): 12–14; "Motley," *Durham (N.C.) Herald-Sun*, 3 June 1998, sec. C, p. 2 (obituary); Kelly Brewington, "Renowned 'Dual Trumpeter' Great Musician, Humanitarian," *Durham (N.C.) Herald-Sun*, 4 June 1998, sec. C, p. 1 (obituary); Jay Bruder, "Frank Motley," *Blues and Rhythm: The Gospel Truth* 131 (August 1998): 21 (obituary).

Mouzon, Alphonse

Drums, piano, trumpet, miscellaneous instruments, singer, composer, arranger
21 November 1948 (Charleston, S.C.)–
S.C. residence: Charleston (1948–1966)

In Charleston, Mouzon received musical instruction from Lonnie Hamilton III and Charles Garner. While in N.Y.C. preparing to be a medical technician, he took drum lessons from Bobby Thomas, who arranged for Mouzon to play in the pit band of the Broadway show *Promises, Promises* (1969). He studied acting in N.Y.C., including at the Lee Strasberg Theatre and Film Institute (1975). A regular with Roy Ayers (1970–1971) and McCoy Tyner (1972–1973), he was a charter member of two important bands that fused jazz and rock, Weather Report (1971–1972) and Eleventh House (1973–1975). With them he helped establish jazz-rock drumming by using jazz polyrhythms and a rock pulse. The first of these groups, which expanded on Miles Davis's fusion music (some members of the group had played with Davis) and

Alphonse Mouzon; photograph by Emma Alexandra Mouzon, permission of Alphonse Mouzon

became popular, featured Joe Zawinul and Wayne Shorter; also admired, but less so than Weather Report, the second was led by Larry Coryell, with whom Mouzon reunited off and on into the 1980s. On his albums as leader he has played various kinds of music, including what might be called funk, rhythm and blues, fusion, pop, disco, new age, jazz, and light jazz. Mouzon, who formed Tenacious Records in 1992, offers drum instruction in Northridge, Calif. He composed the music for the movie *Begleiter* (2006).

Compositions

"All That Jazz," "Angel Face," "Anticipation," "The Baker's Daughter," "Bebop Be Dobop," "Birds on a Wire," "Blues Clues," "By All Means," "Come On and Do It," "The Cover Girl," "Daddy's Little Girl," "Do I Have To," "Early Spring," "Feeling Good," "The Funky Waltz," "Harlem Blues," "If Tomorrow Comes," "I'm Glad That You're Here," "I'm Never Gonna Say Goodbye," "I Wonder Why," "Jean-Pierre," "Just Another Samba," "A Labor of Love," "Love Fantasy," "A Lullaby for Little Alphonse," "Mad about You," "Making Love with You," "Mind Transplant," "More Miles in the Sky," "Morning Sun," "Mystic Crystal," "Never Say Never," "New York City," "The Next Time We Love," "Night for Love," "The Night Is Still Young," "Night Walker," "On Top of the World," "Poobli," "Protocol," "The Sky Is the Limit," "Stepping Stone," "The Survivor," "To Mom with Love," "Undulations," "Virtue," "A Waltz for Emma," "Whatever," "Wish You Were Here," "You're All I Have"

Recordings as Leader

The Essence of Mystery (1972), *Funky Snakefoot* (1973), *Mind Transplant* (1974), *The Man Incognito* (1976), *Virtue* (1976), "Just Like the Sun" (1976), "New York City" (1976), "Without a Reason" (1976), *In Search of a Dream* (1977), *Baby Come Back* (ca. 1979), *By All Means* (1980), *Absolute Greatest Love Songs and Ballads (1981–1998)* (includes previously issued material, plus five remixes and two new selections), *Distant Lover* (1981), *Morning Sun* (1981), *Step into the Funk* (ca. 1982), *The Sky Is the Limit* (1984), *Back to Jazz* (1985), *Love Fantasy* (1986), *Early Spring* (1987), *As You Wish* (1988–1989), *The Survivor* (1992), *On Top of the World* (1994), *The Night Is Still Young* (1996), *Live in Hollywood* (2001), *Jazz in Bel-Air* (2008), *The Main Attraction* (2010), *Angel Face* (2011)

Leaders Recorded With

Gil Evans (1969), Robin Kenyatta (1969, 1974), Roy Ayers (1970), Wayne Shorter (1970), Eugene McDaniels (1970 or 1971), Les McCann (1971), Weather Report (1971), Tim Hardin (ca. 1971), Doug Carn (1972), Norman Connors (1972), Bobbi Humphrey (1972), McCoy Tyner (1972–1973), Larry Coryell (1973–1975, 1977, 1985), John Klemmer (1973), Teruo Nakamura (1973), Buddy Terry (1973), Roberta Flack (1974), Charles Sullivan (1974), Joachim Kühn (1975), Patrick Moraz (1975), Piano Conclave (1975), Jeremy Steig (1975), Donald Byrd (1976), Al DiMeola (1976), Alphonso Johnson (1976), Bill Summers (1976), Carlos Garnett (1977), Jasper van't Hof (1977, 1979), Willie Colón (ca. 1977), Herbie Hancock (1978, 1980–1981), Paul Jackson (1978), Kimiko Kasai (1978), Betty Davis (1979), Rolf Kühn (1980), Arild Anderson (1981), Torsten de Winkel (1984), Secret Message (1984), Klaus Doldinger (ca. 1988), Miles Davis (1990), Final Notice (ca. 1990), Infinity (1991), Just Friends (1991), Coryells (1999), Alphonse Philippe Mouzon (2010)

Films

That Thing You Do! (1996), *First Daughter* (2004), *The Dukes* (2007)

Website

www.tenaciousrecords.com/Home.html (accessed 21 May 2014)

References

PRIMARY: Julie Coryell and Laura Friedman, *Jazz-Rock Fusion: The People, the Music* (Boston: Marion Boyars, 1978), 75–76 (interview); R[alph] T[ee], "Musin' with Mouzon," *Blues and Soul* 415 (11 September 1984): 19 (substantial comments by Mouzon).

SECONDARY: Dan Morgenstern, "Alphonse Mouzon: 'Play Yourself,'" *Down Beat* 40 (12 March 1973): 18–21, 31; Ray Townley, "Funky Fingers a Waltzin'," *Down Beat* 41 (14 March 1974): 13; Marv Hohman, "Do the Funky Renaissance with Alphonse Mouzon," *Down Beat* 42 (4 December 1975): 15–16, 42; Mark Holston, "Alphonse Mouzon," *Jazziz* 5 (February–March 1988): 53; Jonathan Widrin, "Smooth Operator Swings Back," *Down Beat* 63 (October 1996): 41; Bill Milkowski, "Hearsay: Alphonsemouzon [*sic*]," *JazzTimes* 31 (November 2001): 34.

Mulholland, Brian Thomas

Bass
7 November 1978 (Anderson, S.C.)–
S.C. residences: Anderson (1978–2001), Columbia (2001–2002)

Mulholland began playing bass at age ten. He performed in high school bands before matriculating at the University of South Carolina, where he continued playing and from which he received a degree in 2001. Following his master's degree from the University of North Texas in 2005, he toured with Maynard Ferguson and performed at the trumpeter's final recording session. He is currently an adjunct lecturer at the University of Texas at Arlington.

Compositions

"Antipopes," "Bric-a-Brac," "Buy Marvin Gardens," "Deco," "Discipline," "Energon," "McKinley," "Ohm's Law," "Pwned," "Running Riot," "Second Helping," "Shifty," "Shortest Way," "Stoplight Won't Change," "They Make Them Like They Used To"

Recordings as Leader

Deco (2005), *Lower Convergence Bass Trio* (2005; with Jeff Eckels and Lynn Seaton)

Leaders Recorded With

Stockton Helbing (2004, 2006, 2010–2011), Lily Maase (2004), Clay Ross (2004), Ken Edwards (2006), Maynard Ferguson (2006), Kevin Brunkhorst (2008), Dan Cavanagh (2008)

Mulligan, Levy

Trombone
S.C. residence: Charleston (probably by late 1910s–at least into 1920s)

Apparently a ward of Jenkins Orphanage, Mulligan played in its bands in the early 1920s.

Murphy, John

Cornet
Probably 1907 or 1908–?
S.C. residence: Charleston (by 1915–at least into 1920s)

A ward of Jenkins Orphanage, Murphy played in its bands in the 1920s.

John Chilton records Murphy's birth year as 1907; when the musician was enumerated for the census at the orphanage on 9 January 1920, his age was estimated as eleven. Chilton notes that Murphy entered the institution in 1915.

Reference

SECONDARY: John Chilton, *A Jazz Nursery: The Story of the Jenkins' Orphanage Bands of Charleston, South Carolina* (London: Bloomsbury Book Shop, 1980), 57.

Murray, Juggy (Henry, Jr.; "Big Foot," "Juggy Murray Jones")

Record company owner, producer, conductor, singer
Possibly 24 November 1922 (Charleston, S.C.)–probably 20 January 2005 (New York, N.Y.)
S.C. residence: Charleston (possibly 1922–after 1925, but no later than 1930)

Murray moved with his family from Charleston to N.Y.C., where, as a child, he danced on the streets for money. He became known as Juggy because he frequently filled his grandfather's jug with liquor, at the elder's request. Though involved in real estate and inexperienced in music, in 1957 he formed Sue Records, named for his mother and daughter; the next year he established a subsidiary, Symbol Records. Mainly his labels released rhythm and blues. Sue gained popular success in the early 1960s with recordings by Ike and Tina Turner, including "A Fool in Love." Other hits on his labels include "Itchy Twitchy Feeling," by Bobby Hendricks; "Mockingbird," by Inez and Charlie Foxx; and "Let's Stick Together," by Wilbert Harrison. He recorded such jazz musicians as Ray Bryant, Harry Edison, and Jimmy McGriff. In 1968 United Artists assumed ownership of the Sue master recordings and Murray's publishing company Saturn, though Murray remained in the record business. He soon revived the Sue label, released music on it and Juggernaut Records, moved to Calif. in the mid-1970s, and established Jupiter Records. John Broven notes that Murray took rhythm and blues "into the soul age with productions that had an energetic, rhythmic beat with a distinct gospel edge" (352).

Though 1923 is generally considered Murray's birth year, the Social Security Death Index identifies it as 1922. Estimated age six, Murray was enumerated for the census in N.Y.C. on 10 April 1930. Most frequently his death date is recorded as 8 February 2005, though the Social Security Death Index specifies 20 January 2005. The existence of a

Murray vinyl album titled *Built for Speed,* to which many sources refer, has not been confirmed.

Compositions

"As Long as I'm Waltzing with You," "Believe It or Not," "Boss-a-Nova," "Built for Speed," "Buttered Popcorn," "Can't Wait until Tomorrow," "Confusion," "Copy Cat," "Count to Ten," "Disco Extraordinaire," "Discotheque U.S.A.," "Get Your Thing Together," "Hey, Lonely," "Hummingbird," "I Can't Do It," "I Have a Dream," "I'm Coming Home," "I'm Sorry You're Lonely," "Inside America," "It'll Change," "Just a Minute," "Love in My Heart," "Oily," "Oki," "One Love," "Out to Lunch," "Pony Express," "Priscilla's Walk," "She Blew a Good Thing," "Skokie Drive," "The Sneak," "Soul at Sunrise," "So Young and So Innocent," "Spoiler," "Super Positive Delight," "Sure Thing," "Thock It to Me Honi," "Wobble March"

Recordings as Leader (These Are Release Dates, Not Necessarily Recording Dates)

I Have a Dream (1965; as Juggy Murray), "Birmingham Blues" (1965; as Juggy Murray), "March on Washington" (1965; as Juggy Murray), "Just a Minute" (1966; as Juggy), "Soul at Sunrise" (1966; as Juggy), "Oily" (1969; as Juggy), "The Spoiler" (1969; as Juggy), "Buttered Popcorn" (1970; as Juggy), "Thock It to Me Honi" (1970; as Juggy), *Inside America* (1976; as Juggy Murray Jones), *Rhythm and Blues* (1977; as Juggy Murray Jones), "I Apologize" (possibly ca. 1980; as Big Foot), "Watch Your Step" (possibly ca. 1980; as Big Foot), "Love Is a Gamble" (1982; as Juggy Murray Jones, with Cuba Gooding), "What Happened" (1982; as Juggy Murray Jones), "Just You and Me" (possibly early 1980s; as Juggy Jones)

References

SECONDARY: Alan Warner, "Sue: The Sound of Soul," booklet accompanying the 4-CD *Sue Records Story: New York City, the Sound of Soul* (1994; EMI 28093); Pierre Perrone, "Juggy Murray: Astute Founder of Sue Records," *Independent* (London), 20 April 2005, p. 34 (obituary); John Broven, *Record Makers and Breakers: Voices of the Independent Rock 'n' Roll Pioneers* (Urbana: University of Illinois Press, 2009), 352–57; David Edwards and Mike Callahan, "The Sue Records Story," http://www.bsnpubs.com/N.Y.C./sue/suestory.html (2011; accessed 21 May 2014).

Myers, Leon

Probably S.C.

S.C. residence: Charleston (possibly by mid-1920s–at least into late 1920s)

A ward of Jenkins Orphanage, Myers played in its bands in the late 1920s, though his instrument is not known.

Myers might be the Leonard Myers who was enumerated for the census with his family in Charleston on 13 January 1920. Born in S.C., he was then one year, two months old.

Myott, Big Dave (David; "Bo")

Singer

31 March 1918 (Lee County, S.C.)–14 April 1993 (Columbia, S.C.)

S.C. residences: Lee County (1918–possibly late 1930s), Sumter (–1993)

Myott served in the army in 1944 and 1945. He led Big Dave and the House Rockers, for which he composed the two songs the group recorded for Cordé Records in Newark, N.J. With Brownie McGhee he wrote "Washing Dishes," though it has apparently not been recorded. He is buried in the Wayman Chapel A.M.E. Church Cemetery, Sumter, S.C.

Myott's birth and death dates come from his grave marker and the Social Security Death Index.

Compositions

"Goin' on Baby," "Slow Walkin' Down," "Washing Dishes"

Recordings as Leader (Both Late 1950s, as Big Dave)

"Goin' on Baby," "Slow Walkin' Down"

References

SECONDARY: "David Myott," *Sumter (S.C.) Item,* 18 April 1993, sec. A, p. 8 (obituary); "Goin' on Baby," http://oldwax.blogspot.com/2011_09_01_archive.html (12 September 2011; accessed 21 May 2014).

Nesbitt, Blind Gussie

Guitar, singer
12 January 1910 (Spartanburg, S.C.)-?
S.C. residences: Spartanburg (1910-ca. 1925), Union (ca. 1925-)

Primarily a singer of religious music, Nesbitt was familiar with blues musicians in the Union area and apparently influenced at least one, Henry "Rufe" Johnson. Burm Lawson of Union arranged for Nesbitt and Lil McClintock to record on the same day in Atlanta for Columbia Records, which they did in December 1930. The next year in Charlotte, N.C., Nesbitt recorded two selections at a four-song RCA Victor session led by Jack Goudlock; the tunes with Nesbitt have not been released. He recorded once more, in N.Y.C. in 1935 for Decca. He played, but did not record, with Julius Daniels.

Recordings as Leader

"Canaan Land" (1930; as Blind Nesbit), "Pure Religion" (1930; as Blind Nesbit), "God Is Worried at Your Wicked Ways" (1935), "He's the Joy of My Salvation" (1935), "I'll Just Stand and Wring My Hands and Cry" (1935), "Motherless Children" (1935), "Nobody's Fault but Mine" (1935; unissued)

Leader Recorded With

Jack Goudlock (1931; unissued)

References

SECONDARY: Paul Oliver, *Songsters and Saints: Vocal Traditions on Race Records* (Cambridge: Cambridge University Press, 1984), 213, 215; Bruce Bastin, *Red River Blues: The Blues Tradition in the Southeast* (Urbana: University of Illinois Press, 1986), 188–90, 193, 195.

Nesbitt, Joseph

Drums
Ca. 1885-?
S.C. residence: Charleston (by 1895-at least into early 1900s)

Apparently a ward of Jenkins Orphanage, Nesbitt played in its bands from the 1890s into the early 1900s and performed with one of them in England in 1895.

The passenger list of the *Paris,* which transported the orphanage band to England in September 1895, records Nesbitt's age as ten; the list for the *Teutonic,* which returned the group to the United States the next month, specifies it as nine.

References

SECONDARY: John Chilton, *A Jazz Nursery: The Story of the Jenkins' Orphanage Bands of Charleston, South Carolina* (London: Bloomsbury Book Shop, 1980), 57; Howard Rye, "Visiting Fireboys: The Jenkins' Orphanage Bands in Britain," *Storyville* 130 (1987): 137–43.

New, Elliott Lanier

Guitar, singer
16 February 1964 (Atlanta, Ga.)-
S.C. residences: Columbia (1987-2005), Chapin (2005-)

New began playing the guitar at age thirteen, though not seriously until his years at Vanderbilt University. There he became interested in the blues to the degree that he studied various blues styles, learned to play the music, and for three years hosted *Sunday Night Blues* on WRVU, the student radio station. He received a bachelor's degree in

Elliott New; photograph by Mark McLane, permission of Elliott New

1986. Upon moving to Columbia he again hosted a program, this time *Monday Night Blues* on WFMX. Also in Columbia, in 1989 he formed his first band, the Blues Blasters, which, as personnel changed, in a few years became known as Elliott and the Untouchables. Popular in the Southeast, this group has performed at festivals in Ireland and Quebec.

Compositions

"Ain't No Big Thing," "Blues Came Callin'," "Both Ends Burnin'," "Bottle of Blues," "Can't Afford to Keep Her," "Checkout Time," "Crazy 'bout You," "Danger Zone," "Drive These Blues Away," "Empty Heart," "A Girl Like You," "Givin' Up on You," "Got What You Need," "If I Could," "Life without You," "Limo Driver," "More Than That," "Red Hot, Got Me Burnin'," "Shell of a Man," "Sweet Little Woman," "Toss 'n' Turn," "Turned Me Upside Down," "Voodoo Stew," "You're All I Need"

Recordings as Leader

Live at Beulah's (1994), *Last Meal* (1995), *Danger Zone* (1997), *Both Ends Burnin'* (1998), *Smokin' the Blues* (2000), *Voodoo Stew* (2005)

Website

http://www.elliottandtheuntouchables.com/ (accessed 21 May 2014)

Nick, John

Trombone
Saint Petersburg, Fla.-?
S.C. residence: Charleston (by 1921–at least until 1926)

A ward of Jenkins Orphanage beginning in 1921, Nick played in its bands in the mid-1920s.

Reference

SECONDARY: John Chilton, *A Jazz Nursery: The Story of the Jenkins' Orphanage Bands of Charleston, South Carolina* (London: Bloomsbury Book Shop, 1980), 57.

Nine Sizzling Syncopators

Also known as Smiling Billy and His Collegiate Serenaders, this group of Claflin University students performed at least in the mid-1920s.

Reference

SECONDARY: Vivian Glover, *Men of Vision–Claflin College and Her Presidents* (Orangeburg, S.C.: Claflin College, 1995), 103.

Norris the Troubadour

See Mayhams, Norridge Bryant

Odom, King David

Singer
17 April 1918 (S.C., probably Barnwell County)–6 November 1988
S.C. residence: probably Barnwell County (1918–no later than mid-1940s)

In the 1940s Odom led the King Odom Quartet, a rhythm-and-blues group that recorded for Musicraft, was featured on the weekly radio program *Swingtime at the Savoy,* and toured with the singer Savannah Churchill. During the 1950s it recorded for Derby Records, then Abbey, before disbanding in 1954. Odom then made his living repairing machinery.

Odom's birth and death dates come from the Social Security Death Index.

Recordings as Leader (All with the King Odom Quartet or the King Odom Four)

"Down by the Old Mill Stream" (1948), "I Found a Twinkle" (1948), "I Like My Chickens Frying Size" (1948), "I'm Livin' Humble" (1948), "I'm Looking Over a Four Leaf Clover" (1948), "Mary Lou" (1948), "Moonlight Frost" (1948), "Pickin' a Chicken" (1948), "They Put John on the Island" (1948), "Who Struck John?" (1948), "If You Didn't Love Me" (1950), "I'm Glad I Made You Cry" (1950), "Lover Come Back to Me" (1950), "Walkin' with My Shadow" (1950), "All of Me" (1951), "My Heart Cries for You" (1951), "Rain Is the Teardrops of Angels" (1951), "What a Wonderful Feeling" (1951), "Don't Trade Your Love for Gold" (1952), "Lucky" (1952)

References

SECONDARY: "King Odom Quartet Is a New Radio Version of Cinderella," *New York Amsterdam News,* 21 February 1948, p. 23; "Woman Sues Quartette; Asks 25 Gs," *New*

York Amsterdam News, 16 February 1952, pp. 1, 4 (city edition); "Spotlight on the King Odom Four, Part One!," http://www.vocalgroupharmony.com/Lucky.htm (2003; accessed 21 May 2014); "Spotlight on the King Odom Four, Part Two!," http://www.vocalgroupharmony.com/Im_Look.htm (2003; accessed 21 May 2014); Marv Goldberg, "The King Odom Quartet," http://www.uncamarvy.com/KingOdomQuartet/kingodomquartet.html (2009; accessed 21 May 2014); "Spotlight on Savannah Churchill, Part Two of Two," http://www.vocalgroupharmony.com/3ROWNEW/WhyWasIBorn.htm (2010; accessed 21 May 2014); "In Rememberance [*sic*] of . . . Isaiah Bing," http://www.toddbaptista.com/remember.html (2013; accessed 21 May 2014); "Uncommon Labels, Part One," http://www.vocalgroupharmony.com/4ROWNEW/AmazinWillieMays.htm (2013; accessed 21 May 2014); Todd Baptista, "In Rememberance [*sic*] of . . . Cleveland 'Bill' Bing, Baritone with Golden Gate Quartet, King Odom Four, Dies at 91," http://www.toddbaptista.com/remember.html (2014; accessed 21 May 2014).

Old Morrisville Brass Band

Andrews, S.C.

Known as a jump-up band, this group plays in the manner of black community bands ca. 1900 that performed various kinds of music and were precursors of jazz groups. Isaac Davis was its original leader. It performed at the 1992 Black Heritage Festival in Savannah, Ga., and the 1994 New Orleans Jazz & Heritage Festival. About the group Ry Cooder said, "They can't finger these horns and they can't change keys, but they'll blow you right out of your seat. It is good."

Recordings as Leader

"Jump Up" (1990, 2003), *Jumpin' Music* (ca. 2007)

Award

Jean Laney Harris Folk Heritage Award (1993)

Reference

SECONDARY: Jas Obrecht, "Ry Cooder—Talking Country Blues and Gospel," http://jasobrecht.com/ry-cooder-talking-country-blues-and-gospel/ (2010; accessed 21 May 2014).

Orell, Carter

Trombone

S.C. residence: Charleston (at least 1930s)

Apparently a ward of Jenkins Orphanage, Orell played in its bands in the 1930s.

Original Charleston Camp-Meeting Shouters

Charleston, S.C.

At a camp meeting outside Charleston, minstrel impresario Al G. Field heard and hired this group of four men, three women, and six boys. From 1895 until probably 1897 the singers toured with Field's Real Negro Minstrels and Troupe of Arabs, also known as both the Colored Minstrels and the Darkest America Company. In anticipation of the troupe's opening in Columbus, Ohio (Field's residence), a writer for the *New York Clipper* (8 June 1895) noted that the singers' "chants and shouts are very peculiar, and they are expected to be a big surprise." Also in the *Clipper* (13 July 1895), a reviewer of the initial performance noted that "the Charleston Shouters, at the conclusion of the first part, made a distinct hit, especially McIntosh" (290). With Field they were featured in at least two sketches, "Musical Melange" and "The Barber's Picnic," the latter also titled "The Barbers' Holiday." Following its Columbus appearance the troupe was scheduled to tour Canada and then the United States for forty weeks, with the prospect of also performing in England.

The McIntosh who sang with this group has not been identified. Frank M. Hailstock, an associate of the Shouters by virtue of being the leader of Field's orchestra, composed some of the early tunes written in rag time, including "On the Suaunee" and "Zambo's Frolic on the Swanee."

References

SECONDARY: "Variety and Minstrelsy," *New York Clipper,* 8 June 1895, p. 211; "Variety and Minstrelsy," *New York Clipper,* 13 July 1895, pp. 290, 292; program for a Darkest America performance at the Grand Opera House, Hamilton, Ontario, Canada (n.p., ca. 1896) (also available at http://archive.org/details.php?identifier=cihm_36301 [accessed 21 May 2014]); Tim Brooks, *Lost Sounds: Blacks and the Birth of the Recording Industry, 1890–1919* (Urbana: University of Illinois Press, 2004), 500; Bruce Vermazen, *That Moaning Saxophone: The Six Brown Brothers and the Dawning of a Musical Craze* (New York: Oxford University Press, 2004), 32.

Ott, Horace

Composer, arranger, keyboards
15 April 1933 (Saint Matthews, S.C.)–
S.C. residences: Saint Matthews (1933–1955), Union (1955–1956), Myrtle Beach (2010–)

Ott began playing and arranging music while attending high school in Orangeburg; his interest in music intensified at what is now South Carolina State University, from which he received a degree in 1955. While attending these schools he lived at home in Saint Matthews. After teaching for a year in Union he served in the army (1956–1958), playing in one of its bands. Upon discharge he entered the N.Y.C. music scene, soon succeeding with an arrangement of "Tonight's the Night" for the Shirelles. Other successes followed, including arrangements of "Don't Let Me Be Misunderstood" (which he co-composed) for Nina Simone and "Macho Man," "Y.M.C.A.," "In the Navy," and "San Francisco/Hollywood" for the Village People. He arranged music for the musical *Inner City* (1972) and the movies *Gordon's War* (1973), *Lialeh* (1974), and *Can't Stop the Music* (1980). With Danny Holgate he arranged the music for the all-black production of *Guys and Dolls* (1976). He also composed and arranged for—and played with—numerous jazz musicians. Solomon Burke sings Ott's "You're Good for Me" on the sound track of *Light of Day* (1987).

Compositions

"Anything Can Happen," "Ask Me No Questions," "Bootie Bounce," "Call Me Sweet Things," "Chris Cross," "City of Blues," "Dancing Man," "Deep in My Soul," "Don't Drive Me Away," "Don't Let Me Be Misunderstood" (as Gloria Caldwell), "Don't Spoil Our Good Thing," "Down Home," "Everything's Hunky Dory," "For Someone Else," "Hello Lover, Goodbye Tears," "Huckleberry Queen," "I Can't Get Up the Nerve," "If You Get There before I Do," "I Heard What You Said," "I'm Comin' On Back to You," "It's Just Me," "Just to Please You," "Lazy Boy," "Let Me Know in Advance," "Like the Big Guys Do," "Love Trouble," "Message to My Babe," "Miss Poopie," "Moonlight Promises," "My Best Friend," "My Heart Feels These Things," "Night Glider," "Nobody but Betty," "Only Young Once," "Our Love Will Grow," "Playboy," "Prove It," "Room of Memories," "Song for Aretha," "Teach Me the Game of Love," "Tears on My Window," "Thank You Very Much," "Tight Times," "Two Guys from Trinidad," "We're Doing Fine," "When Woman Was Made for Man," "With You," "You Ain't Nothing but Fire," "You Left Me All Alone," "You're Good for Me"

Leaders Recorded With (as Instrumentalist, Arranger, or Both)

Shirelles (1960), Hank Ballard (1961), Gladys Knight (1961), Jackie Wilson (1961), Solomon Burke (1963), Sam Cooke (1963), Doris Troy (1963–1964), Don Covay (1964–1965), Panama Francis (1964), Nina Simone (1964–1965, 1968), Jive Five (1965), Titus Turner (1966), Helena Ferguson (1967), Aretha Franklin (1968), Tamiko Jones (1968), Jimmy McGriff (1969, 1971, 1973–1974), Joe Williams (1970), Houston Person (1971, 1977, ca. 1978, 1980, 1982, 1988), Charlie Brown (1972), Ronnie Foster (1972), Bobbi Humphrey (1972), Bernard Purdie (1972), Gil Scott-Heron (1972), Joe Thomas (1972), Lou Donaldson (1973–1974), Jimmy Witherspoon (1973), Richard "Groove" Holmes (ca. 1973, 1975–1976), Rusty Bryant (1974), Dakota Staton (1974), Shirley Bassey (ca. 1974), Caesar Frazier (1975), Bob Thiele (1975), Marilyn McCoo and Billy Davis, Jr. (1976), Softones (1976), Willy Bridges (1977), Johnny Taylor (1977), Village People (1977–1979), Patrick Juvet (1978), Arthur Prysock (ca. 1978), Leon Thomas (1988), Etta Jones (1989–1990), Joey DeFrancesco (1995)

Reference

PRIMARY: Benjamin Franklin V, *Jazz and Blues Musicians of South Carolina: Interviews with Jabbo, Dizzy, Drink, and Others* (Columbia: University of South Carolina Press, 2008), 86–95.

Palmer, Aaron Huntland, Jr.

Dancer, singer

Probably October 1894 or 29 December 1896 (Charleston, S.C.)–not before 1963

S.C. residence: Charleston (1894 or 1896–no later than 1910)

Primarily a dancer, Palmer performed with the Whitman Sisters from 1910 until 1922. In 1914 a reviewer likened his dancing to that of George Walker, the late partner of Bert Williams. Palmer left the Whitmans to dance in Lew Leslie's *Plantation Revue* (1922), which starred Florence Mills. In the 1930s he teamed with Louise Cox, his second wife, as Aaron Palmer and Peaches. He remained active at least through the 1930s.

Initially married to the dancer Alice Whitman, Palmer, whose given name is sometimes spelled Aron, was the father of dancer Albert "Pops" Whitman, who was not a South Carolinian. Conducted in Charleston on 5 June, the 1900 census records his birth date as October 1894; his 1918 draft registration card specifies the date 29 December 1896, records the middle name, and indicates the birthplace. His age was estimated as forty-nine when Palmer was enumerated for the census in N.Y.C. on 17 April 1930. The 1900 and 1930 censuses use the suffix Jr. In *Jazz Dance*, Marshall Stearns and Jean Stearns indicate that they interviewed Palmer in 1962 and 1963.

References

SECONDARY: "Whitman Sisters Present Fine and Attractive Amusement Bill at Lafayette Theater," *Indianapolis Freeman: An Illustrated Colored Newspaper,* 5 December 1914, p. 5; "Aaron and Kelly Hit," *Chicago Defender,* 22 September 1923, p. 7; "Aaron Protests," *Chicago Defender,* 16 February 1924, p. 6; "May Whitiman [*sic*] Pays New York a Surprise Visit," *New York Amsterdam News,* 9 October 1929, p. 9; "Palmer-Cox Romance Leads to Philly Altar," *Baltimore Afro-American,* 12 November 1932, p. 4; Marshall Stearns and Jean Stearns, *Jazz Dance: The Story of American Vernacular Dance* (New York: Macmillan, 1968), passim (comments by Palmer); Nadine George-Graves, *The Royalty of Negro Vaudeville: The Whitman Sisters and the Negotiation of Race, Gender and Class in African American Theater, 1900–1940* (New York: St. Martin's, 2000), 11, 36, 97.

Palmer, Edmund Perry

Singer

26 June 1896 (Columbia, S.C.)–5 November 1949 (Sumter, S.C.)

S.C. residences: Columbia (1896–early 1910s, mid-1910s–at least into early 1920s), Orangeburg (early 1910s–mid-1910s), Sumter (by mid-1920s–1949)

Palmer sang with the Claflin University Quintet, at least in 1913. In time he attended the Renouard School of Mortuary Science in N.Y.C. (1925) and worked at a funeral home in Sumter before establishing his own Sumter mortuary in 1933. He is buried in Walker Cemetery, Sumter.

Reference

SECONDARY: "E. P. Palmer Dies; Rites Set Tuesday," *Sumter (S.C.) Daily Item,* 7 November 1949, p. 7 (obituary).

Parker, Aaron

See Porter, Aaron

Parmley, Doc(k)

Trumpet, cornet, and possibly other brass instruments

Possibly 5 April 1905 (Horry County, S.C., in or near Conway)–ca. April 1963 (Jackson, Miss.)

S.C. residences: Horry County (possibly 1905–at least until 1920), possibly Charleston (early 1920s)

Probably during the early 1920s Parmley played in brass bands, possibly including ones associated with Jenkins Orphanage. He was with Eddie Heywood, Sr., in 1926, L. B. Holtkamp's Smart Set Minstrels in 1927, and the Royal Mississippians, his own group, by 1929. The Royal Mississippians lasted at least until 1937, though during this period he also toured as sideman, including with the Kansas City Rhythm Kings (1929) and Little Brother Montgomery (probably beginning in the early 1930s). When speaking with Karl Gert zur Heide, Montgomery termed Parmley a "great trumpet player" (45). Probably in the late 1930s Parmley assumed leadership of Montgomery's band, the Southland Troubadours. Saxophonist Teddy Edwards began his professional career with Parmley's band (1936), which later included pianist Paul Gayten (1940).

Parmley was the brother of musician Edmond Parmley. He was enumerated for the 1910 and 1920 censuses in Horry County, S.C.; both identify S.C.

as his birthplace and spell his given name Dock. The 1940 census, conducted in Jackson, Miss., spells the name Doc, indicates that he was born in N.C., states that he lived in Jackson in 1935, and characterizes his occupation as orchestra leader.

References

SECONDARY: "Sylvester Russell's Review," *Pittsburgh Courier,* 28 May 1927, p. 15; Dave Peyton, "The Musical Bunch," *Chicago Defender,* 9 July 1927, p. 6 (national edition); Dave Peyton, "The Musical Bunch," *Chicago Defender,* 25 May 1929, p. 6 (national edition); "The Musical Bunch," *Chicago Defender,* 8 June 1929, p. 6 (national edition); "The Musical Bunch," *Chicago Defender,* 29 June 1929, p. 6 (national edition); "Here and There with Bob Hayes," *Chicago Defender,* 14 December 1929, p. 6 (national edition); Walter Barnes, Jr., "Hittin' High Notes," *Chicago Defender,* 20 June 1931, p. 5 (national edition) (the surname is spelled Parmely); J. E. Conic, "Mississippi State News," *Chicago Defender,* 21 December 1935, p. 20 (national edition); Bob Hayes, "Here and There," *Chicago Defender,* 3 April 1937, p. 21 (national edition); "The Story of Creole George Guesnon as told to Walter Eysselinck," *Storyville* 18 (August–September 1968): 16–22, 33 (see especially 22); Karl Gert zur Heide, *Deep South Piano: The Story of Little Brother Montgomery* (London: Studio Vista, 1970), passim; John Chilton, *A Jazz Nursery: The Story of the Jenkins' Orphanage Bands of Charleston, South Carolina* (London: Bloomsbury Book Shop, 1980), 57; David Griffiths, *Hot Jazz: From Harlem to Storyville* (Lanham, Md.: Scarecrow Press, 1998), 30; Sarah Parkin, "Edwards, Teddy," http://www.encyclopedia.com/doc/1G2-3496200031.html (January 2004; accessed 21 May 2014); Paul Swinton, "The Life and the Music of Arnold Wiley," *The Frog Blues and Jazz Annual: The Musicians, the Records and the Music of the 78 Era* 1 (2010): 71–87 (see especially 78); "Paul Gayten," http://www.ifccom.ch/reperes/jazz_3970.html (2012; accessed 21 May 2014); "Rock Source: Jazz," http://www.rocksourcearchive.com/rs_user1.php?db_user=rs_jazz&day=05&month=Apr (undated; accessed 21 May 2014).

Parmley, Edmond L. ("Lou," "Luke")

Various brass instruments, including mellophone and tuba

28 September 1903 (Horry County, S.C., in or near Conway)–October 1981

S.C. residences: Horry County (1903–at least until 1920), possibly Charleston (early 1920s)

Probably during the early 1920s Parmley played in brass bands, possibly including ones associated with Jenkins Orphanage. He was with the band of L. B. Holtkamp's Smart Set Minstrels in 1927, played with the Kansas City Rhythm Kings in 1929, and from no later than 1929 at least into 1937 was a regular with the Royal Mississippians, led by his brother, Doc(k). Probably beginning in the early 1930s he was also affiliated with the band of Little Brother Montgomery, the Southland Troubadours, and remained with it when his brother assumed leadership, probably in the late 1930s. Edmond was its booking agent.

Parmley's birth and death dates come from the Social Security Death Index. Parmley was enumerated for the 1910 and 1920 censuses in Horry County, S.C.; both identify S.C. as his birthplace. The 1940 census, conducted in Jackson, Miss., indicates that he was born in N.C., states that he lived in Jackson in 1935, shows that in 1940 he resided with his brother and sister-in-law, and characterizes his occupation as musician.

References

SECONDARY: "Sylvester Russell's Review," *Pittsburgh Courier,* 28 May 1927, p. 15; Dave Peyton, "The Musical Bunch," *Chicago Defender,* 9 July 1927, p. 6 (national edition); "The Musical Bunch," *Chicago Defender,* 29 June 1929, p. 6 (national edition) (Parmley is identified as Lou); "Here and There with Bob Hayes," *Chicago Defender,* 14 December 1929, p. 6 (national edition) (Parmley is identified as Edward); Walter Barnes, Jr., "Hittin' High Notes," *Chicago Defender,* 20 June 1931, p. 5 (national edition) (the musician is identified as Tuba Parmely); Karl Gert zur Heide, *Deep South Piano: The Story of Little Brother Montgomery* (London: Studio Vista, 1970), passim (comments by Parmley, who is identified as Luke); John Chilton, *A Jazz Nursery: The Story of the Jenkins' Orphanage Bands of Charleston, South Carolina* (London: Bloomsbury Book Shop, 1980), 57 (Parmley is identified as Luke); David Griffiths, *Hot Jazz: From Harlem to Storyville* (Lanham, Md.: Scarecrow Press, 1998), 30.

Patrick, Edward Robert, Jr. ("Cornetsky," "Fess")

Cornet, trumpet

25 November 1893 (Charleston, S.C.)–?

S.C. residence: Charleston (1893–no later than 1919)

Though Patrick lived with his family as late as 1900, he became a ward of Jenkins Orphanage. He served as the institution's music director ca. 1912 and accompanied its band to England in 1914. By 1919 he lived in Newark, N.J.; that year he again traveled to England, this time with the Southern Syncopated Orchestra. He remained there until 1921, when he moved to Paris, where he lived at least until 1925, when he was playing with the Stratton Jazz Band.

Patrick was the brother of trombonist Jake Patrick. When applying for passports in 1919 and 1923 Patrick identified Newark, N.J., as his permanent residence; when applying for one in 1920 he specified it as Charleston, S.C. Drawing on information provided by Guillermo Olliver, Karl Gert zur Heide reports that in May 1923 Patrick sailed on the *Lutetia* from Bordeaux, France, to Buenos Aires (e-mail from zur Heide, 21 February 2013).

References

SECONDARY: "Newark, N.J.," *New York Age*, 5 July 1919, p. 5; John Chilton, *A Jazz Nursery: The Story of the Jenkins' Orphanage Bands of Charleston, South Carolina* (London: Bloomsbury Book Shop, 1980), 57; Howard Rye, "Visiting Fireboys: The Jenkins' Orphanage Bands in Britain," *Storyville* 130 (1987): 137–43; Howard Rye, "Southern Syncopated Orchestra: The Roster," *Black Music Research Journal* 30 (Spring 2010): 46–47.

Patrick, Jake (Jacob E.; "Trombonesky")

Trombone

18 August of either 1896 or 1897 (Charleston, S.C.)–possibly 1935 or 1936 (possibly Buenos Aires, Argentina)

S.C. residence: Charleston (1896 or 1897–no later than 1919)

Though Patrick lived with his family as late as 1900, he became a ward of Jenkins Orphanage. He performed with its band in England in 1914. By 1919 he lived in Newark, N.J., and played in the greater N.Y.C. area, including with the Steeple Chase Park Band. He was possibly a member of the 369th Regiment Hell Fighters Band. In 1919 he again traveled to England, this time with the Southern Syncopated Orchestra, and performed there into 1922. Independent of this orchestra and at least until 1924, he played in other European countries, including Belgium and, presumably, France, Spain, and Switzerland.

Patrick was the brother of cornetist Edward Patrick. With one exception public documents record 18 August 1897 as Patrick's birth date. The exception is the passenger list of the *St. Louis*, which transported the orphanage band from Liverpool to N.Y.C. in 1914. It specifies the date of 18 August 1896. Because Patrick can be documented as applying for a passport in Paris in 1924, a report that he was killed in a fight in Belgium in 1922 or 1923 is incorrect. In an unpublished letter to Karl Gert zur Heide dated 1 June 1978, musician Gordon Stretton states that Patrick died in Buenos Aires in 1935 or 1936 (e-mail from zur Heide, 21 February 2013).

References

SECONDARY: "Newark, N.J.," *New York Age*, 5 July 1919, p. 5; Howard Rye, "Visiting Fireboys: The Jenkins' Orphanage Bands in Britain," *Storyville* 130 (1987): 137–43; Howard Rye, "Southern Syncopated Orchestra: The Roster," *Black Music Research Journal* 30 (Spring 2010): 47; Horst P. J. Bergmeier and Rainer E. Lotz, "James Arthur Briggs," *Black Music Research Journal* 30 (Spring 2010): 101, 103–4.

Pazant, Al (Alvin Bradford)

Trumpet, flugelhorn, singer

14 February 1942 (Beaufort, S.C.)–

S.C. residence: Beaufort (1942–1959)

After completing high school in Beaufort, Pazant enrolled at Florida A&M University, from which he received a degree in music education (1963). After playing with the Lionel Hampton band for nine months (1963–1964), he settled in N.Y.C., where he began teaching. A year later he established an evening jazz workshop, from which evolved the Al Pazant and the Brothers big band, which played at Smalls Paradise. When his brother, Eddie, joined it, the group became known as the Pazant Brothers,

Al Pazant; permission of Da-Renne P. Westbrook

sometimes with the words "and the Beaufort Express" added to the name. It became the Cotton Club All-Stars in 1978. Pazant toured with the show *Blues in the Night,* backing Della Reese, Eartha Kitt, and others (1985), and was musical director for Melba Moore (late 1980s–early 1990s). Though he played trumpet with the vocal group Manhattans off and on beginning in 1978, he has been its bass singer since 1990. After retiring from the N.Y.C. school system in 1999, he taught music in East Orange, N.J.

Compositions

"Back to Beaufort," "Brandy Foot," "Chick-a-Boom," "Dixie Rock," "Dragon Fly," "Here I Come," "Just for Tonight," "Mr. Crack," "Spooky," "Waterfront Blues," "You've Got to Do Your Best"

Recordings as Leader (All with Eddie Pazant)

Rare New York City Funk 1969–1975, Live at the Museum of Modern Art (1970), *Loose and Juicy* (ca. 1974), *Full Circle* (ca. 1992)

Leaders Recorded With

Pucho Brown (1968–1970, 1993, 1995, 1997, 2000), Kool and the Gang (1973–1974), Monty Guy (1984), Carrie Smith (1992), Manhattans (ca. 1993, and at other times)

References

SECONDARY: Colin Dilnot, "Ed Bland and Pazant Bros," http://indangerousrhythm.blogspot.com/2007/11/pazant-bros_28.html (28 November 2007; accessed 21 May 2014); David Lauderdale, "How Music Sweetened Family's Life," *Hilton Head (S.C.) Island Packet,* 9 October 2010, sec. A, p. 3 (also available as "Joyful Noises: Music Unites Beaufort Family" at http://www.islandpacket.com/2010/10/09/1401983/joyful-noises-music-unites-beaufort.html [accessed 21 May 2014]).

Pazant, Eddie (Edward Theodore)

Saxophone, clarinet, flute, oboe
29 June 1938 (Savannah, Ga.)–
S.C. residences: Beaufort (1940–1955), Orangeburg (1956)

Upon completing high school Pazant attended what is now Virginia State University. The summer following his freshman year (1956), he toured with Lionel Hampton. After a semester at what is now South Carolina State University, he returned to Virginia State before again joining Hampton, this time for fourteen years; he became the band's

Eddie Pazant; permission of Da-Renne P. Westbrook

musical director. Upon leaving Hampton he settled in N.Y.C. as a freelance musician, though he played regularly with the band of his brother, Al. It became known as the Pazant Brothers, sometimes with the words "and the Beaufort Express" added to the name. It became the Cotton Club All-Stars in 1978. Pazant toured with the show *Blues in the Night,* backing Della Reese, Eartha Kitt, and others (1985), and toured with Melba Moore for five years (late 1980s–early 1990s). He played with the vocal group Manhattans off and on beginning in 1978, but regularly beginning in 1990. For several years during the first decade of the twenty-first century, he taught music in the East Orange, N.J.

Compositions

"Back to Beaufort," "Brandy Foot," "Chick-a-Boom," "Dixie Rock," "Dragon Fly," "Here I Come," "Spooky," "Waterfront Blues," "You've Got to Do Your Best"

Recordings as Leader

Rare New York City Funk 1969–1975 (with Al Pazant), *Live at the Museum of Modern Art* (1970; with Al Pazant), *Loose and Juicy* (ca. 1974; with Al Pazant), *Full Circle* (ca. 1992; with Al Pazant), *Home Cookin'* (ca. 2005)

Leaders Recorded With

Lionel Hampton (1958–1961, 1963–1964, 1966–1967), Phil Upchurch (1967), Preston Love (1968), Pucho Brown (1969–1970, 1993, 1995, 1997, 1999–2000), Frank Foster (1969), Dizzy Gillespie (1969 or 1970), Sonny Phillips (1970), Kool and the Gang (1973–1974), Lawrence Lucie (ca. 1979, ca. 1981), Monty Guy (1984), Carrie Smith (1992), Manhattans (ca. 1993, and at other times), Cubana Bop (1996, 1998), George Gee (1997, 1999, 2004), Grant Green, Jr. (1997), Mary Starr (1999), Amy Coleman (2000), Marlena (ca. 2006), Herschel Dwellingham (ca. 2007), Jo Thompson (ca. 2010)

Award

Coastal Jazz Association of Savannah, Georgia, Hall of Fame (1993)

References

SECONDARY: Colin Dilnot, "Ed Bland and Pazant Bros," http://indangerousrhythm.blogspot.com/2007/11/pazant-bros_28.html (28 November 2007; accessed 21 May 2014); David Lauderdale, "How Music Sweetened Family's Life," *Hilton Head (S.C.) Island Packet,* 9 October 2010, sec. A, p. 3 (also available as "Joyful Noises: Music Unites Beaufort Family" at http://www.islandpacket.com/2010/10/09/1401983/joyful-noises-music-unites-beaufort.html [accessed 21 May 2014]) (comments by Pazant); Linda Sickler, "Coastal Jazz Association Presents Duke Ellington Tribute in Savannah," http://m.savannahnow.com/do/2012-04-18/coastal-jazz-association-presents-duke-ellington-tribute-savannah (2012; accessed 21 May 2014) (comments by Pazant).

Peek, Paul Edward, Jr.

Guitar, singer
23 June 1937 (High Point, N.C.)–3 April 2001 (Lithonia, Ga.)
S.C. residence: Greenville (1942–1956)

Peek was from a musical family: His mother, Dessie, played piano, and siblings Libby and Jackie performed as the Peek Sisters, a vocal duo that had a radio program in Greenville. In the early and mid-1950s he played with country groups, including Country Earl's Circle E Ranch Boys and Arthur Smith and His Crackerjacks. He became a member of Gene Vincent's Blue Caps in 1956. Though he remained with Vincent until 1958 or 1959, during this period he also recorded as leader. His first record—"Sweet Skinny Jenny" and "The Rock-a-Round" (1958)—was the initial release by National Recording Corporation in Atlanta; the pianist on these two tunes is Esquerita, whom Peek discovered at the Owl's Club in Greenville ca. 1957. (Later Peek recorded for Mercury, Columbia, and other labels.) After leaving the Blue Caps, Peek continued playing the kind of music he had performed with Vincent, but also country. Beginning in the early 1960s he and his group, the Peek-a-Boos, performed in the Southeast, including Jacksonville, N.C., where they served as house band at the Jazzland Club. He and other former Blue Caps reunited to play in England in 1982 (Vincent died in 1971); they performed in the United States into the 1990s. Peek spent most of his remaining active years playing in clubs in and around Atlanta, where he was popular. Following his death from cirrhosis of the liver, his body was cremated.

Compositions

"Brother-in-Law," "Gee but I Miss That Girl," "Olds-Mo-William," "Pink Thunderbird," "The Rock-a-Round," "Shadow Knows," "Short Shortnin'," "Sweet Skinny Jenny," "Time Will Bring You Everything," "Waikiki Beach," "Yes, I Love You Baby"

Paul Peek; permission of Jacqueline Peek Peace

Recordings as Leader

The NRC Years, 1958–1960, Rockin' through the Teenage Years (1958–1963, 1966), "Out Went the Lights of My World" (1969), "Sweet Lorraine" (1969), "Caught between Love" (1984), "Often Think about You" (1984)

Leader Recorded With

Gene Vincent (late 1950s)

Films (as a Member of Gene Vincent's Blue Caps)

The Girl Can't Help It (1956), *Hot Rod Gang* (1958; also titled *Fury Unleashed*)

Awards

Rockabilly Hall of Fame (1997); Fiddling John Carson Award (2001)

Website

www.rockabillyhall.com/PaulPeekTribute.html (accessed 21 May 2014)

References

SECONDARY: Roger Nunn, "The Rock-a-Round with Paul Peek," part 1, *Now Dig This* 41 (August 1986): 24–28; Roger Nunn, "The Rock-a-Round with Paul Peek," part 2, *Now Dig This* 42 (September 1986): 29–31; Spencer Leigh, "Paul Peek," *Independent* (London), 6 April 2001, independent review sec., p. 6 (obituary); Kay Powell, "Paul Peek Jr., 63, Guitarist, Singer in Rockabilly Hall of Fame," *Atlanta (Ga.) Journal-Constitution*, 7 April 2001, sec. B, p. 4 (obituary).

Peg Leg Sam (Arthur Jackson; "Peg Pete")

Harmonica, singer

28 December 1911 (near Jonesville, S.C.)–27 October 1977 (near Jonesville, S.C.)

S.C. residence: near Jonesville (1911–1977, with absences)

As a youth Jackson learned songs from his mother, who played accordion and organ. He began a life of itinerancy around age ten. He made money in Greenville by dancing, occasionally with Peg Leg Bates. He also performed on harmonica, though he modernized his technique ca. 1927 with the assistance of Elmon Bell. Presumably as a result of falling from a train, he lost his right leg in 1930; thereafter he was known as Peg Leg Sam. For many years beginning in the mid-1930s in Rocky Mount, N.C., he had a radio program during the tobacco season. Also beginning in the 1930s he began working with medicine shows. Among them was W. R. Kerr's Indian Remedy Company, headquartered in Spartanburg. With Kerr he worked as straight man for Pink Anderson, though in time he assumed Anderson's responsibility of attracting customers by playing and singing. He continued with such shows until 1972, when the last one, that of Chief Thundercloud (Leo Kahdot), performed for the final time. Over the years he occasionally spent winters at home. In 1970 Bruce Bastin and Peter Lowry discovered him, were smitten by him, recorded him, and began releasing his music on Flyright (Bastin) and Trix (Lowry). They also arranged for him to perform at colleges and festivals. He is buried in the Thompson Baptist Church Cemetery, Jonesville.

Jackson's birth date (28 December 1911) comes from the Social Security Death Index; some sources indicate that the musician was born ten days earlier. When enumerated for the census on 19 or 20 January 1920 at estimated age eight, he lived with his family in Boganville Township, Union County, S.C.

Peg Leg Sam, near Spartanburg, S.C., 1970; permission of the photographer, Peter B. Lowry

Recordings as Leader

Medicine Show Man (1970, 1972; also titled *Kickin' It*), "Bad Gasoline" (1970; with Baby Tate), *The Last Medicine Show* (1972), "Fox Chase" (1973), *Going Train Blues* (1975; also titled *Early in the Morning* and *Joshua*), "Walking Cane" (1976)

Leader Recorded With

Henry "Rufe" Johnson (1972)

Film

Born for Hard Luck: Peg Leg Sam Jackson (1976) (also available at www.folkstreams.net/film,1, with a transcript and additional information [accessed 21 May 2014])

References

PRIMARY: Bruce Bastin, *The Last Medicine Show* (Bexhill-on-Sea, Sussex, England: Flyright, 1973), passim (this booklet accompanies the vinyl album *The Last Medicine Show* [Flyright 507–8]) (dialogue between Peg Leg Sam and Chief Thundercloud).

SECONDARY: Bruce Bastin, *Crying for the Carolines* (London: Studio Vista, 1971), 82–85; Bruce Bastin and Pete Lowry, "Blues from the South-East (Sequel 3): 'Tricks Ain't Workin' No More,'" *Blues Unlimited* 80 (February–March 1971): 15; Kip Lornell, "Peg Pete and His Pals," *Living Blues* 11 (Winter 1972–1973): 27–29; "Arthur (Pegg) Jackson," *Spartanburg (S.C.) Herald*, 28 October 1977, sec. D, p. 6 (obituary); Kent Cooper, "Peg Leg Sam," *Living Blues* 35 (November–December 1977): 39 (obituary); Bruce Bastin, "From the Medicine Show to the Stage: Some Influences upon the Development of a Blues Tradition in the Southeastern United States," *American Music* 2 (Spring 1984): 34–35, 37; Bruce Bastin, *Red River Blues: The Blues Tradition in the Southeast* (Urbana: University of Illinois Press, 1986), 190–92; Peter Cooper, *Hub City Music Makers: One Southern Town's Popular Music Legacy* (Spartanburg, S.C.: Holocene, 1997), 50–51, 53; Jerry Bledsoe, "Peg Leg Jackson: The Last Medicine Show," in *Making Notes: Music of the Carolinas*, ed. Ann Wicker (Charlotte: Novello Festival Press, 2008), 76–78 (comments by Peg Leg Sam).

Pemberton, Roger Max

Saxophone, clarinet, flute
17 October 1930 (Evansville, Ind.)–
S.C. residence: Columbia (1986–)

Roger Pemberton; photograph by Jane Borgstedt, permission of Roger Pemberton

Beginning in 1945 Pemberton played with bands in the Evansville, Ind., area; he also toured with Ray Anthony. After receiving a degree in music education from the University of Evansville (1953), he was drafted into the army, which he served for two years as performer and band leader at Fort Leonard Wood, Mo. Upon leaving military service he joined Jimmy Palmer's group in Chicago but in 1957 became a member of Woody Herman's Third Herd; a year later he quit Herman to teach school in White County, Ill. Following his 1961 master's degree from Indiana University, he joined its faculty, though he left this position in 1964 to freelance in N.Y.C. That year he toured with Pearl Bailey and Louis Bellson before affiliating with Maynard Ferguson. In 1965 he became a regular with the band of *The Merv Griffin Show*, led by Mort Lindsey; when Griffin moved to Los Angeles in 1970 Pemberton remained in N.Y.C. From there he toured with Sammy Davis, Jr. He joined Ray Bloch's organization and led a band but also worked as a clinician for C. G. Conn, a relationship that continued after his 1972 relocation to Evansville. He became Jazz Artist in Residence at the University of South Carolina in 1986, a position he held until retiring in 2000. During his professorship he led the U.S. Airways Jazz Orchestra from 1995 to 1998. Pemberton remains active on the Columbia jazz scene.

Compositions

"Another Shade of Blue," "Any Way You Slice It," "Ballad for Marvin," "Barely Bossa Nova," "Bean

Blossom Waltz," "Blues in F," "Bobby's Bag," "Bossa Fuego," "Brazil Bound," "Doodlebug," "Gnawbone Stomp," "Here's Merv," "Hoosier," "Latin Liason," "Marshall," "Monk's Mood," "No Vibrato," "October Morn," "Ode to Sister Sue," "Rico Three," "R. P. Blues," "Short Vamp Blues," "Slick Stuff," "Soulful One," "Swingin' at Greenstreet's," "This One's for Neal," "Villa of Mysteries," "Whiskey Waltz"

Recordings as Leader

Chicagojazz (1980), *Carolina Love Moods* (1986)

Leaders Recorded With

Jerry Coker (1955), Woody Herman (1957–1958), Maynard Ferguson (1964), Mort Lindsey (mid-to-late 1960s), Les Hooper (1973, ca. 1977), Rich Matteson (1973), Phil Wilson (1977), Warren Kime (ca. 1980), Illinois All State Jazz Band I (1981), Bill Porter (1982)

Awards

Honorary degree, Newberry College (1976); honorary degree, University of Evansville (2008)

Pennicks, Marion

See Rennicks, Marion

Pergno (?), William

Ca. 1888–?
S.C. residence: Charleston (by 1895–)

Apparently a ward of Jenkins Orphanage, this musician played in its bands at least in the 1890s and performed with one of them in England in 1895. His instrument is not known.

The passenger list of the *Paris,* which transported the orphanage band to England in September 1895, records the musician's name as possibly Perrymid (and his age as eight); the list for the *Teutonic,* which returned the group to the United States the next month, records it as possibly Pergno (and his age as seven).

Reference

SECONDARY: Howard Rye, "Visiting Fireboys: The Jenkins' Orphanage Bands in Britain," *Storyville* 130 (1987): 137–43.

Perry, Ermit V.

Trumpet
Not before 1910 (probably Gainesville or Jacksonville, Fla.)–?
S.C. residence: Charleston (1921–1926)

A ward of Jenkins Orphanage from 1921 to 1926, Perry played in its bands. He became a professional musician, initially with Bubber Applewhite's Florida Troubadours and then the Sunset Royals. Another member of the Sunset Royals, trombonist and arranger Fred Norman, credits Perry with teaching him to count time correctly. Always a sideman, he is best known for his affiliation with Dizzy Gillespie in the mid-1950s. He played in Broadway bands during the 1970s.

Perry was the brother of trumpeter Glenwood Perry. John Chilton notes that Perry was born around 1910 in Jacksonville, Fla. He was born after 20(?) April 1910, when his family, excluding him, was enumerated for the census in Gainesville, Fla.

Leaders Recorded With

Ace Harris (1937), Cootie Williams (1944–1946), Sarah Vaughan (1947), Joe Thomas (1949), Louis Jordan (1951), Dizzy Gillespie (1955–1957), Sammy Lowe (1956 or 1957), Benny Goodman (1958), Reuben Phillips (1960–1961)

Film

Cootie Williams and His Orchestra (1943; series 1, number 2 of *Film Vodvil*)

References

SECONDARY: Stanley Dance, *The World of Swing* (New York: Scribner's, 1974), 1: 232; John Chilton, *A Jazz Nursery: The Story of the Jenkins' Orphanage Bands of Charleston, South Carolina* (London: Bloomsbury Book Shop, 1980), 50, 58.

Perry, Glenwood

Trumpet
Probably 1908 or 1909 (Fla., probably Gainesville)–30 May 1933 (Charleston, S.C.)
S.C. residence: Charleston (probably by early 1920s–1933)

A ward of Jenkins Orphanage, Perry played in its bands from the mid-1920s probably until his death.

Perry was the brother of trumpeter Ermit V. Perry. When Perry was enumerated for the census in Gainesville, Fla., in April 1910, probably on the 20th, his age was estimated as two. His death certificate indicates that at the time of his death from acute dilatation of the heart, he was a musician residing at Jenkins Orphanage. It notes that he was born in 1909.

Reference

SECONDARY: Bruce Bastin, "A Note on the Carolina Cotton Pickers," *Storyville* 95 (June–July 1981): 177–82.

Perrymid, William

See Pergno (?), William

Person, Houston Stafford, Jr.

Saxophone
10 November 1934 (Florence, S.C.)–
S.C. residences: Florence (1934–1952), Orangeburg (1952–ca. 1955)

Person began playing the saxophone during his senior year in high school and continued performing on it at what is now South Carolina State University, where he matriculated in 1952. He left school to join the air force. While stationed in Germany he was encouraged by such army musicians as Eddie Harris and Cedar Walton. Upon discharge he attended Hartt College of Music in Hartford, Conn. (1958–1961). He lived in several cities as a professional musician, including Boston, before settling in Newark, N.J. Most influenced by the large-toned playing of Illinois Jacquet and Gene Ammons, Person is sometimes considered the last saxophonist in their tradition. Known for respecting a tune's melody, he favors standards (such as "Laura") and jazz originals (Gigi Gryce's "Social Call"). From the early 1970s until her death in 2001, he played and recorded with singer Etta Jones. The number and frequency of his recordings indicate the appeal of his music. Despite performing in various modes—including what might be called mainstream jazz, gospel, disco, and soul—and working as sideman in different kinds of groups—including many featuring the organ—his actual playing is largely consistent: a rich tone, a sure sense of rhythm, and, especially at his own sessions, faithfulness to the melody. He is particularly effective on duet recordings with Ran Blake, Ron Carter, and Bill Charlap. His solo on "Shaft," recorded at a Bernard Purdie session (1971), gained a degree of popularity. He plays the saxophone solos on the sound track of *Romance and Cigarettes* (2005).

Compositions

"Brother H.," "Goodness," "Grilled Cheese and Bacon," "Groovin' and a-Groovin'," "Houston's Blues," "The Pimp," "Soul Dance," "Sweet Buns and Barbeque," "Torii Station," "True Blues," "Underground Soul," "Up at Joe's, Down at Jim's," "Why Not"

Recordings as Leader

Underground Soul! (1966), *Chocomotive* (1967), *Trust in Me* (1967), *Blue Odyssey* (1968), *Soul Dance* (1968), *Goodness!* (1969), *Person to Person!* (1970), *Truth!* (1970), *Houston Express* (1971), *Sweet Buns and Barbecue* (1972), *The Real Thing* (1973), *Houston Person '75* (1974), *Get Out'a My Way!* (1975), *The Big Horn* (1976), *Pure Pleasure* (1976), *Stolen Sweets* (1976), *Harmony* (1977), *The Nearness of You* (1977), *Wild Flower* (1977), *The Gospel Soul of Houston Person* (ca. 1978), *Suspicions* (1980), *Very Personal* (1980), *Heavy Juice* (1982), *Always on My Mind* (1985), *Basics* (1987), *The Talk of the Town* (1987), *We Owe It All to Love* (1988), *The Party* (1989), *Something in Common* (1989; with Ron Carter), *Now's the Time* (1990; with Ron Carter), *Why Not!* (1990), *The Lion and His Pride* (1991), *Person-ified* (1996), *The Opening Round* (1997), *My Romance* (1998), *Soft Lights* (1999), *Dialogues* (2000), *In a Sentimental Mood* (2000), *Blue Velvet* (2001), *Sentimental Journey* (2002), *Social Call* (2003), *To Etta with Love* (2004), *You Taught My Heart to Sing* (2004), *All Soul* (2005), *Just between Friends* (2005), *Thinking of You* (2007), *Mellow* (2009), *Moment to Moment* (2010), *Naturally* (2012), *Nice 'n' Easy* (2013)

Leaders Recorded With

Johnny "Hammond" Smith (1963–1970), Don Patterson (1967), Billy Butler (1968, 1970), Gene Ammons (1969), Charles Earland (1969, 1971, 1978, 1982, 1990–1991), Sonny Phillips (1969), Charles Kynard (1970), Horace Silver (1970), Melvin Sparks (1970), Grant Green (1971), Bernard Purdie (1971, 1993), Tiny Grimes (1973), Reuben Wilson (ca. 1974), Etta Jones (1975–1978, 1980, 1983, 1986–1987, 1989–1993, 1995, 1997–2001), Richard "Groove" Holmes (1977, 1980, 1988–1989), Johnny Lytle (1980–1981, 1989, 1991–1992), Ran Blake (1983), Roger Kellaway (1984), Les McCann

(1984), Hank Crawford (1985), Eric Gale (1987), Lena Horne (1988, 1993, 1997), Brother Jack McDuff (1988–1990), Leon Thomas (1988), Shirley Scott (1989), Joey DeFrancesco (ca. 1989, 1993–1994, 1997), Lorez Alexandria (1990, 1993), Della Griffin (1990, 1992, 1996), Jimmy Ponder (1990–1991), Dakota Staton (1990, 1996), Buddy Tate (1990), Dr. Lonnie Smith (1991), Rhoda Scott (early 1990s), Ernie Andrews (1992, 1997, 2000, 2002, 2005), Michael Carvin (1992), Lou Rawls (1992), Sax Legends (1992), Mihoko Uemura (1992, 2007), Freddie Cole (1993, 2006, 2010), Rodney Kendrick (1993), Vanessa Rubin (1993), Carrie Smith (1993), Warren Vaché (1993, 2010), Teddy Edwards (1994, 1996), Junior Mance (1995, 2008), Ron Carter (1999), Stan Hope (1999, 2004), Janis Siegel (2002), Carol Sloane (2003), Ernestine Anderson (2008–2010)

Awards

Eubie Blake Jazz Award (1982); Fred Hampton Scholarship Fund Image Award (1993)

References

PRIMARY: Joao Moreira dos Santos, "Houston Person: Having a Good Time," http://www.allaboutjazz.com/php/article.php?id=18861&page=1#.UJBGRlLpUY5 (2005; accessed 21 May 2014) (interview); Benjamin Franklin V, *Jazz and Blues Musicians of South Carolina: Interviews with Jabbo, Dizzy, Drink, and Others* (Columbia: University of South Carolina Press, 2008), 96–103.

SECONDARY: Keith Shadwick, "Soul Saxophones," in *Masters of the Jazz Saxophone,* ed. Tony Bacon (London: Balafon Books, 2000), 113; Gary Giddins, "Personality: Houston Person Sticks to Your Ribs," *Village Voice,* 28 May 2002, p. 74; Nat Hentoff, "Protector of the Soulful Melody," *Wall Street Journal,* 7 December 2010, sec. D, p. 5 (comments by Person); "Houston Person," http://musicians.allaboutjazz.com/musician.php?id=10237#.UJBExFLpUY4 (2011; accessed 21 May 2014) (comments by Person); Tom Reney, "Houston Person: Timeless, Yet Endangered, Style," http://jazztimes.com/articles/55040-houston-person-timeless-yet-endangered-style (2012; accessed 21 May 2014) (comments by Person).

Phelps, Walter Francis ("Uncle Walt")

Guitar, harmonica, singer

Late 1890s (Laurens County, S.C.)–4 February 1983 (Asheville, N.C.)

S.C. residences: Laurens County (late 1890s–probably early 1910s), Landrum (probably early 1910s–1920s)

An originator of the Piedmont blues, Phelps began playing the harmonica while a grade schooler in Landrum, S.C., though the guitar became his main instrument. He moved to Asheville, N.C., in the 1920s. There during that decade he played with the parents of his wife, Ethel Johnston Phelps; in the 1930s he performed on Asheville streets with Peg Leg Sam (Arthur Jackson) and Henry "Rufe" Johnson. He also played in various parts of N.C. with Pink Anderson, among others. In 1942 Phelps formed a band that was active into the 1950s. Rediscovered in the 1970s, he played at the John Henry Folk Festival (Pence Springs, W.Va.), Shindig on the Green (Asheville, N.C.), and the University of North Carolina (Asheville). He also teamed with his wife as a musical duo, with her singing. For almost two decades he was employed by the city of Asheville. He is buried in Pinedale Memorial Gardens, Greenville, S.C.

Phelps's middle name appears in the obituary published in the *Spartanburg Herald-Journal;* the one in the *Asheville Citizen and Times* records his middle initial as S. Information in the holdings of Warren Wilson College, Swannanoa, N.C., indicates that Phelps was born on 10 April 1896. His obituary states that he died at age eighty-six. The most likely accurate document, the Social Security Death Index, records his birth date as 5 June 1899. Though no recording of Phelps has apparently been released, recordings of his and his wife's performances in Asheville (mid-1970s) and Swannanoa (1980) are preserved on cassette tapes in the library of Warren Wilson College. The couple's performance at the 1978 John Henry Folk Festival is preserved in the Joan Fenton Collection, 1952–1978, in the Southern Folklife Collection, Louis Round Wilson Special Collections Library, University of North Carolina, Chapel Hill. The Fenton collection records Johnston as the maiden name of Ethel Phelps.

References

SECONDARY: "'Uncle Walt' Phelps, 86, Former Band Leader, Dies," *Asheville (N.C.) Citizen and Times,* 5 February 1983, sec. 2, p. 12 (obituary); "Walter F. Phelps," *Spartanburg (S.C.) Herald-Journal,* 8 February 1983, sec. B, p. 8 (obituary).

Pinckney, Thomas Hamilton

Cornet, possibly singer
Probably ca. 1863 (Columbia, S.C.)–27 December 1935 (Columbia, S.C.)
S.C. residence: Columbia (probably ca. 1863–1935)

Pinckney was born on the grounds of what is now the University of South Carolina, where his father was a baker. He attended the preparatory school of the institution from 1874 to 1876. He became a barber, probably in the early 1880s. By 1898 he and his brother William formed a band that included other family members and that played throughout S.C. Around 1910 it included trumpeter Amos M. White. The band was active at least until 1922. In time Pinckney became an undertaker and owned considerable property. According to the *Palmetto Leader* he was, at his death, "one of Columbia's best known business men." He is buried in section 1C, Palmetto Cemetery, Columbia.

Pinckney was a grandfather of Leroy Pinckney Hardy, a professional musician. The census estimates various years for Pinckney's birth, ranging from ca. 1863 to the mid-1870s. The earliest known documentation of his age is in the 1870 census (enumerated on 30 June), which estimates it as seven; South Carolina College Student Registers indicate that he entered the preparatory school of the college in 1874 at age eleven. Though his death certificate notes that he died at age fifty-nine, his death notice in the *Columbia Record* (27 December 1935) states that he died at age seventy-two.

Thomas Pinckney; permission of Leroy Hardy, Jr.

References

SECONDARY: South Carolina College Student Registers, vols. 1–7: 1806–1918 (microfilm housed in the South Caroliniana Library, University of South Carolina, Columbia; Pinckney is documented in the unpaginated vol. 5, years 1874–1876); "Come! Come! Where?," *Columbia (S.C.) Southern Indicator,* 12 August 1922, p. 2; "T. H. Pinckney Dies at Home," *Columbia (S.C.) Record,* 27 December 1935, p. 14 (obituary); "Funeral Today Thomas H. Pinckney: Negro Undertaker Once Led Famous Dance Orchestra, Attended Carolina," *Columbia (S.C.) State,* 29 December 1935, p. 3 (obituary); "Pinckney Services Held at Zion Baptist Church," *Columbia (S.C.) Record,* 30 December 1935, p. 3; "Thousands Attend Funeral Hon. Thos. H. Pinckney," *Columbia (S.C.) Palmetto Leader,* 4 January 1936, p. 1; Amos M. White, interview by William Russell, 23 August 1958, four reels of tape and a typed summary, Hogan Jazz Archive, Tulane University, New Orleans, p. 2 of summary (also available at http://musicrising.tulane.edu/uploads/transcripts/a.%20white%2008-23-1958.pdf [accessed 21 May 2014]).

Pinckney, William

Probably ca. 1867 (Columbia, S.C.)–before 1936
S.C. residence: Columbia (probably ca. 1867–before 1936)

By 1898 Pinckney and his brother Thomas formed a band that included other family members and that played throughout S.C. Around 1910 it included trumpeter Amos M. White, who, when mentioning his time with the band, referred only to Thomas as its leader. The band was active at least until 1922.

When Pinckney was enumerated for the census on 30 June 1870, his age was estimated as three; in June 1880, as ten. Conducted in Columbia on 8 June, the 1900 census indicates that he was born in July 1877, which is impossible. In 1935 the *State* newspaper noted that Pinckney led the 149th Regiment marching band during the Spanish-American War. Though a photograph exists of Pinckney in a military uniform, it has not been confirmed that he served in the military or led a regimental band. As best as can be determined, there was no S.C.

William Pinckney; permission of Leroy Hardy, Jr.

149th Regiment, though other states had one. See *Historical Roster and Itinerary of South Carolina Volunteer Troops Who Served in the Late War between the United States and Spain, 1898, Coupled with Brief Sketches of Their Movements from the Beginning to the Ending of the Conflict,* comp. J. W. Floyd (Columbia, S.C.: R. L. Bryan, 1901). In commenting on the funeral of Thomas Pinckney in 1936, the *Palmetto Leader* stated that William Pinckney, a barber, "died some years ago."

References

SECONDARY: "Come! Come! Where?," *Columbia (S.C.) Southern Indicator,* 12 August 1922, p. 2; "Funeral Today Thomas H. Pinckney: Negro Undertaker Once Led Famous Dance Orchestra, Attended Carolina," *Columbia (S.C.) State,* 29 December 1935, p. 3; "Pinckney Services Held at Zion Baptist Church," *Columbia (S.C.) Record,* 30 December 1935, p. 3; "Thousands Attend Funeral Hon. Thos. H. Pinckney," *Columbia (S.C.) Palmetto Leader,* 4 January 1936, p. 1; Amos M. White, interview by William Russell, 23 August 1958, four reels of tape and a typed summary, Hogan Jazz Archive, Tulane University, New Orleans, p. 2 of summary (also available at http://musicrising.tulane.edu/uploads/transcripts/a.%20white%2008-23-1958.pdf [accessed 21 May 2014]).

Pinkney, (Willie) Bill

Singer

15 August 1925 (Dalzell, S.C.)–4 July 2007 (Daytona Beach, Fla.)

S.C. residences: Dalzell (1925–1943, 1945–1949), Sumter (1970–2007)

While with the army during World War II, Pinkney and four other soldiers formed the U.S. Friendly Five, a gospel group. After his discharge in late 1945 he returned to Dalzell, his hometown, and became an automobile mechanic and truck driver, the latter at Shaw Air Force Base. He also resumed singing, this time with the Singing Cousins, a gospel group he founded. In 1949 he moved to N.Y.C., where he sang with the Jerusalem Stars and Southern Knights. (The former organization included Benjamin Peay, later known as Brook Benton.) He became a member of the second version of Clyde McPhatter's Drifters in 1953. This group had hits with such recordings as "Honey Love," "Money Honey," and "White Christmas"; the first two reached number one on the rhythm-and-blues charts, and the last, featuring Pinkney, is included on the sound tracks of *Home Alone* (1990) and *Mixed Nuts* (1994). When Pinkney argued for increased compensation for the Drifters in 1956, he was fired by George Treadwell, the singers' manager, as he was again in 1958, after having rejoined the group in 1957. Between his affiliations with the Drifters, he led the Flyers. When the Drifters dissolved Pinkney formed the Original Drifters, with which he performed for the remainder of his life, though on its initial recordings the group was identified as Harmony Grits. When not touring with the Original Drifters, he sang occasionally with the Traveling Echoes, a gospel sextet. He died just before a scheduled performance of the Original Drifters. He is buried in Saint Luke A.M.E. Churchyard Cemetery, Sumter, S.C.

Tony Allan, who comments on George Treadwell's 1956 firing of Pinkney, wrote his book with Treadwell's widow. Numerous sources indicate that Pinkney played baseball with the Blue Sox in the New York Negro League. The League had no such team. He pitched for a sandlot team called the Blue Sox that played initially in Central Park in N.Y.C. He returned to S.C. in 1970. Even though he relocated to Nev., he retained a residence in Sumter.

Compositions

"After the Hop," "I Found Some Lovin'," "No Sweet Lovin'," "Sally's Got a Sister"

Recordings as Leader (with Pinkney's Original Drifters, Except as Noted)

"My Only Desire" (1956; with the Flyers), "On Bended Knee" (1956; with the Flyers), "After the Hop" (1958; as Bill Pinky and the Turks), "Sally's Got a Sister" (1958; as Bill Pinky and the Turks), "Am I to Be the One" (1959; with the Harmony Grits), "Gee" (1959; with the Harmony Grits), "I Could Have Told You" (1959; with the Harmony Grits), "Santa Claus Is Comin' to Town" (1959; with the Harmony Grits), "Little School Girl" (1964; with the Teals), "Sugar Girl" (1964; with the Teals), "I Found Some Lovin'" (1967), "The Masquerade Is Over" (1967), "Can You Forgive" (1971), "Millionaire" (1971), "Ol' Man River" (1971, 1988), "I'm the Original" (1970s), "Just Drifting Along" (1970s), "Just Let Your Heart Be Your Guide" (1978), "Plain, Simple, but Sweet" (1978), "Broke Blues" (1979), "Sixty Minute Man" (1979), "I Count the Tears" (1980), "(More Than a Number in My) Little Red Book" (1980), "Get and Hold My Hand" (1988), *A White Christmas* (1989), "Gonna Move across the River" (1989), "W-P-L-J (White Port Lemon Juice)" (1989), "Ain't Got No Money" (1990), "She Felt Too Good" (1992; long and short versions), "Ain't Got No Money" (1993), *Anthology* (released 1997; recording dates unknown, but mostly reissues, with some songs released for the first time), "Tired of Being Your Fool" (1999), *O Holy Night: A Drifters Christmas* (2000), "I Love New Orleans Music" (2001), "Let the Doorbell Ring" (2001; with the Mojo Blues Band), "Some Like It Hot" (2001)

Leaders Recorded With

Drifters (1953–1956), Ruth Brown (1954; as member of the Drifters, who, for the session with Brown, were called the Rhythmakers), Johnny Darrow (1961; Darrow was better known as Johnny Moore), Flashbacks (2001)

Awards

Rock and Roll Hall of Fame (1988; as member of the Drifters); Order of the Palmetto (1993); South Carolina Entertainment and Music Hall of Fame (1994); Carolina Beach Music Awards Hall of Fame (1995; as member of the Original Drifters); Vocal Group Hall of Fame (1998; as member of the Drifters); Joe Pope Pioneer Award (1999); Rhythm & Blues Foundation Pioneer Award (1999); honorary degree, Coastal Carolina University (2001); the stretch of S-43-1342 (old U.S. 521) from S.C. 441 to Charles Jackson Rd. in Dalzell, S.C., named the Bill Pinkney of the Original Drifters Memorial Highway (2008).

Website

www.originaldrifters.com/ (accessed 21 May 2014)

References

PRIMARY: Bill Pinkney, as told to Maxine Porter, *Drifters 1: Bill Pinkney, Celebration 50 Years, 1953–2003* (Las Vegas: BillMax Publishing, 2003).

SECONDARY: Tony Allan, with Faye Treadwell, *Save the Last Dance for Me: The Musical Legacy of the Drifters, 1953–1993* (Ann Arbor: Popular Culture, Ink., 1993), passim; Mike Karvelas, "Original Drifter Gets Order of Palmetto," *Sumter (S.C.) Item,* 16 May 1993, sec. A, p. 8; C. S. Murphy, "Pinkney Park Dedicated," *Sumter (S.C.) Item,* 29 October 1996, sec. A, pp. 1, 12; Otis R. Taylor, Jr., "No Longer Drifting," *Columbia (S.C.) State,* 14 August 2005, sec. E, pp. 1, 4 (comments by Pinkney); Jay Warner, *American Singing Groups: A History from 1940s to Today* (Milwaukee: Hal Leonard, 2006), 159–62; Otis R. Taylor, Jr., "S.C. Music Icon Pinkney Dies," *Columbia (S.C.) State,* 5 July 2007, sec. A, pp. 1, 6 (obituary); "Bill Pinkney, 81, of the Drifters Vocal Group," *New York Times,* 6 July 2007, sec. B, p. 7 (obituary); "Willie Pinkney," *Sumter (S.C.) Item,* 8 July 2007, sec. A, p. 10 (obituary); "Bill Pinkney," *Juke Blues* 64 (late 2007): 68 (obituary); Marv Goldberg, "The Drifters (The Early Years)," www.uncamarvy.com/Drifters/drifters.html (2009); Marv Goldberg, "The Original Drifters," www.uncamarvy.com/OrigDrifters/origdrifters.html (2009; accessed 21 May 2014).

Plantation Melody Quintet

See Claflin University Plantation Melody Quintet

Platt, Robert

French horn, tuba
S.C. residence: Charleston (1930s)

Apparently a ward of Jenkins Orphanage, Platt played in its bands in the 1930s.

Pope, Odean

Saxophone, clarinet, oboe, flute, piccolo, piano, composer
Probably 24 October 1938 (Ninety-Six, S.C.)–
S.C. residence: Ninety-Six (probably 1938–ca. 1948)

As a youth in Ninety-Six, Pope was inspired by various kinds of music, including that at the Baptist church his family attended. He moved to Philadelphia when he was apparently either ten or twelve; there he was smitten by the jazz bands he heard at the Earle Theater. He attended high school with Spanky DeBrest, Jimmy Garrison, and Benny Golson, among other musicians who would become significant. By eighteen he was a professional, playing in Sam Reed's pit band at the Uptown Theater. Soon he met drummer Max Roach (with whom he was a regular in 1967 and 1968) and began associating with such Philadelphia musicians as John Coltrane, Jimmy Heath, and Jimmy Smith. He studied with Hasaan Ibn Ali, Ray Bryant, Kenny Clarke, Jymie Merritt, and other active musicians. Around 1971 he helped form Catalyst, a jazz-funk collective that disbanded in 1976. The next year he established a saxophone choir (nine saxophones plus rhythm section) to re-create sounds he heard in his church in Ninety-Six. During the 1970s he taught for the Model Cities Cultural Arts Association and at summer camps sponsored by the Settlement Music School. In 1979 he again joined Roach, with whom he performed off and on until 2002. He composed and performed *Collective Voices* (1999), a suite that features tap dancers in the role of percussionists. The CD *Serenity* consists of his playing solo soprano saxophone in nature. With combos of various sizes he experiments with multiphonics and free jazz. Francis Davis believes that in "his quasi-spiritual obsession with harmonic theory and instrumental technique" (107), Pope embodies qualities common to Philadelphia musicians of his era.

With one exception all sources consulted indicate that Pope was born on 24 October 1938. The U.S. Public Records Index, vol. 1, states that he was born on 24 October 1930. He has not been located in the 1940 census. Pope told Greg Cahill that he moved to Philadelphia at age ten; David R. Adler writes that Pope located there when he was twelve. *The Funkiest Band You Never Heard* (two CDs) includes all four releases by Catalyst. Selections from *Ninety-Six* and *Ebioto* were reissued on Pope's CD *What Went Before*, vol. 1.

Compositions

"956," "Almost Like Me," "The Binder," "Blues for Eight," "Cis," "Collections," "Convictions," "Custody of the American Spirit," "Doug's Prelude," "Family Portrait," "Fifth House," "Fresh Breeze," "The Garden of Happiness," "Good Question Too," "Gray Hair," "Knot It Off," "Limu," "Mail Order," "Me and You," "Minor Infractions," "Morning Mist," "Mwalimu," "Neapolitan Minor," "Ninety-Six," "Nothing Is Wrong," "Off If Not," "Out for a Walk," "Overture," "Philly in Three," "Phrygian Love Theme," "The Ponderer," "Portrait," "Prince La Sha," "Red River Road," "Rejuvenate," "Saxophone Shop," "Scorpio Twins," "She Smiled Again," "Sis," "Spanish Love Theme," "Speaking to the Clouds," "The Spirit Room," "Suite for Two," "Terrestrial," "To the Roach," "Trilogy," "Voice," "WL," "You Remind Me," "Zip"

Recordings as Leader

Catalyst (1972), *Perception* (1972; by Catalyst), *Unity* (1974; by Catalyst), *A Tear and a Smile* (1975; by Catalyst), *Almost Like Me* (1982), "Improvisation 1" (1983), *The Saxophone Shop* (1985), *Out for a Walk* (1990), *The Ponderer* (1990), *Epitome* (1993), *Ninety-Six* (1995), *Collective Voices* (1996), *Changes and Chances* (1999; with Dave Burrell), *Ebioto* (ca. 1999), *Philadelphia Spirit in New York* (2001; with Byard Lancaster), *Nothing Is Wrong* (2003; with Khan Jamal), *Two Dreams* (2004), *Locked and Loaded: Live at the Blue Note* (2005), *The Mystery of Prince Lasha* (2005; with Prince Lasha), *Serenity* (2006), *To the Roach* (2006), *Fresh Breeze* (2008), *The Misled Children Meet Odean Pope* (2008), *Odeans List* (2008), *Plant Life* (2008), *Universal Sounds* (ca. 2010), *Odean's Three* (2012)

Leaders Recorded With

Hasaan Ibn Ali (1965), John Minnis (1975–1978), Max Roach (1979–1980, 1982, 1984–1986, 1990–1991), Art Davis (1984), Jamaaladeen Tacuma (1986), Bill Cosby (1987), Bobby Zankel (1991), Sunny Murray (1994), Carl Grubbs (2002), Donald Bailey (2006), Khan Jamal (2008)

Film

Pipes of Peace (2008)

Awards

Pew Fellowship in the Arts (1992); Rockefeller Award (1992)

Website

http://www.odeanpope.com/ (accessed 21 May 2014)

References

PRIMARY: Tom Beetz, "De dankbaarheid van Odean Pope," *Nu Jazz* 10 (Juli 1982): 409–11 (interview; in Dutch); Chip Stern, "Odean Pope: Students and Teachers; Tracing Forgotten Tenor Traditions," *Musician* 65 (March 1984): 26, 28, 30 (mainly a narrative by Pope); George W. Harris, "Pope's Authority," http://www.jazzweekly.com/2012/12/popes-authority/ (17 December 2012; accessed 21 May 2014) (substantial comments by Pope).

SECONDARY: Russell Woessner, "Odean Pope," *Down Beat* 50 (March 1983): 46–47 (comments by Pope); Gene Seymour, "Odean Pope: Music First, Then Money," *Philadelphia Daily News,* 18 February 1987, features sec., p. 47 (comments by Pope); Francis Davis, "Odean Pope: This Tenor Saxophonist Shows That Philadelphia-Area Musicians Clearly Share Some Traits," *Philadelphia Inquirer,* 4 April 1987, sec. D, pp. 1, 8 (reprinted in Davis's *Outcats: Jazz Composers, Instrumentalists, and Singers* [New York: Oxford University Press, 1990], 107–10) (comments by Pope); Kevin L. Carter, "Collective Approach for Sax Man," *Philadelphia Inquirer,* 3 December 1999, features weekend sec., p. 21 (comments by Pope); Greg Cahill, "The Seeker," *Northern California Bohemian,* http://www.metroactive.com/papers/sonoma/02.22.01/pope-0108.html (22–28 February 2001; accessed 21 May 2014) (comments by Pope); Nate Chinen, "Odean Pope: The Catalyst," *JazzTimes* 36 (June 2006): 56–64 (also available at http://jazztimes.com/articles/16922-odean-pope-the-catalyst [accessed 21 May 2014]) (comments by Pope); David R. Adler, "Odean Pope Carries Jazz Legacy Gracefully," *Philadelphia Inquirer,* 23 September 2007, sec. H, pp. 1, 6 (comments by Pope); A. D. Amorosi, "The Coolest Cats Come Out to Aid Jazzman Odean Pope," *Philadelphia Inquirer,* 23 March 2011, sec. E, p. 5.

Porter, Aaron

Possibly 1886 (S.C.)-?

S.C. residence: Charleston (at least 1890s–at least until 1900)

A ward of Jenkins Orphanage, Porter played in its bands at least in the 1890s and performed with one of them in England in 1895. His instrument is not known.

The passenger list of the *Paris,* which transported the orphanage band to England in September 1895, records Porter's age as eight; the list of the *Teutonic,* which returned the group to the United States the next month, as seven. Conducted in Charleston on 28 June, the 1900 census indicates that Porter was born in S.C. in September 1886. Howard Rye spells the musician's surname Parker.

Reference

SECONDARY: Howard Rye, "Visiting Fireboys: The Jenkins' Orphanage Bands in Britain," *Storyville* 130 (1987): 137–43.

Porter, Bobby

Singer

S.C. residence: Spartanburg (probably by 1950s–probably at least into early 1960s)

In the mid-1960s Porter recorded two songs for Bobby and Danny Robinson's Enjoy Records in N.Y.C. He was probably the Bobby Porter who performed at the Apollo Theater in 1965; it has not been determined if he was the Bobby Porter who sang at a Wilson Picket concert in Brooklyn (1971).

Recordings as Leader (Both 1965)

"Foxy Devil," "Searching for Love"

References

SECONDARY: Apollo Theater advertisement, *New York Amsterdam News,* 26 June 1965, p. 22; Charles Hobson, "Brooklyn, Home of Soul, Hosts Bad Black Show," *New York Amsterdam News,* 4 December 1971, sec. C, p. 1.

Potter, Chris (Joseph Christopher)

Saxophone, clarinet, flute, organ, singer, composer

1 January 1971 (Chicago, Ill.)-

S.C. residence: Columbia (1975-1989)

Potter entered the Columbia jazz scene as a young teenager. After completing high school in Columbia he attended college in N.Y.C. and received a degree from the Manhattan School of Music (1993). During his collegiate years he played regularly with Red Rodney, who had discovered him in Columbia. Also during these years he began recording, both as leader and sideman with the likes of Paul Motian, Dave Douglas, Dave Holland, and the Mingus Big Band. His performance on "In Vogue" with Joanne Brackeen (1998) was nominated for a Grammy Award. As a result of this activity and his live performances, he was awarded the prestigious Danish Jazzpar Prize, which, from 1990 to 2004, was given annually to an established musician deserving of additional acclaim. At twenty-nine he was its youngest recipient. He began incorporating electric elements into his music around 2004; soon thereafter his group Underground emphasized freedom and funk concurrently. His backing on *Songs for Anyone* includes such classical instruments as cello, viola, and violin; the music on *The Sirens* was inspired by Homer's *The Odyssey*. He tours extensively, including internationally. Ted Panken expresses a view held by many: "Potter has emerged as a leading improvisational voice of his generation" (32). Nate Chinen goes further: Potter is "the most commandingly skilled saxophonist of his generation, an improviser of deft insight and athletic poise" (1).

Compositions

"Abyssinia," "Against the Wind," "The Arc of a Day," "Arjuna," "Azalea," "Big Top," "Celestial Nomad," "Chief Seattle," "Cupid and Psyche," "Dawn," "Estrellas del Sur," "Eurydice," "Facing East," "Gratitude," "High Noon," "Highway One," "Interstellar Signals," "Invisible Man," "Kalypso," "Lift," "Megalopolis," "Migrations," "Mind's Eye," "Narrow Road," "Nausikaa," "New Year's Day," "Next Best Western," "Nudnik," "Okinawa," "Penelope," "Shadow," "The Sirens," "Small Wonder," "Snake Oil," "Song for Anyone," "The Steppes," "Stranger at the Gate," "Sun King," "Time's Arrow," "Train," "Ultrahang," "Underground," "Viva las Vilnius," "Vox Humana," "Washed Ashore," "Wayfinder," "What You Wish," "The Wheel," "Wine Dark Sea," "Zea"

Recordings as Leader

Presenting Chris Potter (1992), *Concentric Circles* (1993), *Sundiata* (1993), *Chris Potter–Kenny Werner* (1994), *Pure* (1994), *Moving In* (1996), "Oh Come All Ye Faithful" (1996), *Unspoken* (1997), *Vertigo* (1998), *Gratitude* (2000), *This Will Be* (2000), *Lift: Live at the Village Vanguard* (2002), *Traveling Mercies* (2002), *Underground* (2005), *Song for Anyone* (2006), *Follow the Red Line: Live at the Village Vanguard* (2007), *Ultrahang* (2009), *The Sirens* (2011), *Imaginary Cities* (2013)

Leaders Recorded With

Red Rodney (1990, 1992), Greg Gisbert (1992, 1994), Bill Warfield (1992), Ryan Kisor (1993, 1999), Marian McPartland (1993), Mingus Big Band (1993–1994, 1997), John Swana (1993, 1997), Gene Harris (1994), Jazz Mentality (1994), Paul Motian (1994, 1996–1998, 2005–2006, 2009), Randy Sandke (1994), Billy Drummond (1995), Ray Drummond (1995), Carol Fredette (1995), Urbie Green (1995), Per Husby (1995), Susannah McCorkle (1995–1997), James Moody (1995), Renee Rosnes (1995, 1997, 2001), Scott Colley (1996–1997, 1999), Al Foster (1996, 2007), Billy Hart (1996), Brother Jack McDuff (1996–1997), Ed Palermo (1996), John Patitucci (1996, 1998–1999, 2001, 2006), Marlena Shaw (1996), Steve Swallow (1996, 1999, 2001), Dave Douglas (1997–1998, 2001, 2003), Arkadia Jazz All-Stars (1998), Joanne Brackeen (1998), Jim Hall (1998), Dave Holland (1998, 2001–2002, 2005, 2007, 2009), David Binney (2000, 2004, 2010), John Fedchock (2000), Nnenna Freelon (2000), Donna Leonhart (2000), Danilo Perez (2000), Joachim Schoenecker (2000), Alex Sipiagin (2000–2001, 2003, 2006, 2011), Mike Gibbs (2001), Joachim Kühn (2001), Wayne Shorter (2002), Kenny Wheeler (2004), Kenny Werner (2006), Patricia Barber (2007), Monterey Quartet (2007), Adam Cruz (2010), Mike Stern (2011), Burak Bedikyan (2012), Pat Metheny (2012–2013)

Awards

Jazzpar Prize (2000); Jazz Journalists Association Tenor Saxophonist of the Year (2004, 2013)

Website

www.chrispottermusic.com (accessed 21 May 2014)

References

PRIMARY: Christopher Porter, "Shop Talk: Chris Potter," *JazzTimes* 31 (June 2001), 97 (as "Chris Potter: Shop Talk," also available at http://jazztimes.com/articles/20549-chris-potter-shop-talk [accessed 21 May 2014]) (interview); Arturo Mora, "Chris Potter: The Challenge Seeker," http://www.tomajazz.com/perfiles/chris_potter_interview.htm (2007; accessed 21 May 2014) (interview); Benjamin Franklin V, *Jazz and Blues Musicians of South Carolina: Interviews with Jabbo, Dizzy, Drink, and Others* (Columbia: University of South Carolina Press, 2008), 206–22; Nate Chinen, "A Word with Chris Potter: Sax Inspiration in a Greek Epic," *New York Times*, 6 February 2013, sec. C, pp. 1, 5 (late edition) (as "Sax Inspiration in a Greek Epic," also available at http://www.nytimes.com/2013/02/06/arts/music/q-and

-a-chris-potter-on-the-sirens.html?pagewanted=all &_r=0 [accessed 21 May 2014]) (interview); Alexandra Heeney, "An Interview with Jazz Saxophonist Chris Potter, Resident Artist at the Stanford Jazz Workshop, *Stanford Daily,* 20 August 2013, intermission sec., p. 1 (also available at http://www.stanforddaily.com/2013/08/20/an-interview-with-jazz-saxophonist-chris-potter-resident-artist-at-the-stanford-jazz-workshop/ [accessed 21 May 2014]).

SECONDARY: Bill Milkowski, "Raising the Bar," *JazzTimes* 27 (December 1997): 82–84, 86, 88 (comments by Potter); Julie Jarema, "Chris Potter's Spin Tale," *Down Beat* 66 (May 1999): 32–33 (comments by Potter); Frank Griffith, "Contemporary Traditionalists," in *Masters of the Jazz Saxophone,* ed. Tony Bacon (London: Balafon Books, 2000), 202–3; Dan Ouellette, "Which Way Up? Chris Potter Develops the Backbone to Ascend to the Marquee," *Down Beat* 73 (February 2006): 40–42 (comments by Potter); David R. Adler, "The Potter Principle," *JazzTimes* 36 (March 2006): 54–58 (comments by Potter); Ted Panken, "Part of the Pantheon," *Down Beat* 75 (February 2008): 30–32, 34–35 (comments by Potter).

Powe, Norman Ptolemey

Trombone

6 April 1917 (Cheraw, S.C.)–17 May 2003 (Cheraw, S.C.)

S.C. residence: Cheraw (1917–at least until 1935, including his time at Laurinburg Institute; by 1945–2003)

Powe received at least rudimentary instruction on the trombone at Robert Smalls School in Cheraw, where his cousin Dizzy Gillespie was also a student. The two received scholarships to Laurinburg Institute in N.C., where they enrolled in 1933, studied classical music, roomed together, and practiced together. At age seventeen he became a professional musician, touring for a few months with King Oliver; in 1937 he joined the organization of Jimmie Gunn of Charlotte, N.C. From Charlotte, he moved to N.Y.C., where he played with Doc Wheeler. After serving in the navy as Musician, Second Class, he joined the band of Louis Armstrong.

Powe's date and place of birth and full name come from his 1945 draft registration card. The 1940 census indicates that Powe then lived in Charlotte and that he had lived in Cheraw in 1935.

Leaders Recorded With

Doc Wheeler (1941–1942), Louis Armstrong (1945–1946)

References

PRIMARY: Dizzy Gillespie, with Al Fraser, *To Be, or Not . . . to Bop: Memoirs* (Garden City, N.Y.: Doubleday, 1979), 44–46 (recollections by Powe).

SECONDARY: Alyn Shipton, *Groovin' High: The Life of Dizzy Gillespie* (New York: Oxford University Press, 1999), passim.

Powell, James

French horn, tuba

Ca. 1916 (S.C.)–?

S.C. residence: Charleston (by late 1920s–at least into 1930s)

A ward of Jenkins Orphanage, Powell played in its bands in the 1930s. Later he toured with Silas Green from New Orleans, a tent show.

At estimated age fourteen Powell was enumerated for the census in Charleston on 2 April 1930. This document indicates that he was born in S.C. Bruce Bastin identifies Wilmington, N.C., as Powell's last known residence.

References

SECONDARY: John Chilton, *A Jazz Nursery: The Story of the Jenkins' Orphanage Bands of Charleston, South Carolina* (London: Bloomsbury Book Shop, 1980), 58; Bruce Bastin, "A Note on the Carolina Cotton Pickers," *Storyville* 95 (June–July 1981): 177–82.

Princeton, David

S.C. residence: Charleston (1910s)

Apparently a ward of Jenkins Orphanage, Princeton played in its bands in the 1910s, though his instrument is not known.

Princeton was probably the brother of musician Sylvester Princeton.

Princeton, Sylvester

S.C. residence: Charleston (1910s)

Apparently a ward of Jenkins Orphanage, Princeton played in its bands in the 1910s, though his instrument is not known.

Princeton was probably the brother of musician David Princeton.

Professor Clark's Brass Band

Charleston

On 26 April 1893 this eighteen-piece band performed in a parade celebrating the fiftieth anniversary of the Odd Fellows of Charleston.

Reference

SECONDARY: "Solving the Race Problem," *Indianapolis Freeman: An Illustrated Colored Newspaper,* 6 May 1893, p. 5.

Pruitt, (Patrick) Shane

Guitar, singer
26 April 1977 (Spartanburg, S.C.)–
S.C. residence: Spartanburg (1977–)

From a musical family, Pruitt began guitar lessons at age eleven. Soon after being graduated from Dorman High School (1995), he went on the road for a year and a half with Patrick Vining, with whom he recorded for the initial time. He then formed Flat Front Tire, which played throughout the Southeast for three years. In 2006 he established the Shane Pruitt Band, which continues, though he plays concurrently with Shampoo Duo, with drummer Tracy Littlejohn. He also freelances. In addition to the blues Pruitt plays gospel music and Southern rock.

Shane Pruitt, at home in Spartanburg, S.C., April 2014; permission of the photographer, Heather Pruitt

Compositions

"Blues for the Southside," "Both Feet over Water," "Done Got Over," "Earl the Squirrel," "Give It to You," "Heart of Stone," "I Love You So," "I Smell It," "It'll Be," "Mama Said Birds Pick Up the Best Fruit," "Resting Place," "Rich Man's Problem," "Sallie Mae," "Thought You Were My Friend," "T.V. Stomp," "Won't Stop," "You Know Where I'm Coming From," "Your Town"

Recordings as Leader

The Shane Pruitt Band (2007–2008), *State of Grace* (2010), *Mill Billy Blues* (2012; with Matthew Knights, Brandon Turner, and Freddie Vanderford)

Leader Recorded With

Patrick Vining (1998)

Award

Metro Magazine (Greenville, S.C.) Instrumentalist of the Year (2005)

Website

http://shanepruittband.com/ (accessed 21 May 2014)

References

PRIMARY: Dan Armonaitis, "Local Guitar Whiz Shane Pruitt on Rock Legends Cruise II, 'Mill Billy Blues' and Jadeveon Clowney's Big Hit," http://soundobservations.blogs.goupstate.com/10963/local-guitar-whiz-shane-pruitt-on-rock-legends-cruise-ii-%E2%80%9Cmill-billy-blues%E2%80%9D-and-jadeveon-clowney%E2%80%99s-monster-hit/ (4 January 2013; accessed 21 May 2014) (interview).

SECONDARY: Dan Armonaitis, "Spartanburg Guitarist Shane Pruitt to Perform on Rock Legends Cruise to the Bahamas," http://soundobservations.blogs.goupstate.com/10465/spartanburg-guitarist-shane-pruitt-to-perform-on-rock-legends-cruise-to-the-bahamas/ (18 November 2011; accessed 21 May 2014) (comments by Pruitt); "The Shane Pruitt Band: Ever-Evolving Blues and Gospel Trio to Play Southern Hops in Florence," http://www.scnow.com/entertainment/article_2d291273-879e-5a63-afbd-ac81aaaefe12.html (16 May 2012, updated 26 December 2012; accessed 21 May 2014).

Prysock, Arthur, Jr.

Singer

1 or 2 January 1924 (Spartanburg, S.C.)–21 June 1997 (outside Hamilton, Bermuda)

S.C. residence: Spartanburg (1924–probably no later than 1926)

Though Prysock probably left Spartanburg for N.C. before turning three, he returned to S.C. to visit relatives and, as he aged, help them farm. Soon after moving to Hartford, Conn., possibly in 1944, he began singing and was discovered by bandleader Buddy Johnson. His first recording with Johnson became popular: "They All Say I'm the Biggest Fool" (1944). Will Friedwald believes that, together, Prysock and Johnson "were the progenitors of . . . the 'soul ballad'" (376). Prysock left Johnson in 1952 to become a single, which he remained for the rest of his career. He was probably most heard by television audiences who viewed Löwenbräu Beer commercials beginning ca. 1978. On them the unidentified Prysock sang "Here's to Good Friends." They became so well known that his next album included a complete performance of the song and was titled *Here's to Good Friends.* He sang in the tradition of baritone virility popularized by Billy Eckstine. The mellifluousness of his voice led to his recording recitations of Ed Bruce's "A Working Man's Prayer" (1967) and poems from Walter Benton's *This Is My Beloved* (1968). He sings on the sound tracks of *The Split* and *The Young Runaways* (both 1968); his recordings of "Teach Me Tonight" (from the album *A Rockin' Good Way*) and "This Guy's in Love with You" (from *This Guy's in Love with You*) received Grammy nominations. During his last years he lived in Bermuda.

Prysock was the brother of saxophonist Wilburt "Red" Prysock, who was not a South Carolinian. Almost all sources consulted identify Arthur Prysock's birth date as 2 January 1929. When he was enumerated for the census in Morehead, Guilford County, N.C., on 9 April 1930, his age was estimated as five. Information about the family in this census is unreliable because it specifies S.C. as Wilburt Prysock's birthplace; he was born in Guilford County, N.C., on 2 February 1926. The date of Wilburt's birth suggests that the Prysocks resided in N.C. before then. When completing his draft registration card in 1942 Arthur Prysock entered his birth date as 2 January 1924 and his age as eighteen; he also indicated that he was born in Spartanburg, that he lived in Pomona, Guilford County, N.C., and that he worked for the Pomona Terra Cotta Company, as did his father. The Social Security Death Index records that the singer was born on 1 January 1924 and died on 21 June 1997. Though the Registry General in Hamilton, Bermuda, officially confirms this death date, some sources state that the singer died on 7 June 1997. The second "Death Notices" notes that Prysock's middle name was William and that he was to be buried in Long Island, N.Y. His middle name has not been confirmed; his grave has not been located. Prysock's draft registration card includes a space for providing a middle name; here Prysock drew a line, probably to indicate that he has none.

Compositions

"Bye Bye Baby," "Every Morning Baby," "My Sweet Woman," "Only for You," "There Goes the Mailman"

Recordings as Leader

"All of Me" (1946), "I'll Always Be in Love with You" (1946), "Jelly, Jelly" (1946), "Makin' a Fool Out of Me" (1946), *Strictly Sentimental* (1951), "I Cover the Waterfront" (1952), "I'm a Sentimental Fool" (1952), "School of Love" (1952), "Jean" (1953), "My Mood" (1953), "Nobody Cares" (1953), "If You Don't, Somebody Will" (1954), "I Have Lived" (1954), "I'll Never Let You Cry" (1954), "I'm in Heaven Tonight" (1954), "Morning, Noon and Night" (1954), "Show Me How to Mambo" (1954), "Take Care of Yourself" (1954), "This I Know" (1954), "Come Home" (1955), "Woke Up This Morning" (1955), "Bye Bye Baby" (ca. 1956), "O-Ho-O-Yeh, What the Heck" (ca. 1956), "There Goes the Mailman" (ca. 1956), "Too Long I've Waited" (ca. 1956), "I Just Want to Make Love to You" (ca. 1958), "All or Nothing at All" (1959), "For Your Love" (1959), "Let There Be Love" (1959), *Arthur Prysock Sings Only for You* (1961), *Coast to Coast* (1962), *A Portrait of Arthur Prysock* (1963), *Intimately Yours* (1964–1965), *Arthur Prysock–Count Basie* (1965), *Art and Soul* (1966), *Love Me* (1967), *To Love or Not to Love* (1967–1968), *Funny Thing* (1968), *I Must Be Doing Something Right* (1968), *This Is My Beloved* (1968), *The Country Side of Arthur Prysock* (1969), *Fly My Love* (1969), *The*

Lord Is My Shepherd (1969), *Where the Soul Trees Grow* (1969), *Unforgettable* (1970), *Arthur Prysock Does It Again!* (ca. 1977), *Here's to Good Friends* (ca. 1978), *A Rockin' Good Way* (1985), *This Guy's in Love with You* (1986), *Today's Love Songs, Tomorrow's Blues* (1987–1988)

Leaders Recorded With

Buddy Johnson (1944–1945, 1947, 1949–1952), Airmen of Note (1968)

Awards

Order of the Palmetto (1983); Rhythm & Blues Foundation Pioneer Award (1995); Spartanburg Music Trail Marker (2011)

References

PRIMARY: Benjamin Franklin V, *Jazz and Blues Musicians of South Carolina: Interviews with Jabbo, Dizzy, Drink, and Others* (Columbia: University of South Carolina Press, 2008), 40–46.

SECONDARY: "Death Notices," *Royal Gazette* (Hamilton, Bermuda), 23 June 1997, p. 23; "Death Notices," *Royal Gazette* (Hamilton, Bermuda), 24 June 1997, p. 25; Stephen Holden, "Arthur Prysock, 68, Rhythm-and-Blues Singer," *New York Times*, 25 June 1997, sec. D, p. 20 (obituary); "Memorial Service for Arthur Prysock," *Bermuda Sun* (Hamilton, Bermuda), 27 June 1997, p. 2; Spencer Leigh, "Arthur Prysock," *Independent* (London), 23 August 1997, p. 16 (obituary); Will Friedwald, *A Biographical Guide to the Great Jazz and Pop Singers* (New York: Pantheon, 2010), 375–79.

Quattlebaum, Doug (Elijah Douglas)

Guitar, singer

Possibly 22 January 1929 (possibly Mott Township, Florence County, S.C.)–1 March 1996 (Philadelphia, Pa.)

S.C. residence: Mott Township, Florence County (probably 1929–ca. 1940)

Quattlebaum sang in a family quartet by age seven and became proficient on guitar shortly after moving to Philadelphia ca. 1940. He toured with gospel groups from the 1940s off and on into the 1960s. These groups included the Haze Quartet of Lake City, S.C., the Charity Gospel Singers, the Bells of Joy, the Harlem Gospel Singers, the Ward Singers, and the Musicalaires. After being discovered by Pete Welding in 1961 he performed both gospel music and blues in various clubs. Peter Lowry characterizes his guitar style as "a staccato, slashing chording with a few single-string runs of short duration; it's a fierce, declamatory sound that blends well with his voice" (11). Quattlebaum reportedly worked as a minister for an undetermined period.

Quattlebaum's birth date is usually recorded as 22 January 1927, though the musician's age was estimated as one year, three months when Quattlebaum was enumerated for the census on 17 April 1930 in Mott Township, Florence County, S.C. His full name and precise dates of birth and death come from the Social Security Death Index. In time his mother married a brother of bluesman Arthur "Big Boy" Crudup. Quattlebaum sings Crudup's "Mama Don't Allow Me" on *Softee Man Blues*. The title of this album derives from the musician's occupation at the time: driver of an ice cream truck in Philadelphia. He attempted to attract customers by playing the guitar at his various stops, as the photograph on the record sleeve documents. Paul Sheatsley announces the forthcoming British 77 Records release of Quattlebaum's recording of Crudup's "Mean Old Frisco Blues," though it apparently remains unissued.

Compositions

"Baby I'm Back," "Come Back Blues," "Don't Be Funny, Baby!," "Jailhouse Blues," "Lizzie Lou," "Love My Baby," "Quattlebaum's Boogie," "Sweet Little Woman," "Worried Mind Blues" (also titled "Worried Life Blues")

Recordings as Leader

"Don't Be Funny, Baby!" (1953; two versions), "Foolin' Me" (1953), "Lizzie Lou" (1953), *If You've Ever Been Mistreated* (1961), *Softee Man Blues* (1961), "Baby I'm Back" (late 1960s), "Jailhouse Blues" (late 1960s)

Leader Recorded With

Presumably the Bells of Joy (ca. 1952)

References

SECONDARY: Paul Sheatsley, "Quattlebaum," *Record Research: The Magazine of Record Statistics and Information* 42 (March–April 1962): 12; Peter Lowry,

"Philadelphia Sound," *Blues Unlimited* 91 (May 1972): 11, 30; Bruce Bastin, *Red River Blues: The Blues Tradition in the Southeast* (Urbana: University of Illinois Press, 1986), 319–20; Chris Smith, "'I'm Your Ice-Cream Man': Doug Quattlebaum," *Blues and Rhythm: The Gospel Truth* 39 (1988): 14.

R

Ramsey, Lewis

Alto horn, mellophone
2 April 1914 (Charleston, S.C.)-?
S.C. residence: Charleston (1914-at least into early 1930s)

A ward of Jenkins Orphanage, Ramsey played in its bands in the late 1920s and early 1930s and performed with one of them in England in 1929.

The passenger list of the *Majestic,* which transported the orphanage band from Plymouth, England, to N.Y.C. in June 1929, records Ramsey's birth date and place.

References

SECONDARY: John Chilton, *A Jazz Nursery: The Story of the Jenkins' Orphanage Bands of Charleston, South Carolina* (London: Bloomsbury Book Shop, 1980), 58; Howard Rye, "Visiting Fireboys: The Jenkins' Orphanage Bands in Britain," *Storyville* 130 (1987): 137–43.

Reddick, Billy

Trumpet
S.C. residence: Charleston (probably 1920s)

A ward of Jenkins Orphanage, Reddick played in its bands, probably in the 1920s.

Reddick was the brother of trombonist James Reddick. Billy Reddick's given name is probably William; the surname is possibly spelled Riddick.

Reddick, James ("Jabbo")

Trombone
S.C. residence: Charleston (at least in 1920s)

A ward of Jenkins Orphanage, Reddick played in its bands. On tour with one of them in Fla. ca. 1921, he and Cladys Smith ran away and joined a band led by Eagle Eye Shields. The institution located them and returned them to Charleston. In time Reddick's nickname, Jabbo, became Smith's.

Reddick was the brother of trumpeter Billy Reddick. John Chilton spells the surname Riddick; Balliett and Deffaa, Reddick.

References

SECONDARY: John Chilton, *A Jazz Nursery: The Story of the Jenkins' Orphanage Bands of Charleston, South Carolina* (London: Bloomsbury Book Shop, 1980), 27, 58; Whitney Balliett, *Jelly Roll, Jabbo, and Fats: 19 Portraits in Jazz* (New York: Oxford University Press, 1983), 69 (reprinted in Balliett's *American Musicians: Fifty-Six Portraits in Jazz* [New York: Oxford University Press, 1986], 64); Jabbo Smith, untitled comments in notes to Smith's *Hidden Treasure,* vol. 2 (mid-1980s; Jazz Art Productions, unnumbered); Chip Deffaa, *Voices of the Jazz Age: Profiles of Eight Vintage Jazzmen* (Urbana: University of Illinois Press, 1990), 191, 194.

Reeder, Eskew

See Esquerita

Rennicks, Marion

Alto horn
3 June 1902 (Greenville, S.C.)-?
S.C. residences: Greenville (1902-no later than early 1910s), Charleston (at least in 1910s)

A ward of Jenkins Orphanage, Rennicks played in its bands in the 1910s, including the one that performed in England in 1914.

Rennicks's date and place of birth come from the passenger list of the *St. Louis,* which transported the orphanage band from Liverpool to N.Y.C. in September 1914. On the list for the *Campania,* which took the group to England in May, Rennicks's surname is spelled Pennicks.

Reference

SECONDARY: Howard Rye, "Visiting Fireboys: The Jenkins' Orphanage Bands in Britain," *Storyville* 130 (1987): 137–43.

Rhoad, Toubo (Herbert Lee)

Singer

1 October 1944 (in or near Bamberg, S.C.)–8 December 1988 (Sacramento, Calif.)

S.C. residence: in or near Bamberg (1944–probably late 1950s)

Rhoad reportedly sang with the Friendship Gospel Singers before helping found the Parisians in 1962. Five years later he and four others formed the Persuasions. After recording for Catamount Records this a cappella group was discovered by Frank Zappa, who arranged for it to record for Straight Records. Thereafter the singers toured regularly and recorded frequently for various companies; they sing on the sound track of *E.T. the Extra-Terrestrial* (1982). They disbanded for a few years in the 1980s, though they reactivated shortly before Rhoad's death and performed on the oldies circuit. The group is known for its eclectic repertoire. Rhoad's body was cremated.

Rhoad's birth and death dates, death place, and middle name come from California, Death Index, 1940–1997. Some sources indicate that the singer died in Davis, Calif. According to his obituary in the *New York Times,* Rhoad moved to Brooklyn, N.Y., as a teenager.

Leaders Recorded With

Parisians (1962), Persuasions (1969, ca. 1970–1974, ca. 1976-ca. 1977, ca. 1979, ca. 1984, 1988), Les McCann (1972; this and all subsequent recordings with the Persuasions), Paul Pena (1973), Don McLean (ca. 1974), Phoebe Snow (ca. 1974), Stevie Wonder (ca. 1974), Joni Mitchell (1979)

References

SECONDARY: Jim Dulzo, "The Persuasions: We're Gonna Sing It Acapella!," *Ann Arbor (Mich.) Sun,* 6 September 1974, p. 11; "Herbert (Toubo) Rhoad, Singer, 44," *New York Times,* 15 December 1988, sec. D, p. 26 (obituary); Rip Rense, "Persuasions' Reunion Goes on Despite Tragedy," *Los Angeles Times,* 15 December 1988, sec. H, p. 5; Rip Rense, "The Persuasions Story," http://thepersuasionslive.com/persstory.htm (2011; accessed 21 May 2014).

Rice, Daryle

See Ryce, Daryle LaMaría

Richardson, C. C. (Clarence Clifford; "Peg")

Guitar, singer, dancer

18 December 1918 (Sumter, S.C.)–30 January 1984 (Kanawah City, W.Va.)

S.C. residence: Sumter (1918–probably 1932)

Despite losing a foot and injuring the other as a result of falling from a train at age nine, Richardson worked, beginning in 1932, as a jitterbug dancer with Silas Green from New Orleans, a tent show; soon he became a tap dancer, modeling his style on that of Peg Leg Bates. Early the next decade he was with Blake's Carnival; later in the 1940s he danced with jazz and blues groups, including the band of Benny Carter. As a dancer he was billed as Peg Richardson. After years on the road, in 1962 he settled in Charleston, W.Va., where he worked for the post office. Though as a youth Richardson learned to play the guitar from a grandfather and uncle (and sang in the Brown Chapel U.M.E. Church in Sumter), he more or less abandoned the instrument until 1969 or 1970, when he not only resumed playing but began recording with it.

Compositions

"C. C.'s Blues," "C. C. Stomp," "Don't Do It"

Recordings as Leader

"C. C.'s Blues" (1970), "Hey Night" (1970), "Don't Do It" (ca. 1972), "What More Can Jesus Do" (ca. 1972), "I Thought I Heard My Backdoor Slam" (ca. 1973), "My Love Is Gone" (ca. 1973), "Just Like a Woman, She'll Do It All the Time" (1970s), "Louise, the Sweetest Gal I Know" (1970s), "I'm Gonna Love You till I Die" (1975), "Same Old Train" (1975), *I Ain't Got Nothing but the Blues* (ca. 1975, ca. 1979)

References

PRIMARY: Roger Meeden, "'Ain't Nothin' but the Blues': C. C. Richardson Interview," *Whiskey, Women, and . . .* 4 (February 1973): 4–6.

SECONDARY: Ray Brack, "City Blues Artist C. C. Richardson Getting Attention from around Globe," *Charleston (W.Va.) Gazette,* 20 January 1973, sec. A, p. 8; Norman Darwen, "C. C. Richardson," *Living Blues* 59 (Spring 1984): 35 (obituary).

Richardson, Joe ("Deacon," "Fender 'Guitar' Slim," "Ground Hog," "Tender Slim")

Guitar, singer

9 February of either 1938 or 1940 (Lykesland, Richland County, S.C.)–

S.C. residences: Lykesland, Richland County (1938 or 1940–1957), Pineville (ca. 1982–)

After being graduated from Hopkins High School in 1957, Richardson moved to N.J. to pursue a career in music; there he played at house parties. The next year he settled in N.Y.C., where he recorded for the initial time (with the Isley Brothers) and became associated with the Chantels; with this group he toured for a month with Dick Clark's Caravan of Stars. Also on the tour was Little Anthony and the Imperials, with whom Richardson soon began playing. Though he continued performing with groups during the 1960s, that decade he also recorded all the music released under his name, or pseudonyms, other than an album probably recorded in 1970 for Sylvia Robinson's Turbo Records and a CD of religious music decades later. When he began working in the computer industry in the late 1960s, he gradually withdrew from the music scene, though he performed regularly in church, which remained his musical venue upon returning to S.C. in the early 1980s.

Joe Richardson, N.Y.C., 1962; permission of Joe Richardson

When enumerated for the census on 12 April 1940 as Joe J. Richardson, the child's age was estimated as two years. Yet when discussing his life during a telephone conversation on 20 July 2013, Richardson insisted that he was born on 9 February 1940 as Joe Richardson, Jr., with no middle name.

Compositions

"American Dollar," "Atomic Blues," "Blues Ain't Nothin' but a Good Woman on Your Mind," "Born Funky," "Cheatin' Love Is Sweeter," "Checkin' Up on My Baby," "Don't Cut Out on Me," "Funky Robot," "Going Back Home," "Groundhog Mood," "Hip Huggin' Mini," "I Got to Get Enough," "Juanita Blue," "Love True Love," "Mississippi Love Boy," "Nobody's Woman," "P's and Q's," "Right On with the Right On," "Sanora Sanora," "Sing and Praise God [*sic*] Name," "Someone Has Taken Your Place," "Sticking Because She's Stuck," "To the Bone," "The Watchman," "We're Still on This Mission and Praising God," "Wig Wearing Mama," "Without You," "You Won't Get Away"

Recordings as Leader (These Are Release Dates, Not Necessarily Recording Dates)

"Atomic Blues" (1960; as Fender "Guitar" Slim), "Hey Joe" (1960; as Tender Slim), "Teenage Hayride" (1960; as Tender Slim), "Tender Rock" (1960; as Fender "Guitar" Slim), "Hip Huggin' Mini" (1968; as Tender Joe Richardson), "I Ain't Going for That" (1968; as Tender Joe Richardson), *Got to Get Enough* (probably 1970; as Ground Hog), *We're Still on This Mission Praising God* (2007; as Deacon Richardson)

Leaders Recorded With

Isley Brothers (1959), Dave "Baby" Cortez (ca. 1960, 1962–1964, 1972), Coasters (1961), King Curtis (1962), Shirelles (1967), Don Covay (1969)

Richardson, John

Trombone, tuba

S.C. residence: Charleston (1919–no later than 1929)

A ward of Jenkins Orphanage beginning in 1919, Richardson played in its bands in the 1920s. Around 1929 he moved to N.Y.C., where he led his own band.

Reference

SECONDARY: John Chilton, *A Jazz Nursery: The Story of the Jenkins' Orphanage Bands of Charleston, South Carolina* (London: Bloomsbury Book Shop, 1980), 58.

Richbourg, John D. ("John R.")

Broadcaster, producer, manager, record company owner, singer/speaker

20 August 1910 (in or near Manning, S.C.)–15 February 1986 (Nashville, Tenn.)

S.C. residences: in or near Manning (1910–no later than 1928), Charleston (1941–1942)

Reared in or near Manning, by 1928 Richbourg lived in Chattanooga, Tenn., where he performed in plays, as he also did (and in radio dramas) subsequently for a dozen years in N.Y.C. After announcing on WTMA in Charleston (1941–1942), he worked for WLAC, Nashville, where he broadcast as John R. until 1973, other than when serving in the navy (1944–1946). In his early years at WLAC he played mainly blues. In the 1950s he began featuring rhythm and blues, music that many listeners, black and white, wanted to hear. As a result—and because his late-night show could be heard throughout much of the United States, as well as into Canada and the West Indies—he became popular as the purveyor of vital music that was generally unavailable elsewhere on radio. The nature of this music, the quality of his voice, and his occasional use of the black vernacular caused many listeners incorrectly to think him black. He supervised recordings for Sound Stage 7 (a subsidiary of Monument Records) and owned the record companies Luna, Rich, Seventy-Seven, and Sound Plus. He operated J. R. Enterprises, managed the singer Joe Simon, taught at the Tennessee School of Broadcasting, and mentored numerous aspiring disc jockeys, including Robert Weston Smith, later known as Wolfman Jack. Late in life Richbourg sold cassette tapes of some of his programs broadcast in the 1960s and 1970s. On 26 March 1985 at the Grand Ole Opry Hall in Nashville, Hank Ballard, James Brown, Ruth Brown, B. B. King, and other notables performed at a concert honoring him.

Jim O'Neal's claim in "John R." that Richbourg was born in Davis Station, S.C., which is near Manning, has not been substantiated. A Richbourg commercial for Ernie's Record Mart is on *Night Train to Nashville: Music City Rhythm and Blues, 1945–1970;* one for Swinging Soul Medallion is on the second volume of this collection.

Recordings as Leader (All 1965; as John R.)

"Keep On Scratching," "Mo Jo Blues," "Night Train," "Stag o'Lee"

Award

Carolina Beach Music Awards Hall of Fame (1995)

References

PRIMARY: Daddy Cool [Dave Booth], "Hey John R.—Whatcha Gonna Do?," *Juke Blues* 7 (Winter 1986): 19–21 (interview).

SECONDARY: "TV and Movie Screen's Personality of the Month: John Richbourg/WLAC/Nashville, Tenn.," *TV and Movie Screen* 19 (April 1972): 47 (comments by Richbourg); Robert K. Oermann, "R&B Greats Pay Tribute to Legendary Deejay John R.," *Nashville Tennessean,* 27 March 1985, sec. D, p. 1; Clarke Canfield, "John R. Eulogized as Music Influence, Friend," *Nashville Banner,* 18 February 1986, sec. A, pp. 1, 4; "John R., a Legendary Disc Jockey," *Nashville Banner,* 18 February 1986, sec. A, p. 6 (obituary); Jim O'Neal, "John R.," *Living Blues* 70 (1986): 14–15 (obituary); Wes Smith, *The Pied Pipers of Rock 'n' Roll: Radio Deejays of the 50s and 60s* (Marietta, Ga.: Longstreet Press, 1989), passim (see especially 106–16); John Broven, *Record Makers and Breakers: Voices of the Independent Rock 'n' Roll Pioneers* (Urbana: University of Illinois Press, 2009), passim (see especially 99–101, 112–14); Dale R. Patterson, "The Daddy of Rhythm and Blues: John R.," http://rockradioscrapbook.ca/johnr1.html (undated; accessed 21 May 2014).

Riddick, Billy

See Reddick, Billy

Riddick, James

See Reddick, James

Riggins, Clyde

Saxophone

S.C. residence: Charleston (at least early 1930s)

Apparently a ward of Jenkins Orphanage, Riggins played in its bands in the early 1930s.

Rivers, Arthur

Singer

Probably S.C.

S.C. residence: Orangeburg (probably at least early-to-mid-1910s)

Rivers sang in and toured with the Claflin University Quintet, at least in 1913.

Rivers, Joe

Singer

1936 or 1937 (Charleston, S.C.)–

S.C. residence: Charleston (1936 or 1937–no later than 1956)

Rivers was discovered by musician Rex Garvin, who paired him with Johnnie Richardson, daughter of Garvin's associate Zelma Sanders, owner of J&S Records. As Johnnie and Joe the duo had several doo-wop/rhythm and blues successes with J&S, "Over the Mountain, across the Sea" paramount among them; it reached the top ten on both the rhythm-and-blues and pop charts. Dick Clark played it on *American Bandstand*. After disbanding in the mid-1960s Rivers and Richardson reunited to record a few singles and an album and to perform on the oldies circuit.

Estimated age three, Rivers was enumerated for the census in Charleston on 15 April 1930. Some sources state that Rivers and Johnnie Richardson established Dice Records. With the assistance of her mother, Richardson created it as a subsidiary of J&S Records in 1958.

Composition

"Why Do You Hurt Me So?"

Recordings as Leader (All by Johnnie and Joe, with Johnnie Richardson; These Are Release Dates, Not Necessarily Recording Dates)

I'll Be Spinning: The J&S Recordings (1956–1960, 1962–1963, 1965, 1969–1970), "Trust in Me" (1958), "I Adore You" (1960), "I Want You Here Beside Me" (1960), "Why Do You Hurt Me So?" (1960), "Your Love" (1960), "You Said It, and Don't Forget It" (1960), "Won't You Come Back to Me" (1962), "The Devil Said No, Gone with Your Bad Self" (1963), "Shortening Bread" (1965), "False Love Has Got to Go" (1970), *Kingdom of Love* (1982)

Leader Recorded With

Climbers (released 1957)

References

SECONDARY: Aaron Fuchs, "Johnnie and Joe: The J&S Records Story," *Goldmine* 81 (February 1983): 10–12 (this issue is also designated volume 9, number 2) (includes discography); Don Miller, "Johnnie and Joe," *Keystone Record Collectors' Recorder* 1 (Winter 1988): 7–8 (includes discography); J. C. Marion, "Zell Sanders and J&S Records," http://home.earthlink.net/~v1tiger/jands.html (2003; accessed 21 May 2014); Mick Patrick, notes to Johnnie and Joe's *I'll Be Spinning: The J&S Recordings* (2006; Ace CD CHD 1138) (includes discography); J. C. Marion, "The Great R&B Duos, Part Two," http://home.earthlink.net/~jaymar41/Great_Duos_part_Two.html (undated; accessed 21 May 2014).

Rivers, Oscar, Jr.

Saxophone, piano

11 August 1940 (Charleston, S.C.)–

S.C. residences: Charleston (1940–1957, 1979–), Orangeburg (1957–1961)

After being graduated from Burke High School in Charleston (1957), Rivers matriculated at what is now South Carolina State University, where he played in its bands. Upon completing his degree (1961), he taught in the Chicago public school system. While in Chicago he performed at the Regal Theater and with such instrumentalists as Gene

Oscar Rivers; permission of George Kenny

Ammons and Sonny Stitt at McKie's Lounge. Also during this period he received a master's degree from Roosevelt University (1974). In 1979 he returned to Charleston, where he taught, as he also did on James Island; concurrent with his teaching he performed locally, as he continues doing. He studied in Morelos, Mexico, in 1987.

Leader Recorded With

Charleston Jazz Initiative Legends Band (2010)

References

SECONDARY: Jack McCray, *Charleston Jazz* (Charleston, S.C.: Arcadia Publishing, 2007), 72, 81; Stratton Lawrence, "Oscar Rivers Trio Chills Out at the Swamp Fox: Charleston's Charlie Parker," *Charleston (S.C.) City Paper,* http://www.charlestoncitypaper.com/charleston/oscar-rivers-trio-chills-out-at-the-swamp-fox/Content?oid=3415236 (1 June 2011; accessed 21 May 2014).

Robinson, Bobby (Morgan Clyde)

Composer, producer, record company owner, record store owner

16 April 1917 (near Union, S.C.)–7 January 2011 (New York, N.Y.)

S.C. residence: near Union (1917–1937)

After serving in the army during World War II, in 1946 Robinson opened a record store, Bobby's Records, in Harlem on 125th St., near the Apollo Theater, though in the early 1990s he moved it to Frederick Douglass Blvd., at 125th St. Its success permitted him and his brother Danny to establish, in 1951, the first of his several record companies, Robin; most folded by 1957, though he soon established new ones. As owner of these labels he became a major producer of rhythm-and-blues, soul, and hip-hop recordings by such performers as Buster Brown ("Fannie Mae"), Dave "Baby" Cortez ("The Happy Organ"), King Curtis ("Soul Twist"), Lee Dorsey ("Ya Ya"), Grandmaster Flash ("Superappin'"), Wilbert Harrison ("Kansas City"), Gladys Knight ("Every Beat of My Heart"), the Shirelles ("Dedicated to the One I Love"), and Packman ("I'm the Packman"). He also produced recordings by bluesmen Arthur "Big Boy" Crudup, Champion Jack Dupree, and Elmore James. Robinson is credited with composing or co-composing well over three hundred tunes, though his involvement with some of them has been called into question, such as "Warm and Tender Love," possibly written by Joe Dean Haywood. Robinson is buried in the Woodson Chapel Baptist Church Cemetery, Union.

Compositions

"All Systems Go," "April in Georgia," "Bad Luck," "Bobby's Boogie," "Body Rock," "Coffee for Mama," "Country Rock and Rap," "Did You Hear What I Say?," "Do You Like That Funky Beat," "Fannie Mae," "Funk Box Party," "Going Back to My Home Town," "Hard Grind," "Here We Go," "Hippy Dippy Do," "Honey Sweet," "Hully Gully Rock," "I Done Somebody Wrong," "I'm Coming Home," "I'm the Packman," "It Takes the Dark to Make You See the Light," "I Wanna Know," "I Would If I Could," "Jack, That Cat Was Clean," "Let Me Take You Out," "Lonesome Drag," "Make the Girl Love Me," "Mother Mojo," "Need Your Lovin'," "Never Turn Back," "Our Love," "Paid the Cost," "Pour the Corn," "Put the Boogie in Your Body," "Rockin' at Midnight," "Rollin' and Tumblin'," "Say It Was a Dream," "Seven Day Fool," "Shame," "Sinner Man's Prayer," "Strong Feeling," "Super Rappin' Theme," "Talk to Me Baby," "They Tried," "Until I Die," "Walking in a Trance," "What Will Become of Me," "With Your Funny Lookin' Self," "Ya Ya," "You Got Me Up Tight"

Film

That Rhythm, Those Blues (1988)

Award

Blues Foundation's Blues Hall of Fame (2006)

References

PRIMARY: Art Turco and Sal Salzano, "Interview: Bobby Robinson," *Record Exchanger* 10 (1972): 4–6, 8–10; Art Turco, "Interview: Bobby Robinson," *Record Exchanger* 11 (1972): 4–6, 8, 10–11; Art Turco, "Interview: Bobby Robinson," *Record Exchanger* 12 (1973): 4, 6–7, 10–11; "Comments from Bobby Robinson," in *The Fire/Fury Records Story,* ed. Diana Reid Haig (N.p.: Capricorn Records, 1993), 6–11.

SECONDARY: John Morthland, "The Fire/Fury Story," in *The Fire/Fury Records Story,* ed. Diana Reid Haig (N.p.: Capricorn Records, 1993), 12–15; Red Kelly, "Grand Master Flash and the Furious Five—Super Rappin' Theme (Enjoy 6009)," http://redkelly.blogspot.com/2007/01/grand-master-flash-and-furious-five.html (2007; accessed 21 May 2014); Timothy Williams, "In Harlem, 2 Record Stores Go the Way of the Vinyl," *New York Times,* 21 January 2008, sec. B, pp. 1, 4; John Broven, *Record Makers and Breakers: Voices of the Independent*

Rock 'n' Roll Pioneers (Urbana: University of Illinois Press, 2009), passim (see especially 341–52) (comments by Robinson); "Morgan Clyde 'Bobby' Robinson," *Union (S.C.) Daily Times,* 11 January 2011, p. 2 (obituary); Douglas Martin, "Bobby Robinson, Harlem Music Impresario," *New York Times,* 12 January 2011, sec. A, p. 17 (obituary); Red Kelly, "The Update Project: Case One—Joe Haywood," http://soul detective.blogspot.com/2012/06/update-project-case-one-joe-haywood.html (2012; accessed 21 May 2014); Larry Benicewicz, "Remembering Bobby Robinson (1917–2011)," http://www.bluesworld.com/bobby robinson.html (undated; accessed 21 May 2014).

Robinson, Danny (Lawrence or Laurence Dwain)

Record company owner, record store owner

23 June 1929 (probably Bogansville Township, Union County, S.C.)–17 April 1996 (New York, N.Y.)

S.C. residence: Union County, S.C. (1929–ca. 1950)

Around 1950 Robinson moved to N.Y.C., where he entered the record business with his brother Bobby. Together they established Robin Records (later, Red Robin), Everlast Records, and Enjoy Records. Mid-decade, Danny alone created Holiday Records, which had a local hit with "Castle in the Sky," by the Bop-Chords. His next venture, in the late 1950s, was Vest Records. His labels generally released doo-wop/rhythm and blues, though they sometimes issued music by such bluesmen as Champion Jack Dupree, Elmore James, Brownie McGhee, and Sonny Terry. He also operated a record store.

Robinson's birth and death dates come from the Social Security Death Index. John Broven provides Robinson's middle name in *Record Makers and Breakers: Voices of the Independent Rock 'n' Roll Pioneers* (Urbana: University of Illinois Press, 2009), 502.

References

SECONDARY: Art Turco and Sal Salzano, "Interview: Bobby Robinson," *Record Exchanger* 10 (1972): 8; Art Turco, "Interview: Bobby Robinson," *Record Exchanger* 12 (1973): 7, 10; John Morthland, "The Fire/Fury Story," in *The Fire/Fury Records Story,* ed. Diana Reid Haig (N.p.: Capricorn Records, 1993), 12; Todd Baptista, "Remembering the Bop Chords," *Goldmine* 798 (April 2011): 94–97 (this issue is also designated volume 37, number 4) (also available as "Harlem's Bop Chords Built Their Own 'Castle in the Sky'" at http://www.goldminemag.com/article/harlems-bop-chords-built-their-own-castle-in-the-sky [accessed 21 May 2014]).

Robinson, George

Trombone

S.C. residences: Charleston (by late 1920s–probably at least into mid-1930s), Dillon (undetermined dates)

Apparently a ward of Jenkins Orphanage, Robinson played in its bands in the late 1920s and early 1930s.

Robinson was the brother of trombonist William "Geechie" Robinson. Bruce Bastin records Dillon as Robinson's last known address.

References

SECONDARY: John Chilton, *A Jazz Nursery: The Story of the Jenkins' Orphanage Bands of Charleston, South Carolina* (London: Bloomsbury Book Shop, 1980), 58; Bruce Bastin, "A Note on the Carolina Cotton Pickers," *Storyville* 95 (June–July 1981): 177–82.

Robinson, T. J. (Timothy James)

Trombone

12 September 1988 (Charleston, S.C.)–

S.C. residence: Charleston (1988–2006)

Robinson, who began playing the trombone at age eight, performed with the S.C. All-State Jazz Ensemble (2003–2004) before being graduated from the Charleston County School of the Arts

T. J. Robinson; permission of T. J. Robinson

(2006). While enrolled at the Manhattan School of Music, which awarded him a degree in 2010, he also studied at the Royal College of Music in London (2009). A freelancer who plays many styles of music, he toured with the ghost band of Artie Shaw and is a regular member of the PitchBlak Brass Band, headquartered in Brooklyn, N.Y.

Compositions

"All to the Ill (Fly)," "It's All Good," "Sunday's Best," "Super Saiyan Seven," "Ulysses," "Wine Dat Gyal"

Leaders Recorded With

Manhattan School of Music Afro-Cuban Jazz Orchestra (2008), Charleston Jazz Initiative Legends Band (2010), PitchBlak Brass Band (2011–2012)

Films

The Notebook (2004), *Nine* (2009)

Robinson, William ("Geechie")

Trombone

Ca. 1913 (N.C.)–?

S.C. residence: Charleston (by late 1920s–probably mid-1930s)

A ward of Jenkins Orphanage, Robinson played in its bands in the late 1920s and early 1930s. After leaving the institution no later than the mid-1930s, he became a professional musician. He played in Tex. with Don Albert, as well as Boots and His Buddies, led by drummer Boots Douglas. Later he performed with such bands as Fletcher Henderson's (that included Edmund Gregory, later known as Sahib Shihab) and Lionel Hampton's (that included Charles Mingus).

Robinson was the brother of trombonist George Robinson. When Robinson was enumerated for the census at the orphanage on 2 April 1930, his birthplace was identified as N.C. and his age was estimated as seventeen. On most of his recordings he is identified as James Robinson; on some, as Geechie Robinson. Because he was enumerated for the 1930 census as William, presumably his full name is William James Robinson.

Leaders Recorded With

Don Albert (1936), Fletcher Henderson (1945), Dinah Washington (1946), Gerald Wilson (1946), Lionel Hampton (1947)

Reference

SECONDARY: John Chilton, *A Jazz Nursery: The Story of the Jenkins' Orphanage Bands of Charleston, South Carolina* (London: Bloomsbury Book Shop, 1980), 58.

Rodney, Linda Sullivan ("Chocolate Thunder")

Singer

5 August 1956 (Simpsonville, S.C.)–30 June 2014 (Simpsonville, S.C.)

S.C. residences: Simpsonville (1956–1981), Greenville (1981–2014)

As a youth Rodney sang in church. In time she discovered blues and soul music and was influenced mostly by Aretha Franklin. After turning professional in 1999 she performed in clubs and at music festivals. She sang in Europe as well as in Canada, including at the 2009 Montreal Jazz Festival. Rodney is buried in M. J. "Dolly" Cooper Veterans Cemetery, Anderson, S.C.

Before marrying, the singer adopted the middle name Jean to distinguish herself from other Linda Sullivans in the S.C. upstate area.

Compositions

"Ain't Gonna Cry," "Are You Sweet or Not?," "Baby, Let's Dance," "Baby, Let's Play the Blues," "Barkin' up the Wrong Tree," "Beggin' Blues," "Blues Don't Come Knockin'," "Bring It On," "Bring My Baby Back," "Carolina Blue," "Caught in My Net," "The Cost of Lovin' You," "Cowboy Heaven," "Ever New," "555-Help," "Get This Monkey off My Back," "Got My Act Together," "Hey, You There," "I Look in the Mirror," "It's All Good," "Just Gotta Tell Ya," "Love Caused It," "Love Sneakin' up on Me," "Love Thang," "Mama, He Left Me," "Mama Was a Pistol," "My Blackberry Patch," "My Georgia Pine," "My Mule," "The Only Male for Me," "Other Side of Memphis," "Power of a Lady," "Round and Round," "Run, Run, Run," "Russell City," "Somebody's Been ah Listenin'," "Strut My Stuff," "Twice Happy," "When a Man Says I Do," "You're Gonna Get Me in Trouble," "Your Lil' Red Wagon"

Recordings as Leader

Linda Sullivan Rodney aka Chocolate Thunder, 1956–2014 (2000 and unknown later dates; privately issued), *Live at the Vintage Blues Club* (2000; privately issued), *Barkin' up the Wrong Tree!*

(2002), *Ear Candy* (2009), *Stone Cold Blues Satisfaction* (2012)

References

PRIMARY: Mike Spain, "Exclusive Interview with Chocolate Thunder," http://voices.yahoo.com/exclusive-interview-chocolate-6259992.html (2010; accessed 21 May 2014).

SECONDARY: "Linda Rodney," http://beasleyfuneralhome.net/pages/obituaries.php?obitid=456 (July 2014; accessed 2 December 2014) (obituary); Vincent Harris, "Linda Rodney, a.k.a. Chocolate Thunder, 1956–2014," http://www.greenvillejournal.com/life-culture/sound-check/3363-linda-rodney-a-k-a-chocolate-thunder.html (July 2014; accessed 20 October 2014).

Rosemond, (Crescent) Clinton

Singer

1 November 1882 (Seneca, S.C.)–10 March 1966 (Sawtelle, Calif.)

S.C. residence: Seneca (1882–probably 1898)

Rosemond sang with the Southern Syncopated Orchestra as early as 1919; that year and for the next three years, he was with the group in Great Britain where, concurrently, he sang with the Royal Southern Singers. He accompanied this organization to Australia in 1923. Back in England in the mid-1920s he sang with the Southern Trio/Royal Southern Three, which also performed in Germany and Denmark and for a time included Mabel Mercer. This group sang in the London production of *Blackbirds of 1926*. With his wife (dancer Corinne Meaux) and their child, he returned to the United States in 1929, settling in Los Angeles. Though he sang there, he worked primarily as an actor. He had roles in over forty movies, including Fred Zinnemann's one-reel *Story of Doctor Carver* (1938), in which he plays the adult George Washington Carver. Late in life he was in charge of press relations for the Los Angeles chapter of the American Association of Afro-American Relations. Rosemond, who served as a private in the Spanish-American War, is buried in the Los Angeles National Cemetery, plot 99, A 10.

C. Clinton Rosemond, London, 1920s; permission of Clint Rosemond

Rosemond was the father of pianist Bertha Hope, later Hope-Booker, who is not a South Carolinian.

Films

The Mask of Fu Manchu (1932), *No Man of Her Own* (1932), *Carolina* (1934), *Camp Meetin'* (1936), *The Green Pastures* (1936), *Hearts in Bondage* (1936), *Dark Manhattan* (1937), *Hollywood Hotel* (1937), *They Won't Forget* (1937), *Accidents Will Happen* (1938), *The Story of Doctor Carver* (1938), *The Toy Wife* (1938), *Young Dr. Kildare* (1938), *Calling Dr. Kildare* (1939), *Golden Boy* (1939), *Midnight Shadow* (1939), *Stand Up and Fight* (1939), *Dark Command* (1940), *Maryland* (1940), *Safari* (1940), *Santa Fe Trail* (1940), *Badlands of Dakota* (1941), *Belle Starr* (1941), *Blossoms in the Dust* (1941), *Are Husbands Necessary?* (1942), *Syncopation* (1942), *The Vanishing Virginian* (1942), *Yankee Doodle Dandy* (1942), *Cabin in the Sky* (1943), *Flesh and Fantasy* (1943), *I Dood It* (1943), *Is Everybody Happy?* (1943), *I Walked with a Zombie* (1943), *Heavenly Days* (1944), *Jungle Queen* (1945), *Voice of the Whistler* (1945), *Colonel Effingham's Raid* (1946), *The Secret Heart* (1946), *Three Little Girls in Blue* (1946), *The Burning Cross* (1947), *The Homestretch* (1947), *Sport of Kings* (1947), *Tonight We Sing* (1953)

References

SECONDARY: Bill Smallwood, untitled piece, *Los Angeles California Eagle*, 6 June 1963, p. 7; Howard Rye, "Southern Syncopated Orchestra: The Roster," *Black Music Research Journal* 30 (Spring 2010): 52–54.

Rosen, Terry (Terence E.)

Guitar, broadcaster

1939, ca. October (Atlanta, Ga.)–28 December 1999 (Columbia, S.C.)

S.C. residence: Columbia (ca. 1944–ca. 1957, early 1970s–1999)

Before becoming a teenager Rosen taught himself to play the guitar; in time he studied at Westlake College of Music in Calif. Following a period backing the Salmas Brothers in Las Vegas, in the early 1960s he became a member of the Harry James band and, subsequently, of the band backing Sammy Davis, Jr.; he toured and recorded with both. Following his tenure with Davis, Rosen freelanced in Detroit before settling in Columbia; there he received undergraduate (1984) and graduate (1987) degrees from the University of South Carolina. He performed regularly in local clubs and used young Chris Potter as a sideman. He hosted *Inside Jazz* on the South Carolina Educational Radio Network (1986–1998) and helped produce Jazz on Main (also known as Main Street Jazz), an annual festival held in Columbia (1987–1997). In a Columbia hotel he died from a gunshot wound to the head, a death the police judged accidental.

When Rosen was enumerated for the census in Atlanta on 8 April 1940, his age was estimated as 6/12 (six months). A claim that he recorded with the Rat Pack (Frank Sinatra and others) has not been substantiated.

Leaders Recorded With

Harry James (1960–1961), Sammy Davis, Jr. (ca. 1963)

References

PRIMARY: Marc Minsker, "My Interview with Terry Rosen," http://www.geocities.ws/eyelounge/ROSEN interview.html (1997; accessed 21 May 2014).

SECONDARY: Norma Autrey, "No Place Like Home," *Columbia (S.C.) Record,* 26 January 1984, neighbors sec., pp. 1, 5; "Guitarist Dies from Gunshot Wound," *Columbia (S.C.) State,* 31 December 1999, sec. B, p. 1; "Terry Rosen," *Columbia (S.C.) State,* 4 January 2000, sec. B, p. 4 (obituary).

Roth, Sylvia

Trumpet

9 February 1926 (Chicago, Ill.)–?

S.C. residences: Greenville (1964), Columbia (1964–1987), Charleston (1987–)

Roth began piano lessons at four and trumpet study at thirteen. In 1940 she joined the Melody Maids, a band of female Chicago high school students. This group evolved into the Sharon Rogers band that played at local hotels and ballrooms. Roth studied piano, improvising, and arranging at the American Conservatory of Music and the Art Shefte School, both in Chicago; she took trumpet lessons from Forrest Nicola, who had been a member of the John Philip Sousa band. She began college as a music major at the University of Michigan but transferred to North Park Junior College in Chicago so she could continue playing with Rogers as the featured trumpeter. In late 1943 or early 1944 the band began touring full-time, playing extensively in the United States and performing in Japan and the South Pacific under the auspices of USO. It did not record, though tapes of its music exist. When the group disbanded in 1947 Roth returned to Chicago to teach trumpet and piano at

Sylvia Roth; permission of Sylvia Roth

the Chicago School of Music and in her own studio. In 1951 she gave up music to pursue a career in aviation. In 1961 she was one of the first twenty-five women invited to take tests to become an astronaut (the Women in Space Program), though she declined because of work commitments.

Most of the biographical information provided here comes from Roth herself. Some of it conflicts with information in Pat McGrath Avery's book.

Award

South Carolina Aviation Hall of Fame (1993)

References

SECONDARY: Bruce Smith, "Lady Fliers with 40,000 Hours Retiring," *Sumter (S.C.) Item,* 15 April 1988, sec. A, p. 11; Carri Karuhn, "Friendship Survives the Sea: All-Female Band from 1940s Holds Reunion, Recalls Crash," *Chicago Tribune,* 27 July 1995, sec. 2, pp. 1, 5; Sherrie Tucker, *Swing Shift: "All-Girl" Bands of the 1940s* (Durham, N.C.: Duke University Press, 2000), passim (comments by Roth); Margaret A. Weitekamp, *Right Stuff, Wrong Sex: America's First Women in Space Program* (Baltimore: Johns Hopkins University Press, 2004), 95; Pat McGrath Avery, *The Sharon Rogers Band: Laughed Together, Cried Together, Crashed and Almost Died Together* (Branson West, Mo.: River Road Press, 2010), 205–6.

Rudy Blue Shoes

See Wyatt, Rudy

Russell, Snookum (Isaac Edward, Jr.)

Piano, bass, singer, arranger
6 April 1913 (Columbia, S.C.)–11 August 1981 (New Orleans, La.)
S.C. residence: Columbia (1913–probably early 1930s)

As a child Russell took piano lessons from a neighbor. In Columbia he led, arranged for, and performed on piano and bass with the Ajax Band. After playing with Hartley Toots in Miami beginning in 1934, he formed Snookum Russell's Rockland Orchestra (1939); the name derived from the Rockland Palace in Miami. His band played in *Harlem Frolics* (1940), a revue headed by Butterbeans and Susie that performed on the Lichtman theater circuit. He moved his organization to Indianapolis, where it engaged in a series of musical battles with Claude Trenier's group (1941). Ray Brown, J. J. Johnson, and Fats Navarro were sidemen with Russell before becoming major figures. In time Russell settled in New Orleans, where he became a regular at the Paddock Lounge. He is buried in Holt Cemetery, New Orleans.

Russell was the brother of pianist Stomp Russell.

Compositions

"Basin Street Ain't Basin Street Anymore," "Juke Box Boogie Boogie Chick"

Recordings as Leader

"(Be Bop) That's the Kick I'm On" (1946), "I'm a Shy Guy" (1946), "Basin Street Ain't Basin Street Anymore" (1954), "Juke Box Boogie Boogie Chick" (1954), *Snookum* (1974)

Leaders Recorded With

Earl Williams (1951), George Lewis (1962), Wallace Davenport and Don Albert (1974)

References

SECONDARY: "Snookum Russell and His Orchestra Are Heading North," *Pittsburgh Courier,* 6 April 1940, p. 20; "Snookum Russell and His Blitzkreig of Swing," *Baltimore Afro-American,* 2 May 1942, p. 17; "From the Unknown Ranks to Fame in One Coast Jump Is Snookum Russell: Gives Hollywood New Kind of Groovy Swing," *Chicago Defender,* 27 November 1943, p. 10 (national edition); Sarah Graydon McCrory, *"Alex": Reminiscences, Columbia, South Carolina, and the Isaac Russell Family, 1910–1980* (N.p.: n.p., 1982), 15, 26–30, 67; Leif Bo Petersen and Theo Rehak, *The Music and Life of Theodore "Fats" Navarro: Infatuation* (Lanham, Md.: Scarecrow Press, 2009), 13–18.

Russell, Stomp (Wilbert Allen)

Piano, singer
18 October 1921 (Columbia, S.C.)–24 December 2011 (Pa., possibly Wynnewood)
S.C. residence: Columbia (1921–probably early 1940s)

Largely self-taught, Russell imitated the playing of notable pianists while performing on Columbia radio station WCOS. In 1942 he formed the Al "Stomp" Russell Trio that toured and recorded; it operated out of Los Angeles until Russell moved to West Philadelphia, Pa., in 1946. The group became known as the Do Ray Me Trio the next year. For six months in 1959 it performed at the Flamingo in Las Vegas, sharing the bill with Harry James. Following the 1978 dissolution of the group, Russell performed as a single. He spent his last days in a

Wynnewood, Pa., nursing home and is buried in section 87, lot 130, east side grave, Fernwood Cemetery, Fernwood, Pa.

Russell was the brother of pianist Snookum Russell. The Social Security Death Index records the birth and death dates of Wilbert A. Russell. He was enumerated as Allen Russell in the 1930 and 1940 censuses. The Do Ray Me Trio is spelled various ways.

Compositions

"A.B.C. Boogie," "By Candlelight," "Cabaret," "Dancing By," "Day Dreaming," "Don't Leave Me Now," "Don't Yield to Temptation," "8, 9, and 10," "Every Joe Needs His Jane," "Give Me My Money Back," "The Good Book," "Holiday Blues," "I Cried Last Night," "(I Found Love) When I Found You," "I'll Never Stop Being Yours," "I Must Forget about You," "It's Like Taking Candy from a Baby," "It's So," "Just Plain Love," "Let's Get Together," "Lying and Crying for You," "A Million Times a Day," "One, Two, Three Kick Blues," "Oo-Wee," "Rhumba Blues," "She Would Not Yield to My Temptation (although All I Wanted Was a Kiss)," "That's How Love Begins," "Until I Met You," "Walk Slow, My Love," "Why Did You Do It, Baby?," "Why Don't You Say What You Mean?," "World War 2 Blues"

Recordings as Leader

"8, 9, and 10" (1945), "It's So" (1945), "Shy Ann" (1945), "Solid Mr. Kelly with the Jelly" (1945), "Blue Prelude" (1946), "Cement Mixer" (1946), "Cynthia" (1946), "Dig, Mister K. Kay Kay" (1946), "Down the Road a Piece" (1946; possibly also titled "Let's Go Down the Road"), "Give Me My Money Back" (1946), "Holiday Blues" (1946), "I Must Forget about You" (1946), "I'm Yours" (1946),"Let's Get Together" (1946), "Mellow Jelly Blues" (1946), "More Than You Know" (1946), "Say It Isn't So" (1946), "Say What You Mean" (1946), "Shy Ann" (1946), "Three Little Words" (1946), "Under the Stars" (1946), "What Kind of Love Is That" (1946), "World War 2 Blues" (1946), "If I Could Steal You (from Somebody Else)" (1946 or 1947), "Ramona" (1946 or 1947), "Strike Blues" (1946 or 1947), "The Trouble with Me Is You" (1946 or 1947), "Just Plain Love" (1947), "Nobody Loves a Fat Man" (1947), "Once in a While" (1947), "Please Be Kind" (1947), "Studebaker" (1947), "The Wise Old Man" (1947; this and all subsequent recordings made with the Do Ray Me Trio), "Wrapped Up in a Dream" (1947), "I Couldn't Help It" (1949), "Only One Dream" (1949), "Rhumba Blues" (1949), "How Can You Say You Love Me" (1950), "May That Day Never Come" (1950), "I Couldn't Help It" (1951), "I Don't Want to Be Alone for Christmas" (1951), "I'll Be Waiting" (1951), "I Want to Be with You" (1951), "No More Dreams" (1951), "I'll Never Stop Being Yours" (1952), "I'm Used to You" (1952), "Oo-Wee" (1952), "She Would Not Yield" (1952), *The Do-Ray-Mi Trio* (1959), *The Exciting Do-Ray-Me Trio* (ca. 1966)

Leaders Recorded With

Timmie Rogers (1945), Harold Conner (1949; with Do Ray Me Trio), Buddy Hawkins (1949–1950, 1958; with Do Ray Me Trio), Mary Del (ca. 1949; with Do Ray Me Trio)

References

SECONDARY: Sarah Graydon McCrory, *"Alex": Reminiscences, Columbia, South Carolina, and the Isaac Russell Family, 1910–1980* (N.p.: n.p., 1982), 26, 29, 67; Tom Reed, *The Black Music History of Los Angeles—Its Roots* (Los Angeles: Black Accent on L.A. Press, 1992), facing 1; Marv Goldberg, "The Al Russell Trio/Do Ray Me Trio," www.uncamarvy.com/DoRayMe/dorayme.html (2009; accessed 21 May 2014); John F. Morrison, "Wilbert 'Al' Russell, 90, R&B and Jazz Performer," *Philadelphia Daily News*, 29 December 2011, local sec., p. 30 (obituary); Todd Baptista, "Obituaries: Al Russell," *Blues and Rhythm: The Gospel Truth* 267 (March 2012): 15; J. C. Marion, "Memories of the Do-Ray-Me Trio," http://home.earthlink.net/~jaymar41/smallgroups.html (undated; accessed 21 May 2014).

Russo, Charlie (Charles)

Saxophone, clarinet, oboe, arranger

27 August 1910 (Bronx, N.Y.)–29 May 1975 (Greenville, S.C.)

S.C. residence: Greenville (1967–1975)

Russo began playing in bands at fifteen. He joined Charlie Spivak's organization in the early 1940s and remained with it until his death, in time serving as its manager. After a performance he was murdered at Ye Olde Fireplace in Greenville, where the band had been in residence since 1967. The crime has not been solved. He is buried in section 2, lot 235, west half, Saint Mary's Cemetery, Cortland, N.Y.

Consulted evidence does not prove that the alto saxophonist Charles Russo who recorded with Willie Farmer in 1938 was the Russo who became affiliated with Charlie Spivak. It has not been confirmed that Russo appears on screen with Spivak's band in the movies *Pin Up Girl* and *Follow the Boys* (both 1944).

Leader Recorded With

Charlie Spivak (1942–1953, 1955–1956, 1958, 1962, 1967–1968, 1972–1973)

References

SECONDARY: "Charles Russo," *Greenville (S.C.) News,* 30 May 1975, p. 19 (obituary); "Charles Russo, Member of Spivak Band, Killed during Restaurant Holdup," *Cortland (N.Y.) Standard,* 30 May 1975, p. 16 (obituary); Bill Higgins, "Tips, Descriptions Only Russo Leads," *Greenville (S.C.) News,* 30 May 1975, pp. 1, 5; Jim McAllister, "For Spivak Now, It's 'Why? Why?,'" *Greenville (S.C.) News,* 30 May 1975, p. 39.

Rutledge, Leroy

Cornet, trumpet
Ca. 1898 (S.C.)-ca. 1978
S.C. residence: Charleston (at least early 1920s)

Apparently a ward of Jenkins Orphanage, Rutledge played in its bands in the early 1920s. As a professional musician headquartered in N.Y.C., he participated in two of the earliest recording sessions by the Washingtonians, the initial band of Duke Ellington.

John Chilton states that Rutledge was born "c. 1900" and died "c. 1978." When enumerated for the census in N.Y.C. on 5 April 1930, the musician's age was estimated as thirty-two; this document, which indicates that Rutledge was born in S.C., identifies him as a cornetist.

Leaders Recorded With

Charlie Johnson (1925), Duke Ellington (1926)

Reference

SECONDARY: John Chilton, *A Jazz Nursery: The Story of the Jenkins' Orphanage Bands of Charleston, South Carolina* (London: Bloomsbury Book Shop, 1980), 58.

Ryce, Daryle LaMaría (Daryle LaMaría Rice)

Singer, guitar, piano, violin
29 September 1953 (Spartanburg, S.C.)-
S.C. residence: Spartanburg (1953-1974, 1977-1978, 2007-)

Rice started piano lessons in fourth grade; at twelve she began studying the violin, and the

Daryle Ryce; photograph by Jim McGuire, permission of Daryle Ryce

guitar two years later. After receiving a degree from Spartanburg High School (1971), she attended Converse College on a violin scholarship and, at eighteen, performed professionally, initially in clubs but also on television. Following her junior year she became a full-time professional musician, as which she ultimately toured internationally. After leaving Spartanburg she lived mainly in Charlotte, N.C., but also in Durham, N.C., and Nashville, Tenn. She changed her surname from Rice to Ryce in the mid-1980s. For Lady Lullaby, a company she established in 1994, she recorded lullabies for children. Primarily a jazz performer, she mostly plays and sings her own compositions and what she considers the best American music from 1940 to 1970.

Compositions

"Aces Don't Come Every Hand," "Chain It Up," "Dance, Dance," "Daryle's Blues," "From Now On," "I Don't Want Nobody," "I'd Rather Have You," "I Love You but I Can't," "I'm Glad," "I've Got to Know," "Jonathan," "Last One to Know," "Let's Start to Love," "Livin' from Day to Day," "Lyin'," "Most of All," "No Room for Goodbyes," "Payday," "Put Me in the Movies," "Same Ol', Same Ol',"

"Saxman," "Shelter for a Homeless Heart," "Should I Call?," "So Long Ago (George's Tune)," "Somebody's Been Cookin'," "Straight Drive," "Sweet Little Annie of May," "Take Me Back to Carolina," "Too Soon," "Way You Touched Me," "What Are We Fightin' For?," "You're My Only Love," "You Walked Away"

Recordings as Leader

I Walk with Music (1980; additional material recorded in 1996 for the CD release), *Lonely Days* (1986), *Hold Me* (1987), *Carolina Blue* (1989), *Unless It's You* (1991), *Rosa's Grandchild* (1992), *From Now On* (1994), *The Heart of Christmas* (ca. 1996; with Loonis McGlohon), *Children of the Earth* (1998), *Nothing Like an Old Friend* (2000), *My Love, My Guitar* (2002)

Leaders Recorded With

Loonis McGlohon (1989–1992), Mercury Dime (1997)

References

SECONDARY: Scott Belford, "Words and Music (and Life) by Daryle Ryce," *Radiance: The Magazine for Large Women* 30 (Spring 1992): pp. 30–31, 44–45 (comments by Ryce); Peter Cooper, *Hub City Music Makers: One Southern Town's Popular Music Legacy* (Spartanburg, S.C.: Holocene, 1997), 39, 152–65 (comments by Ryce); Jose Franco, "Daryle Ryce Comes Home to Perform," http://www.goupstate.com/article/19980327/NEWS/803270331 (27 March 1998; accessed 21 May 2014) (comments by Ryce); womanNshadows, "The Music of Daryle Ryce," http://womannshadows.hubpages.com/hub/The-Music-of-Daryle-Ryce (13 December 2010; accessed 21 May 2014) (comments by Ryce).

Scott, Arthur

June 1888 (S.C.)–?

S.C. residence: Charleston (at least 1890s–at least until 1900)

A ward of Jenkins Orphanage, Scott played in its bands at least in the 1890s and performed with one of them in England in 1895. His instrument is not known.

Scott's birth date comes from the 1900 census, conducted at the orphanage on 28 June.

Reference

SECONDARY: Howard Rye, "Visiting Fireboys: The Jenkins' Orphanage Bands in Britain," *Storyville* 130 (1987): 137–43.

Scott, George

Drums

S.C. residence: Charleston (at least early 1900s)

Apparently a ward of Jenkins Orphanage, Scott played in its bands in the early 1900s.

John Chilton states that "it has been suggested" that Scott changed his name to George Stafford, as which he worked with the Charlie Johnson band in N.Y.C. Chilton's source has not been identified, and the claim has not been substantiated. George Stafford drummed on recordings with Johnson (1925, 1927–1929), Jackson and His Southern Stompers (1928), Eddie Condon (1929), Little Chocolate Dandies (1929), Henry "Red" Allen (1935), Art Karle (1936), and Mezz Mezzrow (1936).

Reference

SECONDARY: John Chilton, *A Jazz Nursery: The Story of the Jenkins' Orphanage Bands of Charleston, South Carolina* (London: Bloomsbury Book Shop, 1980), 58.

Scott, Milford Kenneth

See Blue Scotty

Seabrooks, Thaddeus

Trumpet

Probably 10 June 1912 (Charleston, S.C.)–?

S.C. residence: Charleston (1912–at least into early 1930s)

A ward of Jenkins Orphanage, Seabrooks played in its bands in the late 1920s and early 1930s and performed with one of them in England in 1929. Subsequently he played with the Carolina Cotton Pickers.

The passenger list of the *Columbus,* which transported the orphanage band to Plymouth, England, in April 1929, records Seabrooks's age as sixteen and his given name as Madden. The list of the *Majestic,* which returned the group to N.Y.C. two months later, identifies the precise birth date and place. The musician's age was estimated as sixteen when Seabrooks was enumerated for the census in Charleston on 2 April 1930. Some jazz sources render his surname Seabrook.

Leader Recorded With

Probably Carolina Cotton Pickers (1936–1937)

References

SECONDARY: John Chilton, *A Jazz Nursery: The Story of the Jenkins' Orphanage Bands of Charleston, South Carolina* (London: Bloomsbury Book Shop, 1980), 58; Bruce Bastin, "A Note on the Carolina Cotton Pickers," *Storyville* 95 (June–July 1981): 177–82; Howard Rye, "Visiting Fireboys: The Jenkins' Orphanage Bands in Britain," *Storyville* 130 (1987): 137–43.

Sease, Marvin

Singer, guitar, composer

16 February 1946 (Blackville, S.C.)–8 February 2011 (Vicksburg, Miss.)

S.C. residences: Blackville (1946–ca. 1960), Charleston (ca. 1960–1966)

Sease began singing in Charleston ca. 1960 with the Five Gospel Crowns. Upon moving to N.Y.C. in 1966 he affiliated with other gospel groups, including the Gospel Knights and the Mighty Gospel Crowns. In time he formed his own group, the Soul Keys, which performed mostly gospel music. After committing to rhythm and blues in 1978 he sang with the group named Sease and recorded for his own label, Early Records. He gained success with the re-release of his first album. He composed many of the songs he sang, including "Candy Licker," his signature piece. David Whiteis notes that Sease "honored [the blues] and its heritage." After succumbing to pneumonia, Sease was buried in the Cadedonia Christian Church Cemetery, Ehrhardt, S.C.

Marvin Sease, Charlotte, N.C., 14 February 2009; permission of the photographer, Gene Tomko

Compositions

"Ain't Nobody in the Bedroom," "Anyway You Want It," "The Bitch Git It All," "Candy Licker," "Condom on Your Tongue," "Ditch Diggers," "Don't Go," "Do You Need a Licker?," "Everybody's Diggin on Me," "Everything You Eat Ain't Good," "Funky Christmas," "Ghetto Man," "Greedy Girl," "Hoochie Mama," "I Ate the Whole Thing," "I Ate You for My Breakfast," "I Belong to You," "I Can't Afford to Be Caught," "I Can't Let You Go," "I Got Beat Out," "I Gotta Clean Up," "I Made You a Woman," "I'm Coming Home," "I'm Mr. Jody," "I Wanna Do It with You," "I Wanna Rock You," "Lady," "Let Me Dream," "Let Me Hold and Squeeze You," "Love Is a Game," "Love Machine," "Marvin's Testimony," "Money Is What You Want," "Motel Lover," "Please Take Me," "Power of Coochie," "Rockin' Them Bones," "She's My Baby's Momma," "So Glad You're Mine," "Take Me Back," "Tell Me What to Do," "Thanks for Loving Me," "Two Wrong Shoes," "We Gotta Make a Plan," "We're Still Together," "Who You Been Giving It To?," "You Must Be Crazy," "You're Number One," "You Should Be Grateful," "You Turn Me On"

Recordings as Leader (These Are Release Dates, Not Necessarily Recording Dates)

"Looking for Something for Nothing" (1974), "Thankful for This Life" (1974), "It's Too Early or Too Late" (1979), "Let's Go to a Disco" (1979), *Ghetto Man* (1986; re-released as *Marvin Sease,* with "Candy Licker" added), *Breakfast* (1987), *The Real Deal* (1989), *It's Christmas Time* (1990; extended-play record), *Show Me What You Got* (1991), *The Housekeeper* (1993), *Do You Need a Licker?* (1994), *Please Take Me* (1996), *The Bitch Git It All* (1997), *Hoochie Momma* (1999), *A Woman Would Rather Be Licked* (2001), *I Got Beat Out* (2002), *Playa*

Haters (2004), *Live with the Candy Licker* (2005), *Who's Got the Power* (2008)

Leader Recorded With

Gospel Knights (ca. 1966)

Awards

Southern Soul Blues Song of the Year and Best Slow Jam (2008; awarded to "I'm Coming Home" in the Blues Critic Awards Readers' Poll)

References

PRIMARY: Jim O'Neal, "Marvin Sease: The Candy Licker," *Living Blues* 134 (July–August 2007): 18–27 (interview).

SECONDARY: Heikki Suosalo, "Interview with Marvin Sease," http://www.soulexpress.net/marvinsease_interview.htm (1996; accessed 21 May 2014) (despite the title, this is an article by Suosalo, not an interview with Sease, though it includes comments by him); Sherryl M. Peters, "Blackville Native Who Made R&B Charts Dead at Age 64," *Orangeburg (S.C.) Times and Democrat,* 12 February 2011, sec. A, p. 6; "Marvin Sease," *Orangeburg (S.C.) Times and Democrat,* 16 February 2011, sec. A, p. 4 (obituary); David Whiteis, "Marvin Sease," *Living Blues* 212 (April 2011): 6 (obituary); "Marvin Sease," *Juke Blues* 71 (Summer 2011): 59 (obituary).

Sexton, (Mary) Ann

Singer
5 February 1950 (Greenville, S.C.)–
S.C. residence: Greenville (1950–1980)

During her formative years Sexton, a cousin of singer Chuck Jackson, sang in choirs at church and school. She recorded initially at age seventeen and soon married saxophonist Melvin Burton, with whom she formed the group Masters of Soul. During the 1970s she was affiliated with disc jockey John Richbourg, who produced her recordings for Sound Stage 7 and recorded her for his own Seventy-Seven Records. "You're Gonna Miss Me" and "You're Losing Me" were popular successes. Retired from music, she moved to N.Y.C. in 1980. Late that decade she became a paraprofessional in a Bronx school, where she worked for over two decades as Mary Burton. She resumed performing in 2007. Her recording of "You're Losing Me" is on the sound track of *21 Grams* (2003).

Four compilations of Sexton's recordings have been released: *Loving You, Loving Me* (1978), *Love Trials* (1987), *You're Gonna Miss Me* (1995), and *Anthology* (2004).

Compositions (All as Ann Burton)

"Come Back Home," "I Still Love You," "Keep On Holding On," "You're Losing Me," "You've Been Gone Too Long" (the yellow-label Seventy 7 Records release identifies the composer as Ann Benton)

Recordings as Leader (These Are Release Dates, Not Necessarily Recording Dates)

"Come Back Home" (1972), "I Still Love You" (1972), "You're Letting Me Down" (1972), "You've Been Gone Too Long" (1972), "Have a Little Mercy" (1973), "If I Work My Thing on You" (1973), "It's All Over but the Shouting" (1973), "Let's Huddle Up" (1973), "Loving You, Loving Me" (1973), "You Can't Win" (1973), "You're Gonna Miss Me" (1973), "You're Losing Me" (1973), "Keep On Holding On" (probably early 1970s), "Love, Love, Love" (1974), "Let's Huddle Up and Cuddle Up" (1975), *The Beginning* (1977), "You Got to Use What You Got" (1977), "Santa Claus Is Coming to Town" (2010)

Leaders Recorded With

Elijah and the Ebonies (1967; as Mary Sexton), Ferry Ultra (2009)

Website

http://site.annsexton.net/ (accessed 21 May 2014)

References

SECONDARY: Brendan Greaves and Jason Perlmutter, notes to *Said I Had a Vision: Songs and Labels of David Lee* (2010; Paradise of Bachelors PoB-01); "The Wonderful Ms. Ann Sexton!," http://site.annsexton.net/Ann_s_Story.html (2010; accessed 21 May 2014); Red Kelly, "Ann Sexton—It's All Over but the Shouting (77–125)," http://redkelly.blogspot.com/2011/02/ann-sexton-its-all-over-but-shouting-77.html (2012; accessed 21 May 2014); Sir Shambling [John Ridley], "Elijah and the Ebonies Feat. Mary Sexton," http://www.sirshambling.com/artists_2012/E/elijah_ebonies/index.php (2012; accessed 21 May 2014); Toby Walker, "Ann Sexton," http://www.soulwalking.co.uk/Ann%20Sexton.html (undated; accessed 21 May 2014).

Shelton, Come By

Piano

Probably 1890 or 1891 (probably Union County, S.C., but possibly Union town)–?

S.C. residence: Union County, probably including Cross Anchor and possibly Union town (probably 1890 or 1891–)

Characterized by Pete Lowry and Bruce Bastin as among the Union County party pianists, Shelton helped inspire Henry "Rufe" Johnson to play the piano ca. 1933.

Shelton was probably one of two brothers. Their draft registration cards indicate that Charlie Shelton was born on 18 February 1890 in Union County, S.C., and that Wash Shelton was born on 16 September 1891 in Union, S.C. When they completed the cards on 5 June 1917 in the Cross Keys district of Union County, Charlie lived in Cross Anchor, S.C., while Wash resided at RFD 1, Cross Anchor. The brothers worked as farm laborers.

References

SECONDARY: Pete Lowry, notes to Henry "Rufe" Johnson, *The Union County Flash!* (1973; Trix 3304); Bruce Bastin, *Red River Blues: The Blues Tradition in the Southeast* (Urbana: University of Illinois Press, 1986), 193.

Shepherd, Leo ("The Whistler")

Trumpet, arranger

Ca. 1926 (Charleston, S.C.)–before 1980

S.C. residence: Charleston (ca. 1926–early 1940s)

A ward of Jenkins Orphanage beginning in 1932, Shepherd performed in its bands in the late 1930s and early 1940s. After becoming a professional musician he was affiliated with Lionel Hampton from 1946 into the early 1950s; his playing is much in evidence on "Playboy" (1946) and "Hamp's Boogie No. 2" (1949). For Hampton he arranged "Cobb's Idea" (1946), a feature for saxophonist Arnett Cobb, and possibly other tunes. He is known for playing extremely high notes (which led to his nickname), a skill that influenced Maynard Ferguson.

Conducted in Charleston on 21 May, the 1940 census indicates that Shepherd was born in S.C., estimates his age as fourteen, and notes that he lived in Charleston in 1935. (Ancestry.com transcribes the surname as Sheflurd.) John Chilton states that Shepherd was born in Charleston and had died by the time Chilton completed his manuscript.

Leaders Recorded With

Lionel Hampton (1946–1951), Billie Holiday (1948)

Reference

SECONDARY: John Chilton, *A Jazz Nursery: The Story of the Jenkins' Orphanage Bands of Charleston, South Carolina* (London: Bloomsbury Book Shop, 1980), 58.

Shine, Edward

Saxophone

S.C. residence: Charleston (at least in 1930s)

Apparently a ward of Jenkins Orphanage, Shine played in its bands in the 1930s.

It has not been determined if the musician was the Joseph Shine who was enumerated for the census at the orphanage on 21 May 1940. If so he was a ward of the institution, was born in S.C., and lived in Charleston in 1935; this census estimates his age as fourteen.

Shirley, Jimmy (James Arthur)

Guitar, bass

Probably ca. 1910 (Union, S.C.)–3 December 1989 (New York, N.Y.)

S.C. residence: Union (probably ca. 1910—at least until 1920)

Though born in Union, Shirley apparently spent many of his formative years in Cleveland, Ohio. By the mid-1930s he was a professional musician in Cincinnati. He resided in N.Y.C. by 1937; there he was with the trio of pianist Clarence Profit for a few years before leading his own trio in Philadelphia (1941–1942) and touring with Ella Fitzgerald (1942–1943). For Blue Note in 1944 he led a session that has not been released. For a decade beginning in the mid-1940s he was with the trio of Herman Chittison, though during this period he also led his own trio (it played at the Village Vanguard in 1947) and, as freelancer, performed with other musicians. He made several recordings in Paris in March 1975. He is known for his guitar sound, which might be characterized as quasi-Hawaiian.

All published sources consulted indicate that Shirley was born on 31 May 1913. His age was estimated as nine when he was enumerated for the census in Union on 21 January 1920. It has not been determined if the guitarist was the James A. Shirley who composed "Day and Night," "Don't Change," and "That Girl."

Compositions

"I'm Born with the Blues," "Jimmy's Rock"

Recordings as Leader

"Jimmy's Blues" (1945), "Star Dust" (1945), *China Boy* (1975)

Leaders Recorded With

Wingy Carpenter (1940), Creole George Guesnon (1940, 1946), Clarence Profit (1940), Artie Shaw (1941), Edmond Hall (1943), Coleman Hawkins (1943), Herman Chittison (1944), Sidney DeParis (1944), Art Hodes (1944), James P. Johnson (1944), Clyde Bernhardt (1945, 1972), Cousin Joe (1945–1946), Evelyn Knight (1945), Pigmeat Markham (1945), Earl Bostic (1946–1947, 1952, 1954–1955), Una Mae Carlisle (1946), Sidney Catlett (1946), Ella Fitzgerald (1946), Pat Flowers (1946, 1972, 1975), John Hardee (1946), Billie Holiday (1946), Pete Johnson (1946), Billy Kyle (1946), Ram Ramirez (1946), Kirby Walker (1946), Muriel Adams (1947), Rose Murphy (1949), Wynonie Harris (1950), Little Sylvia (1951), Birmingham Boogie Boys (1952), Jimmy Rushing (1952), Barbara Lea (1955), Screamin' Jay Hawkins (1956–1957), Little Willie John (1957), Bubber Johnson (1957), Julian Dash (1970), Stephane Grappelli (1975), Johnny Guarnieri (1975), Slam Stewart (1975)

References

SECONDARY: "Jimmy Shirley," http://www.classicjazzguitar.com/artists/artists_page.jsp?artist=69 (2005; accessed 21 May 2014); Scott Yanow, "Jimmy Shirley," http://www.allmusic.com/artist/jimmy-shirley-mn0000076191 (undated; accessed 21 May 2014).

Shorts, Etta Nora

Singer

Probably July 1885 (S.C.)–?

S.C. residence: Charleston (by 1900–at least until 1910)

A teacher at Jenkins Orphanage, Shorts soloed in Poughkeepsie, N.Y., with the institution's Orphan Brass Band and Jubilee Concert Company (1909). A reviewer noted her "good contralto voice."

When enumerated for the 1900 census with her family in Charleston, Shorts was identified as having been born in S.C. in July 1885. Her age was estimated as twenty-three when she was enumerated in Charleston on 23 April 1910. The first document provides her middle name; the second, her occupation.

Reference

SECONDARY: "Jenkins Band Makes Big Hit," *Poughkeepsie (N.Y.) Daily Eagle*, 13 July 1909, p. 5.

Shrimp City Slim (Gary Anthony Erwin)

Keyboards, guitar, singer, composer, broadcaster, organizer

10 October 1953 (Chicago, Ill.)–

S.C. residence: Charleston (1983–)

Erwin performed professionally before finishing high school. After studying anthropology at the Universidad de las Americas in Cholula, Puebla, Mexico (1971–1972), he moved to Boston to pursue a career in music. He performed there with various groups. In 1983 he moved to Charleston, where, in time, he hosted the long-running radio programs *Blues in the Night, South to Louisiana, Erwin Music,* and *La Noche Latina,* all aired on the South Carolina Educational Radio Network. In the middle and late 1980s he established the Lowcountry Blues Society, opened a record store, and formed the group Blue Light Special. He became an active organizer of blues events, including the Lowcountry Blues Bash (Charleston), the Carolina Downhome Blues Festival (Camden), the Greenwood Blues Cruise, and the Pee Dee Blues Bash (Florence). He adopted the name Shrimp City Slim in 1992. Either alone or with his band, he has toured extensively, especially internationally.

Compositions

"Ain't No Future in This Town," "Allergic to Mink," "Being Broke," "Big Fish, Small Pond," "Blue Palmetto," "Buy My Music While I'm Still Alive," "Call Me in Carolina," "Can You Handle This?," "Charleston," "Charleston Strut," "Drop in the Bucket," "Enjoy the Ride," "Give Your Face a Rest," "Gnat Bite," "Go Back to New Orleans," "Gone with the Wind," "Good, Good Love," "Hey, Mr. D.J.," "Highway 17 Blues," "Hittin' on You," "Hot Potato," "I Got a Long Way to Go," "It's About

Time," "I Work Nights," "Just Space between Us," "Lay Your Walking Shoes Down," "Leper of the City," "Lovely on the Water," "Lowcountry Mama," "Mama's Recipe," "Money Stupid," "The Moon Song," "Natural Resource," "Older Man," "One Day," "Only a Matter of Time," "Phosphate Woman," "Places I Can't Go No More," "Salina Cruz," "Say Goodbye to Charleston," "She Got Papers," "The Starlite Room," "Star Marina," "Sticky Fingers," "The Supermarket," "Switch Me Over (to Love)," "The Time We Should Have Spent Together," "Wheel Your Love to Me," "You Are the Reason," "Your Side of Town"

Recordings as Leader

Ancestor Worship: The Boston Sessions, 1980–83, Live in Colombia (1989; as Blue Light Special), *Gone with the Wind* (1992; as Blue Light Special), *Blues on the Beach* (1994), *Blue Palmetto* (1996), *I Work Nights* (1998), *Highway 17: Lowcountry Blues Live* (2001), *Dark Road Piano* (2006), *Rio Angie* (2012), *Star Marina* (2012–2013)

Leaders Recorded With

Randy Crowe (1989), Big Boy Henry (1990s), Chicago Bob Nelson (1991), Dave Peabody (1993, 1996), Neal Pattman (1995), Paul Dudley Kershaw (1998), Scott Perry (1999), Wanda Johnson (2003, 2006, 2008), Shelley Magee (2006), Papa Wheel (2010), Professor Bottleneck (2011), Shelly Waters (2012–2013)

Awards

Premio Cultural Circulo Hispanoamericano de Charleston (1997); Unsung Heroes of Afrikan Amerikan Classical Music Awards Lifetime Achievement Award (2006)

Website

www.shrimpcityslim.com (accessed 21 May 2014)

References

PRIMARY: Benjamin Franklin V, *Jazz and Blues Musicians of South Carolina: Interviews with Jabbo, Dizzy, Drink, and Others* (Columbia: University of South Carolina Press, 2008), 160–73.

SECONDARY: Clair Delune, "Gary Erwin: Charleston's 'Shrimp City Slim,'" in *Making Notes: Music of the Carolinas*, ed. Ann Wicker (Charlotte: Novello Festival Press, 2008), 81–82.

Sibley, Doris

Saxophone
Ca. 1926 (Fla.)-?
S.C. residence: Charleston (by 1935-at least into early 1940s)

A ward of Jenkins Orphanage, Sibley played in its bands in the early 1940s.

Sibley's age was estimated as fourteen when the youth was enumerated for the census at the orphanage on 21 May 1940. This document indicates that the Floridian lived in Charleston in 1935. She might be the Doris Sibley, estimated age six, who was enumerated in Gainesville, Fla., on 11 April 1930.

Simmons, Lewis

S.C. residence: Charleston (at least late 1920s)

Apparently a ward of Jenkins Orphanage, Simmons played in its bands in the late 1920s, though his instrument is not known.

Simmons might be the Lewis Simmons who, with his family, was enumerated for the census in Charleston on 3 January 1920; this document estimates his age as ten. This person was probably the Lewis Simmons, a farm laborer estimated age thirty, who was enumerated in Saint James Santee Township, Charleston County, on 16 April 1940.

Simmons, (Samuel) Lonnie

Organ, saxophone, clarinet
14 July of either 1914 or 1915 (probably Charleston, S.C., though possibly Mount Pleasant)-4 February 1995 (Chicago, Ill.)
S.C. residence: probably Charleston, though possibly Mount Pleasant (1914 or 1915-ca. 1930)

In Charleston, Simmons played with a local band, the Nighthawks. Probably around 1930 he left S.C. for N.Y.C., where, mid-decade at the Yeah Man Club, he led a trio that included banjo player Freddie Green, a friend from Charleston. Simmons's group subsequently played at the Exclusive Club and, as either a quintet or sextet, at the Black Cat; during the engagement at the latter Kenny Clarke was the drummer. As a result of his affiliation with Fats Waller in the late 1930s Simmons became enamored of the organ, which soon became his main instrument, though he continued playing the saxophone. He joined the band of Chick Webb in 1939, shortly before the leader's death, but remained with it as it continued under the nominal leadership of Ella Fitzgerald. After leaving this organization he moved to Chicago, where he lived the remainder of his life. He became active on the local music scene, performing solo and leading bands, including a quartet at the Garrick Lounge in 1943. He served as a musician in the navy during World War II, leading a sextet that one writer characterized as "hot but subtle" ("17 Musicians from Noted Orchestras Form Jazz Band That Pleases Personnel at Oahu"). Beginning in 1969 he and his wife operated Lonnie's Organ Rental; from around this time until a month before his death, he performed at Biasetti's Steak House. Simmons also worked as a freelance photographer. He is buried in Oak Woods Cemetery, Chicago.

In "Bronzeville Conversation with Lonnie Simmons and Friend," Simmons states that he was born in Charleston on 14 July 1915; his obituaries note that he died at age eighty. His age was estimated as five when he was enumerated for the census in Charleston on 24 April 1920. The South Carolinian Samuel Simmons who was enumerated for the census on 3 April 1940 in N.Y.C. at estimated age twenty-seven was probably Lonnie Simmons. The Social Security Death Index indicates that the musician was born on 14 July 1914. In an interview with Stanley Dance and Helen Dance, Freddie Green states that Simmons, as a youth, lived in Mount Pleasant, S.C. In the early 1940s Samuel Simmons became known as Lonnie.

Composition

"Lonnie's Blues"

Recordings as Leader (All 1953)

"Black Orchid," "I Can't Get Started," "Lonnie's Blues"

Leaders Recorded With

Hot Lips Page (1938), Jabbo Smith (1938), Fats Waller (1938), Al Cooper (1939–1941), Ella Fitzgerald (1940–1941), Red Saunders (1951), Brother Jack McDuff (1966)

References

PRIMARY: Charles Walton, "Bronzeville Conversation with Lonnie Simmons and Friend," https: //groups.google.com/forum/?fromgroups=#!topic/rec.music.bluenote/l8mtaL__GQc (April 2001; accessed 21 May 2014).

SECONDARY: "Lonnie Simmons, Band Leader, Makes Return Trip to Great Lakes for Recruit Training," *New York Age,* 8 April 1944, p. 10; "17 Musicians from Noted Orchestras Form Jazz Band That Pleases Personnel at Oahu," *New York Age,* 22 July 1944, p. 10; "Chicago's Club DeLisa to Close in February," *Jet* 13 (6 February 1958): 59; Stanley Dance and Helen Dance, "The Freddie Green Interview," www.freddiegreen.org/interviews/dance.html (1977; accessed 21 May 2014); Dave Hoekstra, "Magic of Lonnie Simmons: At 73, Storied Organist Still Pulls Out All the Stops," *Chicago Sun-Times,* 15 January 1988, p. 7 (comments by Simmons); "Lonnie Simmons, 80, Jazz Musician, Sideman to Stars," *Chicago Sun-Times,* 9 February 1995, p. 58 (obituary); "Samuel 'Lonnie' Simmons, 80, Keyboard Artist, Photog Dies," *Jet* 87 (27 February 1995): 52 (obituary); Jim Linderman, "Samuel Lonnie Simmons: The Man Who Never Sleeps," http://vintagesleaze.blogspot.com/2012/12/samuel-lonnie-simmons-man-who-never.html#.UX_R4UpXf_0 (2012; accessed 21 May 2014); Eugene Chadbourne, "Lonnie Simmons," http://www.allmusic.com/artist/lonnie-simmons-mn0001518672 (undated; accessed 21 May 2014).

Singleton, Charlton Pinckney

Trumpet, piano, organ, singer

7 January 1971 (Awendaw, S.C.)–

S.C. residences: Awendaw (1971–1995, 2001–2005), North Charleston (1995–2001, 2005–)

After becoming interested in the piano at age three, Singleton studied it, organ, violin, cello, and trumpet, ultimately focusing on the last of these instruments. He toured Europe with the United States Collegiate Wind Band in 1988, the year before being graduated from Wando High School in Mount Pleasant. Though he initially matriculated at Berklee College of Music in Boston, he transferred to South Carolina State University, from which he received a degree in 1994. Since then he has worked as a teacher at all levels, from elementary through college. He helped found the ska band SKWZBXX in 1995 and played with Plane Jane, a party band, as well as with the group Gradual Lean. In addition to leading a trio, quintet, and big band, he is artistic director of the Charleston Jazz Orchestra.

Charlton Singleton; photograph by Alice Keeney, permission of Charlton Singleton

Compositions

"Eudoranova," "Fantasy," "Lovers for Life," "Machen," "Never Gonna Let You Go," "The New Deal," "Soulmate," "Sweets' Sweets," "Turn the Lights Down"

Recordings as Leader

The New Deal (2011), *Soul Cavern* (2013)

Leaders Recorded With

SKWZBXX (1997–1998), Patrick Davis (ca. 2002), Danielle Howle (2006), Amber Caparas (2010), Charleston Jazz Initiative Legends Band (2010), Mark Sterbank (2010, 2013), Doug Jones (2011)

Films

Rich in Love (1992), *The Notebook* (2004)

Award

South Carolina State University Jazz Hall of Fame

Website

www.charltonsingleton.com (accessed 21 May 2014)

References

SECONDARY: Rob Young, "High Profile: Charlton Singleton," *Charleston (S.C.) Post and Courier,* 12 July 2008, sec. F, pp, 1–2 (comments by Singleton); Jack McCray, "The Jazz Man," *Charleston* 24 (November 2010): 80–85 (also available at http://charlestonmag.com/charleston_magazine/feature/the_jazz_man [accessed 21 May 2014]) (comments by Singleton); Paul Bowers, "Charlton Singleton Escapes the Ska Scene to Emerge as One of Charleston's Jazz Greats," *Charleston (S.C.) City Paper,* http://www.charlestoncitypaper.com/charleston/charlton-singleton-escapes-the-ska-scene-to-emerge-as-one-of-charlestons-jazz-greats/Content?oid=4153934 (5 September 2012; accessed 21 May 2014) (comments by Singleton).

Small, Drink ("Blues Doctor")

Guitar, piano, singer, composer
28 January 1933 (Bishopville area, S.C.)–
S.C. residences: Bishopville area (1933–ca. 1955), Columbia (ca. 1955–)

As a youth Small listened to various kinds of music, including country, blues, gospel, and jazz. He learned to play the piano in church and the guitar from neighbors and itinerant musicians. While still a teenager he formed the gospel group Six Stars; after it broke up he joined the Golden Five. Upon completing high school in 1953 he studied barbering before moving in 1955 to Columbia, where he joined the Spiritualaires, with which he recorded and toured. When he began singing the blues in the late 1950s, he became a popular performer at fraternity parties at the University of South Carolina. As leader he initially recorded for Sharp Records, a subsidiary of Savoy; later he established his own label, Bishopville Records. He has also recorded for, in sequence, Southland, Erwin Music, Mapleshade, Ichiban, and Music Maker. He plays guitar in various styles, but primarily in the Piedmont style of Willie Walker, Gary Davis, and others. Though he performs regularly in the S.C. midlands, he has played at major festivals, including the Smithsonian Folklife Festival, the Chicago Blues Festival, and the New Orleans Jazz & Heritage Festival.

The 1940 census apparently does not include a person named Drink Small. However, the household of the musician's grandmother Emma Small, which included her children Alice, Louis, and Joel, was enumerated that year in May in Ionia Township, Lee County. Then twenty-seven, Alice was the mother of Drink Small. The census indicates that the family also included Emma's seven-year-old grandson, Henry Small. Because he was born around 1933, the year of Drink Small's birth, Henry might be Drink, though Small, unaware of Henry, denies this possibility.

Compositions

"Atlanta Georgia Is a Little New York," "Baby, Leave Your Panties Home," "Bingo Lover," "Bishopville Is My Home Town," "Bishopville Women," "Bowlegged Woman," "Charleston Women Blues," "Coon Dog Blues," "Don't Bump My Stacy Adams Shoes," "Do What the Lord Say Do," "Drinkin' the Wine," "Drink Small Boogie," "D.U.I.," "Fish Fryin' Mama," "Gimme Some Money," "Greenback," "Hunting Coon," "I Got Two Hounds," "I Love You, Alberta," "I'm in Love with a Grandma," "I Want to Make Love," "Jamaican Blues," "Living in a BBQ World," "Mr. Green Is the Barbecue Man," "My Rod," "Never Too Late to Do Right," "Nurse Song," "One Woman," "President Clinton Blues," "Ride Snatchin' Daddy," "Rub My Belly," "Shag My Blues Away," "Slop Job Blues," "So Bad," "Something in the Milk Ain't Clean," "Song with No Name," "So Sweet," "South Carolina Boogie," "Three Rivers Blues," "Tittie Man," "Too Deep," "Tryin' to Survive at 75," "Ugly Woman Blues," "The United States Will Never Be the Same," "Variety Blues," "When You Tell One Lie, You Gotta Tell Another," "Widow Woman," "You Can't Get the Country Out of Me," "You Don't Have to Be Funky," "Y2K Blues"

Recordings as Leader

"Cold, Cold Rain" (1959), "I Love You, Alberta" (1959), *I Know My Blues Are Different, 'Cause I'm the One Who Has Them* (ca. 1972), "Atlanta, Georgia, Is a Little New York," two parts (ca. 1979), *Blues Doctor: Live and Outrageous!* (1986–1988), "I'm in Love with a Grandma" (1987), "Shag My Blues Away" (1987), *Electric Blues Doctor Live!* (1988), *Live at the New Orleans Jazz Festival* (1989), *The Blues Doctor* (1990), *Round Two* (1991), "Bishopville Women" (1991), "Widow Woman" (1991), *Hallelujah Boogaloo* (1997, 1999, 2005), "Drinkin' the Wine" (1997; with Cootie Stark), *Drink Small Does It All* (2003), "Physical Attraction" (2003), "You Don't Have to Be Funky" (2003), *Live at the Whig* (2004), *Tryin' to Survive at 75* (2008; later titled *Tryin' to Survive after 75*), "The United States Will Never Be the Same," two parts (2009), *Drinkism Songs* (2010), "Living in a BBQ World" (2011; two versions)

Leaders Recorded With

Spiritualaires of Columbia, S.C. (1956–1957; also known as the Spiritual Airs), Kip Anderson (1959, 1964, possibly 1982), Shelley Magee (2006)

Film

Toot Blues (2008)

Awards

Jean Laney Harris Folk Heritage Award (1990); Carolina Beach Music Awards Hall of Fame (2008); Jus' Blues Music Award (2013); NEA National Heritage Fellow (2015); South Carolina Entertainment and Music Hall of Fame (date unknown)

References

PRIMARY: Tut Underwood, "Drink Small: Prescription from the Blues Doctor," *Living Blues* 104 (July–August 1992): 13–17 (interview); "Drink Small," in *Music Makers: Portraits and Songs from the Roots of America,* ed. Timothy Duffy (Athens, Ga.: Hill Street Press, 2002), 137 (narrative by Small); Benjamin Franklin V, *Jazz and Blues Musicians of South Carolina: Interviews with Jabbo, Dizzy, Drink, and Others* (Columbia: University of South Carolina Press, 2008), 69–85; Mark Coltrain, "Drink Small: The Way Drink Think!," *Living Blues* 208 (August 2010): 30–31 (interview); Kelly Rae Smith, "Drink Small Is Big on Banter, Drinkism, and the Dirty Blues: The Tittie Man," *Charleston (S.C.) City Paper,* http://www.charlestoncitypaper.com/charleston/drink-small-is-big-on-banter-drinkism-and-the-dirty-blues/Content?oid=5074114 (4 February 2015; accessed 11 June 2015) (substantial comments by Small).

SECONDARY: Chaz Joyner, "Drink Small's Blue's [*sic*]," *Egghead: The Reading Rag for Open-Minded Organisms* 1 (March 1961): 4–5, 19; Gary Erwin, "Part-Preacher, Part-Soulman, Drink Small Plays the Blues," *Charleston (S.C.) News and Courier,* 9 March 1990, sec. C, p. 7; Opal Louis Nations, "The Charles Derrick Story: With Forays into the Careers of Kip Anderson, Drink Small and the Spiritualaires," *Blues and Rhythm: The Gospel Truth* 242 (September 2009): 16–20; Julia Rogers Hook and Julie Jenkins, "Drink Small, Columbia's Own 'Blues Doctor' since the 1950s," *Columbia (S.C.) Star,* 27 January 2012, p. 9; Gail Wilson-Giarratano, *Drink Small: The Life and Music of South Carolina's Blues Doctor* (Charleston, S.C.: History Press, 2014); "NEA Announces Recipients of Nation's Highest Award in the Folk and Traditional Arts," http://arts.gov/news/2015/nea-announces-recipients-nation%E2%80%99s-highest-award-folk-and-traditional-arts (9 June 2015; accessed 11 June 2015); "Local Blues Stalwart Drink Small Honored," *Columbia (S.C.) State,* 10 June 2015, sec. A, p. 2.

Smalls, Cliff (Clifton Arnold)

Piano, trombone, arranger
3 March 1918 (Charleston, S.C.)–8 February 2007 (Brooklyn, N.Y.)
S.C. residence: Charleston (1918–ca. 1935)

The son of a father who gave music lessons, Smalls played trombone before concentrating on piano. While in high school in Charleston, on weekends he played with the Royal Eight, a local group. He left school to tour with the Carolina Cotton Pickers. While a student at the Conservatory of Music of Kansas City, Kans., in 1942, he was discovered by Earl Hines. After playing trombone and second piano with Hines, Smalls became a member of Billy Eckstine's band, then Earl Bostic's. He plays on Bostic's recording of "Flamingo," which became a hit. Badly injured in a 1951 automobile accident, he was confined to bed for over a year. The injury led to his legal action against Bostic, who drove the car in which Smalls was riding. Subsequently he played with groups led by Al Sears (1953) and Bennie Green (1953–1956). He also worked with singers: Clyde McPhatter (performing on the recordings of "A Lover's Question" and "Lovey Dovey"), Brook Benton (for over seven years), and Smokey Robinson. He dubbed Ella Fitzgerald's piano playing in the movie *Let No Man Write My Epitaph* (1960). Beginning in 1968 he was a regular in the band of Ernie Wilkins. He performed with the New York Repertory Company and, in the 1980s, toured Europe with Oliver Jackson's group.

Smalls's birth and death dates come from the Social Security Death Index. At least one source records his death year as 2008.

Compositions
"Blues in the Afternoon," "Cliff Dweller," "Cliffo," "You're Never Too Young"

Recordings as Leader
"Blues in the Afternoon" (1970), "God Bless the Child" (1970), "The Hour of Parting" (1970), "What Is This Thing Called Love?" (1970), *Swing and Things* (1976), *Caravan* (1978 or 1979; also titled *The Man I Love*)

Leaders Recorded With
Carolina Cotton Pickers (probably 1936–1937), Earl Hines (1944–1948), Melrose Colbert (1947), Earl Bostic (1950–1951), Lucky Thompson (1950), Annisteen Allen (1951), Gene Redd (1951–1952), Bennie Green (1953–1956), Al Sears (1953), Bobbie and Ronald (1956), Earl King (1956), Paul Williams (1956), Lord Essex (1957), Clyde McPhatter (1958), Julian Dash (1970), Sy Oliver (1972–1973, 1976), Eddie Barefield (1973), Ella Fitzgerald (1973), Paul Gonsalves (1973), Chick Webb Orchestra (1973), Buddy Tate (1975), Norris Turney (1975), Milt Hinton (1976), Oliver Jackson (1977–1979, 1982), Bunny Briggs (1978), Jimmy Powell (1978)

References
PRIMARY: Stanley Dance, *The World of Earl Hines* (New York: Scribner's, 1977), 261–72 (narrative by Smalls); "Sue Terry Interviews Clifton Smalls," *Jazz Artist* 3 (August 1999): 1, 3 (*Jazz Artist* was published by Local 802, American Federation of Musicians AFL-CIO).
SECONDARY: "New York Beat," *Jet* 13 (7 November 1957): 63; Alain Balalas, "Cliff Smalls," *Bulletin du Hot Club de France* 271 (May 1979): 5–6 (in French); John Chilton, *A Jazz Nursery: The Story of the Jenkins' Orphanage Bands of Charleston, South Carolina* (London: Bloomsbury Book Shop, 1980), 46 (comments by Smalls); Bruce Bastin, "A Note on the Carolina Cotton Pickers," *Storyville* 95 (June–July 1981): 177–82; Jack McCray, *Charleston Jazz* (Charleston, S.C.: Arcadia Publishing, 2007), 55.

Smalls, Ed (Edwin Alexander)

Nightclub proprietor
1880s, possibly 22 September 1884 (S.C., possibly Columbia)–13 October 1974 (New York, N.Y.)
S.C. residences: possibly Columbia (1880s–no later than 1900), Charleston (by 1900–no later than 1910)

Apparently the son of an organ teacher, Smalls moved to N.Y.C. by 1910. In Harlem he opened a pool hall on Fifth Ave. in 1919, but the next year he turned its basement into a cafeteria that provided entertainment. In 1925 he moved his establishment to a larger facility at 135th St. and Seventh Ave. and made it into a nightclub, which he named Smalls Paradise. One of the most popular Harlem clubs during the Jazz Age, it catered to wealthy blacks and whites, unlike the other two major clubs—Connie's Inn and the Cotton Club—which were owned by and admitted only whites. Smalls Paradise was noted for its dancing waiters and early morning breakfast dances; the latter were popular with patrons of establishments that closed by around 4:00 A.M. For a decade beginning in 1925 its band was led by Charlie Johnson, whose sidemen included Benny Carter and Jabbo Smith. Johnson recorded with groups named the Paradise Orchestra and the Paradise Ten. In 1939 a writer for the *New York Age,* William E. Clark, considered Ed Smalls "Harlem's leading business man." Smalls sold the club in 1959, though it operated until 1986, including briefly in the early 1960s under the ownership of Wilt Chamberlain, the basketball player. It was the longest-lived Harlem nightclub. Smalls was interested in boxing to the degree that he managed the fighter George Brothers in the late 1930s. He is buried in Woodlawn Cemetery, Bronx, N.Y.

Smalls's date and place of birth have not been confirmed. "Oldest Negro Night Club" notes that Smalls was born in Columbia, S.C., while C. Gerald Fraser claims that he was "from Charleston, S. C.," which does not mean that he was born there. Conducted in Charleston on 7 or 8 June, the 1900 census states that Smalls was born in September 1884; the Social Security Death Index confirms this date and specifies the day as the 22nd. When enumerated on 22 April 1910 he was an elevator operator living in N.Y.C.; this document estimates his age as twenty-six. His draft registration card, completed on 12 September 1918, indicates that he was born in February 1884 and that he worked as a shipping clerk. Conducted in N.Y.C. on 10 January, the 1920 census records that Smalls, estimated age thirty-two, managed a pool hall. When he was enumerated in N.Y.C. on 15 April 1940 his age was estimated as fifty-two. C. Gerald Fraser believes that Smalls was born on 12 September 1882. Abraham D. Sofaer contends that Smalls was a grandson of Robert Smalls, famous for his daring escape from slavery; Kathleen Drowne and Willie Hamilton think that Smalls was descended from Robert Smalls. In his study of Robert Smalls's families Andrew Billingsley does not mention Ed Smalls. The first word in the name of Ed Smalls's club is rendered variously: Smalls, Small's, Smalls', and Smalls's. On the club's marquee it was spelled "Smalls," the spelling used here. A group called Small's Paradise Entertainers performs in the movie short *Smash Your Baggage* (1933). In 1943 Malcolm Little (later Malcolm X) worked as a waiter at Smalls's establishment.

References

SECONDARY: Travelle Swift, "Speakin' o' Ed. Smalls," *New York Amsterdam News,* 17 October 1928, p. 7 (comments by Smalls); Errol Aubrey Jones, "George Brothers Challenges Bob Pastor for Fight," *New York Age,* 16 January 1937, p. 8; William E. Clark, "Sports of the Age," *New York Age,* 11 February 1939, p. 8; "Oldest Negro Night Club," *Ebony* 4 (October 1949): 44–46; James Booker, "Ed Smalls Planning to Retire in April," *New York Amsterdam News,* 6 February 1954, p. 1 (comments by Smalls); Amos M. White, interview by William Russell, 23 August 1958, four reels of tape and a typed summary, Hogan Jazz Archive, Tulane University, New Orleans, p. 18 of summary (also available at http://musicrising.tulane.edu/uploads/transcripts/a.%20white%2008-23-1958.pdf [accessed 21 May 2014]); C. Gerald Fraser, "Ed Smalls, Whose Club Brought the Famous to Harlem, Is Dead," *New York Times,* 18 October 1974, p. 44 (late Jersey edition) (obituary); Willie Hamilton, "Big Ed Smalls' Death Marks End of an Era," *New York Amsterdam News,* 19 October 1974, sec. A, p. 1 (obituary); "Ed Smalls Dies at Age 92; Owned Famous Harlem Spot," *Jet* 47 (November 1974): 29–30 (obituary); Kathleen Drowne, "Small's Paradise," in *Encyclopedia of the Harlem Renaissance,* ed. Cary D. Wintz and Paul Finkelman (New York: Routledge, 2004), 2: 1120–21; Andrew Billingsley, *Yearning to Breathe Free: Robert Smalls of South Carolina and His Families* (Columbia: University of South Carolina Press, 2007); Abraham D. Sofaer, "The National Jazz Museum in Harlem," http://www.abesofaer.com/2011-pdfs/THE-NATIONAL-JAZZ-MUSEUM-Ind.-HARLEM.pdf (2011; accessed 21 May 2014).

Smalls, Edward

Saxophone

S.C. residence: Charleston (1920s)

Apparently a ward of Jenkins Orphanage, Smalls played in its bands in the 1920s.

Smalls, Joseph

Trumpet, trombone

6 October 1913 (probably West Palm Beach, Fla.)–?

S.C. residence: Charleston (probably by 1920–probably at least into early 1930s)

Apparently a ward of Jenkins Orphanage, Smalls played in its bands at least in the 1920s and performed with one of them in England in 1929.

The passenger list of the *Columbus,* which transported the orphanage band to Plymouth, England, in April 1929, records Smalls's age as fourteen. The list of the *Majestic,* which returned the group to N.Y.C. in June, identifies his specific birth date and place. Smalls was never enumerated for the census at the institution. He is probably the Joseph Smalls who was enumerated with his mother in Charleston on 9 or 10 January 1920 (estimated age seven) and on 7 April 1930 (seventeen). The first document records his birthplace as S.C.; the second, as Fla.

References

SECONDARY: John Chilton, *A Jazz Nursery: The Story of the Jenkins' Orphanage Bands of Charleston, South Carolina* (London: Bloomsbury Book Shop, 1980), 14–15, 27, 31–32, 58–59; Howard Rye, "Visiting Fireboys: The Jenkins' Orphanage Bands in Britain," *Storyville* 130 (1987): 137–43.

Smalls, Julius ("Geech")

Trumpet, trombone
-1977 (Newark, N.J.)
S.C. residence: Charleston (at least into 1920s)

Apparently a ward of Jenkins Orphanage, Smalls played in its bands in the 1920s. That decade he settled in Newark, N.J., where he performed at least into the 1930s, including with Duke Anderson, the Blue Rhythm Syncopators, and Pittman's Plaza Four.

Reference

SECONDARY: Barbara J. Kukla, *Swing City: Newark Nightlife, 1925–50* (Philadelphia: Temple University Press, 1991), 218.

Smiling Billy and His Collegiate Serenaders

See Nine Sizzling Syncopators

Smith, Albert

Piano, singer
25 November 1915 (Rembert, S.C.)-19 February 2003 (Rembert, S.C.)
S.C. residence: Rembert (1915-2003)

Smith, who began experimenting with the piano around age five, played the blues and gospel music. He was assisted by the Music Maker Relief Foundation, which gave him a piano and released his only recordings. He is buried in the New Haven United Methodist Church Cemetery, Bishopville, S.C.

Smith's birth date comes from the Social Security Death Index. The article "Albert Smith" in *Music Makers* indicates that at the time it was written Smith was "in his nineties" (139).

Recordings as Leader (All 1990s)

"Big Belly Mamma," "Learning to Play Piano," "Walk on Water"

References

SECONDARY: Joel Dyes, "The Piano Man," *Sumter (S.C.) Item,* 21 November 1993, sec. C, p. 1; "Albert Smith," in *Music Makers: Portraits and Songs from the Roots of America,* ed. Timothy Duffy (Athens, Ga.: Hill Street Press, 2002), 138–39; "Albert Smith," *Sumter (S.C.) Item,* 20 February 2003, sec. A, p. 7 (obituary).

Smith, Alton

Guitar, singer
3 June 1902 (rural Calhoun County, S.C.)-27 October 1960 (Saint Matthews, S.C.)
S.C. residences: rural Calhoun County (1902-no later than 1920), Saint Matthews (by 1920-1960)

The guitar playing of Smith, a laborer, inspired James "Blood" Ulmer, a young neighbor. Following his death from heart trouble, Smith was buried in Mount Carmel Cemetery, Saint Matthews.

Smith's dates and places of birth and death, cause of death, occupation, and burial place come from his death certificate. When Smith was enumerated for the 1910 census, he lived with his family in Caw Caw Township, Calhoun County; by the time of the 1920 census he resided in Saint Matthews, where he dwelled for the remainder of his life.

Reference

SECONDARY: Walter Hetfield, "Rare Blood," *Guitar Player* 24 (May 1990): 90–94, 156.

Smith, Arthur ("Guitar Boogie")

Guitar, banjo, mandolin, violin, trumpet, composer
1 April 1921 (Clinton, S.C.)-3 April 2014 (Charlotte, N.C.)
S.C. residences: Clinton (1921-1927), Kershaw (1927-1941), Spartanburg (1941-1943)

As a youth Smith played the trumpet, though he left it and Dixieland for stringed instruments and country music. He performed on radio and, while a teenager, signed a contract with RCA Victor; he and his group, the Crackerjacks, recorded initially in 1938. Despite his many recordings, including blues, he is probably best known for writing "Guitar Boogie," which he recorded for the first time in 1944, and "Feudin' Banjos," which he recorded with Don Reno in 1955. As "Dueling Banjos," the latter tune became popular from its performance in the movie *Deliverance* (1972). Broadcast for over three decades beginning in the early 1950s, *The Arthur Smith Show* was the first nationally syndicated country music television program. Later that decade Smith established the first recording studio in the Carolinas. Such musicians as Johnny Cash, Lester Flatt, and Earl Scruggs recorded in it; there James Brown recorded "Papa's Got a Brand New Bag." Smith also wrote and recorded religious music, composed music for a dozen movies, owned a chain of groceries, and sponsored fishing tournaments. He is buried in Evergreen Cemetery, Charlotte, N.C.

Compositions

"Acres of Diamonds," "Bach Boogie," "Banjo Boogie," "Banjo Rag," "Beach Boogie," "Blue, Blue Blues," "Blue Guitar," "Blues for Caroline," "Blues on Guitar," "Boogie Battle," "Boogie Blues," "Boomerang," "British Back Beat," "Carolina Cotton," "Carolina Maid," "Cotton Patch Rag," "Cracker Boogie," "Cripple Creek Shuffle," "Deep Sea Blues," "Empty Bottle Blues," "Express Train Boogie," "Feudin' Banjos" (also titled "Dueling Banjos"), "Fiery Guitar," "Fingers on Fire," "Five-String Banjo Boogie," "Guitar and Piano Boogie," "Guitar Boogie," "Hard-Boiled Boogie," "Hi-Lo Boogie," "Honky Tonk Queen," "In Memory of Hank Williams," "Maggie's Blues on Guitar," "Mandolin Boogie," "Midnight Rag," "More Guitar Boogie," "Ole Man Blues," "Raindrops and Teardrops," "Red Wing Boogie," "Rhumba Boogie," "Rinky Tinky Rhythm," "River Rag," "Rocking the News," "Smith's Rag," "Sweet Candy Man," "Teen-Age Rebel," "Texas Hop," "Three-D Boogie," "Travelin' Blues," "Troubled Mind Blues," "Who Shot Willie?"

Recordings as Leader

"I'm Going Back to Old Carolina" (1938), "Old Santa Claus Is Leavin' Just Because" (1938), "Beaty Steel Blues" (1944), "Each Night at Nine" (1944), "Guitar Boogie" (1944, 1945), "Please Come Back to Me, Daddy" (1944), "After You've Gone" (1945), "Blue Boogie" (1945), "Fingers on Fire" (1945), "South" (1945), "Stompin' at the Savoy" (1945), "Twelfth Street Rag" (1945, 1948), "More Guitar Boogie" (1946), "The Corset Song" (1947), "Guitar and Piano Boogie" (1947), "Banjo Boogie" (1948, 1959), "Foolish Questions" (1948), "New Look Blues" (1948), "Be Bop Rag" (late 1940s), "Mountain Be Bop" (late 1940s), "Chicken Strut" (1952), "All Night Blues" (1953), "Oklahoma Polka" (1953), "Feudin' Banjos" (1955; also titled "Dueling Banjos"), "Blue Rock" (1956), "Guitar Bustin'" (1958), *36 Best Loved Hymns* (ca. 1960), *Mister Guitar* (1961), *In Times Like These* (early 1960s), *Arthur "Guitar Boogie" Smith Goes to Town* (1962), *Arthur [Guitar] Smith and Voices* (1962), *Down Home with Arthur "Guitar Boogie" Smith* (1962–1963), *The Fourth Man and Other Beautiful Songs of Grace* (1962), *The Arthur Smith Show Live—On Stage from King's Mountain, N.C.* (1963; the title is from the label, not the cover, which identifies the album as *In Person: The Arthur Smith Show: Don't You Dare Miss It!*), *Blue Guitar* (1963), *The Arthur Smith Show: Wolverton Mountain and Other Mountain Songs* (1964), *The Original Guitar Boogie* (1964), *Town and Country Guitar Hits* (1964), *Great Country and Western Hits* (1965), *Singing on the Mountain* (1965), *The Arthur Smith Show Presents a Tribute to Jim Reeves* (1966), *Something Old, Something New* (1966), *The Guitars of Arthur "Guitar Boogie" Smith* (1967), *Arthur Smith Plays Bach Bacharach Bluegrass and Boogie* (1970), *Battling Banjos* (1973), *Our Favorite Hymns* (1973; also titled *Singin' on the Mountain*), *Guitars Galore* (1974; by Smith and Son, the son being Clay Smith), *Oldgrass, Newgrass, Bluegrass* (1976; by the Smith Bros. Bluegrass Orchestra), *Feudin' Again!* (1979; with Don Reno), *Swinging on the Swinging Bridge* (ca. 1992; with Raymond Fairchild)

Awards

Honorary degree, Steed College (1978); Hall of Fame, North Carolina Association of Broadcasters (1990); North Carolina Folk Heritage Award (1998); South Carolina Entertainment and Music Hall of Fame (1998); Lifetime Achievement Award, South Carolina Broadcasters Association (2006); North Carolina Music Hall of Fame (2010)

References

PRIMARY: Arthur Smith, *Apply It to Life* (Nashville: T. Nelson, 1991).

SECONDARY: Ed Davis, "Arthur Smith," *Muleskinner News:*

The Blue Grass Music Magazine 6 (February 1975): 9–11; Don Rhodes, "Arthur Smith: A Wide and Varied Musical Career," *Bluegrass Unlimited* 12 (July 1977): 20–23; Charles Wolfe, "The Odyssey of Arthur Smith," *Bluegrass Unlimited* 13 (August 1978): 50–57; Duncan Brantley, "Country Music's Arthur Smith Has a New Hit in Fishing Tournaments," *Sports Illustrated* 61 (10 December 1984): unnumbered pages between 100 and 113; Frye Gaillard, "Duelin' Banjos: Arthur Smith and Don Reno," in *Making Notes: Music of the Carolinas,* ed. Ann Wicker (Charlotte: Novello Festival Press, 2008), 29–31 (comments by Smith); Will Schultz, "Arthur 'Guitar Boogie' Smith (1921–)," http://www.northCarolinahistory.org/encyclopedia/458/entry (2012; accessed 21 May 2014); Daniel E. Slotnik, "Arthur Smith, 93; Wrote 'Dueling Banjos,'" *New York Times,* 9 April 2014, sec. B, p. 19 (also available as "Arthur Smith, Musician Who Wrote 'Dueling Banjos,' Dies at 93" at http://www.nytimes.com/2014/04/09/arts/music/arthur-smith-dies-at-93-wrote-dueling-banjos.html [accessed 21 May 2014]) (obituary); Ralph Grizzle, "Guitar Man: Arthur Smith," http://www.kenilworthmedia.com/cv/ourstate/people/arthur_smith.htm (undated; accessed 21 May 2014).

Smith, Chris (Christopher)

Composer, piano, singer

12 October 1879 (Charleston, S.C.)–4 October 1949 (New York, N.Y.)

S.C. residence: Charleston (1879–ca. 1895)

As a youth Smith, who apprenticed as a baker, played guitar and piano at functions in Charleston. In the 1890s he and Theodore Bowman, a Charleston friend, performed on the road with a medicine show and then went to N.Y.C. as a vaudeville team no later than 1900. They collaborated on many songs, beginning with "Coon's Day in May" (1898). Smith and Bowman worked together for approximately a decade, though Smith also had a songwriting and vaudeville relationship with another Bowman, Elmer. Additionally Smith had vaudeville acts with Billy Harper and Billy B. Johnson. He wrote over three-hundred tunes. His collaborators included Jimmy Durante, Sterling Grant, W. C. Handy, Walter Hirsch, Cecil Mack (R. C. McPherson), Bob Schafer, Henry Troy, and Clarence Williams. His compositions, often syncopated, were sung or played by notable performers, including Louis Armstrong, Sidney Bechet, Eubie Blake, Fanny Brice, Alberta Hunter, Jelly Roll Morton, Bessie Smith, Clara Smith, Willie "The Lion" Smith, and Sophie Tucker. Smith's most popular composition, "Ballin' the Jack" (1913), written with Jim Burris, inspired a dance that was used in the N.Y.C. musical *The Girl from Utah* (1914) and in the movies *For Me and My Gal* (1942) and *On the Riviera* (1951); it has been recorded hundreds of times and mentioned in such a recording as Chuck Berry's "Oh Baby Doll" (1957). Smith and Sterling Grant's "Lookin' for Another Sweetie" (1929) was retitled "I'm Confessin'" and credited to Al J. Neiburg, Doc Daugherty, and Ellis Reynolds.

Smith's birth date comes from his two World War I draft registration cards and his sole card for World War II. The death date is recorded in "Chris Smith, Dies." Conducted on 12 June, the 1900 census indicates that Smith then resided in N.Y.C.

Compositions

"Ain't Dat an Awful Feeling!," "All in Down and Out," "Any Old Place in Yankee Land Is Good Enough for Me," "Ballin' the Jack," "The Barn-Yard Rag," "Beans! Beans!! Beans!!!," "The Blues," "Boom, Turn, Ta-Ra-Ra, Zing Boom," "Bye Bye My Eva Bye Bye," "Cake Walkin' Babies from Home," "Cindy Lee," "Coon's Day in May," "Darktown Reveille," "Down among the Sugar Cane," "Down in Honky-Tonk Town," "The Farm Yard Blues," "Good-Bye, I'll See You Some More," "Good-Bye Ma Honey I'm Gone," "Good Morning Carrie!," "He's a Cousin of Mine," "Honky Tonky Monkey Rag," "The Humming Coon," "If We Were Alone," "I'll Do as Much for You," "In the Shadows of the Silv'ry Moon," "Is Julia Home?," "It Takes a Good Man to Do That," "I've Got de Blues," "I've Got My Habits On," "I Want to Know Where Tosti Went," "Junk Man Rag," "Let's Agree to Disagree," "Long Gone," "Lookin' for Another Sweetie," "Love, Honor, and Obey," "Mame, or the Mountain Maid," "Mister Moon, Kindly Come Out and Shine," "Monkey Rag," "My Country! Right or Wrong," "Never Let the Same Bee Sting You Twice," "Oh, So Sweet," "Only One Waltz More," "San Francisco Blues," "Scaddle-De-Mooch," "Shame on You," "That Puzzlin' Rag," "That Sneaky Snakey Rag," "Two Is Company and Three Is a Crowd," "You're in the Right Church but the Wrong Pew," "Yo' Wasting Time"

References

PRIMARY: Chris Smith, "Is Ragtime Dead?," *New York Age,* 8 April 1909, p. 6.

SECONDARY: Edward B. Marks, *They All Sang: From Tony Pastor to Rudy Vallée* (New York: Viking, 1935), passim; "Chris Smith," *Billboard* 61 (11 June 1949): 38–39; "Chris Smith, Dies," *New York Amsterdam News*, 8 October 1949, p. 2 (obituary); Tom Fletcher, *100 Years of the Negro in Show Business* (New York: Burdge, 1954), 145, 147–48, 169; Samuel B. Charters and Leonard Kunstadt, *Jazz: A History of the New York Scene* (Garden City, N.Y.: Doubleday, 1962), 45–47; Paul Oliver, *Songsters and Saints: Vocal Traditions on Race Records* (Cambridge: Cambridge University Press, 1984), passim; Eunmi Shim, "Chris Smith and the Ragtime Song" (master's thesis, University of Illinois at Urbana-Champaign, 1993); David A. Jasen, *Tin Pan Alley: An Encyclopedia of the Golden Age of American Song* (New York: Routledge, 2003), 374–75, 1768; Peter C. Muir, *Long Lost Blues: Popular Blues in America, 1850–1920* (Urbana: University of Illinois Press, 2010), passim; Benjamin Franklin V, "Chris Smith and the Bowmans," *Music Reference Services Quarterly* 15 (2012): 240–62.

Smith, Clara ("Queen of the Moaners," "Songbird of the South")

Singer

Probably September 1892 (S.C., probably Spartanburg)–2 February 1935 (Detroit, Mich.)

S.C. residence: probably Spartanburg (probably 1892–no later than ca. 1910)

Along with Ma Rainey, Bessie Smith, Mamie Smith, and a few others, Clara Smith was among the first blues singers to record. Beginning ca. 1910, she sang in vaudeville throughout the South and in time became a headliner on the Theater Owners' Booking Association circuit. She mentored a young entertainer who became famous as Josephine Baker. Within a few months of settling in N.Y.C. in early 1923, Smith began recording for Columbia, a relationship that lasted until 1932. This company released all but a few of her 125 recordings, including three under the leadership of Bessie Smith, two in 1923 and one (though another was not released) in 1925. These duets by the two Smiths were the only ones recorded by Bessie Smith, which, given her prominence, indicates how highly Columbia valued Clara Smith. (Gunther Schuller believes that "on her finest recordings she was very close to Bessie's equal" [239].) Of all the blues singers active during the 1920s, only Bessie Smith recorded more than Clara Smith. "My Doggone Lazy Man," which Clara Smith recorded in 1924, is the earliest example of a black harmonica player (Herbert Leonard) playing on a blues recording. Her recording of Harold Grey's "Done Sold My Soul to the Devil" (1924) is the first recorded blues to detail what the title describes, an action most famously invoked in the blues by Robert Johnson when telling of supposedly selling his soul to the devil in exchange for the ability to play the guitar masterfully. In singing about the devil as trickster, she initiated a rich blues tradition. Also in 1924 she established the Clara Smith Theatrical Club in N.Y.C., which she operated until 1932. She often recorded with jazz musicians. Among the highlights of her career are songs recorded in 1925 with the backing of Louis Armstrong, such as "Court House Blues" and ""Shipwrecked Blues." Following her 1926 marriage to baseball player Charles Wesley, she appeared in revues and other musical productions, including her own *Black Bottom Revue* and *Clara Smith Revue* (both 1927), as well as *Dream Girls and Candied Sweets* (1929), *Dusty Lane Revue* (1930), *January Jubilee Revue* (1931), and the all-black Western musical *Trouble on the Ranch* (1931). She was well enough known among blacks that in 1929 Chester L. Washington asked his readers, in one of ten questions about racial awareness published in the *Pittsburgh Courier*, "Who is Clara Smith?" (The answer: "Well-known blues singer—stage and record-recording artist.") Paul Oliver characterizes her singing: "Smith's work overall is a story of continued progression from moderate beginnings through successive stages until, by 1925, her flowering as a Classic Blues singer virtually without peer. She had a musical voice, clear enunciation, considerable range of expression, great vocal flexibility, warmth in her singing and above all, a real, innate feeling for the blues . . ." (11). Smith, who succumbed to heart disease, is buried in Lincoln Memorial Park Cemetery, Macomb County, Mich.

When Smith was enumerated for the census in Spartanburg on 7 June 1900, her birth date was recorded as September 1892. Her death certificate, which indicates that she died at age forty-two, estimates that she was born in 1893. Smith's obituary in the *Chicago Defender* states that the singer was "born 40 years ago in Spartanburg, S. C."

Compositions

"Black Woman's Blues," "Court House Blues," "Deep Blue Sea Blues," "Pictures on the Wall," "So Long, Jim"

Recordings as Leader

Complete Recorded Works in Chronological Order (1923–1932; six CDs)

Leader Recorded With

Bessie Smith (1923, 1925)

Award

Spartanburg Music Trail Marker (2011)

References

PRIMARY: Clara Smith, "Letters," *Chicago Defender,* 28 June 1924, p. 8 (national edition).

SECONDARY: Carl Van Vechten, "Negro 'Blues' Singers," *Vanity Fair* 26 (March 1926): 67, 106, 108; Chester L. Washington, "How Much Do You Know about Your Own Race?," *Pittsburgh Courier,* 15 June 1929, first sec., p. 8 (the answers are on p. 12); "Clara Smith, Popular Blues Singer, Dies," *Chicago Defender,* 9 February 1935, p. 9 (obituary); Paul Oliver, "'Clara Voce': A Study in Neglect," *Jazz Monthly* 2 (April 1958): 8–11, 24; Gunther Schuller, *Early Jazz: Its Roots and Musical Development* (New York: Oxford University Press, 1968), 239–40; Derrick Stewart-Baxter, *Ma Rainey and the Classic Blues Singers* (New York: Stein and Day, 1970), 64–68; Sally Placksin, *American Women in Jazz, 1900 to the Present: Their Words, Lives, and Music* (N.p.: Wideview Books 1982), 39–40; Eric Townley, "The Forgotten Ones: Clara Smith," *Jazz Journal International* 38 (July 1985): 16–17; Guido van Rijn, "Clara Smith: Eyewitness Account, 1926," *Juke Blues* 46 (Spring 2000): 52–53; Scott Yanow, *Classic Jazz* (San Francisco: Backbeat Books, 2001), 212–13; Ayana Smith, "Blues, Criticism, and the Signifying Trickster," *Popular Music* 24 (2005): 179–91; Pat Missin, "Who Was the First Blues Harp Player to Record? (Plus a Few Other Blues Harp 'Firsts')," http://patmissin.com/ffaq/q5.html (undated; accessed 21 May 2014).

Smith, Grace ("Bahama Mama")

Singer

1 January 1908 (Columbia, S.C.)–26 October 1989 (Newark, N.J.)

S.C. residence: Columbia (1908–probably 1922)

Probably in 1922 Smith moved from Columbia to Newark, N.J., where she began her career in the mid-1930s as a dancer at the Nest Club. She soon sang in local clubs, with "Easy Livin'" as her signature song, though "I Cried for You" and "Them There Eyes" were also favorites. She was the vocalist with Freddie Howard and His Swingsters in 1939. She sang in various N.Y.C. clubs, including Smalls Paradise. With other entertainers from Newark, ca. 1940 she performed in the Bahamas (thus her nickname), then Canada in 1944. Teamed with comedian Johnny Berry, she was with a USO show in 1945; subsequently she toured with Wynonie Harris. Smith is backed by the Snub Mosely band on two of the four songs she recorded for National Records in 1947. She turned to gospel music in the 1970s.

Recordings as Leader (All 1947)

"Baby, You're Just My Speed," "Competition Blues," "Get Your Fat Man Now," "What's on the Rail for the Lizards?"

Leader Recorded With

Bill Johnson (1946)

Reference

SECONDARY: Barbara J. Kukla, *Swing City: Newark Nightlife, 1925–50* (Philadelphia: Temple University Press, 1991), 47–48, 218 (comments by Smith).

Smith, Jabbo (Cladys)

Trumpet, cornet, euphonium, trombone, piano, singer

24 December 1908 (Pembroke, Ga.)–16 January 1991 (New York, N.Y.)

S.C. residences: Ladson (ca. 1915–ca. 1916), Charleston (ca. 1916–ca. 1924, with absences)

A ward of Jenkins Orphanage beginning in 1915, Smith learned to play several instruments but focused on the trumpet; his early style on this instrument was influenced by Gus Aiken and, more significantly, Horace Holmes. He became a professional musician with the band of Harry Marsh in Philadelphia, probably in 1924; next he was with Gus Aiken in Atlantic City and then Charlie Johnson there and in N.Y.C. (1925–1926). He began recording in 1926 and the next year soloed on two takes of "Black and Tan Fantasy" with the Duke Ellington band, though he was not a regular member of this organization. Smith, Garvin Bushell, James P. Johnson, and Fats Waller were among the musicians in the pit band of *Keep Shufflin'* (1928); these four men recorded as the Louisiana Sugar Babes. After moving to Chicago in 1928 Smith formed the Rhythm Aces, which was usually a quintet; its twenty recordings were all made in 1929. Modeled on groups led by Louis Armstrong, the Rhythm Aces featured Smith's playing and occasional singing. After the last of its recordings

Smith largely dropped from sight. He was twenty years old. Thereafter he played for a few years in Chicago and Milwaukee before affiliating with the Claude Hopkins band in N.Y.C. (1936–1938), but he made only a few recordings. In time he settled in Milwaukee. Rediscovered in the 1970s, he was honored at the 1975 Newport Jazz Festival, toured Europe, and performed in the musical *One Mo' Time* (1979–1980). When speaking with Chip Deffaa, trumpeter Johnny Letman stated, "Other than Louis [Armstrong], I think the greatest trumpet player I ever heard was . . . Jabbo Smith" (*Jazz Veterans,* 14). Gunther Schuller characterizes Smith as "a musician's musician" (*Early Jazz,* 210), notes that Smith influenced Roy Eldridge, and believes that Louis "Armstrong's trumpet skills, both musical and technical, could not be matched by *any* other trumpeter in his time (except perhaps Jabbo Smith)" (*The Swing Era,* 169). Whitney Balliett considers the Rhythm Aces recordings "among the best of the early jazz recordings" (*Jelly Roll, Jabbo, and Fats,* 66).

Smith's birth and death dates come from the Social Security Death Index. Upon leaving the orphanage around 1924 Smith reportedly briefly attended what is now South Carolina State University, though school records do not include his name. He was enumerated for the 1930 census in the House of Corrections, Chicago. Conducted in Newark, N.J., the 1940 census specifies his occupation as orchestra musician and indicates that in 1935 he lived in N.Y.C.

Compositions

"Absolutely," "Ace of Rhythm," "Band Box Stomp," "Boston Skuffle," "Croonin' the Blues," "Decatur Street Tutti," "How Can Cupid Be So Stupid?," "I Got the Stinger," "I Took My Little Daughter to the Zoo," "Jazz Battle," "Just Play the Blues for Me," "Let's Get Together," "Lina Blues," "Little Willie Blues," "Michigander Blues," "Moanful Blues," "More Rain, More Rest," "Rhythm in Spain," "Sau-sha Stomp," "Sleepy Time Blues," "Sweet and Low Blues," "Take Me to the River," "Take Your Time," "Tanguay Blues," "Till Times Get Better"

Recordings as Leader

"Ace of Rhythm" (1929), "Band Box Stomp" (1929), "Boston Skuffle" (1929), "Croonin' the Blues" (1929), "Decatur Street Tutti" (1929), "I Got the Stinger" (1929), "Jazz Battle" (1929), "Let's Get Together" (1929), "Lina Blues" (1929), "Little Willie Blues" (1929), "Michigander Blues" (1929), "Moanful Blues" (1929), "Sau-sha Stomp" (1929), "Sleepy Time Blues" (1929), "Sweet and Low Blues" (1929), "Take Me to the River" (1929), "Take Your Time" (1929), "Tanguay Blues" (1929), "Till Times Get Better" (1929), "Weird and Blue" (1929), "Absolutely" (1938, 1983), "How Can Cupid Be So Stupid?" (1938), "More Rain, More Rest" (1938), "Rhythm in Spain" (1938), *Hidden Treasure,* two vols. (1961), "Sweet Georgia Brown" (1974), "The Apex Blues" (1976), "Blues in G" (1976), "Moneda from Breda" (1976), "Sweet Sue, Just You" (1976), "Tin Roof Blues" (1976), "Love" (1980), *European Concerts* (1982)

Leaders Recorded With

Thomas Morris (1926), Duke Ellington (1927), Georgia Strutters (1927), Charlie Johnson (1927–1928), Eva Taylor (1927), Louisiana Sugar Babes (1928), Ikey Robinson (1929), Trombone Red (1931), Charles LaVere (1935), Claude Hopkins (1937), Sidney Bechet (1939), Hot Dogs (1976–1977, 1979), South Jazz Band (1976), Jens "Jesse" Lindgren (1978), New Orleans Joymakers (1978)

Award

Coastal Jazz Association of Savannah, Georgia, Hall of Fame (1991)

References

PRIMARY: Mike Joyce, "Jabbo Smith: Interview," *Cadence* 8 (May 1982): 11–13, 57; Whitney Balliett, *Jelly Roll, Jabbo, and Fats: 19 Portraits in Jazz* (New York: Oxford University Press, 1983), 63–73 (reprinted in Balliett's *American Musicians: Fifty-Six Portraits in Jazz* [New York: Oxford University Press, 1986], 59–65) (narrative by Smith); "Jabbo Smith: Eddie Cook Talks to the Mystery Man of the Jazz Trumpet," *Jazz Journal International* 37 (April 1984): 6–8; Jabbo Smith, untitled comments in notes to Smith's *Hidden Treasure,* vol. 2 (1985; Jazz Art Productions, unnumbered); Benjamin Franklin V, *Jazz and Blues Musicians of South Carolina: Interviews with Jabbo, Dizzy, Drink, and Others* (Columbia: University of South Carolina Press, 2008), 17–23.

SECONDARY: "Roy Eldridge," in *The Jazz Makers,* ed. Nat Shapiro and Nat Hentoff (New York: Rinehart, 1957), 299–301; Gunther Schuller, *Early Jazz: Its Roots and Musical Development* (New York: Oxford University Press, 1968), 210–14; John Chilton, *A Jazz Nursery: The Story of the Jenkins' Orphanage Bands of Charleston, South Carolina* (London: Bloomsbury Book Shop, 1980), 14–15, 27–29, 31–32, 41, 50, 58–59 (comments by Smith); untitled essay in notes to Smith's *Hidden*

Treasure, vol. 1 (1985; Jazz Art Productions, unnumbered); Gunther Schuller, *The Swing Era: The Development of Jazz, 1930–1945* (New York: Oxford University Press, 1989), passim; Chip Deffaa, *Voices of the Jazz Age: Profiles of Eight Vintage Jazzmen* (Urbana: University of Illinois Press, 1990), 188–217, 229–30; Chip Deffaa, *Jazz Veterans: A Portrait Gallery* (Fort Bragg, Calif.: Cypress House, 1996), 3–4, 14; Scott Yanow, *Classic Jazz* (San Francisco: Backbeat Books, 2001), 213–14; Scott Yanow, *The Trumpet Kings: The Players Who Shaped the Sound of Jazz Trumpet* (San Francisco: Backbeat Books, 2001), 338–40; Jack McCray, *Charleston Jazz* (Charleston, S.C.: Arcadia Publishing, 2007), 83–84, 86–87.

Smith, Lloyd F. ("Fatman")

Broadcaster, singer, trumpet, saxophone, bass, manager
4 October 1921 (Spartanburg, S.C.)–10 March 1989 (Philadelphia, Pa.)
S.C. residence: Spartanburg (1921–no later than late 1930s)

Smith left S.C. for Philadelphia while a teenager. He is best known as a disc jockey on WHAT, Philadelphia, from the mid-1950s to 1988; he broadcast mostly jazz and blues. At least in 1951 he toured with Louis Jordan and presumably managed him. Beginning in 1955 he managed the vocal group known sequentially as the Chants, the Equadors, the Modern Ink Spots, and the Cardinals. Smith's recording career as a rhythm-and-blues singer was limited to the 1950s; Leroy Kirkland's band is one of the groups that backed him. He also performed in clubs as an emcee. He is buried in Ivy Hill Cemetery, Philadelphia.

Smith's dates of birth and death come from the Social Security Death Index.

Compositions

"Bambalaya," "Cold Blooded," "Forgive Then Forget," "Get By," "Giddy Up, Giddy Up," "I Am the Man," "I Love, I Love You Babe," "I Work So Hard," "Miracle of Love," "Missles on Target," "Miss Mushmouth," "My Appointment Day," "My Clock Stopped," "My Lonely Girl," "No Better for You," "Sad Girl," "Sad Man," "Sad, Sad Lover," "Sex Driver," "Ship On," "Shy Girl"

Recordings as Leader

"Bambalaya" (1952; as the Bayou Boys, with Eddie Jefferson), "Dinah" (1952; as the Bayou Boys, with Eddie Jefferson), "Giddy Up, Giddy Up" (1952), "Why, Oh Why" (1952), "My Clock Stopped" (1953), "No Better for You" (1953), "Part Time Sweetheart" (1956), "Where You Been?" (1956), "Good Gracious" (1957), "Miss Mushmouth" (1957)

Leaders Recorded With

Frank Motley (1951), Tiny Grimes (1952), Manhattans (ca. 1959)

References

SECONDARY: Jim Detjen, "Lloyd 'Fatman' Smith, 67, Phila. Disc Jockey," *Philadelphia Inquirer*, 14 March 1989, sec. F, p. 5 (also available at http://articles.philly.com/1989-03-14/news/26131367_1_disc-jockey-cowboy-boots-administrative-assistant [accessed 21 May 2014]) (obituary); Gina Boubion, "'Fatman' Smith, 67," *Philadelphia Daily News*, 16 March 1989, local sec., p. 28 (obituary); "Lloyd 'Fatman' Smith (1922–1989)—Updated," http://gladdrags.blogspot.com/2009/10/lloyd-fatman-smith-1922-1989.html (13 October 2009; accessed 21 May 2014).

Smith, Ray (Raymond Arthur)

Broadcaster, drums
13 April 1922 (Malden, Mass.)–26 February 2010 (Savannah, Ga.)
S.C. residence: Bluffton (1997–2010)

After World War II, during which he served with the 568th Battalion on Iwo Jima, Smith worked in graphic arts and advertising until retiring in 1988. Beginning in 1958 he broadcast *Jazz Decades* in Framingham, Mass., but in 1972 moved the program to WGBH, Boston. After establishing a residence in S.C., he recorded his program there for continued airing on WGBH. He played drums in traditional jazz bands, including two he led, the Jazz Decades and the Paramount Jazz Band.

Recordings as Leader (All by the Paramount Jazz Band)

Ain't Cha Glad? (1989), *. . . And They Called It Dixieland* (1990–1991), "Jubilee Stomp" (1995), "How Could I Be Blue" (1996), *March of the Hoodlums* (1998)

Leaders Recorded With

Yankee Rhythm Kings (1975–1979), Reggie Phillips (1976), Banu Gibson (1982), Johnny Mince (1982), Rent Party Revelers (1982, 1985–1990)

References

PRIMARY: Arnold Rosen, *Before It's Too Late: Our Aging Veterans Tell Their Stories* (N.p.: Xlibris, 2009), 220–32 (interview).

SECONDARY: Russ Priestley, "Meet Ray Smith—Radio Personality," *Melrose (Mass.) Mirror,* http://melrosemirror.media.mit.edu/servlet/pluto?state=30303470616765303037576562506167653030326964303034343 23139 (1 September 2000; accessed 21 May 2014); David Lauderdale, "Ray Smith Had a Passion for Music, Abhorrence for War," *Hilton Head (S.C.) Island Packet,* 4 March 2010, sec. A, p. 3; Bryan Marquard, "Ray Smith, at 87; Hosted 'Jazz Decades' on WGBH," *Boston Globe,* 7 March 2010, sec. B, p. 12 (final edition); Charles Winokoor, "Ray Smith and His Jazz Decades Will Ever Be Forever Young," *Taunton (Mass.) Daily Gazette,* 7 March 2010, sec. A, p. 4 (as "Ray Smith and His Jazz Decades Are Forever Young," available at http://www.tauntongazette.com/opinions/opinion_columnists/x1224399090/CHARLES-WINOKOOR-Ray-Smith-and-his-Jazz-Decades-are-forever-young [accessed 21 May 2014]).

Smith, Willie (William McLeish)

Saxophone, clarinet, arranger, singer

25 November 1908 (Charleston, S.C.)–7 March 1967 (Los Angeles, Calif.)

S.C. residence: Charleston (1908–ca. 1923)

Smith reportedly played clarinet, his initial instrument, with bands from Jenkins Orphanage, though he was not a ward of the institution. After attending a technical school, he, a good student, majored in chemistry at Fisk University. There he met Jimmie Lunceford, who later formed a band that Smith joined in 1929, serving as arranger, soloist, and leader of the saxophone section. This organization gained popular and critical success. Upon leaving Lunceford in 1942 Smith played with Charlie Spivak until joining the navy the next year. He served at the Great Lakes Naval Training Station, where he trained bands and led one that included Ernie Royal, Clark Terry, and Gerald Wilson. After discharge in 1944 he affiliated with the band of Harry James, with which he played off and on into the mid-1960s. He toured with Jazz at the Philharmonic, replaced Johnny Hodges in the Duke Ellington band, and performed with Charlie Barnet and Billy May, among other leaders. He was influenced by Hodges and Benny Carter; the three of them are generally considered the major alto saxophonists of the swing era. Smith's notable solos include those on "What's Your Story, Morning Glory?" (on clarinet, with Lunceford in 1940), "I'm Confessin'" (with James in 1944), "Tea for Two" (part of a medley also featuring alto saxophonists Benny Carter and Charlie Parker with Jazz at the Philharmonic in 1946), and "Don't Let It Go to Your Head," "Just You, Just Me," and "You're Looking at Me" (with Nat Cole in 1956). Stanley Dance believes that Smith was "probably the greatest leader of a saxophone section that the [jazz] business has known" (93). He is buried in section 10, Angelus Rosedale Cemetery, Los Angeles.

Seemingly all published sources record Smith's birth date as 25 November 1910. His age was estimated as two when he was enumerated in Charleston for the census on 29 April 1910; a decade later (enumerated on 2 February 1920), as eleven. The passenger list of the *Hansa,* which transported the Lunceford band from Southampton, England, to N.Y.C. in March 1937, and the California Death Index, 1940–1997, indicate that he was born on 25 November 1908. His grave marker identifies 1908 as his birth year.

Willie Smith (saxophone), with Juan Tizol (valve trombone); reproduced from the William P. Gottlieb Collection, Library of Congress, Music Division

Compositions

"Never on Friday," "Not So Bop Blues"

Recordings as Leader

"All the Things You Are" (1945), "Body and Soul" (1945), "Honeysuckle Rose" (1945), "I Never Knew" (1945), "It's the Talk of the Town" (1945), "I've Found a New Baby" (1945), "Lover Come Back to Me" (1945; also titled "Experiment Perilous"), "Moten Swing" (1945), "September in the Rain" (1945), "Skylark" (1945), "Sweet Georgia Brown" (1945), "Tea for Two" (1945, 1947), "These Foolish Things" (1945), "Uncle Willie" (1945), "Willie Weep for Me" (1945), "Windjammer" (1945), "You Ought to Be in Pictures" (1945), "Not So Bop Blues" (1947), "Sophisticated Lady" (1947), *Alto Saxophonist Supreme!* (1965; also titled *The Best of Willie Smith*)

Leaders Recorded With

Jimmie Lunceford (1930, 1933–1942), Roy Eldridge (1940), Tab Smith (1941), Charlie Spivak (1942), Tommy Dorsey (1944), Harry James (1944–1951, 1954–1962, 1965), Al Casey (1945), Harry Edison (1945), Esquire All Stars (1945), Slim Gaillard (1945), Bobby Hackett (1945), Eddie Heywood (1945), Billie Holiday (1945, 1954), Helen Humes (1945), Jazz at the Philharmonic (1945–1947, 1952–1953), Jubilee All Stars (1945), Peggy Lee (1945), Johnny Otis (1945), André Previn (1945; also released as by Smith and by the Sunset All Stars), Trummy Young (1945), Ivie Anderson (1946), Wilbert Baranco (1946), Russell Jacquet (1946), Herb Jeffries (1946), Keynoters (1946), Charles Mingus (1946), Charlie Parker (1946), Juan Tizol (1946), Charlie Ventura (1946), Lester Young (1946), Lionel Hampton (1947), Woody Herman (1947), Mills Blue Rhythm Band (1947), Gene Norman (1947), Gerald Wilson (1947, 1954), Amos Milburn (1949–1950, 1952), Duke Ellington (1951–1952), Al Hibbler (1951), Louis Bellson (1952–1954, 1957), Billy May (1952, 1957, 1966), Billy Eckstine (1953–1955), Gene Krupa (1953), Oscar Peterson (1953), Charlie Barnet (1954, 1956, 1966–1967), Buddy Rich (1954), Dizzy Gillespie (1955), Nat Cole (1956), Red Norvo (1958), Nancy Wilson (1959, 1966), Ella Fitzgerald (1964)

References

PRIMARY: Stanley Dance, *The World of Swing* (New York: Scribner's, 1974), 1: 93–110 (substantial comments by Smith).

SECONDARY: "Willie Smith," *Ebony* 4 (June 1949): 41–43; John Chilton, *A Jazz Nursery: The Story of the Jenkins' Orphanage Bands of Charleston, South Carolina* (London: Bloomsbury Book Shop, 1980), 59; Gunther Schuller, *The Swing Era: The Development of Jazz, 1930–1945* (New York: Oxford University Press, 1989), 208, passim; Richard Cook, "Swinging Out," in *Masters of the Jazz Saxophone,* ed. Tony Bacon (London: Balafon Books, 2000), 27–28.

South Carolina Jubilee Singers

In 1876 this group appeared with the Charles Howard Combination, which performed *Uncle Tom's Cabin.* After touring on its own, apparently including two years in Europe during the mid-1880s, the singers participated in another production of *Uncle Tom's Cabin,* this time one billed as *Abbey's Double Mammoth Uncle Tom's Cabin* (1887–1888). During the 1890s they sang at the N.Y. revival meetings of evangelist Elizabeth Lavender (born a slave in S.C.), including in 1898 when Rev. W. H. Davis led the vocalists. In 1896 they were affiliated with the Lowry Institute of Mayesville, S.C., presumably as fundraisers. The South Carolinians toured at least until 1901, when they performed in Maine.

Because "Dancing with Sherman's Soldiers" notes that "the troupe claims to be the original band of South Carolina Jubilee Singers," a theater program for *Abbey's Double Mammoth Uncle Tom's Cabin* characterizes the group as "the original troupe of South Carolina Jubilee Singers," and an advertisement for this production in the *Lewiston (Maine) Saturday Journal* identifies the vocalists as "the only genuine South Carolina Jubilee Singers," more than one organization so named might have existed. If so, the one described here might not have been the group that manipulated audiences at concerts in Hartford, Conn., and Lowell, Mass., in 1877. The performers distributed complimentary tickets that were valid only for a couple, male and female. When the patrons arrived they were directed to the gallery, which was small, hot, and generally unsatisfactory. Having dressed well for the occasion they were forced, because of these conditions, to buy tickets for reserved seats on the main floor. The group described here also might not have been the South Carolina Jubilee Singers that gave a drunken performance at an 1884 concert in Bedford, Ohio.

References

SECONDARY: "Dramatic. Managers, Agents, Doorkeepers, and Others," *New York Clipper*, 7 October 1876, p. 222; untitled article, *Lowell (Mass.) Daily Courier*, 9 August 1877, p. 2; "Silly Dead-Heads in Hartford," *New York Times*, 20 August 1877, p. 5; untitled article, *Lowell (Mass.) Daily Courier*, 23 August 1877, p. 2; "Dancing with Sherman's Soldiers," *Syracuse (N.Y.) Standard*, 10 April 1884, p. 4; "A Bogus Band of Jubilee Singers," *New York Times*, 28 December 1884, p. 5; theater program for *Abbey's Double Mammoth Uncle Tom's Cabin* (probably 1887; available at http://archive.org/details/cihm_48581 [accessed 21 May 2014]); advertisement for *Abbey's Double Mammoth Uncle Tom's Cabin*, *Lewiston (Maine) Saturday Journal*, 28 April 1887, p. 4; "Jubilee Singers," *Poughkeepsie (N.Y.) Daily Eagle*, 14 October 1896, p. 6; "Colored Camp Meeting," *Rome (N.Y.) Citizen*, 16 August 1898, p. 1; "Lewiston and Auburn," *Lewiston (Maine) Daily Sun*, 18 January 1901, p. 8.

Sowell, Richard

Harmonica

13 November 1905 (presumably Buffalo, S.C.)–January 1980 (Jefferson, S.C.)

S.C. residences: Buffalo (1905–at least until 1930), Jefferson (–1980)

With guitarist William Francis, Sowell recorded two songs for Vocalion in 1927.

Sowell's birth and death dates and place of death come from the Social Security Death Index. The musician resided in Buffalo at least until 1930, when he was enumerated there for the census.

Recordings as Leader (Both 1927; with William Francis)

"John Henry Blues," "Roubin Blues"

Spearman, Toni (Ethel Louise)

Singer

5 December 1947 (Greenwood, S.C.)–

S.C. residence: Greenwood (1947–1965, 1968)

Growing up in Greenwood, Spearman sang in church and played saxophone in the high school band. A week after finishing high school in 1965 she moved to N.Y.C., where she took evening classes at City College of New York for a year and a half and sang in clubs on weekends. With the army military police from 1974 until 1988, she served in such countries as Germany, Japan, and Korea, often singing in clubs when off duty. Upon leaving the military she worked for Volkswagen in Germany from 1988 until 1997, when she retired to pursue a career in music, with Munich as her home base. She has performed at numerous blues festivals and has toured with B. B. King and Luther Allison.

Compositions

"Ain't No Fun," "Can't Get No Loving over the Telephone," "The Day You Got Married," "Dining Room Blues," "Do What You Wanna Do," "Freedom," "Going to Have a Party," "Hard Working Man," "I Like to Move," "I'll Be Your Lover," "I Love You No Matter What," "I Need You Tonight," "It Ain't Easy," "Knife in My Back," "Love Kills Pain," "Make It on Our Own," "My Apple on

Toni Spearman (left), with Beverly Guitar Watson, 2011 Rowan Blues & Jazz Festival, Salisbury, N.C.; permission of the photographer, Jan Jenson

a Tree," "My Lord and Me," "The Only Way Out," "Party Funk," "Right to Love Your Lover," "Rock to the Rhythm and Blues," "Rock with Mama," "So-Called Friends," "So Deep in Love with You," "Street Running Man," "Take It Easy, Baby," "Toni's Groove," "Treat Me Like a Clown," "Turn It Up," "Until You," "Voodoo Woman," "The Way You Make Me Feel," "Who Do You Think You Are?," "Who Is She?," "With You," "The World Has Colors," "You Know It Ain't Right"

Recordings as Leader

Rock with Mama! (1986), *Do What You Wanna Do!* (1989), *Freedom* (1992), *People* (1994), *Live in Concert* (1998), *So Called Friends* (2005), *Can't Get No Loving over the Telephone* (2010)

Film

Terror im Namen der Liebe (1997)

Award

Ambassador and Great Blues Artist, Blues Hall of Fame (2013)

References

PRIMARY: "Lady Blues Toni Spearman and Aron Burton—'A Love Affair with the Blues': Blues Life Interview," *Blues Life* 32 (1985): 6–10 (this issue is also designated volume 8, number 4) (also available at http://www.bluesart.at/NeueSeiten/2005BL32.html [accessed 21 May 2014]); Fritz Svacina and Gerhard Blazek, "Interview with Toni Spearman, Vienna 2009," *Blues Art Journal* 2, http://www.bluesart.at/NeueSeiten/2009+Toni+Spearman+Kurzinterview.html (May–July 2009; accessed 21 May 2014); Toni Spearman, "Interview with Rick 'The Train' Dettman from The Train Show, and Pad McKeage from 'Windows on Main,'" *Blues Art Journal*, http://www.bluesart.at/NeueSeiten/1-2010-Toni%20Spearman%20Interview-.html (undated; accessed 21 May 2014).

SECONDARY: Gerald Pazdernik, "Blues Lady Toni Spearman and Aron Burton, Live in Vienna," *Blues Life* 32 (1985): 30–31 (this issue is also designated volume 8, number 4) (also available at http://www.bluesart.at/NeueSeiten/2005BL32.html [accessed 21 May 2014]); "Toni Spearman," http://www.zoominfo.com/#!search/profile/person?personId=1186497761&targetid=profile (2005; accessed 21 May 2014) (though written in the third person, this text is possibly by Spearman); Joseph Sitarz, "Toni Spearman: 'We're Going to Be Rockin' Greenwood,'" *Blues Art Studio* 8, http://www.bluesart.at/NeueSeiten/TONI%20SPEARMAN%20usa.html (2006; accessed 21 May 2014) (comments by Spearman); Nathan Christophel, "Rockin' the House, German Style," *Newberry (S.C.) Observer*, 28 September 2011, pp. 1, 3 (comments by Spearman).

Spencer, Prince

Dancer, singer

Late 1910s (probably Jenkinsville, S.C.)–?

S.C. residence: Jenkinsville (probably late 1910s–ca. 1921)

Spencer, who began dancing in 1932, toured with the band of Ben Bernie and then with Major Bowes and Ted Mack; from 1935 at least until 1937 he teamed with Henry Coleman as the Two Taps. He then performed as a single before joining the Four Step Brothers in 1941. This group was known for challenge dancing: one man danced while the others provided rhythmic accompaniment by clapping; each solo dancer tried to outdo the others. He remained with the Four Step Brothers until the mid-1960s, when he became a grocer in Chicago. Spencer was the unofficial manager of comedian Redd Foxx, a longtime friend.

Some sources indicate that Spencer was born on 3 September 1917 in Jenkinsville, S.C. When enumerated for the census in Township 11 (Jenkinsville), Fairfield County, S.C., on 5 January 1920, his age was estimated as two years; in Toledo, Ohio, on 14 April 1930, as ten; in Boston on 12 April 1940, as twenty-two. Though Spencer's middle initial has been identified as C., the 1920 census records it as A. A 2007 video interview with the dancer is housed at HistoryMakers, 1900 S. Michigan Ave., Chicago, Ill. 60616.

Films

That's My Gal (1947; with the Four Step Brothers), *Here Come the Girls* (1953; with the Four Step Brothers), *The Patsy* (1964; with the Four Step Brothers), *Harlem Nights* (1989)

Awards

Hollywood Walk of Fame (1988; as member of the Four Step Brothers); honorary degree, Oklahoma City University (2002); Flo-Bert Award (2009)

References

PRIMARY: Rusty E. Frank, *Tap! The Greatest Tap Dance Stars and Their Stories, 1900–1955* (New York: William Morrow, 1990), passim (see especially 223–30) (mainly a narrative by Spencer).

SECONDARY: "A Wow on Major Bowes' Hour," *Chicago Defender*, 11 September 1937, p. 7 (national edition);

"Sensational," *Pittsburgh Courier,* 30 March 1940, p. 21; Frank Cullen, *Vaudeville Old and New: An Encyclopedia of Variety Performers in America* (New York: Routledge, 2007), 1: 398–400.

Spivak, Charlie (Charles)

Trumpet, arranger

Probably ca. 1905 (probably Russia)-1 March 1982 (S.C., below Caesar's Head, N.C.)

S.C. residences: Greenville (1967-1976), below Caesar's Head, N.C. (1976-1982)

After studying trumpet as a youth in New Haven, Conn., Spivak became a professional musician before the mid-1920s. As a lead trumpeter with a full, sweet sound, he was in demand, as indicated by the number of recordings he made in the 1930s. His longest affiliation was with the Ben Pollack band; other sidemen included, at one time or another, Jimmy Dorsey, Harry James, Glenn Miller, and Jack Teagarden. Within a jazz context he is best known for his playing on Bob Crosby's recording of "South Rampart Street Parade" (1937). Backed financially by Miller, he organized his own band in 1940. Over time notable personnel included Larry Elgart, Les Elgart, Willie Smith, and Dave Tough. Manny Albam, Sonny Burke, Neal Hefti, Jimmy Mundy, Sy Oliver, and Nelson Riddle were among its arrangers. Vocalists included June Hutton, Tommy Lynn (Leonetti), and Irene Daye, who became his second wife. Beginning in the mid-1950s Spivak was headquartered in Miami. In 1967 he moved to Greenville, where an engagement of several weeks at Ye Olde Fireplace lasted the remainder of his life. Dubby Spivak, his third wife, was the vocalist. Following his death from cancer he was buried in Garden of the Cross lot 109, Grandview Memorial Gardens, Travelers Rest, S.C.

The trumpeter's date and place of birth are in dispute. Some sources, including his widow, indicate that Spivak was born in Kiev, Ukraine; others, New Haven, Conn. One source identifies the place as Talies, Russia, a town that seems never to have existed. His age was estimated as fifteen when he was enumerated for the census in New Haven on 10 January 1920; this document records his birthplace as Russia. His age was estimated as twenty-five when he was enumerated in Bronx, N.Y., on 15 April 1930; this census identifies Russia as his birthplace and notes that his family immigrated to the United States in 1910. In *Conversations with Jazz Musicians,* Zane Knauss states that "Charlie Spivak isn't exactly sure of his birth date, but he's positive he was born in 1907, in Eastern Europe" (178). The Social Security Death Index records 17 February 1907 as the trumpeter's birth date. Sources indicate that Spivak lived in Cleveland, S.C., from 1976 until his death. During these years he lived in a gated community in an unincorporated area; the nearest post office was in Cleveland.

Charlie Spivak, N.Y.C. (?), ca. October 1946; reproduced from the William P. Gottlieb Collection, Library of Congress, Music Division

Compositions

"Charlie Horse," "Daisy Chain," "Even Steven," "Stardreams"

Recordings as Leader (Limited to Those with Possible Jazz Content)

"Autumn Nocturne" (1941), "Charlie Horse" (1941), "Don't Cry" (1941), "I Surrender Dear" (1941), "Let's Go Home" (1941), "Move Over" (1941), "Slap-Slap" (1941), "Stardreams" (1941), "A Weekend in Havana" (1941), "What's Cookin'" (1941), "Brother Bill" (1942), "I Left My Heart at the Stage Door Canteen" (1942), "I'll Remember April" (1942), "I Wonder What's Become of Sally" (1942), "My Devotion" (1942), "Serenade in Blue" (1942), "Daisy Chain" (1943), "Besame Mucho" (1944), "Deed I Do" (1944), "The General Jumped at Dawn" (1944), "I Can't Give You Anything but Love" (1944), "I Got Plenty o' Nothin'" (1944), "Laura" (1944), "Marianne" (1944), "Mean to Me"

(1944), "Solitude" (1944), "Summertime" (1944), "Trav'lin' Light" (1944), "It's Been a Long, Long Time" (1945), "My Baby Said Yes" (1945), "Penthouse Serenade" (1945), "Solid Steven" (1945), "You Go to My Head" (1945), "Blue Champagne" (1946), "Flat Feet" (1946), "Gimme a Little Kiss" (1946), "Linda" (1946), "Stomping Room Only" (1946), "Born to Be Blue" (1947), "Diggin' a Groove" (1947), "The Gentleman Is a Dope" (1947), "Space Jumper" (1947; also titled "Charlie's Diner"), "Stop Throwin' Rocks at the Devil" (1947), "Swingin' the Blues" (1947), "Tennessee" (1947), "Just Friends" (1948), "One Way Passage" (1948), "April in Paris" (1950), "Loveless Love" (1950), "Moonlight on the Ganges" (1950)

Leaders Recorded With

Paul Specht (1924, 1926–1927), Georgians (1925, 1927, 1929), Annette Hanshaw (1929–1930), Ruth Etting (1930), Ben Pollack (1930, 1933–1934, 1936), Gil Rodin (1930–1931), Cornell Smelser (1930), Jack Teagarden (1930–1931, 1939), Ozzie Nelson (1931–1932), New Orleans Ramblers (1931), Dorsey Brothers Orchestra (1934–1935), Ethel Waters (1934), Bing Crosby (1935), Glenn Miller (1935, 1937), Ray Noble (1935–1936), Clark Randall (1935), Larry Clinton (1937), Bob Crosby (1937–1938), Mills Swingphonic Orchestra (1937), Chauncey Morehouse (1937), Claude Thornhill (1937), Johnny Williams (1937), Tommy Dorsey (1938), Casper Reardon (1938), All Star Band (1939), Metronome All Stars (1940), Dubby Spivak (1978)

Films

Follow the Boys (1944), *Pin Up Girl* (1944)

Award

Order of the Palmetto (1978)

References

PRIMARY: Zane Knauss, "Charlie Spivak," in *Conversations with Jazz Musicians* (Detroit: Gale Research, 1977), 178–201.

SECONDARY: "Spivak Gets Crown from TD, Duke Wins, Bing Is New Voice," *Down Beat* 12 (1 January 1945): 1, 13; George T. Simon, *The Big Bands* (New York: Macmillan, 1967), passim (see especially 426–29); George T. Simon, *Simon Says: The Sights and Sounds of the Swing Era, 1935–1955* (New York: Galahad Books, 1971), passim (see especially 437–38); "Four-Week Stint Lasts 10 Years," *Canton (Ohio) Repository,* 26 December 1976, p. 32; "Charlie Spivak, Bandleader Renowned for 'Sweetest Trumpet in the World,' Dies," *Greenville (S.C.) News,* 2 March 1982, sec. A, pp. 1, 7 (obituary); "Charlie Spivak, 77; Big-Band Leader of the 40's," *New York Times,* 2 March 1982, sec. D, p. 23 (obituary); George H. Buck, Jr., "Charlie Spivak, 1907–1982," *C.R.C. Newsletter* 8 (16 August 1982): verso of cover page; Bob Harrington, "When Charlie Spivak Blew Hot!," *Jazz Journal* 52 (March 1999): 10–11 (comments by Spivak); Scott Yanow, *The Trumpet Kings: The Players Who Shaped the Sound of Jazz Trumpet* (San Francisco: Backbeat Books, 2001), 348.

Spivak, Dubby (Wilma Hayes)

Singer, leader

20 February 1933 (Chattanooga, Tenn.)–

S.C. residences: Greenville (1972–1976), below Caesar's Head, N.C. (1976–1984)

Born Wilma Hayes, this singer began performing professionally in Calif. around 1953. Later she lived in Charlotte, N.C., and Atlanta. For approximately a decade beginning ca. 1963 she sang with the group of her second husband, pianist Jerry Lambert. In the early 1970s she performed at the Charcoal Steak House in Greenville. She met Charlie Spivak in 1972, married him in 1974, and sang with his band during its long engagement at Ye Olde Fireplace in Greenville. Upon the death of her husband she led his group for two years (1982–1984).

Dubby Spivak; permission of Dubby Spivak

She performed several times at the Manassas (Va.) Jazz Festival, initially in 1982.

From 1976 until 1984 Spivak lived with her husband in a gated community in an unincorporated area just south of the N.C.-S.C. border. When she remarried in Ala. in 2007 she assumed her husband's surname, Giles.

Recordings as Leader

It's So Peaceful in the Country (1978), *Dubby Swings Lightly* (ca. 1984), *Stardreams* (1986; this CD includes Charlie Spivak's *Now! 1981*)

Leader Recorded With

Charlie Spivak (1978–1981)

Stafford, Alexander

Tuba

(S.C.)

S.C. residence: Charleston (early 1900s–at least until 1910)

Apparently a ward of Jenkins Orphanage, Stafford played in its bands in the early 1900s. He became a music tutor.

Stafford's birthplace is recorded in the 1910 census, for which the youth was enumerated at the orphanage on 22 April 1910; this document does not record his estimated age.

Reference

SECONDARY: John Chilton, *A Jazz Nursery: The Story of the Jenkins' Orphanage Bands of Charleston, South Carolina* (London: Bloomsbury Book Shop, 1980), 59.

Staggers, Jake (Jacob C.; "J. C.")

Banjo, singer

Possibly 28 November 1898 (probably Tugaloo Township, Oconee County, S.C.)–17 June 1984 (Toccoa, Ga.)

S.C. residence: probably Tugaloo Township, Oconee County (possibly 1898–possibly 1928, but no later than 1930)

Around age ten Staggers learned to play the banjo on instruments made from tin pans and animal skins. Though he worked in construction, on the railroads, and as a truck driver, in Georgia—where he moved probably in the late 1920s—he played at dances, as well as at such events as hog killings and corn shuckings. In addition to dance tunes he performed spirituals, railroad songs, and pre-blues, usually unaccompanied. Regarded by Fred J. Hay as "the best banjo picker, black or white, in northeast Georgia and the adjacent part of South Carolina" (8), Staggers is credited with having helped expose white Appalachians to the black banjo tradition, "upon which the blues developed," as Cecelia Conway observes in "Black Banjo Songsters in Appalachia" (156). Staggers is buried in Saint Mark Church Cemetery, Madison, S.C.

The 1900 census is the earliest document located that details realities relating to Staggers's life. Conducted in Tugaloo Township, Oconee County, on 26 or 27 June, it indicates that Jacob C. Staggers was born in S.C. in November 1898. Conducted in Tugaloo Township on 28 April, the 1910 census records his name as John C. Stagers and estimates his age as ten. When, as J. C. Staggers, he registered for the draft in Madison, Oconee County, on 12 September 1918, he stated that he was born on 11 October 1900, worked in farming outside Madison, and lived at RFD 1, Madison. His age was estimated as twenty-one when he was enumerated for the census in Oconee County as John C. Stagers on 23 January 1920. It was estimated as thirty when, as Jake C. Staggers, he was enumerated in Toccoa, Ga., on 17 April 1930. His age was estimated as forty when he was enumerated as J. C. Staggers at Militia District 440, Stephens County, Ga., on 2 April 1940. This census notes that in 1935 he resided in rural Stephens County. The Social Security Death Index records his birth date as 28 November 1898. When speaking with Art Rosembaum in 1981, Staggers identified his birth date as 20 June 1898. At least one source specifies Walhalla, S.C., as Staggers's birthplace. Staggers's unissued recordings are in the Georgia Folklore Collection, Walter J. Brown Media Archives & Peabody Awards Collection, University of Georgia Special Collections Libraries.

Recordings as Leader (All 1981)

"Garfield" (two versions), "Goin' down One Road Feelin' Bad," "How Long the Train Been Gone?," "Sally Ann," "Shout Lulu"

References

PRIMARY: Art Rosenbaum, *Folk Visions and Voices: Traditional Music and Song in North Georgia* (Athens: University of Georgia Press, 1983), 73–86 (interview).

SECONDARY: Art Rosenbaum, notes to the CD *Folk Visions and Voices: Traditional Music and Song in Northern*

Georgia, vol. 2 (1984; Folkways FE-34162); Cecelia Conway, *African Banjo Echoes in Appalachia: A Study of Folk Traditions* (Knoxville: University of Tennessee Press, 1995), passim; Cecelia Conway, "Black Banjo Songsters in Appalachia," *Black Music Research Journal* 23 (Spring–Autumn 2003): 149–66 (see especially 158–59); Fred J. Hay, "Black Musicians in Appalachia: An Introduction to Affrilachian Music," *Black Music Research Journal* 23 (Spring–Autumn 2003): 1–19 (see especially 3, 8).

Staley, Elijah

See Carolina Slim

Stallings, Big Daddy (Charles Edward)

Guitar, singer, composer
8 May 1945 (Columbia, S.C.)-
S.C. residence: Columbia (1945)

At age six months Stallings moved with his parents from Columbia, S.C., to Hobbsville, N.C., where he was reared. Growing up he was exposed to the blues by listening to WLAC, Nashville, and to the electric guitar playing of Fred Hill and Buddy Mitchell, local musicians. After being discharged from the army in 1967 he settled in Baltimore, Md., where he worked as a truck driver. Beginning ca. 1969 he played locally for a dozen years with Antoine, a funk band, after which he performed off and on with other groups. In time he produced his initial CD as a memento for his grandchildren; on it and his subsequent releases he plays his own compositions. Because of the response these releases generated, he began performing at blues festivals.

Big Daddy Stallings, Pennsylvania Blues Festival, Palmerton, Pa., 31 July 2011; permission of the photographer, Gene Tomko

Compositions

"Beulah Mae," "Blues Cowboy," "Blues in Your Funk," "Blues Line Dance," "Blues Party," "Blues Train Express," "Boody Pop and Lock," "Booty Slappin'," "Call Me Big Daddy," "City Life," "Doggone Shame," "Don't Cry," "Down on the Farm," "E-Groove," "Fine Lady," "Four-by-Four Woman," "Funky Farm," "Getting Old," "Goin' Down South," "Hand Dance," "Hard Times, Good Times," "Hobbsville, N.C.," "Hola, Senorita," "Horny Bee," "I'm Gone, Gone," "In Love by Yourself," "I've Got the Blu Hoos," "I Wanna Dance," "Knocked Up," "Last Exit," "Latin Girls," "Let's Boogie," "Levine's Boogie," "Lost and Found," "Lucky Number," "Million Dollars," "My New Chevy Van," "Old Dog," "One Night Lover," "Ragged Sam," "Ronnie Love," "Rubb," "She Devil," "She's Gone," "Soul Rock 'n' Roll," "Strange Things," "Thank You," "Thank You Boogie," "Thank You, Jesus," "Young Boy, Young Man"

Recordings as Leader

One Night Lover (2004), *Blues Evolution* (2007), *Blues Party* (2009), *I Like It When They Call Me Big Daddy* (2013)

Website

http://www.bigdaddystallings.com/ (accessed 21 May 2014)

Reference

PRIMARY: Scott M. Bock, "Charles 'Big Daddy' Stallings: The People Is What Drives You," *Living Blues* 224 (April–May 2013): 28–33 (narrative by Stallings).

Stark, Cootie (Johnny Miller)

Guitar, singer

Possibly 9 December 1926 (Abbeville County, S.C.)–14 April 2005 (Greenville, S.C.)

S.C. residences: Abbeville County (possibly 1926–ca. 1941), Anderson County (ca. 1941–ca. 1942), Greenville (ca. 1942–ca. 1946, 1980s–2005), Columbia (late 1940s–possibly early 1950s)

As a child Miller worked in cotton fields. Known as Cootie from an early age, he was mostly sightless by the time he was a teenager and totally blind by thirty. He began playing guitar around age fourteen. After locating to Greenville he met Baby Tate, who taught him tunes, whereupon Miller sang and played Piedmont blues on Greenville streets. An itinerant musician beginning in the mid-1940s, he resumed living in Greenville in the 1980s after residing in Boston for over a quarter century. In the mid-1990s he was discovered by musicologist Tim Duffy, who, through the Music Maker Relief Foundation, provided him with a new guitar, scheduled performances for him, and recorded him. At this point he became known professionally as Cootie Stark, the surname being a shortened version of the last name of his stepfather, John Henry Starks. He is buried in Greenville Memorial Gardens, Piedmont, S.C.

Cootie Stark, King Biscuit Blues & Gospel Festival, Helena, Ark., 8 October 2004; permission of the photographer, Gene Tomko

Stark was born Johnny (some sources say Johnie; others, James) Miller to Lola Miller; his father is not known. The 1930 census indicates that Miller's mother was then the wife of John Starks and that Johnny Miller lived with them; he is identified as Starks's stepson. The Millers and Starkses had been next-door neighbors. Though Johnny Miller's year of birth is sometimes recorded as 1927, the Social Security Death Index indicates that it was 1926.

Recordings as Leader

"Black Gal" (1996), *Sugar Man* (1997), "Drinkin' the Wine" (1997; with Drink Small), "High Yellow" (1997), "Keep On Walkin'" (1997), *Raw Sugar* (ca. 2002), *Christmas with Cootie* (ca. 2004)

Leaders Recorded With

Neal Pattman (1998), Kenny Wayne Shepherd (2005)

Films

Toot Blues (2008), *Living the Blues* (2010)

Award

Jean Laney Harris Folk Heritage Award (2005)

References

PRIMARY: "Cootie Stark," *Living Blues* 137 (January–February 1998): 23–25 (also available at www.ibiblio.org/musicmakers/mm4000b/mm4008.html [accessed 21 May 2014]) (narrative by Stark).

SECONDARY: Peter Cooper, "Payback Time," *Oxford American* 21–22 (May 1998): 10–11 (comments by Stark); Scott M. Bock, "Cootie Stark: Before the Sugar Man," *Juke Blues* 46 (Spring 2000): 26–29 (comments by Stark); "Johnny Miller," *Greenville (S.C.) News*, 18 April 2005, sec. B, p. 4 (obituary); Dave Peabody, "Neal Pattman and Cootie Stark," *Juke Blues* 59 (Late Summer 2005): 66–67 (obituary); Mark Coltrane, "Cootie Stark," *Living Blues* 180 (September–October 2005): 85–86 (obituary).

Starks, Booker T.

Saxophone

-before 1981

S.C. residence: Charleston (by late 1920s–at least into early 1930s)

Apparently a ward of Jenkins Orphanage, Starks performed in its bands in the late 1920s and early 1930s. He then played with the Carolina Cotton Pickers.

Bruce Bastin indicates that Starks had died by the time Bastin completed his manuscript.

Leader Recorded With

Carolina Cotton Pickers (1936–1937)

References

SECONDARY: John Chilton, *A Jazz Nursery: The Story of the Jenkins' Orphanage Bands of Charleston, South Carolina* (London: Bloomsbury Book Shop, 1980), 59; Bruce Bastin, "A Note on the Carolina Cotton Pickers," *Storyville* 95 (June–July 1981): 177–82.

Stephens, James

See Guitar Slim

Sterbank, Mark John

Saxophone, clarinet, flute
21 February 1966 (Cleveland, Ohio)-
S.C. residence: Charleston (1997-)

Sterbank, who began playing the saxophone at age nine, started performing professionally at sixteen. He focused on jazz and classical music at the Eastman School of Music, from which he received a bachelor's degree in saxophone performance in 1988. He moved to New Orleans to study with Ellis Marsalis; there he received a master's degree in saxophone performance from the University of New Orleans (1991). After living in N.Y.C., where he performed mainly at the Times Square Church, in 1997 he accepted a position at Charleston Southern University, where he teaches saxophone and jazz studies. He is active on the local jazz scene as leader and sideman. He also plays in symphony orchestras.

Compositions

"Along the Way," "Blues in the Key of Fred," "By Faith," "Contrary Motion," "Dayspring," "For unto Us," "Foursight," "Happenstance," "Images," "In This Day and Age," "Leah's Lament," "Leap of Faith," "Little Joy," "Nomad," "Peter's Denial," "Seventy Times Seven," "Slidin'," "Taking Turns," "Tub of Blues"

Recordings as Leader

Hymns and Spirituals (2010), *Hymns and Spirituals 2* (2011), *Dayspring* (2013)

Leaders Recorded With

Charleston Jazz Initiative Legends Band (2010), Charlton Singleton (2011, 2013)

Award

National Endowment for the Arts Jazz Study Grant (1989)

Website

http://www.marksterbank.com/ (accessed 21 May 2014)

References

PRIMARY: Adam Parker, "Sterbank Group Offers 'Hymns and Spirituals,'" *Charleston (S.C.) Post and Courier,* 13 January 2013, sec. E, pp. 1, 3 (interview).

SECONDARY: Jack McCray, "Sterbank Offers 6th 'Hymns and Spirituals,'" *Charleston (S.C.) Post and Courier,* 14 January 2010, sec. F, p. 8; Jack McCray, "'Hymns and Spirituals' Hitting Its Stride," *Charleston (S.C.) Post and Courier,* 13 January 2011, sec. E, p. 8 (comments by Sterbank).

Stewart, Timothy

Alto horn
Ca. 1907-?
S.C. residences: Charleston (by 1920-probably 1926), Orangeburg (1926-at least into 1930)

A ward of Jenkins Orphanage, Stewart played in its bands in the 1920s. In 1930 he received a degree from what is now South Carolina State University.

Stewart's age was estimated as twelve when the youth was enumerated for the census at the orphanage on 9 January 1920.

Reference

SECONDARY: John Chilton, *A Jazz Nursery: The Story of the Jenkins' Orphanage Bands of Charleston, South Carolina* (London: Bloomsbury Book Shop, 1980), 33, 59.

Still, Cleveland

Singer
Possibly October 1934 (possibly rural Lexington County, S.C.)-
S.C. residences: possibly Lexington County (possibly 1934-no later than 1940), possibly Shaw Township, Edgefield County (not before 1935-possibly 1943)

At age nine Still moved from S.C. to N.Y.C. There, in 1955, he sang with the Scale-Tones, a gospel group, before affiliating the next year with the

Marvels, which evolved into the Five Wings. Apparently at Still's suggestion, the group changed its name to the Dubs; this doo-wop/rhythm-and-blues group had hits with "Could This Be Magic" and "Don't Ask Me." Though it disbanded in 1958, three years later Still joined the reconstituted Dubs, which he left in 1963. Around 1970 he helped reestablish the group, which performed on the oldies circuit. After leaving it in 1983 he sang with the Cleveland Still Dubs. With the various Dubs groups Still sang the falsetto parts.

The 1940 census is the only public document found that documents what appears to be Still's family, one headed by a Cleveland Still, age twenty-four. Conducted in Shaw Township, Edgefield County, S.C., on 3 April, it indicates that in 1935 the family lived in rural Lexington County, S.C. However, Cleveland Still, Jr., was not enumerated with this family (or with any other family) for this census, though one of its members could have been born in 1934, the birth year assigned to Cleveland Still, Jr., by Todd R. Baptista in *Group Harmony*. This was Edgar Still, whose age was estimated as five. If the singer was of this family and was born in 1934, he could then have been known as Edgar. Still's birth date has not been confirmed.

Compositions

"Everlasting Love," "Please the Crowd"

Recordings as Leader (with the Cleveland Still Dubs)

"Could This Be Magic" (1984), "Teddy Bear" (1984), "Beside My Love" (1986)

Leaders Recorded With

Marvels (1956), Scale-Tones (1956), Dubs (1957–1958, 1961–1963, 1971, 1973), Five Wings (1957)

Award

United in Group Harmony Association Hall of Fame (1993; as member of the Dubs)

References

SECONDARY: Todd R. Baptista, *Group Harmony: Behind the Rhythm and the Blues* (New Bedford, Mass.: TRB Enterprises, 1996), 28–40, 165 (comments by Still); Marv Goldberg, "The Dubs," http://www.uncamarvy.com/Dubs/dubs.html (2009; accessed 21 May 2014); Frank Fazio, "The Dubs," http://www.soulfulkindamusic.net/dubs.htm (undated; accessed 21 May 2014).

Stirling, Joshua

Tuba

S.C. residence: Charleston (probably at least late 1920s–probably at least into mid-1930s)

Apparently a ward of Jenkins Orphanage, Stirling played in its bands ca. 1930.

Stone, Angie (Angela Laverne Brown; "Angie B.")

Singer, keyboards, composer

Probably 18 December 1961 (Columbia, S.C.)–

S.C. residence: Columbia (probably 1961–possibly ca. 1980)

Angie Brown began her career as Angie B. in 1979 with the trio Sequence, possibly the first female group to record rap. Upon marrying Lil' Rodney C in the mid-1980s she assumed his surname, Stone. She sang with Vertical Hold before beginning a solo career. James M. Manheim believes that her CD *Black Diamond* "exuded a raw power of a kind not often heard in the increasingly electronics-dominated world of urban music" (179). Generally considered a rhythm-and-blues and soul singer with roots in gospel music, Stone has been nominated for Grammy Awards and has had albums reach the top ten on the rhythm-and-blues charts. She sings on the sound tracks of at least a dozen movies, beginning with *Money Talks* (1997).

Some sources record Stone's birth year as ca. 1965, a date that seems unlikely because the singer initially recorded in 1979.

Compositions

"Africa," "All for Me," "Baby," "Baby Cries Ah Yah," "Backup Plan," "Beating of My Heart," "Bring Your Heart," "Brother" (also titled "Brotha"), "Call on Me," "Different Directions," "Everyday," "Excuse Me," "Go Back to Your Life," "Greatdayindamornin'," "Half a Chance," "Happy Being Me," "Here We Go Again," "Hold Me Down," "I Don't Care," "I Found a Keeper," "I Got What You Need," "I Wanna Thank You," "I Wasn't Kiddin'," "Jam for the Ladies," "Jones in My Bones" (also titled "Jonz in My Bonz"), "Kiss All Over Your Body," "Let It Go," "Lovers' Ghetto," "Mahogany Soul," "Make It Last," "Makin' Me Feel," "My People," "No More Rain in This Cloud," "Playa Playa," "Play with It," "Pop Pop," "Send It On," "Shadows of Your Love,"

"Sit Down," "Slippery Shoes," "Something Inside," "Sometimes," "Stay for a While," "Stone Love," "Take Everything In," "Tell Me," "Think Sometimes," "U Lit My Fire," "Wait for Me," "Why Is It?"

Recordings as Leader (These Are Release Dates, Not Necessarily Recording Dates)

Black Diamond (1999), *Mahogany Soul* (2001), *Stone Love* (2004), *The Art of Love and War* (2007), *Unexpected* (2009), *Rich Girl* (2012)

Leaders Recorded With (These Are Release Dates, Not Necessarily Recording Dates)

Sequence (1979–1985), Spoonie Gee (1980; with Sequence), Jill Jones (1987), Buckwheat Zydeco (1992), Lenny Kravitz (1993, 1998), Vertical Hold (1993, 1995), Debelah (1994), D'Angelo (1995, 1998, 2000), Maysa (1995), Devox (1996), Solo (1998), Alex Bugnon (2000), Terry Ellis (2000), Guru (2000), Macy Gray (2001), Boney James (2001), Omar (2001, 2006), Prince (2001), Josh Groban (2002), Knagui (2002), Moby (2002), Raphael Saadiq (2002), Shabazz (2002), Styles P (2002), Erykah Badu (2003), Blue (2003), Joss Stone (2003–2004), Toshi (2004), Roy Tyler (2004), Ray Charles (2005), Al Di Meola (2006), Dionne Warwick (2006), Groove Armada (2007)

Films

The Hot Chick (2002), *The Fighting Temptations* (2003), *Pastor Brown* (2009), *School Gyrls* (2009), *Baby Mama's Club* (2010), *A Cross to Bear* (2012), *Wonder Girls* (2012), *Dreams* (2013), *Love n Success* (2013), *Scary Movie* (2013)

Awards

Soul Train Lady of Soul Award (2000; for best rhythm-and-blues, soul, or rap new artist); Edison Award (The Netherlands) (2004; for the CD *Stone Love*)

References

PRIMARY: Jancee Dunn, "Angie Stone," *Rolling Stone* 836 (16 March 2000): 31 (interview); Asha Bandele, "Been There, Done That," *Essence* 33 (March 2003): 130–34 (dialogue between Stone and Chaka Khan); Marti Parham, "Singer Angie Stone Schools Listeners on Music Industry Battles and 'Art of Love and War,'" *Jet* 112 (17 December 2007): 56 (interview); Pete Lewis, "Angie Stone: Hard Act to Follow," *Blues and Soul* 1061, http://www.bluesandsoul.com/feature/500/hard_act_to_follow/ (2010; accessed 21 May 2014) (interview); Joyce E. Davis, "Chatting With: Angie Stone," *Jet* 121 (6 August 2012): 29.

SECONDARY: Gail Mitchell, "Stone Warms Up on 'Mahogany,'" *Billboard* 113 (3 November 2001): 18 (comments by Stone); Lorraine Ali, "Princess of Soul," *Newsweek* 138 (12 November 2001): 66 (comments by Stone); James M. Manheim, "Angie Stone, 1965–," in *Contemporary Black Biography: Profiles from the International Black Community*, ed. Ashyia N. Henderson (Detroit: Gale, 2002), 31: 178–80; Brenna Sanchez, "Angie Stone," in *Contemporary Musicians: Profiles of the People in Music*, ed. Leigh Ann DeRemer (Detroit: Thomson/Gale, 2002), 37: 202–4 (also available at http://www.encyclopedia.com/topic/Angie_Stone.aspx [accessed 21 May 2014]); Chris Willman, "Everybody Must Get Stone," *Entertainment Weekly* 635 (18 January 2002): 36–37 (comments by Stone); JayQuan, "Ladies First—The Story of the Sequence, Part 1: With Blondy," http://www.thafoundation.com/sequence.htm (2007; accessed 21 May 2014).

Stone, Evelyn McGee

30 July 1920 (Anderson, S.C.)–27 May 2011 (Winter Springs, Fla.)
Singer, drums
S.C. residence: Anderson (1920–1939 or 1940)

When the International Sweethearts of Rhythm performed in Anderson in 1939 or 1940, Evelyn McGee was permitted to sing with the band. She so impressed the instrumentalists that they invited

Evelyn McGee (later Stone), with the International Sweethearts of Rhythm, 1940s; permission of Nancy Bolin

her to join them as featured vocalist. She toured with the group for approximately six years, including in Europe in 1945 (and possibly 1946). Her featured songs included "Candy" and "Rum and Coca Cola." After a two-decade hiatus from music she returned to it in 1966, performing with the composer Jesse Stone, whom she knew from his time as musical director for the International Sweethearts of Rhythm. With their group, the Jesse Stone Duo, she sang and played drums. Around 1970 she married him as her second husband; they moved to Fla. in 1984. Though she sang at the 1980 Women's Jazz Festival in Kansas City, accompanied by Marian McPartland, she did not begin recording until a decade later. She is buried in grave 65, plot M, range 43, block 5, section 70, Garden of Hope, Pinelawn Memorial Park, Farmingdale, N.Y.

Recordings as Leader (These Are Release Dates, Not Necessarily Recording Dates)

It's My Time (1990), *Jump Back* (1998), *When I Grow Too Old to Dream* (2002)

Film

International Sweethearts of Rhythm (1986)

Award

Blue Cross Blue Shield Ageless Heroes Award (1999)

References

PRIMARY: Sally Placksin, *American Women in Jazz, 1900 to the Present: Their Words, Lives, and Music* (N.p: Wideview Books 1982), 138–41 (substantial comments by Stone).

SECONDARY: Ali Stanton, "'Shake, Rattle 'n' Roll' Composer Has Early Birthday," *New York Amsterdam News*, 29 August 1981, p. 25; Linda Dahl, *Stormy Weather: The Music and Lives of a Century of Jazzwomen* (New York: Pantheon, 1984), 54–55 (comments by Stone); Elizabeth Maupin, "A Sound That Just Won't Quit: Jesse and Evelyn Stone Helped Make Music What It Is Today," *Orlando (Fla.) Sentinel*, 15 June 1985, sec. E, pp. 1, 4 (comments by Stone); Marian McPartland, *All in Good Time* (New York: Oxford University Press, 1987), 137–59 (see especially 140, 144, 150–51) (comments by Stone); D. Antoinette Handy, *The International Sweethearts of Rhythm: The Ladies Jazz Band from Piney Woods Country Life School*, revised edition (Lanham, Md.: Scarecrow Press, 1998), passim (comments by Stone); "Newsmakers: Ageless Heroes," *Jet* 96 (7 June 1999): 36; Sherrie Tucker, *Swing Shift: "All-Girl" Bands of the 1940s* (Durham, N.C.: Duke University Press, 2000), passim (comments by Stone); "Evelyn McGee Stone," *Orlando (Fla.) Sentinel*, 31 May 2011, sec. B, p. 6 (obituary); Gary Taylor, "Evelyn McGee Stone: Her Singing Delighted Many for Years," *Orlando (Fla.) Sentinel*, 1 June 2011, sec. B, p. 8; Paul de Barros, *Shall We Play That One Together? The Life and Art of Jazz Piano Legend Marian McPartland* (New York: St. Martin's, 2012), 307–8.

Sullivan, Reggie (Grady Reginold, Jr.)

Bass, singer
15 June 1982 (Travelers Rest, S.C.)-
S.C. residences: Travelers Rest (1982-2002), Columbia (2002-)

Interested in music from childhood, Sullivan played drums before turning to the bass in 1993.

Reggie Sullivan (foreground), with Zach Bingham (left), Art Bar, Columbia, S.C., 2013; photograph by Mike Bull, permission of Reggie Sullivan

After being graduated from Blue Ridge High School in Greer (2000), he attended North Greenville University (2000–2002), where his formal music lessons began. While pursuing an undergraduate degree in jazz studies at the University of South Carolina, which he received in 2006, he performed professionally. Since then he has been a mainstay on the Columbia scene, including as leader of his own band, which he assembled in 2011.

Compositions

"Battle Song," "Beautiful Criminal," "Big Words," "Brother Brother," "Double Cross," "Every Beat of My Heart," "Freedom," "High Five," "Luck of a Clover," "Nobody's Home," "Say Anything," "S.C.," "Small Stuff," "Sociable High," "The Way That I Am"

Recordings as Leader

Together (2012), *Nobody's Home* (2013)

Leaders Recorded With

Mary Ann Hurst (2007), Jeff Lofton (2007), Anne MacCallum (2009, 2011), Pete Neighbour (2009), Robert Gardiner (2010), John Wesley Satterfield (2010), Justin Smith (2010), Charlton Singleton (2011), Cumberland Collective (2012), Lori Mullwee Sealy (2012)

Film

Scattered City (2012)

Website

http://reggiesullivanband.com/ (accessed 21 May 2014)

References

SECONDARY: Patrick Wall, "Reggie Sullivan's Global Soul Revolution," *Columbia (S.C.) Free Times*, 29 February–6 March 2010, p. 42 (comments by Sullivan); Andy Bell and Kyle Petersen, "A Tale of 2 Basses: Craig Butterfield and Reggie Sullivan," *Jasper* 2 (May–June 2013): 28–34 (comments by Sullivan).

Summers, Joseph B.

Drum major

Ca. 1926 (S.C., possibly Columbia)-?

S.C. residences: possibly Columbia (ca. 1926–no later than 1935), Charleston (by 1935–at least into early 1940s)

A ward of Jenkins Orphanage, Summers performed with its bands in the mid-1930s.

Summers's age was estimated as three when the child was enumerated for the census in Columbia on 9 April 1930. It was estimated as fourteen when he was enumerated at the orphanage on 2 April 1940; this document indicates that he lived in Charleston in 1935. It has not been determined if this person was the blues singer J. B. Summers who recorded several times in 1949.

T

Taggart, Joel Washington ("Blind Joel," "Blind Joe Donnell," "Blind Tim Russell," "Blind Jeremiah Taylor")

Guitar, singer

16 August 1892 (in or near Abbeville, S.C.)-15 January 1961 (Chicago, Ill.)

S.C. residences: in or near Abbeville (1892–ca. 1910), Cedar Spring (at least 1910), Greenville (by early 1920s—no later than mid-1920s)

Though he was not totally blind until ca. 1940, Taggart attended South Carolina School for the Deaf and the Blind, at least in 1910. By 1917 he lived in Atlanta, Ga.; around 1919 he probably moved to Winston-Salem, N.C. He resided in Greenville by the early 1920s, though he soon relocated to the Charleston, W.Va., area, where he worked as an evangelist who played and sang religious songs. He became, in 1926, one of the first guitar-playing preachers to record. By 1927 he was in Chicago, where he lived the remainder of his life. There, at one of his recording sessions, Josh White, Taggart's lead boy, or guide, made his first recordings in 1928. The two had met in Greenville in the early 1920s. During his recording career, which lasted from 1926 to 1948, though he recorded nothing between 1934 and 1948, Taggart was affiliated with several labels—including Decca, Paramount, and Vocalion—and used different names. Despite his apparent desire to record the blues, recording companies limited him almost exclusively to religious music, which today might be considered country blues. During the 1930s and 1940s he performed occasionally in Fla. and Detroit. He is buried in Saint Mary's Cemetery, Evergreen Park, Ill.

Taggart was identified as Joe, not Joel, when enumerated for the census at the South Carolina School for the Deaf and the Blind in Cedar Spring on 26 April 1910; this document estimates his age as seventeen. World War I and World War II draft registration cards indicate that he was born in Abbeville on 16 August 1892. The earlier card notes that he has an artificial eye. He might have recorded as Blind Joe Amos, Blind Percy, and Six Cylinder Smith. From 1996 to 1998 Ken Earl, Taggart's grandson, played Captain Joel Taggert on the television series *The Sentinel.*

Composition

"Narcotic Blues"

Recordings as Leader

Complete Recorded Works in Chronological Order, Vol. 1 (1926–1928), Complete Recorded Works in Chronological Order, Vol. 2 (1929–1934), "Little Black Train" (1948), "Preshious Lord" (1948)

References

SECONDARY: Robert Shelton and Walter Raim, *The Josh White Song Book* (Chicago: Quadrangle Books, 1963), 18–20; Max Jones, "Josh White Looks Back 2," *Blues Unlimited* 56 (September 1968): 15–16; Bruce Bastin, *Crying for the Carolines* (London: Studio Vista, 1971), 74; Dorothy Schainman Siegel, *The Glory Road: The Story of Josh White* (San Diego: Harcourt Brace Jovanovich, 1982), 31, 37, 39–40; Paul Oliver, *Songsters and Saints: Vocal Traditions on Race Records* (Cambridge: Cambridge University Press, 1984), 208–10, 214, 217, 228; Bruce Bastin, *Red River Blues: The Blues Tradition in the Southeast* (Urbana: University of Illinois Press, 1986), 167–68; Keith Briggs, "Separating the Wheat from the Tares," *Blues and Rhythm: The Gospel Truth* 33 (December 1987): 9–12 (includes discography); Elijah Wald, *Josh White: Society Blues* (Amherst: University of Massachusetts Press, 2000), 16, 18–19, 21–25, 240, 302; Alex van der Tuuk, "Blind Joel Taggart: Fifty Years Gone, but Not Forgotten," *The Frog Blues and Jazz Annual: The Musicians, the Records and the Music of the 78 Era* 2 (2011): 9–24; Alex van der Tuuk, "The Story of Blind Joel Taggart's Presto Record," *Blues and Rhythm: The Gospel Truth* 265 (Christmas 2011): 18–19.

Tarlton, Jimmie (Johnny James Rimbert)

Guitar, singer

8 May 1892 (Chesterfield County, S.C.)–29 November 1979 (Phenix City, Ala.)

S.C. residences: Chesterfield County (1892–ca. 1904), probably in or near Cheraw (probably 1920s)

Though as a child Tarlton played banjo, harmonica, and possibly accordion, by age eight he focused on guitar. As a teenager he became an itinerant, working various jobs and performing as a street musician before teaming with Tom Darby as a duo in 1926. By this time Tarlton played the steel guitar exclusively. The next year the two recorded their biggest seller and most enduring composition, "Columbus Stockade Blues," with "Birmingham Jail" ("Down in the Valley") on the flipside. When the team dissolved in 1933 Tarlton became a farmer, though he continued playing; he and Darby reunited for a performance in 1963. At the 1966 Newport Folk Festival, Tarlton was on a program with Pete Seeger, the Clancy Brothers, and Ramblin' Jack Elliot. Tony Russell believes that Tarlton's "singing was always excellent, and attained a depth of feeling in [Darby and Tarlton's blues] which was rarely matched among white country singers" (*Blacks Whites and Blues,* 71). Tarlton, whose playing influenced the Dixon Brothers, is buried in Riverdale Cemetery, Columbus, Ga., as is Darby.

Tarlton's full name and dates of birth and death come from his grave marker; the Social Security Death Index confirms the dates (though it omits the day of death) and identifies him as John Tarlton. When enumerated for the 1900 census as Johnnie, Tarlton resided in the west part of ED 20 Court House Township, Chesterfield County. This was probably his residence from birth until leaving home.

Compositions

"Administration Blues," "After the Sinking of the Titanic," "All Bound Down in Birmingham Jail," "Birmingham Jail," "Columbus Stockade Blues," "Cowboy Johnny," "Down in Florida on a Hog," "Fort Benning Blues," "Joe Bowers," "Never Get Drunk Anymore," "New Birmingham Jail," "Pretty Little Girl," "Put-Together Blues," "Rollie Dixon," "Uncle Joe and His Hounds"

Recordings as Leader

Tom Darby and Jimmie Tarlton (1927–1930, 1932–1933; three CDs of a four-CD set comprising the complete released recordings of Darby and Tarlton and all the recordings released only under Tarlton's name through 1933), *Steel Guitar Rag* (1963, 1965)

References

SECONDARY: Norm Cohen and Anne Cohen, "The Legendary Jimmie Tarleton [*sic*]," *Sing Out!* 16 (August–September 1966): 16–19 (comments by Tarlton); Tony Russell, *Blacks Whites and Blues* (New York: Stein and Day, 1970), passim; Pat Harrison, notes to *Tom Darby and Jimmie Tarlton* (2005; JSP Records JSP 7746-A-C); Tony Russell, *Country Music Originals: The Legends and the Lost* (New York: Oxford University Press, 2007), 63–64; Larry Birnbaum, *Before Elvis: The Prehistory of Rock 'n' Roll* (Lanham, Md.: Scarecrow Press, 2013), 199–200.

Tate, Baby (Charles Henry)

Guitar, bass, singer

Probably 28 January of either 1919 or 1920 (probably Abbeville, S.C., though possibly Elberton, Ga.)–17 August 1972 (Columbia, S.C.)

S.C. residences: Abbeville (probably 1919 or 1920–1926), Greenville (1926–1954), Spartanburg (1954–1972)

Reared in Greenville, Tate became an able guitarist by ca. 1930. He performed with such bluesmen as Blind Boy Fuller (a major influence), Brownie McGhee, and Joe Walker; with McKinley Ellis and Washboard Willie Young, he was part of the first band of black musicians (the Carolina Blackbirds) to play on the local radio station (1932). He served in the army from January 1944 until early 1946. In the early 1950s he reportedly recorded for Dave Kapp in Atlanta, though the music was never released. Upon settling in Spartanburg he formed a musical relationship with Pink Anderson that lasted into the 1970s. In 1961 Samuel Charters recorded Tate in Spartanburg; this music was released on the only album solely by Tate, *The Blues of Baby Tate* (Bluesville). The following year Charters again recorded Tate in Spartanburg; three selections were included in Charters's film documentary *The Blues* and released on an Asch album of the same title. Tate next recorded in Spartanburg during 1970–1972; though most of this music remains unissued, some from 1970 was released on Flyright, some on Trix. Tate is important for having introduced Bruce Bastin and Peter Lowry to blues musicians in the Spartanburg area. As a result of their field work, such performers as Peg Leg Sam (Arthur Jackson) and Henry "Rufe" Johnson are now documented.

Tate was reportedly a cousin of guitarist Larry Threaks. Sources indicate that Tate was born on 28 January 1916 in Elberton, Ga. Military records indicate that he was born in Abbeville, S.C., on 28 January 1919. The Social Security Death Index identifies the birth date as 28 January 1920, with the birthplace unspecified. His obituary, which characterizes him as a "native of Greenville County," states that he died at age fifty-two. If this age is

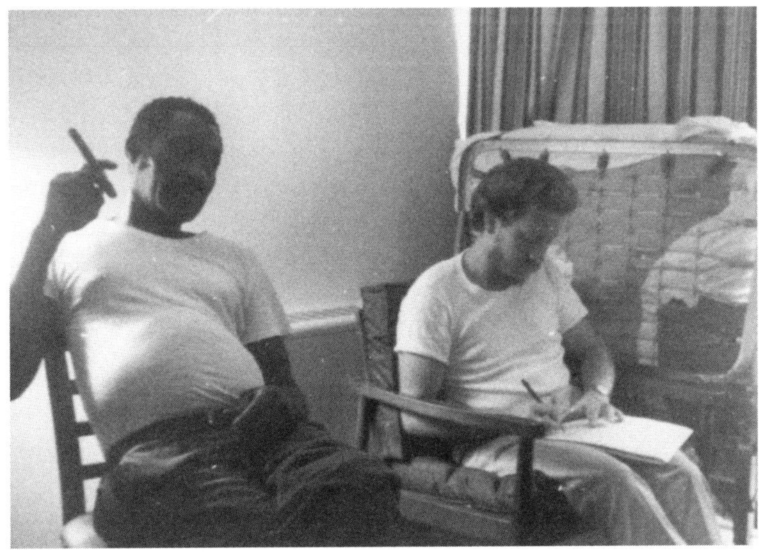

Baby Tate (left), with Bruce Bastin, Spartanburg, S.C., 1970; permission of the photographer, Peter B. Lowry

correct, Tate was born around 1920. Sources record that during his military service Tate was wounded at Omaha Beach on D-Day, that he recovered stateside, and that he was later wounded at the Battle of the Bulge. Military records reveal that he served in the European–African Middle Eastern Theatre from July 1944 into December 1945 and was discharged soon thereafter. He was awarded the European–African Middle Eastern Campaign Medal and the World War II Victory Medal. Records consulted do not mention his having received the Purple Heart.

Compositions

"Late in the Evening," "See What You Done Done"

Recordings as Leader

The Blues of Baby Tate: See What You Done Done (1961), "Bad Blues" (1962), "If I Could Holler Like a Mountain Jack" (1962), "When I First Started Hoboing" (1962), "Bad Gasoline" (1970; with Peg Leg Sam), "Late in the Evening" (1970), "See What You Done Done" (1970; with Peg Leg Sam), "You Can Always Tell" (1970; with Peg Leg Sam)

Leaders Recorded With

Baby Brooks (1970; unissued), Peg Leg Sam (1970)

Film

The Blues (1963)

References

SECONDARY: Bruce Bastin and Pete Lowry, "Tricks Ain't Workin' No More: Blues from the South-East," *Blues Unlimited* 78 (December 1970): 11; Bruce Bastin, *Crying for the Carolines* (London: Studio Vista, 1971), 74–75; Bruce Bastin and Pete Lowry, "Blues from the South-East (Sequel 5): 'Tricks Ain't Workin' No More,'" *Blues Unlimited* 82 (June 1971): 14; "Charles H. Tate," *Spartanburg (S.C.) Herald-Journal,* 19 August 1972, sec. B, p. 6 (obituary); Bruce Bastin, brochure accompanying the album *Another Man Done Gone . . .* (1978; Flyright 528), 4; Bruce Bastin, *Red River Blues: The Blues Tradition in the Southeast* (Urbana: University of Illinois Press, 1986), 177–78.

Taylor, Virgil

Multiple instruments

Ca. 1928 (S.C.)-?

S.C. residences: Georgetown (possibly ca. 1928, but by 1935–no later than 1940), Charleston (by 1940–at least into early 1940s)

A ward of Jenkins Orphanage, Taylor played in its bands in the 1940s.

Taylor was estimated as age twelve when enumerated for the census in Charleston on 22 May 1940; this document notes that he was born in S.C. and lived in Georgetown in 1935.

Thayer, George

French horn

25 December of either 1901 or 1902 (Charleston, S.C.)-?

S.C. residence: Charleston (1901 or 1902–1919)

A ward of Jenkins Orphanage beginning in 1907, Thayer played in its bands in the 1910s, including with ones that performed in *Uncle Tom's Cabin* in N.Y.C. (1913) and at the Anglo-American Exposition in London (1914). As a professional musician he was affiliated with, among other groups, the Rabbit's Foot Minstrels, Holtkamp's Georgia Smart Set, Hunt's Georgia Minstrels, and the Barnum and Bailey circus.

John Chilton quotes seventy-six-year-old Thayer as stating that he was born on 25 December 1901. The passenger list of the *St. Louis,* which transported the orphanage band from Liverpool to N.Y.C. in September 1914, indicates that he was born in Charleston on 25 December 1902. His age was estimated as thirty-five when he was enumerated for the census in West Palm Beach, Fla., on 12 April 1940; this document identifies his highest grade of schooling as the eighth and states that he is a musician. He is probably the George Thayer, estimated age nine, who was enumerated in Charleston on 14 May 1910.

References

SECONDARY: John Chilton, *A Jazz Nursery: The Story of the Jenkins' Orphanage Bands of Charleston, South Carolina* (London: Bloomsbury Book Shop, 1980), 14, 17, 23, 59 (comments by Thayer); Howard Rye, "Visiting Fireboys: The Jenkins' Orphanage Bands in Britain," *Storyville* 130 (1987): 137–43.

Thomas, William

Cornet

8 January 1903 (Charleston, S.C.)-?

S.C. residence: Charleston (1903–at least until 1914)

A ward of Jenkins Orphanage, Thomas played in its bands in the 1910s.

Thomas's date and place of birth come from the passenger list of the *St. Louis,* which transported the orphanage band from Liverpool to N.Y.C. in September 1914. His name is absent from the passenger list of the *Campania,* on which the group sailed from N.Y.C. four months earlier.

Reference

SECONDARY: Howard Rye, "Visiting Fireboys: The Jenkins' Orphanage Bands in Britain," *Storyville* 130 (1987): 137–43.

Thompson, Lucky (Eli, Jr.)

Saxophone, composer, arranger

Possibly 16 June of either 1923 or 1924, though possibly 31 August 1923 (Columbia, S.C.)-30 July 2005 (Seattle, Wash.)

S.C. residence: Columbia (probably only 1923, but possibly also 1924)

After completing high school in Detroit, Thompson went on the road with Erskine Hawkins and then Lionel Hampton. He was also a regular in bands led by Billy Eckstine and Count Basie. In the mid-1940s he began affiliating with combos and leading his own groups of seldom more than eight musicians. He appeared as sideman on his three most historically important recording dates: one, led by Charlie Parker, produced "Moose the Mooche," "Night in Tunisia," "Ornithology," and "Yardbird Suite" (1946); another, headed by Thelonious Monk, featured Monk's first recordings of "Let's Cool One" and "Skippy," as well as the leader's only recording of "Carolina Moon" (1952); and the last, led by Miles Davis, generated "Blue 'n' Boogie" and "Walkin'" (1954). Thompson was one of the first modern musicians to perform frequently on soprano saxophone, recording on it initially in 1959. Disgusted with realities relating to the music business, he lived abroad for extended periods (from the late 1950s into the early 1960s in Paris and from 1968 into 1970 in Lausanne). During his second period in Europe he recorded in France, Germany, Poland, Spain, Switzerland, and Yugoslavia. Between his residences abroad he recorded three impressive albums for Prestige in successive years beginning in 1963. After teaching at Dartmouth College in 1973 and 1974, he drifted into obscurity, lived in unfortunate circumstances, and developed Alzheimer's disease. A transitional figure in the sense that he was comfortable in the swing and bebop contexts, Thompson was influenced initially by Lester Young but later and more strongly by Coleman Hawkins, Ben Webster, and Don Byas. Noal Cohen notes that Thompson "ingeniously [updated] those earlier influences harmonically and rhythmically to create a most original sound and conception that could be adapted to almost any musical context." Charlie Barnet's band plays Thompson's "Smooth Sailing" in the movie *Bright and Breezy* (1956). Thompson reportedly composed music for the movie *Machine, mon ami* (1961).

Thompson is named Eli Thompson, Jr., in the 1940 census and, the next year, on SS-5, the form used for requesting Social Security numbers. Because his death certificate identifies his father as Elijah Thompson, the musician's given name is probably Elijah. Thompson's death certificate and unofficial sources state that the saxophonist was born on 16 June 1924. His Form SS-5 records the date as 16 June 1923; the Social Security Death Index, as 31 August 1923. Until he stated in a 1981 interview (published in 1982) that he was born in

Lucky Thompson (saxophone), with bassist Al McKibbon and singer Hilda A. Taylor (seated), Three Deuces, N.Y.C., ca. July 1948; reproduced from the William P. Gottlieb Collection, Library of Congress, Music Division

Columbia, Detroit was considered his birthplace. Though his identification of Columbia was accepted at face value, it can be corroborated. The 1940 census (for which he was enumerated in Detroit on 10 April at estimated age sixteen) notes that he was born in S.C. For Form SS-5, completed in Detroit on 27 May 1941, he specified Columbia as his birthplace; this same city (spelled Columbus) is entered on his death certificate.

Compositions

"Aliyah," "Angel Eyes," "Boppin' the Blues," "Bunny," "Check Out Time," "Coolin' with Collins," "Dancing Sunbeam," "Deep Passion," "A Distant Sound," "Easy Going," "Fine and Lucky," "Fly with the Wind," "Home Comin'," "Home Free," "I'll Wait Forever," "It's Thursday," "Kinfolk's Corner," "Lord, Lord, Am I Ever Gonna Know," "A Minor Delight," "Minuet in Blues," "Monsoon," "The Night Hawk," "No More," "Nothin' from Nothin'," "Notorious Love," "Once upon a Time," "On Easy Street," "Passin' Time," "The Plain but Simple Truth," "Prey Loot," "Rainbow Inn," "Safari," "The Scene Is Clean," "Seeing Is Believing," "The Shy One," "Slow Drag," "Smooth Sailing," "Sorry Woman Blues," "Soul Lullaby," "Spanish Rails," "Still Waters," "Street Scene," "Thin Ice," "Tight Squeeze," "Velvet Rain," "While You Are Gone," "Will You or Won't You?," "Yesterday's Bottle," "Yesterday's Child," "You Move, You Lose"

Recordings as Leader

"Test Pilots" (1944), "Irresistible You" (1945), "No Good Man Blues" (1945), "Phace" (1945), "Short Day" (1945), "Why Not?" (1945), "Commercial Eyes" (1946), "Dodo's Bounce" (1946), "Dodo's Lament" (1946), "Shuffle That Riff" (1946), "Slim's Mishap" (1946), "Smooth Sailing" (1946), "Boppin' the Blues" (1947), "Boulevard Bounce" (1947), "Just One More Chance" (1947), "Buck-De-Hoodle" (1949), "Nothin' from Nothin'" (1949), "Slow Drag" (1949), "You Must Be Out of Your Mind" (1949), "Coolin' with Collins" (1950), "Over the Rainbow" (1950), "Paradise Valley" (1950), "Stay in There" (1950), "Flamingo" (1953), "Mambo in Blues" (1953), "The Scene Is Clean" (1953), *Accent on Tenor* (1954), "Bunny" (1954), "Moonlight in Vermont" (1954), "The Night Hawk" (1954), *Lucky Plays for the Club* (1956), *Lucky Strikes!* (1956; also released under different titles), *Lucky Thompson Featuring Oscar Pettiford*, 2 vols. (1956), *Lucky Thompson with Gérard Pochonet and His Orchestra* (1956), *Modern Jazz Group* (1956; also titled *Lucky Thompson in Paris 1956*), *Thompson Plays for Thomson* (1956; also released under different titles), *Sammy Price and Lucky Thompson* (1957; also titled *Paris Blues*), *Bongo Jazz* (1959; also titled *Fascinatin' Rhythm*), *Lucky in Paris* (1959), *Lord, Lord, Am I Ever Gonna Know?* (1961), *Lucky Thompson Plays Jerome Kern and No More* (1963), *Lucky Strikes* (1964), *New York City, 1964–65*, *Lucky Thompson Plays Happy Days Are Here Again* (1965), *Lucky Is Back! (Then So Is Love)* (ca. 1965), *A Lucky Songbook in Europe* (1969), *Soul's Nite Out* (1970; also titled *Body and Soul*), *Friday the 13th—Cook County Jail* (1972), *Goodbye Yesterday* (ca. 1972), *I Offer You* (ca. 1973)

Leaders Recorded With

Count Basie (1944–1945, 1951), Erroll Garner (1944), Lucky Millinder (1944), Hot Lips Page (1944), Slim Gaillard (1945–1946), Karl George (1945), Freddie Green (1945), Boyd Raeburn (1945–1946), Willie Smith (1945), Dinah Washington (1945, 1956), David Allyn (1946), Ivie Anderson (1946), Louis Armstrong (1946–1947, 1956–1957), Wilbert Baranco (1946), Ralph Burns (1946), Dizzy Gillespie (1946, 1954), George Handy (1946), Russell Jacquet (1946), Dodo Marmarosa (1946), Charles Mingus (1946), Jimmy Mundy (1946), Charlie Parker (1946, 1949), Ernie Andrews (1947), Ike Carpenter (1947, 1949), Benny Carter (1947, 1952, 1965), Mills Blue Rhythm Band (1947), Phil Moore (1947), Frances Wayne (1947), Miles Davis (1949, 1954), Fletcher Henderson (1950), Gene Redd (1951–1952), Thelonious Monk (1952), Little Jimmy Scott (1952), Jimmy Hamilton (1954), King Pleasure (1954), Terry Pollard (1954), Jack Teagarden (1954), Clark Terry (1954), Jimmy Cleveland (1955), Jo Jones (1955–1956), Chris Connor (1956), Lionel Hampton (1956, 1965, 1977), Johnny Hartman (1956), Milt Jackson (1956–1957), Quincy Jones (1956, 1964), Stan Kenton (1956), Oscar Pettiford (1956, 1959), Kenny Clarke (1957), Harry Arnold (1961), Art Blakey (1965)

Films

New Orleans (1947), *Goodbye Again* (1961; originally titled *Aimez-vous Brahms?*), *Miss April* (1963; originally titled *Frøken April*)

Award

New Jersey Jazz Society American Jazz Hall of Fame (1997)

References

PRIMARY: Nat Hentoff, "Lucky Thompson: In Which an Underrated Musician Talks Strongly about Seamier Side of Jazz," *Down Beat* 23 (4 April 1956): 9 (substantial comments by Thompson); Nat Hentoff, "Call Him Lucky (?): Part Two of the Saga of a Guy Whose Fortunes Belie His Happy Nickname," *Down Beat* 23 (2 May 1956): 14 (substantial comments by Thompson); Valerie Wilmer, "Lucky Thompson Talks to 'Jazz Monthly,'" *Jazz Monthly* 8 (September 1962): 12–15; Burt Korall, "Lucky's Back in Town," *Down Beat* 30 (4 July 1963): 16–17 (substantial comments by Thompson); Dan Morgenstern, "Lucky Thompson Says Later for Music Business," *Down Beat* 33 (13 January 1966): 11, 38 (substantial comments by Thompson); Christopher Kuhl, "Lucky Thompson: Interview," *Cadence* 8 (January 1982): 10–12.

SECONDARY: Mark Gardner, "Lucky Thompson in the Sixties," *Coda* 9 (June 1969): 3–8 (comments by Thompson); Raymond Horricks, *Count Basie and His Orchestra: Its Music and Its Musicians* (Westport, Conn.: Negro Universities Press, 1971), 180–81; Richard Palmer, "Bebop Saxophones," in *Masters of Jazz Saxophone,* ed. Tony Bacon (London: Balafon Books, 2000), 56; Scott Yanow, *Bebop* (San Francisco: Miller Freeman, 2000), 122–24; Lars Bjorn, with Jim Gallert, *Before Motown: A History of Jazz in Detroit, 1920–1960* (Ann Arbor: University of Michigan Press, 2001), 81–83, 96; Tad Shull, "When Backward Comes Out Ahead: Lucky Thompson's Phrasing and Improvisation," in *Annual Review of Jazz Studies 12,* ed. Edward Berger et al. (Lanham, Md.: Scarecrow Press and Institute of Jazz Studies, 2002), 63–83; Ben Ratliff, "Lucky Thompson, Jazz Saxophonist, Is Dead at 81," *New York Times,* 5 August 2005, sec. B, p. 7 (obituary); Philip Coady, "Remembering Lucky Thompson (1924–2005)," *Earshot Jazz: A Mirror and Focus for the Jazz Community* 21 (September 2005): 4–5, 18–19; Marcus Printup, "A Lucky Awakening," *Down Beat* 73 (May 2006): 22; Noal Cohen, notes to Lucky Thompson, *New York City, 1964–65* (2009; Uptown UPCD 27.57/27.58); Todd S. Jenkins, "Lucky Thompson: Bebop Tenor and Soprano Saxophonist," www.jazzhouse.org/gone/lastpost2.php3?edit=1137519707 (2009; accessed 21 May 2014); Ben Ratliff, "A Jazz Pianist Pays Tribute to a Neglected Composer," *New York Times,* 17 December 2009, sec. C, p. 5; Noal Cohen and Chris Byars, "Lucky Thompson in Paris: The 1961 Candid Records Session," *Current Research in Jazz* 2, http://crj-online.org/v2/CRJ-LuckyThompson.php (2010; accessed 21 May 2014).

Threaks, Larry

Guitar

Probably 1905, though possibly 1906 (Laurens, S.C.)–26 June 1970 (Spartanburg, S.C.)

S.C. residences: Laurens (probably 1905 or 1906–ca. 1940), Greenville (ca. 1940–ca. 1942), Spartanburg (ca. 1942–1970)

Threaks, who never recorded, played so impressively that he was the best guitarist McKinley Ellis ever heard. He is buried in Mount Zion Cemetery, Spartanburg.

Threaks was reportedly a cousin of guitarist Baby Tate. His age was estimated as twenty-three when he was enumerated for the census in Laurens on 28 April 1930; at that time he worked as a laborer, as he did for most if not all of the remainder of his life. Bruce Bastin states that Threaks was born on 10 August 1905; the Social Security Death Index records the date as 15 July 1905. His name appears in the Greenville city directories for 1940 and 1941. He is listed in the Spartanburg city directory for the initial time in the volume for 1943–1944.

References

SECONDARY: "Larry Threaks," *Spartanburg (S.C.) Herald,* 29 June 1970, p. 13 (obituary); Bruce Bastin, *Red River Blues: The Blues Tradition in the Southeast* (Urbana: University of Illinois Press, 1986), 187.

Tolbert, Skeets (Campbell Arelius)

Saxophone, clarinet, singer, arranger

14 February 1909 (Calhoun Falls, S.C.)–30 November 2000 (Houston, Tex.)

S.C. residence: Calhoun Falls (1909–no later than 1915)

While a student majoring in biology at Johnson C. Smith University (class of 1931) in Charlotte, N.C., Tolbert toured with one of its bands, Dave Taylor's Dixie Serenaders. In 1934 he moved to N.Y.C., where he played in groups led by Charlie Alexander, Danny Logan, Snub Mosley, and Fats Waller, as well as with a band fronted by the athlete Jesse Owens. In time he assumed leadership of Mosley's organization and named it the Gentlemen of Swing. Usually a sextet, it played in the jump style of the day and included, at one time or another, such musicians as Al Hall, Freddie Jefferson, Buddy Johnson, Lem Johnson, Red Richards, and Carl Smith. It made four soundies in 1944. Giving up life as a professional musician in the mid-1940s because of difficulties in the band business (including low wages caused by the influx of musicians returning from military service), Tolbert became an educator. He was prepared to teach because he received a master's degree in music education from Teachers College, Columbia University, in February 1943. (He continued his education at Juilliard, where he studied music theory during the 1945 spring semester, and at Columbia as a non-degree student in 1951.) For a year he directed bands at two high schools in Charlotte before affiliating with what is now Texas Southern University (1949–1972), where he taught arranging and music theory, gave woodwind instruction, and led the stage band. He composed the school's alma mater. In Houston he helped establish the black musicians' union, which he served as president (1950–1965), and operated the Pied Piper Music Company, where he repaired instruments beginning in 1953. One of his compositions, "Hit That Jive, Jack," became popular in the 1940s in a recording by Nat Cole; Slim Gaillard and, much later, Diana Krall, are among others who recorded it.

Tolbert's birth and death dates come from the Social Security Death Index and the *Houston Chronicle* obituary. Tolbert was enumerated for the 1910 census in Magnolia Township, Anderson County, S.C. (Calhoun Falls is in Magnolia Township); for the 1920 census, in Lincoln County, N.C. In the first part of Nigel Haslewood's article about Tolbert, the author indicates that Tolbert and his family left Calhoun Falls for N.C. before he was "old enough to go to school" (220). He was enumerated for the 1940 census in N.Y.C., where he also lived in 1935. Though Tolbert told interviewers Louis J. Marchiafava and Charles Stephenson that he taught at Texas Southern University from 1949 until 1976, university records indicate that he last worked there in 1972.

Compositions

"Big Fat Butterfly," "Bouncing Rhythm," "Delta Land Blues," "Get Up," "Hail! Hail! Hail! to Texas Southern," "Hit That Jive, Jack," "Hole Holy Roly-Poly," "I Can't Go for You," "Jumpin' Like Mad," "Lazy Gal Blues," "Raz Ma Taz," "The Rhumba Blues," "Ride On," "Sammy's Choppin' Block," "Skin 'Em Back," "That's That Messy Boogie," "This Is the End," "What Is the Matter Now?," "You're My Meat" (also titled "Fat and Forty")

Recordings as Leader

Skeets Tolbert and His Gentlemen of Swing, 1931–1940, Skeets Tolbert and His Gentlemen of Swing, 1940–1942, "No No Baby" (mid-1940s)

Leaders Recorded With

Dave Taylor (1931), Jimmie Gunn (1936)

Award

Houston Community Music Center Golden Note Music Award (1993)

References

PRIMARY: Campbell A. Tolbert, interview by Louis J. Marchiafava and Charles Stephenson, 16 November 1989 and 22 November 1989, Campbell Tolbert Collection, Houston Metropolitan Research Center, Houston Public Library, Houston, Tex. (uncorrected transcript available at http://digital.houstonlibrary.org/oral-history/campbell-tolbert.php [accessed 21 May 2014]).

SECONDARY: John Hammond, with Irving Townsend, *John Hammond on Record* (New York: Summit Books, 1977), 175–77; W. O. Smith, *Sideman: The Long Gig of W. O. Smith, a Memoir* (Nashville: Rutledge Hill Press, 1991), 107–8, 192–93; Nigel Haslewood, "The Jump Bands—No. 3, Part 1: Skeets Tolbert and His Gentlemen of Swing," *Storyville* 156 (6 December 1993): 220–31 (comments by Tolbert); Nigel Haslewood, "The Jump Bands—No. 3, Part 2: Skeets Tolbert and His Gentlemen of Swing," *Storyville* 157 (1 March 1994): 16–19, 22–27 (comments by Tolbert); "Services Set for Tolbert, Composer of TSU Song," *Houston Chronicle,* 8 December 2000, sec. A, p. 40; "Tolbert," *Houston Chronicle,* 8 December 2000, sec. B, p. 21 (obituary); Dave Penny, "Skeets Tolbert," *Blues and Rhythm: The Gospel Truth* 157 (March 2001): 25 (obituary); Larry Birnbaum, *Before Elvis: The Prehistory of Rock 'n' Roll* (Lanham, Md.: Scarecrow Press, 2013), 169, 404nn81–82; Mark Cantor, "Celluloid Improvisations: Filmcraft Session #44—Skeets Tolbert and His Orchestra + Tosh Hammed," *IAJRC Journal* 46 (September 2013): 11–14.

Townsend, Lonnie (Alonzo Gray, Jr.)

Cornet

1 May 1887 (probably Orangeburg, S.C.)–31 October 1913 (Charleston, W.Va.)

S.C. residence: Orangeburg (probably 1887–possibly 1913, other than when touring)

Though he performed professionally for a few years before 1913, in that year Townsend toured with the band of the Rabbit's Foot Minstrels. While with the group he contracted typhoid fever in May, was hospitalized in Charleston, W.Va., and died there five months later. A writer for the *Indianapolis Freeman* considered him "a cornet player of exceptional ability." He is buried in Orangeburg Cemetery.

Townsend's full name and birth and death dates come from the family marker in Orangeburg Cemetery. On an undetermined date Townsend was enumerated for the 1910 census in Birmingham, Ala., presumably while on tour with a musical organization. Lynn Abbott and Doug Seroff state that Townsend was hospitalized in Charlestown, W.Va. Their source, the *Indianapolis Freeman* article, identifies the location as Charleston, W.Va.

References

SECONDARY: "From F. S. Wolcott's Rabbit Foot Company: Decease of Lonnie Townsend," *Indianapolis Freeman: An Illustrated Colored Newspaper,* 13 December 1913, p. 6 (obituary); Lynn Abbott and Doug Seroff, *Ragged but Right: Black Traveling Shows, "Coon Songs," and the Dark Pathway to Blues and Jazz* (Jackson: University Press of Mississippi, 2007), 272; Richard Reid, "Honor Denied: USC Alumni Snubbed Townsend Despite His Many Accomplishments," *Orangeburg (S.C.) Times and Democrat,* 31 July 2011, sec. A, p. 2 (this article about Townsend's father mentions the elder man's children, though not by name).

Trappier, Traps (Arthur Benjamin)

Drums

Possibly 28 May 1908 (Georgetown, S.C.)–17 May 1975 (probably Brooklyn, N.Y.)

S.C. residence: Georgetown (possibly 1908–probably no later than 1919)

Though born in Georgetown, Trappier spent some of his formative years in N.Y.C., where he became a professional musician by 1925. He played with the bands of such leaders as Blanche Calloway and Buddy Johnson before becoming a regular with Fats Waller. He drums on the initial recording of Waller's "Jitterbug Waltz" (1942), which has since been recorded hundreds of times. Primarily a freelancer, he performed with many major musicians, including Louis Armstrong, Hot Lips Page, and Teddy Wilson. Beginning in the late 1950s he led his own trio. His playing was most influenced by that of Sidney Catlett.

Trappier was enumerated for the census in Brooklyn, N.Y., on 7 January 1920; this document estimates his age as ten and indicates that he was born in S.C. Conducted in Brooklyn on 1 June, the 1925 N.Y. state census identifies him as a musician and estimates that he was born in 1909. The 1940 federal census (conducted in Brooklyn on 5 April) estimates his age as thirty and states that he was born in S.C. The Social Security Death Index records his birth date as 28 May 1908 and identifies Brooklyn as his last residence. It has not been determined if the Arthur Trapier enumerated for the census in Charleston on 20 April 1910 at estimated age ten was the musician. A report that Trappier recorded with Skeets Tolbert in 1939 has not been confirmed.

Leaders Recorded With

Fats Waller (1941–1942), Edmond Hall (1944), Billie Holiday (1944), James P. Johnson (1944), New World a-Coming (1944; radio broadcast), Billy Moore (1945), Josh White (1945), WNEW Second Annual American Swing Festival (1945), Pat Flowers (1947), Punch Miller (1947), Tony Parenti (1949), WPIX-TV Stage Show (1949), Sidney Bechet (1950–1951), Ralph Sutton (1950), Henry "Red" Allen (1952), Conrad Janis (ca. 1953), New Orleans Shufflers (1955), The Seven (1956), Willie "The Lion" Smith (1956–1957), Rex Stewart (1958)

Ulmer, Blood (James, Jr.)

Guitar, flute, singer, composer

2 or 8 February 1940 (Calhoun County, S.C.)–

S.C. residence: Calhoun County, including Cameron and Saint Matthews (1940–1958)

When Ulmer was approximately four years old, his father taught him to play the guitar. The guitar playing of neighbors Alton Smith (gospel) and especially Johnny Wilson (blues) inspired him. From age seven to thirteen he sang with the Southern Sons, a gospel group. In 1958 he left S.C. for Pittsburgh, where he backed doo-wop groups and acquired the nickname Youngblood, which eventually was shortened to Blood. He joined the trio of Ernie Goldsmith (1961) and then became a member of the Swing Kings, the band of singer Jewel Bryner (1962–1965). He played with Hank Marr in the mid-

Blood Ulmer, Ponderosa Stomp, New Orleans, La., 26 April 2005; permission of the photographer, Gene Tomko

1960s. Tired of performing conventionally, he soon began playing atonally during an extended stay in Detroit, beginning in 1967. After moving to N.Y.C. in 1971 he became influenced by the musical concepts of Ornette Coleman, with whom Ulmer roomed for almost a year. He led his first recording session in 1977, though the music was not released until over a decade later. He performed and recorded frequently, becoming so valued that Columbia Records signed him to a three-record contract. He made the last of these records with his group Odyssey. In time he recorded with other bands he established: Music Revelation Ensemble, Phalanx (co-led with George Adams), and Third Rail (co-led with Bill Laswell). Though he became more popular in Europe than the United States, the release of *Memphis Blood* bolstered his reputation in his own country, which *Birthright,* a solo recording, solidified. He performs on the sound track of the movie *The End of Violence* (1997).

The musician's birth certificate indicates that Ulmer was born on 2 February 1940; his mother insisted that he was born on the 8th. When enumerated for the census in April 1940, the Ulmer family resided in Cameron, nine miles from Saint Matthews. This document records his name as James W. M. Ulmer and estimates his age as two months.

Compositions

"After Dark," "Arena," "Are You Glad to Be in America?," "Bad Blood in the City," "Birthright," "Black and Blues," "Blues Allnight," "Blues Preacher," "Cheering," "Church," "Convulsion," "Cross Fire," "Dance in the Dark—Music Is My Life," "The Day Of," "The Elephant," "First Blood," "Forbidden Blues," "Freelancing," "Happy Time," "House People," "I Can't Take It Anymore," "I Need Love," "In the Name of . . . ," "Layout," "Let Me Take You Home," "Light Eyed," "Love Dance," "Love Nest," "Moon Shine" (also titled "Moons Shine"), "Morning Bride," "Noise and Clamor," "No Other Option," "Nothing to Say," "No Wave," "Overtime," "Part Time," "Pressure," "Rap Man," "Raw Groove," "Revealing," "Revelation March," "Satisfy (Story of My Life)," "The Scandal Monger," "See-Through," "Street Bride," "Theme from Captain Black," "Timeless," "Time Out," "TV Blues," "Woman Coming"

Recordings as Leader

Revealing (1977), *Tales of Captain Black* (1978), *Are You Glad to Be in America?* (1980), *No Wave* (1980; by Music Revelation Ensemble), *Free Lancing* (1981), *Black Rock* (1982), *Odyssey* (1983), *Part Time* (1983; by Odyssey), "Blues Don't Fail Me Now" (1984), "Eyelevel" (1984), *Phalanx: Got Something Good for You* (1985), *America—Do You Remember the Love?* (1986), *Live at the Caravan of Dreams* (1986), *Original Phalanx* (1987), *In Touch* (1988; by Phalanx), *Music Revelation Ensemble* (1988), *Wings* (1988), *Blues Allnight* (1989), *Black and Blues* (1990), *Elec. Jazz* (1990; by Music Revelation Ensemble), *After Dark* (1991; by Music Revelation Ensemble), "House on Fire" (1991), "Peace and Happiness" (1991), *Blues Preacher* (1992), *Harmolodic Guitar with Strings* (1993), *In the Name of . . .* (1993; by Music Revelation Ensemble), *Live at Bayerischer Hof* (1994), *Knights of Power* (1995; by Music Revelation Ensemble), *Music Speaks Louder Than Words* (1995), *South Delta Space Age* (1995; by Third Rail), *Cross Fire* (1996; by Music Revelation Ensemble), *Forbidden Blues* (1996), *Reunion* (1998; by Odyssey), *Blue Blood* (2001), *Memphis Blood: The Sun Sessions* (2001), *Guitar Music* (2002; with Rodolphe Burger), *No Escape from the Blues* (2003), *Blues and Grass* (2004; by 52d Street Blues Project), *Back in Time* (2005; by Odyssey), *Birthright* (2005), *Bad Blood in the City: The Piety Street Sessions* (2006), *In and Out* (2008)

Leaders Recorded With

Hank Marr (1964), Big John Patton (1969–1970), Joe Henderson (1973), Larry Young(1973), Rashied Ali (ca. 1973), Ornette Coleman (1974), Frank Wright (1977), Juma Sultan (1978), Arthur Blythe (ca. 1978, 1980), Jamaaladeen Tacuma (1982–1983), David Murray (1984, 1986), Cornell Rochester (1985), Grant Calvin Weston (1988), Karl Berger (1994), Liu Sola (1994), Roots (ca. 2001), Jayne Cortez (2003), Hakim Jami (2004), James Carter (ca. 2005), World Saxophone Quartet (2006), Allman Brothers (2010)

Films

The Soul of a Man (2003), *Lightning in a Bottle* (2004)

Award

Down Beat Readers' Poll blues album of the year (2005; for *Birthright*)

Website

http://www.jamesbloodulmer.com/ (accessed 21 May 2014)

References

PRIMARY: Jason Gross, "James Blood Ulmer," www.furious.com/perfect/bloodulmer.html (April 1998; accessed 21 May 2014) (interview); Mark Camarigg, "James Blood Ulmer: There Is Power in the Blues," *Living Blues* 192 (October 2007): 10–13, 16–19 (narrative by Ulmer).

SECONDARY: Clifford Jay Safane, "The Harmolodic Diatonic Funk of James 'Blood' Ulmer," *Down Beat* 47 (October 1980): 22–23, 64 (comments by Ulmer); Jim Miller, "Captain Blood," *Newsweek* 98 (7 December 1981): 89 (comments by Ulmer); Stanley Crouch, "The Boss of Harmolodic House," *Village Voice,* 9 November 1982, p. 58; Gary Giddins, "First Phalanx and Other Naturals," *Village Voice,* 22 May 1984, p. 77; Gary Giddins, *Rhythm-a-ning: Jazz Tradition and Innovation in the '80s* (New York: Oxford University Press, 1985), 235–49; Walter Hetfield, "Rare Blood," *Guitar Player* 24 (May 1990): 90–94, 156 (comments by Ulmer); Stuart Nicholson, "The Deconstructionists," in *Masters of Jazz Guitar,* ed. Charles Alexander (London: Balafon Books, 1999), 136–37; Patrick Ambrose, "Jazz Lessons with James 'Blood' Ulmer," *Morning News,* http://www.themorningnews.org/article/jazz-lessons-with-james-blood-ulmer (11 June 2007; accessed 21 May 2014) (comments by Ulmer); Matthew Brown, "James Blood Ulmer Biography," www.musicianguide.com/biographies/1608003684/James-Blood-Ulmer.html (2012; accessed 21 May 2014); "James Blood Ulmer—Blues—USA," www.3dfamily.org/biography-JAMES_BLOOD_ULMER-Blues-24.html (undated; accessed 21 May 2014).

Vanderford, Freddie (George Frederick)

Harmonica, guitar, washboard
7 October 1953 (Buffalo, S.C.)–
S.C. residence: mostly Buffalo (1953–)

By age twelve Vanderford played the guitar and sang well enough that he performed on television programs in Asheville, N.C., and Spartanburg, S.C. At sixteen he befriended Peg Leg Sam (Arthur Jackson), who taught Vanderford to play the blues on a harmonica. He joined the Mountain Ashe Band in 1974 and in the late 1970s formed the country-rock group Bighorn, which evolved into the Shades; this group backed Nappy Brown in the early 1990s. Vanderford and Little Pink Anderson teamed as the Legacy Duo in 1997; in time Vanderford and Brandon Turner established the New Legacy Duo. Though Vanderford resided in places other than Buffalo, identifying them and determining the dates he lived in them has proven difficult. He always returned to Buffalo.

Compositions

"Big Wheel," "Don't Let Your Mouth Write a Check Your Butt Can't Cash," "Everything Chicken but the Bill," "Trouble Come Knockin'"

Recordings as Leader

Blues Legacy (1997; with Little Pink Anderson; privately issued), *Down Home Southern Fried Blues* (1997; by the Shades), *New Legacy Duo* (1999; with Brandon Turner), "Crazy with a Frying Pan" (2005; with Brandon Turner), "Greasy Greens" (2005; with Brandon Turner), *Greasy Greens* (2010), *Mill Billy Blues* (2012; with Matthew Knights, Shane Pruitt, and Brandon Turner), "Deep Ellum Blues" (2013; with Mill Billy Blues), "Drop Down Mama" (2013; with Mill Billy Blues)

Leader Recorded With

Nappy Brown (1990–1991)

Freddie Vanderford, at the grave of his mentor, Peg Leg Sam; permission of the photographer, Derik Vanderford

Film

The Lot (2011)

Award

Jean Laney Harris Folk Heritage Award (2010)

Website

www.reverbnation.com/freddievanderfordpiedmontblues (accessed 21 May 2014)

References

PRIMARY: Dan Armonaitis, "Q&A: Vanderford Carries Blues' Legacy," *Spartanburg (S.C.) Herald-Journal*, 7 June 2012, sec. E, p. 2 (interview); Derik Vanderford, "A Founding Father of the Piedmont Blues," *Union (S.C.) Daily Times*, 7 February 2013, sec. A, p. 1 (substantial comments by Vanderford).

SECONDARY: Steve Wong, "Profile: The Shades," *Spartanburg (S.C.) Herald-Journal*, 22 August 1997, sec. D, pp. 9, 13 (comments by Vanderford); Jules Corriere, "Freddie Vanderford, Last of the Piedmont Blues Artists," http://www.squidoo.com/freddie-vanderford-last-of-the-piedmont-blues-artists (2011; accessed 21 May 2014).

Vanderhorst, Samuel

Trombone

Probably 3 April 1901 (probably Charleston, S.C.)–?

S.C. residence: Charleston (probably 1901–at least into 1930s)

Apparently a ward of Jenkins Orphanage, Vanderhorst played in its bands in the 1920s and 1930s.

The musician is probably the Samuel Vanderhorst who was born to Louisa and Samuel Vanderhorst in Charleston on 3 April 1901, according to his delayed birth certificate. A Samuel Vanderhorst, born in S.C., was enumerated for the census in May 1910 in Charleston, where he, estimated age eight, and William Vanderhorst, estimated age thirty-five, then lived as boarders. These two young Samuel Vanderhorsts are probably the same person.

Van Vynckt, Raney (Raniel Bruno)

Accordion

Probably either 22 June 1894 or 14 April 1899 (Ghent, Belgium)–10 December 1972 (Durham, N.C.)

S.C. residence: Greenville (by 1918–at least into mid-1920s)

A Greenville resident in the 1910s and 1920s, Van Vynckt recorded country tunes with Homer Christopher in 1927. As a duo that occasionally played the blues, they performed together until 1934. Bruce Bastin implies that in going with Christopher from Greenville to Atlanta to record for Columbia, Van Vynckt might have helped establish a connection that resulted in the Atlanta recordings of Spartanburg residents Pink Anderson and Simmie Dooley. Van Vynckt is buried in the New Hope Presbyterian Church Cemetery, Chapel Hill, N.C.

Van Vynckt's World War I draft registration card identifies the musician's birth date (22 June 1894), birthplace, and first name. The accordionist's death certificate records the middle name, date of birth (14 April 1899), and date and place of death. The Social Security Death Index confirms 14 April 1899 as the birth date. Labels of Van Vynckt's records identify the musician as Raney Vanvink (or Van Vink).

Compositions

"Going Slow," "Lost Mamma Blues," "Spartanburg Blues"

Recordings as Leader (All 1927; with Homer Christopher)

"Alabama Jubilee," "Drifting Back to Dreamland," "Farewell to Thee," "Going Slow" (two versions), "Hilo March," "Hometown Rag," "Lost Mamma Blues" (two versions), "March in D," "Old Fashioned Waltz," "Red Wing," "Sleep, Baby, Sleep," "Spartanburg Blues," "Waiting for the Robert E. Lee"

References

SECONDARY: Tony Russell, "Homer Christopher and the Rise and Fall of the Piano Accordion," *Old Time Music* 33 (Summer 1979–Spring 1980): 15–17; Bruce Bastin, *Red River Blues: The Blues Tradition in the Southeast* (Urbana: University of Illinois Press, 1986), 184.

Vaughn, James

Saxophone

S.C. residence: Charleston (probably late 1930s–at least into mid-1940s)

Apparently a ward of Jenkins Orphanage, Vaughn played in its bands ca. 1940.

Joseph Vaughn, Jr., was enumerated for the census at the orphanage on 21 May 1940. If he was James Vaughan (no evidence has been discovered to indicate that he was), then James, estimated age twelve, was born in N.C.; lived in Asheville, N.C., in 1935; and was the brother of trombonist Richard Vaughn. John Chilton identifies the musician as James in *A Jazz Nursery: The Story of the Jenkins' Orphanage Bands of Charleston, South Carolina* (London: Bloomsbury Book Shop, 1980), 59.

Vaughn, Richard

Trombone

Ca. 1930 (N.C.)–

S.C. residence: Charleston (not before 1935–at least into mid-1940s)

A ward of Jenkins Orphanage, Vaughn played in its bands ca. 1940.

Vaughn was possibly the brother of saxophonist James Vaughn. Conducted at the orphanage on 21 May 1940, the census indicates that Vaughn was born in N.C. and that he lived in Asheville, N.C., in 1935; it estimates his age as ten.

Walker, Barry A. ("Fatback")

Guitar, singer, restaurant owner

4 April 1961 (Atlanta, Ga.)–

S.C. residences: Blythewood (1990), Irmo (1990–)

Reared in Norwalk, Conn., Walker received music instruction in high school, where he played in a jazz band. Though he abandoned the guitar during his years as a mathematics major at the University of Connecticut, he resumed playing soon after receiving his degree in 1983. Upon moving to S.C. in 1990 he formed Fatback and the Groove Band, which has been active ever since; it performed at the 2013 Julius Daniels Blues Festival. From 1999 until 2013 Walker owned and operated Mac's on Main, a Columbia restaurant that featured live music, mostly blues, including occasionally by Walker and his group. An Irmo city councilman, he was initially elected in 2004.

Blues Had a Baby and *The Next Best Thing* are on Fatback and the Groove Band's CD *Anthology,* with some tunes omitted.

Compositions

"Blues Had a Baby," "Bow Wow," "Cobbler Man," "C.O.D.," "Drum Interlude," "Everyday Blues," "Found Your Man," "Funk Ville," "G Funk," "G Jam," "Hey Now," "I'd Rather Go Blind," "If You Don't Love Me," "I Tried To," "Jump Rope," "Little Girl," "Mind Travel," "The Next Best Thing," "Slow Down," "Soup de' Jour"

Recordings as Leader (All by Fatback and the Groove Band)

Blues Had a Baby (1996), *The Next Best Thing* (2001), "Jump Rope" (ca. 2006), *Cobbler Man* (2009)

References

PRIMARY: Benjamin Franklin V, *Jazz and Blues Musicians of South Carolina: Interviews with Jabbo, Dizzy, Drink, and Others* (Columbia: University of South Carolina Press, 2008), 174–84.

SECONDARY: Tim Flach, "Many Paths Lead to Success," *Columbia (S.C.) State,* 11 January 2005, sec. B, p. 6; John Temple Ligon, "Chef Fatback Wears Many Hats at Mac's on Main," *Columbia (S.C.) Star,* 26 August 2005, sec. B, pp. 1–2.

Walker, Joe ("Blind Joe")

Guitar

Possibly ca. 1904 (N.C. or S.C.)–after 1968

S.C. residence: Greenville (by 1926–at least until 1969)

By all accounts an accomplished guitarist, Walker did not record. This street musician directly influenced the playing of Josh White, who served the blind Walker as lead boy, or guide. Baby Brooks later served Walker in this capacity.

Though sources indicate that Walker was the brother of guitarist Willie Walker, no public document has been located indicating that this is the case. No census identifies Joe Walker as being part of the family of father George W., mother Lucy Irene, son George, son Willie, and daughter Lena Walker. Estimated age seven when enumerated for the census in Fairview Township, Greenville County on 22 April 1910, a Joe Walker then lived with his mother, Lee; he was born in S.C. Conducted on 14 April, the 1930 census documents a Joe Walker, estimated age twenty-five and a S.C. native, as living in Greenville as a roomer. Estimated age thirty-six when enumerated on 4 April 1940, a Joe Walker was living in Greenville with his wife, Belvah. It reveals that he was born in N.C., attended school through second grade, was unemployed, and lived in Greenville by 1935. Because Bruce Bastin, in *Red River Blues,* identifies Walker's wife as Beulah (probably a misunderstanding of Belvah, or the 1940 census enumerator might have mistakenly identified Beulah as Belvah), this Joe Walker was probably the musician. In this same book Bastin notes that Walker was alive in Greenville in 1969. It has not been determined definitively if any or all of these enumerated Joe Walkers were the musician.

References

SECONDARY: Max Jones, "Josh White Looks Back (Part 1)," *Blues Unlimited* 55 (July 1968): 16–17; Bruce Bastin, *Crying for the Carolines* (London: Studio Vista, 1971), 68; Bruce Bastin, *Red River Blues: The Blues Tradition in the Southeast* (Urbana: University of Illinois Press, 1986), passim; Elijah Wald, *Josh White: Society Blues* (Amherst: University of Massachusetts Press, 2000), 19, 33.

Walker, Otis

Drums

Possibly 6 June 1914 (Cedar Key, Fla.) or ca. 1915 (S.C.)–before 1980

S.C. residence: Charleston (1926–at least until 1933)

A ward of Jenkins Orphanage from 1926 until 1933, Walker played in its bands in the late 1920s and early 1930s. Subsequently he performed with the Carolina Cotton Pickers.

Bruce Bastin states that Walker was born on 6 June 1914. John Chilton indicates that Walker was born in 1914 in Cedar Key, Fla. If Chilton is correct, then Walker might be the Otis Walker enumerated for the census in Miami on 5 January 1920; this person, born in Fla., was then estimated as age six. For certain the musician was enumerated for the census at the orphanage on 2 April 1930. This document estimates his age as fifteen and records S.C. as his state of birth. The 1940 census enumerates an Ottis Walker living in Levy County, Fla. He was probably the Otis Walker who died in Marion, Fla., in August 1969, according to the Florida, Death Index, 1877–1998. It has not been determined if this person was the musician. John Chilton indicates that Walker had died by the time Chilton completed his manuscript.

Leader Recorded With

Carolina Cotton Pickers (1936–1937)

References

SECONDARY: John Chilton, *A Jazz Nursery: The Story of the Jenkins' Orphanage Bands of Charleston, South Carolina* (London: Bloomsbury Book Shop, 1980), 59; Bruce Bastin, "A Note on the Carolina Cotton Pickers," *Storyville* 95 (June–July 1981): 177–82.

Walker, Samuel

Cornet, trumpet

Ca. 1910 (Fla. or S.C.)–possibly 1930 or 1931 (possibly Princeton, Maine)

S.C. residence: Charleston (by 1920–at least until 1930)

In 1920 Walker lived at Jenkins Orphanage, possibly as a ward, where he helped teach Freddie Green to read music. In Charleston he played with the Nighthawks. He reportedly drowned while on tour with one of the orphanage bands.

Walker's age was estimated as eleven when the youth was enumerated for the census at the orphanage on 9 January 1920; this document indicates that he was born in Fla. His age was estimated as nineteen when he was enumerated in Saint Andrews Township, outside Charleston, on 28 April 1930; this census notes that he was born in S.C. and indicates that he then lived with Jessie Walker and Lucy Walker, presumably his parents, who worked at the orphanage. Jessie was probably the J. J. Walker who oversaw some touring orphanage bands. See Delilah L. Beasley, "Activities among Negroes," *Oakland (Calif.) Tribune*, 19 October 1924, sec. B, p. 3, wherein J. J. Walker is identified as professor. Julius Watson, a former orphanage ward, told John Chilton in 1979 that Samuel Walker died during the 1929–1930 tour of an orphanage band overseen by Walker's father, Reverend Walker, who was probably J. J. Walker. Unless the tour was discontinuous and extended beyond April 1930, Watson's statement is incorrect: Samuel Walker was enumerated for the census that month in Charleston.

References

SECONDARY: Stanley Dance and Helen Dance, "The Freddie Green Interview," www.freddiegreen.org/interviews/dance.html (1977; accessed 21 May 2014); John Chilton, *A Jazz Nursery: The Story of the Jenkins' Orphanage Bands of Charleston, South Carolina* (London: Bloomsbury Book Shop, 1980), 41, 59; Stanley Dance, *The World of Count Basie* (New York: Scribner's, 1980), xvii; Bruce Bastin, "A Note on the Carolina Cotton Pickers," *Storyville* 95 (June–July 1981): 177–82.

Walker, Willie ("Blind Willie")

Guitar, singer

Probably mid-1890s (S.C., possibly Greenville)–4 March 1933 (Greenville, S.C.)

S.C. residence: Greenville (probably mid-1890s–1933)

The best guitarist Josh White ever heard, the most impressive one from the Greenville-Spartanburg area encountered by Pink Anderson, and admired by Ted Bogan and Gary Davis, the blind Walker amazed guitarists with his fast, clean playing. In the early 1910s he performed in a Greenville string band that included Davis. Walker recorded but once, in Atlanta for Columbia in 1930. Accompanied by Sam Brooks, his first cousin and guide, he recorded four tunes, though only two have been released. "South Carolina Rag" is, in the opinion of Elijah Wald, "among the crowning masterpieces of ragtime-blues guitar playing" (19); Walker's performance on this recording reportedly sometimes intimidated other guitarists. Stephen Calt et al. note that "Dupree Blues" is "one of the earliest recorded versions of the 'blues ballad.'" Walker is buried in Richland Cemetery, Greenville.

Walker's age was estimated as fourteen when the musician was enumerated for the census in Austin Township, Greenville County, on 22 April 1910; this document records Walker's name as William. The 1920 (enumerated 6 or 7 January) and 1930 (19 April) censuses note that Walker lived in Greenville Township, refer to him as Willie, and indicate that he has no occupation; in 1920 his age was estimated as twenty-four, while in 1930 it was estimated as thirty-two. His death certificate reveals that he died of congenital syphilis on 4 March 1933 at age thirty-seven. "Dupree Blues" tells of Frank Dupree, a jewel thief from Abbeville, S.C., who, in 1922, was possibly the last person to be legally hanged in Ga. No evidence has been located to prove that Walker was the brother of guitarist Joe Walker, as has sometimes been suggested.

Recordings as Leader (All 1930)

"Da Da Da" (unissued), "Dupree Blues," "Rider Blues" (unissued), "South Carolina Rag"

References

SECONDARY: Stephen Calt et al., notes to *East Coast Blues, 1926–1935* (1968; Yazoo L-1013); Max Jones, "Josh White Looks Back (Part 1)," *Blues Unlimited* 55 (July 1968): 16–17; Max Jones, "Josh White Looks Back 2," *Blues Unlimited* 56 (September 1968): 15–16; Bruce Bastin, *Crying for the Carolines* (London: Studio Vista, 1971), 71–73; Bruce Bastin, *Red River Blues: The Blues Tradition in the Southeast* (Urbana: University of Illinois Press, 1986), 173–76; *"Oh, What a Beautiful City": A Tribute to the Reverend Gary Davis (1896–1972) Gospel, Blues and Ragtime*, ed. Robert Tilling (Jersey, Channel Islands: Paul Mill Press, 1992), 8; Elijah Wald, *Josh White: Society Blues* (Amherst: University of Massachusetts Press, 2000), 19, 32.

Wallace, Frank

Cornet

S.C. residence: Charleston (early 1900s)

Apparently a ward of Jenkins Orphanage, Wallace played in its bands in the early 1900s. He became a music tutor.

Reference

SECONDARY: John Chilton, *A Jazz Nursery: The Story of the Jenkins' Orphanage Bands of Charleston, South Carolina* (London: Bloomsbury Book Shop, 1980), 59.

Ward, Henry

Saxophone

S.C. residence: Charleston (probably by late 1920s–probably at least into mid-1930s)

Apparently a ward of Jenkins Orphanage, Ward played in its bands ca. 1930.

Ward, Marv (Marvin Landon; "Rev. Marv")

Guitar, bass, drums, singer

17 February 1947 (Lorton, Va.)–

S.C. residences: Myrtle Beach (1980–1984), Columbia (1984–)

In Lorton, Va., Ward played guitar in his high school band, performed professionally with Sonny Skillman, and formed the Pohick Valley Boys, which played at the Cellar Door in Washington, D.C., the University of Maryland, and elsewhere. After serving in the navy he began a solo career but also performed with other musicians, including Roger Sprung at the Newport Folk Festival (1968–1969). Subsequently he continued performing solo and with groups, including with the Jon Robinson Expression, the Little Royal Band, and Toyzz. He has appeared at numerous blues festivals. An ordained minister, he works as a television producer and director.

Marv Ward; photograph by Libby Gamble, permission of Marv Ward

Compositions

"Another Slow Twist of the Knife," "Big Medicine," "Blues in the Morning," "Chase These Blues Away," "Come Down to the River," "Come On Over," "Every Time I Look at You I Get the Blues," "Hard Times," "Heart of Stone," "I Can't Give Up on You," "I Dreamed You Were My Lover," "I Need Your Kiss," "I Should Know Better," "It Ain't about You," "It's Just You," "Kindred Souls," "Love Is Calling," "Love Like You Never Been Burned," "Medieval Lady," "Myrtle Beach Cruisers," "Ole Mule," "On Down the Road," "Railroad Gal," "Ridin' on a Daydream," "Silver Crescent," "Tennessee Whiskey," "Unabashed Carnivore," "Virginia," "Wallflower," "Why You Do Me Like You Do"

Recordings as Leader

"High Flying Bird" (1973), *High Flying Bird* (2002), *Come On Out and Get You Some: Live at the Double Door* (2005), *Love Like You Never Been Burned* (2009), *I Should Know Better* (2012)

Leaders Recorded With

Roger Sprung (1969), Bryan Fustukian (1974), Charlie Whyde (1987), Shelley Magee (1999)

Website

www.marvward.com (accessed 21 May 2014)

References

PRIMARY: Otis R. Taylor, Jr., "The Blues, Brothers and Sisters! Say 'Amen'!," *Columbia (S.C.) State*, 22 April 2005, sec. E, p. 12 (interview).

SECONDARY: Kevin Oliver, "Rev. Marv Ward," *Columbia (S.C.) Free Times*, 1–7 February 2012, p. 42.

Washboard Doc (Joseph Doctor)

Washboard, miscellaneous instruments
Probably 8 September 1911 (S.C., probably John's Island)–probably 15 September 1988 (Brooklyn, N.Y.)
S.C. residence: John's Island (probably 1911–ca. 1935)

Doctor began performing with string bands in the Charleston area ca. 1925. In time he became known as Washboard Doc. Possibly in 1935 he moved to N.Y.C., where he was a street musician and where he resided for the remainder of his life. He performed with Ralph Willis in the 1940s; in the 1960s, with John Whitner. Beginning in 1969 he recorded occasionally for Spivey Records, the company of singer Victoria Spivey, and in 1980 performed in Europe.

Doctor's birth and death dates come from the Social Security Death Index, which indicates that the musician died on 15 September 1988; all other sources consulted state that he died a day later. His age was estimated as eight years when he was enumerated for the census in John's Island Township on 9 January 1920.

Recordings as Leader

"Doctor of the Washboard" (1970), "Headless Boogie" (1970s), "Mean Mistreatin' Mama" (1970s), "No Body!" (1970s), "Please Throw a Poor Dog a Bone" (1970s), "Under Your Hood" (1970s), *Washboard Doc and His Hep 3* (1979), *Early Morning Blues* (1980)

Leaders Recorded With

Possibly Ralph Willis (ca. 1950), possibly Sonny Terry (early 1950s), Alec Seward (1966), Smokey Hogg (1969), Roosevelt Sykes (1969), Victoria Spivey and Piano Tuner Papa (1970), Spivey's Blues Paraders (1970), Big Joe Turner (1977), Eunice Davis (1978), Cab Lucky (1979), Screamin' Jay Hawkins (1981)

References

SECONDARY: Norbert Hess, "Obituaries," *Juke Blues* 14 (Winter 1988–1989): 21; Beth Josephic, "Washboard Doc," *Living Blues* 85 (March–April 1989): 35 (obituary).

Washington, Aaron George

Guitar, singer
2 January 1902 (probably Willington, S.C., though possibly Williston, S.C.)–July 1980 (Albany, N.Y.)
S.C. residence: probably Willington, though possibly Williston (1902–ca. 1912)

Around age ten Washington moved from Willington or Williston to the Asheville, N.C., area, where he learned to play the guitar and performed with a string band by ca. 1919. There, in the early 1920s, he befriended Gary Davis, with whom he traveled in the Southeast. In addition to the blues, he performed spirituals, at Davis's suggestion. In the mid-1920s Washington settled in Catskill, N.Y., where he remained until the mid-1940s, when he moved to Hudson, N.Y.; after relocating to Troy, N.Y., he made Albany, N.Y., his home, probably in the early or mid-1950s. Though he largely abandoned music after moving to Catskill, he resumed it in Albany for a few years before giving it up in the late 1950s.

Washington's birth date and date and place of death come from the Social Security Death Index. Kip Lornell states that Washington was born in Willington, S.C., "near the state line about halfway between Athens, Georgia and Columbia, South Carolina" ("Part Two: Albany Blues," 25). This detailed description suggests its accuracy. Yet Bruce Bastin notes that Washington was born in Williston, S.C., which is not located in relation to Athens and Columbia as Lornell describes Washington's birthplace. Both men spoke with Washington.

References

PRIMARY: Kip Lornell, "Part Two: Albany Blues," *Living Blues* 15 (Winter 1973–1974): 22–26 (substantial comments by Washington).

SECONDARY: Christopher Lornell, "The Effects of Social and Economic Changes on the Uses of the Blues," *JEMF Quarterly* 11 (Spring 1975): 43–48 (comments by Washington); Bruce Bastin, *Red River Blues: The Blues Tradition in the Southeast* (Urbana: University of Illinois Press, 1986), 241–42 (comments by Washington).

Washington, Baby (Justine)

Singer
Possibly 13 November 1940 (Bamberg, S.C.)–
S.C. residence: Bamberg (1940–1941)

At age two months Washington was taken from Bamberg to Harlem, where she was reared. She sang with the vocal group Hearts (also known as Jaynetts) in the mid-1950s before recording under her own name. Usually characterized as a soul singer, her biggest hits were "Only Those in Love" and "That's How Heartaches Are Made," both in the 1960s, when she recorded most frequently. She became well enough known to tour with a stage production headed by Sam Cooke (1963) and with the Cavalcade of Stars (1965). After retiring from music in 1971 she returned to it two years later; her last recording to chart was "Can't Get Over Losing You" (1975). Despite popularity evidenced by recording in four decades, her recording career apparently ended in the late 1980s. Robert Pruter notes that Washington "combined down-to-earth gospel soulfulness with a stately uptown elegance" (56).

Though the singer sometimes recorded as Jeanette Washington, she is not the performer of this name who sang back-up with such vocalists as James Brown and George Clinton. On the label of "Ah-Ha," Washington is given composer credit as J. Wash. Other than *That's How Heartaches Are Made* and *With You in Mind,* all of Washington's vinyl albums and CDs consist of previously issued material.

Compositions

"Ah-Ha," "Care Free," "The Clock," "Come On In," "Crying in the Midnight Hour," "Hush Heart," "I'm Not Letting You Go," "Is Our Love Worth Holding On," "I've Got a Feeling," "I've Got to Break Away," "I Wanna Dance," "Lazy Mood," "Let Love Go By," "Money's Funny," "Move On," "Move On, Drifter," "My Time to Cry," "Nobody Cares about Me," "Or Leave Me Alone," "Pedesta," "Standing on the Pier," "Tear after Tear," "The Time," "Train, Car, Boat or Plane," "Who's Gonna Take Care of Me?," "Why Did My Baby Put Me Down?," "Work Out," "You," "You Never Could Be Mine," "Your Fool"

Recordings as Leader (These Are Release Dates, Not Necessarily Recording Dates)

"Congratulations, Honey" (1957), "Every Day" (1957), "There Must Be a Reason" (1957), "Ah-Ha" (1958), "Been a Long Time Baby" (1958), "Hard Way to Go" (1958), "You Never Could Be Mine" (1958), "The Bells (on Our Wedding Day)" (1959), "I Hate to See You Go" (1959), "Let's Love in the Moonlight" (1959), "Why Did My Baby Put Me Down?" (1959), "Workout" (1959), "Medicine Man" (1960; as Jeanette B. Washington), "Move On" (1960; as Jeanette "Baby" Washington), "Tears Fall" (1960; as Jeanette B. Washington), "Too Late" (1960; as Jeanette "Baby" Washington), "Deep Down Love" (ca. 1960), "Your Mama Knows What's Right" (ca. 1960), "Money's Funny" (1961; as Jeanette "Baby" Washington), "Nobody Cares about Me" (1961; as Jeanette "Baby" Washington), "No Tears" (1962), *That's How Heartaches Are Made* (1963), "Hey, Lonely" (1963), "I Can't Wait until I See My Baby's Face" (1963; as Justine Washington), "There He Is" (1963), "Who's Gonna Take Care of Me?" (1963; as Justine Washington), "The Clock" (1964), "It'll Never Be Over for Me" (1964), "Move On, Drifter" (1964), "Run, My Heart" (1964), "Your Fool" (1964), "No Time for Pity" (1965), "Only Those in Love" (1965), "There He Is" (1965), "Silent Night" (1966), "White Christmas" (1966), "Either You're with Me (or Either You're Not)" (1967), "You Are What You Are" (1967), *With You in Mind* (1968), "I Know" (1968), "Baby, Let Me Get Close to You" (1973; with Don Gardner), "Forever" (1973; with Don Gardner), "Can't Get Over Losing You" (1974, 1978; the latter as Jeanette "Baby" Washington), "Care Free" (1974), "Either You Love Me or Leave Me" (1976; as Jeanette "Baby" Washington), "I Wanna Dance" (1978; as Jeanette "Baby" Washington), "Come See about Me" (1980), "You Are Just a Dream" (1980), "Crying in the Midnight Hour" (1988), "Pedestal" (1988)

Leaders Recorded With (These Are Release Dates, Not Necessarily Recording Dates)

Hearts (1956–1958), Jaynetts (1956), Jive Five (1982)

Award

Rhythm & Blues Foundation Pioneer Award (1995)

References

SECONDARY: "Ex-quartet Singer Headed for Stardom," *Chicago Daily Defender,* 25 November 1958, sec. A, p. 18; "Baby Washington Arrives as Star," *Chicago Defender,* 11 March 1961, p. 18 (national edition); Bruce Huston, "Baby Washington," *Soul Survivor* 9 (Summer 1988): 8–12; Bruce Huston, "Baby Washington, Part Two: Her Soul Years," *Soul Survivor* 10 (Spring 1989): 12–15; Robert Pruter, "That's How Heartaches Are Made: The Baby Washington Story," *Goldmine* 525 (8 September

2000): 56, 58, 60 (this issue is also designated volume 26, number 18) (comments by Washington).

Watson, Joseph

Trombone
S.C.
S.C. residence: Charleston (1910s)

A ward of Jenkins Orphanage, Watson played in its bands in the 1910s, including the one that performed in *Uncle Tom's Cabin* in N.Y.C. in 1913.

Conducted at the orphanage on 22 April, the 1910 census indicates that Watson was born in S.C. but does not estimate his age.

Reference

SECONDARY: Edward Ball, *The Sweet Hell Inside: A Family History* (New York: William Morrow, 2001), 105–6.

Watson, Julius ("Hawk")

Trombone, singer
Possibly 11 October 1911 or 10 October 1912 (S.C.)–25 December 1984
S.C. residence: Charleston (by 1920–early 1930s)

A ward of Jenkins Orphanage beginning in 1928, Watson played in its bands in the early 1930s. For the remainder of the decade he performed with the Carolina Cotton Pickers. He is best known for his years with the band of Buddy Johnson (1949–1957), with which he and two other instrumentalists occasionally performed as the Bee Jays, a vocal group, at least in the mid-1950s. An army veteran (he served from 1943 to 1946), he is buried in plot 10, 0, 10912, Calverton National Cemetery, Calverton, N.Y.

Watson's age was estimated as eight when the youth was enumerated for the census in Charleston on 3 January 1920; as sixteen when enumerated at the orphanage on 2 April 1930. The Social Security Death Index indicates that Watson was born on 11 October 1911 and last resided in N.Y.C.; Department of Veterans Affairs BIRLS Death File, 1850–2010, records a birth date of 10 October 1912. Bruce Bastin allows for the possibility that Watson also played drums in the orphanage band.

Leaders Recorded With

Carolina Cotton Pickers (1936–1937), Ace Harris (1937), Doc Wheeler (1941–1942), Cootie Williams (1946–1947), Buddy Johnson (1949–1955, 1957)

References

SECONDARY: Stanley Dance, *The World of Earl Hines* (New York: Scribner's, 1977), 262; John Chilton, *A Jazz Nursery: The Story of the Jenkins' Orphanage Bands of Charleston, South Carolina* (London: Bloomsbury Book Shop, 1980), 32, 40–44, 46, 59 (comments by Watson); Bruce Bastin, "A Note on the Carolina Cotton Pickers," *Storyville* 95 (June–July 1981): 177–82.

Wesley, Fred Alonzo, Jr.

Trombone, composer, arranger
4 July 1943 (Columbus, Ga.)–
S.C. residence: Manning (ca. 1992–)

Perhaps best known for his tenure with James Brown, whom he served as musical director begin-

Fred Wesley; permission of the photographer, Marcos Hermes, and Joya Wesley

ning in 1971 and left in 1975, Wesley has had a varied career. Initially wanting to play jazz, in time he did with Count Basie, whose band he joined in 1978. He also made jazz recordings under his own name. He is adept at the blues, as evidenced by his recordings with Hank Crawford and Dr. John, among others. He played rhythm and blues with the likes of Hank Ballard. He is most important for his involvement with funk, a genre that evolved from James Brown's music and was primarily disseminated by several of Brown's musicians: Bootsy Collins, Pee Wee Ellis, Maceo Parker, and Wesley. In addition to his involvement with such funk groups as Parliament and the P-Funk All-Stars, Wesley led the funk groups the J. B.'s, the New J. B.'s, and the Horny Horns, as well as the J. B. Horns in conjunction with Ellis and Parker. Wesley's compositions have been performed on movie sound tracks, including those of *Black Caesar* (1973), *The Return of Superfly* (1990), *Dead Presidents* (1995), *Snatch* (2000), *The Woodsman* (2004), and *Django Unchained* (2012).

Compositions

"All for One," "Belinda," "Blasters of the Universe," "Blessed Blackness," "Blind Man Can See It," "Blow Your Head," "Blues and Pants," "Bop to the Boogie," "The Boss," "Check Your Body," "Children of Africa," "Christmas Is 4 Ever," "Damn Right I'm Somebody," "Def Do Us Part," "Everything," "Everywhere Is Out of Town," "Feels So Good," "Funky Music Is My Style," "Get Down," "Get Up off Me," "Here We Come," "Here We Go Again," "Hot Pants," "I Can't Say Goodbye," "I Love My Family," "I Make Music," "Incredible," "J. B. Shout," "Keep It Going," "Keep On Doin' What You're Doin'," "King Slaughter," "Learn Chinese," "Let's Play House," "Make It Good to Yourself," "Makin' Love," "Mind Power," "Moon over Brixton," "Never Get Enough," "On the Spot," "Papa Don't Take No Nonsense," "Payback," "Perfect Harmony," "Reality," "Soul Men," "Sweet and Tangy," "That's the Way Love Goes," "To the Beat, Y'all," "Undaground," "Wine Spot," "You Played Yourself"

Recordings as Leader

The Lost Album (1972), *Breakin' Bread* (1974), *A Blow for Me, a Toot to You* (1977), *The Final Blow* (late 1970s), *Say Blow by Blow Backwards* (1979), *House Party* (1980), *The J. B. Horns* (1989–1990; with Pee Wee Ellis and Maceo Parker), *New Friends* (1990), *Comme Ci Comme Ça* (1991), *Swing and Be Funky* (1992), "Last Chance" (1992), "Streets of New York" (1992), "Waiting for You" (1992), *To Someone* (1993), *Amalgamation* (1994), "Give Fred a Chance" (1996), *Full Circle: From Be Bop to Hip Hop* (1998), *Wuda Cuda Shuda* (2002), *It Don't Mean a Thing If It Ain't Got That Swing* (2005), *Funk for Your Ass* (2007; remixed as *The Godfather of Soul Train*), *With a Little Help from My Friends* (2010)

Leaders Recorded With

Vicki Anderson (1966, 1968–1969, 1971, 1975), Hank Ballard (1967–1969), James Brown (1968–1975), Marva Whitney (1968–1969, 1971), Bill Doggett (1969), Bobby Byrd (1970, 1988–1989, 1991, 1995–1996, 2005), Lyn Collins (1971–1973, 1975), Charles Sherrell (1974), George Benson (1975, ca. 1984), Hank Crawford (1975–1976, 1978), David Matthews (1976), Parliament (mid-to-late 1970s), Larry Williams (1977–1978), Count Basie (1978), Milt Jackson and Count Basie (1978), Bernie Worrell (1978, 1992–1993), Bootsy Collins (1979–1980, 1988, 1990, 1994, 1997, 2002, 2005–2006), Jean Carn (possibly 1980s), George Clinton (1982, 1984, 1986, 1993, 1995), P-Funk (1983, 1995), Bobby Womack (1984), Maceo Parker (ca. 1986, 1990–1994, 1996–1998, 2001), Nils Lundgren (between 1988 and 1999), Deee-Lite (1990, 1992), Material (ca. 1991), Phil Upchurch (1992), Cecil Parker (1994), Robert Trowers (1994), Pee Wee Ellis (1996–1997, 2001), James Taylor (1996), Pucho Brown (1999–2000), Bozo Allegro (2000), Carla Cook (2000), Marcus Miller (2000), Space Cowboys (2000), Dr. John (2001), Soulive (2001), Randy Brecker (2002), Javon Jackson (2002), Barry McAll (ca. 2002), Thomas E. Taylor, Jr. (ca. 2002), Pancho Sanchez (2003), Brian Nova (2005), Lenny Kravitz (2007), Susanne Alt (2008), Robin McKelle (ca. 2009), Gerald Albright (2010), Apples (2010), Mop Mop (2011)

Film

My First Name Is Maceo (1996)

References

PRIMARY: Fred Wesley, Jr., *Hit Me, Fred: Recollections of a Sideman* (Durham, N.C.: Duke University Press, 2002); The Dood [Michael J. Edwards], "Fred Wesley JR: From Sideman to Front Man," http://archive.today/MXVnl (2008; accessed 21 May 2014) (interview);

The Dood [Michael J. Edwards], "Fred Wesley JR 2010," http://ukvibe.org/interviews/fred-wesley-jr_2010/ (2010; accessed 21 May 2014) (interview).

SECONDARY: Mike Zwerin, "Fred Wesley: The Importance of a Groove: 'Wuda, Cuda, Shuda,'" http://www.culturekiosque.com/jazz/portrait/fredwesley.html (2003; accessed 21 May 2014); Ann Wicker, "Fred Wesley Jr.: Sideman Extraordinaire," in *Making Notes: Music of the Carolinas,* ed. Ann Wicker (Charlotte: Novello Festival Press, 2008), 108–10 (comments by Wesley); R. J. Smith, *The One: The Life and Music of James Brown* (New York: Gotham Books, 2012), passim.

Westray, Ron (Ronald Kenneth, Jr.)

Trombone, euphonium, composer, arranger
13 June 1970 (Columbia, S.C.)-
S.C. residences: Columbia (1970-1988, 1994-1997), Orangeburg (1988-1992)

Westray joined the Marcus Roberts nonet while a student at South Carolina State University. Following his 1992 graduation he enrolled at Eastern Illinois University; as a graduate student he became a regular with the Lincoln Center Jazz Orchestra (later, Jazz at Lincoln Center Orchestra), an affiliation that continued after receiving his master's degree (1994) and upon returning to his hometown of Columbia. There he operated the Wooden Flute Performance Studio (1995–1996). From 1997 to 2005 he lived in Harlem and was active on the N.Y.C. jazz scene, including as arranger and lead trombonist with the Jazz at Lincoln Center Orchestra. He left N.Y.C. in 2005 to begin his academic career as a professor in the Jazz Studies Program at the University of Texas, Austin. In 2009 he became the Oscar Peterson Chair in Jazz Performance at York University, Toronto.

Compositions

"Baby Walks," "Bird Schtick," "Boogaloo Flu," "Bumpsie's Got It," *Chivalrous Misdemeanors* (score to *Don Quixote,* with twenty-two tunes), "Coming Is Going," "Easy Green," "Esoteric Advent," "Ever Seen a Grown Man Cry," "Exile," "Feel the Pressure," "Fuzzy Dice," "Garments," "I'm You," "Inside Out," "The Jiggy," "Jimmy," "Leaving Home Again," "Liberia in Three Parts," "Like Ronny," "Loop de Loop," "Makin' Happy," "Maybe Later," "Mayfest Junction," *Medical Cures* (suite of nine tunes), "Modern Nostalgia," "Mr. Personality," "Papo Vasquez," "Pow Wow," "Procrastination," "Satarello Shuffle," "Satarello Sunshine," "Scritchum Scratchum," "Scriven, Ga.," "Simple America," "Sista Pie's Echo," "Straight Laced," "Stumble Up!," "Summer Is Coming," "Sun Day," "Swan Gaze," "Twitt-Twoo-Yoo-Hoo!," "Two Words," "Upper Manhattan Jump," "Way Back When," "The Whippy Dipp," "Ye Olde Routine," "Yesterday Night's Mourning," "You Are Out of Sight," "You Shan't See Me in the Morning"

Recordings as Leader

Bone Structure (1996; with Wycliffe Gordon), *Westray Digs In* (2000), *Medical Cures for the Chromatic Commands of the Inner City* (2008), *Live from Austin* (2011; with Thomas Heflin), *Jimi Jazz* (2013), *Magisteria* (2013)

Leaders Recorded With

Marcus Roberts (1991, 1995–1997), Lincoln Center Jazz Orchestra (1993–1995, 1998, 2003), Wynton Marsalis (1993, 1995–1999), Dennis Jeter (1998), Wycliffe Gordon (1999), Veronica Nunn (2000), Travis Shook (2000, 2003), Pete Rodriguez (2005), University of Texas Faculty Jazz (2007), Austin Jazz Workshop (2009), Kate Edmondson (2009), New Orleans Jazz Orchestra (ca. 2009), Richard Underhill (2010)

Award

Outstanding Graduate Alumnus, Eastern Illinois University (2011)

Reference

PRIMARY: Benjamin Franklin V, *Jazz and Blues Musicians of South Carolina: Interviews with Jabbo, Dizzy, Drink, and Others* (Columbia: University of South Carolina Press, 2008), 185–205.

Wheeler, Leroy, Jr. ("Brother," "Shahees")

Singer
13 February 1943 (Sumter, S.C.)-14 September 2008 (Summit, N.J.)
S.C. residence: Sumter (1943-ca. 1959)

Wheeler sang with the Novatones, George Kerr's Serenaders, and the Magnificent Four before affiliating with the Del-Larks (ca. 1961–ca. 1963). He joined the reconstituted Del-Larks in 2006 and remained with the group until his death. He is buried in Rosedale and Rosehill Cemetery, Linden, N.J.

Recordings as Leader

Unidentified songs (probably mid-to-late 1960s; as Shahees Wheeler)

Leader Recorded With

Jackie and the Perigents (mid-1960s)

References

SECONDARY: Charlie Horner, with Pamela Horner, "Doo Wop and Soul in the Birthplace of Funk: The Story of Sammy and the Del Larks," *Echoes of the Past* 86 (Winter 2008): 11–20 (also available at www.classicurbanharmony.net/Del%20Larks%20Story%20edit.pdf [accessed 21 May 2014]); "Leroy Wheeler Jr.," *Newark (N.J.) Star-Ledger,* 17 September 2008, p. 30 (obituary).

White, Amos Mordecai

Cornet

Probably 1889 or early 1890s (Kingstree, S.C.)–2 July 1980 (Alameda, Calif.)

S.C. residences: Kingstree (probably 1889 or early 1890s–ca. 1897), Charleston (ca. 1897–possibly 1910, possibly 1911–1913, at least 1917), possibly Columbia (1910–1911)

By ca. 1897 White had become a ward of Jenkins Orphanage, where he was taught the art of printing and learned to play the alto horn, on which he performed in the institution's bands. Upon completing his wardship in 1906 he remained at the orphanage as teacher. If he attended Benedict College in Columbia (1910–1911), as he claimed, he returned to Charleston and resumed teaching at the institution. Among his students was the drummer Herbert Wright. In 1913 he married Roxie Jenkins, daughter of Lena James Jenkins and Daniel Joseph Jenkins, founders of the orphanage, though he left her to tour as a professional musician. He played cornet in minstrel shows (including Franc's New York Minstrels of Birmingham, Ala.) and circuses (Cole Brothers and Ringling Brothers). Without success he courted another Cole Brothers entertainer, Lizzie Miles, later known as a blues singer. After joining the army in 1918 he led the 816th Pioneer Regiment Brass Band, which played in England and France. Following his 1919 discharge he settled in New Orleans, where he remarried and worked as a printer. He led a band and performed with several groups, including ones led by Papa Celestin, Fate Marable, and Harrison Verrett. He played with Marable on the steamer *Capitol* and on Marable's only two recordings. White's New Orleans Creole Jazz Band, mainly a septet, performed at Anderson's Annex, Spanish Fort, and West End in the early and mid-1920s; its members included Wilhelmina Bart, Barney Bigard, and Bob Ysaguirre. Upon leaving New Orleans in 1926 he toured with Mamie Smith. In 1928 he led what he termed the Original Georgias (possibly the Georgia Minstrels). He settled in Tucson, Ariz., in 1929; there he played with the bands of Gregorio Boyer and Felipe Lopez and led a group called the Rhythm Kings. After leaving Tucson in 1934 he resided in Oakland, Calif., where he owned a print shop, played and taught music occasionally, married again, and spent the remainder of his life.

John Chilton records White's name as Amos Earl Mordecai White; on his 1917 and 1942 draft registration cards the musician identified himself as Amos Mordecai White. His birth date cannot be established with certainty. When recounting his career in 1965 he identified it as 6 November 1889, which is confirmed by the Social Security Death Index and California, Death Index, 1940–1997. His 1917 draft registration card indicates that he was born on 6 November 1890; the 1942 card, on 6 November 1893. His age was estimated as thirty-seven when he was enumerated for the census in Tucson on 10 April 1930; as forty-six when enumerated in Oakland a decade later. California, Marriage Index, 1960–1985, estimates that he was born in 1890. Chilton maintains that White entered the orphanage in 1900; the musician believed that he was placed there at age eight or nine. He said that he taught there for approximately two years after concluding his term as ward in 1906. He was affiliated with the institution as late as 1913, when he married Roxie Jenkins and, according to Chilton, played in its band. Yet his 1917 draft registration card, completed in Charleston, indicates that he considered the orphanage his home while working as a traveling musician with Chas. E. Van Horn. White's assertion that the cornetist recorded with Mamie Smith has not been confirmed.

Leaders Recorded With

Fate Marable (1924), Frank Goudie (1960)

References

PRIMARY: Amos M. White, interview by William Russell, 23 August 1958, four reels of tape and a typed summary,

Hogan Jazz Archive, Tulane University, New Orleans (also available at http://musicrising.tulane.edu/uploads/transcripts/a.%20white%2008-23-1958.pdf [accessed 21 May 2014]); Amos White, as told to Bertrand Demeusy, "The Amos White Musical Career," *Record Research: The Magazine of Record Information and Statistics* 69 (July 1965): 3, 10.

SECONDARY: "Tucson, Ariz.," *Los Angeles California Eagle,* 2 February 1934, p. 9; Grayson Mills, "Amos White and His New Orleans Ragtime Band," *Eureka: The Bimonthly Magazine of New Orleans Jazz* 1 (September–October 1960): 5–7; Samuel Barclay Charters IV, *Jazz: New Orleans, 1885–1963: An Index to the Negro Musicians of New Orleans,* revised edition (New York: Oak Publications, 1963), 101–3; John Chilton, *A Jazz Nursery: The Story of the Jenkins' Orphanage Bands of Charleston, South Carolina* (London: Bloomsbury Book Shop, 1980), 13–14, 49, 59 (comments by White); Jeffrey P. Green, *Edmund Thornton Jenkins: The Life and Times of an American Black Composer, 1894–1926* (Westport, Conn.: Greenwood, 1982), 22, 27.

White, Bill (William)

Singer

Probably December 1918 (Greenville, S.C.)–?

S.C. residence: Greenville (probably 1918–ca. 1936)

In the mid-1930s White left Greenville for N.Y.C. There he sang with his brother Josh, including on the work song "Monday, Tuesday, Wednesday," a recording released on Musicraft (1940). Also that year he recorded with Josh White and His Carolinians for Columbia. After military service during World War II, he toured occasionally with his brother; for Decca they recorded "Josh and Bill Blues" (1947). White also sings on the Period album *Josh White Comes a-Visitin'* (1956). Beginning in 1950 and at least until 1953 he served as factotum for Eleanor Roosevelt at her residence in Hyde Park, N.Y., where his brother occasionally visited as her guest.

White's age was estimated as one year, one month when the child was enumerated for the census in Greenville on 5 January 1920. Josh White recorded three songs for Decca in 1945 with Billy White on drums. It has not been determined if the percussionist was Josh's brother.

Leader Recorded With

Josh White (1940, 1947, 1956)

References

SECONDARY: Eleanor Roosevelt, "Some of My Best Friends Are Negro," *Ebony* 8 (February 1953): 16–20, 22, 24–26 (see especially 22); Dorothy Schainman Siegel, *The Glory Road: The Story of Josh White* (San Diego: Harcourt Brace Jovanovich, 1982), passim; Elijah Wald, *Josh White: Society Blues* (Amherst: University of Massachusetts Press, 2000), passim.

White, Josh (Joshua Daniel; "Tippy Barton," "Pinewood Tom," "The Singing Christian," "Jimmy Walker")

Guitar, singer

Possibly 11 February 1914 (Greenville, S.C.)–5 September 1969 (Manhasset, N.Y.)

S.C. residence: Greenville (possibly 1914–ca. 1921, 1929–1932)

Reared in a religious, musical family, White was exposed to the soulful music of a sanctified church in Greenville. During the 1920s he learned to play the guitar primarily from blind musicians he served as lead boy, or guide, initially John Henry Arnold but also Blind Joel Taggart and Blind Lemon Jefferson, among others. In 1928 he recorded for the first time, backing Taggart in Chicago. Upon returning to Greenville he concluded his formal education

Josh White, with Mary Lou Williams, WMCA, N.Y.C., ca. October 1947; reproduced from the William P. Gottlieb Collection, Library of Congress, Music Division

by attending the eighth grade at Sterling High School during the 1931–1932 school year. After being discovered by a representative of American Record Corporation, White traveled to N.Y.C. in 1932; there he recorded for the initial time as a featured artist, performing twenty songs. Settling there, he played at Harlem rent parties and, in the late 1930s, appeared on *Harlem Fantasy,* a radio program featuring black musicians. As Pinewood Tom he recorded with Leroy Carr and Scrapper Blackwell in 1934; he recorded with Lucille Bogan and Buddy Moss the next year. In 1936 he injured his right hand to the degree that it almost required amputation; during convalescence, he worked odd jobs and became superintendent of an apartment building. Again able to use his hand, he performed in the musical *John Henry* (1940), starring Paul Robeson, who became godfather of White's daughter Beverly. A 1940 recording session was released partly on Blue Note Records (backed by Sidney Bechet) and partly on Musicraft. He formed Josh White and His Carolinians, which included Sam Gary, Carrington Lewis, Bayard Rustin, and White's brother Bill. For Columbia this group recorded a session produced by John Hammond (1940). White appeared regularly on the CBS radio program *Back Where I Come From* (1940–1941), produced by Alan Lomax and Nicholas Ray. With the Golden Gate Quartet he performed at the 1941 inauguration of President Franklin D. Roosevelt; he also sang at a presidential command performance later that year and at Roosevelt's 1945 inauguration. (He became so friendly with the Roosevelts that Mrs. Roosevelt became the godmother of Josh White, Jr., who had a career in music.) White began singing about social issues, especially racial ones. In 1941 he recorded such music at his own sessions and with the leftist Almanac Singers (Lee Hays, Millard Lampell, and Pete Seeger). He appeared with Leadbelly at the Village Vanguard for three months (1941–1942). In 1942 he formed a duo with Libby Holman after teaching her to sing folk music and blues. For much of the 1940s he performed at Café Society Downtown, which welcomed both white and black patrons. He hosted his own radio program in 1944, the year he recorded "One Meat Ball," which became a hit. During that decade he toured and appeared in stage shows and movies; he acted off-Broadway in *A Long Way from Home* (1948) and starred on Broadway in *How Long till Summer* (1949–1950). He accompanied Eleanor Roosevelt to Scandinavia (1950). After being blacklisted for having served as a friendly witness before the House Committee on Un-American Activities in 1950, White spent 1951 in Europe. Headquartered in England, he gave concerts and appeared on BBC. His American reputation revived after releasing albums on Elektra Records, beginning in 1955. He performed at colleges and universities beginning in the late 1950s and sang at the 1963 Capitol Mall event that included Martin Luther King's "I Have a Dream" speech. Some music lovers who favored the authenticity of blues and folk music perceived White's singing as too facile. Yet in *Josh White,* Elijah Wald notes that White, who knew the real sounds of work gangs, for example, intentionally sang clearly so listeners would understand the lyrics and therefore could comprehend the experiences about which he sang. Bruce Bastin observes that White's "fast finger-picking style both epitomized the music of his region and became a role model for future bluesmen" ("Truckin' My Blues Away," 214). White, who died during heart surgery, is buried in Cypress Hills Cemetery, Brooklyn, N.Y.

Compositions

"Bad Housing Blues," "Defense Factory Blues," "Greenville Sheik," "Hard Times Blues," "Jim Crow Train," "Little Brother," "Southern Exposure," "Uncle Sam Says"

Recordings as Leader

Complete Recorded Works in Chronological Order (1929–1945; six CDs), "Broad Players Blues" (1932), "Big House Blues" (1933), "Black Man" (1935), "Cherry Picker" (1935), "Gone Dry Blues" (1935), "Tweet Tweet Mama Blues" (1935), "You Got to Give Me Some of It" (1935), "How Long" (1940), "I Want Jesus to Walk with Me" (1940), "John Henry" (1940), "Lord Have Mercy" (1940), "Moan, Chillun, Moan" (1940), "Mr. Rabbit, You Ear's Mighty Long" (1940), "Old Dan Tucker" (1940), "Rock My Soul in the Bosom of Abraham" (1940), "Run, Sinner, Run" (1940), "Silicosis Blues" (1940), *Josh White Sings* (1949; also titled *Strange Fruit*), *A Josh White Program* (1950; also titled *Ballads*), "Foggy, Foggy Dew" (1950), "Hard Time Blues" (1950), "I'm Gonna Move to the Outskirts of Town" (1950), "Like a Natural Man" (1950), "Take a Gal Like You" (1950), "T.B. Blues" (1950), "Wanderings" (1950), "Black Gal"

(1951), "He Never Said a Mumbling Word" (1951), "I Want You and I Need You" (1951), "The Lass with the Most Delicate Air" (1951), "Lonesome Road" (1951), "On Top of Old Smokey" (1951), *The Story of John Henry . . . a Musical Narrative: Ballads, Blues and Other Songs* (1954–1955), *Josh at Midnight* (1955), *Blues And* (1956), *Josh White* (1956; also titled *Blues*), *Josh White Comes a-Visitin'* (1956), *Josh White Sings Ballads—Blues* (1956), *The Josh White Stories,* vol. 1 (1956), *The Josh White Stories,* vol. 2 (1957; also titled *Good Morning Blues*), *Chain Gang Songs* (ca. 1958), *Blues-Singer and Balladeer* (1959), *Empty Bed Blues* (1960), *The House I Live In* (1960), *Spirituals and Blues* (1960), *Josh White at Town Hall* (1961), *Live!* (1961), *The Beginning* (1963), *The Beginning,* vol. 2 (1963)

Leaders Recorded With

Joel Taggart (1928), Carver Boys (1929), probably Charlie Spand (1929), Scrapper Blackwell (1934), Leroy Carr (1934), Lucille Bogan (1935), Buddy Moss (1935), Walter Roland (1935), Golden Gate Quartet (1940), Almanac Singers (1941), Libby Holman (1942), Leadbelly (Huddie Ledbetter) (1944), Union Boys (1944), Mary Lou Williams (1944), Fletcher Henderson (1950), Memphis Slim (1961)

Films

The Crimson Canary (1945), *Dreams That Money Can Buy* (1948), *The Walking Hills* (1949)

Awards

Honorary degree, Fisk University (1949); Best Blues Singer, *Cavalier* magazine (1965); Josh White postage stamp issued in the Legends of American Music series (1998)

References

PRIMARY: Josh White, "I Was a Sucker for the Communists," *Negro Digest* 9 (December 1950): 26–31; Josh White, with Ivor Mairants, *The Josh White Guitar Method* (London: Hawkes, 1956); "Josh White Talks to Teens: The Wish to Understand," *Seventeen* 24 (April 1965): 172, 257; Max Jones, "Josh White Looks Back (Part 1)," *Blues Unlimited* 55 (July 1968): 16–17 (narrative by White); Max Jones, "Josh White Looks Back 2," *Blues Unlimited* 56 (September 1968): 15–16 (narrative by White); Chris Van Ness, "Josh White Retrospective," *Los Angeles Free Press,* 18 September 1970, p. 58 (interview from 1964).

SECONDARY: Georgina Campbell, "Josh White: A Study in Blues," *Hobo News,* 3 September 1945, p. 6 (abridged as "Study in White and Blues," *Negro Digest* 4 [November 1945]: 7–9); Avery S. Denham, "Preacher in Song," *Collier's* 118 (16 November 1946): 44, 72–73 (comments by White); Robert Shelton and Walter Raim, *The Josh White Song Book* (Chicago: Quadrangle Books, 1963) (comments by White); Carter B. Horsley, "Josh White, Folk Singer, Dead; Known for Spirituals and Blues," *New York Times,* 6 September 1969, p. 29 (obituary); Bruce Bastin, *Crying for the Carolines* (London: Studio Vista, 1971), 66–68; Dorothy Schainman Siegel, *The Glory Road: The Story of Josh White* (San Diego: Harcourt Brace Jovanovich, 1982); James A. McGowan, *Hear Today! Here to Stay!* (Saint Petersburg, Fla.: Sixth House, 1983), 163–69; Jon Bradshaw, *Dreams That Money Can Buy: The Tragic Life of Libby Holman* (New York: William Morrow, 1985), passim; Bruce Bastin, *Red River Blues: The Blues Tradition in the Southeast* (Urbana: University of Illinois Press, 1986), 167–71, 322–24; Bruce Bastin, "Truckin' My Blues Away: East Coast Piedmont Styles," in *Nothing but the Blues: The Music and the Musicians,* by Lawrence Cohn et al. (New York: Abbeville, 1993), 205–31 (see especially 213–15); Elijah Wald, *Josh White: Society Blues* (Amherst: University of Massachusetts Press, 2000); Elijah Wald, "Josh White and the Protest Blues," *Living Blues* 158 (July–August 2001): 36–42; John L. Williams, *America's Mistress: The Life and Times of Eartha Kitt* (London: Quercus, 2012), passim.

Williams, Columbus

Guitar, singer

S.C. residence: possibly the Greenville-Spartanburg area (at least early 1920s)

A street musician, Williams performed in and around Greenville in the early 1920s. Blind, he required a lead boy, or guide, one of whom was Josh White.

A Columbus Williams, estimated age fifty-nine, was enumerated for the census in Cherokee Township, Spartanburg County, S.C., on 13 January 1920. It indicates that he was a farmer, born in S.C., who could neither read nor write. It has not been determined if this man was the musician.

References

SECONDARY: Max Jones, "Josh White Looks Back (Part 1)," *Blues Unlimited* 55 (July 1968): 16–17; Bruce Bastin, *Crying for the Carolines* (London: Studio Vista, 1971), 67–68; Dorothy Schainman Siegel, *The Glory Road: The Story of Josh White* (San Diego: Harcourt Brace Jovanovich, 1982), 21; Bruce Bastin, *Red River Blues: The Blues Tradition in the Southeast* (Urbana: University of Illinois Press, 1986), 167; Elijah Wald, *Josh White:*

Society *Blues* (Amherst: University of Massachusetts Press, 2000), 19.

Williams, Eddie (Edward David)

Trumpet, flugelhorn

28 May 1928 (Charleston, S.C.)–30 December 1985 (Bronx, N.Y.)

S.C. residences: Charleston (1928–ca. 1948), Orangeburg (ca. 1948–ca. 1950)

As a young teenager in Charleston, Williams played with local groups, possibly including bands of Jenkins Orphanage, though he was not a ward of the institution. By fifteen he performed professionally. After being graduated from Burke High School, he matriculated at what is now South Carolina State University ca. 1948 but joined the army around 1950 before completing a degree. He played in the army concert band. Following discharge he settled in N.Y.C., where he became a freelance musician, though he toured with Lionel Hampton in the late 1950s and early 1960s. He fronted an occasional combo for club work, was affiliated for an extended period with a group led by Bobby Green, and played on Broadway in *Hair* and *The Wiz*. Eugene Chadbourne identifies Williams's playing on Lou Donaldson's *Everything I Play Is Funky* and *Hot Dog* as "high points of the Williams recording legacy." Williams is buried in plot 10, 0, 13169, Calverton National Cemetery, Calverton, N.Y.

Composition

"Blondelle"

Leaders Recorded With

Jesse Powell (1955, 1959–1960), Lionel Hampton (1958–1959), Frankie Dunlop (1964), Earl Coleman (1967), Freddie McCoy (1967–1968), Pee Wee Russell (1967), Lou Donaldson (1969, 1971), Galt MacDermot (1970), Oscar Brown, Jr. (1972), Lawrence Lucie (ca. 1981)

References

SECONDARY: John Chilton, *A Jazz Nursery: The Story of the Jenkins' Orphanage Bands of Charleston, South Carolina* (London: Bloomsbury Book Shop, 1980), 59; Eugene Chadbourne, "Eddie Williams," http://www.allmusic.com/artist/eddie-williams-mn0001232278 (undated; accessed 21 May 2014) (includes some incorrect information).

Williams, Ermitt Valgen ("Mr. Blues")

Singer

11 January 1939 (New York, N.Y.)–

S.C. residence: John's Island (2004–)

Williams spent most of his life in N.Y.C., where he worked as an insurance agent. Musical from youth, he sang in his high school choir and took private singing lessons. Over the years he performed in clubs in and around N.Y.C.; in Harlem he created the Unsung Heroes of Afrikan Amerikan Classical Music Awards (2000). Upon moving to S.C. he sang—and continues singing—in venues primarily in the Charleston area. He wrote, produced, and starred in *The Day I Met Joe Williams* (1999) and *The Mr. Blues Story* (2009). He produced the 2011 awards show sponsored by the Gold Key Jazz Society of Myrtle Beach, S.C.

Recordings as Leader

Just for You (1997), *A Tribute to Joe Williams: Live at Cobi's Place*, vol. 1 (2002)

Website

www.ermittmrblueswilliams.com (accessed 21 May 2014)

Reference

SECONDARY: Jack McCray, "Mr. Blues Walks the Walk," *Charleston (S.C.) Post and Courier*, 26 November 2009, sec. F, p. 7.

Ermitt Williams; photograph by Anthony Bell, permission of Ermitt Williams

Williams, Horace ("Spoons")

Spoons, bones, miscellaneous instruments
Possibly 9 May 1910, or 1911 (Newberry County, S.C.)–25 September 1986 (Philadelphia, Pa.)
S.C. residence: Newberry County (possibly 1910 or 1911–no later than early 1940s)

Born to sharecroppers, Williams created music, as a child, on jugs and pie pans. Though he failed to fulfill his dream of dancing in carnivals and tent shows, he ultimately played bones and performed as a comic in carnivals. Over time he accompanied blues musicians, brass bands, and gospel groups on spoons and bones. He served in the army during World War II. Ultimately he settled in Philadelphia, where, in the early 1950s, he and Washboard Slim (Robert Young) briefly operated a carnival. Subsequently he made a living shining shoes and doing odd jobs. He participated in the National Black Story-Telling Festival in Philadelphia (1984). Williams gained such a reputation as a poet/monologist commenting on racial issues in rhyme—as well as for playing bones and jug—that he was awarded a fellowship by the National Endowment for the Arts. In addition to performing on the streets he played music and recited poems in such venues as the Smithsonian Institution (1984) and the Carnegie Recital Hall (1985). He appears in episode 5 of *The Story of English* (1986), a television miniseries broadcast on BBC and PBS.

Williams's birth date of 9 May 1910 comes from Alan Govenar; the obituary in *Living Blues* states that Williams was born in 1911 and specifies 25 September 1986 as his death date. More than once Williams indicated that he left home at thirteen, laboring in various capacities as he worked his way to Philadelphia. However, a Horace Williams was enumerated for the census while a member of the Newberry County Farm chain gang on 19 April 1940; this document estimates his age as thirty and indicates that in 1935 he lived in rural Newberry County. If this person was the bones player, as seems likely, then Williams probably did not leave S.C. until he joined the army.

Compositions

"A Black Man Talks to God," "My Saddest Experience," "Thankful," "This Is My Birthplace but This Is Not My Home"

Award

National Endowment for the Arts National Heritage Fellowship (1985)

References

SECONDARY: Kathy Hacker, "Spoon Tunes: Preserving the Music That Chased the Clouds Away," *Philadelphia Inquirer,* 28 January 1983, sec. C, p. 1 (comments by Williams); Terry E. Johnson, "And the Storytelling Goes On," *Philadelphia Inquirer,* 10 November 1984, sec. C, p. 1 (comments by Williams); Jon Pareles, "Rural South's Rich Culture Is Explored in Concerts," *New York Times,* 18 January 1985, sec. C, p. 20; "'Southern Roots' of Blues at Carnegie," *New York Amsterdam News,* 2 February 1985, p. 23; Gerald B. Jordan, "A Spoon Artist Scoops up a $5,000 National Prize: Philadelphian Wins One of 12 Awards," *Philadelphia Inquirer,* 21 June 1985, sec. E, p. 1 (comments by Williams); Gene Seymour, "He Tried His Hands at Spoons," *Philadelphia Daily News,* 21 June 1985, p. 16 (comments by Williams); Robert McCrum et al., *The Story of English* (New York: Viking, 1986), 226–29; "Obituaries," *Living Blues* 70 (1986): 45; David O'Reilly, "TV's Ode to the Vigor of the English Language," *Philadelphia Inquirer,* 18 September 1986, sec. C, p. 1; Joseph Daniel Sobol, *The Storytellers' Journey: An American Revival* (Urbana: University of Illinois Press, 1999), 138–39 (comments by Williams); Alan Govenar, *Masters of Traditional Arts: A Biographical Dictionary, Volume Two K–Z* (Santa Barbara: ABC Clio, 2001), 677–79 (comments by Williams).

Williams, Horace

Ca. 1913 (Wilmington, N.C.)–1928 (New York, N.Y.)
S.C. residence: Charleston (probably mid-1910s–1928)

Williams was a ward of Jenkins Orphanage from an undetermined date until his death. He drowned while in N.Y.C. to perform in *Porgy* with the institution's band.

John Chilton, who identifies Williams's birthplace, notes that when Williams died in 1928, he was fourteen years old (39); he also states that Williams was born "c. 1912" (60).

Reference

SECONDARY: John Chilton, *A Jazz Nursery: The Story of the Jenkins' Orphanage Bands of Charleston, South Carolina* (London: Bloomsbury Book Shop, 1980), 39, 60.

Williams, John Calvin, Jr.

Saxophone, clarinet

31 October 1936 (Orangeburg, S.C.)-

S.C. residence: Orangeburg (1936-1958, 1981-)

After receiving a degree from what is now South Carolina State University in 1958, Williams attended graduate school, first at Indiana University (1958–1960) and then at California State University (1960–1962). After serving with the music program in the army (1962–1965), he resided in Los Angeles, where he became a professional musician, initially with Ike and Tina Turner and then with Ray Charles. He was with the Count Basie band for six months in 1970, then from 1971 to 1975, and finally from 1980 until 2013. During the years between his last two affiliations with Basie, Williams played in Los Angeles with such musicians as Louis Bellson, Marvin Gaye, and Gerald Wilson, as well as the Capp-Pierce Juggernaut. Following Jack Washington and Charlie Fowlkes, he was the third (and last) of Basie's long-tenured baritone saxophonists.

Leaders Recorded With

T-Bone Walker (1968), Quincy Jones (1969), Count Basie (1971–1973, 1980–1984, 1986, 1989, 1992, 1994, 1996, 1998–1999, 2005, ca. 2009), Joe Williams (1971, 1992), Bing Crosby (1972), Ella Fitzgerald (1972), Paul Jeffrey (1972), Teresa Brewer (1973), Billie Harris (1979), Horace Tapscott (1979), Sarah Vaughan (1981), Caterina Valente (1986), Diane Schuur (1987), George Benson (1990), Lena Horne (1994), Tito Puente (1996), Rosemary Clooney (1997–1998), Michel Leeb (2001), Tony Bennett (2008), Charleston Jazz Initiative Legends Band (2010)

Film

The Last of the Blue Devils (1979)

Awards

South Carolina State University Jazz Hall of Fame (1986); Notable Jazz Orchestra Musician, Gold Key Jazz Society of Myrtle Beach, S.C. (2012)

References

PRIMARY: David J. Gibson, "Count Basie Saxophone Section Celebrates Its 50th Anniversary," *Saxophone Journal* 11 (Fall 1986): 40–48 (see especially 46–48) (narrative by Williams); David J. Gibson, "Count Basie Saxophone Section Celebrates 50th Anniversary, Part II," *Saxophone Journal* 11 (Winter 1987): 39–48 (see especially 45–48) (narrative by Williams); Greg Banaszak, "A Private Lesson with Johnny Williams," *Saxophone Journal* 17 (January–February 1993): 46–48 (though characterized as an interview, this is a narrative by Williams); Benjamin Franklin V, *Jazz and Blues Musicians of South Carolina: Interviews with Jabbo, Dizzy, Drink, and Others* (Columbia: University of South Carolina Press, 2008), 130–42.

Williams, John Henry

Trumpet

-before 1981

S.C. residence: Charleston (at least early 1930s)

Apparently a ward of Jenkins Orphanage, Williams played in its bands in the early 1930s. He then performed with the Carolina Cotton Pickers.

Bruce Bastin states that Williams had died by the time Bastin completed his manuscript.

Leader Recorded With

Carolina Cotton Pickers (1936–1937)

References

SECONDARY: John Chilton, *A Jazz Nursery: The Story of the Jenkins' Orphanage Bands of Charleston, South Carolina* (London: Bloomsbury Book Shop, 1980), 60; Bruce Bastin, "A Note on the Carolina Cotton Pickers," *Storyville* 95 (June–July 1981): 177–82.

Williams, Joseph

Trombone

S.C. residence: Charleston (probably mid-1910s-at least into early 1920s)

Apparently a ward of Jenkins Orphanage, Williams played in its bands in the 1910s and early 1920s. After becoming a professional musician he performed in N.Y.C. with groups led by Willie Gant (1926) and June Clark (1926–1927), as well as those of Billy Fowler, Bob Fuller, and Freddy Moore.

It has not been determined if this musician was the Joe Williams who played with the Jimmie Lunceford band in the mid-1940s.

Leader Recorded With

Bessie Smith (1928)

Reference

SECONDARY: John Chilton, *A Jazz Nursery: The Story of the Jenkins' Orphanage Bands of Charleston, South Carolina* (London: Bloomsbury Book Shop, 1980), 59.

Williams, Joseph M.

Trumpet
-before 1981
S.C. residence: Charleston (by 1930–no later than mid-1930s)

Apparently a ward of Jenkins Orphanage, Williams played in its bands in the early 1930s. He then performed with the Carolina Cotton Pickers.

Bruce Bastin indicates that Williams had died by the time Bastin completed his manuscript.

Leader Recorded With

Carolina Cotton Pickers (1936–1937)

References

SECONDARY: John Chilton, *A Jazz Nursery: The Story of the Jenkins' Orphanage Bands of Charleston, South Carolina* (London: Bloomsbury Book Shop, 1980), 59; Bruce Bastin, "A Note on the Carolina Cotton Pickers," *Storyville* 95 (June–July 1981): 177–82.

Williams, Maurice

Singer, piano, composer
26 April 1940 (Lancaster, S.C.)-
S.C. residence: Lancaster (1940–1961)

Active around Lancaster as a teenager with a group originally named the Royal Charms but later the Gladiolas and later still the Zodiacs, Williams and his group became successful in 1960 when they recorded "Stay," which he had written several years earlier. It is the shortest song (1:38) ever to reach number one on the popular-music charts. He also wrote "Little Darlin'," which he recorded with the Gladiolas but which gained greatest popularity in a version by the Diamonds (1957). These two recordings are on the sound tracks of, respectively, *Dirty Dancing* (1987) and *American Graffiti* (1973). Probably beginning in the early 1970s Williams led the Zodiacs on the oldies circuit. After releasing new material in the late 1960s Williams apparently did not record again for almost three decades.

Maurice Williams; permission of Maurice Williams

Williams's birth date comes from the musician himself. He has not been located in the 1940 census, possibly because he had not been born by the time his family was enumerated for it.

Compositions

"Always," "Anything," "Baby, Baby," "Beach Carol on a Night Like This," "Being without You," "Brothers," "College Girl," "Come Along," "Come Out Tonight," "Comin' Home to You," "Dance, Dance, Dance," "Do I," "Do You Believe," "Emily," "First Love," "Forever Beach," "Hey, Little Girl," "I'll Be There," "I Remember," "I Wanta Know," "Leah," "Little Darlin'," "Little Mama," "Little Sally Walker," "Look My Way," "Lover (Where Are You?)," "May I," "Morning Love," "My Baby's Gone," "Nobody Knows," "No More Tears," "Old Heart Breaker," "Please," "Return," "Running Around," "Say Yeah," "Say You'll Be Mine," "She's Mine," "Shoop Shoop," "Some Day," "Stay," "Stay the Way You Are," "Sweet Bobbie Jean," "Sweetheart, Please Don't Go," "This Feeling," "Try," "Want to Go to Memphis," "We're Lovers," "Wonder," "You've Got It"

Recordings as Leader (These Are Release Dates, Not Necessarily Recording Dates)

"College Girl" (1959), "Golly Gee" (1959), "Lover (Where Are You?)" (1959), "Say Yeah" (1959), "She's Mine" (1959), "T Town" (1959), "Another Little Darling" (1960), "Anything" (1960), "Lita" (1960), "Little Sally Walker" (1960), *Stay* (1961), "Come and Get It" (1961), "Do I" (1961), "Here I Stand" (1961), "High Blood Pressure" (1961), "It's Alright" (1961), "Please" (1961), "Some Day" (1961), "Funny" (1963), "Loneliness" (1963), *At the Beach* (1965), "I Know" (1965), "Nobody Knows" (1965), "So Fine" (1965), "The Wind" (1965), "Lollipop" (1966, 1967), "May I" (1966), "Baby, Baby" (1967), "Being without You" (1967), "This Feeling"

(1967), "Dance, Dance, Dance" (1968), "Don't Be Half Safe" (1968), "Don't Ever Leave Me" (1968), "How to Pick a Winner" (1968), "Ooh Poo Pah Do" (1968), "Stay" (1968), "Surely" (1968), "The Four Corners" (1969), "I'd Rather Have a Memory Than a Dream" (1969), "My Baby's Gone" (1969), "My Reason for Living" (1969), "Return" (1969), "Try" (1969), *Let This Night Last* (1997), *Back to Basics* (2000), *Christmas with Maurice Williams* (2007), *50 Years . . .* (2010), *Merry Christmas* (2010)

Leaders Recorded With

Gladiolas (1957–1958), Ospreys (1958)

Awards

Carolina Beach Music Awards Hall of Fame (1995; with the Zodiacs); South Carolina Entertainment and Music Hall of Fame (1999); Order of the Palmetto (2001); Bill Pinkney Legend Award (2004); Hennessy Privilege Award (2004); Vocal Group Hall of Fame (2007; with the Zodiacs); North Carolina Music Hall of Fame (2010)

References

PRIMARY: Joe Montague, "Legendary Singer-Songwriter Maurice Williams," www.rivetingriffs.com/Maurice%20Willams%20and%20the%20Zodiacs%20Interview.html (2011; accessed 21 May 2014) (interview).

SECONDARY: Arnold Shaw, *Honkers and Shouters: The Golden Years of Rhythm and Blues* (New York: Macmillan, 1978), 457–58; Ann Wicker, "Maurice Williams," in *Making Notes: Music of the Carolinas,* ed. Ann Wicker (Charlotte: Novello Festival Press, 2008), 95–96 (comments by Williams); Todd Baptista, "Stay . . . Just a Little Bit Longer . . . ," *Goldmine* 796 (February 2011): 94–96 (this issue is also designated volume 37, number 2) (also available as "Maurice Williams' Lifetime of Beautiful Melodies" at http://www.goldminemag.com/article/maurice-williams-lifetime-of-beautiful-melodies [accessed 21 May 2014]).

Williams, Sandy (Alexander Balos)

Trombone

24 October 1906 (Summerville, S.C.)–25 March 1991 (New York, N.Y.)

S.C. residence: Summerville (1906–into 1910s)

Williams moved with his family from Summerville to Washington, D.C., sometime during the 1910s. When his parents died within a few months of each other in the late 1910s (from influenza, during an epidemic), he was placed in Saint Joseph's Industrial School in Clayton, Del., where he learned to read music and began playing the trombone. After two years there he ran away, returning to Washington. Around 1923 he became a professional musician in Washington, initially with a theater band before working with Claude Hopkins (1927) and other leaders. Trombonist Jimmy Harrison was his idol. As a regular with Fletcher Henderson (1932–1934), Williams played on some of the band's major recordings, such as "Queer Notions" (1933). He performed longest—most of the 1930s—with Chick Webb; the band's recording of "Blue Minor" (1934) includes one of his notable solos. Chip Deffaa believes that of the musicians in this organization, Williams was "arguably the most impressive soloist." As a member of the Cootie Williams band, he is on the initial recording of Thelonious Monk's "Epistrophy" (1942). He played with Duke Ellington in 1943. A few years later he toured Europe with Rex Stewart's septet (1947–1948), which performed at the first significant jazz festival, the one held in Nice, France, in 1948. Poor health and loss of teeth in the 1950s essentially ended his career, though he played a few subsequent engagements in N.Y.C., where he had freelanced since at least 1935 and lived until his death. Stanley Dance considers Williams "one of the best trombonists of the Swing Era" (63). He is buried in Woodlawn Cemetery, Bronx, N.Y.

Williams's birth and death dates come from the Social Security Death Index. It has not been determined how long Williams lived in Summerville. Using information the musician provided, Stanley Dance records that Williams departed "while he was still very young" (64). In "Confessions of a Trombonist," Williams indicates that he left S.C. when he "was around 5 or 6" (12). He told Johnny Simmen that his family moved from Summerville "in the late teens" ("Sandy Williams: A Portrait," 51).

Compositions

"Let's Go Home," "Sandy's Blues," "Tea for Me"

Recordings as Leader

"After Hours on Dream Street" (1945), "Chili con Carney" (1945), "Mountain Air" (1945), "Sumpin' Jumpin' 'round Here" (1945), "Frost on the Moon" (1946), "Gee, Baby, Ain't I Good to You?" (1946), "Sam-Pan" (1946), "Sandy's Blues" (1946), "Tea for Me" (1946)

Leaders Recorded With

Jelly Roll Morton (1930), Fletcher Henderson (1932–1933, 1941), Chick Webb (1933–1939), Ethel Waters (1934), Ella Fitzgerald (1936–1940), Gotham Stompers (1937), Stuff Smith (1937), Sidney Bechet (1940–1942), Benny Carter (1940, 1946), Coleman Hawkins (1940), Lucky Millinder (1941), Cootie Williams (1942), Duke Ellington (1943), Don Redman (1943), Roy Eldridge (1944), Art Hodes (1944), Brick Fleagle (1945), Bunk Johnson (1945), Pigmeat Markham (1945), Hot Lips Page (1945), Jazz at Town Hall (1946), Rex Stewart (1946–1948), Really the Blues Concert (1947), Gloria Mae (1949), Henry "Red" Allen (1951)

References

PRIMARY: Stanley Dance, *The World of Swing* (New York: Scribner's, 1974), 1: 63–77 (mostly a Williams narrative from 1968); Sandy Williams, "Confessions of a Trombonist," *Jazz Journal* 28 (February 1975): 12–14; Johnny Simmen, "The Sandy Williams Story: Sandy Parle," *Bulletin du Hot Club de France* 316 (Mai 1984): 2–6 (narrative, in French, by Williams); Johnny Simmen, "The Sandy Williams Story," *Bulletin du Hot Club de France* 317 (Juin 1984): 4–7 (mostly a narrative, in French, by Williams).

SECONDARY: Johnny Simmen, "Sandy Williams," *Bulletin du Hot Club de France* 315 (Mars–Avril 1984): 3–6 (in French); Johnny Simmen, "The Sandy Williams Story," *Bulletin du Hot Club de France* 318 (Juillet 1984): 7–9 (comments, in French, by Williams); Johnny Simmen, "The Sandy Williams Story," *Bulletin du Hot Club de France* 319 (Aout–Septembre 1984): 1–4 (in French); Johnny Simmen, "The Sandy Williams Story," *Bulletin du Hot Club de France* 320 (Octobre 1984): 20–23 (comments, in French, by Williams); Johnny Simmen, "Sandy Williams: A Portrait," *Storyville* 116 (December 1984–January 1985): 48–69 (English translation of Simmen's continuous article in *Bulletin du Hot Club de France*, with a modified text); Chip Deffaa, *Jazz Veterans: A Portrait Gallery* (Fort Bragg, Calif.: Cypress House, 1996), 29.

Williams, Walter Bernard

Singer

3 January of either 1888 or 1890 (Columbia, S.C.)–9 October 1921 (at sea, off Corsewall Point, Wigtownshire, Scotland)

S.C. residence: Columbia (1888 or 1890–no later than 1917)

Williams lived in N.Y.C. by 1917, when he registered there for the draft. A corporal with the 367th Infantry (the Buffaloes), he sang with the Enlisted Men's Quartet and was the main vocal soloist at the Manhattan Opera House when the Infantry's band performed there in 1918. After being discharged he sang around town, including as soloist at the Mother A.M.E. Zion Church. His employer, the postal service, granted him a leave of absence to perform in Europe with the Southern Syncopated Orchestra, with which he sang "Oh, Listen to the Lambs" and probably other songs. He departed N.Y.C. in May 1921 and died when the ship transporting the musicians from Scotland to Ireland (the *Rowan*) was struck by two ships and sank.

The 1888 birth year comes from Williams's draft registration card; the 1890, from the singer's 1921 passport application. Both documents indicate that Williams was born in Columbia on 3 January.

References

SECONDARY: Lester A. Walton, "367th in Dance and Song," *New York Age,* 30 March 1918, p. 6; "Young New York Singer Is Lost in Wreck off Scotland," *New York Age,* 15 October 1921, pp. 1, 5; "Members of Syncopated Saved," *Chicago Defender,* 29 October 1921, p. 8; Howard Rye, "Southern Syncopated Orchestra: The Roster," *Black Music Research Journal* 30 (Spring 2010): 64; Howard Rye, "The Southern Syncopated Orchestra," *Black Music Research Journal* 30 (Spring 2010): 212.

Wilson, Benjamin

Saxophone

S.C. residence: Charleston (probably late 1920s–at least into early 1930s)

Apparently a ward of Jenkins Orphanage, Wilson played in its bands ca. 1930.

Wilson, Clyde

See Mancha, Steve

Wilson, John ("Shadow")

Alto horn

29 July 1909 (Charleston, S.C.)–?

S.C. residence: Charleston (1909–at least until 1929)

Apparently a ward of Jenkins Orphanage, Wilson played in its bands in the late 1920s and performed with one of them in England in 1929.

Wilson's birth date and place come from the passenger list of the *Majestic,* which transported the orphanage band from Plymouth, England, to N.Y.C. in June 1929.

Reference

SECONDARY: Howard Rye, "Visiting Fireboys: The Jenkins' Orphanage Bands in Britain," *Storyville* 130 (1987): 137–43.

Wilson, Johnny

Guitar, singer

Ca. 1907 (probably Ga.)–17 July 1954 (Saint Matthews, S.C.)

S.C. residence: Saint Matthews (–1954)

The blues guitar playing of Wilson, a laborer, inspired young James "Blood" Ulmer. Forbidden by his parents to listen to the blues, Ulmer sat under Wilson's house to hear his neighbor play. Wilson is buried in the Friendship Church Cemetery, Saint Matthews.

Wilson's occupation, date and place of death, and burial place come from the musician's death certificate, as do his probable birthplace and approximate age at death (forty-seven).

References

SECONDARY: Walter Hetfield, "Rare Blood," *Guitar Player* 24 (May 1990): 90–94, 156; Matthew Brown, "James Blood Ulmer Biography," www.musicianguide.com/biographies/1608003684/James-Blood-Ulmer.html (2012; accessed 21 May 2014).

Wilson, Ruby

Ca. 1926 (N.C.)–?

S.C. residence: Charleston (not before 1935–at least into early 1940s)

A ward of Jenkins Orphanage, Wilson played in its bands in the early 1940s, though her instrument is not known.

Estimated age fourteen, Wilson was enumerated for the census at the orphanage on 21 May 1940; this document indicates that she was born in N.C. and lived in Asheville, N.C., in 1935.

Wilson, Thomas

Trumpet

S.C. residence: Charleston (probably late 1930s–at least into early 1940s)

Apparently a ward of Jenkins Orphanage, Wilson played in its bands ca. 1940. It has not been determined if he was the Thomas Wilson who recorded with Ernie Fields and Preston Love in the 1950s.

Woods, Pearl (Lily Pearl Woodard)

Singer, composer, producer

24 September 1933 (Saint Matthews, S.C.)–19 March 2010 (Arlington, Tex.)

S.C. residences: Saint Matthews (1933–1951), Columbia (1973–1979, 1982–1983)

Woods moved from S.C. to N.Y.C. in 1951 to live with her godmother and attend college. Instead of continuing her education she entered the Harlem music scene, singing with groups on street corners before establishing herself. In 1966 she affiliated with Duke/Peacock Records, promoting its recordings to East Coast radio stations, producing recording sessions, and writing songs. She and her husband, pianist Fred Johnson, established Pearl-Tone Records and FrePea Music Publishing (both 1969), soon thereafter opened the Soul Shack record store, and in 1973 moved to Columbia, S.C. She and Johnson were affiliated with the Jimmy Swaggart Ministries in Baton Rouge, La., from 1979 until 1982, after which they resided for a year in

Pearl Woods; permission of Fred Johnson

Columbia before settling permanently in Arlington, Tex. There she served as a lay minister and hosted *Beautiful Truth,* a television talk show that focused on religious issues. Her composition "Something's Got a Hold on Me" is performed on the sound tracks of *Blue Sky* (1994; by Etta James), *What Love Is* (2007; by James), and *Burlesque* (2010; by Christina Aguilera). The rapper Flo Rida samples the introduction to this song on "Good Feeling" (2011), which went platinum. The singer is buried as Pearl W. Johnson in site 72, section 107, Dallas-Fort Worth National Cemetery, Dallas, Tex.

Compositions

"Ain't Love a Sweet Thing," "Anything Can Be Fixed," "Baby, Give Me You," "Be My Baby," "Bring Your Fine Self on Home," "Changes," "Disappointment Valley," "Don't Tell It All" (also titled "Keep Your Business to Yourself"), "Feel Good All Over," "Good Enough," "Happy Hearts," "I Can't Break Away from You," "I Don't Want to Suffer," "If I Knew Then," "I'll Be a Crybaby from Now On," "I Loved You Too Much," "I'm Gonna Stick with You," "I'm the Same Old Fool," "I Play Dirty," "It Ain't Like That No More," "It's a Man's World," "It's Loving Time," "It's You," "Joogie Boogie," "Let Nature Take Its Course," "Little Piece of Gold," "Lollipop Baby," "My Love Is Your Love," "Next Door to the Blues," "Nothing Like Love," "One More Time," "Pretty Baby," "Right Now," "Sippin' Sorrow (with a Spoon)," "Sloppin'," "Something's Got a Hold on Me," "Something Touched Me," "Stickum Up, Baby," "Stop the Wedding," "Tell It Like It Is," "That Ain't Right," "That's Where It's At," "Think of Poor Me," "Walkin' Slow," "Why Did You Do It?," "You Can't Hide It," "You Got Soul," "You're All I Need," "Your Replacement," "You've Got Her"

Recordings as Leader

Sippin' Sorrow (with a Spoon) (1956, 1960–1962, 1965), "Let the Good Things Start" (1956), "My Donkey Wouldn't Walk" (1956), "You're Getting Old, Charlie" (1956), "I Loved You Too Much" (1961), "Keep Your Business to Yourself" (1961; also titled "Don't Tell It All"), "Right Now" (1961), "Raindrop Blues" (1970)

Film

Rockin' the Blues (1956)

References

SECONDARY: "Duke Peacock Disk Signs Pearl Woods," *New York Amsterdam News,* 9 April 1966, p. 22; Kevin Goins, notes to *Sippin' Sorrow (with a Spoon)* (2005; Night Train CD-7147); Charles Farley, *Soul of the Man: Bobby "Blue" Bland* (Jackson: University Press of Mississippi, 2011), 134–35.

Wright, Herbert

Drums

Probably ca. 1895 (S.C., probably Charleston)-?

S.C. residence: Charleston (probably ca. 1895–1917)

A ward of Jenkins Orphanage, Wright played in its bands until 1917. That year he joined the organization of James Reese Europe, though he became a good drummer only after Europe improved him, according to Europe's widow. In Europe during World War I, the band became famous as the 369th Regiment Hell Fighters; Wright remained with the group after it returned to the United States. In it he and Steven Wright were known as the percussion twins because of their feature performance with the band. During intermission at a 1919 concert at Mechanics Hall in Boston, Herbert Wright slashed Europe's jugular vein, killing him. Sentenced to prison for manslaughter, he was released in April 1927. While incarcerated he organized the prison band, with which he played. Later he gave drum lessons to Roy Haynes, who became a significant musician.

Wright is probably the Herbert Wright, born in November 1895, who was enumerated for the census with his family in Charleston on 6 June 1900. Probably in 1917 a Herbert Wright (born in December 1895 and a resident of Orangeburg, S.C.) registered for the draft in Williamsport, Pa. Because this person was then on tour with Dobyns Shows, a carnival, he could have been the drummer. Wright's age was estimated as twenty-five when the musician was enumerated for the census at the Massachusetts State Prison on 12 January 1920. A Herbert B. Wright was enumerated in Boston on 19 April 1940; a South Carolinian, he was estimated to be forty-three. It has not been determined if he was the musician. No available evidence proves that the drummer was the Herbert Wright who, according to the Social Security Death Index, was born on 18 July 1897 and died in Massachusetts in October 1965.

Leader Recorded With

James Reese Europe (1919)

References

SECONDARY: "Jim Europe Killed in Boston Quarrel," *New York Times,* 10 May 1919, p. 1; "All 'Little Africa' Mourns Killing of 'Jazz King' Europe," *New York Herald,* 11 May 1919, p. 5; "Wright Held without Bail on Charge of Murder, Hearing May 15," *New York Herald,* 11 May 1919, p. 5; "Drummer Denies Murder of Lieutenant Europe," *New York Herald,* 15 May 1919, p. 3; "Lt. James Reese Europe Buried with Honors," *New York Age,* 17 May 1919, pp. 1, 6 (second edition); "Herbert Wright Sentenced from 10 to 15 Years," *New York Age,* 14 June 1919, p. 1 (home edition); "Jas. Reese Europe's Slayer Freed," *New York Amsterdam News,* 6 April 1927, p. 3 (comments by Wright); "Drummer Who Killed Europe Gets Freedom," *Baltimore Afro-American,* 9 April 1927, p. 9; Noble Lee Sissle, "Memoirs of Lieutenant 'Jim' Europe," typescript, ca. 1942, African American Odyssey, American Memory Collection, Library of Congress, 1–6, 223–36, http://memory.loc.gov/cgi-bin/query/r?ammem/aaodyssey:@field(NUMBER+@band(musmisc+odyo717)) (accessed 21 May 2014); John Chilton, *A Jazz Nursery: The Story of the Jenkins' Orphanage Bands of Charleston, South Carolina* (London: Bloomsbury Book Shop, 1980), 23–24; Reid Badger, *A Life in Ragtime: A Biography of James Reese Europe* (New York: Oxford University Press, 1995), passim; Roy Haynes, "I'm Not a Metronome," *JazzTimes* 37 (November 2007): 50–55, 126–27 (see especially 52).

Wright, Steven or Stephen

Drums
27 June 1897 (Charleston, S.C.)-?
S.C. residence: Charleston (1897-1917)

A ward of Jenkins Orphanage, Wright helped teach Tommy Benford to play drums and performed in the institution's bands until 1917. He was in the one that performed in *Uncle Tom's Cabin* in N.Y.C. (1913) and the one that played in London the next year. In 1917 he became a member of James Reese Europe's band known, during World War I in Europe, as the 369th Regiment Hell Fighters. When it returned to the United States, Wright remained with the organization. In it he and Herbert Wright were known as the percussion twins because of their feature performance with the band. In the 1919 trial of Herbert Wright, accused of murdering James Reese Europe, Steven Wright testified against the defendant. In 1929 he led a group that substituted for Duke Ellington at the Cotton Club in N.Y.C., an engagement that caused problems with the musicians' union because Wright, new to town, had not deposited his union card with Local 802.

Wright's date and place of birth come from the passenger list of the *St. Louis,* which transported the orphanage band from Liverpool to N.Y.C. in September 1914. It has not been determined if he was the Stephen Wright who led the Jewel Orchestra at least in 1938.

Leaders Recorded With

James Reese Europe (1919), Noble Sissle (1921)

References

SECONDARY: Percival Outram, "Activities among Union Musicians," *New York Age,* 26 January 1929, p. 7; "Jenkins Orphan Band in Revue; Play at Smalls," *New York Amsterdam News,* 23 July 1938, p. 5; Noble Lee Sissle, "Memoirs of Lieutenant 'Jim' Europe," typescript, ca. 1942, African American Odyssey, American Memory Collection, Library of Congress, 223–36, http://memory.loc.gov/cgi-bin/query/r?ammem/aaodyssey:@field(NUMBER+@band(musmisc+odyo717)) (accessed 21 May 2014); John Chilton, *A Jazz Nursery: The Story of the Jenkins' Orphanage Bands of Charleston, South Carolina* (London: Bloomsbury Book Shop, 1980), 14; Howard Rye, "Visiting Fireboys: The Jenkins' Orphanage Bands in Britain," *Storyville* 130 (1987): 137–43; Reid Badger, *A Life in Ragtime: A Biography of James Reese Europe* (New York: Oxford University Press, 1995), 222.

Wyatt, Rudy (J. Rudolph; "Blue Shoes")

Piano, bass, guitar, drums, singer
19 October 1947 (Greenville, S.C.)-
S.C. residences: Greenville (from 1947 off and on until 1966, 1971, 1980-1983, 1997-) Travelers Rest (1971-1975), Columbia (1975-1980), Charleston (1983-1997)

As a child Wyatt played piano, drums, and guitar; ever since he has been a multi-instrumentalist. During his junior year at Greenville High School, he began playing in local clubs and recorded with the Snowmen, also known as the Uptowners; these recordings were released by Major Bill Smith of Fort Worth, Tex. After high school he played in Atlanta (1966–1967) before spending two years in the navy as an electrician. Following his discharge he performed in San Francisco and Los Angeles

Rudy Wyatt, Columbia, S.C., 4 Oct 2012; permission of the photographer, Benjamin Franklin V

before returning to S.C. in 1971. Proficient at the blues, rhythm and blues, rock and roll, and other styles of music, he is most adept at New Orleans-style piano and boogie-woogie; in the latter mode he was inspired by the likes of Albert Ammons, Pete Johnson, and Meade Lux Lewis. Over the years he has performed internationally.

Compositions

"Big Toy Box," "Boogie Dr.," "Boogie-Woogie Santa Claus," "Cuttin' the Groove," "Dance to the Boogie Beat," "Fast Life," "Fly by Nighter," "Guitar Daze," "If I Had It," "If'n," "I Found a Do Lolly Lolly Down," "In 'D' Groove," "It's Been a Long Journey," "Kitty Kat Song," "L. B.'s Boogie," "Let Me Be Your Toy Boy," "Lost One," "My Girl Ran Off with the Garbage Man," "New Thunderbird," "On the Spot," "Red Hot Mama," "Spin on a Dime," "Suwannee River Boogie," "You're Mine"

Recordings as Leader

"Dance to the Boogie Beat" (1985), "You're Mine" (1985), "Cuttin' the Groove" (1991), "Mohair Sam" (1991), *Rule of Thumb* (1997), *From the Roots* (2001), "Thunderbird" (ca. 2001; also titled "New Thunderbird")

Leaders Recorded With

Snowmen (1964), Wyld (1966–1967), Linda Rodney (Chocolate Thunder) (2002), Mac Arnold (2005), Rickey Godfrey (2005)

Website

http://rudyblueshoes.com/ (accessed 21 May 2014)

References

SECONDARY: Lisa Dennis, "There's More to 'Blue Shoes' Wyatt Than Boogie-Woogie Piano," *Charleston (S.C.) News and Courier,* 13 September 1985, sec. D, p. 1; Edward O. Marshall, "Rudy 'Blue Shoes' Wyatt Plays His Own Brand of Boogie Woogie," *Charleston (S.C.) News and Courier,* 23 May 1986, sec. F, p. 11; Michael B. Smith, *Carolina Dreams: The Musical Legacy of Upstate South Carolina* (Beverly Hills, Calif.: Marshall Tucker Entertainment, 1997), 32–34.

Young, Herbert

S.C. residence: Charleston (probably late 1920s–at least into early 1930s)

Apparently a ward of Jenkins Orphanage, Young played in its bands ca. 1930, though his instrument is not known.

Young, Washboard Willie

Washboard

Possibly 1910s (probably S.C., possibly Greenville area)–?

S.C. residence: possibly Greenville area (possibly 1910s–at least into 1930s)

Young played with Baby Tate and McKinley Ellis in the Carolina Blackbirds, the first group of black musicians to perform on radio in Greenville (1932).

References

SECONDARY: Bruce Bastin, *Crying for the Carolines* (London: Studio Vista, 1971), 74–75; Bruce Bastin, *Red River*

Blues: The Blues Tradition in the Southeast (Urbana: University of Illinois Press, 1986), 177.

Young, Webster English

Trumpet, singer

3 December 1932 (Columbia, S.C.)–13 December 2003 (Vancouver, Wash.)

S.C. residence: Columbia (1932–ca. 1933)

Young was reared and spent much of his life in Washington, D.C. Inspired by Louis Armstrong, he chose the trumpet as his instrument and began lessons around age ten. Soon his major influences became Roy Eldridge and Dizzy Gillespie, though in time his playing most resembled that of Miles Davis. After serving in the air force (ca. 1951–1955), he entered the jazz scene in N.Y.C., where he associated with such musicians as Davis, John Coltrane, and Jackie McLean. With the exception of apparently unauthorized recordings from 1961, Young made all his recordings in 1957, including the one date he led, a session dedicated to Billie Holiday. Thereafter he lived and played in Washington, New Haven, Boston, Saint Louis, Kansas City, Los Angeles, San Francisco, and Portland, Oreg., before returning to Washington in the mid-1960s; there he remained active in music primarily as a teacher.

Compositions

"House of Davis," "The Lady," "Millie's Pad," "Terry Anne"

Recordings as Leader

For Lady (1957), *Webster Young Plays the Miles Davis Songbook,* three vols. (1961)

Leaders Recorded With (All 1957)

Jackie McLean, Prestige All Stars (with additional material, this session was later released with John Coltrane identified as leader)

Film

7th and T (1987)

References

PRIMARY: Benjamin Franklin V, *Jazz and Blues Musicians of South Carolina: Interviews with Jabbo, Dizzy, Drink, and Others* (Columbia: University of South Carolina Press, 2008), 55–68.

SECONDARY: Adam Bernstein, "D.C. Jazz Trumpeter Webster Young Dies at 71," *Washington Post,* 18 December 2003, sec. B, p. 6 (obituary); Michael Gillespie, "Remembering Webster Young," http://www.msnbc.msn.com/id/3830945/ns/us_news-life/t/remembering-webster-young/ (29 December 2003; accessed 21 May 2014) (obituary).